Lecture Notes in Computer Science 2623

Edited by G. Goos, J. Hartmanis, and J. van Leeuwen

Springer
Berlin
Heidelberg
New York
Hong Kong
London
Milan
Paris
Tokyo

Lecture Notes in Computer Science 2623
Edited by G. Goos, J. Hartmanis, and J. van Leeuwen

Springer
Berlin
Heidelberg
New York
Hong Kong
London
Milan
Paris
Tokyo

Oded Maler   Amir Pnueli (Eds.)

Hybrid Systems:
Computation and Control

6th International Workshop, HSCC 2003
Prague, Czech Republic, April 3-5, 2003
Proceedings

 Springer

Series Editors

Gerhard Goos, Karlsruhe University, Germany
Juris Hartmanis, Cornell University, NY, USA
Jan van Leeuwen, Utrecht University, The Netherlands

Volume Editors

Oded Maler
CNRS-VERIMAG
2 avenue de Vignate, 38610 Gières, France
E-mail: Oded.Maler@imag.fr

Amir Pnueli
Weizmann Institute of Science
Rehovot 76100, Israel
E-mail: amir@wisdom.weizmann.ac.il

Cataloging-in-Publication Data applied for

A catalog record for this book is available from the Library of Congress

Bibliographic information published by Die Deutsche Bibliothek
Die Deutsche Bibliothek lists this publication in the Deutsche Nationalbibliografie;
detailed bibliographic data is available in the Internet at <http://dnb.ddb.de>.

CR Subject Classification (1998): C.3, C.1.m, F.3, D.2, F.1.2, J.2, I.6

ISSN 0302-9743
ISBN 3-540-3-540-00913-2 Springer-Verlag Berlin Heidelberg New York

Springer-Verlag Berlin Heidelberg New York
a member of BertelsmannSpringer Science+Business Media GmbH

http://www.springer.de

© Springer-Verlag Berlin Heidelberg 2003
Printed in Germany

Typesetting: Camera-ready by author, data conversion by PTP-Berlin GmbH
Printed on acid-free paper   SPIN 10872996   06/3142   5 4 3 2 1 0

Preface

This volume contains the proceedings of the *Sixth Workshop on Hybrid Systems: Computation and Control* (HSCC 2003), which was held in Prague, during April 3–5, 2003. The Hybrid Systems workshops attract researchers interested in the modeling, analysis, control, and implementation of systems which involve the interaction of both discrete and continuous state dynamics. The newest results and latest developments in hybrid system models, formal methods for analysis and control, computational tools, as well as new applications and examples are presented at these annual meetings.

The Sixth Workshop continued the series of workshops held in Grenoble, France (HART'97), Berkeley, California, USA (HSCC'98), Nijmegen, The Netherlands (HSCC'99), Pittsburgh, Pennsylvania, USA (HSCC 2000), Rome, Italy (HSCC 2001), and Stanford, California, USA (HSCC 2002). Proceedings of these workshops have been published by Springer-Verlag in the Lecture Notes in Computer Science (LNCS) series.

This year we assembled a technical program committee with a broad expertise in formal methods in computer science, control theory, applied mathematics, and artificial intelligence. We received a set of 75 high-quality submitted papers. After detailed review and discussion of these papers by the program committee, 36 papers were accepted for presentation at the workshop, and the final versions of these papers appear in this volume.

As is the tradition established by previous workshops, the accepted papers span an exciting range of topics, including the "hybridization" of traditional control concepts such as identification, observability and stability, computational techniques for verifying hybrid systems by numerical as well as symbolic methods, new formalisms for expressing systems and their specifications, and an impressive list of papers demonstrated the applicability of hybrid technology to domains such as automotive control, the immune system, electrical circuits, operating systems, and human brains. We hope the reader will find them interesting.

We thank our Program Committee for their technical support in reviewing the papers. Other people who helped us include Ewa Maja Miliszewska who helped in the design of the web page, Nicolas Kowalski who maintained the Start server for submission and evaluation of papers, Jaroslav Dolezal and Tatana Machova from Honeywell Laboratories at Prague who took care of the local organization and, last but not least, Eugene Asarin for his help in editing this volume. Much of the work appearing in these proceedings was done in the framework of European IST projects on hybrid systems and we would like to thank Alkis Konstantellos from the European Commission for his ongoing support for the hybrid cause.

April 2003   Oded Maler
                                                                                                                   Amir Pnueli

Organization

HSCC 2003 was organized by Verimag laboratory of Grenoble together with Honeywell Prague laboratories.

Steering Committee

Maria Di Benedetto (University of Rome "La Sapienza")
Mark Greenstreet (University of British Columbia)
Bruce Krogh (chair)(Carnegie Mellon University)
Oded Maler (Verimag, Grenoble)
Manfred Morari (ETH, Zurich)
Amir Pnueli (Weizmann Institute, Rehovot)
Anders Ravn (DTU, Lyngby)
Alberto Sangiovanni-Vincentelli (University of California at Berkeley)
Claire Tomlin (Stanford University)

Program Committee

Rajeev Alur (University of Pennsylvania)
Eugene Asarin (Verimag, Grenoble)
Alberto Bemporad (University of Siena)
Jennifer Davoren (University of Melbourne)
Sebastian Engell (University of Dortmund)
Mark Greenstreet (University of British Columbia)
Bruce Krogh (Carnegie Mellon University)
Benjamin Kuipers (University of Texas at Austin)
Kim Larsen (University of Aalborg)
John Lygeros (University of Cambridge)
Oded Maler (Co-chair) (Verimag, Grenoble)
Manfred Morari (ETH, Zurich)
George Pappas (University of Pennsylvania)
Amir Pnueli (Co-chair) (Weizmann Institute, Rehovot)
Anders Rantzer (University of Lund)
Alberto Sangiovanni-Vincentelli (University of California at Berkeley)
Shankar Sastry (University of California at Berkeley)
Olaf Stursberg (Carnegie Mellon University, University of Dortmund)
Ashish Tiwari (SRI International)
Paolo Traverso (IRST, Trento)
Howard Wong-Toi (Cadence Berkeley Labs)

Additional Referees

Andrea Balluchi	Gregor Goessler	Anders Ravn
Calin Belta	Pascal Grieder	Manuel Remelhe
Marco Benedetti	Vineet Gupta	Marco Roveri
Luca Benvenuti	Tom Henzinger	Shawn Schaffert
Piergiorgio Bertoli	Jianghai Hu	Henrik Schiøler
Francesco Borrelli	Franjo Ivančić	Roberto Sebastiani
Patricia Bouyer	Saso Jezernik	Miguel Silva
Marco Bozzano	T. John Koo	Slobodan Simic
Linda Brodo	Salvatore La Torre	Maria Sorea
Paul Caspi	Yassine Lakhnech	Paulo Tabuada
Amedeo Cesta	Jean-Pierre Lepeltier	Herbert Tanner
Alessandro Cimatti	Ian Mitchell	Fabio Torrisi
Thao Dang	John Moondanos	Stavros Tripakis
Cătălin Dima	Peter Niebert	Rene Vidal
Michael Drew	Simone Paoletti	Adolfo Villafiorita
Gianni Ferrari-Trecate	Jonathan Paxman	Rafael Wisniewskj
Goran Frehse	Luigi Palopoli	Sergio Yovine
Yan Gao	Claudio Pinello	Shannon Zelinski
Nicolò Giorgetti	Marco Pistore	Jun Zhang
Antoine Girard	S. Ramamoorthy	

Table of Contents

Abstracts of Invited Presentations

Regular Contributions

The Mathematics of Matter and the Mathematics of Mind
(Invited Talk)

David Berlinski

david@berlinski.com

Abstract. It has been the rich body of continuous mathematics that has made possible the development of physical theories. In Newtonian mechanics, the theory of the electromagnetic field, general relativity and quantum electrodynamics, things are continuous. Were it not for the fact that things must be measured – no small consideration, of course – each theory could be formulated in a way that dispenses with numbers entirely. The rewards of continuity have been considerable. Quantum electrodynamics, is accurate to more than ten decimal places, and general relativity, under certain circumstances, accurate to more than thirteen. On the other hand, our reflections about mathematics have for more than sixty years been expressed in an entirely different language. In proof theory, model theory, recursion theory, and automata theory, things are discrete. Were it not for the fact that limits must occasionally be investigated – no small consideration, of course – each theory could be formulated in a way that dispenses with continuous functions entirely. What holds for meta-mathematics holds in a more general way for psychology. Our most sophisticated linguistic theory suggests that every human language is the expression of a unique computational system, one that is entirely discrete. What holds for linguistics is often claimed to hold for molecular biology as well; indeed, the analogies between linguistic and cellular computational systems have seemed as suggestive as they are elusive. The division of ordinary experience between material and mental objects thus finds itself mirrored in the division between continuous and discrete mathematics. In this talk, I should like to investigate the basis for the distinction, asking first whether the distinction may be expressed in terms of certain invariants, and second whether the distinction is itself an artifact, one resulting from the peculiar circumstances in which various sciences have been undertaken. I shall discuss minimalism in linguistics, the Smale-Shub theory of calculability, the use of K-theory in the evaluation of D-branes, and Stephen Wolfram's recent work in cellular automata.

O. Maler and A. Pnueli (Eds.): HSCC 2003, LNCS 2623, p. 1, 2003.
© Springer-Verlag Berlin Heidelberg 2003

A Grand Challenge: Full Reactive Modeling of a Multi-cellular Animal

(Invited Talk)

David Harel

Dept. of Computer Science and Applied Mathematics
Weizmann Institute of Science
Rehovot 76100, Israel
dharel@weizmann.ac.il

Abstract. Biological systems exhibit the characteristics of reactive systems remarkably, and on many levels; from the molecular, via the cellular, and all the way up to organs, full organisms, and even entire populations. Thus, a different brand of bioinformatics arises, in which, rather than "we" solving "their" computational problems, we use "our" languages, methods and tools to model and analyze "their" complex systems. This talk proposes a grand challenge for computer scientist and biologists: to model a full multi-cellular animal as a reactive system. We would like to construct a full, true-to-all-known-facts 4-dimensional model, that would be animated, flexible and comprehensive, and would enable full and realistic simulation of the animal's development and behavior over time (the fourth dimension). It should help uncover gaps in our knowledge, correct errors, suggest new experiments and help predict unobserved phenomena. We actually have a particular organism in mind, the C. elegans nematode worm, a suggestion that is in line with the extraordinarily insightful proposal of Sydney Brenner, co-recipient of the 2002 Nobel Prize, who chose this organism 30 years ago to challenge biologists with the task of discovering the entire development and neurobiology of a living creature. The talk will argue the (long-term) feasibility of the challenge, by describing two pieces of preliminary modeling work: (i) T-cell behavior in the thymus, using statecharts with Rhapsody, linked with Flash animation, and (ii) parts of the vulval development of C. elegans, using LSCs with the Play-Engine.

O. Maler and A. Pnueli (Eds.): HSCC 2003, LNCS 2623, p. 2, 2003.

Developing Home Robotics Products: Challenges and Lessons Learned

(Invited Talk)

Udi Peless

Friendly Robotics
1 Hayassur Street, POB 3777
Hasharon Industrial Park
Kadima 60920, Israel
udi.peless@friendlyrobotics.co.il

Abstract. Developing practical and commercially successful home robotics applications has proven to be a bigger challenge than it may seem, both technologically and commercially. During the last seven years we have gone through several product development and introduction cycles on several different platforms, including robotic lawn mowers and vacuum cleaners. In this talk I will portray our experience so far, and highlight the main lessons learned.

O. Maler and A. Pnueli (Eds.): HSCC 2003, LNCS 2623, p. 3, 2003.
© Springer-Verlag Berlin Heidelberg 2003

Progress on Reachability Analysis of Hybrid Systems Using Predicate Abstraction*

Rajeev Alur[1], Thao Dang[2], and Franjo Ivančić[1]

[1] University of Pennsylvania
[2] VERIMAG

Abstract. Predicate abstraction has emerged to be a powerful technique for extracting finite-state models from infinite-state systems, and has been recently shown to enhance the effectiveness of the reachability computation techniques for hybrid systems. Given a hybrid system with linear dynamics and a set of linear predicates, the verifier performs an on-the-fly search of the finite discrete quotient whose states correspond to the truth assignments to the input predicates. To compute the transitions out of an abstract state, the tool needs to compute the set of discrete and continuous successors, and find out all the abstract states that this set intersects with. The complexity of this computation grows exponentially with the number of abstraction predicates. In this paper we present various optimizations that are aimed at speeding up the search in the abstract state-space, and demonstrate their benefits via case studies. We also discuss the completeness of the predicate abstraction technique for proving safety of hybrid systems.

1 Introduction

Automated verification of hybrid systems offers the promise of revealing subtle errors in high-level models of embedded controllers [1,6,9,14,17,19]. Verification tools compute symbolic representations of the set of reachable states of a model. Dealing with continuous dynamics is a major computational challenge. Contemporary tools for verification of hybrid systems, such as CHECKMATE [9] and d/dt [6], approximate the set of reachable states by polyhedra. Recently, we have shown that effectiveness of these techniques can be enhanced using predicate abstraction [4], a powerful technique for extracting finite-state models from complex, potentially infinite state, discrete systems (see, for instance, [8,11,16]). This paper presents various optimizations to the abstraction and search strategy, discusses completeness of the technique, and presents experimental results.

The input to our verification tool consists of the concrete system modeled by a hybrid automaton, the safety property to be verified, and a finite set of predicates over system variables to be used for abstraction. We require that all

* This research is also presented in [3] and was supported in part by ARO URI award DAAD19-01-1-0473, DARPA Mobies award F33615-00-C-1707, NSF award ITR/SY 0121431, and European IST project CC (Computation and Control).

O. Maler and A. Pnueli (Eds.): HSCC 2003, LNCS 2623, pp. 4–19, 2003.

invariants, switching guards, and discrete updates of the hybrid automaton are specified by linear expressions, the continuous dynamics is linear, possibly with bounded input, and the property as well as the abstraction predicates are linear. An abstract state is a valid combination of truth values to the predicates corresponding to a polyhedral set of the concrete state-space. The verifier performs an on-the-fly search of the abstract system by symbolic manipulation of polyhedra, where the computation of continuous successors of abstract states uses strategies inspired by the techniques used in CHECKMATE and d/dt. There are two significant benefits of postulating the verification problem as a search problem in the abstract system compared to the traditional approach of computing approximations of reachable sets of hybrid systems. First, the continuous reachability computation is applied only to an abstract state, instead of intermediate sets of arbitrary complexity generated during fixpoint computation. Second, while tools such as d/dt are designed to compute a "good" approximation of the continuous successors, we are interested only in checking if this set intersects with a new abstract state, permitting many optimizations. If the initial choice of predicates is too coarse, the search finds abstract counter-examples that are infeasible in the original hybrid system. We have also shown how to analyze such counter-examples to discover new predicates that will rule out related spurious counter-examples [5]. This strategy of iterative refinements of abstractions guided by counter-examples has also been incorporated in our verification tool, which is an integrated component of the modeling and analysis toolkit CHARON [2].

After reviewing the previous work in Section 2, we present a variety of optimizations of the abstraction and search strategy in Section 3. If the original hybrid system has m locations and we are using k predicates for abstraction, the abstract state-space has at most $m \cdot 2^k$ states. To compute the abstract successors of an abstract state A, we need to compute the discrete and the continuous successor-set of A, and check if this set intersects with any of the abstract states. This can be expensive as the number of abstraction predicates grows, and our heuristics are aimed at speeding up the search in the abstract space. The first optimization implements a search constraint based on the additivity of flows of hybrid systems. A second optimization uses the BSP (Binary space partition) technique to impose a tree structure on abstract states so that invalid states (that is, inconsistent combinations of truth values to linear predicates) can be detected easily. A third optimization implements a guided search strategy. Since initial abstraction is typically coarse, the abstract search is likely to reach the target (i.e. unsafe states). During depth-first search, after computing the abstract successors of the current state, we choose to examine the abstract state whose distance to the target is the smallest according to an easily computable metric. We have experimented with a variety of natural metrics that are based on the shortest path in the discrete location graph of the hybrid system as well as the Euclidean distance between the polyhedra corresponding to abstract states and the target. Such a search improves the efficiency significantly in the initial iterations. Another optimization allows a location-specific choice of predicates for abstraction. Instead of having a global pool of abstraction predicates, each location is tagged with a relevant set of predicates, thereby reducing the size of the abstract state-space. The final optimization uses qualitative analysis of vector fields to rule out reachability of certain abstract states from a given abstract state *a priori* before applying the continuous reachability computation.

In Section 4, we address the completeness of our abstraction-based verification strategy for hybrid systems. Given a hybrid system H with linear dynamics, an initial set X_0, and a target set of unsafe states B, the verification problem is to determine if there is an execution of H starting in X_0 and ending in B. If there is such an execution, then even simulation can potentially demonstrate this fact. On the other hand, if the system is safe (i.e., B is unreachable), a symbolic algorithm that computes the set of reachable states from X_0 by iteratively computing the set of states reachable in one discrete or continuous step, cannot be guaranteed to terminate after a bounded number of iterations. Consequently, for completeness, we are interested in errors introduced by, first, approximating reachable sets in one continuous step using polyhedra, and second, due to predicate abstraction. We show that if the original system stays at least δ distance away from the target set for any execution involving at most n discrete switches and up to total time τ, then there is a choice of predicates such that the search in the abstract-space proves that the target set is not reached up to those limits. This shows that predicate abstraction can be used at least to prove bounded safety, that is, safety for all executions with a given bound on total time and a bound on the number of discrete switches.

In Section 5, we present case studies and experimental results. Our first example concerns a parametric version of Fischer's timing-based protocol for mutual exclusion. This model has 4 continuous variables, 23 locations, and we use 7 predicates for abstraction. We show that during initial iterations, guided search works quite well, and improves the time and space requirements. On the other hand, for establishing safety, location-specific choice of abstraction predicates reduces the number of reachable abstract states from 54 to 24. Our second example is an adaptive cruise controller that maintains a safe distance between cars based on communicated acceleration. The model has 5 continuous variables, 8 locations, and we use 17 predicates for abstraction. It can be completely analyzed using our verifier. We are also applying the tool to a design of an electronic throttle controller from DARPA's MoBIES project. The model has 9 continuous variables and 18 locations. Using all the 29 predicates mentioned in the model for the purpose of abstraction, our tool finds counter-examples. Since the model is incomplete, rigorous analysis of this example was not yet possible, but its size is a good indicator of the complexity that our tool can handle.

2   Predicate Abstraction for Hybrid Systems

In this section, we briefly recap the definitions of predicate abstraction for hybrid systems and the search strategy in the abstract state-space as outlined in [4].

2.1 Mathematical Model

We denote the set of all n-dimensional linear expressions $l : \mathbb{R}^n \to \mathbb{R}$ with Σ_n and the set of all n-dimensional linear predicates $\pi : \mathbb{R}^n \to \mathbb{B}$, where $\mathbb{B} := \{0, 1\}$, with $\mathcal{L}_n$. A linear predicate is of the form $\pi(x) := \sum_{i=1}^{n} a_i x_i + a_{n+1} \sim 0$, where $\sim \in \{\geq, >\}$ and $\forall i \in \{1, \dots, n+1\} : a_i \in \mathbb{R}$. Additionally, we denote the set of finite sets of n-dimensional linear predicates by $\mathcal{C}_n$, where an element of $\mathcal{C}_n$ represents the conjunction of its elements.

Definition 1 (Linear Hybrid System). *An n-dimensional* **linear hybrid system** *is a tuple $H = (\mathcal{X}, L, X_0, I, f, T)$ with the following components:*

- $\mathcal{X} \subset \mathbb{R}^n$ *is a convex polyhedron representing the* **continuous state-space.**
- L *is a finite set of* **locations.** *The* **state-space** *of H is $X = L \times \mathcal{X}$. Each state thus has the form (l, x), where $l \in L$ is the discrete part of the state, and $x \in \mathcal{X}$ is the continuous part.*
- $X_0 \subseteq X$ *is the set of* **initial states.** *We assume that for all locations $l \in L$, the set $\{x \in \mathcal{X} \mid (l, x) \in X_0\}$ is a convex polyhedron.*
- $I : L \to \mathcal{C}_n$ *assigns to each location $l \in L$ a finite set of linear predicates $I(l)$ defining the* **invariant** *conditions that constrain the value of the continuous part of the state while the discrete location is l. The hybrid automaton can only stay in location l as long as the continuous part of the state x satisfies $I(l)$, i.e. $\forall \pi \in I(l) : \pi(x) = 1$. We write $\mathcal{I}_l$ for the invariant set of location l, that is the set of all points x satisfying all predicates in $I(l)$.*
- $f : L \to (\mathbb{R}^n \to \mathbb{R}^n)$ *assigns to each location $l \in L$ a* **continuous vector field** *$f(l)$ on x. While at location l the evolution of the continuous variable is governed by the differential equation $\dot{x} = f(l)(x)$. We restrict our attention to hybrid automata with linear continuous dynamics, that is, for every location $l \in L$, the vector field $f(l)$ is linear, i.e. $f(l)(x) = A_l x$ where A_l is an $n \times n$ matrix. The reachability analysis can also be applied to hybrid systems having linear continuous dynamics with uncertain, bounded input of the form: $\dot{x} = A_l x + B_l u$.*
- $T \subseteq L \times L \times \mathcal{C}_n \times (\Sigma_n)^n$ *is a relation capturing discrete transition jumps between two discrete locations. A transition $(l, l', g, r) \in T$ consists of an initial location l, a destination location l', a set of* **guard** *constraints g and a linear* **reset** *mapping r. From a state (l, x) where all predicates in g are satisfied the hybrid automaton can jump to location l' at which the continuous variable x is reset to a new value $r(x)$. We write $\mathcal{G}_t \subseteq \mathcal{I}_l$ for the guard set of a transition $t = (l, l', g, r) \in T$ which is the set of points satisfying all linear predicates of g and the invariant of the location l.*

2.2 Transition System Semantics

We define the semantics of a linear hybrid system by formalizing its underlying transition system. The underlying transition system of H is $T_H = \{X, \to, X_0\}$. The state-space of the transition system is the state-space of H, i.e. $X = L \times \mathcal{X}$. The transition relation $\to \subseteq X \times X$ between states of the transition system is defined as the union of two relations $\rightarrow_C, \rightarrow_D \subseteq X \times X$. The relation $\rightarrow_C$ describes transitions due to continuous flows, whereas $\rightarrow_D$ describes transitions due to discrete jumps.

$$(l, x) \rightarrow_C (l, y) \quad \text{iff} \quad \exists t \in \mathbb{R}_{\geq 0} : \Phi_l(x, t) = y \wedge \forall t' \in [0, t] : \Phi_l(x, t') \in \mathcal{I}_l.$$
$$(l, x) \rightarrow_D (l', y) \quad \text{iff} \quad \exists (l, l', g, r) \in T : x \in \mathcal{G}_t \wedge y = r(x) \wedge y \in \mathcal{I}_{l'}.$$

2.3 Discrete Abstraction

We define a discrete abstraction of the hybrid system $H = (\mathcal{X}, L, X_0, I, f, T)$ with respect to a given k-dimensional vector of n-dimensional linear predicates $\Pi = (\pi_1, \pi_2, \ldots, \pi_k) \in (\mathcal{L}_n)^k$. We can partition the continuous state-space $\mathcal{X} \subseteq \mathbb{R}^n$ into at most 2^k states, corresponding to the 2^k possible boolean evaluations of Π; hence, the infinite state-space X of H is reduced to $|L|2^k$ states in the abstract system. From now on, we refer to the hybrid system H as the *concrete system* and its state-space X as the *concrete state-space*.

Definition 2 (Abstract state-space). *Given an n-dimensional hybrid system $H = (\mathcal{X}, L, X_0, f, I, T)$ and a k-dimensional vector $\Pi \in (\mathcal{L}_n)^k$ of n-dimensional linear predicates, an* **abstract state** *is a tuple (l, b), where $l \in L$ and $b \in \mathbb{B}^k$. The abstract state-space is $Q_\Pi := L \times \mathbb{B}^k$. The* **concretization function** $C_\Pi :$ $\mathbb{B}^k \rightarrow 2^{\mathcal{X}}$ *for a vector of linear predicates $\Pi = (\pi_1, \ldots, \pi_k) \in (\mathcal{L}_n)^k$ is defined as $C_\Pi(b) := \{x \in \mathcal{X} \mid \forall i \in \{1, \ldots, k\} : \pi_i(x) = b_i\}$. If $C_\Pi(b) = \emptyset$, then the vector $b \in \mathbb{B}^k$ is infeasible with respect to Π.*

Definition 3 (Discrete Abstraction). *Given a hybrid system $H = (\mathcal{X}, L, X_0, f, I, T)$, its abstract system with respect to a vector of linear predicates Π is the transition system $H_\Pi = (Q_\Pi, \overset{\Pi}{\rightarrow}, Q_0)$ where*

- *the abstract transition relation $\overset{\Pi}{\rightarrow} \subseteq Q_\Pi \times Q_\Pi$ is defined as the union of the following two relations $\overset{\Pi}{\rightarrow}_D, \overset{\Pi}{\rightarrow}_C \subseteq Q_\Pi \times Q_\Pi$. The relation $\overset{\Pi}{\rightarrow}_D$ represents transitions in the abstract state-space due to discrete jumps, whereas $\overset{\Pi}{\rightarrow}_C$ represents transitions due to continuous flows:*

$$(l, b) \overset{\Pi}{\rightarrow}_D (l', b') \quad \text{iff} \quad \exists (l, l', g, r) \in T, x \in C_\Pi(b) \cap \mathcal{G}_t :$$
$$(l, x) \rightarrow_D (l', r(x)) \wedge r(x) \in C_\Pi(b');$$

$$(l, b) \overset{\Pi}{\rightarrow}_C (l, b') \quad \text{iff} \quad \exists x \in C_\Pi(b), t \in \mathbb{R}_{\geq 0} : \Phi_l(x, t) \in C_\Pi(b') \wedge$$
$$\forall t' \in [0, t] : \Phi_l(x, t') \in \mathcal{I}_l;$$

- *the set of initial states is $Q_0 = \{(l, b) \in Q_\Pi \mid \exists x \in C_\Pi(b) : (l, x) \in X_0\}$.*

A **trace** *in the abstract state-space is a sequence of abstract states $a_0, a_1, \ldots, a_n$, such that $a_0 \in Q_0$, and $a_i \overset{\Pi}{\rightarrow} a_{i+1}$ for $0 \leq i < n$.*

2.4   Searching the Abstract State-Space

Given a hybrid system H we want to verify safety properties. We define a property by specifying a set of *unsafe locations* $U \subseteq L$ and a convex set $\mathcal{B} \subseteq \mathcal{X}$ of *unsafe continuous states*. The property is said to hold for the hybrid system H iff there is no valid trace from an initial state to some state in $\mathcal{B}$ while in an unsafe location. We implemented an on-the-fly DFS search of the abstract state-space. In case we find an abstract state that violates the property, the current trace stored on a stack represents a counter-example. If the abstract system satisfies the property, then so does the concrete system. However, if a violation is found in the abstract system, then the resulting counter-example may or may not correspond to a counter-example in the concrete state-space.

Computing discrete successors is relatively straightforward, and involves computing weakest preconditions, and checking non-emptiness of intersection of polyhedral sets. For computing continuous successors of an abstract state A, we compute the polyhedral slices of states reachable at fixed times $r, 2r, 3r, \ldots$ for a suitably chosen r, and then, take convex-hull of all these polyhedra to over-approximate the set of all states reachable from A. The search strategy as outlined in [4] gives a priority to computing discrete successors rather than continuous successors, as the computation of discrete successors is generally much faster. During the computation of continuous successors we abort or interrupt the computation when a new abstract state is found. Not running the fixpoint computation of continuous successors to completion may result in a substantial speed-up when discovering a counter-example, if one exists. If the search of the abstract state-space finds that the abstract system is safe, then the concrete system is also safe. However, if the search finds a counter-example in the abstract state-space, then this counter-example may or may not correspond to a counter-example in the concrete state-space.

2.5   Counter-Example Analysis

If the predicate abstraction routine returns a counter-example, then this counter-example may not correspond to a counter-example in the concrete hybrid system. Such a counter-example is called *spurious*. We can analyze a counter-example and check whether it corresponds to a concrete one. If we find that the counter-example is indeed spurious, we can compute a set of new predicates based on this counter-example that ensures that a *refined* counter-example is not possible in the refined abstract state-space. Refinement of abstract states is based on the inclusion of the continuous concretizations, and refinement of paths additionally on following the same transitions. For more details about the analysis of counter-examples we refer the reader to [5].

3   Optimizations

If the original hybrid system has m locations and we are using k predicates for abstraction, the abstract state-space has $m \cdot 2^k$ abstract states. To compute the abstract successors of an abstract state A, we need to compute its discrete and continuous successors, and check if this set intersects with the other abstract states. This can be expensive as the number of abstraction predicates grows. We present optimizations in this section that are aimed at speeding up the discovery of counter-examples in the abstract state-space given a reachability property.

We include an optimization technique in the search strategy. Consider a counter-example in the concrete hybrid system. There exists an equivalent counter-example that has the additional constraint that there are no two consecutive transitions due to continuous flow. This is due to the additivity of flows of hybrid systems, namely: $(l, x) \to_C (l, x') \wedge (l, x') \to_C (l, x'') \Rightarrow (l, x) \to_C (l, x'')$. We are hence searching only for counter-examples in the abstract system that do not have two consecutive transitions due to continuous flow. By enforcing this additional constraint we eliminate some spurious counter-examples that could have been found otherwise in the abstract transition system.

Another optimization concerns the construction of the abstract state-space. Since the predicates decompose the continuous state-space into polyhedral regions, instead of computing a polyhedron for each abstract state independently, we can use the Binary Space Partition (BSP) technique to incrementally construct the abstract state-space. The polyhedra resulting from partitioning the continuous state-space by one predicate after another are stored in a BSP tree as follows. First, the root of the tree is associated with the whole set $\mathcal{X}$. A predicate π_i is chosen from Π to partition $\mathcal{X}$ into 2 convex polyhedral subsets and create two child nodes: a left node is used to store the intersection of $\mathcal{X}$ with the half-space $\mathcal{H}(\pi_i)$ (which contains all points in $\mathcal{X}$ satisfying π_i) and a right node to store the intersection with the half-space $\overline{\mathcal{H}(\pi_i)}$. Then the non-empty polyhedra are partitioned recursively at the new nodes. Once all the predicates in Π have been considered, the non-empty polyhedra at the leaves of the tree correspond to the closure of the concretizations of all possible consistent abstract states. This construction is illustrated by figure 1 where the continuous state-space $\mathcal{X}$ is a rectangle in two dimensions and the vector of initial predicates $\Pi = (\pi_1, \pi_2, \pi_3)$. The predicate π_1 partitions $\mathcal{X}$ into 2 polygons P_1 and $P_{\bar{1}}$. Next, splitting P_1 and $P_{\bar{1}}$ by the predicate π_2 gives P_{12}, $P_{1\bar{2}}$ and $P_{\bar{1}2}$, $P_{\bar{1}\bar{2}}$. Then, only the interior of the polygon $P_{\bar{1}\bar{2}}$ intersects with the hyperplane of the predicate π_3 while all other polygons in the current decomposition lie entirely inside $\overline{\mathcal{H}(\pi_3)}$; therefore, only $P_{\bar{1}\bar{2}}$ is split. This BSP tree provides simultaneously a geometric representation of the state-space and a search structure. Note that the amount of splitting depends on the order of predicates and the abstract states. This order is determined by the search strategy, more precisely, the tree is built on-the-fly, based on the decision which abstract state to explore next. This BSP construction allows fast detection of combinations of predicates that give inconsistent abstract states and thus saves a significant amount of polyhedral computations.

3.1   Guided Search

The predicate abstraction implementation performs an on-the-fly depth-first search. Since an abstract state has many successors, the performance of the

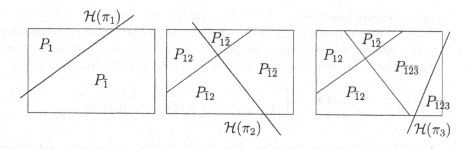

Fig. 1. BSP-based construction of the abstract state-space

search depends on which successor is examined next to continue the search at every step. We present three guided search strategies that we have recently implemented in our tool. In each case, we define a priority function $\rho : Q_\Pi \to \mathbb{R}$ that tells us how "close" each abstract state is to the set of unsafe states. As we are trying to minimize the time it takes to discover a counter-example, we prefer states that are "closer" to the set of unsafe states.

Given a hybrid system $H = (\mathcal{X}, L, X_0, I, f, T)$, we can define a graph $G_H = (V, E)$ such that $V = L$ and $(l, l') \in E$ iff $\exists (l, l', g, r) \in T$. Given the set of unsafe locations $U \subseteq L$, we define a priority function $\rho_D : L \to \mathbb{N}$ on locations as:

$$\rho_D(l) = \begin{cases} 0 & : \quad l \in U, \\ \text{shortest path length from } l \text{ to } U \text{ in } G_H & : \quad l \notin U \land \text{path exists}, \\ \infty & : \quad \text{otherwise}. \end{cases}$$

It is clear that $\forall l \in L : \rho_D(l) \neq \infty \Rightarrow 0 \leq \rho_D(l) \leq |L| - 1$. We use ρ_D in all three guided search strategies that we introduce in the following.

Mask Priority. The mask priority guided search strategy is based on the boolean vector representation of the continuous part of an abstract state. We define a mask $m \in \mathbb{T}^k$ that represents a compact description of the continuous part of all abstract states that intersect with the set of unsafe continuous states $\mathcal{B}$. Given a predicate π, $\mathcal{H}(\pi)$ denotes the half-space defined by π and $\overline{\mathcal{H}(\pi)}$ denotes the complement of $\mathcal{H}(\pi)$. Then we define $m = (m_1, \ldots, m_k)$ as:

$$m_i = \begin{cases} 1 & : \quad \mathcal{B} \subseteq \mathcal{H}(\pi_i), \\ 0 & : \quad \mathcal{B} \subseteq \overline{\mathcal{H}(\pi_i)}, \\ * & : \quad \text{otherwise}. \end{cases}$$

We then define a comparator function $\delta : \mathbb{B} \times \mathbb{T} \to \mathbb{B}$ as

$$\delta(b, t) = \begin{cases} 1 & : \quad t = 1 \land b = 0 \lor t = 0 \land b = 1, \\ 0 & : \quad \text{otherwise}, \end{cases}$$

and a priority function $\rho_1 : \mathbb{B}^k \to \mathbb{N}$ as Clearly, $\forall b \in \mathbb{B}^k : 0 \le \rho_1(b) \le k$. The value $\rho_1(b)$ represents the number of positions in the vector representation b that contradict the corresponding position in the mask m. To combine ρ_1 with ρ_D to form a priority function $\rho_M : Q_\Pi \to \mathbb{N}$ over abstract states we define

$$\rho_M(l, b) = \begin{cases} \infty & : \quad \rho_D(l) = \infty, \\ (k+1)\rho_D(l) + \rho_1(b) & : \quad \text{otherwise.} \end{cases}$$

Euclidean Distance Priority. The Euclidean distance priority guided search strategy differs from the mask priority one because it does not rely on the boolean vector representation enforced by the chosen predicates for the abstraction. Instead, it measures the Euclidean distance from the continuous part of the abstract state to the set of unsafe states. To do so, we define the distance between two non-empty convex polyhedral sets $P \subseteq \mathcal{X}$ and $Q \subseteq \mathcal{X}$ as follows: $d(P, Q) = \inf\{d(p-q) \mid p \in P \wedge q \in Q\}$ where $d(\cdot)$ denotes the Euclidean distance. Then the priority function $\rho_2 : \mathbb{B}^k \to \mathbb{R}$ can be computed as $\rho_2(b) = d(C_\Pi(b), \mathcal{B})$. As $\mathcal{X}$ is bounded, we can compute the limit for any two non-empty convex subsets of $\mathcal{X}$, and we denote that value with $d_\mathcal{X}$. We can then combine ρ_2 with ρ_D to form the priority function $\rho_E : Q_\Pi \to \mathbb{R}$ by defining:

$$\rho_E(l, b) = \begin{cases} \infty & : \quad \rho_D(l) = \infty, \\ (d_\mathcal{X} + 1)\rho_D(l) + \rho_2(b) & : \quad \text{otherwise.} \end{cases}$$

Reset Distance Priority. The Euclidean distance priority does not consider the effects of resets of the continuous variable x enforced by switches in the concrete system. The reset distance priority guided search strategy favors abstract states in any location which are close to the set of unsafe states in an unsafe location after appropriate resets are taken into consideration. Appropriate resets are those that lead the current abstract state to an unsafe location. We define the reset distance priority function $\rho_R : Q_\Pi \to \mathbb{R}$ by $\rho_R(l, b) = \rho_3(l, C_\Pi(b))$ and $\rho_3 : L \times 2^\mathcal{X} \to \mathbb{R}$ by

$$\rho_3(l, X) = \begin{cases} d(X, \mathcal{B}) & : \quad \rho_D(l) = 0, \\ \min\limits_{\substack{(l,l',g,r)\in T \\ \rho_D(l')=\rho_D(l)-1}} \rho_3(l', r(X)) & : \quad \text{otherwise.} \end{cases}$$

The reset distance represents the smallest Euclidean distance of the current abstract state to the unsafe set in a shortest path to an unsafe location, if no more transitions due to continuous flow occur.

3.2   Generalized Predicate Abstraction

We present a formal framework of abstractions of predicate abstraction –generalized predicate abstraction, which allows clustering of abstract states. For illustrative purposes, we use a location-specific predicate abstractor: The main idea of the location-specific predicate abstraction routine is the fact that certain predicates are only important in certain locations. Consider for example guards and invariants. A specific predicate representing an invariant may be important in one location of the hybrid automaton, but may not be relevant in the other locations. Considering this predicate only in the location it is really needed, may reduce the number of reachable abstract states considerably. This is similar to optimizations in predicate-abstraction based tools for model checking of C programs, such as Cartesian predicate abstraction [7]. We define a tri-valued domain $\mathbb{T} := \{0, 1, *\}$, and a function $c : \mathbb{T}^k \to 2^{\mathbb{B}^k}$ as $c(t) = \{b \in \mathbb{B}^k | t_i \neq * \Rightarrow b_i = t_i\}$.

Definition 4. *The generalized predicate abstract state-space is defined as $\hat{Q}_\Pi := L \times \mathbb{T}^k$, such that $(l, t) \to_G (l', t')$ iff $\exists b \in c(t), b' \in c(t') : (l, b) \overset{\Pi}{\to} (l', b')$. The set of initial abstract states is $\hat{Q}_0 := \{(l, t) \in \hat{Q}_\Pi | \exists b \in c(t) : (l, b) \in Q_0\}$.*

The above definition allows a concrete state $(l, x) \in \mathcal{X}$, as well as an abstract state $(l, b) \in Q_\Pi$, to be represented by many states in $\hat{Q}_\Pi$. Hence, we restrict our attention to a subset of $\hat{Q}_\Pi$ that is both a partition and a cover of $\mathbb{B}^k$.

Definition 5. *A subset of abstract states $Q \subseteq \hat{Q}_\Pi$ is called **location-specific**, iff $\forall l \in L, b \in \mathbb{B}^k \exists t \in \mathbb{T}^k : b \in c(t) \wedge (l, t) \in Q$, and $\forall (l, t_1), (l, t_2) \in Q : t_1 \neq t_2 \Rightarrow c(t_1) \cap c(t_2) = \emptyset$. The set of transitions for a location-specific Q is the restriction of $\to_G$ to Q. The set of initial states is the restriction of $\hat{Q}_0$ to Q.*

The search in the generalized abstract state-space needs only slight modifications. The computation of the continuous successor-set of a generalized abstract state does not need any alteration, as transitions due to continuous flow do not change the location of the states and, therefore, the set of predicates remains the same. On the other hand, we need to modify the computation of the discrete successor-set. The weakest precondition computation for a particular discrete switch needs to accommodate for the fact that the set of predicates in the locations before and after the switch are not necessarily the same anymore. The following theorem stating the soundness of this approach is based on the soundness of the predicate abstraction algorithm [4].

Theorem 1. *If the generalized predicate abstraction routine terminates and reports that the system is safe, then the corresponding concrete system is also safe.*

3.3 Vector Field Analysis

In order to construct the discrete abstraction of a hybrid system, we need to compute the continuous successors of an abstract state, and check if this set intersects with the other abstract states. In this section we present a method, based on a qualitative analysis of the vector fields, that avoids the test for feasibility of some transitions. This allows to obtain a first rough over-approximation of the transition relation which is then refined using reachability computations. Similar ideas of qualitative analysis of vector fields have been used in [18].

Geometrically speaking, the concretizations $C_\Pi(b)$ for all $b \in \mathbb{B}^k$ form a convex decomposition of the concrete state-space $\mathcal{X}$. Hence, for any two non-empty abstract states (l, b) and (l, b'), the closures of their concretizations $cl(C_\Pi(b))$ and $cl(C_\Pi(b'))$ are either disjoint or have only one common facet. We now focus on the latter case and denote by F the common facet. We assume that F is a $(n-1)$-dimensional polyhedron. Let n_F be the normal of F which points from $C_\Pi(b')$ to $C_\Pi(b)$. If for all points on the face F the projection of f_l on n_F is non-negative, that is,

$$\forall x \in F \ \langle f_l(x), n_F \rangle \geq 0, \tag{1}$$

then there exists a trajectory by continuous dynamics f_l from $C_\Pi(b')$ to $C_\Pi(b)$. Moreover, any trajectory from $C_\Pi(b)$ to $C_\Pi(b')$ by f_l, if one exists, must cross another polyhedron $C_\Pi(b'')$. In the context of predicate abstraction, this means that the transition from (l, b) to (l, b') is feasible. Furthermore, we need not consider the transition by f_l from (l, b) to (l, b') because this transition, if possible, can be deduced from the transitions via some other intermediate states. Note that when the dynamics f_l is affine, in order for the condition (1) to hold, it suffices that $\langle f_l(x), n_F \rangle$ is non-negative at all the vertices of F.

On the other hand, if the dynamics f_l is stable, we can use the standard Lyapunov technique for linear dynamics to rule out some abstract states that cannot be reached from (l, b) as follows. Let P be the solution of the Lyapunov equation of the dynamics f_l and $\mathcal{E}$ be the smallest ellipsoid of the form $\mathcal{E} = \{x \mid x^T P x \leq \alpha\}$ that contains the polyhedron $C_\Pi(b)$. We know that $\mathcal{E}$ is invariant in the sense that all trajectories from points inside $\mathcal{E}$ remain in $\mathcal{E}$. Consequently, all the abstract states (l, b') such that $C_\Pi(b') \cap \mathcal{E} = \emptyset$ cannot be reached from (l, b) by continuous dynamics f_l.

4   Bounded Completeness

Given a hybrid system H with linear dynamics, an initial set X_0, and a target set $\mathcal{B} \subseteq X$, the verification problem is to determine if there is an execution of H starting in X_0 and ending in $\mathcal{B}$. If there is such an execution, then even simulation can potentially demonstrate this fact. On the other hand, if the system is safe (i.e., $\mathcal{B}$ is unreachable), a *complete* verification strategy should be able to demonstrate this. However, a symbolic algorithm that computes the set of reachable states from X_0 by iteratively computing the set of states reachable in one discrete or continuous step, cannot be guaranteed to terminate after a bounded number of iterations. Consequently, for completeness, we focus on errors introduced by approximating reachable sets in one continuous step using polyhedra, as well as due to predicate abstraction. We show that predicate abstraction is complete for establishing bounded safety; that is, unreachability of unsafe states for a specified number of discrete switches and time duration.

4.1   Completeness for Continuous Systems

We can present a completeness result if we focus on purely continuous systems first. We use two additional assumptions for this result. We only consider systems that exhibit a separation of the reachable state-space and the unsafe states. In addition we use the knowledge of the optimization of the search strategy which prohibits multiple successive continuous successors.

We assume a purely continuous system such that we can specify the initial convex region $\mathcal{X}_0 := \{x \in \mathcal{X} | (l_0, x) \in X_0\}$ and the set of unsafe states $\mathcal{B}$ respectively using the conjunction of a finite set of predicates. In addition, assume a separation of the set $\mathtt{Post}(\mathcal{X}_0)$ of continuous states reachable from $\mathcal{X}_0$, and $\mathcal{B}_{\mathcal{X}}$, the projection of $\mathcal{B}$ onto $\mathcal{X}$, that is $d(\mathtt{Post}(\mathcal{X}_0), \mathcal{B}_{\mathcal{X}}) \geq \epsilon$. Following [12], we know that we can find a small enough time-step that ensures that the over-approximation error due to the computation of convex hulls will not result in an overlap of the over-approximation of $\mathtt{Post}(\mathcal{X}_0)$ with $\mathcal{B}_{\mathcal{X}}$. Additionally, we assume that the set of predicates used for predicate abstraction entails all the predicates corresponding to the linear constraints needed to specify the polyhedral sets $\mathcal{X}_0$ and $\mathcal{B}_{\mathcal{X}}$. Given the optimization of our search strategy it is clear that any abstract refinement of $\mathcal{B}$ will not be declared reachable by the search.

4.2 (n, τ, δ)-Safety

We can prove that our predicate abstraction model checker is complete to establish safety up to a fixed number of discrete switches and time duration. Note that the recent research on *bounded model checking* [10] can be viewed as establishing safety of discrete systems up to a fixed number of transitions. We first define this notion of bounded safety for hybrid systems formally. For this purpose, we define a distance function $d : X \times X \to \mathbb{R}_{\geq 0}$ on X as

$$ d((l, x), (l', x')) = \begin{cases} d(x, x') & : \quad l = l', \\ \infty & : \quad \text{else}; \end{cases} $$

and generalize over sets of states by $d(S, S') = \min_{(l,x) \in S, (l', x') \in S'} d((l, x), (l', x'))$.

Definition 6. *A hybrid system* $H = (\mathcal{X}, L, X_0, I, f, T)$ *is called* (n, τ, δ)-**safe** *for the unsafe set* $\mathcal{B}$, *iff the set of states* $R_{(n, \tau)}(X_0)$ *that is reachable using at most n discrete switches and combined flow of at most τ time-units from the initial states X_0 has a distance of at least δ to the set of unsafe states* $\mathcal{B}$: $d(R_{(n, \tau)}(X_0), \mathcal{B}) > \delta$.

The proof, which is omitted here for the sake of brevity, shows that if the original system stays at least δ distance away from the target set for the first n discrete switches and up to total time τ, then there is a choice of predicates such that the search in the abstract space proves that the target set is not reached up to those limits. This shows that predicate abstraction can be used at least to prove bounded safety, that is, safety for all execution with a given bound on total time and a bound on discrete switches.

Theorem 2 (Bounded Completeness). *The predicate abstract model checker is complete for the class of* (n, τ, δ)-safe hybrid systems.

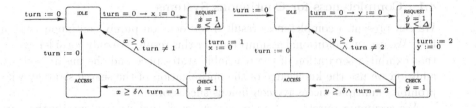

Fig. 2. The two processes for the mutual exclusion example

5   Implementation and Experimentation

The optimizations discussed in this paper have been incorporated in our verification tool. The current prototype implementation of the predicate abstraction model checking tool is implemented in C++ using library functions of the hybrid systems reachability tool d/dt [6]. We implemented a translation procedure from CHARON [2] source code to the predicate abstraction input language which is based on the d/dt input language. A detailed overview of a verification case study starting from CHARON source code is given in [15]. Our tool uses the polyhedral libraries CDD and QHull. It also includes a counter-example analysis and predicate discovery tool as described in more detail in [5].

5.1   Fischer's Mutual Exclusion

We first look at an example of mutual exclusion which uses time-based synchronization in a multi-process system. We want to implement a protocol that allows a shared resource to be used exclusively by at most one of two processes at any given time. The state machines for the two processes are shown in Figure 2. The possible execution traces depend on the two positive parameters Δ and δ. If the parameters are such that $\Delta \geq \delta$ is true, we can find a counter-example that proves the two processes may access the shared resource at the same time. On the other hand, if $\delta > \Delta$, then the system preserves mutual exclusive use of the shared resource. We present a flattened version of the two-process protocol in Table 1. We use the flat model in the following sections to illustrate the mask priority guided search strategy and the generalized predicate abstraction.

Mask Priority. We consider Fischer's two-process protocol example for the case that $\Delta \geq \delta$. As the set of unsafe states corresponds to any continuous state in location 22 (see Table 1), we have $\rho_M(l, b) = \rho_D(l)$. Starting in the abstract state "$l = 0, 0 \leq x < \delta \leq \Delta, 0 \leq y < \delta$" with priority 6, the guided search tries to find a path that leads to a state with priority 0 by reducing the priority as much as possible at each step. In this example, this means that the search tries to reduce the priority of the next abstract state by exactly one at each step. In the case that this is not possible, a continuous transition is considered as this

Table 1. The two-process Fischer's protocol as a flat model: The locations l are numbered from 0 to 22. P_1 specifies the local location of the first process: I represents the Idle location, R the Request location, C the Check location, and A the Access location. P_2 specifies the location of the second process, whereas turn specifies the value of the turn variable in the composed system. Location 0 is the initial location. Location 22 violates the mutual exclusion property regardless of the value of the turn variable.

l	0	1	2	3	4	5	6	7	8	9	10	11	12	13	14	15	16	17	18	19	20	21	22
P_1	I	R	C	A	I	R	C	A	I	R	C	A	C	I	R	C	I	C	C	A	C	R	A
P_2	I	I	I	I	R	R	R	R	C	C	C	C	C	A	A	A	C	I	A	C	R	C	A
turn	0	0	1	1	0	0	1	1	2	2	2	2	1	2	2	2	0	0	1	1	0	0	—
$\rho_D(l)$	6	5	8	7	5	4	3	2	8	3	9	1	9	7	2	8	7	7	1	8	6	6	0

does not affect the priority. It can easily be seen that a valid counter-example can be constructed just by following this decrease of ρ_D. This is in contrast to our previous search algorithm, which always prefers discrete transitions over continuous ones. This leads the search away from a shortest path to a counterexample. Even in this small example, the previous search finds more than 10 other abstract states first.

Generalized Predicate Abstraction. We also consider the verification of Fischer's protocol to illustrate the advantage of the location-specific predicate abstraction routine. The verification using the regular predicate abstraction technique finds 54 reachable abstract states (see [4]), whereas, if we use the location-specific predicates as described in Table 2, we only reach 24 abstract states.

Table 2. Location-specific predicates for the 2-process Fischer's protocol example. The predicates $0 \leq \Delta, 0 \leq \delta, 0 \leq x, 0 \leq y, \Delta < \delta$ are supposed to be present in all locations.

l	Π	l	Π	l	Π
0	—	8	$y \geq \delta$	16	$y \geq \delta$
1	$x \leq \Delta$	9	$x \leq \Delta, y \geq \delta, x \geq y$	17	$x \geq \delta$
2	$x \geq \delta$	10	$x \geq \delta, y \geq \delta, x \geq y$	18	$x \geq \delta$
3	—	11	$y \geq \delta$	19	$y \geq \delta$
4	$y \leq \Delta$	12	$x \geq \delta, y \geq \delta, x \leq y$	20	$x \geq \delta, y \leq \Delta$
5	$x \leq \Delta, y \leq \Delta$	13	—	21	$x \leq \Delta, y \geq \delta$
6	$x \geq \delta, y \leq \Delta, x \leq y$	14	$x \leq \Delta$	22	—
7	$y \leq \Delta$	15	$x \geq \delta$		

5.2   Coordinated Adaptive Cruise Control

We have also successfully applied our predicate abstraction technique to verify a model of the *Coordinated Adaptive Cruise Control* mode of a vehicle-to-vehicle coordination system. This case study is provided by the PATH project. Let us first briefly describe the model (see [13] for a detailed description). The goal of this mode is to maintain the car at some desired speed v_d while avoiding collision with a car in front. Let x and v denote the position and velocity of the car. Let x_l, v_l and a_l denote respectively the position, velocity and acceleration of the car in front. Since we want to prove that no collision happens regardless of the behavior of the car in front, this car is treated as disturbance, more precisely, the derivative of its acceleration is modeled as uncertain input ranging in the interval $[da_{lmin}, da_{lmax}]$. The dynamics of the system is described by the following differential equations: $\dot{x} = v$, $\dot{v} = u$, $\dot{x}_l = v_l$, $\dot{v}_l = a_l$, $\dot{a}_l \in [da_{lmin}, da_{lmax}]$, where u is the input that controls the acceleration of the car. In this mode, the controller consists of several modes. The control law to maintain the desired speed is as follows:

$$
u_1 = \begin{cases} 0.4\varepsilon_v & : \quad a_{cmin} \leq 0.4\varepsilon_v \leq a_{cmax}, \\ a_{cmin} & : \quad 0.4\varepsilon_v < a_{cmin}, \\ a_{cmax} & : \quad 0.4\varepsilon_v > a_{cmax}, \end{cases}
$$

where $\varepsilon_v = v - v_d$ is the error between the actual and the desired speed; a_{cmin} and a_{cmax} are the maximal comfort deceleration and acceleration.

In addition, in order for the car to follow its preceding car safely, another control law is designed as follows. A safety distance between cars is defined as $D = \max\{G_c v_l, D_d\}$ where G_c is the time gap parameter; D_d is the desired sensor range given by $D_d = 0.5 v_l^2 (-1/a_{min} + 1/a_{lmin}) + 0.02 v_l$; a_{min} and a_{lmin} are the maximal decelerations of the cars. Then, the control law allowing to maintain the safety distance with the car in front is given by $u_{follow} = a_l + (v_l - v) + 0.25 (x_l - x - 5 - D)$. Since the acceleration of the car is limited by its maximal breaking capacity, the control law to avoid collision is indeed $u_2 = \max\{a_{min}, u_{follow}\}$. The combined switching control law is given by $u = \min\{u_1, u_2\}$. This means that the controller uses the control law u_1 to maintain the desired speed if the car in front is far and travels fast enough, otherwise it will switch to u_2.

The closed-loop system is modeled as a hybrid automaton with 5 continuous variables (x, v, x_l, v_l, a_l) and 8 locations corresponding to the above described switching control law. The invariants of the locations and the transition guards are specified by the operation regions and switching conditions of the controller together with the bounds on the speed and acceleration. In order to prove that the controller can guarantee that no collision between the cars can happen, we specify an unsafe set as $x_l - x \leq 0$. To define initial predicates, in addition to the constraints of the invariants and guards, we use the predicate of the unsafe set allowing to distinguish safe and unsafe states and another predicate on the difference between the speed and acceleration of the cars. The total number of the initial predicates used to construct the discrete abstraction is 17. For an initial set specified as $x_l - x \geq 100 \wedge v \geq 5$, the tool found 55 reachable abstract states and reported that the system is safe. For this model, in a preprocessing step using the Binary Space Partition technique, the tool found that the chosen set of initial predicates partitions the continuous state space into 785 polyhedral regions, and this enables to reduce significantly the computation time.

References

1. R. Alur, C. Courcoubetis, N. Halbwachs, T.A. Henzinger, P. Ho, X. Nicollin, A. Olivero, J. Sifakis, and S. Yovine. The algorithmic analysis of hybrid systems. *Theoretical Computer Science*, 138:3–34, 1995.
2. R. Alur, T. Dang, J. Esposito, Y. Hur, F. Ivančić, V. Kumar, I. Lee, P. Mishra, G. Pappas, and O. Sokolsky. Hierarchical modeling and analysis of embedded systems. *Proceedings of the IEEE*, 91(1), January 2003.
3. R. Alur, T. Dang, and F. Ivančić. Reachability analysis of hybrid systems using counter-example guided predicate abstraction. Technical Report MS-CIS-02-34, University of Pennsylvania, November 2002.
4. R. Alur, T. Dang, and F. Ivančić. Reachability analysis of hybrid systems via predicate abstraction. In *Hybrid Systems: Computation and Control, Fifth International Workshop*, LNCS 2289, pages 35–48, March 2002.
5. R. Alur, T. Dang, and F. Ivančić. Counter-example guided predicate abstraction of hybrid systems. In *Ninth International Conference on Tools and Algorithms for the Construction and Analysis of Systems*, April 2003.
6. E. Asarin, O. Bournez, T. Dang, and O. Maler. Approximate reachability analysis of piecewise-linear dynamical systems. In *Hybrid Systems: Computation and Control, Third International Workshop*, LNCS 1790. Springer, 2000.
7. T. Ball, A. Podelski, and S. Rajamani. Boolean and Cartesian abstraction for model checking C programs. In *Tools and Algorithms for the Construction and Analysis of Systems*, LNCS 2031. Springer, 2001.
8. T. Ball and S. Rajamani. Bebop: A symbolic model checker for boolean programs. In *SPIN 2000 Workshop on Model Checking of Software*, LNCS 1885. 2000.
9. A. Chutinan and B.K. Krogh. Verification of polyhedral-invariant hybrid automata using polygonal flow pipe approximations. In *Hybrid Systems: Computation and Control, Second International Workshop*, LNCS 1569. Springer, 1999.
10. E.M. Clarke, A. Biere, R. Raimi, and Y. Zhu. Bounded model checking using satisfiability solving. *Formal Methods in Systems Design*, 19(1):7–34, 2001.
11. P. Cousot and R. Cousot. Abstract interpretation: a unified lattice model for static analysis of programs by construction or approximation of fixpoints. In *Proc. of the 4th ACM Symposium on Principles of Programming Languages*, 1977.
12. T. Dang. *Verification and Synthesis of Hybrid Systems*. PhD thesis, Institut National Polytecnique de Grenoble, 2000.
13. A.R. Girard. *Hybrid System Architectures for Coordinated Vehicle Control*. PhD thesis, University of California at Berkeley, 2002.
14. T.A. Henzinger, P. Ho, and H. Wong-Toi. HYTECH: the next generation. In *Proceedings of the 16th IEEE Real-Time Systems Symposium*, pages 56–65, 1995.
15. F. Ivančić. Report on verification of the MoBIES vehicle-vehicle automotive OEP problem. Technical Report MS-CIS-02-02, University of Pennsylvania, March 2002.
16. C. Loiseaux, S. Graf, J. Sifakis, A. Bouajjani, and S. Bensalem. Property preserving abstractions for the verification of concurrent systems. *Formal Methods in System Design Volume 6, Issue 1*, 1995.
17. I. Mitchell and C. Tomlin. Level set methods for computation in hybrid systems. In *Hybrid Systems: Computation and Control*, LNCS 1790. Springer, 2000.
18. O. Stursberg, S. Kowalewski, and S. Engell. Generating timed discrete models of continuous systems. In *Proc. 2nd IMACS Symposium on Mathematical Modeling*, pages 203–209, 1997.
19. A. Tiwari and G. Khanna. Series of abstractions for hybrid automata. In *Hybrid Systems: Computation and Control, Fifth Intern. Workshop*, LNCS 2289, 2002.

Reachability Analysis of Nonlinear Systems Using Conservative Approximation[*]

Eugene Asarin[1], Thao Dang[1], and Antoine Girard[2]

[1] VERIMAG
2 avenue de Vignate, 38610 Gières, France
[2] LMC-IMAG
51 rue des Mathématiques, 38041 Grenoble, France
{Eugene.Asarin,Thao.Dang,Antoine.Girard}@imag.fr

Abstract. In this paper we present an approach to approximate reachability computation for nonlinear continuous systems. Rather than studying a complex nonlinear system $\dot{x} = g(x)$, we study an approximating system $\dot{x} = f(x)$ which is easier to handle. The class of approximating systems we consider in this paper is piecewise linear, obtained by interpolating g over a mesh. In order to be conservative, we add a bounded input in the approximating system to account for the interpolation error. We thus develop a reachability method for systems with input, based on the relation between such systems and the corresponding autonomous systems in terms of reachable sets. This method is then extended to the approximate piecewise linear systems arising in our construction. The final result is a reachability algorithm for nonlinear continuous systems which allows to compute conservative approximations with as great degree of accuracy as desired, and more importantly, it has good convergence rate. If g is a C^2 function, our method is of order 2. Furthermore, the method can be straightforwardly extended to hybrid systems.

1 Introduction

Reachability computation is required by a variety of safety verification, analysis, and design problems for hybrid systems. The importance of the problem has motivated much research on reachability analysis of such systems (see [5, 14]). For a class of hybrid systems with piecewise constant derivatives, methods and tools for (exact) computation of reachable sets are well-developed [26,20, 16]. For systems involving non-trivial continuous dynamics (described by differential equations), exact reachability computation is difficult, and even for linear differential equations it is feasible only for certain classes of matrices, depending on eigenstructure [19,2]. Alternatively, several approximate methods have been developed, and some of them can be used for nonlinear continuous systems, such as [13,8,7,22]. Basically, these methods numerically approximate reachable sets using a variety of set representations (such as polyhedra, level sets). A common

---

[*] Research supported by European IST project "CC - Computation and Control" and CNRS project MathStic "Squash - Analyse Qualitative des Systèmes Hybrides".

O. Maler and A. Pnueli (Eds.): HSCC 2003, LNCS 2623, pp. 20–35, 2003.
© Springer-Verlag Berlin Heidelberg 2003

point of these methods is that they work directly with the nonlinear differential equations, more precisely, they track the evolution of the reachable sets according to the flows of the nonlinear equations. In this work, we take an approach which differs from these methods in this aspect. The main idea of the approach is as follows.

Rather than studying a complex nonlinear system $\dot{x} = g(x)$, we study an *approximating system* $\dot{x} = f(x)$ which is easier to handle. The class of approximating systems we consider in this paper is *piecewise linear*, obtained by interpolating the function g over a mesh built on the state space of the system. Moreover, in order to be conservative, we add an input u to account for the error inherent in approximating g with f, and the result is a system with (bounded) input $\dot{x} = f(x) + u$. This construction gives rise to the question of how to deal with the input in the approximating system efficiently. We thus consider the relation between a system with input and the corresponding autonomous system in terms of reachable sets, and this study leads us to an abstract reachability algorithm for systems with input, which can then be extended to deal with the approximate interpolating systems. The final result is a reachability method for nonlinear systems which allows to compute conservative approximations with as great degree of accuracy as desired, and more importantly, it has good convergence rate. As we shall see later, if g is a C^2 function our method is of order 2. Furthermore, the method can be straightforwardly extended to hybrid systems and readily integrated in a verification tool.

The 'hybridization' approach has previously been explored in [25,17,24] where the approximating systems are systems with piecewise constant slopes or rectangular inclusions. The idea of defining piecewise linear approximation based on interpolation has been used for numerical integration of nonlinear differential equations [9,11]; in this paper, we exploit this idea for reachability computation purposes. In [13], linear approximation is also used in each integration step to obtain better approximations of the reachable sets in 2 dimensions. On the other hand, our reachability method for systems with uncertain input has some similar flavor with the method of approximation of viability kernels of differential inclusions in [23]. Recently, in [15], a control problem for a class of piecewise linear systems, similar to our approximating systems, is solved in terms of reachability conditions.

The paper is organized as follows. Section 2 is devoted to definitions and notations. In Section 3 we consider the reachability problem for (general) continuous systems with input. In Section 4 we present a method to approximate reachable sets of nonlinear systems by means of piecewise linear approximation. The theoretical result of Section 3 is the basis for the proof of the convergence of the method. Section 5 contains some examples illustrating our approach.

2   Basic Definitions

We consider a nonlinear system

$$\dot{x}(t) = g(x(t)), \ x \in \mathcal{X} \subset \mathbb{R}^n. \tag{1}$$

As mentioned in the introduction, we approximate the system (1) with another system (which is easier to solve):

$$\dot{x}(t) = f(x(t)), \ x \in \mathcal{X} \subset \mathbb{R}^n. \tag{2}$$

Let μ be the bound of $||f - g||$, i.e. $||f(x) - g(x)|| \le \mu$ for all $x \in \mathcal{X}$ where $|| \cdot ||$ is some norm on $\mathbb{R}^n$. We assume that the function f is L-Lipschitz. In order to be able to capture all the behaviors of the original system (1), we introduce in the system (2) an input to account for the approximation error.

$$\begin{cases} \dot{x}(t) = s(x(t), u(t)) = f(x(t)) + u(t), \\ u(\cdot) \in \mathcal{U}_\mu \end{cases} \tag{3}$$

where $\mathcal{U}_\mu$ is the set of admissible inputs which consists of piecewise continuous functions u of the form $u : \mathbb{R}^+ \to \mathbb{R}^n$ such that $||u(\cdot)|| \le \mu$. It is not hard to see that the system (3) is an overapproximation of the original system (1) in the sense that all trajectories of (1) are contained in the set of trajectories of (3).

Given an initial point $x \in \mathcal{X}$, let $\Phi_f(t, x)$ be the trajectory starting from x of the system (2) and let $\Phi_s(t, x, u(\cdot))$ be the trajectory starting from x of the system (3) under input $u(\cdot) \in \mathcal{U}_\mu$. For a set of initial points $X_0 \subset \mathcal{X}$ and $T > 0$, the reachable sets of the autonomous system (2) during the interval $[0, T]$ is defined as: $K_f(T, X_0) = \{ y = \Phi_f(t, x) \mid t \in [0, T], x \in X_0 \}$. Similarly, the reachable set of the system (3) from X_0 during the interval $[0, T]$ is defined as: $K_s(T, X_0) = \{ y = \Phi_s(t, x, u(\cdot)) \mid t \in [0, T], x \in X_0, u(\cdot) \in \mathcal{U}_\mu \}$.

3   Reachability Analysis for Systems with Input

As mentioned earlier, with a view to deal with the input in the approximating system, we first consider the problem of deriving the reachable set of a system with input from the reachable set of the corresponding autonomous system. More concretely, our goal is to compute the reacheable set $K_s(T, X_0)$ of the system with input (3), assuming that we are able to compute the image of a set $X \subset \mathcal{X}$ by the flow Φ_f of the autonomous system (2) for a given time $t \ge 0$, denoted by $\Phi_f(t, X)$.

We first describe an abstract algorithm to do so and then discuss the properties of the algorithm concerning conservativeness and convergence of the approximation. It is important to emphasize that these theoretical results are key to the validation of the reachability method for nonlinear systems, developed in the next section.

The idea to solve this problem relies on the following result, which is a consequence of the Fundamental Inequality theorem from the theory of dynamical systems (see Appendix).

Lemma 1. *For all $t \ge 0$ and for all $u(\cdot) \in \mathcal{U}_\mu$,*

$$||\Phi_f(t, x) - \Phi_s(t, x, u(\cdot))|| \le \frac{\mu}{2}(e^{Lt} - 1).$$

Hence, to approximate the reachable set of the system with input, we can appropriately expand the reachable set of the autonomous system by the amount given on the right hand side of the inequality of Lemma 1. We thus define an 'expanding' operation as follows: for a set $S \subset \mathbb{R}^n$ and a real number $\epsilon \geq 0$, the expanded set is $\mathcal{N}(S, \epsilon) = S \oplus \epsilon B$ where B is the unit ball at the origin, and $\oplus$ is the Minkowski sum. Our reachability computation procedure is summarized in Algorithm 1.

Input: Initial set X_0, **Result:** Approximation of $K_s(T, X_0)$
$N = \frac{T}{r}$; $\epsilon = \frac{\mu}{L}(e^{Lr} - 1)$ /* r is the time step */
/* –Initialization */
$P_1 = K_f(r, X_0)$
$Q_1 = \mathcal{N}(P_1, \epsilon)$
$R_1 = Q_1$
/* –Main loop */
for $i \leftarrow 1$ to $N - 1$ do
$\quad$ $P_{i+1} = \Phi_f(r, Q_i)$
$\quad$ $Q_{i+1} = \mathcal{N}(P_{i+1}, \epsilon)$
$\quad$ $R_{i+1} = R_i \cup Q_{i+1}$
end
return R_N

Algorithm 1: Approximating the reachable set of the system with input

In Algorithm 1, r is the time step and the set Q_i represents an overapproximation of the reachable set during time interval $[(i-1)r, ir]$ of the system with input (3). The algorithm consists of the following two phases. The goal of the first phase is to initialize Q_1. This is done by computing P_1, which is indeed the reachable set of the autonomous system (2) for the first time interval $[0, r]$, and then expanding P_1 by the amount ϵ (which is the bound from Lemma 1). In the main loop, each iteration i takes Q_i as input and computes Q_{i+1} as follows. The set P_{i+1} is first computed as the image of Q_i by the flow Φ_f of the autonomous system, and Q_{i+1} is then obtained by expanding P_{i+1} by ϵ. The result R_N is simply the union of all Q_i.

Properties of the Approximation

We now present two properties concerning the conservativeness and convergence of the approximation produced by Algorithm 1.

Theorem 1. *Let R_N be the set computed by Algorithm 1. Then,*

- P1. (Conservative approximation) $K_s(T, X_0) \subseteq R_N$.
- P2. (Convergence of the approximation) $d_H(K_s(T, X_0), R_N) \leq 2\mu r e^{LT}$, *where d_H is the Hausdorff distance.*

As we can see from the theorem, the approximate set produced by Algorithm 1 is guaranteed to be an overapproximation of the exact reachable set. Moreover, it converges to the exact set with regard to the Hausdorff distance. The proof of the theorem can be found in Appendix.

4 Reachability Computation for Nonlinear Systems Using Piecewise Linear Approximation

In this section, we focus on the main problem of the paper, which is the computation of reachable sets for nonlinear continuous systems. Following the 'hybridization' idea, our method consists of two steps. We first approximate the (complex) nonlinear system by a piecewise (simple) linear system. A bound on the approximation error is estimated and then added to the piecewise linear system as uncertain input, which guarantees that the resulting system is indeed an overapproximation of the original system. The second step involves extending Algorithm 1, which is designed for continuous systems with input, to piecewise linear systems. We first describe the two steps of the method and then discuss the convergence results.

4.1 Construction of Approximating Systems

We consider the nonlinear system

$$\dot{x}(t) = g(x(t)), \ x \in \mathcal{X} \subset \mathbb{R}^n \qquad (4)$$

We assume that g is Lipschitz and the state space $\mathcal{X}$ is a bounded convex polyhedron in $\mathbb{R}^n$. To define an approximating system, we decompose the state space into polyhedral regions and then associate with each region a linear system using interpolation. The procedure of decomposition of the state space is called mesh generation. In the sequel, we will define these concepts formally.

Piecewise Linear Approximations Using Interpolation

Definition 1 (Mesh). *A mesh* $\mathcal{M}$ *of the set* $\mathcal{X}$ *is a finite set of full-dimensional convex polyhedra in* $\mathbb{R}^n$, *called* cells, *satisfying the following conditions: (1) The union of all cells* $\bigcup_k C_k = \mathcal{X}$, *and (2) If* C_j *and* C_k *are cells with non-empty intersection, then their intersection lies within the boundaries of both; we say that* C_j *and* C_k *are adjacent and we denote their intersection by* $\partial(C_j, C_k)$.

For a cell $C_k \in \mathcal{M}$, we denote by $V(C_k)$ the set of its vertices and by ∂C_k the boundary of C_k. The size of C_k is $h(C_k) = \max\{ \|x - y\| \mid x, y \in C_k \}$. Then, the *size* (or granularity) of $\mathcal{M}$ is defined as $h(\mathcal{M}) = \max\{ h(C_k) \mid C_k \in \mathcal{M} \}$. Two types of meshes are of practical interest: rectangular and simplicial. A mesh is called *rectangular* if its cells are all boxes in $\mathbb{R}^n$. If all the cells are simplices, then we say that $\mathcal{M}$ is a *simplicial mesh* or a *triangulation* of $\mathcal{X}$. We recall that a simplex in $\mathbb{R}^n$ is the convex hull of $(n+1)$ affinely independent points in $\mathbb{R}^n$, and $h(C_k)$ is simply the maximum edge length.

Given a mesh $\mathcal{M}$ of $\mathcal{X}$, we can derive a piecewise linear approximation of the function g, using interpolation over the mesh. We restrict our attention to simplicial meshes and the motivation will become clear in subsequent development. A discussion on mesh construction is deferred to the end of this section.

Definition 2 (Piecewise linear approximation). *For each cell $C_k \in \mathcal{M}$, let $l_k : \mathbb{R}^n \to \mathbb{R}^n$ be an affine map of the form $l_k(x) = A_k x + b_k$ which interpolates g on the vertices of C_k, that is, $g(v) = l_k(v)$ for all $v \in V(C_k)$. Then, the piecewise linear approximation of g is defined as: $l(x) = l_k(x)$ if $x \in C_k$.*

The advantage of using simplicial meshes lies in the fact that the linear interpolant l_k can be defined uniquely since each cell C_k has $(n+1)$ vertices and, moreover, for any two adjacent cells C_k and C_j, we have $\forall x \in \partial(C_k, C_j)$ $l_k(x) = l_j(x)$. This important property allows us to obtain the following approximating system:

$$\dot{x}(t) = l(x(t))$$

which is continuous and Lipschitz. This not only guarantees the existence and uniqueness of solutions, but also allows to derive a priori bound on the error of approximation, as we will show in the following. This bound will then be used to define a conservative approximating system.

Estimating interpolation error. The error in the approximation of g by the abovedescribed linear interpolation is defined by the bound η of $\|g(x) - l(x)\|$ for $x \in \mathcal{X}$. We will estimate this bound for two cases: g is Lipschitz and g is a C^2 function. For brevity, we denote by h the size of the underlying mesh $\mathcal{M}$.

Lemma 2. *If g is Lipschitz, then*

$$\eta \leq h \frac{2nL}{n+1}$$

where L is the Lipschitz constant of the function g.

We remark is that the second partial derivatives of the linear approximation vanish; therefore, if g is a C^2 function, we can obtain a better error bound.

Lemma 3. *If g is a C^2 function with a second derivative bound K, then*

$$\eta \leq h^2 \frac{n^2 K}{2(n+1)^2}.$$

As we can see from the above lemmas, the bound η is of order $O(h)$ if g is Lipschitz, and it is of order $O(h^2)$ if g is a C^2 function with bounded second derivative. The proofs of these results are presented in Appendix.

Defining conservative approximating systems. We can now use the bound η from the above lemmas to define an overapproximation of the nonlinear system (4), which has the form of the system with bounded input studied in Section 3:

$$\begin{cases} \dot{x}(t) = s(x(t), u(t)) = l(x(t)) + u(t), \\ u(\cdot) \in \mathcal{U}_\eta \end{cases} \tag{5}$$

Before continuing, we mention that it is straightforward to extend this method to a nonlinear systems with input of the form $\dot{x}(t) = g(x(t)) + u(t)$ where $u(\cdot) \in \mathcal{U}_\mu$ by defining an overapproximation of this system as: $\dot{x}(t) = l(x(t)) + u_1(t)$ where $u_1(\cdot) \in \mathcal{U}_\nu$ with $\nu = \eta + \mu$.

Using Lemma 1, we can show that the solution the approximate system (5) converges to the solution of the original system (4) and, moreover, the convergence is of the same order as the convergence of the interpolating function l to g. Indeed, for all $t \geq 0$ and for all $u(\cdot) \in \mathcal{U}_\eta$, we have

$$\|\Phi_g(t, x) - \Phi_s(t, x, u(\cdot))\| \leq \frac{\eta}{2}(e^{Lt} - 1) \tag{6}$$

where $\Phi_g(t, x)$ and $\Phi_s(t, x, u(\cdot))$ are respectively the flows of the system (4) and of the system (5) under input $u(\cdot) \in \mathcal{U}_\eta$.

4.2   Reachability Algorithm for Piecewise Linear Systems

This section is concerned with the problem of computing reachable sets of the piecewise linear systems resulting from the above approximation. Naturally, such systems can be thought of as a special class of hybrid automata [1], for which existing reachability tools (such as [7,6,4]) can be used. In this work, we exploit the particular structure of these approximating systems in order to achieve better efficiency. Our reachability algorithm is an extension of Algorithm 1 for continuous systems with bounded input, and the convergence result is preserved.

When the system stays inside a cell, to compute the reachable sets we can combine Algorithm 1 with one of the available methods (e.g. [7,6,19,4]) for the linear autonomous system. The remaining problem is to handle the changes in the dynamics that happen when the system moves from one cell to another.

Without loss of generality, we assume that initial set X_0 is a convex polyhedron inside the cell C, and let ∂C be the boundary of C. We thus focus on the problem of computing the *set of exit points*, that is, the set of points on ∂C which the system, starting from X_0, can reach to enter an adjacent cell. At these points the system changes the dynamics, and therefore it is important to detect this boundary crossing event.

Given a point $x_0 \in C$, let $t^*(x_0)$ be the smallest time at which the system, starting at x_0, reaches the boundary ∂C. More precisely,

$$t^*(x_0) = \min\{ t \geq 0 \mid \exists u(\cdot) \in \mathcal{U}_\eta \ \Phi_s(x_0, t, u(\cdot)) \in \partial C \}$$

We can generalize the above definition to set X_0 of initial points as follows: $t^*(X_0) = \min\{ t^*(x) \mid x \in X_0 \}$. A method to underapproximate $t^*(x)$ is proposed in [12]. We first extend this method to linear systems with uncertain, bounded input [3]. Moreover, in order to envision the event of boundary crossing we can estimate $t^*(X_0)$ by considering only the trajectories from the vertices of X_0. If no trajectories from X_0 can leave C, we denote this by $t^*(X_0) = +\infty$. Details on these extensions can be found in [3]. On the other hand, in two dimensions considering only the trajectories from the vertices is sufficient to determine the set of exit points on the common boundary of two adjacent cells since it is indeed an interval. In higher dimensions, we need to combine the estimation of t^* with reachability computation, as shown in Algorithm 2.

Input: Initial set X_0 inside cell C
Result: E = Set of exit points on ∂C, R = Reachable set in cell C
$t_{min} = t^*(X_0)$
if $t_{min} = +\infty$ **then**
  $\quad E = \emptyset; \quad R = K_s(T, X_0)$
  $\quad$ **return** E, R
end
$R_0 = K_s(t_{min}, X_0); \quad E = \emptyset; \quad i = 0$
repeat
  $\quad R_{i+1} = K_s(r, R_i) \cap C$
  $\quad E = E \cup (R_{i+1} \cap \partial C)$
  $\quad i = i + 1$
until $R_i = R_{i-1}$;
return $E, R = R_i$

Algorithm 2: Reachability computation for a cell

The algorithm first checks whether the system will always remain inside C, indicated by $t_{min} = +\infty$. If it is not the case, the switching from the dynamics of C to the dynamics of an adjacent cell can happen only at time $t \geq t_{min}$. Therefore, the reachable set on the time interval $[0, t_{min})$ is computed as for a system without switching. The advantage of estimating t^* is that during the interval $[0, t_{min})$ we do not need to check the intersection with the boundary. After time t_{min}, in each step we compute the intersection of the reachable set with the boundary of the current cell until no new reachable states inside C is found. Once the computation for the cell C terminates, to propagate the reachable set inside a new cell C', we use Algorithm 2 starting from the intersection of the exit points E with C'.

Convergence result. In order to show that our method is convergent, again we consider the approximation error in terms of the Hausdorff distance.

Let $K_g(T, X_0)$ be the reachable set of the nonlinear system (4) (which we want to compute), and let $\hat{K}_s(T, X_0)$ be the set computed by using Algorithm 2 for the piecewise linear system (5), as shown above.

Theorem 2.

$$d_H(K_g(T, X_0), \hat{K}_s(T, X_0)) \leq \eta(\frac{e^{LT} - 1}{L} + 2\, r\, e^{LT}).$$

The sketch of proof is as follows. The distance between the (exact) reachable sets of (4) and (5) is the bound given in (6). In addition, for the piecewise linear system we can prove that the distance between the approximate set $\hat{K}_s(T, X_0)$ and the exact set $K_s(T, X_0)$ is indeed the error of Algorithm 1, given by Theorem 1. Then, using the triangle inequality we obtain the inequality of Theorem 2.

As we have seen earlier, if g is a C^2 function with a second derivative bound, η is of order $0(h^2)$ where h is the size of the underlying mesh $\mathcal{M}$. Therefore by choosing appropriate time step r (depending on h), we can guarantee a *quadratic* error bound.

It is worth to mention that the continuity of the approximating systems is key to the convergence results. There are different choices for approximating functions allowing to achieve better convergence. Bilinear interpolation over quadrilaterals may offer a higher order approximation on a well-designed mesh. Another possibility is to use higher degree approximants (such as piecewise quadratic). This, however, requires the ability to deal with more complex autonomous systems.

Simplicial mesh construction. We finish this section by a brief discussion on implementation issues. We have shown earlier a bound on the interpolation error which depends on the mesh size. However, it should be noted that the orientation and shape of the mesh may yield an order of magnitude significant improvement in approximation accuracy. The problem of finding an optimal mesh can be formulated as to minimize the interpolation error. However, the optimal meshes may have complex geometric structures which are expensive in storage and computation costs. In this work, we use a simple triangulation which offers important advantages regarding the operations required by our reachability algorithm.

We construct a simplicial mesh by triangulating an underlying rectangular grid. Indeed, a n-dimensional rectangle can be dissected into $n!$ simplices as follows. It can be assumed that the rectangle is a cube $[0, 1]^n$. We consider a permutation $\pi = (i^1, i^2, \ldots, i^n)$ of $(1, 2, \ldots, n)$ and let S_π be the simplex defined by $0 \leq x_{i^1} \leq x_{i^2} \ldots \leq x_{i^n} \leq 1$. It is not hard to see that such $n!$ simplices S_π form a triangulation of the cube. More elaborated schemes allow to obtain a smaller number of simplices [21]. However, the advantage of this method is that it allows a compact representation of the resulting mesh and thus efficient manipulation. Indeed, we need just to store the coordinates of the grid, and all adjacency information (necessary to propagate the reachable set from one cell to another) can be encoded based on the permutations. In addition, an adaptive mesh can be generated on-the-fly during the progress of the reachability computation by considering the derivative variation locally.

5   Experimentation

Our reachability method was implemented and is being integrated in the tool d/dt in order to analyze hybrid systems. We have experimented the method on various examples. We now present some examples for illustrative purposes.

The Vanderpol equation. The first example is the Vanderpol equation, given below. Here, we are interested in detecting limit cycles of the system.

$$\begin{cases} \dot{x}(t) = y(t) \\ \dot{y}(t) = y(t)(1 - x^2(t)) - x(t). \end{cases}$$

We approximate the system by a piecewise linear interpolating system using a uniform triangular mesh of size $h = 0.05$. We add an input to the latter whichs account for the interpolation error. For a time step $r = 0.05$ and the initial set $X_0 = \{(x,y)|(x-2)^2 + (y-2)^2 \le 0.25\}$, the reachable set is shown in Figure 1. We can see that the final reachable set (plotted on the right) contains the limit cycle.

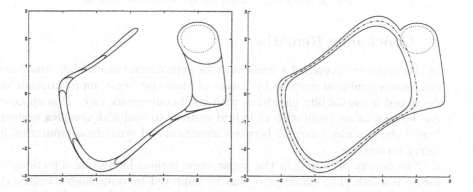

Fig. 1. Left: successive computations of the reachable set. Right: the final reachable set containing the limit cycle.

Zermelo's problem. To illustrate the behavior of our algorithm on a nonlinear system with bounded input, we consider a classical problem of optimal control (Zermelo's problem). The dynamics of the system is as follows:

$$\begin{cases} \dot{x}(t) = y(t) - y^2(t) + u_x(t) \\ \dot{y}(t) = u_y(t) \\ \sqrt{u_x(t)^2 + u_y(t)^2} \le 0.1 \end{cases} \tag{7}$$

We perform the reachability computation with a time step $r = 0.01$ and the result can be seen in Figure 2.

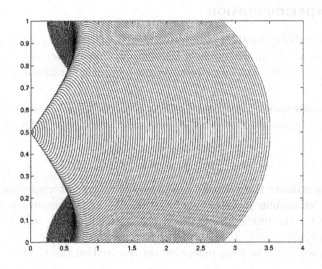

Fig. 2. Successive computations of the reachable set

6   Concluding Remarks

In this paper, we proposed a framework for approximate reachability analysis of continuous nonlinear systems by means of piecewise linear approximation and developed a reachability algorithm with good convergence rate. This approach can be seen as an application of hybrid systems to deal with complex systems. It also shows a nice interplay between numerical and symbolic computation for safety verification.

The results presented in the paper open various interesting directions for future research. The convergence can be improved by using higher degree approximants, such as piecewise quadratic, and a reachability method for such approximating systems would be of great interest. Additionally, using rectangular meshes reduces significantly the complexity of reachability computation and thus the use of a mixed rectangular-simplicial mesh could allow to achieve a good trade-off between accuracy and computation cost. On the other hand, an important question to address is to find conditions or classes of hybrid system for which the convergence result of our method is preserved.

References

1. R. Alur, C. Courcoubetis, N. Halbwachs, T.A. Henzinger, P.-H. Ho, X. Nicollin, A. Olivero, J. Sifakis and S. Yovine. The Algorithmic Analysis of Hybrid Systems, *Theoretical Computer Science* 138, 3–34, 1995.
2. H. Anai and V. Weispfenning. Reach Set Computations Using Real Quantifier Elimination, *Hybrid Systems: Computation and Control*, in M.D. Di Benedetto and A. Sangiovanni-Vincentelli (Eds), 63–75 LNCS 2034, Springer-Verlag, 2001.

3. E. Asarin, T. Dang and A. Girard. Reachability Analysis of Nonlinear Systems using Conservative Approximations, Technical Report IMAG Oct 2002, Grenoble http://www-verimag.imag.fr/~tdang/piecewise.ps.gz.
4. E. Asarin and T. Dang and O. Maler. d/dt: A tool for Verification of Hybrid Systems, *Computer Aided Verification*, Springer-Verlag, LNCS, 2002.
5. M.D. Di Benedetto and A. Sangiovanni-Vincentelli. *Hybrid Systems: Computation and Control*, LNCS 2034, Springer-Verlag, 2001.
6. O. Botchkarev and S. Tripakis. Verification of Hybrid Systems with Linear Differential Inclusions Using Ellipsoidal Approximations, *Hybrid Systems: Computation and Control*, in B. Krogh and N. Lynch (Eds), 73–88 LNCS 1790, Springer-Verlag, 2000.
7. A. Chutinan and B.H. Krogh. Verification of Polyhedral Invariant Hybrid Automata Using Polygonal Flow Pipe Approximations, *Hybrid Systems: Computation and Control*, in F. Vaandrager and J. van Schuppen (Eds), 76–90 LNCS 1569, Springer-Verlag, 1999.
8. T. Dang and O. Maler. Reachability Analysis via Face Lifting, *Hybrid Systems: Computation and Control*, in T.A. Henzinger and S. Sastry (Eds), 96–109 LNCS 1386 Springer-Verlag, 1998.
9. J. Della Dora, A. Maignan, M. Mirica-Ruse, and S. Yovine. Hybrid Computation, *Proc. of ISSAC'01*, 2001.
10. J. Dieudonné. Calcul Infinitésimal, *Collection Méthodes*, Hermann Paris, 1980.
11. A. Girard. Approximate Solutions of ODEs Using Piecewise Linear Vector Fields, *Proc. CASC'02"*, 2002.
12. A. Girard. Detection of Event Occurence in Piecewise Linear Hybrid Systems, *Proc. RASC'02*, December 2002, Nottingham, UK.
13. M.R. Greenstreet and I. Mitchell. Reachability Analysis Using Polygonal Projections, *Hybrid Systems: Computation and Control*, in F. Vaandrager and J. van Schuppen (Eds), 76–90 LNCS 1569 Springer-Verlag, 1999.
14. M. Greenstreet and C. Tomlin. *Hybrid Systems: Computation and Control*, LNCS, Springer-Verlag, 2002.
15. L.C.G.J.M. Habets and J.H. van Schuppen. Control of Piecewise-Linear Hybrid Systems on Simplices and Rectangles, *Hybrid Systems: Control and Computation*, in M.D. Di Benedetto and A. Sangiovanni-Vincentelli (Eds), 261–273 LNCS 2034, Springer-Verlag, 2001.
16. T.A. Henzinger, P.-H. Ho and H. Wong-Toi. HyTech: A Model Checker for Hybrid Systems, *Software Tools for Technology Transfer* 1, 110–122, 1997.
17. T.A. Henzinger, P.-H. Ho, and H. Wong-Toi. Analysis of Nonlinear Hybrid Systems, *IEEE Transactions on Automatic Control* 43, 540–554, 1998.
18. J. Hubbard and B. West. Differential Equations: A Dynamical Systems Approach, Higher-Dimensional Systems, *Texts in Applied Mathematics*, 18, Springer Verlag, 1995.
19. G. Lafferriere, G. Pappas, and S. Yovine. Reachability computation for linear systems, *Proc. of the 14th IFAC World Congress*, 7–12 E, 1999.
20. , K. Larsen, P. Pettersson, and W. Yi. Uppaal in a nutshell, *Software Tools for Technology Transfert* 1, 1997.
21. T.H. Marshall. Volume formulae for regular hyperbolic cubes, *Conform. Geom. Dyn.*, 25–28, 1998.
22. I. Mitchell and C. Tomlin. Level Set Method for Computation in Hybrid Systems, *Hybrid Systems: Computation and Control*, in B. Krogh and N. Lynch, 311–323 LNCS 1790, Springer-Verlag, 2000.

23. P. Saint-Pierre. Approximation of Viability Kernels and Capture Basin for Hybrid Systems, *Proc. of European Control Conference ECC'01*, 2776–2783, 2001.
24. O. Stursberg, S. Kowalewski and S. Engell. On the generation of Timed Approximations for continuous systems, *Mathematical and Computer Modelling of Dynamical Systems* 6–1, 51–70, 2000.
25. A. Puri and P. Varaiya. Verification of Hybrid Systems using Abstraction, *Hybrid Systems II*, in P. Antsaklis, W. Kohn, A. Nerode, and S. Sastry (Eds), LNCS 999, Springer-Verlag, 1995.
26. S. Yovine. Kronos: A Verification Tool for Real-time Systems, *Software Tools for Technology Transfer* 1, 123–133, 1997.

Fundamental Inequality Theorem (see e.g. [18,10]) Let f be a function with values in $\mathbb{R}^n$, continuous and L-Lipschitz on a set $D \subset R^n$. Let $x_1(t)$ and $x_2(t)$ be functions with values in $\mathbb{R}^n$ continuous, piecewise differentiable on an interval $I \subset \mathbb{R}$ containing 0 such that $\forall t \in I$, $x_1(t) \in D$, $x_2(t) \in D$, and $\|\dot{x}_1(t) - f(x_1(t))\| \leq \epsilon_1$, $\|\dot{x}_2(t) - f(x_2(t))\| \leq \epsilon_2$. Then,

$$\forall t \in I, \ \|x_1(t) - x_2(t)\| \leq \|x_1(0) - x_2(0)\| e^{L|t|} + \frac{\epsilon_1 + \epsilon_2}{L}(e^{L|t|} - 1).$$

Proof of Theorem 1 We start by proving the first property. To show that $K_s(T, X_0) \subseteq R_N$, we first observe that, by definition, $R_N = \bigcup_{1 \leq i \leq N} Q_i$. Hence, it suffices to show that for all $i \in \{0, \ldots, N-1\}$

$$\forall x \in X_0 \ u(\cdot) \in \mathcal{U}_\mu \ t \in [ir, (i+1)r] \ \Phi_s(t, x, u(\cdot)) \in Q_{i+1}. \tag{8}$$

We will prove (8) by induction. We begin by the base case ($i = 0$). Let x be an element of X_0, $u(\cdot)$ an admissible control, and $t \in [0, r]$. We denote $y_s = \Phi_s(t, x, u(\cdot))$ and $y_f = \Phi_f(t, x)$. Using the Fundamental Inequality, we have $\|y_f - y_s\| \leq \frac{\mu}{L}(e^{Lt} - 1) \leq \frac{\mu}{L}(e^{Lr} - 1)$. It is easy to see that y_f is an element of P_1; therefore y_s is an element of Q_1, which implies that (8) holds for $i = 0$. We now assume that the formula (8) holds for some $i \geq 0$. Given $x \in X_0$, $u(\cdot) \in \mathcal{U}_\mu$ and $t \in [(i+1)r, (i+2)r]$ we denote $y_s = \Phi_s(t, x, u(\cdot))$ and $z_s = \Phi_s(t - r, x, u(\cdot))$. Since (8) holds for i, we have $z_s \in Q_{i+1}$. Let $y_f = \Phi_f(r, z_s)$. Again, by the Fundamental Inequality, $\|y_f - y_s\| \leq \frac{\mu}{L}(e^{Lr} - 1)$. In addition, $y_f \in P_{i+2}$. It then follows that $y_s \in Q_{i+2}$, which shows that (8) holds for $i + 1$. $\square$

We now prove the convergence property, i.e. $d_H(K_s(T, X_0), R_N) \leq 2\mu r e^{LT}$. We denote by δ_i the Hausdorff semi-distance from the set R_i, computed in iteration i of Algorithm 1, to the corresponding exact set $K_s(ir, X_0)$: $\delta_i = \sup_{x \in R_i} \inf_{y \in K_s(ir, X_0)} \|x - y\|$. To estimate the error bound, we determine the relation between δ_i and δ_{i+1}.

Let x_f^* be an element of R_{i+1} with $i \geq 1$. There are two cases: (1) $x_f^* \in R_i$, and (2) $x_f^* \notin R_i$. For the first case where $x_f^* \in R_i$, it is not hard to see that there exists x_s^* in $K_s(ir, X_0) \subseteq K_s((i+1)r, X_0)$ such that $\|x_f^* - x_s^*\| \leq \delta_i$. We now focus on the second case where $x_f^* \notin R_i$. Then, there exists $y_f^* \in P_{i+1}$ such that

$$\|y_f^* - x_f^*\| \leq \frac{\mu}{L}(e^{Lr} - 1). \tag{9}$$

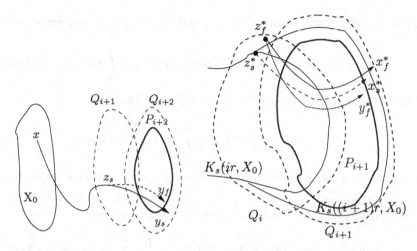

Fig. 3. Idea of the proof of theorem 1: conservativeness property (left) and convergence property (right). The approximate reachable sets Q_i of the system with input are drawn in dotted line and the reachable sets P_i of the autonomous system in bold line.

Let z_f^* be the 'predecessor' of y_f^* by the autonomous system such that $y_f^* = \Phi_f(r, z_f^*)$. Since P_{i+1} is obtained by applying Φ_f to the set Q_i, therefore $z_f^* \in Q_i$, which means that $z_f^* \in R_i$. Then, there exists z_s^* in the exact reachable set $K_s(ir, X_0)$ of the system with input such that $||z_f^* - z_s^*|| \le \delta_i$.

We consider a point x_s^* defined as: $x_s^* = \Phi_s(r, z_s^*, u^*(\cdot))$ where $u^*(\cdot)$ is defined as follows:

$$u^*(t) = \frac{L(x_f^* - y_f^*)}{(e^{Lr} - 1)}.$$

It is easy to see that $u^*(\cdot)$ which is an admissible input of the system (3). In other words, x_s^* is the successor of z_s^* by the system with input, and hence x_s^* is an element of $K_s((i + 1)r, X_0)$. In the following we will determine δ_{i+1} by estimating an upper bound of $||x_f^* - x_s^*||$.

Let $z_f(t)$ and $z_s(t)$ be the solutions of the following equations:

$$\begin{cases} \dot{z}_f(t) = f(z_f(t)), & z_f(0) = z_f^*, \\ \dot{z}_s(t) = f(z_s(t)) + u^*(t), & z_s(0) = z_s^*. \end{cases}$$

We also define two functions $x_f(t)$ and $x_s(t)$ as follows:

$$\begin{cases} x_f(t) = z_f(t) + \frac{t}{r}(x_f^* - y_f^*), \\ x_s(t) = z_s(t). \end{cases}$$

Using the Fundamental Inequality and the bound μ on the input, we have

$$||z_f(t) - z_s(t))|| \le ||z_f^* - z_s^*||e^{Lt} + \frac{\mu}{L}(e^{Lt} - 1) \le \delta_i\, e^{Lt} + \frac{\mu}{L}(e^{Lt} - 1). \tag{10}$$

On the other hand, since $x_f(r) = x_f^*$ and $x_s(r) = x_s^*$, we can write:

$$x_f^* - x_s^* = x_f(r) - x_s(r) = (x_f(0) - x_s(0)) + \int_0^r (\dot{x}_f(s) - \dot{x}_s(s))ds.$$

In addition, $||x_f(0) - x_s(0)|| = ||z_f^* - z_s^*|| \le \delta_i$. Therefore,

$$||x_f^* - x_s^*|| \le \delta_i + ||\int_0^r (\dot{x}_f(s) - \dot{x}_s(s))ds||. \tag{11}$$

We now focus on the term inside the integral of (11). Note that $||\dot{x}_f(s) - \dot{x}_s(s)|| = ||f(z_f(s)) + \frac{(x_f^* - y_f^*)}{r} - f(z_s(s)) - u^*(s)||$. Since f is L-Lipschitz, $||f(z_f(s)) - f(z_s(s))|| \le L\,||z_f(s) - z_s(s)||$. Using (9) and (10) yields

$$||\dot{x}_f(s) - \dot{x}_s(s)|| \le ||x_f^* - y_f^*||(\frac{1}{r} - \frac{L}{e^{Lr} - 1}) + L\,||z_f(s) - z_s(s)||$$
$$\le \frac{\mu}{2}e^{Lr}Lr + L\,(\delta_i\,e^{Ls} + \frac{\mu}{L}(e^{Ls} - 1)).$$

Combining the above inequality with (11) and developing the integral gives

$$\delta_{i+1} \le \delta_i\,e^{Lr} + \frac{\mu}{2}e^{Lr}Lr^2 + \frac{\mu}{L}\,(e^{Lr} - 1 - Lr).$$

Observe that $e^{Lr} - 1 - Lr \le \frac{1}{2}e^{Lr}\,(Lr)^2$, thus $\delta_{i+1} \le \delta_i\,e^{Lr} + \mu\,L\,e^{Lr}\,r^2$. Then,

$$\delta_N \le \delta_1\,e^{L(N-1)r} + \mu\,L\,e^{Lr}\,r^2 \sum_{i=0}^{N-2} e^{iLr} = \delta_1\,e^{L(N-1)r} + \mu\,L\,e^{Lr}\,r^2\,\frac{e^{L\,(N-1)\,r} - 1}{e^{Lr} - 1}.$$

Since $e^{Lr} - 1 \ge Lr$ and, in addition, we can prove that $\delta_1 \le \mu\,r\,e^{Lr}$. The above thus leads to $\delta_N \le 2\,\mu\,r\,e^{LT}$. This completes the proof of the theorem. $\square$

Proof of Lemma 2 We first estimate an upper bound of $||g(x) - l_k(x)||$ for all points x inside a cell $C_k \in \mathcal{M}$. Let v be a vertex of C_k. By triangle inequality, we have $||g(x) - l_k(x)|| \le ||g(x) - g(v)|| + ||g(v) - l_k(x)||$. By definition, $g(v) = l_k(v)$. In addition, g is L-Lipschitz, it then follows that

$$||g(x) - l_k(x)|| \le ||g(x) - g(v)|| + ||l_k(v) - l_k(x)|| \le 2\,L||x - v||. \tag{12}$$

Note that the above inequality holds for any vertex $v \in V(C_k)$. In order to get a tight upper bound on $||g(x) - l_k(x)||$, we can estimate a bound on $||x - v||$ for each vertex v and then choose the smallest bound. Let $V(C_k) = \{v_1, v_2, \dots, v_n\}$ be the set of vertices of C_k. A point $x \in C_k$ can be written as:

$$\begin{cases} x = \sum_{i=1}^n \alpha_i\,v_i \\ \sum_{i=1}^n \alpha_i = 1 \text{ and } \forall i \in \{1, \dots, n\}\ \alpha_i \ge 0. \end{cases} \tag{13}$$

We observe, from the conditions (13), that there exists $j \in \{1, \dots, n\}$ such that $\alpha_j \geq \frac{1}{n+1}$. Since $\sum_{i=1}^{n} \alpha_i v_j = v_j$, we can write $x - v_j = \sum_{i=1, i \neq j}^{n} \alpha_i (v_i - v_j)$. Additionally, $\|v_i - v_j\| \leq h(C_k)$; therefore,

$$\|x - v_j\| \leq h(C_k) \sum_{i=1, i \neq j}^{n} \alpha_i = h(C_k)(1 - \alpha_j) \leq h(C_k) \frac{n}{n+1}. \qquad (14)$$

Using this bound in (12) we get $\forall x \in C_k$ $\|g(x) - l_k(x)\| \leq h(C_k) \frac{2nL}{n+1}$. Note that $\forall C_k \in \mathcal{M}$, $h(C_k) \leq h(\mathcal{M}) = h$, which yields the result of the lemma. $\qquad \square$

Proof of Lemma 3 For a given cell $C_k \in \mathcal{M}$, we define the function $e(x) = g(x) - l_k(x)$ and let $x^* = \arg \max_{x \in C_k} \|e(x)\|$ (note that the simplex C_k is compact). Let v be a vertex of C_k, and all points in the line segment connecting x^* and v can be written as: $x(\gamma) = x^* + \gamma(v - x^*)$, $\gamma \in [0,1]$. To determine a bound on $e(x^*)$, we define a function $z(\gamma) = e(x(\gamma))$ for $\gamma \in [0,1]$. Expanding z with respect to γ gives

$$z(1) = z(0) + \frac{dz}{d\gamma}(0) + \int_0^1 \frac{d^2 z}{d\gamma^2}(s)(1-s)ds. \qquad (15)$$

The ith coordinate of a point $y \in \mathbb{R}^n$ is denoted by y_i. We can see that $dx_i/d\gamma = (v_i - x_i^*)$. Additionally, $\partial^2 l_k / \partial x_i \partial x_j$ vanish for all $i, j \in \{1, 2, \dots, n\}$. Thus,

$$\frac{dz}{d\gamma}(\gamma) = \sum_{i=1}^{n} \frac{\partial e}{\partial x_i}(x(\gamma))(v_i - x_i^*), \quad \frac{d^2 z}{d\gamma^2}(\gamma) = \sum_{i=1}^{n} \sum_{j=1}^{n} \frac{\partial^2 e}{\partial x_i \partial x_j}(x(\gamma))(v_i - x_i^*)(v_j - x_j^*)$$

Since $\partial^2 l_k / \partial x_i \partial x_j$ vanish for all $i, j \in \{1, \dots, n\}$, then $\partial^2 e / \partial x_i \partial x_j = \partial^2 g / \partial x_i \partial x_j$. Similar to the inequality (14) established in the proof of Lemma 2, we can show that there exists $v \in V(C_k)$ such that $\forall i \in \{1, \dots, n\}$ $\|v_i - x_i^*\| \leq h(C_k) n/(n+1)$. Then, using the bound K on the second derivatives of the function g, we obtain $\|\frac{d^2 z}{d\gamma^2}(\gamma)\| \leq (h(C_k))^2 \frac{n^2 K}{(n+1)^2}$. In addition, $\|e(x^*)\|$ is maximum, which implies that $\frac{dz}{d\gamma}(0) = 0$. By definition of the interpolating function, $g(v) = l_k(v)$, then $z(1) = 0$. Therefore, (15) becomes: $g(x^*) - l_k(x^*) + \int_0^1 \frac{d^2 z}{d\gamma^2}(s)(1-s)ds = 0$. Using the above bound on $\|\frac{d^2 z}{d\gamma^2}(\gamma)\|$, we get

$$\|g(x^*) - l_k(x^*)\| \leq (h(C_k))^2 \frac{n^2 K}{(n+1)^2} \int_0^1 (1-s)ds = (h(C_k))^2 \frac{n^2 K}{2(n+1)^2}.$$

Hence, $\forall x \in \mathcal{X}$ $\|g(x) - l(x)\| \leq h^2 \frac{n^2 K}{2(n+1)^2}$, and the proof is complete. $\qquad \square$

Mode Reconstruction for Source Coding and Multi-modal Control*

Adam Austin and Magnus Egerstedt

Georgia Institute of Technology
School of Electrical and Computer Engineering
Atlanta, GA 30332, USA
{austin,magnus}@ece.gatech.edu

Abstract. In this paper we take the point of view that control procedures have an information theoretic content that can be more or less effectively coded. Of particular interest are control procedures for navigation and obstacle avoidance for mobile robots, and we show how tokenized instructions can be used for understanding how computer generated inputs to robotics systems should be defined, selected, and coded. To this end, a dynamic programming algorithm is developed for generating control procedures that are useful in given robotics applications.

1 Introduction

In this paper we continue the development begun in [7,8,9] of viewing control procedures as having an information theoretic content, i.e. as being symbols that can be more or less effectively coded. Of particular relevance to this paper are control procedures for navigation and obstacle avoidance for mobile robots. When humans instruct each other how to carry out navigation tasks, only a limited number of tokenized instructions are used, which can be contrasted with classic control theory where a control action is specified at each time instant. We will show that such tokenized instructions are useful for understanding how computer generated inputs to robotics systems should be defined, selected, and coded. To this end, an information theoretic approach to control theory has been developed in [8], serving as a useful tool not only for source coding of control signals, but also for describing how symbolic instructions should be interpreted and operated on by continuous systems.

In this paper we model the way linguistic control signals affect mechanical devices using *trigger based hybrid systems* [5], serving as an abstraction between the symbolic computer programs and the continuous device dynamics. By combining this type of model with the notion of a *motion description language* (MDL) [4,16], used for representing idealized motions, a model for linguistic control is arrived at in which a cost criterion for evaluating the control laws can be introduced, corresponding to the *description length* [17] of the control procedure.

* The support from NSF through the program EHS NSF-01-161 (grant # 0207411) is gratefully acknowledged.

O. Maler and A. Pnueli (Eds.): HSCC 2003, LNCS 2623, pp. 36–49, 2003.

This cost can be interpreted as the number of bits needed for uniquely coding a given control procedure.

However, the description length only provides the optimal code length if all control modes, or elements in the MDL, are equally likely. It would thus be desirable to generate a probability distribution over the set of modes, which would enable the use of optimal coding strategies. The construction of an algorithm that generates the shortest string of modes from strings of output-input pairs is thus the main contribution of this paper. This furthermore enables us to produce a probability distribution over the empirically obtained modes. This probability distribution can be put to work when coding the control procedures, since, by virtue of Shannon's source coding theorem [18], a more common mode should be coded using fewer bits than an uncommon one. This work has a number of potential applications from teleoperated robotics, control over communication constrained networks, to minimum attention control.

This paper is structured as follows: In Section 2 we introduce motion description languages defined both with respect to continuous machines and finite automata. In Section 3 we show how to pick control laws with short description lengths, followed by a discussion, in Section 4, about how to establish probability distributions over MDLs. A dynamic programming algorithm is proposed in Section 5 for solving this problem by generating control procedures from empirical data, which is applied in Section 6 to the problem of robot control.

2   Motion Description Languages

The primary objects of study in this paper are so called *motion description languages* (MDLs). Given a finite set, or alphabet, A, by $A^\star$ we understand the set of all strings of finite length over A, with the binary operation of concatenation defined on $A^\star$. Relative to this operation, $A^\star$ is a semigroup, and if we include the empty string in $A^\star$ it becomes a monoid, i.e. a semigroup with an identity, and a *formal language* is a subset of thee free monoid over a finite alphabet. (See for example [13] for an introduction to this subject.)

The concept of a *motion alphabet* has been proposed recently in the literature as a finite set of symbols representing different control actions that, when applied to a specific machine, define segments of motion [4,8,11,14,16]. A MDL is thus given by a set of strings that represent such idealized motions, i.e. a MDL is a subset of a free monoid over a given motion alphabet. Particular choices of MDLs become meaningful only when the language is defined relative to the physical device that is to be controlled. One such physical device is the so-called *quantized input-output machine*, given by $M = (U, X, Y, f, h)$, where U is a finite set of admissible inputs, Y is a finite set of outputs, $X \subset \Re^n$ is the state space of the system, $f : X \times U \to TX$ defines the system evolution, and $h : X \to Y$ is a measurable output function. The evolution of the machine is given by $\dot{x} = f(x, u)$, $y = h(x)$, and from [9] we get the following definition:

Definition 1 (Motion Description Language). *Given a quantized input-output machine M. Relative to M we let a motion description language be given by a subset of the free monoid over the set $\Sigma = U \times U^{Y \times U} \times \{0,1\}^Y$.*

In other words, we let the letters in the motion alphabet be triples of the form (u, k, ξ), where $u \in U$, $k : Y \times U \to U$, and $\xi : Y \to \{0,1\}$. If, at time t_0, M receives the input string $(u_1, k_1, \xi_1), \ldots, (u_p, k_p, \xi_q)$, then x evolves according to

$$\dot{x} = f(x, k_1(y, u_1)); \quad t_0 \leq t < T_1$$
$$\vdots \qquad \qquad \vdots$$
$$\dot{x} = f(x, k_q(y, u_q)); \quad T_{q-1} \leq t < T_q,$$

where T_i denotes the time at which the interrupt ξ_i changes from 0 to 1.

Navigation Example

In order to make matters somewhat concrete, we illustrate these ideas with a navigation example, found in [10]. What makes the control of mobile robots particularly challenging is the fact that the robots operate in unknown, or partially unknown environments. Any attempt to model such a system must take this fact into account. We achieve this by letting the robot make certain observations about the environment, and we let the robot dynamics be given by

$$\dot{x} = v, \, x, v \in \Re^2$$
$$y_1 = o_d(x), \, y_2 = c_f(x),$$

where o_d is a quantized, odometric position estimate of x, and c_f is the quantized contact force from the environment. The contact force could either be generated by tactile sensors in contact with the obstacle or by range sensors such as sonars, lasers, or IR-sensors.

Relative to this robot it is now possible to define a MDL for executing motions that drive the robot toward the goal when the robot is not in contact with an obstacle. On the other hand, when the robot is in contact with an obstacle, it seems reasonable to follow the contour of that obstacle in a clock-wise or counter clock-wise fashion, as suggested in [12]. We let the MDL be given by the free monoid over the set

$$\{(u, k, \xi) \mid u = x_F, \, k(y_1, y_2, u) \in \{\kappa(u - y_1), cR(-\pi/2)y_2\}, \, \xi \in \{\xi_{GA}, \xi_{OA}\}\}.$$

The idea here is that the goal is located at x_F, and when the robot is not in contact with an obstacle, the open-loop part of the instruction basically provides x_F as a set-point. Furthermore, the closed-loop mapping $k(y_1, y_2, u) = \kappa(u - y_1)$ can thus be thought of as a simple, proportional feedback law. When the robot is in contact with an obstacle, no set-point is needed, and $k(y_1, y_2, u) = cR(-\pi/2)y_2$, where $c > 0$, $R(\theta)$ is a rotation matrix, and the choice of $\theta = -\pi/2$ corresponds to a clockwise negotiation of the obstacle.

In other words, the multi-modal control sequence used for negotiating obstacles is thus an element in the set $\sigma_{GA} \cdot (\sigma_{OA} \cdot \sigma_{GA})^\star$, where GA and OA denotes "goal-attraction" and "obstacle-avoidance" respectively, and where $a^\star = \{\emptyset, a, aa, aaa, ...\}$. The individual modes $\sigma_{GA} = (u_{GA}, k_{GA}, \xi_{GA})$ and $\sigma_{OA} = (u_{OA}, k_{OA}, \xi_{OA})$ are furthermore given by

$$
\begin{cases}
u_{GA} = x_F \\
k_{GA}(y_1, y_2, u) = \kappa(u - y_1) \\
\xi_{GA}(y_1, y_2) = \begin{cases} 0 \text{ if } \langle y_2, x_F - y_1 \rangle \geq 0 \\ 1 \text{ otherwise} \end{cases} \\
u_{OA} = x_F \\
k_{OA}(y_1, y_2, u) = cR(-\pi/2)y_2 \\
\xi_{OA}(y_1, y_2) = \begin{cases} 0 \text{ if } \langle y_2, x_F - y_1 \rangle < 0 \text{ or } \angle(x_F - y_1, y_2) < 0 \\ 1 \text{ otherwise.} \end{cases}
\end{cases}
$$

Here $\angle(\alpha, \beta)$ denotes the angle between the vectors α and β.

An example of using this multi-modal control sequence is shown in Figure 1.

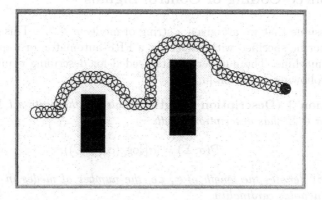

Fig. 1. A multi-modal input string is used for negotiating two rectangular obstacles. Depicted is a simulation of a Nomadic Scout in the Nomadic `Nserver` environment.

Now, in [8], a finite automata version of the quantized input-output machine was introduced, called a *Free-Running, Feedback Automaton* (FRF automaton) in order to arrive at an abstract model of, for example, a landmark-based navigation system for mobile robots [7,14]. If we let X, U, Y be finite sets, and let $\delta \in X^{X \times U}$, $\gamma \in Y^X$, then we can identify $(X, Y, U, \delta, \gamma)$ with an *output automaton*, whose operation is given by $x_{k+1} = \delta(x_k, u_k)$ and $y_k = \gamma(x_k)$.

However, in order to let finite automata read strings of control modes, the model must be modified in such a way that instruction processing is akin to the way in which differential equations "process" piecewise constant inputs. The idea is to let the automaton read an input from a given alphabet, and then advance the state of the automaton repeatedly (free-running property) without reading any new inputs until an interrupt is triggered. Additional structure is furthermore imposed on the input set to allow for feedback signals to be used. Hence a FRF-automaton is a free-running automaton whose input alphabet admits the structure $\Sigma = U \times K \times \Xi$, where, as before, U is a finite set, $K = U^{Y \times U}$, and $\Xi = \{0,1\}^Y$. Hence, the input to a FRF-automaton is a triple (u, k, ξ), where $u \in U$, $k : Y \times U \to U$, and $\xi : Y \to \{0,1\}$.

Definition 2 (Free-Running, Feedback Automaton [8]). *Let X, Y, U be finite sets and let $\delta : X \times U \to X$, $\gamma : X \to Y$ be given functions. Let $\Sigma = U \times K \times \Xi$, where U is a finite set, $K = U^{Y \times U}$, and $\Xi = \{0,1\}^Y$. We say that $(X, \Sigma, Y, \delta, \gamma)$ is a free-running, feedback automaton whose evolution equation is*

$$x_{k+1} = \delta(x_k, k_{l_k}(y_k, u_{l_k})), \ y_k = \gamma(x_k)$$
$$l_{k+1} = l_k + \xi_{l_k}(y_k),$$

given the input string $(u_1, k_1, \xi_1) \cdots (u_p, k_p, \xi_p) \in \Sigma^\star$.

3 Source Coding of Control Signals

Now, assume that we are given a string of modes $\sigma \in \Sigma^\star$. This mode sequence can either be specified with respect to a FRF-automaton or a quantized input-output machine. The number of bits needed for describing σ uniquely is given by the following definition [6,17]:

Definition 3 (Description Length). *Consider the finite set Σ. We say that a word $\sigma \in \Sigma^\star$ has description length*

$$\mathcal{D}(\sigma, \Sigma) = |\sigma| \log_2(card(\Sigma)),$$

where $|\sigma|$ denotes the length of σ, i.e. the number of modes in the string, and card$(\cdot)$ denotes cardinality.

The description length thus tells us how complicated σ is, i.e. how many bits we need for describing it, and since $\Sigma = U \times U^{Y \times U} \times \{0,1\}^Y$ we directly see that a higher resolution measurement results in a larger Y than what is the case for a lower resolution measurement. A better sensor might thus make the control procedures significantly more complicated while only providing marginally better performance. This trade-off between complexity and performance is something that can be capitalized on when designing control laws, which was done in [8] for FRF-automata, and in [7] for quantized input-output machines.

However, the description length does not tell the whole story. It may be a natural measure of the complexity of the control procedure, but if the string of modes is to be sent over a communication channel, which is the case for instance in teleoperated robotics, it would be desirable if a more effective representation of the mode string could be obtained. If we assume that we have been able to establish a probability distribution over Σ we can use optimal coding schemes, such as the Huffman code [15], for finding the shortest expected number of bits

$l^*(\Sigma)$ needed for coding an element drawn at random from Σ. Shannon's classic source coding theorem [18] tells us that $\mathcal{H}(\Sigma) \leq l^*(\Sigma) < \mathcal{H}(\Sigma) + 1$, where the *entropy* $\mathcal{H}(\Sigma)$ is given by

$$\mathcal{H}(\Sigma) = - \sum_{i=1}^{card(\Sigma)} p_i \log_2 p_i.$$

Here the interpretation is that the control triple $\sigma_i \in \Sigma$ occurs with probability p_i, and it should be noted, already at this point, that a probability distribution over Σ corresponds to a specification of what modes are potentially useful. But, to establish such a probability distribution over a structured set, such as the set of modes, is not a trivial task, and in the following sections we study the problem of recovering modes from empirical data. The idea is thus to observe how human operators instruct mobile robots, or how biological systems are structured, and reconstruct the modes from the experimental data.

4   Mode Recovery

As shown in the previous section, in order to employ optimal source coding strategies we first need to establish a probability distribution over Σ, i.e. over the set of modes. For this, a characterization of what modes are potentially useful is needed. In this section we show how such a characterization can be obtained by reconstructing mode-strings from empirical data. The main idea is to collect data, i.e. output-input strings, from real-world systems and then recover an appropriate multi-modal structure that is consistent with the data.

Regardless of whether the dynamic device model is a FRF-automaton or a kinematic machine, we assume that the given output-input string is a collection of pairs

$$(y(1), u(1)), (y(2), u(2)), \dots, (y(q), u(q)) \in (Y \times U)^q \subset (Y \times U)^*,$$

which we, with a slight abuse of notation, denote by $(\mathbf{y}, \mathbf{u})$, where $\mathbf{y} = y(1), y(2), \dots, y(q)$ and $\mathbf{u} = u(1), u(2), \dots, u(q)$. That a system evolving on a FRF-automaton would produce finite length strings of output-input pairs is clear, but some comments must be made in the continuous time case. In this case, one could sample the output-input data temporally, or generate a new pair whenever either the output or the input changes values, which corresponds to a so called *Lebesgue sampling*, in the sense of [2].

Now, given a collection of output-input pairs, the problem that we are interested in is how to produce mode strings that can generate this data. There are a number of ways in which one can conceivably achieve this, and in this paper we take the point of view that any numerically tractable algorithm that achieves the goal is useful. Once such mode strings have been obtained, the empirical probability distribution can simply be computed by letting p_i (the probability of using mode i) be equal to the number of times mode i was used over the total number of modes used. This construction would furthermore be of importance as a multi-modal control synthesis tool, since empirical data would guide our selection of mode strings for accomplishing certain tasks.

In this paper we are interested in the problem of generating the *shortest* mode string $\sigma = \sigma_1 \cdots \sigma_M \in \Sigma^*$ that is consistent with the data, i.e. to find σ that solves

$$\mathcal{P}(\Sigma, \mathbf{y}, \mathbf{u}) : \begin{cases} \min_{\sigma} |\sigma| \\ \text{subject to} \\ \begin{cases} \sigma_{l_k} = (u_{l_k}, k_{l_k}, \xi_{l_k}) \in \Sigma, \; k = 1, \ldots, q \\ k_{l_k}(y(k), u_{l_k}) = u(k), \; k = 1, \ldots, q \\ l_{k+1} = l_k + \xi_{l_k}(y(k)), \; k = 1, \ldots, q, \; l_1 = 1, \end{cases} \end{cases}$$

where the last two constraints ensure that σ is in fact consistent with the data.

We say that $\sigma \in sol(\mathcal{P}(\Sigma, \mathbf{y}, \mathbf{u}))$ if σ solves $\mathcal{P}(\Sigma, \mathbf{y}, \mathbf{u})$. The reason for the inclusion is that we can not hope for a unique solution. We furthermore let $length(\mathcal{P}(\Sigma, \mathbf{y}, \mathbf{u}))$ denote the unique string length of the solutions to $\mathcal{P}(\Sigma, \mathbf{y}, \mathbf{u})$.

Lemma 1. *For any output-input string* $(\mathbf{y}, \mathbf{u}) \in (Y \times U)^q$ *it holds that* $\emptyset \neq sol(\mathcal{P}(\Sigma, \mathbf{y}, \mathbf{u}))$ *as well as* $length(\mathcal{P}(\Sigma, \mathbf{y}, \mathbf{u})) \leq q$.

Proof: We can always find a string of modes, containing q elements, that is consistent with the data by simply using modes that interrupt on every y-value. In other words, $\sigma = \sigma_1 \cdots \sigma_q$ is consistent with the data if

$$\begin{cases} \sigma_i = (u_i, k_i, \xi_i) \\ u_i \text{ arbitrary} \\ k_i(u, y(i)) = u(i), \; \forall u \in U \\ \xi_i(y) = 1, \; \forall y \in Y. \end{cases}$$

$\square$

If we now assume that our primary concern is to construct *feedback laws*, i.e. we limit our focus to mode sets of the form $\Sigma_{cl} = \{u_{cl}\} \times U^{\{u_{cl}\} \times Y} \times \{0,1\}^Y$, where u_{cl} is any arbitrary member of U, we can directly note the following fact:

Lemma 2. $length(\mathcal{P}(\Sigma, \mathbf{y}, \mathbf{u})) = length(\mathcal{P}(\Sigma_{cl}, \mathbf{y}, \mathbf{u}))$.

Proof: Assume that $\sigma = \sigma_1 \cdots \sigma_m \in sol(\mathcal{P}(\Sigma, \mathbf{y}, \mathbf{u}))$, i.e. that $length(\mathcal{P}(\Sigma, \mathbf{y}, \mathbf{u})) = M$, where $\sigma_i = (u_i, k_i, \xi_i)$, $i = 1, \ldots, M$. By Lemma 1 we know that such a σ exists.

Now, form $\sigma' \in \Sigma_{cl}^*$ as $\sigma' = \sigma_1' \cdots \sigma_M'$, where

$$\begin{cases} \sigma_i' = (u_{cl}, k_i', \xi_i'), \; i = 1, \ldots, M \\ k_i'(u_{cl}, y) = k_i(u_i, y), \; i = 1, \ldots, M \\ \xi_i'(y) = \xi_i(y), \; i = 1, \ldots, M. \end{cases}$$

Now, since $\Sigma_{cl} \subset \Sigma$ it is clear that $length(\mathcal{P}(\Sigma, \mathbf{y}, \mathbf{u})) \leq length(\mathcal{P}(\Sigma_{cl}, \mathbf{y}, \mathbf{u}))$. But, by construction, σ and σ' are both consistent with the data, and hence $length(\mathcal{P}(\Sigma_{cl}, \mathbf{y}, \mathbf{u})) = M$. $\square$

What Lemma 2 tells us is that we can search for the shortest closed-loop multi-modal instruction that is consistent with the data and by doing so solve the original problem directly since the lemma furthermore tells us that

$$sol(\mathcal{P}(\Sigma_{cl}, \mathbf{y}, \mathbf{u})) \subset sol(\mathcal{P}(\Sigma, \mathbf{y}, \mathbf{u})).$$

However, we can restrict the search further by only investigating interrupt functions with a special structure, and we define $\hat{\Xi}$ as

$$\hat{\Xi} = \{\xi : Y \to \{0,1\} \mid \xi(y) = 1 \text{ for exactly one } y \in Y\} \subset \{0,1\}^{Y},$$

i.e. $\hat{\Xi}$ is the set of interrupts that trigger for exactly one output value. By using this restricted set of interrupts, we can define an even smaller set of modes as $\hat{\Sigma}_{cl} = \{u_{cl}\} \times U^{\{u_{cl}\} \times Y} \times \hat{\Xi} \subset \Sigma_{cl} \subset \Sigma$, and state the following lemma:

Lemma 3. $length(\mathcal{P}(\Sigma_{cl}, \mathbf{y}, \mathbf{u})) = length(\mathcal{P}(\hat{\Sigma}_{cl}, \mathbf{y}, \mathbf{u}))$.

Proof: We directly note that $length(\mathcal{P}(\Sigma_{cl}, \mathbf{y}, \mathbf{u})) \leq length(\mathcal{P}(\hat{\Sigma}_{cl}, \mathbf{y}, \mathbf{u}))$ since $\hat{\Sigma}_{cl} \subset \Sigma_{cl}$. Now, assume that $\sigma = \sigma_1 \cdots \sigma_M \in sol(\mathcal{P}(\Sigma_{cl}, \mathbf{y}, \mathbf{u}))$, where $\sigma_i = (u_{cl}, k_i, \xi_i)$, $i = 1, \ldots, M$. If we let $trig(i, \sigma, \mathbf{y}) \in Y$ denote the element in the output string that σ_i interrupts on, i.e. the $y \in \mathbf{y}$ that triggers a transition from σ_i to σ_{i+1} when $\xi_i(y) = 1$. We can then form $\hat{\sigma} = \hat{\sigma}_1 \cdots \hat{\sigma}_M \in \hat{\Sigma}_{cl}^{\star}$, with

$$\begin{cases} \hat{\sigma}_i = (u_{cl}, \hat{k}_i, \hat{\xi}_i), \ i = 1, \ldots, M \\ \hat{k}_i(u_{cl}, y) = k_i(u_{cl}, y), \ i = 1, \ldots, M \\ \hat{\xi}_i(y) = \begin{cases} 1 & \text{if } y = trig(i, \sigma, \mathbf{y}) \\ 0 & \text{otherwise,} \end{cases} \ i = 1, \ldots, M. \end{cases}$$

It is clear that $\hat{\sigma}$ is consistent with the data, and hence $\hat{\sigma} \in sol(\mathcal{P}(\hat{\Sigma}_{cl}, \mathbf{y}, \mathbf{u}))$.   □

Corollary 1. $\emptyset \neq sol(\mathcal{P}(\hat{\Sigma}_{cl}, \mathbf{y}, \mathbf{u})) \subset sol(\mathcal{P}(\Sigma, \mathbf{y}, \mathbf{u}))$.

As a direct consequence of Corollary 1 we can focus our attention on the solutions to the reduced problem $\mathcal{P}(\hat{\Sigma}_{cl}, \mathbf{y}, \mathbf{u})$ directly. Without loss of generality we, in the next section, will use this observation as a basis for searching for strings of pairs $(k, \xi) \in U^{Y} \times \hat{\Xi}$, with the understanding that these pairs can be directly augmented to produce triples in $\hat{\Sigma}_{cl}$ in a straightforward manner.

Remark 1. It should be noted that Lemma 3 would no longer hold if we were interested in finding the mode string that contained the least number of distinct modes instead of the shortest strings, e.g. $\sigma_1 \cdot \sigma_2 \cdot \sigma_1 \cdot \sigma_2$ would be preferred over $\sigma_1 \cdot \sigma_2 \cdot \sigma_3$. This might arguably be a more natural way of selecting the modes, but in that case, it is potentially beneficial to use a mode that interrupts on multiple output values, and not only on one distinct y-value, which would contradict Lemma 3.

5 Dynamic Programming

By restricting the search to finding solutions in $\mathcal{P}(\hat{\Sigma}_{cl}, \mathbf{y}, \mathbf{u})$ we note that the closed loop components are directly given by the output-input strings, i.e. that $k_{l_k}(y(k)) = u(k)$ is given by the output-input string $(y(1), u(1)), \ldots, (y(q), u(q))$. All that remains is thus to construct the correct interrupts. Since the interrupts are members of $\hat{\Xi}$, and the output-input string has length q, we can formulate the problem as a *dynamic programming* problem, where the *cost-to-go* satisfies *Bellman's equation*:

$$\mathcal{V}_k(\xi) = \min_{\xi' \in \hat{\Xi}} \{ \mathcal{C}_k(\xi, \xi') + \mathcal{V}_{k-1}(\xi') \},$$

where $\mathcal{C}_k(\xi, \xi')$ is the transition cost associated with using ξ as interrupt at time k and letting ξ' be the interrupt at time $k - 1$, $k = 2, \ldots, q$. It is clear that $\mathcal{C}_k(\xi, \xi') \in \{0, 1, \infty\}$ since a mode switch corresponds to increasing the number of modes by one, no mode switch corresponds to keeping the cost constant, and an infinite cost is incurred if the absence of a mode switch leads to inconsistencies with respect to the data.

The cost-to-go $\mathcal{V}_k(\xi)$ thus specifies the minimum number of modes that are needed for producing a mode sequence consistent with the data $(y(1), u(1)), \ldots, (y(k), u(k))$ when the interrupt at time k is given by $\xi \in \hat{\Xi}$. In other words, we solve the mode recovery problem, i.e. solve $\mathcal{P}(\Sigma, \mathbf{y}, \mathbf{u})$, by computing

$$\begin{cases} \min_{\xi \in \hat{\Xi}} \mathcal{V}_q(\xi) \\ \mathcal{V}_1(\xi) = 1, \ \forall \xi \in \hat{\Xi}. \end{cases}$$

Now, in order to be able to define $\mathcal{C}_k(\xi, \xi')$ it is vitally important that we have a characterization of when the lack of mode switches produce inconsistencies with respect to the data. To this end, we will introduce a set $\mathcal{M}$ that contains the feedback mappings associated with the current mode. The idea now is to capture inconsistencies by comparing the mapping $k(y(k)) = u(k)$ to the feedback mappings present in the current mode, i.e. to the members of $\mathcal{M}$. To make this observation concrete, we first note that we can construct a bijective mapping $\Pi : \hat{\Xi} \to Y$ by letting

$$\xi(\Pi(\xi')) = \begin{cases} 0 & \text{if } \xi \neq \xi' \\ 1 & \text{if } \xi = \xi'. \end{cases}$$

If we, at time k, use interrupt ξ then we note that a mode switch occurs if and only if $\Pi(\xi) = y(k)$. In that case we should "reset" the description of the current mode. If we let $\mathcal{M}_k(\xi) \subset (Y \times U)^*$, $k \in \{1, \ldots, q\}$, $\xi \in \hat{\Xi}$, we can update $\mathcal{M}$ as

$$\mathcal{M}_k(\xi) = \begin{cases} \{(y(k), u(k))\} & \text{if } \Pi(\xi) = y(k) \\ \{(y(k), u(k))\} \bigcup \mathcal{M}_{k-1}(\xi) & \text{otherwise.} \end{cases}$$

The reason why we use the same ξ as argument to $\mathcal{M}_k$ and $\mathcal{M}_{k-1}$ above is that when $\Pi(\xi) \neq y(k)$ an interrupt is not triggered and the same interrupt is used at time k and time $k - 1$.

Now, what remains to be done is to define the transition costs and we first define a mapping η from $Y \times (Y \times U)^*$ to $U \times \{\epsilon\}$, where ϵ is any symbol not in U. The idea is to use $\eta(y, \mathcal{M}_k(\xi))$ to produce the $u \in U$ that the current mode maps y to, i.e. to let

$$\eta(y, \mathcal{M}_k(\xi)) = \begin{cases} u & \text{if } (y, u) \in \mathcal{M}_k(\xi) \\ \epsilon & \text{otherwise.} \end{cases}$$

The transition cost $\mathcal{C}$ can thus be given by

$$\mathcal{C}_k(\xi, \xi') = \begin{cases} 1 & \text{if } \Pi(\xi) = y(k) \\ \infty & \text{if } \Pi(\xi) \neq y(k) \wedge \left(\xi \neq \xi' \vee \eta(y(k), \mathcal{M}_{k-1}(\xi)) \notin \{\epsilon, u(k)\} \right) \\ 0 & \text{otherwise.} \end{cases}$$

From Lemma 1 we know that $\mathcal{P}(\Sigma, \mathbf{y}, \mathbf{u})$ has a finite solution, i.e. that the dynamic programming problem is guaranteed to produce the optimal solution [3] since, by construction, $\mathcal{C}$ and $\mathcal{M}$ are designed in such a way that by solving Bellman's equation we recover the shortest string of modes consistent with the data.

Proposition 1. *If*

$$\xi(q) = \mathrm{argmin}_{\xi \in \hat{\Xi}} \{ \mathcal{V}_q(\xi) \}$$
$$\xi(k-1) = \mathrm{argmin}_{\xi' \in \hat{\Xi}} \{ \mathcal{C}_k(\xi(k), \xi') + \mathcal{V}_{k-1}(\xi') \}, \quad k = q, \dots, 2,$$

then $length(\mathcal{P}(\Sigma, \mathbf{y}, \mathbf{u})) = \mathcal{V}_q(\xi(q)) = card\Big(\{ k \in \{2, \dots, q\} \mid \Pi(\xi(k)) = y(k) \} \Big) + 1.$

Furthermore, we can bound the computational effort involved in solving Bellman's equation in a straightforward manner:

Proposition 2. *Given the output-input string* $(y(1), u(1)), \dots, (y(q), u(q))$. *The number of operations needed for solving the Bellman equation is bounded above by* $\mathcal{O}(qcard(Y)^3)$.

Proof: When solving the dynamic programming problem a total number of $card(\hat{\Xi}) = card(Y)$ possible interrupts must be investigated at each step $k = 1, \dots, q$, i.e. a total number of $qcard(Y)$ nodes must be investigated in the dynamic programming graph. For each node the transition cost $\mathcal{C}_k(\xi, \xi')$ must be computed for all $\xi' \in \hat{\Xi}$, which is obtained by searching through $\mathcal{M}_{k-1}(\xi)$ for inconsistencies. But, $\mathcal{M}$ can at most contain $card(Y)$ consistent output-input pairs, i.e. the total number of computations needed for obtaining $\mathcal{C}_k(\xi, \xi')$ is bounded by $\mathcal{O}(card(Y))$, and the proof follows. $\qquad\square$

Example

As an illustrative example, consider the problem of recovering the mode string when the data $(y(1), u(1)), \dots , (y(6), u(6))$ is given by

y	0 0 1 2 0 1
u	2 0 0 2 1 0

We note that $Y = U = \{0, 1, 2\}$ and we let $\xi_i \in \hat{\Xi}$ denote the interrupt such that $\xi_i(i) = 1$, $i = 0, 1, 2$. We also switch the order of the data string in the dynamic programming algorithm for notational convenience. Hence $(y(1), u(1)) = (1, 0)$, $(y(2), u(2)) = (0, 1)$, and so on.

Step 1:
$\mathcal{V}_1(\xi_i) = 1$ and $\mathcal{M}_1(\xi_i) = \{(y(1), u(1))\} = \{(1, 0)\}$, $\forall i \in \{0, 1, 2\}$.

Step 2:
Since $\Pi(\xi_0) = y(2) = 0$ we get that $\mathcal{C}_2(\xi_0, \xi) = 1$, $\forall \xi \in \hat{\Xi}$, and hence $\mathcal{M}_2(\xi_0) = \{(y(2), u(2))\} = \{(0, 1)\}$. Furthermore, $\eta(y(2), \mathcal{M}_1(\xi)) = \epsilon, \forall \xi \in \hat{\Xi}$ since $y(2) = 0$ is not present in any output-input pairs in $\mathcal{M}_1$, and hence, for $i = 1, 2, \mathcal{C}_2(\xi_i, \xi) = 0$, $\forall \xi \in \hat{\Xi}$, which gives us that

$$\mathcal{V}_2(\xi_0) = 2, \quad \mathcal{V}_2(\xi_1) = 1, \quad \mathcal{V}_2(\xi_2) = 1,$$

as shown in Figure 2. Furthermore, for $i = 1, 2, \mathcal{M}_2(\xi_i) = \{(y(1), u(1)), (y(2), u(2))\}$ which is equal to $\{(1, 0), (0, 1)\}$.

This procedure can be repeated until Step 6, at which point $\min_{\xi \in \hat{\Xi}} \{\mathcal{V}_6(\xi)\} = 3$, as shown in Figure 2. The optimal mode string is thus given by the mode triple $(k_1, \xi_1), (k_2, \xi_2), (k_3, \xi_3)$ where the subscript denotes the order in the string, and where

$$\begin{cases} k_1(0) = 2, \ \xi_1(0) = 1 \\ k_2(0) = 0, \ k_2(1) = 0 \\ \quad \xi_2(0) = 0, \ \xi_2(1) = 1 \\ k_3(0) = 1, \ k_3(1) = 0, \ k_3(2) = 2 \\ \xi_3(0) = 0 \ \xi_3(1) = 1, \ \xi_3(2) = 0. \end{cases}$$

6   Autonomous Robots

The interest in constructing control procedures that could be coded using few bits was originally triggered by a desire to teleoperate mobile robots in communication constrained environments. We therefore report on our findings when collecting empirical data from an experiment where we let an autonomous robot navigate through a cluttered environment using a behavior-based control algorithm [1]. The key observation to be made is that for the dynamic programming algorithm to be applicable, the cardinality of Y and U as well as the length of the string of output-input pairs must be finite. In this example we therefore quantize the temporally sampled measurements and control actions made by the

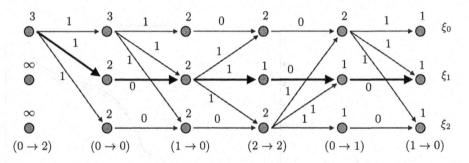

Fig. 2. Depicted is the dynamic programming graph associated with the example. The number over each node gives the cost-to-go, and the arc-number is the transition cost. The solid arrows furthermore show one, of many, optimal solutions.

robot. In particular, we let the robot be of a unicyle-type, i.e. its dynamics is given by

$$\dot{x}_1 = v \cos \phi$$
$$\dot{x}_2 = v \sin \phi$$
$$\dot{\phi} = \omega,$$

where (x_1, y_2) is the position and ϕ is the heading of the robot. The translational and angular velocities (v, ω) are the controlled variables, and we quantize them according to $u \in \{(v, \omega) \mid v \in V, \ \omega \in \Omega\}$, where

$$V = \{\text{slow, medium, fast}\}$$
$$\Omega = \{\text{fast left, slow left, straight, slow right, fast right}\}.$$

In a similar manner the measurements made by the robot are sampled and quantized to produce an output string. We let $y \in \{(y_1, y_2, y_3) \mid y_1 \in Y_1, \ y_2 \in Y_2, \ y_3 \in Y_3\}$, where y_1 gives the distance to the closest obstacle, y_2 gives the relative angle to the closest obstacle, and y_3 gives the relative angle to the goal. By letting the angular quantization be given by the positions of the individual sonars on the sonar-ring, as shown in Figure 3(a), we get

$$Y_1 = \{\text{close, medium, far}\}$$
$$Y_2 = \{1, 2, \dots, 8\}$$
$$Y_3 = \{1, 2, \dots, 8\}.$$

In the experiment, we let the actual robot be controlled using

$$v = v_0 \min\{1, (d_{ob}/D)^2\}$$
$$\omega = C_{ob}(d_{ob})(\phi_{ob} + \pi - \phi) + C_g(\phi_g - \phi),$$

where D is a prespecified safety distance, d_{ob}, ϕ_{ob} is the distance and direction to the closest obstacle, ϕ_g is direction to the goal, and $C_{ob}(d_{ob}) = 0$ if $d_{ob} \geq D$ and $(d_{ob} - D)/d_{ob}^3$ otherwise.

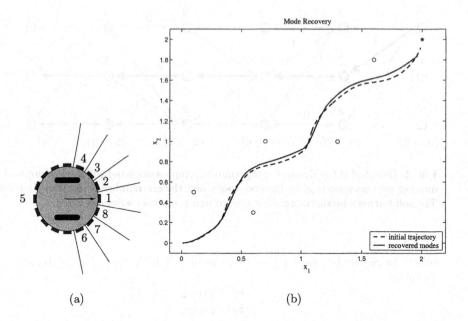

(a)   (b)

Fig. 3. In the left figure, the angular quantization is depicted, while the right figure shows the effect of controlling the robot using a recovered mode string.

The results from applying the dynamic programming algorithm to the data obtained from one string of output-input pairs is shown in Figure 3(b). There the real execution (dashed) is shown together with the effect of controlling the robot using the recovered mode string (solid). In the example, $card(Y) = 192$, $card(U) = 15$, $q = 233$, and the total number of modes is three, i.e. $length(\mathcal{P}(\varSigma, \mathbf{y}, \mathbf{u})) = 3$.

7   Conclusions

In this paper we present a numerically tractable solution to the problem of recovering modes from empirical data. Given a string of output-input pairs, the shortest string of mode triples that is consistent with the data is computed using dynamic programming. This has implications for how to generate multi-modal control laws by observing real systems, but also for the way the control procedures should be coded. The dynamic programming algorithm can be thought of as providing a description of what modes are useful for solving a particular task, from which an empirical probability distribution over the set of modes can be obtained. This probability distribution can be put to work when coding the control procedures, since a more common mode should be coded using fewer bits than an uncommon one. This work has thus a number of potential applications from teleoperated robotics, control over communication constrained networks, to minimum attention control.

References

1. R.C. Arkin. *Behavior Based Robotics*. The MIT Press, Cambridge, MA, 1998.
2. K.J. Åström and B.M. Bernhardsson. Comparison of Riemann and Lebesgue Sampling for First Order Stochastic Systems. In *IEEE Conference on Decision and Control*, pp. 2011–2016, Las Vegas, NV, Dec. 2002.
3. D.P. Bertsekas. *Dynamic Programming and Optimal Control, Vol. 1*. Athena Scientific, Belmont, MA, 1995.
4. R.W. Brockett. On the Computer Control of Movement. In the *Proceedings of the 1988 IEEE Conference on Robotics and Automation*, pp. 534–540, New York, April 1988.
5. R.W. Brockett. Hybrid Models for Motion Control Systems. In *Perspectives in Control*, Eds. H. Trentelman and J.C. Willems, pp. 29–54, Birkhäuser, Boston, 1993.
6. T.M. Cover and J.A. Thomas. *Elements of Information Theory*, John Wiley & Sons, Inc., New York, 1991.
7. M. Egerstedt. Some Complexity Aspects of the Control of Mobile Robots. *American Control Conference*, Anchorage, Alaska, May, 2002.
8. M. Egerstedt and R.W. Brockett. Feedback Can Reduce the Specification Complexity of Motor Programs. To appear in *IEEE Transactions on Automatic Control*, 2002.
9. M. Egerstedt. On the Specification Complexity of Linguistic Control Procedures. *International Journal of Hybrid Systems*, Vol. 2, No. 2, 2002.
10. M. Egerstedt. Motion Description Languages for Multi-Modal Control in Robotics. In *Control Problems in Robotics, Springer Tracts in Advanced Robotics* (A. Bicchi, H. Cristensen and D. Prattichizzo Eds.), Springer-Verlag, pp. 75–90, Las Vegas, NV, Dec. 2002.
11. T.A. Henzinger. Masaccio: A Formal Model for Embedded Components. *Proceedings of the First IFIP International Conference on Theoretical Computer Science*, Lecture Notes in Computer Science 1872, Springer-Verlag, 2000.
12. J.E. Hopcroft and G. Wilfong. Motion of Objects in Contact. *The International Journal of Robotics Research*, Vol. 4, No. 4, pp. 32–46, 1986.
13. J.E. Hopcroft, R. Motwani, and J.D. Ullman. *Introduction to Automata Theory, Languages, and Computation, 2nd Ed.*, Addison-Wesley, New York, 2001.
14. D. Hristu and S. Andersson. Directed Graphs and Motion Description Languages for Robot Navigation and Control. *Proceedings of the IEEE Conference on Robotics and Automation*, May. 2002.
15. D.A. Huffman. A Method for the Construction of Minimum Redundancy Codes. *Proceedings of IRE*, Vol. 40, pp. 1098–1101, 1952.
16. V. Manikonda, P.S. Krishnaprasad, and J. Hendler. Languages, Behaviors, Hybrid Architectures and Motion Control. In *Mathematical Control Theory*, Eds. Willems and Baillieul, pp. 199–226, Springer-Verlag, 1998.
17. J. Rissanen. *Stochastic Complexity in Statistical Inquiry*. World Scientific Publishing Company, River Edge, NJ, 1989.
18. C.E. Shannon. A Mathematical Theory of Communication. *Bell Systems Technical Journal*, Vol. 27, pp. 379–423, 1948.

Hybrid Control Design for a Wheeled Mobile Robot

Thomas Bak[1], Jan Bendtsen[1], and Anders P. Ravn[2]

[1] Department of Control Engineering, Aalborg University, Fredrik Bajers Vej 7C,
DK-9220 Aalborg, Denmark, {tb,dimon}@control.auc.dk
[2] Department of Computer Science, Aalborg University, Fredrik Bajers Vej 7E,
DK-9220 Aalborg, Denmark, apr@cs.auc.dk

Abstract. We present a hybrid systems solution to the problem of trajectory tracking for a four-wheel steered four-wheel driven mobile robot. The robot is modelled as a non-holonomic dynamic system subject to pure rolling, no-slip constraints. Under normal driving conditions, a nonlinear trajectory tracking feedback control law based on dynamic feedback linearization is sufficient to stabilize the system and ensure asymptotically stable tracking. Transitions to other modes are derived systematically from this model, whenever the configuration space of the controlled system has some fundamental singular points. The stability of the hybrid control scheme is finally analyzed using Lyapunov-like arguments.

1 Introduction

Wheeled mobile robots is an active research area with promising new application domains. Mobile robots are mechanical systems characterized by challenging (nonintegrable) constraints on the velocities which have led to numerous interesting path tracking control solutions, see [16], [13], [4], and the recent survey of non-holonomic control problems in [11]. Recently, [3] and [1] have addressed the robot path tracking problem from a hybrid systems perspective. In this paper, we consider a problem of similar complexity and develop a systematic approach to derivation of a hybrid automaton and to stability analysis.

Our work is motivated by a project currently in progress, where an autonomous four-wheel driven, four-wheel steered robot (Figure 1) is being developed. The project needs a robot that is able to survey an agricultural field autonomously. The vehicle has to navigate to certain waypoints where measurements of the crop and weed density are obtained. This information is processed and combined into a digital map of the field, which will eventually allow the farm manager to deal with weed infestations in a spatially precise manner. The robot is equipped with GPS, gyros, magnetometer and odometers, which will not only help in the exact determination of the location where each image is taken, but also provide measurements for an estimate of the robot's position and orientation for a tracking algorithm. Actuation is achieved using independent steering and drive on four wheel assemblies (8 brushless DC motors in total). The robot navigates from waypoint to waypoint following spline-type trajectories between

O. Maler and A. Pnueli (Eds.): HSCC 2003, LNCS 2623, pp. 50–65, 2003.
© Springer-Verlag Berlin Heidelberg 2003

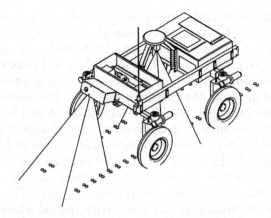

Fig. 1. Schematic model of the experimental platform. The robot is equipped with 8 independent steering and drive motors. Localization is based on fusion of GPS, gyro, magnetometer, and odometer data.

the waypoints to minimize damage to the crop. From a control point of view, this is a tracking problem. To solve this problem a dynamical model of the vehicle subject to pure rolling, no-slip constraints has been developed, following the approach taken in [5] and [6]. Based on this nonlinear model, we design a path tracking control law based on feedback linearization.

Feedback linearization designs have the potential of reaching a low degree of conservativeness, since they rely on explicit cancelling of nonlinearities. However, such designs can also be quite sensitive to noise, modelling errors, actuator saturation, etc. As pointed out in [8], uncertainties can cause instability under normal driving conditions. This instability is caused by loss of invertibility of the mapping representing the nonlinearities in the model. Furthermore, there are certain wheel and vehicle velocity configurations that lead to similar losses of invertibility. Since these phenomena are, in fact, linked to the chosen control strategy rather than the mechanics of the robot itself, we propose in this paper to switch between control strategies such that the aforementioned stability issues can be avoided. This idea is also treated in [15], where singularities in the feedback linearization control law of a ball-and-beam system is treated by switching to an approximate control scheme in the vicinity of the singular points in state space.

In this paper, we intend to motivate the rules for when and how to change between the individual control strategies directly from the mathematical-physical model. We will consider the conditions under which the description may break down during each step in the derivation of the model and control laws. These conditions will then define transitions in a hybrid automaton that will be used as a control supervisor.

However, introducing a hybrid control scheme in order to improve the operating range where the robot can operate in a stable manner comes at a cost:

The arguments for stability become more complex. Not only must each individual control scheme be stable; they must also be stable under transitions (refer to e.g., [12] and the references therein for further information on stability theory for switched systems). A straightforward analysis will show that the system can always be rendered unstable: Just vary the reference input such that transitions are always taken before the transition safe state. We therefore intend to apply the generalized Lyapunov stability theory as introduced by Branicky in [2] to add a second automaton that can constrain the change of the reference input (the trajectory) such that the resulting system remains stable.

We abstract the Lyapunov functions to constant rate functions, where the rates are equivalent to the convergence rate. Each mode or state of the original automaton is then replaced by three consecutive states. The first of these states models the initial transition cost and settling period where the function may increase, albeit for a bounded time, while the second and third state models the working mode with the local Lyapunov function. The third state is the transition safe state, where the Lyapunov function has decreased below its entry value. All three states are guarded by the original conditions for a mode change; but it is potentially unsafe to leave before the third state is entered.

This automaton thus defines safe operating conditions, or put another way: Constraints to be satisfied by the trajectory planner. The composed automaton is in a form where model checking tools can be employed for the analysis. The robot thereby has a tool for determining online whether or not a given candidate trajectory is safe from a stability point of view.

2   Dynamic Model and Linearization

In the following we derive the model and the normal mode control scheme. During the derivation we note conditions for mode changes.

We consider a four-wheel driven, four-wheel steered robot moving on a horizontal plane, constructed from a rigid frame with four identical wheels. Each wheel can turn freely around its horizontal and vertical axis. The contact points between each of the wheels and the ground must satisfy pure rolling and non-slip conditions.[1]

Consider a reference ('field') coordinate system (X_F, Y_F) in the plane of motion as illustrated in Figure 2. The robot position is then completely described by the coordinates (X, Y) of a reference point within the robot frame, which without loss of generality can be chosen as the center of mass, and the orientation θ relative to the field coordinate system of a ('vehicle') coordinate system (X_v, Y_v) fixed to the robot frame. These coordinates are collected in the *posture* vector $\xi = [X\ Y\ \theta]^{\mathrm{T}} \in \mathbb{R}^2 \times \mathbb{S}^1$.

---

[1] The pure rolling and non-slip conditions can obviously not be satisfied in the real-life application, where the robot drives in a muddy field. They are primarily employed here in order to enable us to derive control laws that minimize the amount of slip and the degree by which the wheels 'work against each other.'

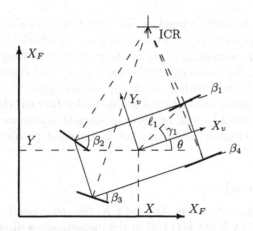

Fig. 2. Definition of the field coordinate system (X_F, Y_F), vehicle coordinate system (X_v, Y_v), vehicle orientation θ, distance ℓ_1, and direction γ_1 from the center of mass (X, Y) to wheel 1. Each wheel plane is perpendicular to the Instantaneous Center of Rotation (ICR).

The position of the i'th wheel $(1 \leq i \leq 4)$ in the vehicle coordinate system is characterized by the angle γ_i and the distance ℓ_i. As the wheels are not allowed to slip, the planes of each of the wheels must at all times be tangential to concentric circles with the center in the Instantaneous Center of Rotation (ICR). The orientation of the plane of the i'th wheel relative to X_v is denoted β_i. The vector $\beta = [\beta_1 \ \beta_2 \ \beta_3 \ \beta_4]^T \in \mathbb{S}^4$ define the wheel orientations.

From an operational point of view a relevant specification of the ICR is to give the orientation of two of the four wheels. We therefore partition β into $\beta_c \in \mathbb{S}^2$ containing the coordinates used to control the ICR location and $\beta_o \in \mathbb{S}^2$ containing the two remaining coordinates that may be derived from the first.

Cross Driving (Singular Wheel Configuration). An important ambiguity (or singular wheel configuration), is present in the approach taken above. For $\beta_1 = \pm\pi/2$ and $\beta_2 = \pm\pi/2$ the configuration of wheels 3 and 4 is not defined. The situation corresponds to the ICR being located on the line through wheel 1 and 2. The wheel configuration $\beta_c = [\beta_3 \ \beta_4]^T$ result in similar problems and both configurations fail during cross driving as all wheels are at $\pm\pi/2$. To ensure safe solutions to the trajectory tracking problem we must ensure that the singular configurations are avoided at all times. Based on this discussion we identify three discrete control modes, q_1, q_2 and q_3:

q_1: Trajectory tracking with $\beta_c = [\beta_1 \ \beta_2]^T$. This mode is conditioned on $|\beta_1| < (\frac{\pi}{2} - e_\beta) \vee |\beta_2| < (\frac{\pi}{2} - e_\beta)$.

q_2: Trajectory tracking with $\beta_c = [\beta_3 \ \beta_4]^T$. This mode is conditioned on $|\beta_3| < (\frac{\pi}{2} - e_\beta) \vee |\beta_4| < (\frac{\pi}{2} - e_\beta)$.

q_3: Cross Driving with $\beta_1 = \beta_2 = \beta_3 = \beta_4$. This mode is conditioned on $(|\beta_1| \geq (\frac{\pi}{2} - e_\beta) \vee |\beta_2| \geq (\frac{\pi}{2} - e_\beta)) \wedge (|\beta_3| \geq (\frac{\pi}{2} - e_\beta) \vee |\beta_4| \geq (\frac{\pi}{2} - e_\beta))$.

where e_β is a small positive number. The two first modes cover the situations where the ICR is governed by wheels 1 and 2 and by wheel 3 and 4, respectively. The last covers the remainder of the configuration space where ICR is approximately at infinity. For brevity of the exposition, we will consider $\beta_c = [\beta_1 \; \beta_2]^T$ in the following; the case with $\beta_c = [\beta_3 \; \beta_4]^T$ is analogous.

In general, no set of two variables is able to describe all wheel configurations without singularities [14]. The problem of singular configurations is hence not due to the representation used here, but is a general problem for this type of robotic systems.

2.1   Vehicle Model

Following the argumentation in Appendix A, the robot posture can be manipulated via one velocity input $\eta(t) \in \mathbb{R}$ in the instantaneous direction of the wheel orientation state $\Sigma(\beta_c) \in \mathbb{R}^3$, which is constructed to meet the pure-roll constraint. Similarly, it is possible to manipulate the orientation of the wheels via an orientation velocity input $\zeta(t) = [\dot\beta_1 \; \dot\beta_2]^T \in \mathbb{R}^2$. The no-slip condition on the wheels that constrain $\eta(t)$ is handled (see Appendix A) by applying Lagrange formalism and computed torque techniques. The result is the following extended dynamical model:

$$\dot\chi = \begin{bmatrix} \dot\xi \\ \dot\eta \\ \dot\beta_c \end{bmatrix} = \begin{bmatrix} 0 & R^T(\theta)\Sigma(\beta_c) & 0 \\ 0 & 0 & 0 \\ 0 & 0 & 0 \end{bmatrix} \chi + \begin{bmatrix} 0 & 0 \\ 1 & 0 \\ 0 & I \end{bmatrix} \begin{bmatrix} \nu \\ \zeta \end{bmatrix} \tag{1}$$

where ν is a new exogenous input that is related to the torque applied to the drive motors, and $R^T(\theta)$ is a coordinate rotation matrix. In equation (1) it is assumed that the β dynamics can be controlled via local servo loops, such that we can manipulate $\dot\beta$ as an exogenous input to the model.

2.2   Normal Trajectory Tracking Control

Provided we avoid the singular wheel configurations the standard approach from here on is to transform the states into normal form via an appropriate diffeomorphism followed by feedback linearization of the nonlinearities and a standard linear control design. We choose the new states

$$x_1 = T(\chi) = \begin{bmatrix} \xi_{ref} - \xi \\ \dot\xi_{ref} - \dot\xi \end{bmatrix}, \tag{2}$$

which yields the following dynamics:

$$\dot x_1 = A_1 x_1 + B_1 \left(\delta(\chi) \begin{bmatrix} \nu \\ \zeta \end{bmatrix} - \alpha(\chi) \right), \quad A_1 = \begin{bmatrix} 0 & I \\ 0 & 0 \end{bmatrix}, \quad B_1 = \begin{bmatrix} 0 \\ I \end{bmatrix}. \tag{3}$$

Using the results from Appendix A, $\delta(\chi)$ and $\alpha(\chi)$ may be found to

$$\delta(\chi) = R^T(\theta) \left[\Sigma(\beta_c) \; N(\beta_c)\eta \right] \tag{4}$$

and

$$\alpha(\chi) = \sin(\beta_1 - \beta_2)\eta^2 \begin{bmatrix} -\ell_1 \sin\beta_2 \cos(\beta_1 - \gamma_1) + \ell_2 \sin\beta_1 \cos(\beta_2 - \gamma_2) \\ \ell_1 \cos\beta_2 \cos(\beta_1 - \gamma_1) - \ell_2 \cos\beta_1 \cos(\beta_2 - \gamma_2) \\ 0 \end{bmatrix} \quad (5)$$

where $N(\beta_c) = [N_1 \ N_2]$ is specified in equations (20) and (21). When we apply
the control law

$$\begin{bmatrix} \nu \\ \varsigma \end{bmatrix} = \delta(\chi)^{-1}(\alpha(\chi) - K_1 x_1) \quad (6)$$

we obtain the closed-loop dynamics $\dot{x}_1 = (A_1 - B_1 K_1)x_1$, which tends to 0
as $t \to \infty$ if K_1 is chosen such that $A_1 - B_1 K_1$ has eigenvalues with negative
real parts. Similar dynamics can be obtained for the mode with $\beta_c = [\beta_3 \ \beta_4]^T$,
resulting in closed-loop dynamics $\dot{x}_2 = (A_2 - B_2 K_2)x_2$.

2.3 Cross Driving Control

The normal trajectory tracking cannot be applied in the singular wheel configurations and a specific control must hence be derived that is able to control the
vehicle when all wheels are parallel. Fortunately, the dynamics of the robot becomes particularly simple in this case. With $\dot{\theta} = 0$ the dynamics are immediately
linear; hence, choosing the states

$$x_3 = T\chi = \begin{bmatrix} \xi_{ref} - \xi \\ \dot{\xi}_{ref} - \dot{\xi} \end{bmatrix}, \quad (7)$$

where T is an appropriate invertible matrix, yields the dynamics

$$\dot{x}_3 = A_3 x_3 + B_3 \begin{bmatrix} \nu \\ 0 \end{bmatrix}, \quad A_3 = \begin{bmatrix} 0 & I \\ A_{31} & A_{32} \end{bmatrix}, \quad B_3 = \begin{bmatrix} 0 \\ I \end{bmatrix} \quad (8)$$

which can be controlled by applying the feedback $\nu = -K_3 x_3$. Note that this
controller does perform any control on the wheel orientation. In order not to
remain in the mode q_3 we impose a new condition, based on the error in orien-
tation, $|\theta_{ref} - \theta|$ ¡ a, where a is a small positive number.

2.4 Rest Configurations

During the feedback linearization design we detect another interesting condition
due to the inversion of $\delta(\chi)$. If $\delta(\chi)$ looses rank, the control strategy breaks down
and the control input grows to infinity. If we avoid the rest configuration, $\eta = 0$,
then $\Sigma(\beta_c)$ specifies the current direction of movement and the column vectors
N_1 and N_2 are perpendicular to this direction and to each other. To avoid an
ill-conditioned $\delta(\chi)$ we must impose a new condition, $|\eta| \geq n$, where n is a small
positive number, on our trajectory tracking modes.

To complete the construction, we add additional modes to handle the rest
configuration. First assume that the robot is started with $\beta_1 = \beta_2 = \beta_3 = \beta_4$. We

may then utilize the controller defined for the cross driving (q_3) mode, choosing ξ_{ref} as an appropriate point on the straight line originating from the center of mass in the direction defined by β along with

$$\dot{\xi}_{ref} = \begin{bmatrix} \eta_{ref} \\ \zeta_{ref} \end{bmatrix} = \begin{bmatrix} 2n \\ 0 \end{bmatrix} \tag{9}$$

This mode (q_0) allows the robot to start from rest. Finally we add a mode q_4 to handle a stop. Again we assume that the wheels have been oriented by the control laws in mode q_1 or q_2 such that the waypoint lies on the straight line from the center of mass in the direction defined by β. We may then apply the same state transformation as in equation (7) along with the same state feedback, and choosing ξ_{ref} as the target waypoint along with $\dot{\xi}_{ref} = 0$.

3   Hybrid Automaton Supervisor

The trajectory tracking problem for this particular robot may be solved by applying the different control laws, as outlined above for different modes. The conditions for exiting the modes have been defined as well. For each of these modes, we defined special control schemes, and conditions. Given that there are two modes where the robot is at rest, and three modes where the robot is driving, it is straightforward to introduce two super-modes, *Rest* and *Driving*. This gives rise to the hierarchical hybrid automaton implemented using Stateflow as shown in Figure 3.

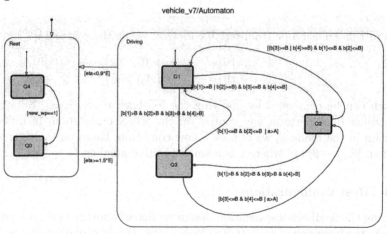

Here b[i] is β_i, B is $\frac{\pi}{2} - e_\beta$ a is $|\theta_{ref} - \theta|$, and A, E, are small positive numbers.

Fig. 3. Stateflow representation of Automaton.

The hybrid automaton [10] consists of five discrete states, $\mathcal{Q} = \{q_0, q_1, q_2, q_3, q_4\}$ as defined during the model and controller derivation. The continuous state x defined by equation (2) or (7) belongs to the state space $\mathcal{X} \subseteq \mathbb{R}^2 \times \mathbb{S}^1 \times \mathbb{R}^3$. The corresponding hybrid state space is $\mathcal{H} = \mathcal{Q} \times \mathcal{X}$. The vector fields are defined by

$$f(q, x) = \begin{cases} (A_3 - B_3 K_3)x_0 & \text{if } q = q_0, \\ (A_1 - B_1 K_1)x_1 & \text{if } q = q_1, \\ (A_2 - B_2 K_2)x_2 & \text{if } q = q_2, \\ (A_3 - B_3 K_3)x_3 & \text{if } q = q_3, \\ (A_3 - B_3 K_3)x_4 & \text{if } q = q_4. \end{cases} \tag{10}$$

Conditions and guards are given in Figure 3 based on the derivations in Section 2. The system including the supervisor was simulated in Simulink and the tracking of an example trajectory is shown in Figure 4. The system is clearly

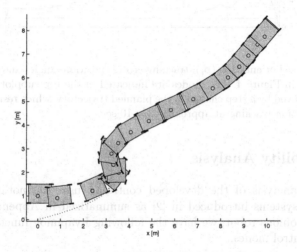

Fig. 4. Tracking a reference trajectory. The vehicle is initially at rest offset from the trajectory by 1 meter in the y-direction.

able to start from a rest configuration, track the trajectory and stop at a rest configuration. In this example the controller starts in the mode q_4, switches to a new waypoint and trajectory information becomes available. As η grows the mode is changed to q_3 and eventually q_1. As the conditions on steering wheels (β_c) are violated the control switches to mode q_2. Finally as the vehicle approaches the end waypoint the mode returns q_4 and stops. As the endpoint is defined by the direction of $\Sigma(\beta_c)$, and the orientation of the wheels are near parallel (and without control) the vehicle reaches the final waypoint with a small error.

Mode changes, tracking errors and wheel positions are given in Figure 5.

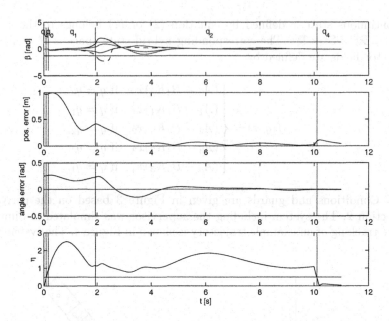

Fig. 5. Wheel orientation (β_i), tracking errors (position, angle) and the input η for the case given in Figure 4. The modes are indicated in the top subplot. The transition to rest is achieved by a step change in the planned trajectory, which result in a disturbance in the position tracking at approximately 10 sec.

4   Stability Analysis

Stability analysis of the developed controller uses the notion of stability of switched systems introduced in [2] as summarized in Appendix B. In case of the autonomous robot, we have the following Lyapunov functions for the individual control modes.

q_0: Starting from rest with $\beta_1 = \beta_2 = \beta_3 = \beta_4$: $V_0(x_0) = x_0^T P_3 x_0$.
q_1: Trajectory tracking with $\beta_c = [\beta_1 \ \beta_2]^T$: $V_1(x_1) = x_1^T P_1 x_1$
q_2: Trajectory tracking with $\beta_c = [\beta_3 \ \beta_4]^T$: $V_2(x_2) = x_2^T P_2 x_2$
q_3: Cross driving with $\beta_1 = \beta_2 = \beta_3 = \beta_4$: $V_3(x_3) = x_3^T P_3 x_3$
q_4: Stopping with $\beta_1 = \beta_2 = \beta_3 = \beta_4$: $V_4(x_4) = x_4^T P_3 x_4$.

In each of the cases listed above, $P_j = P_j^T > 0$ is the positive definite solution to the Lyapunov equation $P_j(A_j - B_j K_j) + (A_j - B_j K_j)^T P_j = -I$. Note that for modes q_0 and q_4, the same state feedback K_3 and solution matrix P_3 as in mode q_3 are used. Elementary calculations now yield

$$V_j = \dot{x}_j^T P_j x_j + x_j^T P_j \dot{x}_j = -x_j^T x_j.$$

With this in place, we can now attempt to analyze the combination of the Lyapunov functions using a hybrid automaton. We note that since we focus on stability only, we can in each mode abstract from the concrete evolution of the state and replace it by the evolution of the Lyapunov function. For each discrete state $q_j, j = 0, \ldots, 4$ in the automaton in Figure 3 we introduce three consecutive states $q'_{j,k}, k = 0, 1, 2$, which evaluate a constant rate variable Λ_j that dominates the j'th Lyapunov function. These states are: An *entry* state $q'_{j,0}$, which represents the gain in the Lyapunov function $V_j(x_j)$ at the instant the hybrid control law switches to mode j; an *active* state $q'_{j,1}$, which represents the period where the feedback control $[\nu \ \zeta^T]^T = -K_j x_j$ is active, and where $V_j(x_j)$ is decreasing toward 0; and a state $q'_{j,2}$, where $V_j(x_j)$ has decreased below the entry level. The basic idea is depicted in Figure 4. When the control enters mode

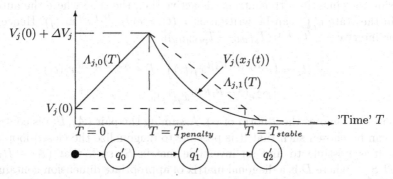

Fig. 6. *Three-state automaton abstracting the Lyapunov function of mode j. The entry, active and stabilized states are indicated below the figure.*

j at time t_j, the Lyapunov function will have gained an amount ΔV_j since the last time it was active. This is modelled abstractly as a constant rate function $\Lambda_{j,0}(T) = T + V_j(t_j), 0 \le T \le T_{penalty}$, where the 'time' $T_{penalty}$ is determined as $\Delta V_j = T_{penalty}$. Here, T is an abstract time used for the evaluation of the constant rate function that dominates the j'th Lyapunov function, and which is reset to 0 every time mode q_j is entered. At $T = T_{penalty}$, the system enters the *active* state, in which $\dot{V}_j$ is negative definite. Consequently, $V_j(x_j(t)), t_j \le t \le t + T_{stable} - T_{penalty}$ is bounded from above by the function $\Lambda_{j,1}(T) = -\alpha_o T + \Delta V_j + V_j(0), T_{penalty} \le T \le T_{stable}, \alpha_o \ge 0$, i.e., another constant rate automaton. T_{stable} is the time where $\Lambda_{j,1}(T) = V_j(0)$; at this point the state changes to $q'_{j,2}$. In order to complete the construction, we must, for each mode change, find the maximal transition penalty ΔV_j which determines $T_{penalty}$, and a suitable α_o.

In general, the transition penalty is the difference between two Lyapunov functions, at the transition point x_j from mode q_i to q_j. In our case, we note that the domains of the Lyapunov functions for the driving modes q_1, q_2, q_3 are identical, cf. equations (2) and (7). Thus the transition penalty is of the form $x_j^T(P_j - P_i)x_j$. Here, we can choose to use the minimum of the P-matrices for all three Lyapunov functions, thus overapproximating the larger ones. This results in a transition penalty of zero, and we can conclude that the system is stable irrespective of the transition pattern while driving. For the transitions to stop mode q_4 and from start mode q_0, the domains are different, cf. equation (9). In the stop transition mode, we can safely ignore the term from the driving Lyapunov function, thus we get a penalty less than $x_4^T P_3 x_4$, where the magnitude of x_4 is determined by the difference $\xi_{ref} - \xi$ and the velocity $\dot{\xi}$. Assuming that the vehicle is stopped only after it has found the trajectory, the first term is close to zero, and the second term is of the order of n. A similar analysis applies to the start to drive mode transition.

The slope α_0 can be evaluated from the entry value $V_j(0)$ and the growth ΔV_j of the j'th Lyapunov function as follows. The solution of the linearized system during the time the j'th controller is active (i.e., the time where the automaton is in the state $q'_{j,k}$) can be written as $x_j(t) = e^{(A_j - B_j K_j)t} x_j(t_j)$. Hence, in the time interval $t \in [t_j; t + (T_{stable} - T_{penalty})]$,

$$V_j(t) = \left(e^{(A_j - B_j K_j)t} x_j(t_j) \right)^T P_j e^{(A_j - B_j K_j)t} x_j(t_j)$$

$$= \| P^{\frac{1}{2}} e^{(A_j - B_j K_j)t} x_j(t_j) \|$$

where $\| \cdot \|$ denotes the 2-norm of $(\cdot)$. Assuming the pair (A_j, B_j) is controllable, K_j can be chosen such that it is possible to diagonalize the closed-loop matrix, i.e., it is possible to find an invertible matrix S_j such that $(A_j - B_j K_j) = S_j D_j S_j^{-1}$, where D is a diagonal matrix of appropriate dimension containing the eigenvalues of $(A_j - B_j K_j)$ in the main diagonal. Thus we have

$$V_j(t)^{\frac{1}{2}} = \| P_j^{\frac{1}{2}} e^{(A_j - B_j K_j)t} x_j(t_j) \|$$

$$= \| P_j^{\frac{1}{2}} S_j e^{D_j t} S_j^{-1} x_j(t_j) \|$$

$$\leq \| P_j^{\frac{1}{2}} S_j \| \, \| S_j^{-1} x_j(t_j) \| \, \| e^{D_j t} \|$$

$$\leq \| P_j^{\frac{1}{2}} S_j \| \, \| S_j^{-1} x_j(t_j) \| \dim(x_j) e^{\lambda_{max}(D_j)}$$

where $P^{\frac{1}{2}}$ is the uniquely determined square matrix satisfying $P = P^{\frac{1}{2}} P^{\frac{1}{2}}$. All the terms in front of the exponential are constants that can be evaluated at time t_j, implying that $(T_{stable} - T_{penalty})$ and α_0 can easily be found once $x_j(t_j)$ is known, i.e., at the transition to mode q_j. As indicated on Figure 4, using the upper bound constant rate functions allows for a certain margin to the actual Lyapunov function, which can be considered a form of 'robustness' of the scheme.

When evaluating the stability of the system for a given trajectory, it is clear that only control transitions from the stabilized state are guaranteed safe. To check for unsafe transitions due to the input we propose to add a second automaton constraining the change of the reference input (the trajectory). This automaton has three states, *startup*, *constant_speed* and *stop* which allows us to specify the basic operation of the path planning. The trajectory planner transitions conditions are guarded by the transitions in the automation describing the Lyapunov function. Mode transitions from the two unsafe states (*entry*, *stabilized*) are redirected to an error mode. When a composition with the path planner has error as an unreachable state – the system is safe. This analysis may be done offline, when trajectories are preplanned, or online, in the case of dynamic trajectory planning.

In the concrete case, the driving modes are safe throughout, while stop and start introduce a jump in the error and thus must be separated by some driving period.

5 Conclusion

We have developed a hybrid control scheme for a path-tracking four-wheel steered mobile robot, and shown how it can be analyzed for stability.

The basis for controller development is standard non-slipping and pure rolling conditions, which are used to establish a kinematic-dynamical model. A normal mode path tracking controller is designed according to feedback linearization methods. Other modes are introduced systematically, where the model has singularities. For each such case a transition condition and a new control mode is introduced. Specialized controllers are developed for such modes.

With the control automaton completed, we found for each mode, Lyapunov-like functions, which combine to prove stability. In order to simplify the analysis, we bound the Lyapunov functions by constant rate functions. This allows us to show stability by analyzing a version of the control automaton, where each mode contains a simple three state automaton that evaluates the constant rate functions.

Discussion and Further Work. In the systematic approach to deriving modes, we list conditions when the normal mode model fails. Some of these, e.g. Cross Driving, are rather obvious; but others, e.g. the Rest Configuration, are less clear, because they are conditions that make the controlled system ill conditioned. Such problems are usually detected during simulation. Thus a practical rendering of the systematic approach is to use a tool like Stateflow and build the normal mode model. When the simulation has problems, one investigates the conditions and defines corresponding transitions. This is an approach that we believe is widely applicable to design of supervisory or mode switched control systems.

Such an approach is evidently only safe to the extent that it is followed by a rigorous stability analysis. The approach we develop is highly systematic. It ends up with a constant rate hybrid automaton which should allow model checking of its properties. In particular, whether it avoids unsafe transitions when composed with an automaton modelling the reference input. A systematic analysis of this combination is, however, future work.

Another point that must be investigated is, how the wheel reference output is made bumpless during mode transitions. Finally, the idealized non-slip and pure rolling conditions are of course impossible to meet in real-life applications (especially the non-slip condition), and the effect of such perturbations must be studied.

Acknowledgement. The authors wish to express their sincere gratitude to the reviewers for their insightful comments. Part of this work was performed at UC Berkeley, and the first author wishes to thank Prof. Shankar Sastry for supporting his visit.

References

1. C. Altafini, A. Speranzon, K.H. Johansson. Hybrid Control of a Truck and Trailer Vehicle, In C. Tomlin, and M. R. Greenstreet, editors, *Hybrid Systems: Computation and Control* LNCS 2289, p. 21ff, Springer-Verlag, 2002.
2. M. S. Branicky. Analyzing and Synthesizing Hybrid Control Systems In G. Rozenberg, and F. Vaandrager, editors, *Lectures on Embedded Systems*, LNCS 1494, pp. 74–113, Springer-Verlag, 1998.
3. A. Balluchi, P. Souères, and A. Bicchi. Hybrid Feedback Control for Path Tracking by a Bounded-Curvature Vehicle In M.D. Di Benedetto, and A.L. Sangiovanni-Vincentelli, editors, *Hybrid Systems: Computation and Control*, LNCS 2034, pp. 133–146, Springer-Verlag, 2001.
4. G. Bastin, G. Campion. Feedback Control of Nonholonomic Mechanical Systems, *Advances in Robot Control*, 1991
5. B. D'Andrea-Novel, G. Campion, G. Bastin. Modeling and Control of Non Holonomic Wheeled Mobile Robots, in *Proc. of the 1991 IEEE International Conference on Robotics and Automation*, 1130–1135, 1991
6. G. Campion, G. Bastin, B. D'Andrea-Novel. Structural Properties and Classification of Kinematic and Dynamic Models of Wheeled Mobile Robots, *IEEE Transactions on Robotics and Automation* Vol. 12, 1:47–62, 1996
7. L. Caracciolo, A. de Luca, S. Iannitti. Trajectory Tracking of a Four-Wheel Differentially Driven Mobile Robot, in *Proc. of the 1999 IEEE International Conference on Robotics and Automation*, 2632–2838, 1999
8. J.D. Bendtsen, P. Andersen, T.S. Pedersen. Robust Feedback Linearization-based Control Design for a Wheeled Mobile Robot, in *Proc. of the 6th International Symposium on Advanced Vehicle Control*, 2002
9. H. Goldstein. Classical Mechanics, Addison-Wesley, 2nd edition, 1980
10. T. A. Henzinger. The Theory of Hybrid Automata, In *Proceedings of the 11th Annual IEEE Symposium on Logic in Computer Science* (LICS 1996), pp. 278–292, 1996.
11. I. Kolmanovsky, N. H. McClamroch. Developments in Nonholonomic Control Problems, *IEEE Control Systems Magazine* Vol. 15, 6:20–36, 1995
12. D. Liberzon, A. S. Morse. Basic Problems in Stability and Design of Switched Systems, *IEEE Control Systems Magazine* Vol. 19, 5:59–70, 1999.
13. C. Samson. Feedback Stabilization of a Nonholonomic Car-like Mobile Robot, In *Proceedings of IEEE Conference on Decision and Control*, 1991.
14. B. Thuilot, B. D'Andrea-Novel, A. Micaelli. Modeling and Feedback Control of Mobile Robots Equipped with Several Steering Wheels, *IEEE Transactions on Robotics and Automation* Vol. 12, 2:375–391, 1996.
15. C. Tomlin, S. Sastry. Switching through Singularities, *Systems and Control Letters* Vol. 35, 3:145–154, 1998.
16. G. Walsh, D. Tilbury, S. Sastry, R. Murray, J.P. Laumond. Stabilization of Trajectories for Systems with Nonholonomic Constraints *IEEE Trans. Automatic Control* 39: (1) 216–222, 1994.

A   Vehicle Dynamics

Denote the rotation coordinates describing the rotation of the wheels around their horizontal axes by $\phi = [\phi_1 \ \phi_2 \ \phi_3 \ \phi_4]^T \in \mathbb{S}^4$ and the radii of the wheels by $r = [r_1 \ r_2 \ r_3 \ r_4] \in \mathbb{R}^4$. The motion of the four-wheel driven, four-wheel steered robot is then completely described by the following 11 generalized coordinates:

$$\kappa = \begin{bmatrix} X \ Y \ \theta \ \beta^T \ \phi^T \end{bmatrix}^T = \begin{bmatrix} \xi^T \ \beta^T \ \phi^T \end{bmatrix}^T \tag{11}$$

and we can write the pure rolling, no slip constraints on the compact matrix form

$$\mathcal{A}(\kappa)\dot{\kappa} = \begin{bmatrix} J_1(\beta)R(\theta) \ 0 \ J_2 \\ C_1(\beta)R(\theta) \ 0 \ 0 \end{bmatrix} \dot{\kappa} = 0 \tag{12}$$

in which

$$J_1(\beta) = \begin{bmatrix} \cos\beta_1 \ \sin\beta_1 \ \ell_1\sin(\beta_1 - \gamma_1) \\ \cos\beta_2 \ \sin\beta_2 \ \ell_2\sin(\beta_2 - \gamma_2) \\ \cos\beta_3 \ \sin\beta_3 \ \ell_3\sin(\beta_3 - \gamma_3) \\ \cos\beta_4 \ \sin\beta_4 \ \ell_4\sin(\beta_4 - \gamma_4) \end{bmatrix} , \quad J_2 = rI_{4\times4},$$

$$C_1(\beta) = \begin{bmatrix} -\sin\beta_1 \ \cos\beta_1 \ \ell_1\cos(\beta_1 - \gamma_1) \\ -\sin\beta_2 \ \cos\beta_2 \ \ell_2\cos(\beta_2 - \gamma_2) \\ -\sin\beta_3 \ \cos\beta_3 \ \ell_3\cos(\beta_3 - \gamma_3) \\ -\sin\beta_4 \ \cos\beta_4 \ \ell_4\cos(\beta_4 - \gamma_4) \end{bmatrix} , \quad \text{and} \quad R(\theta) = \begin{bmatrix} \cos\theta \ \sin\theta \ 0 \\ -\sin\theta \ \cos\theta \ 0 \\ 0 \ \ 0 \ \ 1 \end{bmatrix} .$$

Following the argumentation in [6], the posture velocity $\dot{\xi}$ is constrained to belong to a one-dimensional distribution here parametrized by the orientation angles of two wheels, say, β_1 and β_2. Thus,

$$\dot{\xi} \in \text{span}\{\text{col}\{R(\theta)^T \Sigma(\beta_c)\}\}$$

where $\Sigma(\beta_c) \in \mathbb{R}^3$ is perpendicular to the space spanned by the columns of C_1, i.e., $C_1(\beta)\Sigma(\beta_c) \equiv 0 \ \forall\beta$. Σ can be found by combining the expression for $C_1(\beta)$ with equations for the orientation of wheels 3 and 4 to

$$\Sigma = \begin{bmatrix} \ell_1\cos\beta_2\cos(\beta_1 - \gamma_1) - \ell_2\cos\beta_1\cos(\beta_2 - \gamma_2) \\ \ell_1\sin\beta_2\cos(\beta_1 - \gamma_1) - \ell_2\sin\beta_1\cos(\beta_2 - \gamma_2) \\ \sin(\beta_1 - \beta_2) \end{bmatrix} .$$

The discussion above implies that the robot posture can be manipulated via one velocity input $\eta(t) \in \mathbb{R}$ in the instantaneous direction of $\Sigma(\beta_c)$, that is, $R(\theta)\dot{\xi}(t) = \Sigma(\beta_c)\eta(t) \ \forall t$. Similarly, it is possible to manipulate the orientations of the wheels via an orientation velocity input $\zeta(t) = [\dot{\beta}_1 \ \dot{\beta}_2]^T \in \mathbb{R}^2$.

The constrained dynamics of η are handled by applying Lagrange formalism and computed torque techniques as suggested in [5] and [6]. The Lagrange equations are written on the form [9]

$$\frac{d}{dt}\left(\frac{\partial T}{\partial \dot{\kappa}_k}\right) - \frac{\partial T}{\partial \kappa_k} = c_k(\kappa)^T \lambda + Q_k$$

in which T is the total kinetic energy of the system and κ_k is the k'th generalized coordinate. On the left-hand side, $c_k(\kappa)$ is the k'th column in the kinematic constraint matrix $A(\kappa)$ defined in (12), λ is a vector of Lagrange undetermined coefficients, and Q_k is a generalized force (or torque) acting on the k'th generalized coordinate.

The kinetic energy of the robot is calculated as

$$T = \frac{1}{2}\kappa^\mathrm{T}\begin{bmatrix} R(\theta)^\mathrm{T}MR(\theta) & R(\theta)^\mathrm{T}V & 0 \\ V^\mathrm{T}R(\theta) & J_\beta & 0 \\ 0 & 0 & J_\phi \end{bmatrix}\dot{\kappa} \tag{13}$$

with appropriate choices of M, J_β and J_ϕ. In the case of the wheeled mobile robot we can derive the following expressions:

$$M = \begin{bmatrix} m_f + 4m_w & 0 & -m_w \sum_{i=1}^{4} \ell_i \sin\gamma_i \\ 0 & m_f + 4m_w & m_w \sum_{i=1}^{4} \ell_i \cos\gamma_i \\ -m_w \sum_{i=1}^{4} \ell_i \sin\gamma_i & m_w \sum_{i=1}^{4} \ell_i \cos\gamma_i & \mathcal{I}_f + m_w \sum_{i=1}^{4} \gamma_i^2 \end{bmatrix}. \tag{14}$$

Here, $\mathcal{I}_f$ is the moment of inertia of the frame around the center of mass, and m_f and m_w are the masses of the robot frame and each wheel, respectively. We note that since the wheels are placed symmetrically around the x_v and y_v axes, the off-diagonal terms should vanish. However, this may not be possible to achieve completely in practice, due to uneven distribution of equipment within the robot.

We denote the moment of inertia of each wheel by $\mathcal{I}_w$ and find

$$J_\beta = \frac{1}{2}\mathcal{I}_w I_{4\times 4} \quad \text{and} \quad J_\phi = \mathcal{I}_w I_{4\times 4} \tag{15}$$

and

$$V = \begin{bmatrix} 0 & 0 & 0 & 0 \\ 0 & 0 & 0 & 0 \\ \mathcal{I}_w & \mathcal{I}_w & \mathcal{I}_w & \mathcal{I}_w \end{bmatrix}. \tag{16}$$

The Lagrange undetermined coefficients are then eliminated in order to arrive at the following dynamics:

$$h_1(\beta)\dot{\eta} + \Phi_1(\beta)\zeta\eta = \Sigma^\mathrm{T}E\tau_\phi \tag{17}$$

in which $E = J_1^\mathrm{T}J_2^{-1} \in \mathbb{R}^{3\times 4}$ and $\tau_\phi \in \mathbb{R}^4$ is a vector of torques applied to drive the wheels. The quadratic function $h_1(\beta)$ is given by

$$h_1(\beta) = \Sigma^\mathrm{T}(M + EJ_\phi E^\mathrm{T})\Sigma > 0 \tag{18}$$

and $\Phi_1(\beta) \in \mathbb{R}$ is given by

$$\Phi_1(\beta) = \Sigma^\mathrm{T}(M + EJ_\phi E^\mathrm{T})N(\beta_c) \tag{19}$$

and $N(\beta_c) = [N_1 \ N_2]$, where

$$N_1 = \begin{bmatrix} -\ell_1 \cos \beta_2 \sin(\beta_1 - \gamma_1) + \ell_2 \sin \beta_1 \cos(\beta_2 - \gamma_2) \\ -\ell_1 \sin \beta_2 \sin(\beta_1 - \gamma_1) - \ell_2 \cos \beta_1 \cos(\beta_2 - \gamma_2) \\ \cos(\beta_1 - \beta_2) \end{bmatrix} \qquad (20)$$

$$N_2 = \begin{bmatrix} -\ell_1 \sin \beta_2 \cos(\beta_1 - \gamma_1) + \ell_2 \cos \beta_1 \sin(\beta_2 - \gamma_2) \\ \ell_1 \cos \beta_2 \cos(\beta_1 - \gamma_1) + \ell_2 \sin \beta_1 \sin(\beta_2 - \gamma_2) \\ - \cos(\beta_1 - \beta_2) \end{bmatrix} \qquad (21)$$

Equation (17) can be linearized by using a computed torque approach and choosing τ_ϕ appropriately. The torques are simply distributed evenly to each wheel; we observe that

$$\Sigma^T E \tau_\phi = [a_1 \, a_2 \, a_3 \, a_4][\tau_1 \, \tau_2 \, \tau_3 \, \tau_4]^T = L$$

where L is the left-hand side of equation (17). Then we set $\tau_\phi = H\tau_0$, $H \in \mathbb{R}^4$ and choose $H_i = L\,\mathrm{sign}(a_i)/\sigma$, where σ is the sum of the four entries in the vector $\Sigma^T E$. This distribution policy ensures that the largest torque applied to the individual wheels is as small as possible. By now applying the torque

$$\tau_0 = \frac{1}{\Sigma^T E H} \left(h_1(\beta)\nu + \Phi_1(\beta)\zeta\eta \right), \qquad (22)$$

we obtain $\dot{\eta} = \nu$, where ν is a new exogenous input. The result of the extension is the dynamical model given in equation (1).

B   Stability of Switched Systems

Consider a dynamic system whose behavior at any given time $t \geq t_0$, where t_0 is an appropriate initial time, is described by one out of several possible individual sets of continuous-time differential equations $\Sigma_0, \Sigma_1, \ldots, \Sigma_\mu$, and let $x_0(t), x_1(t), \ldots, x_\mu(t)$ denote the corresponding state vectors for the individual systems:

$$\Sigma_j : \quad \dot{x}_j = f_j(x_j(t)), \quad j = 0, 1, \ldots, \mu$$

The governing set of differential equations is switched at discrete instances t_i, $i = 0, 1, 2, \ldots$ ordered such that $t_i < t_{i+1} \forall i$. That is, the system behavior is governed by Σ_j in the time interval $t_i < t \leq t_{i+1}$, then by Σ_k in the time interval $t_{i+1} < t \leq t_{i+2}$, and so forth. Assume furthermore that for each Σ_j there exists a Lyapunov function, i.e., a scalar function $V_j(x_j(t))$ satisfying $V_j(0) = 0, V_j(x_j) \geq 0$, and $\dot{V}(x_j) \leq 0$ for $x_j \neq 0$. It is noted that, by the last requirement, V_j is a nonincreasing function of time in the interval where Σ_j is active. Hence, it can be deduced that the switched system governed by the sequence of sets of differential equations is stable if it can be shown that

$$V_j(x_j(t_q)) \geq V_j(x_j(t_r))$$

for all $0 \leq j \leq \mu$ and $t_q, t_r \in \{t_i\}$, where $t_q < t_r$ are the last and current switching time where Σ_j became active, respectively.

Modeling and Control of SMT Manufacturing Lines Using Hybrid Dynamic Systems*

L.G. Barajas[1], A. Kansal[2], A. Saxena[2], M. Egerstedt[1], A. Goldstein[1], and E.W. Kamen[1]

[1] Georgia Institute of Technology, Electrical and Computer Engineering, Center for Board Assembly Research Atlanta, GA 30332, USA {lbarajas,magnus,alex.goldstein,ed.kamen}@ece.gatech.edu http://www.cbar.marc.gatech.edu
[2] Georgia Institute of Technology, Textile and Fibre Engineering Atlanta, GA 30332, USA {gtg982b,gtg989b}@mail.gatech.edu

Abstract. In this paper we show how hybrid control and modeling techniques can be put to work for solving a problem of industrial relevance in Surface Mount Technology (SMT) manufacturing. In particular, by closing the loop over the stencil printing process, we obtain a robust system that can recover from faulty initial settings, adapt to environmental changes and unscheduled interrupts, and remove discrepancies associated with bidirectional printing machines. Moreover, a timed Petri net argument is invoked for bounding the control effort in such a way that the throughput of the system is unaffected by the introduction of the closed-loop controller. The soundness of the approach is verified on a real SMT manufacturing line.

1 Introduction

To close the loop around the Stencil Printing Process (SPP) in Surface Mount Technology (SMT) manufacturing has long been a desirable yet evasive goal in the industry [2,7,12,15,14]. By closing the loop it is envisioned that the system will recover from faulty initial settings, adapt to environmental changes and unscheduled interrupts, and remove discrepancies associated with bidirectional printing machines. However, the reason why this problem is particularly challenging is threefold. First, as of yet, no detailed process models have been derived [7,12,14], which implies that traditional, model-based control algorithms are of limited use. Secondly, the high noise levels in the process, combined with aggressive temporal variations in performance due to environmental factors such as humidity and temperature, make data-driven models unsuitable as a basis for control. Thirdly, due to the prohibitive cost (both temporal and monetary) associated with printing a large number of boards, sufficient excitation is a luxury that can not be afforded, i.e. system identification techniques can not be applied.

* This work was supported in part by the Georgia Institute of Technology Manufacturing Research Center Grant No. B01D07.

O. Maler and A. Pnueli (Eds.): HSCC 2003, LNCS 2623, pp. 66–80, 2003.

In this paper we report on our findings when designing a closed-loop control algorithm that overcomes all of these difficulties by switching between different modes of operation as the performance of the process changes. In particular, a coarse search algorithm is used for driving the system to a desired operating band, at which point a statistical, least-squares based controller is introduced for managing the mean and variance of the process. However, additional constraints are put on the controller that can be derived from a higher-level process management point of view. It is vitally important that the introduction of a closed-loop control module does not affect the throughput of the process. Furthermore, by printing boards concurrently the control value obtained when inspecting board k will not necessarily affect board $k+1$. Instead a careful trade-off between delay times, throughput, and control performance must be made, for which a timed Petri net model of the process will be used.

The contribution of this paper can thus be thought of as the development of hybrid process models at both the process management and the process dynamics levels, as well as a solution to an industrially relevant control problem in SMT manufacturing, and the outline of this paper is as follows: In Sect.2 a description of the SPP is given in some detail and in particular the performance objectives and process constraints are presented, followed by a Petri net based analysis of the system in Sect.3. In Sect.4 the hybrid control algorithm is given, and the experimental results are presented in Sect.5.

2   Stencil Printing

The goal of the SPP in SMT manufacturing of Printed Circuit Boards (PCB) is to apply an accurate and repeatable volume of solder paste deposits at precise locations [8,10,18]. It has been shown that a majority of the defects in the final boards can be attributed to the SPP [2,14,16], which makes this step the most critical in the process. Therefore, any attempt to enhance the performance of the line should start with the SPP. Furthermore, a defect that occurs in the early stages of the process will propagate, causing reworking over-costs at each additional step in the process that the PCB goes through without being detected as defective. This stresses the importance of early detection not only of obvious printing errors (e.g., extreme lack or excess of solder paste in a solder brick), but also of possible causes of other defects resulting from degradation of solder paste quality, loss of the working viscosity point, or even machine-related failures.

A simplified version of the SMT manufacturing process is illustrated in Fig.1. In order to solder components to a PCB, it is necessary to "print" solder paste bricks over the metallic contact pads on the board. Once this is successfully achieved and verified by optical or laser inspection, the components are placed on top of the solder bricks and their leads are pushed into the solder paste. When the components have been attached, the solder paste is melted using either reflow soldering or vapor-phase soldering to create the electro-mechanical junctures. Finally, the manufactured PCBs are inspected and tested.

The SPP is illustrated in Fig.2. In the first phase, a metallic stencil is placed over the PCB and solder paste is kneaded on one side of the stencil. During the second phase, the squeegee is pushed over the stencil and is moved from one

Fig. 1. SMT manufacturing line

side to the other of the stencil with a speed and pressure that can be set by the operator. (This squeegee speed is furthermore the control parameter that we adjust in our proposed closed-loop control algorithm.) This procedure makes the solder paste roll to fill the apertures in the stencil. In the final phase, before components, such as BGAs, QFPs, and, 0201s are placed over the solder bricks, a squeegee blade is used for removing excess material from the stencil, and then separate the stencil from the PCB.

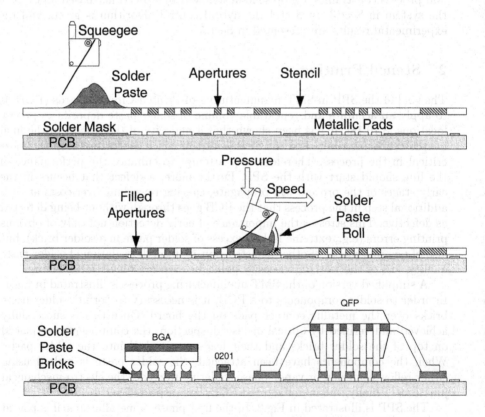

Fig. 2. Stencil printing process

The performance of the SPP can heuristically be characterized by how well the solder bricks are being printed. The objective of a closed-loop control law is thus to adapt the machine settings in such a way that the solder bricks satisfy certain regularity conditions. The industry standard for measuring the quality characteristics of the process is solder-paste-volume deposition [3,11,6,9]. Commonly, a direct sample mean of such values is used as quality characteristics, while a more elaborated approach would be to assign different weights to each solder brick type so that problematic components can be given more importance in the quality characteristics generation process. Such a weighted scheme can be represented by a weighted sample mean

$$\overline{H}_W(n) = \sum_{i=1}^{Q} w_i h(n, i), \quad \sum_{i=1}^{Q} w_i = 1, \quad w_i \geq 0, \tag{1}$$

where Q is the number of solder bricks present in the nth board, $h(n, i)$ is the height of the ith solder brick, and w_i is the weight assigned to that particular brick.

The SPP depicted in Fig.2 is a high-noise process corrupted by two types of noise: measurement inaccuracies and internal system variability. The former can normally be disregarded when 3-D laser measurement techniques are used, while the latter has a six-sigma interval of approximately $\pm 30\%$ of the mean of the probability distribution function of the signal [3], making the process outputs highly variable even under constant conditions. (A typical output histogram of the process can be seen in Fig.8a.) We can thus assume that the process is given by $y = F(C) + v$, where C is the control action corresponding to the squeegee speed and y is the weighted sample mean of the brick height. Furthermore, F is an unknown function of the control variable C, and v is the process noise.

Now, given some value H_d for the desired brick height, the objective is to determine an appropriate squeegee speed C_d such that $||F(C_d) - H_d||$ is suitably small. In particular, what we want to achieve is to reach a desirable process performance while printing as few boards as possible, i.e. using few measurements. Secondly, for the SPP, no dynamical models are as of yet available due to the highly complex process dynamics [7,12,14] and we need to bound the control variability in order to suppress the transient effects associated with changing the control value. The third constraint that we impose is that we want the control law to rapidly reach a desired operating point and then remain close to that point for all future control values. If F is known this problem can be solved using dynamic programming (see for example [4]), but for the problem under consideration in this paper, no such assumptions can be made. Hence only suboptimal solutions can be obtained.

The suboptimal yet effective solution proposed in Sect.4 consists of a hybrid control law that satisfies the constraints, while achieving fast convergence. However, before we can start investigating the details of this control law, some words about higher-level issues must be made. In particular, it must be decided how much computation time is available to the control module without affecting the throughput of the system, which can be done based on a timed Petri net model of the SPP.

3   Timed Petri Net Models

In order to analyze the temporal behavior of the SPP, a timed Petri net model of the stencil printing machine, the inspection machine, and the control module is depicted in Fig.3, where transitions t_1, t_2, t_3 define the operation of the stencil printer, where solder paste is deposited on the board. The inspection machine, in which the measurement of the quality of the solder bricks is conducted, is given by transitions t_4 and t_5. The place p_3 is the buffer in between the two machines, and $M_0(p_9)$ corresponds to the capacity of the buffer. (This capacity is 1 in Fig.3, but it is in fact one of the parameters that should be chosen when designing a control strategy.) Transition t_6 corresponds to the computation of control values, and $M_0(p_6)$ indicates the "board-delay" imposed by the control law. The interpretation is as follows: If $M_0(p_6) = 1$ then the control value obtained from board k directly affects board $k+1$, i.e. no boards are being printed until a control value has been computed. However, the stencil printer is in fact operating in two decoupled directions, i.e. board k is printed with the squeegee blade moving forward, while board $k + 1$ is printed in a backwards direction.

Due to the discrepancies in performance in the two printing directions shown in Fig.8a, where Dir 0 and Dir 1 denote forward and backward directions respectively, we will assume that $M_0(p_6) = 2c$, $c = 1, 2, \ldots$, or in other words, that the control values computed from boards printed in the forward direction only affects other boards printed in that direction and vice versa for backwards boards. What we want to do in this section is thus to compute the throughput and cycle time of the Petri net, and then design the intermediary buffer size $M_0(p_9)$ and controller look-back $c = M_0(p_6)/2$ in such a way that the control delay is as small as possible.

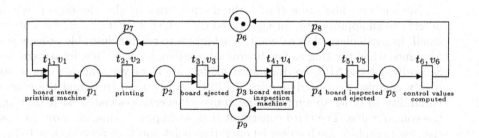

Fig. 3. Timed Petri net model for the SPP with online controller.

3.1   Timing and Buffer Size Considerations

The model in Fig.3 is a so-called *marked graph* [17], i.e. the weights are all equal to one and each place in the Petri net has a unique input and output transition. For such marked graphs, the following equations describe the temporal behavior of the Petri net:

$$\begin{cases} \pi_{i,k+M_0(p_i)} = \tau_{r,k}, \quad \text{where } {}^\circ p_i = \{t_r\} \\[2mm] \tau_{j,k} = \max \left\{ \tau_{j,k-1}, \max_{p_i \in {}^\circ t_j} \{\pi_{i,k}\} \right\} + v_{j,k}, \end{cases} \tag{2}$$

where $\pi_{i,k}$ denotes the time at which place p_i receives its kth token, $M_0(p_i)$ is the initial marking of p_i, ${}^\circ p_i$ denotes the set containing the unique input transition to p_i. Furthermore, $\tau_{j,k}$ denotes the time at which transition t_j fires its kth time, ${}^\circ t_j$ denotes the set of input places to t_j, and $v_{j,k}$ defines the delay-time between t_j becoming fireable for the kth time and its firing.

We first note that the inspection machine is the bottle-neck machine in the SPP, i.e. that $v_1 + v_2 + v_3 < v_4 + v_5$. We do not want the introduction of a control law to slow down the process, i.e. reduce the throughput, so an initial assumption is that

$$v_1 + v_2 + v_3 + v_6 < v_4 + v_5. \tag{3}$$

In order to simplify the computations we furthermore assume initially that $M_0(p_9) = \infty$, i.e. that the buffer capacity is infinite, which corresponds to removing the loop containing p_9 in Fig.3. Under this assumption the timing equations give that $\tau_{5,k} = \tau_{5,k-1} + v_4 + v_5$, when k is large enough to suppress the effects caused by the initial markings. What this means is that the throughput, ρ, of the system is $\rho = 1/(v_4 + v_5)$, i.e. that the cycle time of the PN is $CT_{PN} = 2c(v_4 + v_5)$, since a total number of $2c = M_0(p_6)$ tokens are cycling through the PN. An additional relevant measure is the process cycle time, i.e. the time that a board spends in the SPP, which is given by $CT = CT_{PN} - v_6$, since the $(k+2c)^{th}$ control evaluation takes place after the kth board has left the SPP.

Under the infinite buffer capacity assumption and the assumption that $v_4 + v_5 > v_1 + v_2 + v_3 + v_6$, an accumulation of printed boards occurs in the buffer p_3. It furthermore follows that $M(p_3) \in \{2c - 2, 2c - 1\}$, i.e. that the actual number of tokens in the buffer changes between $2c - 2$ and $2c - 1$ for durations T_1 and $v_5 + v_4 - T_1$ respectively, where T_1 can be computed as follows:

$$\begin{aligned} T_1 &= \tau_{3,2c-1+k} - \tau_{4,k} = \tau_{1,2c-1+k} + v_2 + v_3 - \tau_{4,k} \\ &= \pi_{6,k-1+M_0(p_6)} + v_1 + v_2 + v_3 - \tau_{4,k} \\ &= \tau_{6,k-1} + v_1 + v_2 + v_3 - \tau_{4,k}. \end{aligned} \tag{4}$$

But, since t_4 and t_6 become fireable simultaneously, i.e. $\tau_{6,k-1} - v_6 = \tau_{4,k} - v_4$, we get $T_1 = v_1 + v_2 + v_3 + v_6 - v_4$, and the following relation holds:

$$M(p_3) = \begin{cases} 2c - 2 & \text{for a duration of } v_1 + v_2 + v_3 + v_6 - v_4 \\ 2c - 1 & \text{for a duration of } v_5 + 2v_4 - v_1 - v_2 - v_3 - v_6. \end{cases} \tag{5}$$

If we now assume that the buffer capacity is finite then it is clear that the case when $M_0(p_9) \geq 2c - 1$ is identical to the case when $M_0(p_9) = \infty$ due to the fact that no more than $2c - 1$ boards are present in the buffer at any given time.

However, when $M_0(p_9) < 2c - 1$, the process dynamics change in the following manner: The inspection time is now long enough for the accumulation of the boards to occur at p_3, while the accumulation is restricted by the bound on the capacity of the buffer. Thus the place p_6 will always contain $2c - M_0(P_9) - 2$ tokens, since two tokens are in the inspection and printing machine. We would expect the buffer to be full after transients, i.e. that $M(p_3) = M_0(p_9)$. But, there are instances of duration v_3 when $M(p_3)$ drops to $M_0(p_9) - 1$. This happens when the buffer p_3 is full and t_3 is waiting for a token in p_9. As soon as t_4 fires, p_3 looses one token but t_3 becomes fireable.

Hence, for any value of controller look-back c, we get the number of boards in the buffer p_3 after transients as

$$M(p_3) = \begin{cases} M_0(p_9) - 1 & \text{for a duration of } v_3 \\ M_0(p_9) & \text{for a duration of } v_4 + v_5 - v_3. \end{cases} \quad (6)$$

The inspection machine is still the bottleneck machine, which implies that the throughput of the PN remains the same. But the SPP cycle time becomes $CT = (M_0(p_9) + 1)(v_4 + v_5) + v_5 - v_3$, since the printed board has to wait inside the printing machine before ejecting as the buffer p_3 is full.

3.2   Discussion

The controller look-back c directly affects the process performance. The response time increases with increasing c as the process control values for the nth board are computed based on the inspection data of the $(n - c)^{th}$ board printed in the same direction. But the process performance also depends on the time available to compute the process control values, i.e. on v_6. As the available computation time increases, more complex statistical computations can be carried out in order to achieve higher accuracy. Since the throughput is limited by the inspection time, we can decrease the waiting time of the boards in p_3 and make this time available for computation instead, without affecting throughput. Thus, if we increase v_6 (assuming that $v_1 + v_2 + v_3 \leq v_4 + v_5$, i.e. printing takes less time than inspection), then the maximum value to which v_6 can be increased ($\hat{v}_6$) without affecting the throughput can be found as follows:

If we increase computation time s.t. $v_6 > v_4 + v_5$, then $M(p_5)$ increases due to accumulation of tokens in p_5 and once the effect of transients is suppressed, $M(p_5) \in \{2c - 2, 2c - 1\}$. The time taken to suppress the transients depends on the magnitude of v_6 and the controller look-back c. This accumulation in p_5 leads to idling of the inspection machine causing a decrease in the throughput. Thus, $\hat{v}_6 = v_4 + v_5$. But, if the controller look-back is one, the control value of the kth inspected board should be generated and the $(k + 2)^{th}$ board should be printed before the inspection of the $(k+1)^{th}$ board completes, meaning that $\tau_{6,k}$, $\tau_{1,k+2}$, $\tau_{2,k+2}$ and $\tau_{3,k+2}$ should occur before $\tau_{5,k+1}$, i.e. before the inspection machine goes idle. Thus, we obtain the maximum time available to compute the control values as shown in Fig.4(a) and calculated as

$$\hat{v}_6 = \begin{cases} v_4 + v_5 - (v_1 + v_2 + v_3) & \text{if } c = 1 \\ v_4 + v_5 & \text{if } c > 1. \end{cases} \quad (7)$$

An interesting point to note here is that, until $v_6 \leq \hat{v}_6$, inspection time is the bottleneck and governs the throughput of the system. But once v_6 increases beyond $\hat{v}_6$, computation becomes the bottleneck, i.e. the throughput of the system is reduced. The throughput ρ, for $v_6 \geq \hat{v}_6$, and as a function of the controller look-back is depicted in Fig.4(b) and is given by

$$\rho = \begin{cases} \frac{1}{v_6 + v_1 + v_2 + v_3} & \text{if } c = 1 \\ \frac{1}{v_6} & \text{if } c > 1. \end{cases} \tag{8}$$

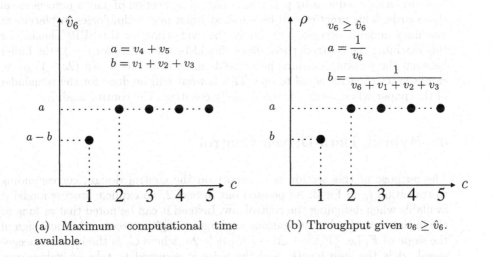

(a) Maximum computational time available.

(b) Throughput given $v_6 \geq \hat{v}_6$.

Fig. 4. In the left figure, the maximum available computation time $\hat{v}_6$ is depicted as a function of the controller look-back. The right figure shows the relationship between the throughput ρ and the controller look-back.

To summarize: The performance of the process depends on the controller look-back c and the available computation time v_6. A small c ensures lower response time whereas larger v_6 provides more time for computations, generating better control values, which can improve the process quality and efficiency. Thus, ideally we should keep the controller look-back as small as possible, i.e. let c be equal to one, and have $v_6 = \hat{v}_6$. However, if $c = 1$, the response time improves but $\hat{v}_6$ decreases by $v_1 + v_2 + v_3$. This tradeoff can be decided on the basis of the relative magnitudes of the v_i values. For instance, if the inspection time is significantly larger than the printing time ($v_4 + v_5 \gg v_1 + v_2 + v_3$) then one can expect that sufficient time to compute good control values is available. As a consequence, the controller look-back should be kept equal to one.

For the SMT manufacturing line at the Center for Board Assembly Research (CBAR) at the Georgia Institute of Technology, the v_i-values are of the order of $v_1 = 8s; v_2 = 20s; v_3 = 2s; v_4 = 2s; v_5 = 180s$. Thus, if we keep $c = 1$, the computation time available is

$$v_6 = (v_4 + v_5) - (v_1 + v_2 + v_3) = 150s. \tag{9}$$

On the other hand, the control law proposed in Sect.4 requires 15s to compute the control values with a 1GHz Intel Pentium III processor using Matlab compiled code. It may seem unnecessary to go through all these calculations to find out that the available time for computation is one order of magnitude larger than the current computation time of the algorithm. However, new technology in post-printing inspection machines is reducing v_5 below 60s in which case, v_6 will be heavily limited by the inspection time v_5. Also, the inspection time can be considerably reduced by performing partial inspection of only a percentage of the boards. This practice will be required when new technologies in placement machines make it necessary to reduce the cycle time for the SPP. Thence, for this machine, the controller look-back should be one. Also, for $c = 1$, the buffer between the printing machine never holds more than one board ($2c - 1$) so we can keep its capacity equal to one. This is what will be done for the remainder of this paper when we go on and actually construct the control module.

4   Hybrid, Data-Driven Control

The purpose of this section is to report on the control design, corresponding to transition t_6 in Fig.3. As pointed out in Sect.2, no explicit process model is available when designing the control law. Instead it can be noted that as long as the initial control value separations are large enough to recover the local sign of the slope of F, i.e. $\|F(C_0 + \Delta) - F(C_0)\| \geq 2a$, where C_0 is the initial squeegee speed, Δ is the step length, and the noise is assumed to take on values over $[-a, a]$, we recover a conjugated gradient direction. By using a fixed step length descent along the recovered direction, a locally optimal (over the quantized set of control values $\{C \in \Re \mid C = C_0 + k\Delta, \ k \in \mathbb{Z}\}$) control value can be obtained in a fixed number of steps, i.e. while printing few boards, as shown in [1]. Under additional assumptions about the unimodality of F, a globally optimal control value can furthermore be obtained over the quantized set.

Once the conjugated gradient search has terminated, a statistical fine-tuning of the squeegee speed (over $\Re$) can be used. We choose to work with a windowed version of a least-squares affine estimator of F, which can then be directly used to compute the control values.

In other words, given the static input-output map $y = F(C) + v$, we want to find an affine estimate of F as $F(C) = \theta_0 + \theta_1 C$ using the last N output values. With a slight abuse of notation we denote these by $y_1, \ldots, y_N$ and let $C_1, \ldots, C_N$ denote the corresponding N last inputs. What this implies is that N defines the size of the sample window. Thence, in order to recover the affine estimator parameters $\theta = [\theta_0 \ \theta_1]^T$, the standard basis, given by the N×2-matrix M, can be formed from the unitary N-vector $b = [1 \ 1 \ \ldots \ 1]^T$ and the control values vector $\mathbf{C} = [C_1 \ C_2 \ \ldots \ C_N]^T$, arranged side by side such that $M = [b \vdots \mathbf{C}]$.

Now, the classic LS solution [13] to the over-determined problem, $M\theta = \mathbf{y}$, where $\mathbf{y} = [y_1 \; y_2 \; \cdots \; y_N]^{\mathrm{T}}$, was shown in [3] to satisfy the following equation

$$\theta = \frac{\mathbf{C}^{\mathrm{T}}\left[\left(\dfrac{\mathbf{C}b^{\mathrm{T}} - \mathbf{C}^{\mathrm{T}}b\mathbb{I}_N}{N\mathbb{I}_N - bb^{\mathrm{T}}}\right) \otimes \mathbf{y}\right]}{\mathbf{C}^{\mathrm{T}}(N\mathbb{I}_N - bb^{\mathrm{T}})\mathbf{C}} , \tag{10}$$

where $\mathbb{I}_N$ is the $N \times N$ identity matrix. Equation (10) can thus be used to calculate the parameters θ of the affine estimator, and for the sake of clarity, it should be noticed that

$$\left(\frac{\mathbf{C}b^{\mathrm{T}} - \mathbf{C}^{\mathrm{T}}b\mathbb{I}_N}{N\mathbb{I}_N - bb^{\mathrm{T}}}\right)$$

is a partition matrix which operates (using the Kronecker product ($\otimes$)) on the vector $\mathbf{y}$ of data samples. An extensive explanation of the complete controller can be found in [3], and the switched control law that we propose in this paper is thus given by two distinct stages:

1. A constrained conjugated-gradient search for reaching the desired operational band is used in the first part of the control law.
2. A least-squares affine estimator for maintaining and fine-tuning the process constitutes the second part.

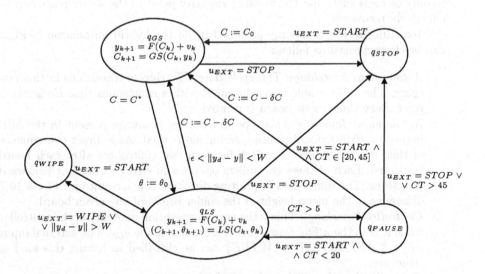

Fig. 5. Stencil printing process hybrid automaton.

The switched control strategy is depicted in Fig.5 as a directed graph, or hybrid automaton, and the interpretation of the process dynamics, transition guards, and resets are as follows: The two main states are q_{GS} and q_{LS} corresponding to the gradient-search and least-squares parts respectively. A transition from the machine idling (q_{STOP}) to q_{GS} occurs when the external control variable u_{EXT} is equal to $START$, at which point the squeegee speed is set to C_0. (We used $C_0 = 0.5$in/sec in the experiments in Sect.5). Once the locally optimal control value C^* is obtained, a transition occurs to the least-squares part of the algorithm, at which point a reset initializes the least-squares parameters θ. If the performance of the least-squares algorithm deteriorates, a new gradient search is conducted. However, if the performance is too poor ($\|y_d - y\| > W$), for some error bound W, then this is an indication that the stencil needs to be manually wiped. The last state of the hybrid automaton (q_{PAUSE}) is entered if the process cycle time, CT, as defined in the previous section, exceeds 5min. If, after the pause state is entered, the process is restarted within 20min, no gradient search is needed, while $CT \in [20, 45]$min indicates that a new search is needed. These additional states are required in order to capture the complex nature of the process, and in order to be able to adapt to external events affecting the process. The most important one of them being the pause of the production line due to a external input. Depending on the duration of the disturbance, the process should be recovered, restarted or stopped in order to maintain or restore the printing quality.

The choice of the guards based on the temporal variable CT is critical for the correct operation of the hybrid automaton. The guards have been empirically chosen using the parameters and materials stated in Sect.5. For very a low viscosity solder paste, these values should be reduced from the order of minutes to only seconds such that the working viscosity point of the solder paste can be effectively recovered.

According to the taxonomy proposed in [5] the hybrid automaton in Fig.5 can be characterized as follows:

- *Autonomous Switchings*: The *cycle time CT* triggers transitions in this category. The CT-variable is synchronized with a continuous time clock but is reset every time a new board is printed.
- *Autonomous Impulses*: This type of behavior is always present in the SPP because a bidirectional printing technique is used. As a direct consequence of this, it is necessary to switch between two controllers after each board is printed. Each of these controllers operates in either forward or backward directions. The differences in printing direction can account up to for a 10% difference in the mean height of the solder bricks of any given board.
- *Controlled Switchings*: This is the normal operation modality of the controller while it is in the *affine least-squares* estimator mode q_{LS}. The external input $u_{EXT} \in \{START, STOP, WIPE\}$ can be classified as having this kind of structure.
- *Controlled Impulses*: This is the standard operation modality of the controller while in the *gradient search* mode q_{GS}.

In the following section we will illustrate the usefulness of the proposed switched control strategy by applying it to the SPP at the CBAR SMT manufacturing line.

5   Experimental Results

The hybrid control algorithm proposed in this paper is used for generating control values for the stencil printing process. The input control variable is squeegee speed and the output is the weighted sample mean of the height of the deposited solder bricks. A 12in metallic blade at a constant pressure setting of $12lb/in^2$ was used to perform the procedure over a laser-cut 5mil ($127\mu m$) stencil, using non-clean 63/37 (tin/lead%) solder paste Type IV.

The experimental setup used for this paper includes a Speedline MPM-3000 stencil printer and a CyberOptics Sentry-2000 3D-Laser inspection system which are part of one of the Surface Mount Technology (SMT) manufacturing lines at the Center for Board Assembly Research (CBAR) at the Georgia Institute of Technology.

Figure 6 shows the control values as the hybrid algorithm goes through the different operational modes. Additionally, the case when a large disturbance is introduced is considered. In this case, the output setting is changed by -25% after the 13th iteration, and Fig.7 shows how the algorithm is able to adapt to this sudden set-point change in only a few iterations.

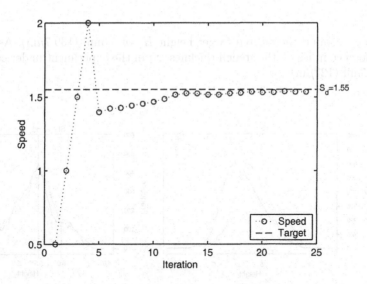

Fig. 6. Constant desired height.

Figure 8 shows the effect of the controller over the process in a real production run. This plot demonstrates how the controller discriminates between printing directions and by adjusting the weighted sample mean on a board-by-board basis independently in each direction it aligns the solder brick height distributions to the desired mean height. Depicted are the output histograms generated with and without the controller. It should be noted that the distribution in Fig.8b is

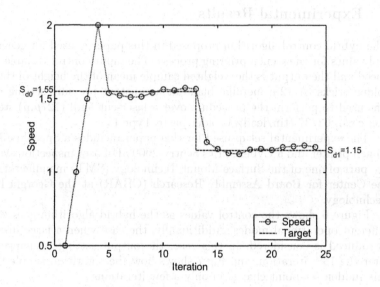

Fig. 7. Step applied to desired height.

center around the desired target height H_d of 5.5mil (139.7μm). As marked for reference in Fig.8, the stencil thickness S_t in the experiment under consideration is 5mil (127μm).

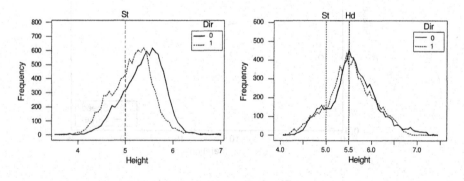

(a) Without closed-loop control.   (b) With closed-loop control.

Fig. 8. Process histograms.

6 Conclusions

In this paper we show how hybrid control and modeling techniques can be put to work for solving a problem of industrial relevance in SMT manufacturing by closing the loop over the stencil printing process. A timed Petri net argument is invoked for bounding the control effort in such a way that the throughput of the system is unaffected by the introduction of the closed-loop controller. The actual control law is comprised of a switched algorithm that, in stage one, quickly reaches a desirable band of operation using a constrained, conjugated gradient search. In stage two, a windowed version of a least squares algorithm is applied to shape the distributions of the solder brick heights around the desired brick height, and the soundness of the approach is verified on a real SMT manufacturing line.

References

1. Barajas, L.G., Egerstedt, M., Kamen, E.W., Goldstein, A.: Process control in a high-noise environment with limited number of measurements. To appear in: *2003 American Control Conference*, Denver, CO (2003)
2. Barajas, L.G., Kamen, E.W., Goldstein, A.: On-line enhancement of the stencil printing process. *Circuits Assembly* (2001) 32–36
3. Barajas, L.G., Kamen, E.W., Goldstein, A., Egerstedt, M., Small, B.: A closed-loop hybrid control algorithm for stencil printing. In: *Surface Mount Technology Association International Conference (SMTA02)*, Boston, MA (2002) 51–58
4. Bertsekas, D.P.: *Dynamic programming and optimal control*. Athena Scientific (1995)
5. Branicky, M., Borkar, V., Mitter, S.: A unified framework for hybrid control: model and optimal control theory. *IEEE Transactions on Automatic Control*, **43** (1998) 31–45
6. Burr, D.: Solder paste inspection: process control for defect reduction. In: *Test Conference, 1997. Proceedings., International*, CyberOpt. Corp., USA (1997) 1036
7. Durairaj, R., Nguty, T.A., Ekere, N.N.: Critical factors affecting paste flow during the stencil printing of solder paste. *Soldering & Surface Mount Technology* **13** (2001) 30–34
8. Fujiuchi, S.: Fundamental study on solder paste for fine pitch soldering. In: *Electronics Manufacturing Technology Symposium, 1991., Eleventh IEEE/CHMT International*, IBM Japan, Shiga, Japan (1991) 163–165
9. Gopalakrishnan, L.: Continuous improvement of the solder paste deposition process through designed experiments. *IPC/SMTA Electronics Assembly Expo. Proceedings of the Technical Program* (1998)
10. Gopalakrishnan, L., Srihari, K.: Solder paste deposition through high speed stencil printing for a contract assembly environment. *Journal of Electronics Manufacturing* **8** (1998) 89–101
11. Husman, M.S., Rukavina, J.P., Yuan, G.: A study of solder paste volumes for screen printing. *Proceedings of the Technical Program. NEPCON West'93* (1993)
12. Johnson, A., Flori, A.: High density/fine feature solder paste printing. In: *Proceedings of APEX.* (2001)
13. Kamen, E.W., Su, J.: *Introduction to optimal estimation*. Advanced textbooks in control and signal processing. Springer, London; New York (1999)

14. Lau, F.K.H., Yeung, V.W.S.: A hierarchical evaluation of the solder paste printing process. *Journal of Materials Processing Technology* **69** (1997) 79–89
15. Lotfi, A., Howarth, M.: *An intelligent closed-loop control of solder paste stencil printing stage of surface mount technology.* Nottingham Trent University. Department of Mechanical and Manufacturing Engineering, Nottingham (1998)
16. Pan, J., Tonkay, G., Storer, R., Sallade, R., Leandri, D.: Critical variables of solder paste stencil printing for micro-BGA and fine pitch QFP. In: *Electronics Manufacturing Technology Symposium, 1999. Twenty-Fourth IEEE/CPMT*, Dept. of Ind. & Manuf. Syst. Eng., Lehigh Univ., Bethlehem, PA, USA (1999) 94–101
17. Proth, J.M., Xie, X.: *Petri nets : a tool for design and management of manufacturing systems.* Wiley, New York (1996)
18. Venkateswaran, S., Srihari, K., Adriance, J., Westby, G.: A realtime process control system for solder paste stencil printing. In: *Electronics Manufacturing Technology Symposium, 1997., Twenty-First IEEE/CPMT International*, Dept. of Syst. Sci. & Ind. Eng., State Univ. of New York, Binghamton, NY, USA (1997) 62–67

Hybrid Control of an Automotive Robotized Gearbox for Reduction of Consumptions and Emissions

Alberto Bemporad[1], Pandeli Borodani[2], and Massimo Mannelli[1]

[1] Dip. Ingegneria dell'Informazione
Università di Siena
Via Roma 56, 53100 Siena, Italy
bemporad@dii.unisi.it, massimo.mannelli@PSD.Invensys.com
[2] FIAT Research Center
Vehicle Control Systems
Strada Torino 50 , 10043 Orbassano(TO), Italy
p.borodani@crf.it

Abstract. This paper describes the application of hybrid modeling and receding horizon optimal control techniques for supervising an automotive robotized gearbox, with the goal of reducing consumptions and emissions, a problem that is currently under investigation at Fiat Research Center (CRF). We show that the dynamic behavior of the vehicle can be easily approximated and captured by the hybrid model, and through simulations on standard speed patterns that a good closed loop performance can be achieved. The synthesized control law can be implemented on automotive hardware as a piecewise affine function of the measured and estimated quantities.

1 Introduction

The automotive market analysts forecast for the automatic transmission system a relevant growth in the near future [1]. Conventional automatic transmissions provide a good level of comfort, but evidence significant drawbacks concerning other aspects: fuel economy, cost, weight, and size. Also, many customers (particularly in European countries) associate with the manual gearbox a significant value in terms of driving feeling and expectation.

Recent technological developments try to satisfy the increasing demand of the automotive market for automatic transmissions, matching at the same time the conflicting requirements of comfort, performance, fuel economy and cost reduction. An extremely promising system is the automated gearbox, named in this paper "robotized gearbox" (Fig. 1); it is based on servo actuators applied to a standard mechanical gearbox. The new transmission system with both automatic and semiautomatic operating modes [2,3,4,5] is directly derived from a standard manual gearbox by adding electronically controlled small servo-hydraulic actuators, capable to move better than the human driver the gearshift mechanisms [6].

O. Maler and A. Pnueli (Eds.): HSCC 2003, LNCS 2623, pp. 81–96, 2003.
© Springer-Verlag Berlin Heidelberg 2003

Fig. 1. Robotized gearbox

The introduction of the robotized gearbox gives the opportunity to transfer the driver's request to a higher level and to use automatic criteria for optimizing the lower level. An automatic system supervisor can in fact control the gear shifting and the torque regulators with the duty of choosing the gear and the engine torque, satisfying the requests of the driver, the constraints, and optimizing the powertrain behavior, reducing consumptions and emissions. Emissions are of particular interest, as in recent years the European Community has stressed the noxious effects of emissions, and is trying to drastically reduce them in the near future.

In this paper we show how the whole system (vehicle and robotized gearbox) can be modeled as a hybrid one in order to synthesize a supervisor that brings the engine torque close to the Optimal Operating Line (OOL), while minimizing consumptions and emissions. The system is indeed intrinsically hybrid, as once the gear (a discrete input) is selected, a different continuous dynamics results.

Current CRF control strategies are mainly based on static maps, as in most automatic gear shifting schemes nowadays in production. Such control schemes are motivated by the fact that the system is nonlinear. The presence of nonlinearities and constraints on one hand, and the simplicity needed for real-time implementation on the other, have discouraged the design of optimal control strategies for this kind of problem. Recently, a new framework for modeling hybrid systems was proposed in [7], and an algorithm for synthesizing piecewise affine optimal controllers for such systems in [8]. In this paper we describe how the hybrid framework [7] and the optimization-based control strategy [8] can be successfully applied for solving this problem in a systematic way. More in detail, for solving the gearbox control problem we need to design a supervisor (depicted as MPC Controller in Fig. 2) that in real-time decides the best gear that minimizes consumptions and emissions and, at the same time, guarantees a good tracking of the desired traction power. As these are conflicting objectives, besides the gear the supervisor is allowed a second degree of freedom, namely to deviate the desired requested engine torque $T_E(\omega_{engine})$ by a quantity Δ_{Torque}. The idea is to solve the posed control problem by formulating a model-based receding

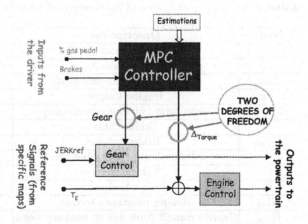

Fig. 2. Hybrid supervisor for a robotized gearbox with two degrees of freedom

horizon optimal control problem which minimizes consumptions, emissions, and the deviation Δ_{torque} from the desired torque. We show, through simulations on a simplified model and for a set of parameters provided by CRF, that good performances can be achieved, particularly comparing our results with the ones obtained by CRF and with the ones provided by the European Union on standard speed patterns. Furthermore, the resulting optimal controller consists of a piecewise affine function of the measurements, that can be easily implemented.

2   Vehicle Model

With the objective in mind of controller design, the vehicle model considered here is highly simplified, although it still allows the synthesis of a reasonably performing control action, as will be shown in Section 5. The model consists of the equations [9, 10]

$$\dot{\omega}_{sec} = \frac{1}{J_P(\tau_c)}\left(T_E\tau_c - \beta_2\omega_{sec} - \frac{2}{\tau_p}T_{axle}\right) \tag{1a}$$

$$\dot{V}_X = \frac{1}{m}\left(\frac{2}{R_e}(T_{axle} - T_{brake} - T_{rot}) - F_{friction} + F_{slope}\right) \tag{1b}$$

$$\dot{T}_{axle} = K_{sa}\left(\frac{\omega_{sec}}{\tau_p} - \frac{V_X}{R_e}\right) + \beta_1\frac{d\left(\frac{\omega_{sec}}{\tau_p} - \frac{V_X}{R_e}\right)}{dt} \tag{1c}$$

with

$$F_{friction} = \frac{1}{2}\rho\,V_X^2\,S\,C_x, \tag{1d}$$

Table 1. Physical quantities and parameters of the vehicle model

Name	Description	
ω_{sec}	Secondary shaft speed	rpm
V_X	Vehicle velocity	m/s
T_{axle}	Torque about the axle shaft	Nm
T_E	Engine torque	Nm
τ_c	Gear ratio (when gear engaged)	
τ_p	Bridge ratio	
T_{brake}	Brake torque	Nm
$J_P(\tau_c)$	Equivalent primary inertia	kgm^2
m	Vehicle mass	m
R_e	Rolling wheel radius	m
T_{rot}	Rolling resistance torque	Nm
F_{slope}	Gravity contribution due to roadway slope	N
β_1	Axle coefficient	kgm^2/s
K_{sa}	Axle coefficient	kgm^2/s^2
β_2	Combustion dynamic coefficient	kgm^2/s
ρ	Air density	kg/m^3
S	Frontal area of the vehicle	m^2
C_x	Aerodynamic drag coefficient	
$JERK_{ref}$	Reference jerk during gear shifting	m/s^3

where the involved physical quantities and parameters are described in Table 1. The first equation represents the engine dynamics, the second one describes the longitudinal motion dynamics of the vehicle, the third equation is referred to the axle dynamics. The friction force is approximated as a linear function of the velocity, based on a best fit on the range [15, 120] km/h, which is the range where the gear is most often shifted. The rolling resistance torque is approximated as constant, as this force, compared to the other friction forces, has no meaningful variations. Terms like $J_P(\tau_c)$ show that those parameters depend on the gear ratio τ_c, as there are indeed five different linear dynamics, one for each gear. Fig. 3 shows the position of the open loop poles for each one of them. Moreover, we assume that the requested engine torque is immediately applied (therefore neglecting the delay due to the torque control loop) and that it corresponds to the actual torque delivered by the engine.

3   Hybrid Model

Hybrid systems provide a unified framework for describing processes evolving according to continuous dynamics, discrete dynamics, and logic rules [11,12,13,14]. The interest in hybrid systems is mainly motivated by the large variety of practical situations, for instance embedded control systems, where physical processes interact with digital controllers. Several modeling formalisms were developed by various researchers to describe hybrid systems, among them the class of Mixed

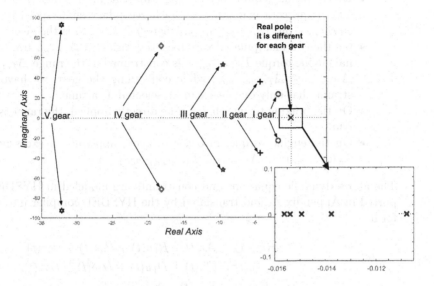

Fig. 3. Position of the poles for each gear

Logical Dynamical (MLD) systems introduced in [7]. Examples of real-world applications that can be naturally modelled within the MLD framework are listed in [15], where the authors describe the language HYSDEL (Hybrid System Description Language) for obtaining an MLD model from a high level textual description of the hybrid dynamics. HYSDEL is used here to "hybridize" the vehicle model (1), as reported in Appendix A. Such a model is obtained through the following steps:

- Discretize the model with sampling time $T_s = 0.3$ s. This value corresponds to the average synchronization time of the robotized gearbox.
- Introduce a Boolean input $gear^i \in \{0, 1\}$ for each gear $i = 1, \ldots, 4$, with $\delta^i = 1$ if and only if the corresponding gear #i is engaged. The condition "gear #5 engaged" is then represented by $gear^1 = gear^2 = gear^3 = gear^4 = 0$.
- Introduce an auxiliary continuous variable $\omega_{sec}(j)$ for each gear #j, $j = 1, \ldots, 5$, and set $\omega_{sec} = \sum_{j=1}^{5} \omega_{sec}(j)$, where only one variable $\omega_{sec}(j)$ is nonzero at a time.
- Reduce the order of the linear dynamics (1b) [1] and get a model with only one state, in order to simplify the control algorithm.
- Add the following constraints in order to guarantee the correct operation of the engine:

---

[1] Order reduction is achieved by first obtaining a balanced realization using the MATLAB® function `balreal`, and then by reducing the order using the MATLAB® function `modred`.

- On the primary shaft speed, ω_{engine} must be in the range $[700, 6000]$ rpm. This requires a constraint on each secondary shaft speed of the form $\omega(j)_{min} < \omega(j)_{sec} < \omega(j)_{max}$, where $j = 1, \dots, 5$ is the gear.
- On the two manipulated variables: the variation Δ_{Torque} from the nominal engine torque $T_E(\omega_{engine})$ is constrained in the range $\Delta_{Torque,min} \leq \Delta_{Torque} \leq \Delta_{Torque,max}$, while concerning the gear, we have the constraint that only one gear can be selected at a time.
- On the braking torque that can be directly applied, the range is $[0, 1150]$ Nm.
- On the engine torque, in order to avoid applying an excessive torque, $T_E(\omega_{engine}) + \Delta_{Torque} < T_{available}(\omega_{engine})$.

The above dynamic equations and constraints are modeled in HYSDEL, as reported in Appendix A, and translated by the HYSDEL compiler into the MLD form

$$x(t+1) = Ax(t) + B_1u(t) + B_2\delta(t) + B_3z(t) \tag{2a}$$

$$y(t) = Cx(t) + D_1u(t) + D_2\delta(t) + D_3z(t) \tag{2b}$$

$$E_2\delta(t) + E_3z(t) \leq E_1u(t) + E_4x(t) + E_5, \tag{2c}$$

where $x \in \mathbb{R}^4$, $(x_1 = x_{red}, x_2 = T_{ref}, x_3 = T_{brake}, x_4 = $ road slope, $u \in \mathbb{R} \times \{0,1\}^4$, $(u_1 = \Delta_{torque} \in \mathbb{R}, u_{j+1} = gear^j \in \{0,1\}, j = 1, \dots, 4)$, $y \in \mathbb{R}^2$, $(y_1 = \omega_{engine}, y_2 = T_E)$, $\delta \in \{0,1\}^2$ and $z \in \mathbb{R}^{12}$. The state x_{red} is the state of the reduced-order model, the other states are actually just measured variables, and all the inputs are manipulated variables.

In order to validate the model, in Fig. 4 we compare the open-loop evolution of the discrete-time MLD model (2) and of the nonlinear continuous time model (1), under the same inputs (% of gas pedal and gear). It is apparent that the MLD model captures in discrete time the hybrid behavior of the system quite satisfactorily. It may be noted that there is a small offset due to the approximation of the friction term: this is not a problem, as the offset will be compensated by the feedback control action from actual measured values. The validity of the hybrid MLD model is also confirmed by the fact that the "ground power"[2] requested by both models is practically the same (Fig. 5).

4   Optimization-Based Control Design

We describe how receding horizon optimal control for hybrid systems [7,8] can be usefully employed here to design a control law for the robotized gearbox control problem. The main idea is to setup a finite-horizon optimal control problem for the hybrid MLD system by optimizing a performance index under constraints,

---

[2] The ground power is the total power that the vehicle receives from the external environment (the ground). Given the engine torque request T_E, it is computed using the following relations: $T_G = T_E\eta_t\tau_p\tau_c$ and $P_GR_e = T_GV_X$, where T_G, η_t, and P_G are respectively ground torque, engine efficiency, and ground power.

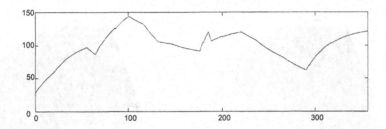

Fig. 4. Comparison of speed profiles: nonlinear model (1) vs. hybrid MLD model (2)

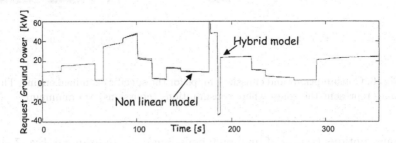

Fig. 5. Comparison of requested ground power: nonlinear model (1) vs. hybrid MLD model (2)

with the goal of minimizing consumptions and emissions and, at the same time, of guaranteeing a good tracking of the desired traction power.

The performance index we attempt at minimizing will contain a term that penalizes the input command Δ_{torque} (=deviation of the requested engine torque from the nominal one) and two functions $f_1(C)$ and $f_2(E)$ that express the value of consumptions and emissions, respectively. These functions, as shown in Fig. 6, are highly nonlinear. In order to use linear programming solvers, we need to approximate $f_1(C)$ and $f_2(E)$ as piecewise affine maps. With the goal of minimizing consumptions and emissions, the supervisor should bring the outputs of the MLD system (engine speed and engine torque[3]) as close as possible to the zone where the consumptions/emissions are lowest. As can be seen from Fig. 6(a), the zone of minimum consumption is located near the zone where the engine torque is maximum[4]. This means that minimizing consumptions does not necessary imply a lower efficiency. On the contrary, if the right gear is chosen, it is possible to maintain the same speed without loosing efficiency. We approximate function $f_1(C)$ ($f_2(E)$) as a piecewise affine function on the difference between the system outputs and the coordinates of the point y_{cons} of minimum

---

[3] In the maps the ordinate is expressed in BMRP: it represents the ratio between the engine torque and the swept volume; the second term depends on the volume of the engine, once the engine is engaged, it is a constant.

[4] The engine torque is maximum on the range [1500,2500] rpm; it is the same range where BMRP is maximum because of the relation $T_E = BMRP \cdot swept\ volume$

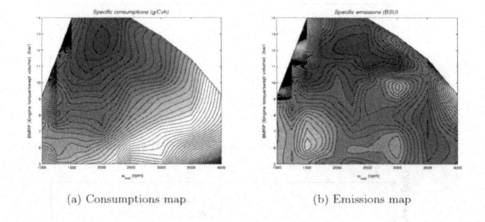

(a) Consumptions map   (b) Emissions map

Fig. 6. Consumptions and emissions maps for the specific examined engine. The darkest zones represent the zones where consumptions (emissions) are minimum

consumptions (y_{emiss} of minimum emissions). As an example, Fig. 7 shows the resulting piecewise affine approximation for $f_1(C)$.

The resulting finite-time hybrid optimal control problem is the following:

$$\min_{u_0^{T-1}, \delta_0^{T-1}, z_0^{T-1}} J(u_0^{T-1}, x_0) \triangleq \sum_{k=0}^{T-1} \rho \cdot \|(\Delta_{torque}(t+k|t))\|_\infty +$$

$$\rho_c \cdot \left\| \begin{bmatrix} q_{c_1} & q_{c_2} \\ q_{c_3} & q_{c_4} \end{bmatrix} \left(\begin{bmatrix} y_1(t+k|t) \\ y_2(t+k|t) \end{bmatrix} - y_{cons} \right) \right\|_\infty + \rho_e \cdot \left\| \begin{bmatrix} q_{e_1} & q_{e_2} \\ q_{e_3} & q_{e_4} \end{bmatrix} \left(\begin{bmatrix} y_1(t+k|t) \\ y_2(t+k|t) \end{bmatrix} - y_{emiss} \right) \right\|_\infty$$

$$(3)$$

$$\text{subject to} \begin{cases} x_0 = x(t) \\ x_{k+1} = Ax_k + B_1u_k + B_2\gamma_k + B_3z_k \\ y_k = Cx_k + D_1u_k + D_2\gamma_k + D_3z_k \\ E_2\gamma_k + E_3z_k \le E_1u_k + E_4x_k + E_5, \end{cases}$$

where $x(t)$ is the state of the MLD system at time t, and $\| \cdot \|_\infty$ is the standard ∞-norm. Matrices $Q_1 = \begin{bmatrix} q_{c_1} & q_{c_2} \\ q_{c_3} & q_{c_4} \end{bmatrix}$ and $Q_2 = \begin{bmatrix} q_{e_1} & q_{e_2} \\ q_{e_3} & q_{e_4} \end{bmatrix}$ are the weighting matrices needed for the approximated piecewise affine consumption and emission functions. By varying the weights ρ_c, ρ_e we are able to emphasize the reduction of consumptions or emissions.

In (3) we assume that possible physical and/or logical constraints on the variables of the hybrid system are already included in the mixed-integer linear constraints of the MLD model, as they can be conveniently modeled through the language HYSDEL. Receding horizon control (RHC) amounts to repeatedly computing the optimal solution to (3) at each time t, and applying only the first optimal control move u_0^* as the input $u(t)$ to the system. Problem (3) can be translated into a mixed integer linear problem (MILP), i.e., into the minimization of a

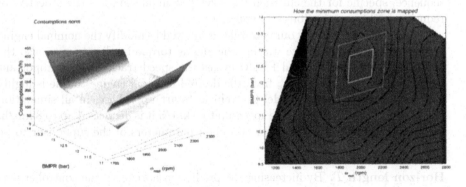

Fig. 7. Piecewise affine approximation of the consumptions map

linear cost function subject to linear constraints, where some of the variables are constrained to be binary, see [8] for details.

5 Simulations

The receding horizon optimal controller based on the hybrid MLD model (2) is simulated in closed loop with a more accurate nonlinear model provided by CRF. The reported simulations are performed using standard speed patterns for emission test cycles, namely the ECE and EUDC patterns[5].

- The ECE cycle is an urban driving cycle, also known as UDC. It was devised to represent city driving conditions, e.g., in Paris or Rome. It is characterized by low vehicle speed, low engine load, and low exhaust gas temperature.
- The EUDC (Extra Urban Driving Cycle) segment has been added after the fourth ECE cycle to account for more aggressive, high speed driving modes. The maximum speed of the EUDC cycle is 120 km/h.

We investigate the behavior of the nonlinear model provided by CRF in closed-loop with three different types of controllers: (1) receding horizon hybrid optimal controller, (2) controller based on static maps (provided by CRF), and (3) gear shifting sequence provided by the EU standard.

The first controller, as described in Section 4, has two degrees of freedom: the gear and the deviation from the nominal requested engine torque. By varying the weights ρ_c and ρ_e it is possible to emphasize the reduction of consumptions or emissions, or in general to trade off between them. The second one is based on a static map provided by CRF that is mainly designed for minimizing consumptions (other maps may be available for minimizing emissions). The third simulation is obtained by feeding the gear shifting sequence provided by the EU standard to the nonlinear vehicle model. Such a sequence represents an ideal

---

[5] The cycles definition can be found in the EEC Directive 90/C81/01.

sequence, specific for the emission test cycles at hand, and has the objective of reducing both consumptions and emissions.

We underline that only our controller is allowed to modify the nominal engine torque. Unfortunately, since varying the engine torque implies to vary also the speed and since in ECE and EUDC cycles the speed tracking is an important aspect, the deviation Δ_{Torque} from the desired nominal engine torque is highly penalized. As we did not model the vehicle "start up" phase, in all simulation tests rather than decreasing the speed up to 0 km/h it is decreased up to 8 km/h.

Besides the weights, the other two main parameters of the supervisor to be tuned are:

Horizon length T. By increasing the prediction horizon T the controller performance improves, but, at the same time, the number of constraints in (3) (and the complexity of the piecewise affine controller) increases. Therefore, tuning T amounts to find the smallest value which leads to a satisfactory closed-loop behavior. In our case, since the requested engine torque is immediately applied (see Section 2), the engine torque dynamics is neglected, so that the difference in performance using different horizons T (we tested $T = 1, \ldots , 4$) is minimal. Hence, for the benefit of computational simplicity, we chose $T = 1$.

Control signal Δ_{Torque}. While this should be as much as possible close to zero for the reasons mentioned above, it improves the performance of the MPC controller, as it gives the possibility of further reducing consumptions and emissions, at the price of a loss of perfect power tracking, as shown in Fig. 8.

In Fig. 8 and in Fig. 9 we show the simulation results on the ECE and EUDC cycles. In simulating the MPC controller, rather than looking for a trade off between consumptions and emissions, we emphasize the performance where the goal is only to reduce consumptions or only to reduce emissions, as requested by CRF for a comparison between the MPC controller and the one based on static maps.

The MPC controller has a good performance in both cases: clearly, in Fig. 9 the results on the left side are obtained using a high ratio ρ_c/ρ_e (controller MPC_C), on the contrary, with a low ρ_c/ρ_e we obtained the results shown on the right side (controller MPC_E), by consequently reducing only emissions. By properly choosing the weights we would have a behavior very similar to the one that used the ideal gear shifting sequence.

As expected, when we emphasize the performance where the goal is only to reduce consumptions (MPC_C) or emissions (MPC_E), the other variable (emissions or consumptions, respectively) sensibly increases, as shown in Fig.10. We remark again that in the present MPC setup one directly selects the desired tradeoff between consumptions and emissions by simply choosing the ratio ρ_c/ρ_e.

The results discussed above were simulated in about 220 s (ECE cycle) and 440 s (EUDC cycle) on a PC Pentium III 1 GHz running MATLAB/Simulink and the MILP solver of Cplex [16], using a prediction horizon $T = 1$ (see [17] for more simulation results). Therefore, the controller is not directly suitable for

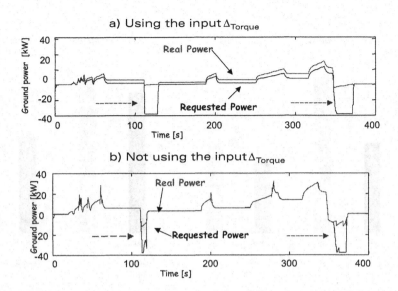

Fig. 8. Comparison between the track traction power with or without using the control signal Δ_{torque}. Dashed arrows show the points, during both simulations, where it was impossible for the engine to reach the desiderate ground power.

implementation on automotive hardware, both for excessive CPU requirements and software complexity. This problem is dealt with in next section.

6   Implementation as a Piecewise Affine Control Law

Once the tuning of the MPC controller is done in simulation, the explicit piecewise affine form of the control law can be computed off-line by using a multiparametric mixed integer linear programming (mp-MILP) solver, according to the approach of [8], [18]. Rather than solving the MILP (3) *on line* for the given current states and reference signals, the idea is to use the mp-MILP solver to compute *off line* the solution of the MILP (3) for all the states and reference signals within an (overestimate of the) expected range of values.

As shown in [8], the control law has the piecewise affine form

$$u(t) = F_i \Theta(t) + g_i \quad \text{if } H_i \Theta(t) \leq k_i, \ i = 1, ..., n_r, \tag{4}$$

where for our model $u = [\Delta_{torque}, gear^6]'$ and the set of parameters $\Theta = [speed, \%gas\ pedal]'^7$. Therefore, the set of states+references is partitioned into n_r polyhedral cells, and an affine control law is define in each one of them.

---

[6] It is a real variable; it easy to translate it in the form presented in Section 3.

[7] These parameters can be translated into the state vector by using suitable transformation maps.

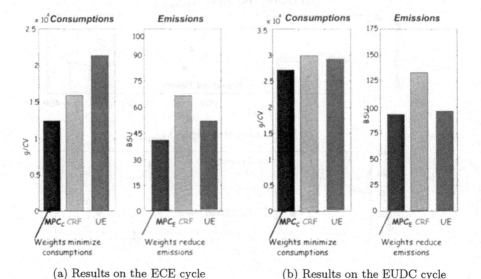

(a) Results on the ECE cycle   (b) Results on the EUDC cycle

Fig. 9. Comparison of resulting consumptions and emissions using the three different strategies (ECE and EUDC cycles)

We remark that for any given $\Theta(t)$ the on-line solution of RHC via MILP and the explicit off-line solution (4) provide the same result. Therefore, a good design strategy consist of tuning the MPC controller using simulation and on-line optimitazion, and then to convert the controller to its piecewise affine explicit form. The explicit controller will behave in exactly the same way at a much lower computational cost. The control law can in fact be implemented on-line in the following simple way:

  i. determine the i-th region that contains the current vector $\Theta(t)$;
 ii. compute the $u(t) = F_i\Theta(t) + g_i$ according to the corresponding i-th control law.

More efficient ways of evaluating piecewise affine control law, based on the organization of the controller gains an a balanced search tree, are reported in [19]. At this stage the complexity of the explicit piecewise affine control low (4) has not been yet analyzed. This will be the subject of future research.

Acknowledgements. We thank Domenico Mignone, Fabio D. Torrisi, Nicolò Giorgetti, and Francesco Borrelli for their help with the simulation setup, and A.T.A. (Automotive Technical Association) and the Automatic Control Laboratory at ETH Zurich for the support of Massimo Mannelli.

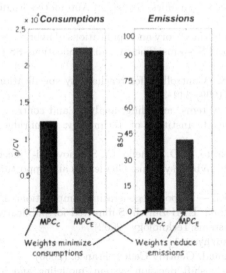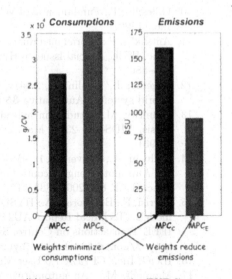

(a) Comparison on the ECE cycle

(b) Comparison on the EUDC cycle

Fig. 10. Comparison of resulting consumptions and emissions in the MPC controller using different weights (ECE and EUDC cycles)

References

1. Borodani, P., Gianoglio, R., Giuliano, F., Ippolito, L., Lupo, M.: The interactive robotized gearbox improves fuel economy and driver expectations. In: Proc. Fédération Internationale des Sociétés d'Ingénieurs des Techniques de l'Automobile (FISITA), Paris (1998)
2. Ippolito, L., Rovera, G.: Potential of robotized gearbox to improve fuel economy, Certosa di Pontignano (SI), Italy (1996)
3. Hoio, Y., Iwatsuki, K.: Toyota five speed automatic transmission with application of modern control theory. SAE Paper 920610 (1992)
4. Naruse, T., Nakashima, Y.: A study on evaluation method and improvement of shift quality of automatic transmission. SAE Paper 930673 (1993)
5. Yamaguchi, H., Takahashi, H.: Automatic transmission gear change control using fuzzy logic. (Nissan Motor Company Ldt.)
6. Borodani, P., Gianoglio, R., Giuliano, F., Lupo, M.: Gear change control system according to driving style in a motor vehicle provided with servo assisted gears. European patent nr. EP 0950839 (1999) International Application Number: 99107256.2 3.
7. Bemporad, A., Morari, M.: Control of systems integrating logic, dynamics, and constraints. Automatica **35** (1999) 407–427
8. Bemporad, A., Borrelli, F., Morari, M.: Piecewise linear optimal controllers for hybrid systems. In: Proc. American Contr. Conf., Chicago, IL (2000) 1190–1194
9. Genta, G.: Motor Vehicle Dynamics: Modeling and Simulation. Volume 43 of Series on Advances in Mathematics for Applied Sciences. World Scientific Pub Co (1997)

10. Gillespie, T.: Fundamental of Vehicle Dynamics. Society of Automotive Engineers, Inc. (1992)
11. Antsaklis, P.: A brief introduction to the theory and applications of hybrid systems. Proc. IEEE, Special Issue on Hybrid Systems: Theory and Applications **88** (2000) 879–886
12. Lygeros, J., Tomlin, C., Sastry, S.: Controllers for reachability specifications for hybrid systems. Automatica **35** (1999) 349–370
13. Branicky, M.: Studies in hybrid systems: modeling, analysis, and control. PhD thesis, LIDS-TH 2304, Massachusetts Institute of Technology, Cambridge, MA (1995)
14. Balluchi, A., Benvenuti, L., Benedetto, M.D., Pinello, C., Sangiovanni-Vincentelli, A.: Automotive engine control and hybrid systems: Challenges and opportunities. Proc. IEEE **88** (2000) 888–912
15. Torrisi, F., Bemporad, A.: HYSDEL — A tool for generating computational hybrid models. Technical Report AUT02-03, ETH Zurich, Submitted for publication on IEEE Transactions on Control Systems Technology (2002) `http://control.ethz.ch/~hybrid/hysdel`.
16. ILOG, Inc.: CPLEX 7.0 User Manual, Gentilly Cedex, France. (2000)
17. Mannelli, M.: An automotive gear-shift decision system: modeling and hybrid control (2002) Master thesis. University of Florence, Italy. In Italian.
18. Bemporad, A., Morari, M., Dua, V., Pistikopoulos, E.: The explicit linear quadratic regulator for constrained systems. Automatica **38** (2002) 3–20
19. Tøndel, P., Johansen, T., Bemporad, A.: Evaluation of piecewise affine control via binary search tree. Automatica (2003) In press.

A   Appendix

Below we report the HYSDEL model of the vehicle, from which we obtain the MLD model. Note that T_{ref}, T_{brake}, slope are treated here as measured constant states, as their value is updated at every step.

```
/* Model 8: model for the control release 8.5
27.02.02(M.S.G)-01.03.02(N.S.G.) M.p.T */

SYSTEM MODEL8 {
 INTERFACE
 {
  STATE
  {
   REAL wsec, Cref, brake, slope;
   /* wsec = The only state in the reduced-order model: it has not a physical meaning
      Cref = Engine reference torque at time t
      brake = Braking torque
      slope = Slope*/
  }
  INPUT
  {
   REAL DC;
   /* DC= Engine torque variation*/
   BOOL gear1,gear2,gear3,gear4;
   /*gear(i)= i-th gear; gear 5 is obtained when each input is zero*/
  }
  OUTPUT
  {
   REAL wmot, torque;
   /* wmot = Primary shaft speed in rpm*
      torque= Real torque applied*/
  }
  PARAMETER
  {
   REAL T1 = 3.909;
   REAL T2 = 2.238;
   REAL T3 = 1.444;    /*Gear ratio (for each gear engaged)*/
   REAL T4 = 1.029;
```

```
        REAL T5 = 0.767;
        REAL Tp = 3.15;      /*Bridge ratio*/
        REAL wmin=700;       /*Minimum primary shaft speed*/
        REAL wmax=6000;      /*Maximum primary shaft speed*/

        REAL C1=0.8874;
        REAL C2=1.0026;
        REAL C3=1.0442;      /*coefficients for the outputs re-establish from the state (of the
                               reduced-order model) wsec*/
        REAL C4=1.0601;
        REAL C5=1.0676;
        .
        .                    /*other parameters are omitted for lack of space*/
        .
        REAL pi= 3.14159;
        REAL e = 1e-6;       /*precision*/
    }
}
IMPLEMENTATION
{
  AUX
  {
    REAL  wsec1, wsec2, wsec3, wsec4, wsec5, Cm1, Cm2, Cm3, Cm4, Cm5, Cwmax1, Cwmax3;
    BOOL w1, w2;   /*auxiliary variables*/
  }
  AD
  {
    w1 = wmax1-(60/2/pi)*(C1*wsec1*T1+C2*wsec2*T2+C3*wsec3*T3+C4*wsec4*T4+C5*wsec5*T5)<=0
                         [wmax1-wmin,wmax1-wmax,e];
    w2 = wmax2-(60/2/pi)*(C1*wsec1*T1+C2*wsec2*T2+C3*wsec3*T3+C4*wsec4*T4+C5*wsec5*T5)<=0
                         [wmax2-wmin,wmax2-wmax,e];
    /*w3 = wmax3-wsec1*T1+wsec2*T2+wsec3*T3+wsec4*T4+wsec5*T5<=0 [wmax3-wmin,wmax3-wmax,e];*/
  }
  DA
  {
    wsec1 = {IF (gear1)              THEN a111*wsec+b111*rend*(T1*Cref+DC)+b112*slope+b113*brake+b114*Crot+b115
                         [(wmax*pi*2)/(60*T5),0,e]};
    wsec2 = {IF (gear2)              THEN a211*wsec+b211*rend*(T2*Cref+DC)+b212*slope+b213*brake+b214*Crot+b215
                         [(wmax*pi*2)/(60*T5),0,e]};
    wsec3 = {IF (gear3)              THEN a311*wsec+b311*rend*(T3*Cref+DC)+b312*slope+b313*brake+b314*Crot+b315
                         [(wmax*pi*2)/(60*T5),0,e]};
    wsec4 = {IF (gear4)              THEN a411*wsec+b411*rend*(T4*Cref+DC)+b412*slope+b413*brake+b414*Crot+b415
                         [(wmax*pi*2)/(60*T5),0,e]};
    wsec5 = {IF ~(gear1|gear2|gear3|gear4)  THEN
    a511*wsec+b511*rend*(T5*Cref+DC)+b512*slope+b513*brake+b514*Crot+b515 [(wmax*pi*2)/(60*T5),0,e]};

    Cm1 = {IF (gear1)                THEN Cref+DC/T1      [Cmax,-70,e]};
    Cm2 = {IF (gear2)                THEN Cref+DC/T2      [Cmax,-70,e]};
    Cm3 = {IF (gear3)                THEN Cref+DC/T3      [Cmax,-70,e]};
    Cm4 = {IF (gear4)                THEN Cref+DC/T4      [Cmax,-70,e]};
    Cm5 = {IF ~(gear1|gear2|gear3|gear4)  THEN Cref+DC/T5  [Cmax,-70,e]};

    Cwmax1 = {IF (~w1) THEN  /* Maximum Engine torque in the range [700, w1] rpm*/
    Tcmax1*((C1*wsec1*T1+C2*wsec2*T2+C3*wsec3*T3+C4*wsec4*T4+C5*wsec5*T5)-(wmax1)*(2*pi/60))+Cmax
                         [9000,-5,e]};

    Cwmax3 = {IF w2 THEN     /* Maximum Engine torque in the range [w2, 6000] rpm*/
    Tcmax3*((C1*wsec1*T1+C2*wsec2*T2+C3*wsec3*T3+C4*wsec4*T4+C5*wsec5*T5)-(wmax2)*(2*pi/60))+Cmax
                         [500,-50,e]};

  }

  CONTINUOUS
  {

    wsec=wsec1+wsec2+wsec3+wsec4+wsec5;  /*in rad/s*/
    Cref=Cref;                   /*Nm*/
    brake=brake;                 /*Nm*/
    slope=slope;                 /*N*/
  }

  OUTPUT
  {
    wmot=(C1*wsec1*T1+C2*wsec2*T2+C3*wsec3*T3+C4*wsec4*T4+C5*wsec5*T5)*60/2/pi;
    /*Primary shaft speed in rpm*/
    torque=4*pi*(Cm1+Cm2+Cm3+Cm4+Cm5)/(100*1.91);
    /*Engine Torque/swept volume in BMRP*/
  }
  MUST
  {
    -brake<=0;          /* Minimum brake torque*/
    brake<=maxbrake;    /* Maximum brake torque*/
    /*~((~w1)&(~(gear1|gear2|gear3|gear4)));*/
    w2->w1;
    /*w3->w2;
    w3->w1*/

    -((REAL gear1)+(REAL gear2)+(REAL gear3)+(REAL gear4)+1)<=-0.9999;
    (REAL gear1)+(REAL gear2)+(REAL gear3)+(REAL gear4)<=1.0001;

    /* Check the Primary shaft speed*/
```

```
   -(C1*wsec1*60*T1+C2*wsec2*60*T2+C3*wsec3*60*T3+C4*wsec4*60*T4+C5*wsec5*60*T5)/(2*pi)<=-wmin;
   C1*wsec1<=((wmax-1000)*pi*2)/(60*T1);
   C2*wsec2<=(wmax*pi*2)/(60*T2);
   C3*wsec3<=(wmax*pi*2)/(60*T3);
   C4*wsec4<=(wmax*pi*2)/(60*T4);
   C5*wsec5<=(wmax*pi*2)/(60*T5);

   /*Maximum Engine Torque*/
   Cm1<=Cwmax1+Cmax*((REAL w1)+(1-(REAL w2))-1)+Cwmax3;
   Cm2<=Cwmax1+Cmax*((REAL w1)+(1-(REAL w2))-1)+Cwmax3;
   Cm3<=Cwmax1+Cmax*((REAL w1)+(1-(REAL w2))-1)+Cwmax3;
   Cm4<=Cwmax1+Cmax*((REAL w1)+(1-(REAL w2))-1)+Cwmax3;
   Cm5<=Cwmax1+Cmax*((REAL w1)+(1-(REAL w2))-1)+Cwmax3;

   /*Constraints for Delta Torque*/
    DC<=DCmax;
    -DC<=-DCmin;
  }
 }
}
```

A Greedy Approach to Identification of Piecewise Affine Models

Alberto Bemporad, Andrea Garulli, Simone Paoletti, and Antonio Vicino

Università di Siena, Dipartimento di Ingegneria dell'Informazione,
Via Roma 56, 53100 Siena, Italy
{bemporad,garulli,paoletti,vicino}@dii.unisi.it

Abstract. This paper addresses the problem of identification of piecewise affine (PWA) models. This problem involves the estimation from data of both the parameters of the affine submodels *and* the partition of the PWA map. The procedure that we propose for PWA identification exploits a greedy strategy for partitioning an infeasible system of linear inequalities into a minimum number of feasible subsystems: this provides an initial clustering of the datapoints. Then a refinement procedure is applied repeatedly to the estimated clusters in order to improve both the data classification and the parameter estimation. The partition of the PWA map is finally estimated by considering pairwise the clusters of regression vectors, and by finding a separating hyperplane for each of such pairs. We show that our procedure does not require to fix a priori the number of affine submodels, which is instead automatically estimated from the data.

1 Introduction

Black-box identification of nonlinear systems has been widely addressed in different contexts. A large number of model classes have been considered and their properties deeply investigated (see the survey papers [1,2] and references therein). In this paper, we deal with the problem of identifying a piecewise affine (PWA) model of a discrete-time nonlinear system from input-output data. PWA systems have become more and more popular in recent years, thanks to their equivalence with several classes of hybrid systems [3,4]. However, estimation of hybrid models from data has not received the attention it deserves in the control community, except for few very recent contributions [5,6,7].

Identification of PWA models involves the simultaneous estimation of both the parameters of the affine submodels *and* the partition of the PWA map. The first issue is closely related to the problem of classifying the data, *i.e.*, the problem of correctly assigning each datapoint to an affine submodel. In [5] a two-phase approach for the classification of the datapoints and the estimation of the parameters has been proposed. The classification problem is reduced to an optimal clustering problem, in which the number of clusters is fixed. Once the datapoints have been classified, linear regression is used to compute the final submodels. In [6] the attention is focused on two subclasses of PWA models, namely hinging

O. Maler and A. Pnueli (Eds.): HSCC 2003, LNCS 2623, pp. 97–112, 2003.
© Springer-Verlag Berlin Heidelberg 2003

hyperplanes (HHARX) and Wiener piecewise affine (W-PWARX) autoregressive exogenous models. For these classes of models, the identification problem is formulated as a suitable mixed-integer linear (or quadratic, depending on the choice of the cost function) programming problem, which can be solved for the global optimum. Also in [7] the identification problem for a class of hybrid systems is formulated as an optimization problem, and an algorithm which provides an approximation of the optimal solution is developed. It makes it possible to incorporate particular a priori knowledge, such as the level of abstraction, the structure, and the desired accuracy of the model.

The identification procedure proposed in this paper does not require that the number of affine submodels is fixed a priori. Hence, this number must be *estimated* from data, together with the parameters of the submodels and the partition of the map. The key approach here is the selection of a bound on the prediction error. This induces a set of linear inequality constraints on the parameters of the PWA model to be estimated. These constraints are generally infeasible (otherwise a single affine model would fit the data within the given error level). Hence, a suitable strategy is suggested for picking a number of submodels which is compatible with the available data and the selected bound. In particular, the greedy strategy proposed in [8] for partitioning an infeasible system of linear inequalities into a minimum number of feasible subsystems, is exploited in order to provide an initial clustering of the datapoints. To each feasible subsystem a set of feasible parameter vectors is then associated according to the bounded-error assumption [9,10]. After the first classification, a projection algorithm is applied repeatedly to the estimated clusters in order to improve both the classification of the datapoints and the estimation of the parameters. In this phase, the datapoints are grouped together according to the fact that they are fitted by the same affine submodel, so that outliers are automatically rejected. Notice that the final number of submodels and the corresponding parameter vectors will depend on the selected bound on the prediction error, so that this determines both the complexity of the model and the quality of the approximation. The partition of the PWA map is finally estimated by considering pairwise the clusters of regression vectors, and finding a separating hyperplane for each of such pairs. Linear Support Vector Machines [11] are suitable for this aim. In this paper, we show that, given two clusters of points, the problem of finding a generalized separating hyperplane (*i.e.*, a hyperplane that minimizes the number of misclassified points) can be formulated as a maximum feasible subsystem problem, for which computationally efficient methods exist [12].

2   Problem Statement

Let $F : \mathcal{X} \mapsto \mathbb{R}^p$ be a nonlinear map defined over the polyhedron $\mathcal{X} \subseteq \mathbb{R}^n$, and assume that a collection of N samples (y_k, x_k), $k = 1, \ldots, N$, of $F(\cdot)$ is given, where

$$y_k = F(x_k) + e_k ,$$

(1)

and $e_k \in \mathbb{R}^p$ is a perturbation term. The aim is to find, on the basis of the available samples, a Piecewise Affine (PWA) approximation $f(\cdot)$ of $F(\cdot)$,

$$f(x) = \begin{cases} \theta_1' \begin{bmatrix} x \\ 1 \end{bmatrix} & \text{if } x \in \mathcal{X}_1 \\ \vdots & \vdots \\ \theta_s' \begin{bmatrix} x \\ 1 \end{bmatrix} & \text{if } x \in \mathcal{X}_s, \end{cases} \tag{2}$$

where $\theta_i \in \mathbb{R}^{(n+1) \times p}$ are parameter matrices, and $\{\mathcal{X}_i\}_{i=1}^s$ is a polyhedral partition of $\mathcal{X}$ (i.e., $\bigcup_{i=1}^s \mathcal{X}_i = \mathcal{X}$, $\mathcal{X}_i \cap \mathcal{X}_j = \emptyset$ if $i \neq j$, and each *region* $\mathcal{X}_i$ is a convex polyhedron, represented in the form[1] $\mathcal{X}_i = \left\{ x \in \mathbb{R}^n : H_i \begin{bmatrix} x \\ 1 \end{bmatrix} \leq 0 \right\}$, where $H_i \in \mathbb{R}^{q_i \times (n+1)}$).

In the context of nonlinear function approximation, y_k represent values of $F(\cdot)$ obtained at certain points x_k, and e_k is either zero (for instance when $F(\cdot)$ can be computed analytically), or an approximation error (for instance when $F(\cdot)$ is evaluated numerically by iterative procedures, as in the case of implicit functions or optimal value functions).

In the context of system identification, $k \in \mathbb{Z}$ is the time index, x_k is the regression vector (accordingly, $\mathcal{X}$ is called the *regressor set*), y_k is the system output, and e_k is noise. For instance, when identifying state-space models of the form

$$\begin{cases} \xi_{k+1} = F_1(\xi_k, u_k) \\ \eta_k = F_2(\xi_k, u_k), \end{cases} \tag{3}$$

x_k contains the components of the state and input vectors at time k, i.e., $x_k = [\xi_k' \ u_k']'$, whereas $y_k = [\xi_{k+1}' \ \eta_k']'$, assuming that the state vector is measurable. A typical reason for estimating a PWA approximation of (3) is for applying the tools of verification, controller synthesis, and stability analysis developed for linear hybrid systems, to nonlinear processes.

In this paper, we rather focus on identification of PWARX (Piecewise affine AutoRegressive eXogenous) models in the form (2), where $p = 1$, the regression vector is defined as $x_k = [y_{k-1} \cdots y_{k-n_a} \ u_{k-1}' \cdots u_{k-n_b}']'$, and $u_k \in \mathbb{R}^m$ and $y_k \in \mathbb{R}$ denote the system input and output, respectively. In this case, the parameter vectors $\theta_i \in \mathbb{R}^{n+1}$, $i = 1, \ldots, s$, contain the coefficients of the ARX *submodels*. For simplicity of exposition, throughout the paper it is assumed $p = 1$, though the presented approach is easily applicable to the case $p > 1$ by small

---

[1] We do not assume here that $f(\cdot)$ is continuous. Without this assumption, definition (2) is not well posed in general, since the function could be multiply defined over common boundaries of the regions $\mathcal{X}_i$. One could avoid this by replacing some of the "$\leq$" inequalities with "$<$" in the definitions of the polyhedra $\mathcal{X}_i$, although this issue is not of practical interest in the problem at hand.

amendments to the procedures shown in Sections 3 and 4. For a more compact notation, hereafter we will consider the extended regression vector $\varphi_k = [x'_k \ 1]'$.

The key approach of this paper consists in selecting a bound δ on the *prediction error*, i.e., in requiring

$$|y_k - f(x_k)| \leq \delta, \quad \forall k = 1, \ldots, N, \tag{4}$$

for some $\delta > 0$. Notice that the prediction error is the sum of the approximation error $F(x_k) - f(x_k)$ and the perturbation term e_k. Then, the considered identification problem can be formulated as follows:

Problem 1. Given N datapoints (y_k, x_k), $k = 1, \ldots, N$, estimate a positive integer s, a partition $\{\mathcal{X}_i\}_{i=1}^{s}$ and parameter vectors $\{\theta_i\}_{i=1}^{s}$, such that the corresponding PWA model (2) of system (1) is compatible with the available data according to condition (4).

Condition (4) naturally leads to a set-membership or bounded-error approach to the identification problem (see, e.g., [9,10]). Notice that the bound δ is not necessarily given a priori, it is rather a tuning knob of the procedure. A reliable choice of it can often be made a posteriori by performing a series of trials for different values of δ, and then selecting a value that provides a good trade-off between the complexity of the model (in terms of number of submodels) and the quality of the approximation (in terms of mean square error). To clarify this, consider the case of nonlinear function approximation, where the smaller δ, the larger the number s of submodels needed to fit the datapoints (y_k, x_k) to a PWA map (2). On the other hand, the larger δ, the worse the approximation, since large errors are allowed.

The following example will be used throughout the paper to illustrate the mechanism of the proposed identification procedure.

Example 1. Let the data be generated by the PWARX system

$$y_k = \begin{cases} [-0.4 \ 1 \ 1.5] \, \varphi_k + e_k & \text{if } [4 \ -1 \ 10] \, \varphi_k < 0 \\ [0.5 \ -1 \ -0.5] \, \varphi_k + e_k & \text{if } \begin{bmatrix} -4 & 1 & -10 \\ 5 & 1 & -6 \end{bmatrix} \varphi_k \leq 0 \\ [-0.3 \ 0.5 \ -1.7] \, \varphi_k + e_k & \text{if } [-5 \ -1 \ 6] \, \varphi_k < 0, \end{cases}$$

for which $\varphi_k = [y_{k-1} \ u_{k-1} \ 1]'$ and $s = 3$. The input signal u_k and the noise signal e_k are uniformly distributed in $[-5, 5]$ and $[-0.1, 0.1]$, respectively. $N = 200$ estimation datapoints are used. The partition of the regressor set and the set of available regression vectors are depicted in Figure 1. The three regions contain 55, 66 and 79 points, respectively.

3 The MIN PFS Problem

In this section we will describe the greedy algorithm proposed in [8] for partitioning an infeasible system of linear inequalities into a minimum number of feasible

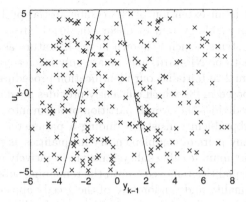

Fig. 1. The partition of the regressor set and the available regression vectors

subsystems. We will also show how to use this algorithm in our identification procedure to obtain an initial classification of the datapoints and a set of feasible parameter vectors for each submodel.

In the first part of our identification procedure, we do not consider the problem of estimating the hyperplanes defining the polyhedral partition of the regressor set. We focus only on classifying the datapoints according to the fact that they are fitted by the same affine submodel. Obviously, in this phase it is reasonable to look for the minimum number of submodels (namely s) fitting all (or most of, due to possible outliers) the datapoints. In other words, we look for the "simplest" PWA model that is consistent with the data and condition (4), where, for a given δ, "simplicity" is measured in terms of the number of affine submodels.

By requiring condition (4), the classification problem can be formulated as follows:

Problem 2. Given $\delta > 0$ and the (possibly infeasible) system of N linear complementary inequalities

$$
\begin{cases}
\varphi_k'\theta \leq y_k + \delta \\
\varphi_k'\theta \geq y_k - \delta
\end{cases}, \quad k = 1, \ldots, N,
\tag{5}
$$

find a partition of this system into a minimum number s of feasible subsystems, under the constraint that two paired complementary inequalities must be included in the same subsystem (i.e., they must be simultaneously satisfied by the same parameter vector θ).

The above formulation makes it possible to address simultaneously the two fundamental issues of data classification and parameter estimation. Given any solution of Problem 2, the partition of the complementary inequalities provides the classification of the datapoints, whereas each feasible subsystem defines the set of feasible parameter vectors for the corresponding affine submodel.

Problem 2 is an extension of the combinatorial problem of finding a Partition of an infeasible system of linear equalities into a MINimum number of Feasible Subsystems, which is known in the literature as MIN PFS. Since MIN PFS turns out to be NP-hard, and we are only interested in a suboptimal solution of Problem 2 to initialize our identification procedure, we adopt the greedy approach proposed in [8], which efficiently provides good approximate solutions. This approach divides the overall partition problem into a sequence of subproblems. Each subproblem consists in finding a parameter vector $\theta \in \mathbb{R}^{n+1}$ that satisfies as many pairs of complementary inequalities as possible. Starting from system (5), maximum feasible subsystems are iteratively extracted (and the corresponding inequalities removed), until the remaining subsystem is feasible. Due to the suboptimality and randomness of the greedy approach [8], this procedure yields a (not necessarily minimal) partition into feasible subsystems.

The problem of finding one $\theta \in \mathbb{R}^{n+1}$ that satisfies as many pairs of complementary inequalities as possible extends the combinatorial problem of finding a MAXimum Feasible Subsystem of an infeasible system of linear inequalities, which is known in the literature as MAX FS. Based on the consideration that also MAX FS is NP-hard, the approach proposed in [8] tackles the above extension of MAX FS using a randomized and thermal variant of the classical Agmon-Motzkin-Schoenberg relaxation method for solving systems of linear inequalities [13,14]. This provides good solutions in a reasonably short computation time.

3.1   The Randomized Relaxation Method for the MAX FS Problem

We now briefly describe the randomized relaxation method proposed in [8] for solving the extension of MAX FS to the setting with pairs of complementary inequalities[2].

First, the algorithm requires the definition of a maximum number of cycles $C > 0$, an initial temperature parameter $T_0 > 0$, and an initial estimate $\theta^{(1)} \in \mathbb{R}^{n+1}$ (e.g., randomly selected, or computed by least squares). During each cycle all the datapoints are selected in the order defined by a prescribed rule (e.g., cyclicly, or uniformly at random without replacement), so that each cycle consists of N iterations. If k is the index of the selected datapoint, and $\theta^{(j)}$ is the current estimate (where $j = 1, \ldots, CN$ is the iteration counter), the corresponding violation is computed as follows:

$$
v_j^k = \begin{cases} \varphi_k' \theta^{(j)} - y_k - \delta & \text{if } \varphi_k' \theta^{(j)} > y_k + \delta \\ y_k - \varphi_k' \theta^{(j)} - \delta & \text{if } \varphi_k' \theta^{(j)} < y_k - \delta \\ 0 & \text{otherwise .} \end{cases}
$$

The basic idea is to favor updates of the current estimate $\theta^{(j)}$ which aim at correcting unsatisfied inequalities with a relatively small violation. Indeed, the

---

[2] The algorithm is illustrated in its first application to the overall system (5), but it can be easily specialized when, in subsequent applications, only a subsystem of system (5) is considered.

correction of an unsatisfied inequality with large violation is likely to corrupt other inequalities that $\theta^{(j)}$ satisfies. A decreasing temperature parameter T, which the violations are compared with, is therefore introduced in order to give decreasing attention to unsatisfied inequalities with large violations. The algorithm can be formalized as follows.

Given: C, T_0, $\theta^{(1)}$;
Set $c = 0$, $j = 1$, $\bar{\theta} = \theta^{(1)}$;
while $c < C$ **do**
Initialize the set of indices $I = \{1, \ldots, N\}$ and set $T = (1 - c/C)T_0$;
repeat
   Pick the index k from I according to the prescribed rule;
   Compute the violation v_j^k and set $\lambda_j = (T/T_0)\exp(-v_j^k/T)$;
   if $\varphi_k'\theta^{(j)} > y_k + \delta$ **then** $\theta^{(j+1)} = \theta^{(j)} - \lambda_j\varphi_k$;
   else if $\varphi_k'\theta^{(j)} < y_k - \delta$ **then** $\theta^{(j+1)} = \theta^{(j)} + \lambda_j\varphi_k$;
   else $\theta^{(j+1)} = \theta^{(j)}$;
   if $\theta^{(j+1)} \neq \theta^{(j)}$ and $\theta^{(j+1)}$ satisfies a larger number of complementary inequalities than $\bar{\theta}$ **then** $\bar{\theta} = \theta^{(j+1)}$;
   Set $I = I - \{k\}$ and $j = j + 1$;
until $I = \emptyset$
Set $c = c + 1$;
end.

All the complementary inequalities satisfied by $\bar{\theta}$ form a feasible subsystem of system (5), which is the solution of the extended MAX FS returned by the algorithm. Notice that this solution is not guaranteed to be optimal, even though $\bar{\theta}$ is the estimate that, during the process, has satisfied the largest number of complementary inequalities.

For the choice of C and T_0, as well as for practical questions concerning the implementation of the algorithm, we refer to [8].

3.2   Comments about the Greedy Approach to MIN PFS

Let us denote by $\hat{s}$ the number of feasible subsystems of system (5) provided by successive applications of the algorithm described in Section 3.1. The estimate of the number of affine submodels needed to fit the data and the classification of the datapoints thus provided suffer two drawbacks. First, it is not guaranteed to yield minimum partitions, *i.e.*, the number of submodels $\hat{s}$ could be larger than the minimum number s needed, *e.g.*, because two subsets of complementary inequalities that could be satisfied by one and the same parameter vector, are extracted at two different iterations. Second, since some datapoints might be consistent with more than one submodel, the cardinality and the composition of the clusters could depend on the order in which the close-to-maximum feasible subsystems are extracted.

In order to cope with these drawbacks, a procedure for the refinement of the estimates will be proposed in the next section. As we will show, such a

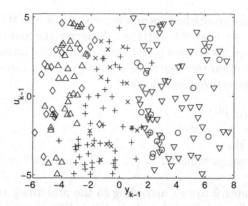

Fig. 2. Initial classification of the regression vectors. Each mark corresponds to a different cluster, for a total of six clusters

procedure improves both the classification of the datapoints and the quality of the fit by properly reassigning the datapoints and selecting pointwise estimates of the parameter vectors that characterize each submodel.

Notice that one could decide to stop the algorithm when the cardinalities of the extracted clusters become too small. This might be useful in order to penalize submodels that account for just a few datapoints (that, most likely, are outliers).

Example 1 (cont'd). We ran the greedy algorithm (with $C = 100$, $T_0 = 100$ and cyclic selection of the datapoints) over the set of datapoints of Example 1. Since the noise was uniformly distributed in $[-0.1, 0.1]$, the bound δ was chosen equal to 0.1 accordingly. We found a complete partition into $\hat{s} = 6$ clusters, containing 52, 61, 35, 17, 20 and 15 datapoints, respectively. The six clusters of regression vectors are depicted in Figure 2. The number of submodels is overestimated, and from the comparison of Figures 1 and 2 it is evident that regression vectors belonging to the same region were extracted at different iterations of the algorithm.

4   Refinement of the Estimates

The initialization of the identification procedure described in Section 3 provides the clusters $\mathcal{D}_i^{(0)}$ which consist of all the datapoints (y_k, x_k) corresponding to the i-th extracted feasible subsystem of system (5), $i = 1, \ldots, \hat{s}$. Moreover, each feasible subsystem defines the set of feasible parameter vectors for the corresponding affine submodel.

As discussed in Section 3.2, a refinement procedure is required in order to improve both the classification of the datapoints and the quality of the fit. The basic procedure that we propose consists of two main steps to be iterated. In the first step, all the datapoints are classified according to the current estimated parameter vectors. In the second step, new pointwise estimates of the parameter vectors are selected on the basis of the previously computed clusters of datapoints. This is performed by using the *projection estimate* defined as

$$\Phi_p(\mathcal{D}) = \arg\min_{\theta} \max_{(y_k, x_k) \in \mathcal{D}} \left| y_k - \varphi_k' \theta \right|, \qquad (6)$$

where $\mathcal{D}$ is a cluster of datapoints (y_k, x_k). Notice that the computation of the projection estimate can be formulated as a suitable *linear programming* (LP) problem. The refinement procedure can be formalized as follows.

0. **Initialization**
   Set $t = 1$ and select a termination threshold $\gamma \geq 0$.
   For $i = 1, \dots, \hat{s}$, set $\hat{\theta}_i^{(1)} = \Phi_p(\mathcal{D}_i^{(0)})$.
1. **Reassignment of the datapoints**
   For each datapoint (y_k, x_k), $k = 1, \dots, N$:
   - If $\left| y_k - \varphi_k' \hat{\theta}_i^{(t)} \right| > \delta$ for all $i = 1, \dots, \hat{s}$, then mark (y_k, x_k) as *infeasible*.
   - If $\left| y_k - \varphi_k' \hat{\theta}_i^{(t)} \right| \leq \delta$ for more than one $i = 1, \dots, \hat{s}$, then mark (y_k, x_k) as *undecidable*.
   - If $\left| y_k - \varphi_k' \hat{\theta}_i^{(t)} \right| \leq \delta$ for only one $i = 1, \dots, \hat{s}$, then assign (y_k, x_k) to $\mathcal{D}_i^{(t)}$ and mark it as *feasible*.
2. **Re-estimation of the parameter vectors**
   For $i = 1, \dots, \hat{s}$, compute $\hat{\theta}_i^{(t+1)} = \Phi_p(\mathcal{D}_i^{(t)})$.
3. **Termination**
   If $\|\hat{\theta}_i^{(t+1)} - \hat{\theta}_i^{(t)}\|/\|\hat{\theta}_i^{(t)}\| \leq \gamma$ for all $i = 1, \dots, \hat{s}$, then exit. Otherwise, set $t = t + 1$ and go to step 1.

In order to avoid that the procedure does not terminate, only a maximum number $t_{\max}$ of refinements is allowed. Convergence properties of the procedure are currently under investigation.

The basic idea of the procedure is that, while the new parameter vectors $\hat{\theta}_i^{(t+1)}$ are computed on the basis of the clusters $\mathcal{D}_i^{(t)}$, some infeasible, as well as undecidable, datapoints may become feasible, *i.e.*, may be assigned to some cluster $\mathcal{D}_i^{(t+1)}$, thus improving the quality of the classification. Notice that the use of the projection estimate in step 2 guarantees that no feasible datapoint at refinement t becomes infeasible at refinement $t + 1$, since

$$\max_{(y_k, x_k) \in \mathcal{D}_i^{(t)}} \left| y_k - \varphi_k' \hat{\theta}_i^{(t+1)} \right| \leq \max_{(y_k, x_k) \in \mathcal{D}_i^{(t)}} \left| y_k - \varphi_k' \hat{\theta}_i^{(t)} \right| \leq \delta, \quad i = 1, \dots, \hat{s}.$$

In step 1 the distinction among infeasible, undecidable, and feasible datapoints is motivated by the following considerations. If the estimated parameter vectors provide a good fit of the data, it is likely that a datapoint (y_k, x_k) considerably violating the inequalities $\left| y_k - \varphi_k' \hat{\theta}_i^{(t)} \right| \leq \delta$, $i = 1, \dots, \hat{s}$, is an outlier. Hence, it is reasonable to expect that neglecting the infeasible datapoints in the parameter re-estimation helps to improve the quality of the fit. The undecidable datapoints are instead consistent with more than one submodel. This indecision (that is inherent with the data) could be solved only by exploiting the partition of the PWA map. In this phase, neglecting the undecidable datapoints helps to reduce the number of misclassifications. As it will be clarified in the next section, this will make possible a better estimation of the PWA partition.

The basic procedure for the refinement of the estimates does not change the estimated number of submodels, so that further steps are required to cope with the case when the greedy algorithm provides an overestimation of the number of submodels needed to fit the data. Recall that this could occur because of the suboptimality of the greedy strategy, and the randomness of the method used to tackle the extended MAX FS problem.

In order to decrease the number of submodels, we can use information about the estimated parameter vectors and the cardinalities of the clusters. In fact, if two subsets of complementary inequalities can be satisfied by one and the same parameter vector, it is likely that the corresponding estimated parameter vectors are very similar (and we possibly have a large number of undecidable datapoints), so that they can be merged into one subset. On the other hand, if during the refinement of the estimates the cardinality of a cluster becomes too small with respect to N, the corresponding submodel can be discarded, since it accounts only for few datapoints (most likely outliers). Additional steps to the basic procedure are thus the following (α and β are fixed nonnegative thresholds):

- **Similarity of the parameter vectors**
  Compute $\alpha_{i^*,j^*} = \min_{1 \leq i < j \leq \hat{s}} \|\hat{\theta}_i^{(t)} - \hat{\theta}_j^{(t)}\| / \min\{\|\hat{\theta}_i^{(t)}\|, \|\hat{\theta}_j^{(t)}\|\}$. If $\alpha_{i^*,j^*} \leq \alpha$, merge the submodels i^* and j^*, update the number of submodels $\hat{s}$, and renumber the submodels from 1 to $\hat{s}$.

- **Cardinality of the clusters**
  Compute $\beta_{i^*} = \min_{i=1,\dots,\hat{s}} \dim(\mathcal{D}_i^{(t)})/N$. If $\beta_{i^*} \leq \beta$, discard the i^*-th submodel, update the number of submodels $\hat{s}$, and renumber the remaining submodels (and, accordingly, the corresponding clusters) from 1 to $\hat{s}$. Then, reassign only the undecidable datapoints as in step 1.

The similarity of the parameter vectors is to be tested before the reassignment of the datapoints. The fusion of two submodels i^* and j^* can be performed in different ways. For instance, the fused parameter vector can be computed as the mean $(\hat{\theta}_{i^*}^{(t)} + \hat{\theta}_{j^*}^{(t)})/2$, or on the basis of the union of the clusters $\mathcal{D}_{i^*}^{(t-1)}$ and $\mathcal{D}_{j^*}^{(t-1)}$, using the projection estimate (6). This latter computation generally provides better performance. The cardinality of the clusters is instead to be tested after the reassignment of the datapoints.

The thresholds α and β should be suitably chosen in order to decrease the number of submodels still preserving a good fit of the data. Indeed, it is clear that, if such thresholds are chosen too large, the number of submodels might decrease under s. In this case, the number of infeasible datapoints increases, since some significant dynamics is no more in the model. One could use this information to adjust α and β, and then repeat the refinement. In general, when the procedure terminates, the number of infeasible datapoints is always an index of the quality of the fit.

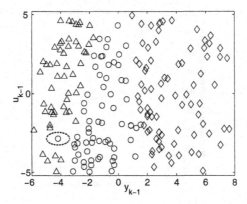

Fig. 3. Classification of the regression vectors (*triangles, circles, diamonds*) after the refinement

Example 1 (cont'd). We performed the refinement procedure with $\alpha = 15\%$, $\beta = 1\%$ and $\gamma = 0.001\%$. The termination condition was reached after six refinements. The number $\hat{s}$ of estimated submodels decreased from 6 to 3. The corresponding three clusters of regression vectors are depicted in Figure 3, and contain 53, 65 and 79 points, respectively. Two datapoints are left infeasible, and only one is undecidable. The finally estimated parameter vectors are

$$\hat{\theta}_1 = \begin{bmatrix} -0.3921 \\ 0.9978 \\ 1.5426 \end{bmatrix}, \quad \hat{\theta}_2 = \begin{bmatrix} 0.4980 \\ -0.9994 \\ -0.4971 \end{bmatrix}, \quad \hat{\theta}_3 = \begin{bmatrix} -0.3000 \\ 0.5005 \\ -1.7011 \end{bmatrix},$$

providing very good estimates of the true submodels. In Figure 3 the highlighted (misclassified) circle shows that the clusters marked with triangles and circles are not linearly separable. It is worth noticing in Figure 4 how the number of undecidable datapoints considerably decreases as the number of refinements increases, *i.e.*, as the number of estimated submodels is reduced.

5   Estimation of the Partition of the Regressor Set

So far we have classified the datapoints and estimated the affine submodels. The final step of the identification procedure consists in estimating the partition of the regressor set. This step can be performed by considering pairwise the clusters $\mathcal{F}_i = \{x_k | (y_k, x_k) \in \mathcal{D}_i\}$ (where $\mathcal{D}_i$, $i = 1, \ldots, \hat{s}$, is the final classification of the feasible datapoints provided by the refinement procedure), and finding a separating hyperplane for each of such pairs.

Given two linearly separable clusters $\mathcal{F}_i$ and $\mathcal{F}_j$, with $i \neq j$, a *separating hyperplane* $x'a + b = 0$, with $a \in \mathbb{R}^n$ and $b \in \mathbb{R}$, is such that, for some $\varepsilon > 0$,

$$\begin{cases} x_k'a + b \leq -\varepsilon & \forall x_k \in \mathcal{F}_i \\ x_k'a + b \geq \varepsilon & \forall x_k \in \mathcal{F}_j . \end{cases} \tag{7}$$

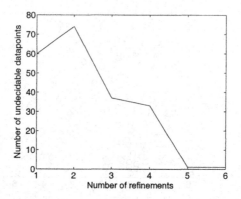

Fig. 4. Number of undecidable datapoints vs the number of refinements

If the two clusters $\mathcal{F}_i$ and $\mathcal{F}_j$ are not linearly separable, a hyperplane that minimizes the number of misclassified points (*i.e.*, points x_k not satisfying (7)) is called *generalized separating hyperplane*. Notice that, even though the true function $F(\cdot)$ were a PWA map defined over a polyhedral partition of the $\mathcal{X}$-domain, two clusters $\mathcal{F}_i$ and $\mathcal{F}_j$ might anyway not be linearly separable due to classification errors. This kind of errors is actually expected to be reduced by the distinction into *infeasible*, *undecidable*, and *feasible* datapoints. Indeed, the infeasible datapoints account mainly for the outliers, whereas the undecidable datapoints are those that most likely could induce misclassifications, since they are consistent with more than one submodel.

Linear Support Vector Machines (SVMs) are a suitable tool for this stage of the identification procedure, since they accomplish simultaneously the distinct tasks of finding the *optimal separating hyperplane* of two clusters of points (*i.e.*, the separating hyperplane that maximizes the distance from the closest point of each cluster), while minimizing the number of misclassified points [11].

In this paper, we show that the problem of finding a generalized separating hyperplane (thus providing also linearly separable clusters of points) can be formulated as a MAX FS problem. Indeed, given two clusters $\mathcal{F}_i$ and $\mathcal{F}_j$, according to (7) a separating hyperplane turns out to be a solution of the system of linear inequalities $\Phi \begin{bmatrix} a \\ b \end{bmatrix} \leq \xi$, where the rows of Φ are the vectors φ_k' for all $x_k \in \mathcal{F}_i$ and $-\varphi_k'$ for all $x_k \in \mathcal{F}_j$, and ξ is a column vector of $-\varepsilon$'s. If such system is infeasible, solving a MAX FS problem clearly corresponds to finding a hyperplane that minimizes the number of misclassified points. The misclassified points, if any, are then removed from $\mathcal{F}_i$ and/or $\mathcal{F}_j$. Since MAX FS is NP-hard, the randomized relaxation method for MAX FS proposed in [12] (of which the algorithm presented in Section 3.1 is a straightforward estension) can be used to provide good solutions in a short amount of computation time.

Optionally, once two linearly separable clusters of points are available, one could look for the optimal separating hyperplane of the two clusters. As detailed in [11], this can be performed by solving a *quadratic programming* (QP) problem:

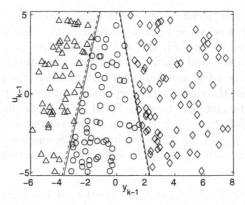

Fig. 5. Final classification of the regression vectors (*triangles, circles, diamonds*), and true (*dashed lines*) and estimated (*solid lines*) partition of the regressor set

$$\min_{(a,b)} \frac{1}{2} \|a\|^2$$
$$\text{subject to} \quad \begin{cases} x_k' a + b \leq -1 & \forall x_k \in \mathcal{F}_i \\ x_k' a + b \geq 1 & \forall x_k \in \mathcal{F}_j . \end{cases} \tag{8}$$

This separating hyperplane is termed *optimal* as it separates the two clusters with the maximal margin[3]. Each estimated region $\hat{\mathcal{X}}_i$, $i = 1, \ldots, \hat{s}$, is then defined by all the optimal hyperplanes separating $\mathcal{F}_i$ from $\mathcal{F}_j$, with $j \neq i$.

The method for the estimation of the PWA partition based on separating hyperplanes has two major drawbacks. First, if the two clusters $\mathcal{F}_i$ and $\mathcal{F}_j$ are not contiguous, the corresponding separating hyperplane possibly does not contribute to delimiting the estimated regions $\hat{\mathcal{X}}_i$ and $\hat{\mathcal{X}}_j$, i.e., we have redundancy in the representation of the partition. Second, when $n > 1$, this method does not guarantee that the estimated regions form a complete partition of the regressor set.

The former drawback can be overcome by eliminating redundant hyperplanes through standard linear programming techniques. The latter drawback is more important, since it causes the model to be not completely defined over the whole regressor set. However, both in simulation and optimization the presence of "holes" in the PWA partition can be often accepted. In simulation, when a regression vector falls into a "hole", it can be reasonably assigned to the nearest region, whereas for optimization purposes, trajectories passing through a "hole" are simply automatically discarded as infeasible, with the only consequent drawback of inducing suboptimal solutions. We are currently investigating how to avoid the presence of such "holes" by partitioning them into additional convex sets.

---

[3] It can be easily shown that, in (8), at least one "$\leq$" and one "$\geq$" constraint are active at the optimum, so that the distance of the closest point of each cluster from the optimal hyperplane is $1/\|a\|$.

The above mentioned techniques generally provide satisfactory results when the number of misclassified points is small with respect to the cardinalities of the two clusters $\mathcal{F}_i$ and $\mathcal{F}_j$. If this is not the case, at least one of $\mathcal{F}_i$ and $\mathcal{F}_j$ needs to be partitioned. Notice that, when a cluster $\mathcal{F}_i$ must be partitioned, this may correspond to nonconnected regions where the parameter vector is the same (recall that the classification procedure groups together the datapoints only according to the fact that they are fitted by the same affine submodel), or to a nonconvex region that needs to be split into convex polyhedra. Techniques for partitioning a cluster $\mathcal{F}_i$ by exploiting the information about the misclassified points while separating $\mathcal{F}_i$ from $\mathcal{F}_j$, with $j \neq i$, are currently under investigation.

Example 1 (cont'd). The final classification of the regression vectors and the estimated partition of the regressor set are depicted in Figure 5. The line separating triangles and diamonds has not been drawn, since it is redundant, whereas the two solid lines are defined by the coefficient vectors

$$\hat{h}_1 = \begin{bmatrix} 4.0036 & -0.9854 & 9.5903 \end{bmatrix}', \quad \hat{h}_2 = \begin{bmatrix} 5.0002 & 0.9990 & -6.2009 \end{bmatrix}',$$

that are very similar to the true ones. Notice that in Figure 3 the clusters marked with triangles and circles are not linearly separable (consider the highlighted circle), so that the pre-separation exploiting MAX FS is actually useful to detect the misclassification and to provide linearly separable clusters. The overall computation of the estimated PWA model took about 7 seconds on an AMD Athlon 1GHz running Matlab 6.1 non-optimized code.

Example 2. The PWA identification algorithm was successfully applied to fit the data generated by a discontinuous PWARX system for which the regression vector was $x_k = [y_{k-1} \ y_{k-2} \ u_{k-1} \ u_{k-2}]'$ (so that $n = 4$), and $s = 4$. The input signal u_k was chosen to be uniformly distributed in $[-5, 5]$, and the noise signal e_k was assumed to be normally distributed with zero mean and variance $\sigma^2 = 0.2$. δ was chosen equal to $3\sigma = 1.34$. $N = 1000$ and $N_V = 500$ datapoints were used for estimation and validation, respectively. The algorithm provided $\hat{s} = s = 4$ submodels. The true and the estimated parameter vectors are shown in Table 1. The validation of the model was performed by computing the prediction error, *i.e.*, the difference between the measured and the predicted output, whose plot is depicted in Figure 6. Notice that it is mostly contained between δ and $-\delta$. Spikes

Table 1. True and estimated parameter vectors for Example 2

θ_1	$\hat{\theta}_1$	θ_2	$\hat{\theta}_2$	θ_3	$\hat{\theta}_3$	θ_4	$\hat{\theta}_4$
-0.05	-0.09	1.21	1.22	1.49	1.48	-1.20	-1.25
0.76	0.77	-0.49	-0.50	-0.50	-0.52	-0.72	-0.65
1.00	1.04	-0.30	-0.28	0.20	0.23	0.60	0.65
0.50	0.45	0.90	0.89	-0.45	-0.36	-0.70	-0.80
0	0.08	0	-0.13	0	0.20	0	0.37

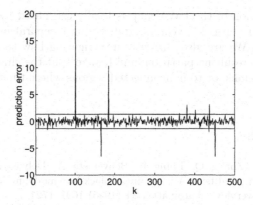

Fig. 6. Plot of the prediction error for Example 2

are due to regression vectors assigned to the wrong submodel because of errors in the estimation of the PWA partition, and to discontinuity of the PWA map. The overall computation of the estimated PWA model took about one minute and half on an AMD Athlon 1GHz running Matlab 6.1 non-optimized code. Notice that this example is quite challenging, due to the quite low signal/noise ratio and the high number of parameters to be estimated with respect to the available data.

6 Conclusions

In this paper we considered the problem of identifying a PWA model of a (possibly non-smooth) discrete-time nonlinear system from input-output data. We proposed a two-stage procedure that first divides the data into clusters and estimates the parameters of the affine submodels, and then estimates the coefficients of the hyperplanes defining the partition of the PWA map.

In order to provide an initial clustering of the datapoints, we adopted the greedy strategy proposed in [8]. The major capability of this strategy is that it also provides an estimate of the number of submodels needed to fit the data. Other approaches could be used to initialize the identification procedure (e.g., the k-plane clustering algorithm proposed in [15]). Then, we proposed an algorithm for improving both the classification of the datapoints and the estimation of the parameters. The algorithm alternates between datapoint reassignment and parameter update. Moreover, the number of submodels is allowed to vary from iteration to iteration. This is made possible by introducing the thresholds α and β, which the similarities of the parameter vectors and the cardinalities of the clusters of datapoints are compared with, respectively. Current research is aimed at deriving rules for the automatic selection and update of α and β, in order to completely automatize the algorithm and to further improve its performance, and at investigating convergence properties of the algorithm.

The partition of the PWA map is finally estimated by considering pairwise the clusters of regression vectors, and finding a separating hyperplane for each of such pairs. We are also currently investigating how to avoid the presence of "holes" in the resulting partition, and how to split the clusters corresponding to nonconvex regions, or to nonconnected regions where the affine submodel is the same.

References

1. Sjöberg, J., Zhang, Q., Ljung, L., Benveniste, A., Delyon, B., Glorennec, P., Hjalmarsson, H., Juditsky, A.: Nonlinear black-box modeling in system identification: a unified overview. Automatica **31** (1995) 1691–1724
2. Juditsky, A., Hjalmarsson, H., Benveniste, A., Delyon, B., Ljung, L., Sjöberg, J., Zhang, Q.: Nonlinear black-box models in system identification: mathematical foundations. Automatica **31** (1995) 1725–1750
3. Bemporad, A., Ferrari-Trecate, G., Morari, M.: Observability and controllability of piecewise affine and hybrid systems. IEEE Trans. Automatic Control **45** (2000) 1864–1876
4. Heemels, W., Schutter, B.D., Bemporad, A.: Equivalence of hybrid dynamical models. Automatica **37** (2001) 1085–1091
5. Ferrari-Trecate, G., Muselli, M., Liberati, D., Morari, M.: A clustering technique for the identification of piecewise affine systems. Automatica **39** (2003) 205–217
6. Bemporad, A., Roll, J., Ljung, L.: Identification of hybrid systems via mixed-integer programming. In: Proc. 40th IEEE Conf. on Decision and Control. (2001) 786–792
7. Münz, E., Krebs, V.: Identification of hybrid systems using apriori knowledge. In: Proc. 15th IFAC World Congress. (2002)
8. Amaldi, E., Mattavelli, M.: The MIN PFS problem and piecewise linear model estimation. Discrete Applied Mathematics **118** (2002) 115–143
9. Milanese, M., Vicino, A.: Optimal estimation theory for dynamic systems with set membership uncertainty: an overview. Automatica **27** (1991) 997–1009
10. Milanese, M., Norton, J.P., Piet-Lahanier, H., (eds.), E.W.: Bounding Approaches to System Identification. Plenum Press, New York (1996)
11. Vapnik, V.: Statistical Learning Theory. John Wiley (1998)
12. Amaldi, E., Hauser, R.: Randomized relaxation methods for the maximum feasible subsystem problem. Technical Report 2001-90, DEI, Politecnico di Milano, Italy (2001)
13. Agmon, S.: The relaxation method for linear inequalities. Canadian J. Math. **6** (1954) 382–392
14. Motzkin, T., Schoenberg, I.: The relaxation method for linear inequalities. Canadian J. Math. **6** (1954) 393–404
15. Bradley, P.S., Mangasarian, O.L.: k-plane clustering. Journal of Global Optimization **16** (2000) 23–32

A Hoare Logic for Single-Input Single-Output Continuous-Time Control Systems[*]

Richard J. Boulton[**], Ruth Hardy, and Ursula Martin

School of Computer Science, University of St Andrews
St Andrews, Fife, Scotland, UK
Ursula.Martin@acm.org

Abstract. This paper presents a Hoare-style logic for reasoning about the frequency response of control systems in the continuous-time domain. Two properties, the gain (amplitude) and phase shift, of a control system are considered. These properties are for a sinusoidal input of variable frequency. The logic operates over a simplified form of block diagram, including arbitrary transfer functions, feedback loops, and summation of signals. Reasoning is compositional, i.e. properties of a system can be deduced from properties of its subsystems. A prototype tool has been implemented in a mechanised theorem prover.

1 Introduction

Many man-made dynamical systems such as cars, planes, CD-players and nuclear reactors are augmented with a control system in hardware or software. The physical system is typically refered to as the *plant*. Some plants are inherently unstable in the absence of a control system (e.g. many fighter aircraft), and the systems are often safety critical or mission critical.

Most control systems are configured as a *closed loop* (a feedback loop) in which the outputs or current behaviour of the plant are measured and subtracted from a reference input (a control value such as desired cruising speed of a car). The resulting difference is used as input to a controller which in turn produces signals to control the plant. There may also be a control component in the feedback path.

Control systems may be modelled in the continuous or discrete time domains. In the former, signals are continuously varying with time, modelled as a real number. In the latter, the signals are sampled at discrete time intervals and so the value of a signal may be discontinuous and time can be modelled using integers. Numerical modelling, simulation, and analysis of control systems are supported by computer software. For example, MathWorks Simulink [4] provides a graphical representation of a control system as the standard engineers' block-diagram, which is obtained from the original dynamical system using Laplace transforms.

---

[*] Research supported by QinetiQ and by an EPSRC studentship to the second author.
[**] Affiliation with the University of St Andrews ceased in June 2002.

O. Maler and A. Pnueli (Eds.): HSCC 2003, LNCS 2623, pp. 113–125, 2003.

While there is a wealth of academic literature on the design of control systems [7], less attention has been paid to design validation, especially of software systems. In practice, visual inspection of numeric plots is widely used: for example, suites of Bode and Nichols plots are used to specify and discharge design requirements for flight control [8], expressed in terms of phase and gain of an input signal.

The use of formal methods and computational logic in the analysis of control systems is of increasing importance, but has thus far largely been confined to hybrid systems and statechart-like models. The widespread use of Simulink suggests that effective formal verification techniques for block diagrams could have significant impact. In general terms one might expect to annotate points in a diagram with assertions stating what was true at that point, for example a property of phase or gain, and use a logic to reason about the assertions. Thus, for example, one might hope to replace the plotting described above with an automated analysis using computational logic.

The work described here constitutes an early step in this programme. We present a Hoare logic for reasoning about assertions in block diagrams involving phase and gain. Hoare logics [3] were originally studied by Hoare, Floyd and others to give an axiomatic basis for programming, and continue to be used for a variety of applications [6]. As far as we know, our work is the first to investigate Hoare-style logics for feedback systems: There has been little other formal methods work at the block-diagram level. Arthan and others developed ClawZ [1], a system that translates discrete-time models, described using Simulink [4], into formal specifications in the Z language. A controller implementation in an Ada-like programming language can then be verified against these Z specifications using the ProofPower mechanised proof assistant. Similarly, Mahony [5] has investigated adding feedback to the DOVE specification environment. Other authors [10] have studied reasoning about diagram languages at a more abstract level. There has also been little work at the dynamical-systems level. An exception is Tiwari et al's work on abstraction for dynamical systems [9].

To simplify matters we chose initially to work with continuous-time rather than discrete models, with a single input and a single output. In practice, the stability, time response, and frequency response of control systems are often analysed: We chose the latter, which treats the amplitude and phase shift of the output signal when the system is presented with a sinusoidal input with a range of frequencies. The key observation, on which the rest of the paper is built, is that gain (amplitude) and phase are properties that behave compositionally as larger control systems are constructed from subsystems. This allows us to build a logic for properties of control systems in the style of Hoare logics.

In the rest of this paper we present gain and phase, our language Cosy for representing block diagrams, our Hoare logic, a simple worked example showing analysis of gain and phase, brief details of our implementation in a theorem proving system, and directions for further work.

2   Composition of Gain and Phase

In this section we develop the aspects of control we need: see a textbook such as the one by Ogata [7] for more details. The Laplace transform is used to transform the dynamical system representation of a continuous control system to a block diagram, essentially a directed graph with edges, corresponding to components, labelled by rational functions over the complex numbers. Assume a component is represented as a function f of time t. Then the Laplace transform maps f to a new function F (the transfer function) that has a complex frequency value, s, as its argument:

$$F(s) = \int_0^\infty f(t)e^{-st}\, dt$$

where $f(t)$ is assumed to be zero for negative values of t. Thus in the block diagram, $f(t)$ corresponds to an edge labelled F, with input s and output $F(s)$. The Laplace transforms have nice properties, e.g. the transform for two components in sequence is the product of the transforms for the components. Similarly, the output signal of a component is represented by the product of the transform of the input signal and the transform for the component.

In frequency analysis, we are interested in the behaviour of sinusoidal signals. The analysis is done by substituting $j\omega$ for the variable s in the Laplace transform, where j is $\sqrt{-1}$ and ω is the (real-valued) frequency of the signal.[1] The result is a complex number which can be written in the form $re^{j\theta}$. When the transform represents a sinusoidal signal, r is its amplitude and θ is its phase. When the transform represents a component in the control system, r is the gain (the factor by which the component increases the amplitude) and θ is the change in phase caused by the component.

The gain and phase-shift values are dependent on the frequency ω, and so would be more properly written as $r(\omega)$ and $\theta(\omega)$, but for notational simplicity, the ω is omitted in what follows. In the logical formulas presented below, the frequency is implicitly *universally quantified*, that is to say, the formulas are intended to hold *for all* values of frequency. By making the frequency explicit, it would also be possible to reason about formulas for restricted ranges of frequency.

Now suppose we have a control (sub)system constructed from two components in sequence, where $G_1(s)$ and $G_2(s)$ are the transfer functions for the components. As indicated above, the transfer function for the combined system is given by $G_1(s)G_2(s)$. Hence, the result of substituting $j\omega$ for s is $G_1(j\omega)G_2(j\omega)$, which equals $(r_1 r_2)e^{j(\theta_1+\theta_2)}$. So, the gain of the combined system is the product of the constituent gains, and the phase shift of the combined system is the sum of the constituent phase shifts.

So, for sequencing of components, gain and phase compose in a straightforward manner. But, there are other structures to be found in the models of control systems, most notably feedback loops and summing points. Consider the following closed loop system:

---

[1] Control engineers conventionally use j rather than i and we follow that practice here.

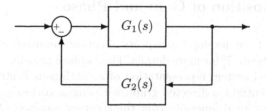

The transfer function of the entire closed loop system is given by $C(s) = \frac{G_1(s)}{1+G_1(s)G_2(s)}$. Manipulation of complex numbers yields the following formulas for the gain and phase shift of the closed loop:

$$|C(j\omega)| = \sqrt{\frac{r_1^2}{1 + 2r_1r_2\cos(\theta_1 + \theta_2) + r_1^2 r_2^2}}$$

$$\arg(C(j\omega)) = \arctan\left(\frac{\sin\theta_1 - r_1 r_2 \sin\theta_2}{\cos\theta_1 + r_1 r_2 \cos\theta_2}\right)$$

So, the gain and phase shift of a feedback loop can be expressed purely in terms of the gains and phase shifts of its subsystems, but in contrast to sequencing, in this case the gain and phase shifts become inter-dependent. As a consequence, in reasoning about frequency response, the gain and phase shift must be taken together.

Apart from feedback loops, the other significant structure in control systems is a summing point. For single-input, single-output systems, it can be assumed that the two signals to be summed ultimately come from the same source:

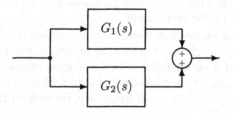

Then the transfer function expressing the relationship between the output and input of this system is $C(s) = G_1(s) + G_2(s)$. Hence, the gain and phase shift are as follows:

$$|C(j\omega)| = \sqrt{r_1^2 + 2r_1r_2\cos(\theta_1 - \theta_2) + r_2^2}$$

$$\arg(C(j\omega)) = \arctan\left(\frac{r_1\sin\theta_1 + r_2\sin\theta_2}{r_1\cos\theta_1 + r_2\cos\theta_2}\right)$$

3   Cosy: A Simple Language for Control Systems

The sequencing, feedback loop, and summation constructs presented in Section 2 can represent a wide range of control systems. All the constructs have a single

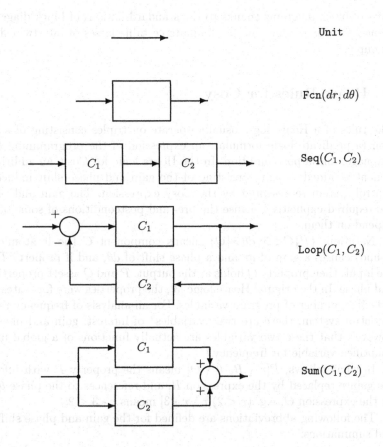

Fig. 1. The Cosy language constructs

input and a single output and are described in terms of subsystems that also have this property. Hence, they give rise to a simple language for control systems, which we shall call Cosy. The abstract syntax of this language is given in Fig. 1, alongside the corresponding block diagrams. In addition to the compound constructs, there are two atomic forms: Unit, which simply represents a wire, and Fcn, which represents a transfer function with gain dr and phase shift $d\theta$. The names dr and $d\theta$ are used instead of r and θ to emphasize that these values represent the *changes* in amplitude and phase caused by the transfer function. C_1 and C_2 are arbitrary subsystems.

We can characterise exactly those block diagrams that can be translated directly into Cosy, as those with a tree-structure reflecting the Cosy constructs. While an arbitrary block diagram can be an arbitrary directed graph, many examples in practice (cf [8]) seem to have this structure, perhaps because good designers build them up recursively from simpler components, and avoid intertwined loops, just as good programmers would. In fact Cosy represents a larger class of block diagrams thanks to the standard notions of block diagram equivalence [7], which allow one to eliminate certain classes of intertwined loops for example.

4   Hoare Rules for Cosy

The rules of a Hoare logic usually operate on triples consisting of a precondition (a predicate logic formula), an expression of the programming (or other) language, and a postcondition. In the Hoare logic for Cosy, an additional component is added: a pair consisting of the gain and phase shift induced by the control system represented by the Cosy expression. The gain and phase shift are required explicitly because the pre- and postconditions of some of the rules depend on them.

Notation: $\{P\}C{<}dr, d\theta{>}\{Q\}$ means component C (be it atomic or compound) causes a gain of dr and a phase shift of $d\theta$, and if property P holds at the input, then property Q holds at the output. P and Q assert properties of gain and phase. In the original Hoare logic [3], the properties were for states involving a flexible number of program variables. For an analysis of frequency response of a control system, there are two "variables" of interest: gain and phase. (Note, however, that these two variables are actually functions of a global universally quantified variable for frequency.)

In what follows, $P[r \setminus R, \theta \setminus \Theta]$ means the property P with references to the gain r replaced by the expression R, and references to the phase θ replaced by the expression Θ, e.g. $(r < 2)[r \setminus r * 3]$ means $r * 3 < 2$.

The following abbreviations are defined for the gain and phase shift of loops and summations:

$$lr(dr_1, d\theta_1, dr_2, d\theta_2) = \sqrt{\frac{dr_1^2}{dr_1^2 dr_2^2 + 2dr_1 dr_2 \cos(d\theta_1 + d\theta_2) + 1}}$$

$$lt(dr_1, d\theta_1, dr_2, d\theta_2) = \arctan\left(\frac{\sin d\theta_1 - dr_1 dr_2 \sin d\theta_2}{\cos d\theta_1 + dr_1 dr_2 \cos d\theta_2}\right)$$

$$sr(dr_1, d\theta_1, dr_2, d\theta_2) = \sqrt{dr_1^2 + 2dr_1 dr_2 \cos(d\theta_1 - d\theta_2) + dr_2^2}$$

$$st(dr_1, d\theta_1, dr_2, d\theta_2) = \arctan\left(\frac{dr_1 \sin d\theta_1 + dr_2 \sin d\theta_2}{dr_1 \cos d\theta_1 + dr_2 \cos d\theta_2}\right)$$

Fig. 2 presents an axiom or rule for each of the Cosy language constructs plus some additional logical rules and a special rule for all components.

In the Unit Axiom, Unit has no effect on the signal, so the postcondition is the same as the precondition. The gain is 1, and the phase shift is 0. The axiom for transfer functions is analogous to the Assignment Axiom for imperative programming languages. If P is true at the input having had the variables r and θ (gain and phase) replaced by the values they have at the output, then P is true at the output. The value of r at the output is equal to the product of the

The Unit Axiom

$$\vdash \{P\}\texttt{Unit}{<}1,0{>}\{P\}$$

The (Transfer) Function Axiom

$$\vdash \{P[r \setminus r * dr, \; \theta \setminus \theta + d\theta]\}\texttt{Fcn}(dr, d\theta){<}dr, d\theta{>}\{P\}$$

The Sequencing Rule

$$\frac{\vdash \{P\}C_1{<}dr_1, d\theta_1{>}\{Q\} \qquad \vdash \{Q\}C_2{<}dr_2, d\theta_2{>}\{R\}}{\vdash \{P\}\texttt{Seq}(C_1, C_2){<}dr_1 * dr_2, d\theta_1 + d\theta_2{>}\{R\}}$$

The Generalised Loop Rule

$$\frac{\vdash \{P\}C_1{<}dr_1, d\theta_1{>}\{Q\} \qquad \vdash \{R\}C_2{<}dr_2, d\theta_2{>}\{S\}}{\begin{array}{c} \vdash \{(P \wedge R)[r \setminus r * lr(dr_1, d\theta_1, dr_2, d\theta_2), \; \theta \setminus \theta + lt(dr_1, d\theta_1, dr_2, d\theta_2)]\} \\ \texttt{Loop}(C_1, C_2){<}lr(dr_1, d\theta_1, dr_2, d\theta_2), lt(dr_1, d\theta_1, dr_2, d\theta_2){>} \\ \{Q[r \setminus r * dr_1, \; \theta \setminus \theta + d\theta_1] \; \wedge \; S[r \setminus r * dr_2, \; \theta \setminus \theta + d\theta_2]\} \end{array}}$$

The Generalised Sum Rule

$$\frac{\vdash \{P\}C_1{<}dr_1, d\theta_1{>}\{Q\} \qquad \vdash \{R\}C_2{<}dr_2, d\theta_2{>}\{S\}}{\begin{array}{c} \vdash \{(P \wedge R)[r \setminus r * sr(dr_1, d\theta_1, dr_2, d\theta_2), \; \theta \setminus \theta + st(dr_1, d\theta_1, dr_2, d\theta_2)]\} \\ \texttt{Sum}(C_1, C_2){<}sr(dr_1, d\theta_1, dr_2, d\theta_2), st(dr_1, d\theta_1, dr_2, d\theta_2){>} \\ \{Q[r \setminus r * dr_1, \; \theta \setminus \theta + d\theta_1] \; \wedge \; S[r \setminus r * dr_2, \; \theta \setminus \theta + d\theta_2]\} \end{array}}$$

Precondition Strengthening

$$\frac{\vdash P' \Rightarrow P \qquad \vdash \{P\}C{<}dr, d\theta{>}\{Q\}}{\vdash \{P'\}C{<}dr, d\theta{>}\{Q\}}$$

Postcondition Weakening

$$\frac{\vdash \{P\}C{<}dr, d\theta{>}\{Q\} \qquad \vdash Q \Rightarrow Q'}{\vdash \{P\}C{<}dr, d\theta{>}\{Q'\}}$$

The Shift Right Rule

$$\frac{\vdash r' \neq 0 \qquad \vdash \{P[r \setminus r * r', \; \theta \setminus \theta + \theta']\}C{<}dr, d\theta{>}\{Q\}}{\vdash \{P\}C{<}dr, d\theta{>}\{Q[r \setminus r/r', \; \theta \setminus \theta - \theta']\}}$$

The Shift Left Rule

$$\frac{\vdash r' \neq 0 \qquad \vdash \{P\}C{<}dr, d\theta{>}\{Q[r \setminus r * r', \; \theta \setminus \theta + \theta']\}}{\vdash \{P[r \setminus r/r', \; \theta \setminus \theta - \theta']\}C{<}dr, d\theta{>}\{Q\}}$$

The Component Rule

$$\frac{\vdash \{Q\}C{<}dr, d\theta{>}\{R\}}{\vdash \{P[r \setminus r * dr, \; \theta \setminus \theta + d\theta]\}C{<}dr, d\theta{>}\{P\}}$$

Fig. 2. Axioms and rules of the Hoare logic for control systems

value of r at the input with the function's gain dr. Similarly, the value of θ at the output is the sum of θ at the input and the function's phase shift $d\theta$.

The sequencing rule simply states that gain and phase compose by multiplication and addition when two components are joined in sequence. Note the connection between the postcondition of C_1 and the precondition of C_2.

For loops and summations, there are many variations the rules could take. The rules given here are quite general, but are arguably less natural for proofs than some of the other possibilities. Note that the substitutions have been normalised to avoid division and subtraction.

The logic features the traditional Hoare rules for strengthening a precondition and weakening a postcondition, but it also has two other logical rules. Arbitrary amounts of gain and phase shift can be moved between the precondition and postcondition and vice versa. There are two rules for this, one for each direction. The only restriction is that the gain factor moved between the two conditions must be non-zero to avoid division-by-zero problems. Semantically, there is no real difference between the two shift rules, because r' is allowed to be a fraction, and θ' is allowed to be negative. However, syntactically one rule may be more convenient than the other when matching rules to formulas in a proof.

The transfer function axiom can be generalised to cover any system. If the gain and phase shift of the system are known, the system can be treated in the same way as an atomic transfer function. The Component Rule achieves that. Observe that only the values of dr and $d\theta$ are required from the hypothesis; the precondition and postcondition are thrown away.

Following Gordon's approach [2], the logic has been mechanised in the HOL98 theorem proving system, allowing goal-directed reasoning, machine assistance in the details of the proof, and automatic generation of verification conditions (VCs). VCs are the logical formulas that must ultimately be proved in a proof within the Hoare logic. The VCs themselves are pure predicate logic formulas, that is, they do not involve the constructs of Cosy.

The rules of the Hoare logic have been proved in HOL98 starting from a definition of the behaviour of gain and phase for the Cosy language constructs. We therefore have good reason to believe that the logic is sound, though it is possible that some side conditions have been masked by defining the behaviour instead of deriving it formally from a theory of Laplace transforms. Furthermore, the fact that we have been able to construct a verification condition generator from the Hoare logic suggests that the logic is complete with respect to the underlying predicate logic. As is usual, the predicate logic itself is not complete.

5   A Sample Proof

As a very simple example, suppose there are two components in sequence, a controller and a plant, and the phase shift of the combined system is required to be greater than $-145°$, as follows:

$$\{\theta = 0\}\, \mathtt{Seq}(\mathtt{Fcn}(dr, d\theta), \mathtt{Fcn}(2, -100°))\!<\!\ldots\!>\!\{\theta > -145°\}$$

The gain and phase shift of the controller have been left as symbolic entities dr and $d\theta$. The aim is to determine constraints on them using the Hoare logic. The proof, using the function axiom and sequencing rule, can be illustrated like this:

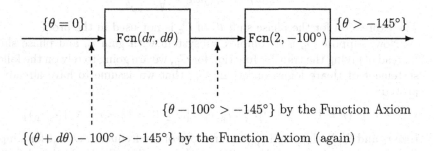

$\{\theta - 100° > -145°\}$ by the Function Axiom

$\{(\theta + d\theta) - 100° > -145°\}$ by the Function Axiom (again)

The sequencing rule is used to combine the two theorems obtained by means of the function axiom. The result is:

$$\vdash \{(\theta + d\theta) - 100° > -145°\}$$
$$\textsf{Seq}(\textsf{Fcn}(dr, d\theta), \textsf{Fcn}(2, -100°)) < dr * 2, d\theta - 100° >$$
$$\{\theta > -145°\}$$

Now, if it can be proved that $(\theta = 0) \Rightarrow ((\theta + d\theta) - 100° > -145°)$, precondition strengthening can be used to obtain the required result. The condition is true if and only if $d\theta > -45°$, which is the required constraint on the controller.

In this example, the constraint on $d\theta$ could have been determined from the compound gain and phase shift $<dr * 2, d\theta - 100°>$, but for large examples, the expressions for the overall gain and phase shift may become too complex to be practical. The next section illustrates how reasoning in terms of the properties of subsystems can ease this problem.

6   A More Complex Example

The Hoare logic can be used as a means to compute expressions for the gain and phase shift of a system. More importantly, it can also be used to prove *properties* of the system from properties of its subsystems. The example below is intended to illustrate that.

Consider the following closed-loop system:

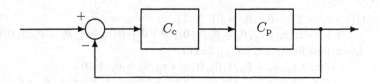

where the controller C_c is specified by the transfer function G_c:

$$G_c(s) = \frac{2s+1}{s}$$

Hence, the gain r_c of C_c is:

$$r_c(\omega) = |G_c(j\omega)| = \sqrt{\frac{4\omega^2 + 1}{\omega^2}}$$

The expression for the phase shift θ_c of C_c is not used in the proof.

Now, suppose C_p is a complex subsystem with gain r_p and phase shift θ_p. Instead of giving the transfer function for C_p, we are going to rely on the following statement of Hoare logic concerning C_p, that we assume to have already been proved:

$$\vdash \{r = 1 \ \wedge \ \theta = 0\}C_p{<}r_p, \theta_p{>}\{\omega \geq 0 \Rightarrow (r = r_p \ \wedge \ 1 < r_p)\} \tag{1}$$

Like r_c and θ_c, both r_p and θ_p are functions of the frequency ω, but for simplicity the dependency is not made explicit in the notation. Similarly, r and θ may be dependent on ω. The postcondition of theorem 1 states that for frequencies greater than or equal to zero, the gain of C_p is greater than 1.

The aim is to prove the following Hoare logic formula about the closed-loop system:

$$\{r = 1 \ \wedge \ \theta = 0\}\text{Loop}(\text{Seq}(\text{Fcn}(r_c, \theta_c), C_p), \text{Unit}){<}\ldots,\ldots{>}\{\omega \geq 0 \Rightarrow r < 2\}$$

The first step is to use the precondition of (1) as the predicate in an application of the Function Axiom on C_c, with a view to sequencing the two components:

$$\vdash \{(r = 1 \ \wedge \ \theta = 0)[r \setminus r * r_c, \ \theta \setminus \theta + \theta_c]\}\text{Fcn}(r_c, \theta_c){<}r_c, \theta_c{>}\{r = 1 \ \wedge \ \theta = 0\}$$

which simplifies to:

$$\vdash \{r * r_c = 1 \ \wedge \ \theta + \theta_c = 0\}\text{Fcn}(r_c, \theta_c){<}r_c, \theta_c{>}\{r = 1 \ \wedge \ \theta = 0\} \tag{2}$$

Combining (2) and (1) using the Sequencing Rule yields the following theorem:

$$\vdash \{r * r_c = 1 \ \wedge \ \theta + \theta_c = 0\} \tag{3}$$
$$\text{Seq}(\text{Fcn}(r_c, \theta_c), C_p){<}r_c * r_p, \theta_c + \theta_p{>}$$
$$\{\omega \geq 0 \Rightarrow (r = r_p \ \wedge \ 1 < r_p)\}$$

Now, in order to reason about the loop, a theorem must be obtained about the unit feedback. This is achieved using the Unit Axiom, with T, the predicate that is always true, as the pre- and postcondition:

$$\vdash \{\text{T}\}\text{Unit}{<}1, 0{>}\{\text{T}\} \tag{4}$$

Applying the Generalised Loop Rule to (3) and (4) produces:

$$\vdash \{((r * r_c = 1 \ \wedge \ \theta + \theta_c = 0) \ \wedge \ \text{T})$$
$$[r \setminus r * lr(r_c * r_p, \theta_c + \theta_p, 1, 0), \ \theta \setminus \theta + lt(r_c * r_p, \theta_c + \theta_p, 1, 0)]\}$$
$$\text{Loop}(\text{Seq}(\text{Fcn}(r_c, \theta_c), C_p), \text{Unit})$$
$$<lr(r_c * r_p, \theta_c + \theta_p, 1, 0), lt(r_c * r_p, \theta_c + \theta_p, 1, 0)>$$
$$\{(\omega \geq 0 \Rightarrow (r = r_p \ \wedge \ 1 < r_p))[r \setminus r * (r_c * r_p), \ \theta \setminus \theta + (\theta_c + \theta_p)] \ \wedge \ \text{T}\}$$

which simplifies to:

$\vdash \{(r * lr(r_c * r_p, \theta_c + \theta_p, 1, 0)) * r_c = 1 \wedge (\theta + lt(r_c * r_p, \theta_c + \theta_p, 1, 0)) + \theta_c = 0\}$
$\quad \text{Loop}(\text{Seq}(\text{Fcn}(r_c, \theta_c), C_p), \text{Unit})$
$\quad\quad <lr(r_c * r_p, \theta_c + \theta_p, 1, 0), lt(r_c * r_p, \theta_c + \theta_p, 1, 0)>$
$\quad \{\omega \geq 0 \Rightarrow (r * (r_c * r_p) = r_p \wedge 1 < r_p)\}$

$$(5)$$

By exploiting the associativity of multiplication and addition, the Shift Right Rule can be applied to (5) to get the precondition into the form we require:

$\vdash \{r = 1 \wedge \theta = 0\}$
$\quad \text{Loop}(\text{Seq}(\text{Fcn}(r_c, \theta_c), C_p), \text{Unit})$
$\quad\quad <lr(r_c * r_p, \theta_c + \theta_p, 1, 0), lt(r_c * r_p, \theta_c + \theta_p, 1, 0)>$
$\quad \{\omega \geq 0 \Rightarrow ((r/(lr(r_c * r_p, \theta_c + \theta_p, 1, 0) * r_c)) * (r_c * r_p) = r_p \wedge 1 < r_p)\}$

This result also relies on r_c and $lr(r_c * r_p, \theta_c + \theta_p, 1, 0)$ both being non-zero. A little rearranging and simplification in the postcondition yields:

$\vdash \{r = 1 \wedge \theta = 0\}$ $\qquad\qquad\qquad\qquad\qquad\qquad\qquad\qquad (6)$
$\quad \text{Loop}(\text{Seq}(\text{Fcn}(r_c, \theta_c), C_p), \text{Unit})$
$\quad\quad <lr(r_c * r_p, \theta_c + \theta_p, 1, 0), lt(r_c * r_p, \theta_c + \theta_p, 1, 0)>$
$\quad \{\omega \geq 0 \Rightarrow (r = lr(r_c * r_p, \theta_c + \theta_p, 1, 0) \wedge 1 < r_p)\}$

The postcondition now clearly states the expected value of the gain of the closed loop in terms of the gain and phase shifts of the subsystems, whilst also retaining the constraint on r_p imposed by (1).

The required result can be obtained by Postcondition Weakening provided we can prove the following formula of pure predicate logic:

$$(\omega \geq 0 \Rightarrow (r = lr(r_c * r_p, \theta_c + \theta_p, 1, 0) \wedge 1 < r_p)) \Rightarrow (\omega \geq 0 \Rightarrow r < 2)$$

So, working under the assumption that $\omega \geq 0$, the facts from which $r < 2$ is to be derived are: $r = lr(r_c * r_p, \theta_c + \theta_p, 1, 0)$ and $1 < r_p$. It is also the case that $r_c > 2$ (from the definition). Expanding the definition of lr gives:

$$r = \sqrt{\frac{r_c^2 r_p^2}{r_c^2 r_p^2 + 2r_c r_p \cos(\theta_c + \theta_p) + 1}}$$

Now, since $r_c r_p \geq 0$, and $\cos(\theta_c + \theta_p) \geq -1$,

$$\frac{r_c r_p}{\sqrt{r_c^2 r_p^2 + 2r_c r_p \cos(\theta_c + \theta_p) + 1}} \leq \frac{r_c r_p}{\sqrt{r_c^2 r_p^2 - 2r_c r_p + 1}}$$

and,

$$\frac{r_c r_p}{\sqrt{r_c^2 r_p^2 - 2r_c r_p + 1}} = \frac{r_c r_p}{\sqrt{(r_c r_p - 1)^2}} = \frac{r_c r_p}{r_c r_p - 1} =$$

$$\frac{r_p \sqrt{\frac{4\omega^2 + 1}{\omega^2}}}{r_p \sqrt{\frac{4\omega^2 + 1}{\omega^2}} - 1} = \frac{\sqrt{4\omega^2 + 1}}{\sqrt{4\omega^2 + 1} - \frac{\omega}{r_p}}$$

Also, since $1 < r_\mathrm{p}$, then $\frac{\omega}{r_\mathrm{p}} < \omega$. Therefore, $\frac{\omega}{r_\mathrm{p}} < \frac{\sqrt{4\omega^2+1}}{2}$, and hence,

$$\frac{\sqrt{4\omega^2+1}}{\sqrt{4\omega^2+1}-\frac{\omega}{r_\mathrm{p}}} < 2$$

Chaining all these facts together gives $r < 2$, as required.

It is likely that, in practice, tighter bounds on the frequency response would be obtained, e.g. by taking phase into consideration, and by deriving a bound in terms of frequency instead of as a simple constant.

7   Conclusions and Future Work

This paper has proposed a framework for formally reasoning about the frequency response of continuous-time control systems. The framework takes the form of a Hoare-style logic, based around expressions for the gain and phase shift of control-system structures in terms of the gain and phase shift of substructures.

The framework can be used to derive expressions for the gain and phase of a control system. This goes beyond usual control engineering practice because it can be used for symbolic values as readily as for numeric values. Furthermore, using a Hoare-style logic offers more than calculation (numeric or symbolic): Constraints (typically inequalities) can be derived. This can be easier than seeking exact values for gain and phase. The approach can also be used in reverse to obtain constraints on the parameters of a controller so as to achieve specified behaviour of the overall system. Constraints may be derived for a particular frequency, a range of frequencies, or for all frequencies. Unlike many frequency response analysis methods, this approach is not limited to constraints that can be expressed graphically. And all this is done within the rigors of a formal proof system.

A fuller development for our work would require a more detailed treatment of dynamical systems, Laplace transforms, block diagrams, an appropriate assertion language, and their associated analytical and logical subtleties: hence this paper is a first step. We believe our logic to be sound with respect to the semantics of block diagrams corresponding to the Laplace transform.

There are many directions for further research: extending our techniques to a wider class of arguments than phase and gain; developing the constraint approach we defined above; extending the class of block diagrams we can handle (for example by extending our logic to handle intertwined loops); development of a suitable assertion language; adaptation to multiple-input/output (MIMO), state-space or discrete-time systems; and finally effective automation as a component of standard toolsets such as Simulink.

Acknowledgements. We are indebted to Manuela Bujorianu, John Hall, Rick Hyde, and Yoge Patel for their insights into control engineering, to Rob Arthan, Tom Kelsey, and Colin O'Halloran for helpful discussions, and to the anonymous referees for their comments.

References

1. R. Arthan, P. Caseley, C. O'Halloran, and A. Smith. ClawZ: Control laws in Z. In *Proc. 3rd IEEE International Conference on Formal Engineering Methods (ICFEM 2000)*, York, September 2000.
2. M. J. C. Gordon. Mechanizing programming logics in higher order logic. In G. Birtwistle and P. A. Subrahmanyam, editors, *Current Trends in Hardware Verification and Automated Theorem Proving*, pages 387–439. Springer-Verlag, 1989.
3. C. A. R. Hoare. An axiomatic basis for computer programming. *Communications of the ACM*, 12(10):576–580, 583, October 1969.
4. The MathWorks. Simulink. http://www.mathworks.com/products/simulink/
5. B. Mahony. The DOVE approach to the design of complex dynamic processes. In *Proc. of the First International Workshop on Formalising Continuous Mathematics*, NASA conference publication NASA/CP-2002-211736, pages 167–187, August 2002.
6. T. Nipkow. Hoare Logics in Isabelle/HOL. In *Proof and System-Reliability*, pages 341–367, Kluwer, 2002.
7. K. Ogata. *Modern Control Engineering*. Prentice-Hall, third edition, 1997.
8. R. W. Pratt, editor. *Flight Control Systems: Practical Issues in Design and Implementation*, volume 57 of *IEE Control Engineering Series*. The Institution of Electrical Engineers, 2000. Copublished by The American Institute of Aeronautics and Astronautics.
9. A. Tiwari and G. Khanna. Series of abstractions for hybrid automata. In *Proc. 5th International Workshop on Hybrid Systems: Computation and Control (HSCC 2002)*, volume 2289 of Lecture Notes in Computer Science, Springer, 2002.
10. C. Gurr and K. Tourlas. Towards the principled design of software engineering diagrams. In *Proc. 22nd International Conference on Software Engineering*, pages 509–520, ACM Press, 2000.

Reachability Questions in Piecewise Deterministic Markov Processes

Manuela L. Bujorianu and John Lygeros

Department of Engineering,
University of Cambridge,
Cambridge, CB2 1PZ, UK
{lmb56,jl290}@eng.cam.ac.uk

Abstract. We formulate a stochastic hybrid system model that allows us to capture a class of Markov processes known as piecewise deterministic Markov processes (PDMPs). For this class of stochastic processes we formulate a probabilistic reachability problem. Basic properties of PDMPs are reviewed and used to show that the reachability question is indeed well defined. Possible methods for computing the reach probability are then concerned.

Keywords: Hybrid systems, reachability, Markov processes, hitting times.

1 Introduction

Hybrid systems generalise both discrete state-transition systems and continuous dynamical systems. Hybrid systems posses continuous dynamics defined within regions of the state space and discrete transitions among the regions. Although the deterministic models for hybrid systems capture many characteristics of real systems, in practice stochastic features arise because of the inherent uncertainty in the environment of most real world applications. Few stochastic hybrid system models have been proposed in the literature (e.g. [8,12]). Different researchers have tried to propose different models from their own perspectives. The most important difference lies in where the randomness is introduced: in the continuous evolution, discrete transition times and discrete transition destinations.

In this paper a class of stochastic processes, called piecewise-deterministic Markov processes, is proposed as a model for studying stochastic hybrid systems. The piecewise-deterministic Markov processes (PDMPs) are an important class of non-linear continuous-time stochastic hybrid dynamical systems which admit theoretical analysis (see [4,5]). PDMPs are stochastic models in which the randomness appears as point events, i.e., there is a sequence of random occurrences at fixed or random times $T_1 < T_2 < T_3 < ...$ but there is no additional component of uncertainty between these times. A PDMP consists of a mixture of deterministic motion along a vector field and random jumps governed by some prescribed probabilistic law. The main properties of PDMPs are that they are

O. Maler and A. Pnueli (Eds.): HSCC 2003, LNCS 2623, pp. 126–140, 2003.

strong Markov processes, they have an exact characterisation of the extended generator and they are right processes. The PDMP viewed as a solution of a martingale problem and the generator-based computations of process distributions and process functional expectations have been well studied in [5].

In this paper, we sketch some approaches for studying the reachability problem for PDMP. In a probabilistic framework, the reachability problem consists of determining the probability that the system trajectories enter some prespecified set starting from a certain set of initial conditions with a given probability distribution. Developing a methodology for the reachability analysis of stochastic hybrid systems will involve dealing with two aspects:

1. the theoretical aspect of the measurability of the reachability sets; and
2. the computational aspect regarding how to estimate the probability of the reachability events and how to quantify the level of approximation introduced.

The PDMP reachability problem approach presented in this paper is based on hitting time expectations. We prove that the reachable sets are events (measurable sets) in the underlying probability space, so we can deal with probabilistic notions in order to estimate their "measure". Also, we develop a formal link between the hitting distributions and some potential theory notions, namely reduced functions and excessive functions.

2 Definitions and Notation

2.1 Background

Evolution will take place in a hybrid state space consisting of discrete and continuous components. The discrete component may take one of countably many values. The continuous component may take values in Euclidean space, $\mathbb{R}^n$, whose dimension may be different for different values of the discrete state. More formally, consider a countable set Q, a map $d : Q \to \mathbb{N}$, and a map $X : Q \to 2^{\mathbb{R}^{d(\cdot)}}$ assigning to each value of $q \in Q$ a subset $X(q) \subseteq \mathbb{R}^{d(q)}$. We will use $q \in Q$ to denote the discrete part of the state and $x \in X(q)$ to denote the continuous part[1]. We will refer to the set

$$\mathbb{S} = \mathbb{S}(Q, d, X) = \bigcup_{q \in Q} \{q\} \times X(q)$$

as the *state space* of the system and its elements $\alpha = (q, x) \in \mathbb{S}(Q, d, X)$ as the *states*. Notice that in order to define the state space one needs to specify three elements, (Q, d, X). We define the *boundary* of $\mathbb{S}(Q, d, X)$ by

---

[1] If the set Q is finite then we can dispense with the additional complication of having the dimension of the continuous state depending on the discrete state. We can embed everything into a single Euclidean space of high enough dimension $\mathbb{R}^m$ where $m = \max_{q \in Q} \{d(q)\}$. This is likely to be the case for most applications.

$$\partial\mathbb{S}(Q,d,X) = \bigcup_{q\in Q}\{q\}\times\partial X(q),$$

where $\partial X(q)$ denotes the boundary of $X(q)$ in the Euclidean topology of $\mathbb{R}^{d(q)}$.

A *vector field*, f, on the hybrid state space, $\mathbb{S}(Q,d,X)$, can be thought as a function $f : \mathbb{S}(Q,d,X) \to \mathbb{R}^{d(\cdot)}$ assigning to each $(q,x) \in \mathbb{S}$ a vector (direction) $f(q,x) \in \mathbb{R}^{d(q)}$. We define the *flow* of the vector field f as a function $\phi : \mathbb{S}(Q,d,X) \times \mathbb{R} \to \mathbb{S}(Q,d,X)$ with $\phi(\alpha,t) = (\phi_q(\alpha,t),\phi_x(\alpha,t))$, $\phi_q(\alpha,t) \in Q$, $\alpha = (q,x)$ and $\phi_x(q,x,t) \in X(q)$, given by

$$\phi_x(q,x,0) = x$$
$$\phi_q(q,x,t) = q \text{ for all } t \in \mathbb{R}$$
$$\frac{d}{dt}\phi_x(\alpha,t) = f(\phi(\alpha,t)) \text{ for all } t \in \mathbb{R}.$$

Notice that, depending on the properties of f and the sets $X(q)$, the flow may not be defined for all $(\alpha,t) \in \mathbb{S}(Q,d,X) \times \mathbb{R}$. This technical point will be ignored for the time being, but will be addressed by appropriate assumptions later on.

Consider now a hybrid state space, $\mathbb{S}(Q,d,X)$ and a vector field f on that state space. If $\partial\mathbb{S}(Q,d,X) \not\subseteq \mathbb{S}(Q,d,X)$ (for example, if $\mathbb{S}(Q,d,X)$ is an open set in the product topology), then certain parts of $\partial\mathbb{S}(Q,d,X)$ may be reachable from points in $\mathbb{S}(Q,d,X)$ under the flow of f and others not. We denote the *former* by $\Gamma((Q,d,X),f)$. In other words,

$$\Gamma((Q,d,X),f) = \{\alpha \in \partial\mathbb{S}(Q,d,X) \mid \exists(\alpha',t) \in \mathbb{S}(Q,d,X) \times \mathbb{R}_+, \alpha = \phi(\alpha',t)\}.$$

Clearly $\partial\mathbb{S}(Q,d,X) \cap \mathbb{S}(Q,d,X) \subseteq \Gamma((Q,d,X),f)$ for all f, and the two sets are equal if $\mathbb{S}(Q,d,X)$ is closed.

Given (Q,d,X), for each $q \in Q$ let $\mathcal{B}(q)$ denote the Borel σ-algebra of $X(q)$ (where $X(q)$ is provided with the trace topology with respect to the Euclidean topology of $\mathbb{R}^{d(q)}$). Define $\mathcal{B}(\overline{\mathbb{S}}) = \sigma(\bigcup_{q\in Q}\{q\}\times\mathcal{B}(q))$, where $\overline{\mathbb{S}} = Q \times \mathbb{R}^\infty$ and $(\overline{\mathbb{S}},\mathcal{B}(\overline{\mathbb{S}}))$ will be a measurable space.

For simplicity we will drop dependencies on Q, d, X whenever they are clear from the context.

2.2 Piecewise Deterministic Markov Processes

Definition 1. *A Piecewise Deterministic Markov Process (PDMP) H is a collection $H = ((Q,d,X),\ f,\ Init,\ \lambda,\ R)$, where*

- *Q is a countable set.*
- *$d : Q \to \mathbb{N}$ is a map giving the dimensions of the continuous state spaces.*
- *$X : Q \to 2^{\mathbb{R}^{d(\cdot)}}$ maps each $q \in Q$ to a subset of Euclidean space of appropriate dimension, $X(q) \subseteq \mathbb{R}^{d(q)}$.*
- *$f : \mathbb{S}(Q,d,X) \to \mathbb{R}^{d(\cdot)}$ is a vector field.*
- *$Init : \mathcal{B}(\overline{\mathbb{S}}) \to [0,1]$ is an initial probability measure on $(\overline{\mathbb{S}},\mathcal{B}(\overline{\mathbb{S}}))$, with $Init(\mathbb{S}^c) = 0$.*

- $\lambda : \mathbb{S}(Q, d, X) \to \mathbb{R}_+$ is a transition rate function.
- $R : \mathcal{B}(\overline{\mathbb{S}}) \times (\mathbb{S}(Q, d, X) \cup \Gamma((Q, d, X), f)) \to [0, 1]$ is a transition probability measure, with $R(\mathbb{S}^c, \cdot) = 0$.

To avoid technical pitfalls we introduce the following standing assumption.

Assumption 1 H satisfies the following well-posedness assumptions:

1. For all $q \in Q$, $f(q, \cdot)$ is a globally Lipschitz continuous function.
2. $X(q) \subset \mathbb{R}^{d(q)}$ is an open set in the Euclidean topology for all $q \in Q$.
3. $\lambda : \mathbb{S} \to \mathbb{R}_+$ is measurable.
4. For all $\alpha \in \mathbb{S}$ there exists $\varepsilon > 0$ such that the functions $t \mapsto \lambda(\phi(\alpha, t))$ is integrable for all $t \in [0, \varepsilon)$.

One can show that under Assumption 1 the space $(\overline{\mathbb{S}}, \mathcal{B}(\overline{\mathbb{S}}))$ is a Borel space (i.e. is homeomorphic to a Borel subset of a complete separable metric space) and $\mathcal{B}(\overline{\mathbb{S}})$ is a sub-σ-algebra of its Borel σ-algebra.

To define an *execution* of the PDMP, consider the *exit time*, $t^* : \mathbb{S} \to \mathbb{R}_+ \cup \infty$ defined by

$$t^*(\alpha) = \inf\{t \geq 0 \; : \; \phi(\alpha, t) \notin \mathbb{S}\}.$$

$t^*(\alpha)$ is the first time when the process hits the boundary. Notice that we may have $t^*(\alpha) = \infty$ for some $\alpha \in \mathbb{S}$. We define the *survivor function*, $F : \mathbb{S} \times \mathbb{R}_+ \to [0, 1]$ by

$$F(\alpha, t) = \begin{cases} \exp(-\int_0^t \lambda(\phi(\alpha, \tau))d\tau) & \text{if } t < t^*(\alpha) \\ 0 & \text{if } t \geq t^*(\alpha) \end{cases}$$

The survivor function is used to define the jump times as random variables. Note that a PDMP allows predictable jumps. The executions of H can now be "generated" using the Algorithm 1. All random extractions in Algorithm 1 are assumed to be independent one of another.

Algorithm 1 (Generation of Executions of H)
    set $T = 0$
    select $\mathbb{S}$-valued "random variable", $\hat{\alpha}$, according to *Init*
    repeat
        select $\mathbb{R}_+$-valued random variable $\hat{T}$ such that $P[\hat{T} > t] = F(\hat{\alpha}, t)$
        set $\alpha_t = \phi(\hat{\alpha}, t - T)$ for all $t \in [T, T + \hat{T})$
        select $\mathbb{S}$-valued "random variable" $\hat{\alpha}$ according to $R(\cdot, \phi(\hat{\alpha}, \hat{T}))$
        set $T = T + \hat{T}$
    until true

To ensure that α is defined on the entire $\mathbb{R}_+$ one needs to exclude the possibility of infinite number of discrete transitions taking place in a finite amount of time (Zeno executions). Let N_t denote the number of discrete transitions in the interval $[0, t]$. The following assumption is introduced in [5].

Assumption 2 *For all* $t \in \mathbb{R}_+$, $\mathbb{E}[N_t] < \infty$.

Other nasties (escape to infinity in finite time, etc.) are excluded by Assumption 1. Under Assumptions 1 and 2, Algorithm 1 defines a function $\alpha : \mathbb{R}_+ \to \mathbb{S}$, which is right continuous with left limits. A *stochastic execution* of H with the starting point $\alpha = (q, x) \in \mathbb{S}$ is a sample path starting with α of the piecewise deterministic Markov process H. Let $\mathcal{H}$ denote the family of all stochastic executions of H. Let $\mathcal{H}_\alpha$ denote the set of all stochastic executions which have $\alpha \in \mathbb{S}$ as starting point. The random events associated with a sample path are:

1. The random extraction of the initial condition;
2. The random extraction of the time of each transition;
3. The random extraction of the destination of each transition.

Overall, if the sample path takes N discrete transitions (possibly with $N = \infty$) one has to deal with N random variables taking values in $\mathbb{R}_+$ and $N + 1$ "random variables" taking values in $\mathbb{S}$. Davis [5] provides a construction for relating all of these random phenomena to a single random extraction from the Hilbert cube. $(\Omega, \mathcal{A}, P)$ will therefore be assumed to be the underlying probability space, where $\Omega = [0, 1]^\infty$ is the Hilbert cube, $\mathcal{A}$ is the product σ-field of the Lebesgue sets of $[0, 1]$ and P is the product of the Lebesgue measures. Recall that a property holds P-*almost sure* $(P - a.s)$ if there exists a set $\Omega' \subset \Omega$ such that $P(\Omega') = 0$ and the property holds everywhere on $\Omega \backslash \Omega'$.

The following fact is shown in [5,4].

Theorem 1 (Strong Markov Property). *Under Assumptions 1 and 2, Algorithm 1 defines a strong Markov process.*

2.3   An Application to Air Traffic Control

To illustrate the possible practical applications of PDMP we provide a high level discussion of how they can be used to model sector transitions in Air Traffic Control (ATC); other possible applications to finance, insurance, etc. are discussed in [5].

Under current ATC procedures, air space is divided into sectors. Different air traffic controllers are responsible for managing air traffic in the different sectors. Therefore, whenever aircraft move between sectors they have to be handed of from one air traffic controller to another. This involves communication between air traffic controllers (and possibly physical movement of air strips from one ATC workstation to another!) Since the hand-off process distracts the attention of the ATC from other tasks (such as maintaining aircraft separation) sector transitions can become safety critical especially in areas where the aircraft density is high, for example the Terminal Maneuvering Areas (TMA).

Piecewise deterministic Markov processes can be used to capture the ATC sector transition process. Sector transitions are characterised by the following types of dynamics:

Continuous Dynamics. Accurate models of continuous dynamics are not particularly important for sector transitions. In certain cases it may also be possible to separate the vertical and horizontal components of the continuous model. Specifically for transitions at the TMA gates the horizontal and vertical may interact, since aircraft may be climbing when leaving the TMA or descending when entering it.

Discrete Dynamics. Sector transitions are intrinsically discrete phenomena. The state of the system undergoes a transition when an aircraft changes sector and is handed of from one ATC to another. One needs to ensure that the aircraft will find itself in a safe configuration in the new sector before the transition is allowed to go ahead. If not (for example, if the traffic density in the new sector is already too high) the transition should be delayed. In this case, one has to ensure that it is safe for the aircraft to remain in its current sector.

Currently all these tasks are performed by ATC based on established procedures. Some flexibility is allowed depending on traffic conditions; for example an air traffic controller may delay accepting a flight coming into a sector if there are more urgent problems to deal with. Introducing automation safely requires full understanding of these procedures. One would have to ensure, for example, that the system does not give rise to situations where an aircraft can neither be handed on nor remain in the current sector safely.

Stochastic Phenomena. There is some uncertainty in the time at which a hand-off from one sector to the other will take place. The exact timing of the transition may depend on the traffic in both sectors. Hand-off may take place earlier if traffic in the current sector is heavy, or may be delayed if traffic in the receiving sector is heavy. The effect of this uncertainty tends to be small in current conditions, but may become more pronounced as traffic densities increase.

The above discussion suggests that it is possible to model sector transitions using a PDMP. Let $X(q)$ with $q \in Q$ denote the area covered by each ATC sector, where Q is the total number of the ATC sectors. Since precise information about continuous motion of the aircraf is not crucial, we can assume that the continuous motion of the aircraft in each sector is deterministic, governed by a given vector field f. The transition rate function λ will have support in a neighbourhood of the sector boundary. The magnitude of λ will depend on the traffic density in the current sector, ρ_c, and the traffic density in the new sector, ρ_n; more specifically λ increases as ρ_c increases or ρ_n decreases. Since the next sector is known, R can be modelled by a simple function.

A central problem in the air traffic context is determining the probability of conflict, i.e. the probability two aircraft come closer than a minimum allowed distance. If this probability can be computed, an alert can be issued when it exceeds a certain threshold. In the context of PDMP, the computation of the conflict probability reduces to a reachability problem: computing the probability that the PDMP modelling the aircraft motion reaches an unsafe part of the state space (one where two aircraft come closer than the minimum allowed distance). Motivated by this observation, problems of reachability for PDMP will be studied in Section 4.

3 Properties of PDMPs

3.1 PDMPs as a Markov Family

Under our assumptions the PDMP H can be thought of as a process defined on Ω or as a Markov family defined on $D_{\mathbb{S}} = D_{\mathbb{S}}[0, \infty)$, where $D_{\mathbb{S}}$ denote the set of right-continuous functions z on $\mathbb{R}_+$ with values in $\mathbb{S}$ and with left limit $\lim_{s \nearrow t} z(s)$ for all $t \in (0, \infty)$ (see [5]). More concretely, let $\tilde{\alpha}_t(z) = z(t)$ for $z \in D_{\mathbb{S}}$. Let $\mathcal{F}_t^0$ denote the natural filtration, $\mathcal{F}_t^0 = \sigma\{\tilde{\alpha}_s, s \leq t\}$ and $\mathcal{F}^0 = \vee_t \mathcal{F}_t^0$. The construction of a PDMP defines for each starting point $\alpha = (q, x) \in \mathbb{S}$ a measurable mapping $\psi_\alpha : \Omega \to D_{\mathbb{S}}$ such that $\tilde{\alpha}_t(\psi_\alpha(\omega)) = \alpha_t(\omega)$. Let P_α denote the image measure, $P_\alpha = P\psi_\alpha^{-1}$. This defines a family of measures $\{P_\alpha, \alpha \in \mathbb{S}\}$. Thus, indeed, a PDMP can be thought of as a Markov family defined on $D_{\mathbb{S}}$. Moreover, every elementary event $\omega \in \Omega$ can be thought of as a stochastic execution of H. So $\mathcal{H}_\alpha$ can be identified with Ω.

Let $\Im$ be the family of all finite stopping times associated to H and $\mathcal{P}(\mathbb{S})$ the lattice of probabilities on $\mathbb{S}$. For all $\mu \in \mathcal{P}(\mathbb{S})$ we define a measure P^μ on $(D_{\mathbb{S}}, \mathcal{F}^0)$ by $P^\mu(E) = \int P_\alpha(E)\mu(d\alpha)$. We then denote by $\mathcal{F}_\infty^\mu$ (resp. $\mathcal{F}_t^\mu$) the completion of $\mathcal{F}_\infty^0$ (resp. of $\mathcal{F}_t^0$) with respect to P^μ. We also set

$$\mathcal{F}_\infty := \bigcap_{\mu \in \mathcal{P}(\mathbb{S})} \mathcal{F}_\infty^\mu \quad \text{and} \quad \mathcal{F}_t := \bigcap_{\mu \in \mathcal{P}(\mathbb{S})} \mathcal{F}_t^\mu$$

Obviously, $\{\mathcal{F}_{t+}^0\}$, $\{\mathcal{F}_t^\mu\}$, $\{\mathcal{F}_t\}$ are *admissible families* [1]. We call $\{\mathcal{F}_t\}_{t \geq 0}$ the *minimum completed admissible family*. For a PDMP we have

$$\mathcal{F}_t = \mathcal{F}_{t+} := \bigcap_{\varepsilon > 0} \mathcal{F}_{t+\varepsilon}$$

(see [5]). Usually, we denote by $p(t, \alpha, E)$ the transition function for H defined for $t \in \mathbb{R}_+, \alpha \in \mathbb{S}$ and $E \in \mathcal{B}(\mathbb{S})$. The measure P_α and the transition function p are related by $P_\alpha[\alpha_t \in E] = p(t, \alpha, E)$, $(t, \alpha, E) \in \mathbb{R}_+ \times \mathbb{S} \times \mathcal{B}(\mathbb{S})$.

3.2 Hitting Times

$\overline{\mathbb{S}}$ is a locally compact separable metric space, and we assume that Δ is adjoined to $\overline{\mathbb{S}}$ as the point at infinity. Let $\mathcal{B}$ (resp. $\mathcal{B}_\Delta$) be the Borel σ-algebra of $\overline{\mathbb{S}}$ (resp. $\overline{\mathbb{S}}_\Delta$). We define $\zeta(\omega) = \inf\{t : \alpha_t(\omega) = \Delta\}$ provided the set in braces is not empty and $\zeta(\omega) = \infty$ if it is empty. ζ is a numerical random variable which is called the *lifetime* of the process H. For $A \subset \mathbb{S}_\Delta$ we define three functions:

$$D_A(\omega) = \inf\{t \geq 0 : \alpha_t(\omega) \in A\}$$
$$T_A(\omega) = \inf\{t > 0 : \alpha_t(\omega) \in A\}$$
$$\hat{T}_A(\omega) = \inf\{t > 0 : \alpha_{t-}(\omega) \in A\}$$

where in all cases the infimum of the empty set is understood to be $+\infty$. We call D_A (resp. T_A) the *first entry* (resp. *hitting*) *time* of A.

Assumption 3 *The given Markov process H has the state space* $(\overline{\mathbb{S}}, \mathcal{B}^*)$, *where*

$$\mathcal{B}^* = \mathcal{B}^*(\overline{\mathbb{S}}) = \bigcap_{\mu \in \mathcal{P}(\overline{\mathbb{S}})} \mathcal{B}^\mu(\overline{\mathbb{S}})$$

is the σ-algebra of all universally measurable sets of $\overline{\mathbb{S}}$, and is quasi-left continuous on $[0, \zeta)$ (i.e. whenever (T_n) is an increasing sequence from $\mathfrak{S}$ with limit T, then almost surely $\alpha_{T_n} \to \alpha_T$ on $[T < \zeta]$).

Assumption 3 is not very restrictive, see [1] for further discussions. At least, if $t^*(\alpha) = \infty$ for all $\alpha \in \mathbb{S}$, $\lambda \in C_b(\mathbb{S})$ and the function $\alpha \to Rf(\alpha)$ is continuous for $f \in C_b(\mathbb{S})$ (where $C_b(\mathbb{S})$ is the of bounded continuous functions on $\mathbb{S}$) then H has a Feller semi-group (see [5]). The Feller property implies the quasi-left continuity on $[0, \infty)$ (see [7]).

A normal Markov process is called *standard process* if its state space is a locally compact space with a countable base, its minimum completed admissible family is right continuous, its paths are Càdlàg and it is a quasi-left continuous strong Markov process.

Proposition 1. *Under Assumptions 1, 2 and 3 the PDMP H is a standard process.*

Proof. The proof follows from Assumption 3 and the construction of a PDMP, all the standard process requirements have been actually stated in [5].

Lemma 1. *Under Assumptions 1, 2 and 3 the hitting times for a PDMP, H, have the following properties:*

1. *If G is open (in $\mathbb{S}_\Delta$) then $D_G = T_G$ and D_G is an $\{\mathcal{F}^0_{t+}\}$ stopping time.*
2. *If $A \subset \mathbb{S}$ we define $d_A = \min(D_A, \zeta) = D_{A \cup \{\Delta\}}$. D_A is an $\{\mathcal{F}_t\}$ stopping time if and only if d_A is.*

Proof. Part 1 follows from [1] Chapter I, Lemma 10.8. Part 2 follows from [1] Chapter I, Lemma 10.9.

For any $A \subset \mathbb{S}$ and $t \geq 0$ let

$$R_t(A) = \{\omega : \alpha_s(\omega) \in A \cup \{\Delta\}, \text{ for some } s, 0 \leq s \leq t\},$$
$$R_t^*(A) = \{\omega : \alpha_s(\omega) \in A, \text{ for some } s, 0 \leq s \leq t\}.$$

Notice that $R_t(G)$ and $R_t^*(G)$ are in $\mathcal{F}_t^0$ if G is open.

Lemma 2. *For any set A, d_A is an $\{\mathcal{F}_t\}$ stopping time if and only if $R_t(A) \in \mathcal{F}_t$ for all t.*

Proof. This result is an immediate consequence of the definitions of d_A and $R_t(A)$.

Lemma 3. *[1] If $K \subset \mathbb{S}$ is compact then*

1. $R_t(K) \in \mathcal{F}_t$ *for all* t.
2. *If $\{G_n\}$ is a decreasing sequence of open subsets of $\mathbb{S}$ with $G_n \supset \overline{G}_{n+1} \supset K$ for all n and such that $K = \cap G_n = \cap \overline{G}_n$, then $d_{G_n} \uparrow d_K$ a.s. and $P^\mu(R_t(G_n)) \downarrow P^\mu(R_t(K))$ for all μ and t.*

Proposition 2. *For any Borel set B, $R_t(B) \in \mathcal{F}_t$.*

Proof. Since every Borel set is the union of a countable increasing sequence of compact sets, then the result is follows directly from Lemma 3.

Corollary 1. D_A *and* T_A *are* $\{\mathcal{F}_t\}$ *stopping times for all Borel subsets A of* $\mathbb{S}_\Delta$.

3.3   Hitting Distributions

For a Borel set $E \in \mathcal{B}(\mathbb{S})$, let us define the $p-$order *hitting distributions* H_p^E by

$$H_p^E(\alpha, f) = \mathbb{E}_\alpha(e^{-pT_E} f(\alpha_{T_E})), p > 0, \alpha \in \mathbb{S}$$

for every universally measurable function f. If $p = 0$, we write H^E instead of H_0^E, this kernel being defined by $H^E(\alpha, f) = \mathbb{E}_\alpha(f(\alpha_{T_E})I_{[T_E < \infty]})$. H_p^E is a Markovian kernel on $(\mathbb{S}, \mathcal{B}^*(\mathbb{S}))$ (see [13]).

3.4   Excessive Functions

Definition 2. *A universally measurable function f on $\mathbb{S}$ is said to be p-excessive $(p > 0)$ w.r.t. the kernel semi-group of PDMP H if*

$$f(\alpha) \geq 0, e^{-pt} p_t f(\alpha) \nearrow f(\alpha) \ P - a.s. \ t \searrow 0, \alpha \in \mathbb{S}, (p > 0).$$

A 0-excessive function is simply called excessive.

A PDMP satisfying the standard conditions is a Borel right process (see [5]). We denote by $B(\mathbb{S})$ the set of all bounded measurable functions $f : \mathbb{S} \to \mathbb{R}$. This is a Banach space under the norm

$$\|f\| = \sup_{\alpha \in S} |f(\alpha)|.$$

The operator semi-group (P_t) associated to a PDMP, H, maps $B(\mathbb{S})$ into $B(\mathbb{S})$. Let $B_0(\mathbb{S})$ be the subset of $B(\mathbb{S})$ consisting of excessive functions. The semi-group (P_t) is said to be *strongly continuous* on $B_0(\mathbb{S})$ and $B_0(\mathbb{S})$ is a closed linear subspace of $B(\mathbb{S})$ (see [5]).

If f is a $p-excessive$ function then $H_p^E(\cdot, f)$ is called the *p-reduced function* (or the reduced function if $p = 0$) of f on E. The p-reduced function of 1 on E

is denoted by e_E^p (or e_E if $p = 0$) and is called the *p-equilibrium potential* of E (or the *equilibrium potential* if $p = 0$). If f is *p-excessive*, then so its *p*-harmonic average $H_p^E(\cdot, f)$ relative to a Borel set E (see [13]).

Given E a Borel set and f a *p*-excessive function ($p > 0$), let $L_{f,E} = \{g \in \mathcal{B}_0, g \geq f \text{ on } E\}$. The inferior envelope of $L_{f,E}$ is equal to $H_p^E f$ with except of at most some irregular points for E which belong to E. The same conclusion is true if $p = 0$ if $\mathbb{S}$ is the union of an increasing sequence (S_n) of measurable sets with bounded potentials $U(S_n)$ (XV T18 [13]). Since $L_{f,E}$ is a closed convex set the computation of $H_p^E(\cdot, f)$ can be approach using convex analysis techniques (see [9]).

4 Reachability

4.1 Reachability Definitions

To address the reachability questions assume that we have a given PDMP, H, and a set $E \in \mathcal{B}(\mathbb{S})$. Let us to define:

$$Reach_T(E) = \{\omega \in \Omega \mid \exists t \in [0, T] : \alpha_t(\omega) \text{ or } \alpha_{t-}(\omega) \in E\}$$
$$Reach_\infty(E) = \{\omega \in \Omega \mid \exists t \geq 0 : \alpha_t(\omega) \text{ or } \alpha_{t-}(\omega) \in E\}$$

Problem 1. Are $Reach_T(E)$ and $Reach_\infty(E)$ really events? In other words, can we define the measure $P[Reach_T(E)]$ and $P[Reach_\infty(E)]$ of these sets in the underlying probability space?

Notice that if $Reach_T(E)$ is an event then so is $Reach_\infty(E)$, since

$$Reach_\infty(E) = \bigcup_{n=0}^{\infty} Reach_n.$$

Problem 2. If it turns out that we can assign a probability to $Reach_T(E)$ and $Reach_\infty(E)$, can we compute these probabilities?

4.2 Reachability Computations

Under the above assumptions, the reachability events for a given PDMP, H, and a set $E \in \mathcal{B}(\mathbb{S})$ become:

$$Reach_T(E) = \{\omega \in \mathcal{H} : \exists t \in [0, T] \; \alpha_t(\omega) \text{ or } \alpha_{t-}(\omega) \in E \cup \{\Delta\}\}$$
$$Reach_\infty(E) = \{\omega \in \mathcal{H} : \exists t \geq 0 \; \alpha_t(\omega) \text{ or } \alpha_{t-}(\omega) \in E \cup \{\Delta\}\}.$$

where $\mathcal{H}$ denote the family of all stochastic executions of H. If the process is supposed to be quasi-left continuous on $[0, \infty)$, we can remove Δ from the above definitions.

Proposition 3. $Reach_T(E) \in \mathcal{F}_T$, $Reach_\infty(E) \in \mathcal{F}_\infty$.

Proof. We have $R_T(E) \in \mathcal{F}_T, R_\infty(E) \in \mathcal{F}_\infty$ (cf. Propostion 2). Since the process H is standard (cf. Proposition 1) then $P^\mu[Reach_T(E) \backslash R_T(E)] = 0$ for all $\mu \in \mathcal{P}(\mathbb{S})$ (see [1]). Therefore, since $Reach_T(E) = [Reach_T(E) \backslash R_T(E)] \cup R_T(E)$ then $Reach_T(E) \in \mathcal{F}_T$. The second part of the proposition follows since

$$Reach_\infty(E) = \bigcup_{n=0}^{\infty} Reach_n.$$

Let α be a given state in $\mathbb{S}$ and E a Borel set in $\mathbb{S}$. We are interested to compute the probability of the set of stochastic executions from $\mathcal{H}_\alpha$ which reach E at least one moment $t \in [0, T]$ or $t \in [0, \infty)$, i.e.,

$$P_\alpha(Reach_T(E)) = P_\alpha(D_E \leq T, \widehat{T}_E \leq T)$$
$$P_\alpha(Reach_\infty(E)) = P_\alpha(D_E < \infty, \widehat{T}_E < \infty)$$

Because the process is standard, the probabilities we should compute become

$$P_\alpha(R_T(E)) = P_\alpha(D_E \leq T) \text{ and } P_\alpha(R_\infty(E)) = P_\alpha(D_E < \infty). \quad (1)$$

To compute the probabilities from (1) one can start with the generator of the process H. Theoretically, it is possible, giving the generator of the process H, to determine the entire probabilities measure P_α. Technical conditions are required make this calculation feasible even in theory, and no one would think of carrying it out in practice except for artificial examples.

Alternatively, one can define the *hitting probabilities* relative to a Borel set E as below:

$$\varphi_E^p(\alpha) = H_p^E(\alpha, 1) = \mathbb{E}_\alpha(e^{-pD_E}) \text{ and } \varphi_E(\alpha) = H_{0+}^E(\alpha, 1) = P_\alpha(D_E < \infty). \quad (2)$$

φ_E^p (resp.φ_E) is a *p-excessive* (resp. *excessive*) function (see [7]).

A possible approach to compute the hitting probabilities of equation (2) is to treat them as excessive functions and invoke approximation results for excessive functions. A very important observation here is that these hitting probabilities relative to a Borel set E are exactly the equilibrium potentials associated to E, so they are equal to 1 for every regular point for E. Let us recall, that a point α is *regular* for E provided it is regular for T_E (i.e. $P_\alpha(T_E = 0) = 1$) and it is *irregular* for E provided it is irregular for T_E (i.e. $P_\alpha(T_E = 0) = 0$). We denote by E^r the set of all points which are regular for the Borel set E ($E^o \subset E^r \subset \overline{E}$). In this context we have to study some exceptional sets of the state space (without regular points) and the case when the process is starting from a point belonging to $\mathbb{S} \backslash E$.

4.3   Approximation of the Hitting Times

In this section, reachability questions are characterised as hitting time problems. Let us consider a fixed start point $\alpha_0 \in \mathbb{S}$ and the sequence $T_1 < T_2 < T_3 < \dots$

of jump times associated to α_0. Let E a Borel subset of $\mathbb{S}$. Let A be the generator of the process H and let $D(A)$ denote the domain of the generator. It is known (see [5]) that the process $(C_t^u)_{t \in \mathbb{R}_+}$ defined by $C_t^u = u(\alpha_t) - u(\alpha_0) - \int_0^t Au(\alpha_s)ds$ is a martingale for each u in the domain $D(A)$. This fact implies that for each $t > 0$ we have $\mathbb{E}[u(\alpha_{t \wedge T_E}) - u(\alpha_0) - \int_0^{t \wedge T_E} Au(\alpha_s)ds] = 0$. Since we supposed that $T_E < \infty$ a.s., letting $t \to \infty$ gives

$$\mathbb{E}[u(\alpha_{T_E})] - \mathbb{E}[u(\alpha_0)] - \mathbb{E}[\int_0^{T_E} Au(\alpha_s)ds] = 0. \tag{3}$$

As in [10], we define the *occupation measure* μ_0 and *hitting distribution* μ_1 by

$$\mu_0(B) = \mathbb{E}[\int_0^{T_E} I_B(\alpha_s)ds] \text{ and } \mu_1(B) = P(\alpha_{T_E} \in B)$$

for all $B \in \mathcal{B}(\mathbb{S})$.

It is clear that if $B \subset E$ then $\mu_0(B) = 0$ and if $B \subset E^c$ then $\mu_1(B) = 0$. Therefore, μ_0 is concentrated in E^c and μ_1 is concentrated in E. With an integrability argument one can obtain from (3) the following equation, so-called *adjoint equation*:

$$\int_{E^c} Au(\alpha)\mu_0(d\alpha) + u(\alpha_0) - \int_E u(\alpha)\mu_1(d\alpha) = 0. \tag{4}$$

It is clear that

$$\mu_0(E^c) = \mathbb{E}(T_E) \text{ and } \mu_1(E^c) = 0. \tag{5}$$

If we take $u = I_{E^c}$ and we suppose that $\alpha_0 \notin E$ then the adjoint equation becomes $\int_{E^c} AI_{E^c}(\alpha)\mu_0(d\alpha) + 1 = 0$. It is known that for every $u \in D(A)$, Au is given by

$$Au(\alpha) = \mathcal{L}_f u(\alpha) + \lambda(\alpha) \int_{\mathbb{S}} (u(\beta) - u(\alpha))R(d\beta, \alpha).$$

Thus, we get $\int_{E^c} \{\lambda(\alpha) \int_{\mathbb{S}} (I_{E^c}(\beta) - I_{E^c}(\alpha))R(d\beta, \alpha)\}\mu_0(d\alpha) + 1 = 0$ and, if we denote $\Lambda_E(\alpha) = \lambda(\alpha) \int_E R(d\beta, \alpha) = \lambda(\alpha)R(E, \alpha)$ then

$$\int_{E^c} \Lambda_E(\alpha)\mu_0(d\alpha) = 1.$$

Thus, once the measure μ_0 has been determined (using for e.g. linear programming methods), the hitting time mean can be obtained from (5).

The following lemma is extremely useful to estimate the expectations of the moments of hitting times.

Lemma 4. *[6] Let E be a Borel subset of $\mathbb{S}$, $T = T_E$ and let $m(t) = \sup\{P_\alpha[T > t], \alpha \in \mathbb{S}\}$. Then, for all $t \geq 0, \alpha \in \mathbb{S}$ we have $\mathbb{E}_\alpha T \leq \frac{t}{1-m(t)}$. Moreover, if $m < 1$, for $0 < p < -\frac{1}{t}\ln m$ then $\mathbb{E}_\alpha e^{pT}$ is an analytic function of p in a neighbourhood of the origin, i.e., we have*

$$\mathbb{E}_\alpha e^{pT} = \sum_{k=1}^\infty \frac{p^k}{k!}\mathbb{E}_\alpha T^k.$$

If we suppose that T_E is finite then there exists T_k such that $T_E \in [T_k, T_{k+1})$. Using lemma 4 and the survivor function from Algorithm 1 we obtain the following estimation for all $k \geq 1$

$$\mathbb{E}_{\alpha_0} T_E \leq \frac{T_{k+1}}{1 - P_{\alpha_{T_k}}[T_E > T_{k+1}]} \leq \frac{T_{k+1}}{\exp(-\int_{T_k}^{T_E} \lambda(\phi(\alpha_{T_k}, \tau))d\tau)}$$

Then we compute the quantities $\tau_k = \frac{T_k}{\mathbb{E}_{\alpha_0} T_E}$, $k = 0, 1, 2, 3, \ldots$ (with the convention $T_0 = 0$) and let τ_{k_0} be the biggest one. Then $T_E \in [T_{k_0}, T_{k_0+1})$, i.e. the number of steps after the set E is reached is k_0.

5 Conclusions and Further Work

In this paper we set up PDMPs, as models for stochastic hybrid systems, and the corresponding reachability problem. An important result is that, under some technical assumptions, a PDMP is a standard Markov process. This fact has as a consequence that the "reach" events are real events in the underlying probability space, for which we can compute the probability measures. This result can be considered as the main result of this paper. It allows us to treat the reachability problem with some well-known tools like hitting times, hitting distributions or hitting time moments. We obtained also a method which allows us to estimate the number of steps after a certain set is reached. In an ongoing work we will develop some randomised algorithms for evaluating the system performance in terms of quantities such as the average time to reach a certain set and we will apply these algorithms to aircraft conflict detection.

Current work focuses on two methods for computing the probabilities of the reach events. In the remaining of this section we summarise the main points of these two approaches.

5.1 Via Capacity Theory

An other approach to study some important properties of "reach" probabilities is via capacity theory. These probabilities can be thought of as Choquet capacities on the state space $\mathbb{S}$ (see [1] for more details about Choquet capacities).

Let $\mathbb{S}$ be a locally compact separable metric space and let $\mathcal{K}$ be the class of all compact subsets of $\mathbb{S}$. A function $\varphi : \mathcal{K} \to \mathbb{R}$ is called a *Choquet capacity* if

1. if $A, B \in \mathcal{K}$ and $A \subset B$, then $\varphi(A) \leq \varphi(B)$;
2. given $A \in \mathcal{K}$ and $\varepsilon > 0$ there exists an open set $G \supset A$ such that for every $B \in \mathcal{K}$ with $A \subset B \subset G$ one has $\varphi(B) - \varphi(A) < \varepsilon$;
3. $\varphi(A \cup B) + \varphi(A \cap B) \leq \varphi(A) + \varphi(B)$ for all $A, B \in \mathcal{K}$ (strongly subaddtive).

Given a Choquet capacity φ one defines the *inner capacity*, $\varphi_*(A)$, of an arbitrary set $A \subset \mathbb{S}$ by $\varphi_*(A) = \sup_{K \subset A} \varphi(K)$ where the supremum is taken over all compact subsets of A. One next defines the outer capacity $\varphi^*(A)$, of an arbitrary set by $\varphi^*(A) = \inf_{G \supset A} \varphi_*(G)$ where the infimum is taken over all open sets containing A.

Let μ (a probability measure on $\mathbb{S}$) and t be fixed; then $\varphi(K) = P^\mu[R_t(K)]$ is a Choquet capacity on the compact subsets of $\mathbb{S}$ (see [1]). In this case it is enough to compute these probabilities only for the compact sets.

A good presentation of the operations on Choquet capacities can be found in [2], Chapter V. In this context very important are the approximation results for the hitting times. For the computation of Choquet capacities we can use similar methods as in the fractal theory (see [14], [15]), where these capacities are very useful. The capacity theory offers us sufficient tools to study the reachability problem for PDMP. It is clear that there is an overlapping between the capacity theory and the theory of hitting times, but the capacity theory is very well studied, richer then the second one and it could be a suitable candidate for our problem.

5.2   Via Optimal Control

An alternative, indirect approach to reachability questions is using optimal control. In this direction we consider the possibility to draw parallels between the computations based on the extended generator of a PDMP and the Hamilton-Jacobi equations. A start point is to consider, for any Borel set, its indicator function $I_E : \mathbb{S} \to \{0,1\}$ and to set

$$P[Reach_T(E)] = \mathbb{E}[\max_{t \in [0,T]} I_E(\alpha_t)]$$
$$P[Reach_\infty(E)] = \mathbb{E}[\max_{t \geq 0} I_E(\alpha_t)].$$

Because $Reach_T(E)$ and $Reach_\infty(E)$ are measurable, it follows that the expectations $E[\max_{t \in [0,T]} I_E(\alpha_t)]$ and $E[\max_{t \geq 0} I_E(\alpha_t)]$ are well-defined. Since I_E is binary the maximum in the last equations exists. Using similar techniques as those developed in [11], we believe that it is possible to characterise the previous probabilities as viscosity solutions to a partial differential equation ([3]).

A further step of our work will be to improve our stochastic hybrid system models, namely the PDMPs, requiring some randomness between jumps. This aim could be accomplished asking the continuous motion between jumps to be led by some "nice" stochastic differential equations.

Acknowledgement. Work was supported by the European Commission under COLUMBUS, IST-2001-38314.

References

1. R.M.Blumenthal, R.K.Getoor, *Markov Processes and Potential Theory*, Academic Press, New York and London, 1968
2. G. Choquet, Theory of Capacities, *Annales de l'Institut Fourier, Grenoble*, 5, p131–291, (1953–1954)

3. M.G. Crandall, P.L. Lions, *Viscosity Solutions of Hamilton-Jacobi Equations*,Transactions of the American Mathemetical Society, 277(1), pp.1–42, May 1983.
4. M.H.A. Davis, *Piecewise-Deterministic Markov Processes: A General Class of Non-Diffusion Stochastic Models,* Journal of the Royal Statistical Society, B, 46(3), pp. 353–388, 1984.
5. M.H.A. Davis, *Markov Models and Optimization,* Chapman & Hall, London, 1993
6. E.B. Dynkin. *Markov Processes.* vol.I, Springer-Verlag, Berlin. Göttingen. Heidelberg,1965
7. M. Fukushima. *Dirichlet Forms and Markov Processes* North Holland, 1980
8. M. K. Ghosh, A. Arapostathis, S. I. Marcus, *Ergodic Control of Switching Diffusions,* Siam J. Control Optim., Vol. 35, No. 6, pp. 1952–1988, November 1997.
9. K. Helmes, R.H. Stockbridge, Numerical Evaluation of Resovents and Laplace Transforms of Markov Processes Using Linear Programming, Math. Meth. of Oper. Res., No.53,
10. K. Helmes, S. Röhl, R.H. Stockbridge, *Computing Moments of the Exit Time Distribution for Markov Processes by Linear Programming,* Math. Meth. of Oper. Res., No.49.
11. J. Lygeros. *On Reachability and Minimum Cost Optimal Control.* Technical Report CUED/F-INFENG/TR.430, Department of Engineering, University of Cambridge, 2002.
12. J. Hu, J. Lygeros, S. Sastry, *Towards a Theory of Stochastic Hybrid Systems,* HSCC 2000, pp.160–173.
13. P.A. Meyer, *Processus de Markov,* Lecture Notes in Mathematics 26, Berlin, Heidelberg, New York: Springer 1967.
14. J.Lévy Véhel, P.Mignot, Multifractal Segmentation of Images, *Fractals,* 2(3), p371–377, 1994.
15. J.Lévy Véhel, R. Vojak, Multifractal Analysis of Choquet Capacities: Preliminary Results, *Rapport de recherche,* 2576, INRIA, 1995.

Automatic Verification of a Turbogas Control System with the Murφ Verifier*

Giuseppe Della Penna[1], Benedetto Intrigila[1], Igor Melatti[1],
Michele Minichino[3], Ester Ciancamerla[3], Andrea Parisse[1], Enrico Tronci[2,**],
and Marisa Venturini Zilli[2]

[1] Dip. di Informatica, Università di L'Aquila, Coppito 67100, L'Aquila, Italy
{dellapenna,intrigila,melatti,parisse}@di.univaq.it
[2] Dip. di Informatica Università di Roma "La Sapienza",
Via Salaria 113, 00198 Roma, Italy
{tronci,zilli}@dsi.uniroma1.it
[3] ENEA , CR Casaccia, Via Anguillarese, 00060 Italy
{minichino,ciancamerlae}@casaccia.enea.it

Abstract. Automatic analysis of *Hybrid Systems* poses formidable challenges both from a modeling as well as from a verification point of view. We present a case study on automatic verification of a *Turbogas Control System* (TCS) using an extended version of the Murφ verifier. TCS is the heart of *ICARO*, a 2MW *Co-generative Electric Power Plant*.

For large hybrid systems, as TCS is, the modeling effort accounts for a significant part of the whole verification activity. In order to ease our modeling effort we extended the Murφ verifier by importing the C language **long double** type (*finite precision real numbers*) into it.

We give experimental results on running our extended Murφ on our TCS model. For example using Murφ we were able to compute an admissible range of values for the variation speed of the *user demand* of electric power to the turbogas.

1 Introduction

Automatic analysis of *Hybrid Systems* poses formidable challenges both from a modeling as well as from a verification point of view. In fact the simultaneous presence of continuous and discrete variables may lead very quickly to *state explosion*, thus preventing completion of the verification process.

Many verification tools (*model checkers*) are available for automatic verification of hybrid systems. Examples are: HyTech [14,2,1] and UPPAAL [17,26]. Also tools originally designed for hardware verification have been used for hybrid systems verification. E.g. in [25] SMV [18,21] has been used for verification of chemical processing systems.

---

* This research has been partially supported by MURST projects MEFISTO and SAHARA

** Corresponding Author: Enrico Tronci. Tel: +39 06 4991 8361 Fax: +39 06 8541 842

In this paper we present a case study on automatic verification of a *Turbogas Control System* (TCS) using an extended version of the Murφ verifier [9,19]. TCS is the main subsystem of *ICARO*, a 2MW *Co-generative Electric Power Plant* in operation at the ENEA Research Center of Casaccia (Italy). TCS is a quite complex control system whose main goal is to regulate the opening of the fuel gas valve of ICARO turbine so that the generated electric power, turbine rotation speed and exhaust smokes temperature are all within given limits notwithstanding changes in the *user demand* for electric power to the turbogas.

We resorted to the Murφ verifier after failing to complete verification using HyTech and SMV. We think Murφ success on this case study can be explained as follows. The transition relations of the many subsystems forming TCS are quite big. This fact is an obstruction for symbolic model checkers as HyTech and SMV. However, when we put such transition relations together the set of reachable states becomes of moderate size. In fact, the controller goal is exactly that of keeping the reachable states within a small neighborhood of the system *setpoint*. An explicit model checker, like Murφ, can easily exploit this fact thus avoiding state explosion.

To ease the hybrid systems modeling activity we decided to *import* within the Murφ verifier the C `long double` type (*finite precision real numbers*). The resulting Murφ verifier still uses a discrete time model. However the C `long double` type is now available for real valued state variables. This turned out to be very useful during the modeling activity, which, in our experience, accounts for a significant part of the whole hybrid system verification activity. Of course our extension to Murφ applies to *Cached* Murφ [23,7], *Disk* Murφ [20] and *Random* Murφ [24] as well.

Our results show that Murφ, enhanced with finite precision real numbers, is definitively to be considered among the candidate tools available for automatic analysis of hybrid control systems. The main contributions of this paper can be summarized as follows.

- We sketch (Section 3) syntax and semantics of the Murφ verifier enhanced with *finite precision real numbers*.
- We present (Section 4) our case study on verification of a *Turbogas Control System* (TCS).
- We show (Section 5) some of our experimental results on using Murφ enhanced with finite precision real numbers on the Murφ model for the system described in Section 4. Using Murφ we were able to compute an admissible range of values for the variation speed of the *user demand* for electric power to the turbogas.

2   The Murφ Verifier

The goal of this section is to give a short overview of the Murφ verifier. For further details we refer the reader to [9,19].

From a conceptual point of view, Murφ takes as input a *Finite State System* S and checks that a given invariant property φ for S is satisfied.

Definition 1. *1. A* Finite State System *(FSS) S is a 4-tuple (S, I, A, R) where: S is a finite set (of states), $I \subseteq S$ is the set of initial states, A is a finite set (of transition labels) and R is a relation on $S \times A \times S$. R is usually called the* transition relation *of S.*

2. Given states $s, s' \in S$ and $a \in A$ we say that there is a transition from s to s' labeled with a iff $R(s, a, s')$ holds. We say that there is a transition from s to s' (notation $R(s, s')$) iff there exists $a \in A$ s.t. $R(s, a, s')$ holds. The set of successors *of state s (notation* next(s)*) is the set of states s' s.t. $R(s, s')$.*

3. The set of reachable states *of S (notation* Reach(S)*) is the set of states of S reachable in zero or more steps from I.*

Formally, Reach(S) *is the smallest set s.t.*

1. $I \subseteq$ Reach(S),

2. for all $s \in$ Reach(S), next(s) $\subseteq$ Reach(S).

In the following we will always refer to a given (once and for all) system $S = (S, I, A, R)$. Thus, e.g., we will write Reach for Reach(S). Also we may speak about the set of initial states I as well as about the transition relation R without explicitly mentioning S.

The core of all automatic verification tools is the *reachability analysis*, i.e. the computation of Reach given a definition of S in some language. In fact checking that *all* reachable states of S satisfy a given (invariant) property φ entails computing Reach. For this reason we focus on the computation of the set of reachable states of S.

Since the transition relation R of a system defines a graph (*transition graph*) computing Reach means visiting (exploring) the transition graph starting from the initial states in I. This can be done, e.g., using a *Depth First* (DF) visit or a *Breadth First* (BF) visit.

For example the automatic verifier SPIN [22] uses a DF visit. Murφ [19] may use a DF as well as a BF visit. However certain compression options can only be used with a BF visit, for this reason here we focus only on BF visit.

Fig. 1 shows the standard BF state space exploration algorithm. Essentially this is the algorithm used by Murφ to visit the state space of a given system S.

Note that since S is a finite state system, the algorithm in Fig. 1 always terminates since we never visit the same state more than once.

```
Queue Q;   Hash Table T;
bfs(init_states, next) {
for s in init_states enqueue(Q, s); /* load Q with initial states */
for s in init_states insert(T, s); /* mark initial states as visited */
while (Q is not empty) { s = dequeue(Q);           /* visit */
 for all s' in next(s)
    if (s' is not in T) {enqueue(Q, s'); insert(T, s');}}}
```

Fig. 1. Explicit Breadth First Visit

The algorithm in Fig. 1 makes use of two main memory data structures: a *Queue*, where states are stored and retrieved (in FIFO order) during the search, and a *Hash Table* used to store all visited states. In Fig. 1 invariants for state s may be checked whenever function enqueue(Q, s) is called.

Note that Murφ (like SPIN) represents states *explicitly*, i.e. each visited state is stored in RAM (namely in the hash table). There are model checkers (e.g. UPPAAL, SMV, HyTech) that represent states *symbolically*. In symbolic model checking the set V of visited states is represented with its characteristic function f (i.e. $f(s) = $ **if** $s \in V$ **then** 1 **else** 0) and suitable data structures (e.g. OBDDs, *Ordered Binary Decision Diagrams* [6]) are used to represent f. Examples of symbolic model checkers are SMV [21], UPPAAL [17,26] (both based on OBDDs) and HyTech [14,2,1] which is based on polyedra in multidimensional real space [13,8,11,12].

Explicit model checkers (e.g. as Murφ and SPIN) typically perform better on *software-like* (i.e. asynchronous) systems [15], whereas *symbolic* model checkers (e.g. as SMV) typically perform better on *hardware-like* (i.e. synchronous) systems.

Murφ input consists of a definition of the system S to be verified and a definition of the property φ to be checked. Both definitions are stored in a file that we call here *Murφ description*.

The Murφ description language for system S is a high-level programming language for finite-state asynchronous concurrent systems (i.e. software like systems). Murφ description language is high-level in the sense that many features found in common high-level programming languages such as Pascal or C are part of Murφ. For example, Murφ has user-defined data types, procedures, and parameterization of descriptions.

A Murφ description consists of: declarations of constants, types, global variables and procedures; a collection of transition rules; a description of the initial states; and a set of invariants.

The behavioral part of Murφ is a collection of transition rules. Each transition rule is a guarded command which consists of a condition (a Boolean expression on global variables) and an action (a statement that can modify the values of the variables).

The condition and the action are both written in a Pascal-like language. The action can be an arbitrarily complex statement containing loops and conditionals. No matter how complex it is, the action is executed *atomically*, i.e. no other rule can change the variables or otherwise interfere with it while it is being executed.

A *Murφ state* is an assignment of values to all of the global variables of the description.

An execution of the description is generated by executing the endless loop in Fig. 2.

```
loop forever {
1. Find all enabled rules, i.e. all rules whose conditions are true
   in the current state;
2. Choose arbitrarily an enabled rule and execute its action,
   thus yielding a new state; }
```

Fig. 2. Murφ execution loop

Note that Murφ descriptions are nondeterministic, because of the arbitrary choice in step 2 in Fig. 2. The user has no control over how this choice is made, so a *correct* Murφ program must do the right thing no matter which rules are chosen. However, once a rule has been chosen, the action is deterministic (there is a unique next state). Note that when using Murφ as a verifier *all* reachable states of a Murφ program are visited.

A small toy example should help to clarify the matter. Let us consider the *Discrete Time System* (DTS) defined by equation 1, where $\mathbf{x}(t)$ is the state value at time t and $\mathbf{d}(t)$ is the disturbance value at time t.

$$\mathbf{x}(t+1) = \begin{cases} \mathbf{x}(t) + \mathbf{d}(t) \text{ if } \mathbf{x}(t) \leq 3 \\ \mathbf{x}(t) - \mathbf{d}(t) \text{ otherwise} \end{cases} \quad \forall t[\mathbf{d}(t) \in \{0,1,2\}], \quad \mathbf{x}(0) = 0. \quad (1)$$

Fig. 3 shows the FSS corresponding to the DTS defined by Equation 1. The initial state $\mathbf{x}(0) = 0$ is shown with an arrow in Fig. 3, where nodes are labeled with state values and edges are labeled with action (disturbance, in our case) values.

Murφ code for the DTS in Equation 1 is given in Fig. 4 where we have examples of (declarations of) constants, types, global variables, functions, initial states, transition rules and invariants.

Fig. 5 summarizes the output of the Murφ verifier when given the input in Fig. 4. Namely, the Murφ verifier returns an *error trace*, i.e. a (loopless) path in the graph in Fig. 3 from an initial state to a state violating the invariant property. If we replace the $<$ sign in the invariant in Fig. 4 with $\leq$ then the invariant property is always satisfied since all reachable states of the DTS defined by Equation 1 have a value less than or equal to 5 (see Fig. 3).

Remark 1. In the BF algorithm in Fig. 1 only reachable states are visited and thus stored in the hash table T. That is the set of reachable states essentially depends only on the *system dynamics*. For example, the set of reachable states for the system defined in Fig. 4 is the integer interval $[0, 5]$. This set does not depend on state_type (the type of variable x in Fig. 4) as long as state_type contains the integer interval $[0, 5]$. For example, if in Fig. 4 we change the state_type declaration to state_type : 0..100, the set of reachable states is still the integer interval $[0, 5]$.

3   Extending Murφ Input Language with Real Numbers

Murφ built-in types are ranges of integers and enumerative types. To ease the hybrid systems modeling activity we also want to be able to handle *finite precision real numbers* within the Murφ verifier. Namely, we want to be able to handle within Murφ numbers of the form $s_M\, d_0.d_1 \cdots d_{m-1} \times 10^{s_E\, e_{n-1} \cdots e_0}$ where: d_i and e_i are decimal digits, $d_0 \neq 0$, s_M, $s_E \in \{'+','-'\}$. As usual we call $s_M\, d_0.d_1 \cdots d_{m-1}$ the *mantissa* and $s_E\, e_{n-1} \cdots e_0$ the *exponent* of the number $s_M\, d_0.d_1 \cdots d_{m-1} \times 10^{s_E\, e_{n-1} \cdots e_0}$.

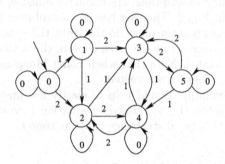

Fig. 3. FSS for the discrete time system in Equation 1.

```
CONST -- constant declarations
MAX_STATE_VALUE : 5;
TYPE    -- type declarations
state_type : 0 .. 10; -- integers from 0 to 10
disturbance_type : 0 .. 2;  -- integers from 0 to 2
VAR    -- (global) variable declarations
x : state_type;  -- x is a variable of type state_type

-- define next state function
function next(x: state_type; d : disturbance_type): state_type;
begin if (x <= 3) then return (x + d); else return (x - d); endif end;

startstate "init" x := 0; end;  -- define initial state

ruleset d : disturbance_type  do  -- define transition rule
   rule "time step" true ==> begin x := next(x, d); end;
end; -- ruleset d

invariant "x is not too big" -- define property to be verified
(x < MAX_STATE_VALUE);
```

Fig. 4. Murφ code for the DTS in Equation 1.

```
Startstate init fired.
x:0
----------
Rule time step, d:1 fired.
x:1
----------
Rule time step, d:2 fired.
x:3
----------
Rule time step, d:2 fired.
The last state of the trace (in full) is:
x:5
----------
```

Fig. 5. Murφ error trace for Murφ model in Fig. 4.

```
const  -- constant declarations
SAMPLING_FREQ : 100.0;  -- Hz. Inverse of the sampling time.
MAX_U: 200.0;     -- Max user demand value (kW)
MAX_D_U: 10.0;    -- Max of time derivative of user demand
MAX_D_P: 0.1;    -- Max of time derivative of compressor pression
MAX_PRES_COMPR: 13.0; -- Max compressor pression (bar)
MIN_PRES_COMPR : 11.0;  -- Min compressor pression (bar)
Power_setpnt : 2000.0;   -- Setpoint of Electric Power (kW)
Texh_setpnt : 552;  -- Setpoint of exhaust smokes temperature(C)
Vrot_setpnt: 75;  -- Setpoint of rotation speed (RPM)
Pow_v_coef : Power_setpnt;        -- valve coefficient in turbogas model
Texh_v_coef : 0.1*Texh_setpnt; -- valve coefficient in turbogas model
Vrot_v_coef : 2*Vrot_setpnt;     -- valve coefficient in turbogas model
FREQ_1 : 100; -- frequency injection disturbances

type  -- type declarations
Disturbance_type : -1..1;
real_type : real(4, 2);  -- used for all real variables
longint_type : -50000 .. +50000;  -- used for counters

var  -- variable declarations
step_counter : longint_type; -- initialized to 0
  -- we do: step_counter := (step_counter + 1)%FREQ_1 at each time step
Power : real_type;   -- Generated Electric Power
```

Fig. 6. A glimpse of the Murφ declarations used in our model.

To this end we add to the Murφ verifier the type `real(m, n)` of real numbers with m digits for the mantissa and n digits for the exponent. Type `real(m, n)` is finite, its cardinality is $2 \times 9 \times 10^{m-1} \times 2 \times 10^n = 36 \times 10^{m+n-1}$. Thus our extension has no impact on Murφ verification algorithms (e.g. as that in Fig. 1) , however makes it easier to model hybrid systems within Murφ.

Note that, as from Remark 1, the huge cardinality of the type `real(m, n)` does not imply, *a priori*, a huge size of the set of reachable states.

The type `real(m, n)` is built on `long double` C type. For this reason the *mantissa* size m and the *exponent* size n in `real(m, n)` must satisfy the following constraints: $1 \leq m \leq$ LDBL_DIG, $2 \leq n \leq \lfloor \log_{10} \text{LDBL\_MAX\_10\_EXP} \rfloor + 1$, where LDBL_DIG is the maximum number of digits for the mantissa of the `long double` C type and LDBL_MAX_10_EXP is the maximum value of the exponent of the `long double` C type. These constants are defined in the C header `float.h`.

Fig. 6 gives an example of variables and constant declarations within our extended Murφ.

We also extended Murφ by importing all functions available in the C `math` library (header `math.h`). Such functions can now be freely used within the Murφ input language.

Our extension to Murφ is implemented by suitably extending Murφ parser and by adding (low level) functions to store and retrieve finite precision real values into the Murφ internal state representation (namely, state byte vector bits, see Murφ documentation [19]).

4 ICARO Turbogas Control System

In this section we will shortly describe the system to be verified and the requirements that we are supposed to verify.

ICARO is a 2MW Electric Co-generative Power Plant, in operation at the ENEA Research Center of Casaccia (Italy), used to provide electricity and heating to the above ENEA Center.

Depending on the operating conditions (e.g. *startup, normal, shutdown*) ICARO models are widely different. Here we only focus on *normal* operating conditions, i.e. the situation in which ICARO is running at its *nominal* (setpoint) power. In particular our model cannot be used to study system behaviour during transient operating modes (e.g. at startup or shutdown).

ICARO plant consists of many subsystems. Here we only focus on one of the many subsystems of ICARO (e.g. see [5,3,4]). Namely we focus on the *Gas Turbine* ICARO subsystem that we call in the following ICARO *Turbogas Control System* (TCS). TCS is the heart of ICARO and is indeed ICARO most critical subsystem. Unfortunately, TCS is also the largest ICARO subsystem, thus making the use of model checking for such hybrid system a challenge.

Unless otherwise stated, all our data (e.g. block diagrams, parameter values, etc) are taken from the ICARO documentation [10].

TCS is a *control system*, that is a (hybrid) system in which we can distinguish two subsystems: the *plant* (i.e. the controlled system) and the *controller* (which sends commands to the plant in order to meet given requirements on the whole system behaviour). Note that many (but not all) hybrid systems are indeed control systems.

Fig. 7 shows the high level block diagram for TCS. The *Turbogas* block in Fig. 7 is the *the plant*. The *Controller* block in Fig. 7 is the *the controller*. In the following we describe the elements of Fig. 7.

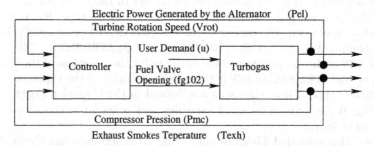

Fig. 7. High level block diagram of ICARO Turbogas Control System

4.1 Turbogas Continuous Time Model

The block named *Turbogas* in Fig. 7 models the *Gas Turbine* module. As a matter of fact this module consists of many subsystems (e.g. the compressor, the combustion chamber, the turbine itself and the generator). For our purposes here we can simply look at its input-output model. The turbogas system has the following input variables.

$fg102$ Variable $fg102$ takes value in the real interval $[0,1]$. This variable gives the opening fraction of the turbogas fuel gas valve (namely valve FG102). For example variable $fg102$ takes value 0 when the valve FG102 is fully closed (no fuel can flow trough the valve) and value 1 when the valve FG102 is fully opened. This is a *control variable*, i.e. a variable whose value can be chosen by the controller so as to achieve predefined goals.

u Variable u models the *User Demand* of electric power. This variable has to be considered as a *disturbance*, i.e. a variable whose value we (i.e. the controller) cannot choose.

The output variables of the turbogas system are the following ones.

P_{el} *Electric power* generated by the alternator.
V_{rot} *Rotation speed* of the gas turbine.
T_{exh} *Temperature* of the exhaust smokes.
P_{mc} *Pression* of the compressor.

The controller goal is to keep the turbogas output variables as close as possible to their *setpoint* notwithstanding variations in the user demand u. The values of the output variables at the setpoint are given in Fig. 8.

- Electric Power setpoint value: $P_{el}^0 = 2000$ (KW).
- Exhaust Smokes Temperature setpoint value: $T_{exh}^0 = 552$ (C).
- Turbine Rotation Speed setpoint value: $V_{rot}^0 = 75$ (RPM)
- Compressor Pression setpoint value: $P_{mc}^0 = 12$ (Bar)

Fig. 8. Turbogas setpoint values.

For the purposes of our analysis we used the ODE (*Ordinary Differential Equation*) model, shown in Fig. 9, to link turbogas input variables with output variables. Of course such a model is only valid in a neighborhood of the setpoint.

Note that, according to the model in Fig. 9, the compressor pression P_{mc} can change value *nondeterministically* as long as it satisfies the constraints given in Fig. 9. We do not need a more detailed model here since the compressor pression is only used as input to the fuel gas valve controller whose requirements do not involve the compressor pression.

We do not know *in advance* the user demand u. However, by making some hypothesis on the user demand u dynamics we can follow for the user demand model in Fig. 9 the same approach we used for the compressor pression. Namely, we simply ask that the user demand $u(t)$ be in the interval $[0, MAX\_U]$ (the user demand is always non-negative since users cannot produce electric power) and the *variation speed* of the user demand $\dot{u}(t)$ be at most MAX_D_U. Note that for the model in Fig. 9 the only *input* variable is $fg102$, all other variables (i.e. $P_{el}, V_{rot}, T_{exh}, P_{mc}, u$) are *state* as well as *output* variables.

$$\dot{P}_{el}(t) = \alpha_{1,1}P_{el}(t) + \alpha_{1,2}fg102(t) + \alpha_{1,3}u(t)$$

$$\dot{T}_{exh}(t) = \alpha_{2,1}T_{exh}(t) + \alpha_{2,2}fg102(t) + \alpha_{2,3}(P_{el}(t) - P_{el}^0) + \alpha_{2,4}(P_{mc}(t) - P_{mc}^0)$$

$$\dot{V}_{rot}(t) = \alpha_{3,1}V_{rot}(t) + \alpha_{3,2}fg102(t) + \alpha_{3,3}(P_{el}(t) - P_{el}^0)$$

$$P_{mc}(t) \in [MIN\_P_{mc}, MAX\_P_{mc}] \qquad | \dot{P}_{mc}(t) | \leq MAX\_D\_P_{mc}$$

$$u(t) \in [0, MAX\_U] \qquad | \dot{u}(t) | \leq MAX\_D\_U$$

Fig. 9. Turbogas ODE model used for our analysis.

4.2   Requirements

The goal of the turbogas controller is to set the turbogas control variable $fg102$ so as to keep the value of turbogas output variables P_{el}, V_{rot}, T_{exh} within given limits notwithstanding variations in the user demand u. Such limits are shown in Fig. 10 and are our requirements, i.e. the properties that we will have to check during verification.

$$1300 \leq P_{el}(t) \leq 2500$$
$$200 \leq T_{exh}(t) \leq 580$$
$$40 \leq V_{rot}(t) \leq 120$$

Fig. 10. Turbogas Control System requirements.

4.3   Turbogas Controller

Fig. 11 shows the block diagram for the fuel gas valve controller (i.e. the controller of Fig. 7).

In the following we describe the controller subsystems.

All the controller subsystems (namely: N1 Governor, Power Limiter, Exhaust Temperature Limiter) are built from the *elementary cell* shown in Fig. 12.

Note that in the *elementary cell* in Fig. 12 we have the simultaneous presence of linear blocks (e.g. the integrator block labeled $1/s$ in Fig. 12), *saturation* blocks, *test for* > 0 and logical (AND) blocks. This makes the elementary cell a hybrid system. Since all subsystems in TCS are based on the cell in Fig. 12, it turns out that TCS itself is a (quite big) hybrid system.

From Fig. 11 it is clear that the turbogas controller output is obtained as the minimum (block MIN) of the outputs of the three subsystems N1 Governor, Power Limiter, Exhaust Temperature Limiter.

The *N1 Governor* block in Fig. 13 computes the power demand with the goal of maintaining the turbine rotation speed within given bounds.

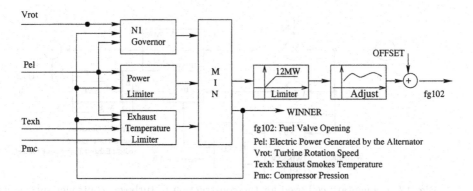

Fig. 11. Turbogas fuel gas valve controller.

The *Power Limiter* block in Fig. 14 computes the power demand with the goal of maintaining the electric power generated within given bounds.

The *Exhaust Temperature Limiter* block in Fig. 15 computes the power demand with the goal of maintaining the temperature of the exhaust smokes within given bounds.

The subsystem MIN in Fig. 11 computes the minimum among its inputs. Moreover, the block MIN returns the name (index) of the winner (i.e. of the input which attained the minimum value) on the output labeled WINNER.

The block *Limiter* in Fig. 11 saturates the power demand to 12MW.

The block *Adjust* together with the OFFSET parameter in Fig. 11 translates the power demand from the Limiter block into a fuel valve opening command, i.e. into a real number in the range [0,1].

5   Experimental Results

We transformed all the continuous time models into discrete time ones using a sampling time T of 10ms, as suggested in [10].

An example of the Murφ code used in the declaration section of our Murφ model is in Fig. 6. Space constraints do not allow us to show more here.

Using Murφ (with real numbers) we ran several experiments modifying the value of the *speed of variation* of the user demand (MAX_D_U in Fig. 6), thus computing an admissible range of values for the variation speed of the user demand.

Intuitively, if MAX_D_U is too big, the controller cannot compensate for the sudden user demand variation and the requirements will not be satisfied.

Fig. 16 shows our experimental results.

The size of each state is 470 bits (rounded up to 60 bytes). In all our experiments we used the --cache option which replaces Murφ hash table with a cache table [23].

When verification fails (rows 3 and 4 of Fig. 16), Murφ returns an error trace. In such cases the diameter of the reachability graph gives the error trace length. Thus it is quite clear that even for the 4th row of Fig. 16 the error trace is too

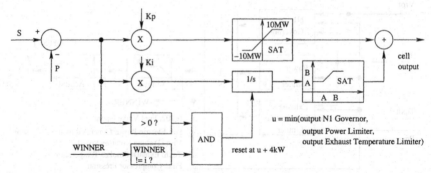

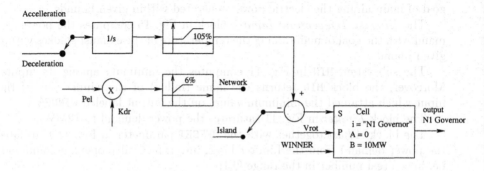

Fig. 12. Elementary cell used for the construction of turbogas controller subsystems: N1 Governor, Power Limiter, Exhaust Temperature Limiter. Cell Inputs: S, P, WINNER. Cell Parameters: i, A, B. Known Constants: Kp, Ki (from [10])

Fig. 13. Turbine Rotation Speed Controller (N1 Governor). The switches Acceleration/Decelaration, Network/Island change the controller *mode*. Their settings are chosen by a higher level controller or by the human operator. Kdr is a known constant (given to us in [10])

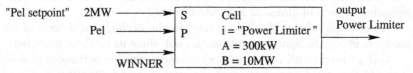

Fig. 14. Electric Power Controller (Power Limiter)

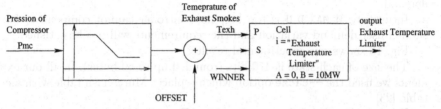

Fig. 15. Exhaust Smoke Temperature Controller (Exhaust Temperature Limiter)

long (804 states) to be shown here. However, in Fig. 17 we show the first and last state of such an error trace.

Note how, in row 1 and 2 of Fig. 16, when MAX_D_U increases, the number of reachable states increases too.

Row Number	MAX_D_U	Reachable States	Rules Fired	Reachability Graph Diameter	CPU Time (sec)	Verification Result
1	10.0	2246328	6738984	12904	16988.18	PASS
2	17.5	7492389	22477167	7423	54012.18	PASS
3	25	1739719	5186047	1533	12548.25	FAIL
4	50	36801	109015	804	271.77	FAIL

Fig. 16. Results on a INTEL Pentium 4, 2Ghz Linux PC with 512M RAM. Murφ options used: -b (bit compression), -c (40 bit hash compaction), --cache (use cache rather than hash table, cached Murφ) -m350 (use 350 MB of RAM for the cache).

From Fig. 16 it is quite clear that only a very small fraction of the 2^{480} states (480 bits are needed to represent a state) is reachable. This is the main reason why we were able to complete verification using Murφ. Note however that if we consider the turbogas model without the controller, the number of reachable states is much higher, out of reach for Murφ. In this respect our findings are similar to those of Kurshan and McMillan in their arbiter verification [16].

The behaviour described above is somehow to be expected. In fact, here we are interested in automatic verification of a control system in a neighborhood of its *setpoint* (i.e. our initial state is the setpoint state). Since the *controller* goal is typically that of keeping the whole system in a (small) neighborhood of the setpoint, we may expect that the set of reachable states from the setpoint is not *too big* (if the controller is well designed).

Taking advantage of this fact, using a symbolic model checker (e.g. as HyTech and SMV are) may be hard. As a result, the representation of the system transition relation can be so large that we may run out of memory even before starting the reachability analysis. Indeed this was our experience when we tried to use HyTech and SMV on our hybrid system verification problem.

For the above reason we decided to try Murφ which is an *explicit state verifier*.

Our experimental results show that for hybrid (control) systems explicit state model checkers (e.g. as Murφ) should be considered among the available verification tools.

6   Conclusions

We showed how the C long double type (*finite precision real numbers*) can be easily imported within the Murφ verifier. This allows us to easily use Murφ for modeling and verification of hybrid systems.

We presented a case study on automatic verification of a *Turbogas Control System* (TCS) using the Murφ verifier. TCS is is a quite large control system and is the main subsystem of *ICARO*, a 2MW *Co-generative Electric Power Plant*.

```
                                      ................
                                      The last state of the trace (in full) is:
Startstate initstate fired.           Power:+1.695e+03
Power:+2.000e+03                       Vrot:+3.999e+01
Vrot:+7.500e+01                        Texh:+5.520e+02
Texh:+5.520e+02                        N1_gov:+1.211e+04
N1_gov:+1.000e+03                      Pow_lim:+2.112e+03
Pow_lim:+1.000e+03                     Temp_lim:+7.294e+03
Temp_lim:+1.000e+03                    valve_fg102:+2.111e-01
valve_fg102:+1.000e-01                 v:+1.050e+02
v:+7.500e+02                           N1_state:+2.115e+03
N1_state:+1.000e+03                    Powlim_state:+1.808e+03
Powlim_state:+1.000e+03                templim_state:+2.115e+03
templim_state:+1.000e+03               minall:+2.112e+03
minall:+1.000e+03                      winner:2
winner:2                               step_counter:5
step_counter:0                         pression:+1.200e+01
pression:+1.200e+01                    user_demand:+1.500e+02
user_demand:+0.000e+00                 modality_value:2
modality_value:1                       ----------
................                       End of the error trace.
                                      ================================================
                                      Result: Invariant "rotation speed ok" failed.
```

Fig. 17. First and last state of the 804 states of Murφ error trace for row 4 of Fig. 16.

We showed experimental results on using Murφ for verification of TCS. Using Murφ we were able to compute an admissible range of values for the variation speed of the *user demand* for electric power to the turbogas.

Our experimental results suggest that Murφ enhanced with finite precision real numbers can be used quite effectively for modeling and for automatic analysis of hybrid control systems.

Testing Murφ on larger hybrid systems is a natural *next step* of our research efforts.

References

[1] url: http://www.eecs.berkeley.edu/~tah/HyTech.
[2] R. Alur, T.A. Henzinger, and P.-H. Ho. Automatic symbolic verification of embedded systems. *IEEE Trans. on Software Engineering*, 22, 1996.
[3] A. Bobbio, E. Ciancamerla, G. Franceschinis, R. Gaeta, M. Minichino, and L. Portinale. Methods of increasing modelling power for safety analysis, applied to a turbine digital control system. In *Proc. of 21st International Conference on "Computer Safety, Reliability and Security" (SAFECOMP)*, LNCS, Catania, Italy, Sept 2002. Springer.
[4] A. Bobbio, E. Ciancamerla, M. Gribaudo, A. Horvath, M. Minichino, and E. Tronci. Model checking based on fluid petri nets for the temperature control system of the icaro co-generative plant. In *Proc. of 21st International Conference on "Computer Safety, Reliability and Security" (SAFECOMP)*, LNCS, Catania, Italy, Sept 2002. Springer.
[5] A. Bobbio, S.Bologna, M. Minichino, E. Ciancamerla, P.Incalcaterra, C.Kropp, and E. Tronci. Advanced tecniques for safety analysis applied to the gas turbine control system of icaro co generative plant. In *Proc. of X Convegno TESEC*, Genova, Italy, June 2001.

[6] R. Bryant. Graph-based algorithms for boolean function manipulation. *IEEE Trans. on Computers*, C-35(8), Aug 1986.

[7] url: http://www.dsi.uniroma1.it/~tronci/cached.murphi.html.

[8] N. V. Chernikova. Algorithm for discovering the set of all solutions of a linear programming problem. *USSR Computational Mathematics and Mathematical Physics*, 8(6):282–293, 1968.

[9] D. L. Dill, A. J. Drexler, A. J. Hu, and C. H. Yang. Protocol verification as a hardware design aid. In *IEEE International Conference on Computer Design: VLSI in Computers and Processors*, pages 522–5, 1992.

[10] ENEA. *Proprietary ICARO Documentation*.

[11] N. Halbwachs. Delay analysis in synchronous programs. In *Proc. of: Computer Aided Verification (CAV)*, number 697 in LNCS, pages 333–346. Springer, 1993.

[12] N. Halbwachs, P. Raymond, and Y.-E. Proy. Verification of linear hybrid systems by means of convex approximation. In *Proc. of: Static Analysis Symposium (SAS)*, number 864 in LNCS, pages 223–237. Springer, 1994.

[13] T. A. Henzinger, P.-H. Ho, and H. Wong-Toi. Hytech: The next generation. In *Proc. of the 16th Annual IEEE Real-time Systems Symposium (RTSS)*, pages 56–65. IEEE, 1995.

[14] T.A. Henzinger, P.-H. Ho, and H. Wong-Toi. Hytech: A model checker for hybrid systems. *Software Tools for Technology Transfer*, 1, 1997.

[15] A. J. Hu, G. York, and D. L. Dill. New techniques for efficient verification with implicitily conjoined bdds. In *31st IEEE Design Automation Conference*, pages 276–282, 1994.

[16] R.P. Kurshan and K.L. McMillan. Analysis of digital circuits through symbolic reduction. *IEEECAD*, 10(11):1356–1371, November 1991.

[17] Kim G. Larsen, Paul Pettersson, and Wang Yi. UPPAAL: Status and developments. In Orna Grumberg, editor, *CAV97*, number 1254 in LNCS, pages 456–459. Springer–Verlag, Jun 1997.

[18] K. L. McMillan. *Symbolic model checking*. Kluwer Academic Publishers, Massachusetts, 1993.

[19] url: http://sprout.stanford.edu/dill/murphi.html.

[20] G. Della Penna, B. Intrigila, E. Tronci, and M. Venturini Zilli. Exploiting transition locality in the disk based murφ verifier. In *Proc. of 4th International Conference on "Formal Methods in Computer Aided Verification" (FMCAD)*, LNCS, Portland, Oregon, USA, Nov 2002. Springer.

[21] url: http://www.cs.cmu.edu/~modelcheck/.

[22] url: http://netlib.bell-labs.com/netlib/spin/whatispin.html.

[23] E. Tronci, G. Della Penna, B. Intrigila, and M. Venturini Zilli. Exploiting transition locality in automatic verification. In *IFIP WG 10.5 Advanced Research Working Conference on: Correct Hardware Design and Verification Methods (CHARME)*. LNCS, Springer, Sept 2001.

[24] E. Tronci, G. Della Penna, B. Intrigila, and M. Venturini Zilli. A probabilistic approach to space-time trading in automatic verification of concurrent systems. In *Proc. of 8th IEEE Asia-Pacific Software Engineering Conference (APSEC)*, Macau SAR, China, Dec 2001. IEEE Computer Society Press.

[25] A. L. Turk, S. T. Probst, and G. J. Powers. Verification of real-time chemical processing systems. In *Hybrid and Real-Time Systems*, number 1201 in LNCS, pages 259–272. Springer, 1997.

[26] url: http://www.docs.uu.se/docs/rtmv/uppaal/.

Modeling the Electrical Activity of a Neuron by a Continuous and Piecewise Affine Hybrid System

Jean-Guillaume Dumas and Aude Rondepierre

Laboratoire de Modélisation et Calcul
Tour IRMA - BP 53, 38041 Grenoble cedex 9. France
{Jean-Guillaume.Dumas,Aude.Rondepierre}@imag.fr
www-lmc.imag.fr/lmc-mosaic/{Jean-Guillaume.Dumas,Aude.Rondepierre}

Abstract. A hybrid system is proposed to model the electrical potential emitted by a neuron as a response to an externally applied DC current. Experimentally, Hodgkin and Huxley built a four-dimensional and non-linear dynamical system to simulate this activity. Our idea is to use a new continuous and piecewise affine approximation as a hybrid model of the Hodgkin-Huxley dynamic. Our new model reproduces the Hodgkin-Huxley features with good accuracy (e.g. including the fact that the incoming current intensity is a bifurcation parameter), and, moreover, still allows an analytic computation of its solutions.

1   Introduction

Neurons communicate with each other by generating electrical signals, called action potentials. Action potentials are the result of currents that pass through ion channels in the cell membrane. Each neuron integrates the incoming signals and, when the stimulation reaches a certain threshold, an output signal is generated and delivered. This paper deals with the dynamics of the membrane potential of a single neuron under a certain stimulus.

As a result of their experiments on a giant squid nerve fiber, Hodgkin and Huxley proposed a first model describing the dynamics of the action potentials [9]. The main idea is that because of active ion transport (mainly sodium, potassium and chloride) through the cell membrane, this membrane acts as a capacitor. From then their measures tended to show that potassium ions can cross the membrane when four similar molecules occupy a certain region of this membrane (so that potassium conductance is considered proportional to the number of sites on the inside of the membrane which are occupied by the four molecules, $g_K \approx \bar{g}_K n^4$). Similarly, the sodium conductance is supposed to be proportional to the number of sites on the inside of the membrane which are occupied simultaneously by three activating molecules and not blocked by an inactivating molecule ($g_{Na} \approx \bar{g}_{Na} m^3 h$). The chloride and other ions conductance is supposed constant. From this assumptions, Hodgkin and Huxley then proposed the following dynamical system as a simplified neuron model:

O. Maler and A. Pnueli (Eds.): HSCC 2003, LNCS 2623, pp. 156–171, 2003.

$$(\text{H-H}) \begin{cases} C_M \frac{dV}{dt} = I(t) - \bar{g}_K n^4 (V - V_K) - \bar{g}_{Na} m^3 h (V - V_{Na}) - \bar{g}_l (V - V_l) \\[2mm] \frac{dn}{dt} = (1-n).\alpha_n(V) - n.\beta_n(V) \\[2mm] \frac{dm}{dt} = (1-m).\alpha_m(V) - m.\beta_m(V) \\[2mm] \frac{dh}{dt} = (1-h).\alpha_h(V) - h.\beta_h(V) \end{cases}$$

- V is the displacement of the membrane potential from its resting value
- n is the proportion of the K^+ activating molecules inside the membrane at time t ; $0 \le n \le 1$
- m is the proportion of the Na^+ activating molecules inside the membrane at time t ; $0 \le m \le 1$
- $1 - h$ is the proportion of the Na^+ inactivating molecules inside the membrane at time t ; $0 \le h \le 1$
- $I(t)$ is the intensity of the current applied to the neuron cell.

The α and β being respectively the transfer rate constants from outside to inside and from inside to outside, the $\bar{g}_X$ and V_X being respectively the conductances and resting potentials of potassium, sodium and chloride ions [11].

Despite the small dimension of the (H-H) system, the mathematical analysis is still quite complex. Therefore only numerical simulations are used and simplified models are required for a better understanding of the neuronal dynamics.

Some simplifications have been proposed [1], models like integrate-and-fire, resonate-and-fire ([13]) or even Hopfield or FitzHugh-Nagumo (see [15, §6.5] or [7, §3.1] for further references) provide different level of relevant informations on the neuronal dynamics. For instance, these models are used to show the existence of a spike (excitable state), or of a threshold potential for the emission of a periodical state (see e.g. [7, §3.3] for more details). Unfortunately, these simplifications give only a few fully analytical results or low quality numerical approximations. Therefore some piecewise linear simplifications have been proposed by Tonnelier [16] to combine analytic results and good numerical approximations. Still there is no complete analytic analysis of the dynamics and Tonnelier's approximations suffer from a non-continuous behavior.

Our approach is to use a hybrid system modeling and to refine Tonnelier's approximation. Indeed the main advantage of an hybrid system is that it combines fully symbolic and multi-scale resolutions. On the one hand, by using continuous and linear approximations, any refinement is possible: the original system is replaced by piecewise linear parts at as many points as needed to ensure any quality of approximation. On the other hand in each resulting "cell" (corresponding to a state of the hybrid system), the system is fully linear and therefore analytically solvable. These two aspects together enable an analytic analysis of most of any system properties, whatever its complexity is.

There are many possible linearization by parts. For instance, one can build a mesh of the phase space and use multi-dimensional interpolation to define a linear approximation of the system in each cell (simplex) of the mesh, see [4,8,2] for more details. We present a few simultations using this approximation in section 5.3. In this paper, we will instead use another idea: we linearize each equation separately by implicit representation and one-dimensional linearization on each variable, see sections 2.2 and 2.3 (using the latter on the Hodgkin-Huxley model, we actually need fewer hybrid states to prove the desired analytic properties).

We therefore propose a new *continuous* and piecewise affine approximation of the Hodgkin-Huxley model. We implicitly build a hybrid automaton defined by the pieces of the approximation within the phase plane of the dynamical system (see figure 6). Now, in each state, the solutions of our model are analytically computable. Moreover, simulations of this automaton show the good quality of our approximations.

In section 2, we give a reduction from the four-dimensional Hodgkin-Huxley model to a two-dimensional continuous and piecewise affine model. We next linearize both equations separately by way of an implicit representation in sections 2.2 and 2.3 and propose the associated hybrid automaton in section 3. We then fully analyze the model dynamics in section 4 and produce some simulations and comparisons between the Hodgkin-Huxley model and our approximation in section 5.

2   Reduction of the Hodgkin-Huxley Model

In this section we propose a reduction from the Hodgkin-Huxley model to our piecewise affine and continuous model. We combine both FitzHugh-Nagumo [7, §3.1.1] and Tonnelier's approaches [16, §1.4.3] and refine them.

2.1   From Four Dimensions to Two Dimensions

The first step is to reduce the dimension. We first rewrite the activating or inactivating molecule equations in the form $X = -\frac{1}{\tau_X(V)}\left(X - \bar{X}(V)\right)$. Then for a fixed potential V, the variable X approaches the value $\bar{X}(V)$ (its asymptotic

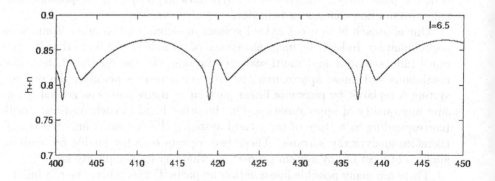

Fig. 1. Simulation of $n + h$ variation with time for a low intensity

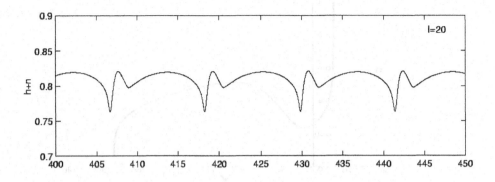

Fig. 2. Simulation of $n + h$ variation with time for a high intensity

value) with a time constant $\tau_X(V)$. Experimental data shows that the variable m always reaches its asymptotic value $\bar{m}(V)$ much faster than the variables n and h do [7, §2.2.1]. The first hypothesis is then that *the m-gate of sodium are instantaneously activated*, so that we can assume $m \approx \bar{m}(V)$. Then, FitzHugh noticed that whatever incoming current intensity, *the n+h quantity remains close to 0.8* as shown on figures 1 and 2 from Jeff Moehlis[1]. We now have a system with only two dimensions : V and n. In the following, we will consider the functions and constants given e.g. in [5]:

$$V_{Na} = 115mV \; ; \; V_K = -12mV \; ; \; V_l = 10.599mV$$

$$\bar{g}_{Na} = 120m\Omega^{-1}cm^{-2} \; ; \; \bar{g}_K = 36m\Omega^{-1}cm^{-2} \; ; \; \bar{g}_l = 0.3m\Omega^{-1}cm^{-2}$$

$$C_M = 1\mu Fcm^{-2} \; ; \; \bar{m}(V) = \frac{25 - V}{25 - V + 40\left(e^{-\frac{7}{4}V + \frac{5}{2}} - e^{-\frac{1}{18}V}\right)}$$

$$\alpha_n(V) = \frac{10 - V}{100\left(e^{\frac{10-V}{10}} - 1\right)} \; ; \; \beta_n(V) = \frac{e^{-\frac{V}{80}}}{8}$$

2.2   The First Equation Approximation

Let φ be the right hand side of the first equation, leaving out the intensity:

$$\varphi \; : \; (V, n) \to -\bar{g}_K n^4 (V - V_K) - \bar{g}_{Na} \bar{m}(V)^3 (0.8 - n)(V - V_{Na}) - \bar{g}_l (V - V_l)$$

Figure 3 shows an example of the value of $\varphi(V, n)$ as an implicit curve $\varphi(V, n) = c$ for some constant c. The implicit curve representing $\varphi(V, n) = c$ (of the form $n = \delta(V)$) has clearly a cubic shape. FitzHugh and Nagumo then proposed to approximate δ by a degree three polynomial p (scaled and shifted to maintain its roots between 0 and 1).

---

[1] http://www.math.princeton.edu/~jmoehlis/APC591/tutorials/tutorial2

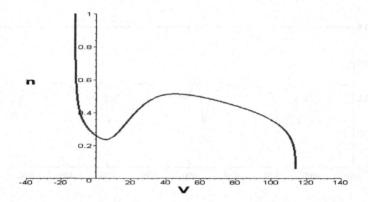

Fig. 3. Implicit representation of the first right hand side, here c=-3

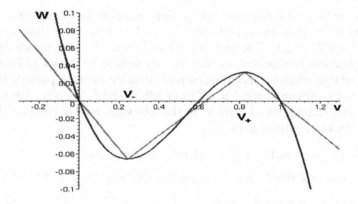

Fig. 4. The piecewise affine p̃ and the degree 3 polynomial approximations of the first right hand side

They obtained the following equation with w corresponding to a scaling and shifting of n, v is a scaling of $C_M V$ and I is modified consequently:

$$\frac{dv}{dt} = v(1-v)(v-a) - w + I = p(v) - w + I, \text{ for } 0 < a < 1. \quad (1)$$

Unfortunately this approximation is still too complex for a fully analytical approach. Consequently we decided to linearize $\varphi(V, n)$ by pieces and care to preserve the continuity of the curve. We also used the previous scalings and shiftings and choose to preserve $(v_-, p(v_-))$ and $(v_+, p(v_+))$, the respective coordinates of the local minimum and maximum of p $(v_- = \frac{a+1-\sqrt{a^2-a+1}}{3}, v_+ = \frac{a+1+\sqrt{a^2-a+1}}{3})$, as well as the two extreme roots. As shown on figure 4, p is now approached by the following continuous and piecewise affine function, p̃ :

$$\tilde{p}(v)=\begin{cases} \frac{p(v_-)}{v_-}v & if\ v<v_- \\ \left[\frac{p(v_+)-p(v_-)}{v_+-v_-}\right]v + \left[p(v_+) - \frac{p(v_+)-p(v_-)}{v_+-v_-}v_+\right] & if\ v_- \le v \le v_+ \quad (2) \\ \frac{p(v_+)}{1-v_+}(1-v) & if\ v>v_+ \end{cases}$$

Finally the first equation of the system becomes: $\frac{dv}{dt} = \tilde{p}(v) - w + I$.

2.3 The Second Equation Approximation

Unlike FitzHugh-Nagumo, we propose to also approach the second equation the same way. Let ψ be the second right hand side, before scaling and shifting: $\psi : (V,n) \to (1-n)\alpha_n(v) - n\beta_n(v)$, for $0 \le n \le 1$. Figure 5 shows the implicit curve $\psi(V,n) = c$, here for $c = 0$. The graph $V = \chi(n)$ of this implicit curve has a logoïde shape.

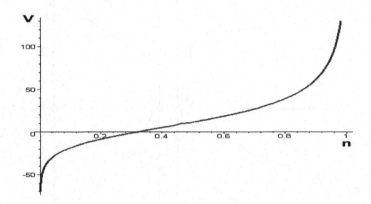

Fig. 5. Implicit representation of the second right hand side

Therefore, we linearize again by pieces and use the scales and shifts of the first approximation. This introduces extra constant factors in this second equation, so that $\psi(V,n)$ is replaced by $bv - \tilde{\chi}(w)$, with $\tilde{\chi}(w)$ the affine approximation chosen: linear for most of its range (indeed equation 1 shows that for no incoming current and with no displacement potential, the neuron must remain inactive, i.e. at $v = 0$ and $I = 0$, $\frac{dv}{dt}$ must be zero and so is w) and with a small slope outside two extreme thresholds w_0 and w_1, as follows:

$$\tilde{\chi}(w) = \begin{cases} \lambda_0(w - w_0) + \gamma w_0 & if\ w \le w_0 \\ \gamma w & if\ w_0 \le w \le w_1 \quad (3) \\ \lambda_1(w - w_1) + \gamma w_1 & if\ w \ge w_1 \end{cases}$$

Finally the second equation of the system becomes: $\frac{dw}{dt} = bv - \tilde{\chi}(w)$.

3   Hybrid Automaton

Now, we have a continuous and piecewise affine system modeling the neuron activity. To study the dynamics of this model (M), we consider it as a hybrid system:

$$\begin{cases} \frac{dv}{dt} = \tilde{p}(v) - w + I \\[2mm] \frac{dw}{dt} = bv - \tilde{\chi}(w) \end{cases} \tag{M}$$

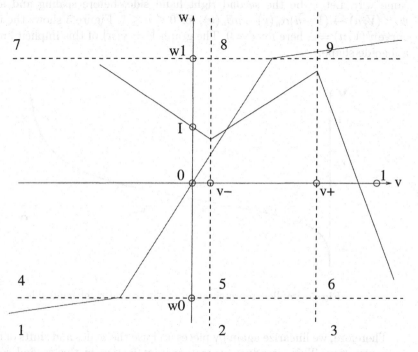

Fig. 6. Hybrid automaton of the continuous and piecewise affine model

As there are 3 different pieces for each equation, this system is a hybrid automaton with nine contiguous states. Inside each state (rectangular cell), the trajectory evolves continuously according to its affine system (defined in sections 2.2, and 2.3). Figure 6 shows these states together with the affine system for a positive incoming current. Next section will study the different possible configurations, and therefore the transitions between the states, depending on the applied DC current I.

4   Analysis of the (M) Model Dynamics

We assume the current intensity I to be constant and positive (we are in the case where the neuron is under an external stimulation). We begin the analysis with the study of the equilibrium points of the system. This enables us to study I as a bifurcation parameter of the system.

4.1   Equilibrium Points

The equilibrium point of the system (M) is an intersection of the two curves induced by the differential equations: (w = p̃(v)+I) and (bv = χ̃(w)).

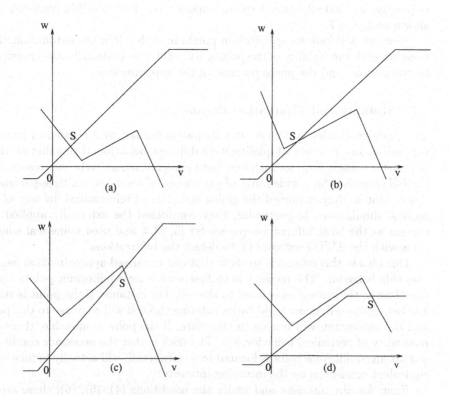

Fig. 7. Some equilibrium points of the system (M) when $I > 0$

In concordance with experimental data, we assume that the linear part of $\tilde{\chi}$ is neither nearly horizontal, nor nearly vertical. Therefore, first, we assume that γ (resp. λ) is small enough (resp. big enough), which means that the middle part of $\tilde{p}$ is is more gentle than the linear part of $\tilde{\chi}$ and steeper than the nearly horizontal parts of $\tilde{\chi}$. Second, as the linear part of $\tilde{\chi}$ is not extremely steep, $\frac{7}{6}w_1 > v_+$. Lastly, we consider that w_0 is negative so that $(v = 0, w = 0)$, the resting point for $I = 0$, is reachable. This together gives us the following conditions:

$$\frac{b}{\lambda_i} < \frac{p(v_+) - p(v_-)}{v_+ - v_-} < \frac{b}{\gamma} \tag{4}$$

$$\frac{b}{\gamma}v_+ < w_1 \tag{5}$$

$$w_0 < 0 \tag{6}$$

By looking at the original system and the graphs of the functions, we see that the experimental data of e.g. [9, Table 3], [10, §3.2.3] or [5, §2] largely fulfill these conditions. Therefore we can consider that they are non-restrictive. Consequently, we actually only have to consider the four possible configurations shown on figure 7.

Now, we will look for equilibrium points in each cell of the automaton. This together with the stability of the points, will enable us to describe the transitions between states and the phase portrait of the approximation.

4.2   Stability and Bifurcation Parameter

The Hodgkin-Huxley system is actually parameterized by a number of parameters and shows a variety of qualitatively different behaviors depending on these parameter values. [5,6], for instance, have explored numerically the dynamics of the HH equations for a wide range of parameter values in the multiple-parameter space, that is, they examined the global structure of bifurcations, by way of numerical simulations. In particular, they considered the externally applied DC current as the basic bifurcation parameter [5, §3.3] and used numerical simulations with the AUTO software [3] to detect the bifurcations.

Our idea in this section is to show that our linearized approximation models also this behavior. The method is to first search for equilibrium points corresponding to the system associated to the cell. For instance, if the point is stable and belongs to cell, many trajectories entering this cell will converge to this point and the automaton will remain in this state. If the point is unstable, there is a possibility of periodical behavior, etc. The trick is that the necessary conditions so that an equilibrium point is located in a certain cell, will actually induce some equivalent conditions on the incoming intensity:

First, for any intensity and under the conditions (4), (5), (6), there are no fixed point in states 1, 2, 3, 7 and 8. In state 4, the equilibrium point verifies the following: $w^* = \frac{p(v_-)}{v_-}v^* + I$; $bv^* = \gamma w^*$. Then a simple computation shows that belonging to cell 4 (i.e. $v^* < v_-$ and $w_0 < w < w_1$)) is equivalent to $I < I_1$ and $I_0 < I < I_1'$, where $I_1 = \frac{\gamma}{b}v_- - p(v_-)$, $I_0 = \frac{\gamma}{b}\left[\frac{b}{\gamma} - \frac{p(v_-)}{v_-}\right]w_0$ and $I_1' = \frac{\gamma}{b}\left[\frac{b}{\gamma} - \frac{p(v_-)}{v_-}\right]w_1$. Now, as $w_0 < 0$, I_0 is negative. Also, using condition 5, we have $I_1 < I_1'$. Moreover, when computing the jacobian of the system at the fixed points one can show that this point is actually stable. So we have the nice condition on I:

– whenever $0 \leq I < I_1$, there exist a stable fixed point inside cell 4 and we are in case (a).

In the same manner, we can show that there exists two other threshold intensities $I_2 = \frac{b}{\gamma}v_+ - p(v_+)$ and $I_3 = w_1 + \frac{p(v_+)}{1-v_+} \left(\frac{\gamma}{b}w_1 - 1\right)$, so that:

– whenever $I_1 < I < I_2$, there exists an unstable fixed point inside cell 5 and we are in case (b).
– whenever $I_2 < I < I_3$, there exists a stable fixed point inside cell 6 and we are the case (c).

And, the last possible fixed points are located in cells 8 and 9 with the condition:

– whenever $I > I_3$ there exists a stable fixed point inside cell 9 and we are in case (d).

In conclusion, we analytically proved that *the neuronal stimulus I (equivalently the externally applied DC current) is a bifurcation parameter* of our linearized system. In the following section we actually prove that when a stable fixed point exists in a cell, the automaton tends to switch to the state containing this fixed point. Therefore the neuron emits one or more spike and then stabilizes at a given potential. On the contrary, in case (b), we will see that the configuration leads to a periodic behavior.

4.3 Phase Portrait

The phase space associated to our model is divided into nine cells defined by the automaton (6). In the previous section, we proved that in cases (a), (c) and (d) the linearized system has only one fixed point. This point is located in a certain cell, so that whenever a trajectory arrives in this cell, it is attracted to the fixed point. Then, the question is: do we have global convergence towards the fixed point ? The idea is to show that for every initial condition (v_i, w_i), the associated trajectory tends to cross the cell containing the fixed point.

Well, as shown on figure 8, the two nullclines of our system divide the plan into four parts. Each one of those four parts has then a different combination of v and w derivative signs. On the smae figure, we show an example trajectory simulated with CONTENT (an environment for continuation and bifurcation analysis of dynamical systems [14]). For instance, in the part defined by ($v' > 0$ and $w' > 0$), the trajectory evolves in concordance, i.e. v and w are increasing. Now, since the third affine part of the v-nullcline decreases in v, the trajectory *must* cross it at some point. When this happens, w keeps increasing while v now starts to decrease as the trajectory is in the ($v' < 0$ and ($w' > 0$) part. The key point is that a trajectory will *always turn anti-clockwise* in the phase space. In conclusion, this together with the analysis of section 4.2 proves the following:

– whenever $0 \leq I < I_1$, all the trajectories collapse to the stable fixed point of cell 4. This correspond to a spike emission followed by a return back to the resting potential.

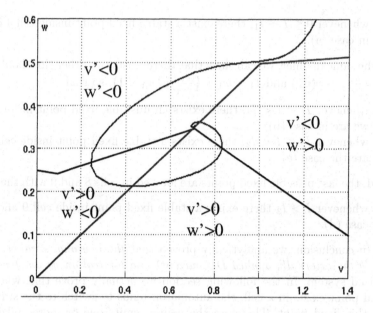

Fig. 8. Trajectory behavior using the sign of the derivatives (here for $I > 0$)

- whenever $I_1 < I < I_2$, all the trajectories keep turning around the unstable fixed point of cell 5. This correspond to oscillations of the potential.
- whenever $I_2 < I$, all the trajectories expand to a stable fixed point inside cell 6, 8 or 9. This correspond to a stimulation by a very high incoming intensity with a spike emission and a stabilization at a high potential.

5   Quality of the Approximation

We now confront the theoretical results of the previous section with the numerical simulations of the Hodgkin-Huxley model. The simulations are done with CONTENT or Matlab. We first produce simulations of the original Hodgkin-Huxley model and compare them with simulations of our hybrid model. Then we present an alternative way of linearizing which gives an even better quality of simulations but no fully analytical analysis yet.

5.1   Hodgkin-Huxley Model

The simulations of the Hodgkin-Huxley model show that there are two main characteristic for the neuronal behavior: a spike solution and a periodic solution shown respectively on figures 9 and 10. Here we used Matlab as the system is too complex for CONTENT (CONTENT had some troubles to draw the trajectory before finding the limit cycle and the trajectory even crossed itself !).

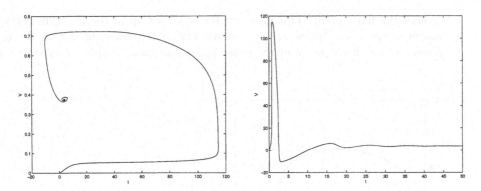

Fig. 9. Excitable state (low incoming intensity) in a simulation of Hodgkin-Huxley model: fixed point in the phase space corresponding to the Spike solution for the displacement current

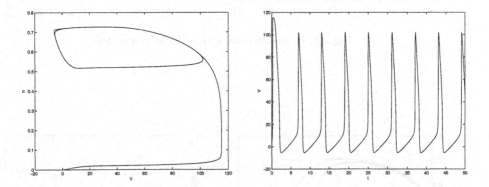

Fig. 10. Periodic state (high incoming intensity) in a simulation of Hodgkin-Huxley model: limit cycle in the phase space corresponding to Oscillations of the displacement current

Next section will produce the simulations of our linearized model for the two equivalent situations.

5.2   The Continuous and Piecewise Affine Model

The analysis of section 4 has shown that our model also produces the two characteristic behaviors: *an excitable state* and *a periodic state*. We here show the good numerical properties of these two states. Indeed, on figure 11, the left simulation is the convergence towards the stable fixed point and the right simulation shows the quality of our approximation of the spike solution. Analytically, within this excitable state (e.g. one of the configurations (a), (c) or (d) holds), the neuron emits actually a finite number of spikes, each one corresponding to a full loop around the fixed point. This does not really shows up in the Hodgkin-Huxley model as the other spikes are very small. On the contrary, in our model, the scales are much smaller and the other spikes are more visible. Moreover our

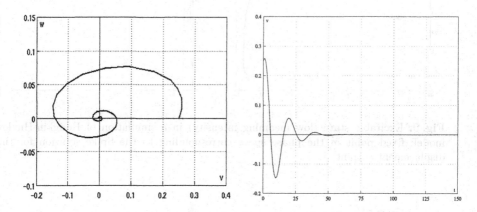

Fig. 11. Excitable state within the hybrid system

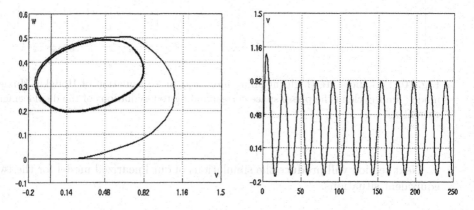

Fig. 12. Periodical state within the hybrid system

model reproduces the main property of the Hodgkin-Huxley model, that is to say the ability to generate oscillations when the current intensity is within an appropriate range. The right simulation of figure 12 shows this oscillatory state, namely the periodic state. Also, the CONTENT simulator can now detect easily the limit cycle, as shown on the left simulation on figure 12.

When comparing with the simulations of the Hodgkin-Huxley model of the previous subsection, we clearly see the good quality of the approximation. Indeed, the continuity and the accuracy of our approximation ensures a good regularity of the new solution.

5.3   Another Linearization for an Hybrid Approach: Multi-dimensional Interpolation

In this section we propose to show the use of multi-dimensional interpolation instead of the scheme of section 2.2 (using implicit representations). The idea is to

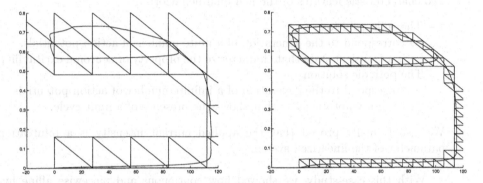

Fig. 13. Matlab Simulations of the periodic state using linear interpolation with 30 and 200 points on the mesh

build a mesh of the phase space (this can be done dynamically as the trajectories evolve). For the Hodgkin-Huxley model we can use either the 4-dimensional or the 2-dimensional version. For the sake of visualization, we produce here figures linearizing in dimension 2. The system of A. Girard [8,2] uses interpolation at each node of the mesh to define a linear approximation of the system in each cell (simplex). Figure 13, shows the periodic trajectory of figure 12 for different mesh sizes. One can check the convergence of the trajectory when the mesh is refining. Indeed, linearization can always be close enough to the original model so that the phase portrait of the linearization reproduces the full original behavior [8]. Also, we are able to automatically compute fixed points or stable and unstable invariants and we can semi-automatically compute e.g. the limit cycles (i.e. a point close enough to the cycle must be provided manually) or even the local attracting sets. Still, this method does not allow us to analyse any property of the system. The study of the Intensity as a bifurcation parameter, for instance, seems still pretty difficult with this approach.

6   Conclusion

The Hodgkin-Huxley model only considers two different ionic species (K+, Na+) and a leakage current. However, even for this four dimensional model, the mathematical analysis is complex and most of the results are numerical. We therefore need simplified models to understand the neuronal dynamics better.

Our approach was first to reduce the dimension of the Hodgkin-Huxley model (using FitzHugh-Nagumo approach) and then to approximate each equation of the reduced system by a continuous and piecewise affine function. Indeed the continuity of our approximation ensures the regularity of the new solution and the piecewise affine approximation allows us to compute the solutions analytically. Both simulations and analytical study of our model bring to the fore the two characteristic features of the neuronal behavior:

- The spike solution
  ↪ correspond to the generation of a finite number of action potentials.
  ↪ is a transient state that characterize the property of neuronal excitability.
- The periodic solution
  ↪ correspond to the generation of a infinite number of action potentials.
  ↪ is an asymptotic state that shows the presence of a limit cycle.

We also formally proved that the applied current intensity is a bifurcation parameter of the linearized system.

With this case-study, we showed how continuous and piecewise affine hybrid systems can be used to analytically compute phase portraits that approach complex dynamical systems with no loss of intrinsic properties. Next step would then be to provide an automatic or quasi-automatic symbolic computation of the phase portrait of piecewise affine systems. Indeed, we are able to automatically compute fixed points or stable and unstable invariants. Still the full automatic analysis is not yet possible as we can only compute e.g. the limit cycles with some manual inputs. Also, a combination of different kind of linearizations would allow multi-resolution and therefore an even higher quality of simulation together with the semi-automatical analysis.

References

1. L.F. Abbott and T. Kepler. Model neurons: From hodgkin-huxley to hopfield. In L. Garrido, editor, *Statistical Mechanics of Neural Networks*, pages 5–18. Springer-Verlag, Berlin, 1990.
2. Eugene Asarin, Thao Dang, and Antoine Girard. Reachability of non-linear systems using conservative approximations. In *Proceedings of the 2003 Hybrid Systems: Computation and Control, Prague, The Czech Republic*, April 2003.
3. E.J. Doedel, R.C. Paffenroth, A.R. Champneys, T.F. Fairgrieve, Yu.A. Kuznetsov, B. Sandstede, and X. Wang. Auto 2000: Continuation and bifurcation software for ordinary differential equations (with homcont). Technical report, California Institute of Technology, February 2001. http://auto2000.sourceforge.net.

4. Jean Della Dora, Aude Maignan, Mihaela Mirica-Ruse, and Sergio Yovine. Hybrid computation. In Bernard Mourrain, editor, *Proceedings of the 2001 International Symposium on Symbolic and Algebraic Computation, London, Ontario, Canada.* ACM Press, New York, July 2001.
5. Hidekazu Fukai, Shinji Doi, Taishin Nomura, and Shunsuke Sato. Hopf bifurcations in multiple-parameter space of the hodgkin-huxley equations i. global organization of bistable periodic solutions. *Biological Cybernetics*, 82:215–222, 2000.
6. Hidekazu Fukai, Shinji Doi, Taishin Nomura, and Shunsuke Sato. Hopf bifurcations in multiple-parameter space of the hodgkin-huxley equations ii. singularity theoretic approach and highly degenerate bifurcations. *Biological Cybernetics*, 82:223–229, 2000.
7. Wulfram Gerstner and Werner M. Kistler. *Spiking Neuron Models: Single Neurons, Populations, Plasticity.* Cambridge University Press, August 2002.
8. Antoine Girard. Approximate solutions of ordinary differential equations using piecewise linear vector fields. In *Proceedings of the 2002 Computer Algebra in Scientific Computing, Big Yalta, Ukraine.* Springer-Verlag, September 2002.
9. A.L. Hodgkin and A.F. Huxley. A quantitative description of membrane current and its application to conduction and excitation in nerve. *Journal of Physiology*, 177:500–544, 1952.
10. Frank C. Hoppensteadt. *An Introduction to the Mathematics of Neurons: Modeling in the Frequency Domain.* Number 14 in Cambridge Studies in Mathematical Biology. Cambridge University Press, 2 edition, 1997.
11. Frank C. Hoppensteadt and Charles S. Peskin. *Modeling and Simulation in Medicine and Life Sciences.* Springer-Verlag, 2 edition, 2002.
12. E.M. Izhikevich. Neural excitability, spiking, and bursting. *International Journal of Bifurcation and Chaos*, 10:1171–1266, 2000.
13. Eugene M. Izhikevich. Resonate-and-fire neurons. *Neural Networks*, 14(6-7):883–894, 2000.
14. Yu.A. Kuznetsov and V.V. Levitin. Content: integrated environment for analysis of dynamical system, 1997. http://www.maths.ex.ac.uk/~hinke/courses/Content.
15. James D. Murray. *Mathematical Biology.* Springer-Verlag, Heidelberg, 3 edition, 1993.
16. Arnaud Tonnelier. *Dynamique non-linéaire et bifurcations en neurosciences mathématiques.* PhD thesis, Université Joseph Fourier, Grenoble, France, October 2001.

Hybrid Control of Parabolic PDEs: Handling Faults of Constrained Control Actuators

Nael H. El-Farra and Panagiotis D. Christofides

Department of Chemical Engineering
University of California
Los Angeles, CA 90095-1592
farra@ucla.edu, pdc@seas.ucla.edu

Abstract. This work proposes a hybrid control methodology that integrates feedback and switching for fault-tolerant constrained control of linear parabolic partial differential equations (PDEs) for which the spectrum of the spatial differential operator can be partitioned into a finite "slow" set and an infinite stable "fast" complement. Modal decomposition techniques are initially used to derive a finite-dimensional system (set of ordinary differential equations (ODEs) in time) that captures the dominant dynamics of the PDE. The ODE system is then used as the basis for the integrated synthesis, via Lyapunov techniques, of a stabilizing nonlinear feedback controller together with a switching law that orchestrates the switching between the admissible control actuator configurations, based on their constrained regions of stability, in a way that respects actuator constraints and maintains closed-loop stability in the event of actuator failure. Precise conditions that guarantee stability of the constrained closed-loop PDE system under actuator switching are provided. The proposed method is applied to the problem of stabilizing an unstable, spatially unifrom steady-state of a linear parabolic PDE under constraints and actuator failures.

1 Introduction

The study of distributed systems in control is motivated by the fundamentally distributed nature of the control problems arising in many chemical and physical systems, such as transport-reaction processes and fluid flows. The distinguishing feature of distributed control problems is that they involve the regulation of distributed variables by using spatially-distributed control actuators and measurement sensors. Several classes of spatially-distributed processes (such as transport-reaction processes) are naturally modeled by parabolic PDE systems that involve spatial differential operators whose spectrum can be partitioned into a finite slow part and an infinite stable fast complement [12]. The traditional approach to the control of parabolic PDEs involves the application of Galerkin's method to the PDE system to derive ODE systems that describe the dynamics of the dominant (slow) modes of the PDE system, which are subsequently used as the basis for the synthesis of finite-dimensional controllers (e.g., [2,16,

O. Maler and A. Pnueli (Eds.): HSCC 2003, LNCS 2623, pp. 172–187, 2003.

6]). A potential drawback of this approach is that the number of modes that should be retained to derive an ODE system that yields the desired degree of approximation may be very large, leading to complex controller design and high dimensionality of the resulting controllers.

Motivated by this, significant recent work has focused on the synthesis of nonlinear low-order controllers on the basis of ODE models obtained through combination of Galerkin's method with approximate inertial manifolds (see the recent book [5] for details and references). In addition to this work, other advances in control of PDE systems include controller design based on the infinite-dimensional system and subsequent use of approximation theory to compute low-order finite dimensional compensators [3], results on distributed control using generalized invariants [15] and concepts from passivity and thermodynamics [18], analysis and control of parabolic PDE systems with actuator saturation [7], and the stabilization of PDE systems using boundary control [14,4].

While the above efforts have led to the development of a number of systematic methods for distributed controller design, these methods focus exclusively on the classical control paradigm, where a fixed control structure (single feedback law, fixed actuator/sensor spatial arrangement) is used to achieve ceratin control objectives (see Fig.1a). There are many practical situations, however, where it is desirable, and sometimes even necessary, to consider a hybrid control paradigm, such as the one depicted in Fig.1b, where the control system consists of a family of controller configurations (e.g., a family of feedback laws and/or a family of actuator/sensor spatial arrangements) together with a higher-level supervisor that uses logic to orchestrate switching between these control configurations. An example, where consideration of hybrid control is necessary, is the problem of control actuator failure. In this case, upon the detection of a fault in the operating actuator configuration, it is often necessary to switch to an alternative, well-functioning actuator configuration, with a different spatial placement of the actuators, in order to preserve closed-loop stability. Switching between spatially distributed actuators in this case provides a means for fault-tolerant control. Due to the use of logic-based switching and the variable structure of the control system, the dynamics of the control system in the hybrid paradigm are an intermix of discrete and continuous components. This is in contrast to the purely continuous dynamics in the classical control paradigm. Furthermore, whereas a fixed control structure can at best achieve a tradeoff between multiple control objectives in classical control, switching in hybrid control allows the accommodation and reconciliation of multiple, possibly conflicting, control objectives.

Motivated by these considerations, this work proposes a hybrid control methodology which integrates feedback and switching for the constrained stabilization of linear of parabolic PDEs. The central idea is the integrated synthesis, via Lyapunov techniques, of a stabilizing nonlinear feedback controller together with a stabilizing switching law that orchestrates the switching between the admissible control actuator configurations, in a way that respects actuator constraints, accommodates inherently conflicting control objectives, and guarantees

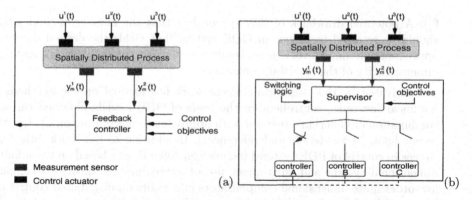

Fig. 1. Comparison between the control structures arising in (a) the classical control, and (b) the hybrid control paradigms of spatially distributed systems.

closed-loop stability at the same time. The rest of the paper is organized as follows. In section 2, we present some mathematical preliminaries to characterize the class of parabolic PDEs considered, and formulate precisely the switching problem. Then in section 3, we initially use modal decomposition to derive an ODE system that captures the dominant dynamics of the PDE. This ODE system is then used as the basis for the integrated synthesis of the feedback and the switching laws. Precise conditions that guarantee stability of the constrained closed-loop PDE system under actuator switching are provided. Finally, the proposed hybrid control method is applied in section 4, through computer simulations, to the problem of fault-tolerant stabilization of the unstable steady-state of a linearized model of a diffusion-reaction process. The proposed hybrid control method has also been extended to the nonlinear case in [8] and applied in [11] to the problem of fault-tolerant constrained stabilization of the Kuramoto-Sivashinsky equation, a fourth-order PDE that describes wavy behavior.

2   Preliminaries

2.1   Class of Systems

In this work, we focus on control of linear parabolic PDEs of the form:

$$\frac{\partial \bar{x}}{\partial t} = b\frac{\partial^2 \bar{x}}{\partial z^2} + \alpha\bar{x} + w\sum_{i=1}^{l}b_i(z)u_i \tag{1}$$

subject to the boundary conditions:

$$\bar{x}(0,t) = 0, \ \ \bar{x}(\pi,t) = 0 \tag{2}$$

and the initial condition:

$$\bar{x}(z,0) = \bar{x}_0(z) \tag{3}$$

where $\bar{x}(z,t) \in \mathbb{R}$ denotes the state variable, $z \in [0, \pi] \subset \mathbb{R}$ is the spatial coordinate, $t \in [0, \infty)$ is the time, $u_i \in [-u_i^{max}, u_i^{max}] \subset \mathbb{R}$ denotes the i-th constrained input, and u_i^{max} is a positive real numbers. $\dfrac{\partial^2 \bar{x}}{\partial z^2}$ denotes the second-order spatial derivative of $\bar{x}$; α, b, and w are constant real numbers with $b > 0$, and $\bar{x}_0(z)$ is the initial condition. The function $b_i(z)$ is a known smooth function of z which describes how the control action $u_i(t)$ is distributed in the finite interval $[0, \pi]$. Whenever the control action enters the system at a single point z_0, with $z_0 \in [0, \pi]$ (i.e. point actuation), the function $b_i(z)$ is taken to be nonzero in a finite spatial interval of the form $[z_0 - \mu, z_0 + \mu]$, where μ is a small positive real number, and zero elsewhere in $[0, \pi]$. Throughout the paper, the notation $|\cdot|$ will be used to denote the standard Euclidean norm in $\mathbb{R}^m$, while the notations $|\cdot|_2$ and $\|\cdot\|_2$ will be used to denote the L_2 norms (as defined in Eq.4 below) associated with a finite-dimensional and infinite dimensional Hilbert spaces, respectively. Finally, we recall the definition of a class $\mathcal{KL}$ function. In particular, a function $\beta(s,t)$ is said to be of class $\mathcal{KL}$ if, for each fixed t, the function $\beta(s, \cdot)$ is continuous, increasing, and zero at zero and, for each fixed s, the function $\beta(\cdot, t)$ is non-increasing and tends to zero at infinity.

For a precise characterization of the class of PDEs considered in this work, we formulate the PDE of Eq.1 as an infinite dimensional system in the Hilbert space $\mathcal{H}([0, \pi]; \mathbb{R})$, with $\mathcal{H}$ being the space of functions defined on $[0, \pi]$ that satisfy the boundary conditions of Eq.2, with inner product and norm:

$$(\omega_1, \omega_2) = \int_0^\pi (\omega_1(z), \omega_2(z))_{\mathbb{R}} dz, \|\omega_1\|_2 = (\omega_1, \omega_1)^{\frac{1}{2}} \qquad (4)$$

where ω_1, ω_2 are two elements of $\mathcal{H}([0, \pi]; \mathbb{R})$ and the notation $(\cdot, \cdot)_{\mathbb{R}}$ denotes the standard inner product in $\mathbb{R}$. Defining the state function x on $\mathcal{H}([0, \pi]; \mathbb{R})$ as:

$$x(t) = \bar{x}(z,t), \qquad t > 0, \qquad z \in [0, \pi], \qquad (5)$$

the operator $\mathcal{A}$ as:

$$\mathcal{A}x = b\frac{\partial^2 \bar{x}}{\partial z^2} + \alpha\bar{x}, \quad x \in D(\mathcal{A}) = \{x \in H^2(0, \pi) : \bar{x}(0, t) = \bar{x}(\pi, t) = 0\} \qquad (6)$$

where $H^2(0, \pi)$ is a Sobolev space, and the input operator as:

$$\mathcal{B}u = w\sum_{i=1}^{l} b_i u_i \qquad (7)$$

the system of Eqs.1-2-3 takes the form:

$$\dot{x} = \mathcal{A}x + \mathcal{B}u, \qquad x(0) = x_0 \qquad (8)$$

where $x_0 = \bar{x}_0(z)$. For $\mathcal{A}$, the eigenvalue problem is defined as:

$$\mathcal{A}\phi_j = \lambda_j \phi_j, \qquad j = 1, \dots, \infty \qquad (9)$$

where λ_j denotes an eigenvalue and ϕ_j denotes an eigenfunction. The eigenvalue problem takes the form

$$b\frac{\partial^2 \phi_j}{\partial z^2} + \alpha\phi_j = \lambda_j\phi_j \tag{10}$$

subject to

$$\phi_j(0) = \phi_j(\pi) = 0 \tag{11}$$

where $b > 0$. A direct computation of the solution of the above eigenvalue problem yields

$$\lambda_j = \alpha - bj^2, \quad \phi_j(z) = \sqrt{\frac{2}{\pi}}sin(j\,z), \quad j = 1,\ldots,\infty \tag{12}$$

The spectrum of $\mathcal{A}$, $\sigma(\mathcal{A})$, is defined as the set of all eigenvalues of $\mathcal{A}$, i.e. $\sigma(\mathcal{A}) = \{\lambda_1, \lambda_2, \cdots\}$. From the expression for the eigenvalues, it is clear that all the eigenvalues of $\mathcal{A}$ are real, and that, for a given α and b, only a finite number of unstable eigenvalues exists, and the distance between two consecutive eigenvalues (i.e., λ_j and λ_{j+1}) increases as j increases. Furthermore, $\sigma(\mathcal{A})$ can be partitioned as $\sigma(\mathcal{A}) = \sigma_1(\mathcal{A})\bigcup\sigma_2(\mathcal{A})$, where $\sigma_1(\mathcal{A}) = \{\lambda_1, \cdots, \lambda_m\}$ contains the first m (with m finite) "slow" (possibly unstable) eigenvalues and $\sigma_2(\mathcal{A}) = \{\lambda_{m+1}, \lambda_{m+2}, \cdots\}$ contains the remaining "fast" stable eigenvalues. This implies that the dominant dynamics of the PDE can be described by a finite-dimensional system, and motivates the use of modal decomposition in section 3.1 to derive a finite-dimensional system that captures the dominant (slow) dynamics of the PDE.

It should be noted here that, while our development in this section has considered only a single PDE (for the purpose of simplifying the notation and the solution of the resulting eigenvalue problem), the results of this paper can be extended to systems with multiple parabolic PDEs.

2.2   Problem Formulation

Consider the spatially distributed system of Eq.1, where the control inputs, u_i, are constrained in the interval $[-u_i^{max}, u_i^{max}]$, and assume that N (with N finite) different spatial arrangements (configurations) of the control actuators are available for possible use in feedback control. The notation $\bar{z}_k$, where $k \in \{1, \cdots, N\}$, is used to represent the vector of spatial locations of the actuators in the k-th configuration. Only one actuator configuration can be active for control, at any time instance, while the rest are kept dormant. To ensure controllability of the system, we allow only a finite number of switches over any finite interval of time. The problem of interest is how to coordinate switching between the different actuator configurations in a way that respects the actuator constraints and guarantees closed-loop stability. To address this problem, we formulate the following three objectives:

1. Initially, modal decomposition is employed to derive a finite-dimensional approximation that captures the dominant dynamics of the infinite-dimensional system of Eq.8.

2. Next, the finite-dimensional system is used as the basis for the synthesis, via Lyapunov-based control techniques [13], of a bounded nonlinear controller that enforces asymptotic stability and provides an explicit characterization of the constrained stability region, associated with each control actuator configuration.
3. Finally, a switching rule is derived to orchestrate the transition between the various actuator configurations. The switching law determines which actuator configuration can be activated at a given moment, i.e. the value of the index k as a function of time.

3   Constrained Hybrid Control of Parabolic PDEs

3.1   Modal Decomposition

In this section, we apply standard modal decomposition to the system of Eq.8 to derive a finite-dimensional system. Let $\mathcal{H}_s$, $\mathcal{H}_f$ be modal subspaces of $\mathcal{A}$, defined as $\mathcal{H}_s = span\{\phi_1, \phi_2, \ldots, \phi_m\}$ and $\mathcal{H}_f = span\{\phi_{m+1}, \phi_{m+2}, \ldots\}$ (the existence of $\mathcal{H}_s$, $\mathcal{H}_f$ follows from the properties of $\mathcal{A}$). Defining the orthogonal projection operators P_s and P_f such that $x_s = P_s x$, $x_f = P_f x$, the state x of the system of Eq.8 can be decomposed as:

$$x = x_s + x_f = P_s x + P_f x \tag{13}$$

Applying P_s and P_f to the system of Eq.8 and using the above decomposition for x, the system of Eq.8 can be written in the following equivalent form:

$$\frac{dx_s}{dt} = \mathcal{A}_s x_s + \mathcal{B}_s u$$
$$\frac{\partial x_f}{\partial t} = \mathcal{A}_f x_f + \mathcal{B}_f u \tag{14}$$
$$x_s(0) = P_s x(0) = P_s x_0, \quad x_f(0) = P_f x(0) = P_f x_0$$

where $\mathcal{A}_s = P_s \mathcal{A}$, $\mathcal{B}_s = P_s \mathcal{B}$, $\mathcal{A}_f = P_f \mathcal{A}$, $\mathcal{B}_f = P_f \mathcal{B}$, and the partial derivative notation in $\frac{\partial x_f}{\partial t}$ is used to denote that the state x_f belongs to an infinite-dimensional space. In the above system, $\mathcal{A}_s$ is a diagonal matrix of dimension $m \times m$ of the form $\mathcal{A}_s = diag\{\lambda_j\}$, and $\mathcal{A}_f$ is an unbounded differential operator which is exponentially stable (following from the fact that $\lambda_{m+1} < 0$ and the selection of $\mathcal{H}_s$, $\mathcal{H}_f$). From the above modal decomposition procedure, we have the following finite-dimensional system

$$\frac{dx_s}{dt} = \mathcal{A}_s x_s + \mathcal{B}_s u \tag{15}$$

which describes the evolution of the m slow modes of the infinite-dimensional system.

Remark 1. We note that the above model reduction procedure which led to the finite-dimensional system of Eq.15 can also be used, when empirical eigenfunctions of the system of Eq.1 computed through Karhunen-Loeve (KL) expansion are used as basis functions in $\mathcal{H}_s$ and $\mathcal{H}_f$ instead of the eigenfunctions of $\mathcal{A}$. For approaches on how to compute empirical eigenfunctions through KL expansion, the reader is referred to [1].

3.2   Integrating Feedback and Switching

Having obtained a finite-dimensional model that describes the dominant dynamics of the infinite-dimensional system, we proceed in this section to describe the proposed procedure for designing the hybrid control system. To this end, and since our objective is the stabilization of the infinite-dimensional, we assume, for simplicity, that the number of inputs is equal to the number of slow modes (i.e. $l = m$). Though not discussed in this paper explicitly, the results can be generalized to address the problem of reference-input tracking. For a clear presentation of our results, we consider the equivalent representation of the slow system of Eq.15 in terms of the evolution of the amplitudes of the eigenmodes. This finite-dimensional ODE system is given by

$$\dot{a}_s(t) = F a_s(t) + G(\bar{z}_k) u(t) \tag{16}$$

where $a_s(t) = [a_1(t) \cdots a_m(t)]^T \in \mathbb{R}^m$, $a_i(t)$ is the amplitude of the i-th eigenmode, $x_s(t) = \sum_{j=1}^{m} a_j(t)\phi_j$, $(x_s(t), \phi_j) = a_j(t)(\phi_j, \phi_j)$, F is an $m \times m$ diagonal matrix of the form $F = diag\{\lambda_j\}$, and $\bar{G}$ is an $m \times m$ matrix whose (i, k)-th element is given by $G_{ik} = \phi_i(\bar{z}_k)$. Using a quadratic Lyapunov function of the form $V = a_s^T \Phi a_s$, where Φ is a positive-definite symmetric matrix that satisfies the Riccati inequality

$$F^T \Phi + \Phi F - \Phi G G^T \Phi < 0 \tag{17}$$

we synthesize the following bounded nonlinear feedback law [13]

$$u = -r(a_s, u_{max}^k, \bar{z}_k) \left(L_G V\right)^T (\bar{z}_k) \tag{18}$$

where

$$r(a_s, u_{max}^k, \bar{z}_k) = \frac{L_F^* V + \sqrt{(L_F^* V)^2 + (u_{max}^k |(L_G V)^T (\bar{z}_k)|)^4}}{|(L_G V)^T (\bar{z}_k)|^2 \left[1 + \sqrt{1 + (u_{max}^k |(L_G V)^T (\bar{z}_k)|)^2}\right]} \tag{19}$$

where $\bar{z}_k = [\bar{z}_{k_1} \ \bar{z}_{k_2} \ \cdots \ \bar{z}_{k_m}]^T$, $k \in \{1, \cdots, N\}$, $L_F^* V = a_s^T (F^T \Phi + \Phi F) a_s + \rho |a_s|^2$, $\rho > 0$, $L_G V(\bar{z}_k) = 2 a_s^T \Phi G(\bar{z}_k)$. The notation u_{max}^k is used to indicate the magnitude of actuator constraints associated with the k-th actuator configuration. This quantity is allowed to vary from one configuration to another. The scalar function $r(\cdot)$ in Eqs.18-19 can be thought of as a nonlinear gain of the $L_G V$ controller. This Lyapunov-based gain, which depends on both the magnitude of actuator constraints, u_{max}^k, and the spatial arrangement of the actuators, $\bar{z}_k$, is shaped in a way that guarantees constraint satisfaction and asymptotic closed-loop stability within a well-characterized region in the state space given in Theorem 1 below.

We are now ready to state the main result of this work. Theorem 1 below provides both the state feedback control law (see the discussion in remark 5 for output feedback controller design and implementation) as well as the necessary switching law, and states precise conditions that guarantee closed-loop stability in the switched closed-loop infinite-dimensional system.

Theorem 1. *1. Consider the system of Eq.16 under the feedback control law of Eqs.18-19 and let δ_s^k be a positive real number such that the compact set $\Omega(u_{max}^k, \bar{z}_k) = \{a_s \in \mathbb{R}^m : a_s^T \Phi a_s \le \delta_s^k\}$ is the largest invariant set embedded within the region described by the following inequality*

$$L_F^* V \le u_{max}^k |(L_G V)^T (\bar{z}_k)| \tag{20}$$

Without loss of generality, assume that $\bar{z}_{k(0)} = \bar{z}_1$ and $a_s(0) \in \Omega(u_{max}^1, \bar{z}_1)$. If, at any given time T, the condition

$$a_s(T) \in \Omega(u_{max}^j, \bar{z}_j) \tag{21}$$

holds, for some $j \in \{1, \cdots, N\}$, then setting $\bar{z}_{k(T+)} = \bar{z}_j$ guarantees that the switched closed-loop system of Eq.15-18-19 is asymptotically stable.

2. Consider the parabolic PDE of Eq.1 under the control law of Eq.18-19 and the switching law of Eq.21. Let Θ_k be the set of all $x_s(0)$ for which $a_s(0) \in \Omega(u_{max}^k, \bar{z}_k)$. Then given any $x_s(0) \in \Theta_k$, for any $k \in \{1, \cdots, N\}$, and given any $x_f(0)$, the infinite-dimensional switched closed-loop system is asymptotically stable.

Remark 2. Owing to the dependence of the input operator $\mathcal{B}_s$ in Eq.15 on the spatial locations of the control actuators (through the actuator distribution functions $b_i(z)$), the inequality of Eq.20 is parameterized by the actuator locations and can therefore be used to explicitly identify the admissible control actuator configurations ($\bar{z}_k$) for which stability of the constrained closed-loop system is guaranteed. For a given actuator configuration (fixed $\bar{z}_k$), the inequality of Eq.20 describes the state space region where the control action satisfies the constraints and enforces the negative-definiteness of the time-derivative of the Lyapunov function along the trajectories of the finite-dimensional closed-loop system. By computing the largest invariant set, $\Omega(u_{max}^k, \bar{z}_k)$, within this region, we obtain an estimate of the stability region associated with each actuator configuration. The requirement that the set $\Omega(u_{max}^k, \bar{z}_k)$ be invariant is needed to ensure that at no time do the closed-loop trajectories violate Eq.20, under any actuator configuration.

Remark 3. Due to the linear structure of the system of Eq.8, and the absence of any nonlinear terms, the only source of coupling between the slow and fast subsystems of Eq.14 (obtained through the application of modal decomposition to the system of Eq.8) is the control input, $u(\cdot)$, which is shared by both subsystems. This fact, together with the fact that the control input is, by design, a function of the slow states only, implies that the evolution of the x_s states, in the closed-loop system, is independent of x_f (note however that the evolution of x_f depends on x_s). An important consequence of this outcome is the fact that the stability region obtained (for each actuator configuration) on the basis of the finite-dimensional system of Eq.15 is exactly the same as the stability region for the slow subsystem in the infinite-dimensional closed-loop system. In other words, the set of initial states that stabilize the constrained switched finite-dimensional closed-loop system of Eq.15 (for a given actuator configuration) is the same as the set of initial slow states needed to stabilize the infinite-dimensional switched closed-loop system of Eq.14 (for the same actuator configuration). It should be noted here that this result is different from its counterpart in the nonlinear case [8], where the dependence of the closed-loop x_s-subsystem on x_f introduces a discrepancy (which can nonetheless be made arbitrarily small) between the stability regions for the finite-dimensional closed-loop slow system (obtained through Galerkin's method) and the slow subsystem of the infinite-dimensional closed-loop system.

Remark 4. The switching law of Eq.21 orchestrates the transition between the various actuator configurations in a way that respects the constraints and guards against any potential instability that may arise due to switching. The basic problem here owes to the limitations imposed by constraints on the set of feasible initial conditions that can be used, for a given actuator configuration, to stabilize the closed-loop system. Different actuator configurations possess different stability regions and, depending on where the state trajectory is at a given moment in time, a switch from one configuration to another may land the state outside the stability region associated with the target configuration, thus leading to instability. To guard against this possibility, the switching law of Eq.21 tracks the temporal evolution of the slow state and allows switching to another actuator configuration only when the state is within the corresponding stability region for that configuration. This determines, implicitly, the earliest safe switching time. This idea of connecting the switching logic with the stability regions was first proposed in [9] for constrained control of switched nonlinear systems. Extensions of this work to switched systems with uncertainty can be found in [10].

4   Simulation Example

In this section, we demonstrate through computer simulations how the concept of coupling feedback and actuator-switching can be used to deal with the problem of constrained stabilization of parabolic PDEs in the presence of actuator failures.

To this end, consider the following parabolic PDE

$$\frac{\partial x}{\partial t} = \frac{\partial^2 x}{\partial z^2} + \left(\beta_T e^{-\gamma}\gamma - \beta_U\right) x + \beta_U b(z)u(t)$$

$$x(0,t) = 0, \quad x(\pi,t) = 0, \quad x(z,0) = x_0(z)$$

(22)

which represents a linearized model of a typical diffusion-reaction process, around the zero steady-state (see [7] for some results on constrained control of the non-linear model), where x denotes the dimensionless temperature in the reactor, β_T denotes a dimensionless heat of reaction, γ denotes a dimensionless activation energy, β_U denotes a dimensionless heat transfer coefficient, $u(t)$ denotes the manipulated input (the temperature of the cooling medium) and $b(z)$ is the corresponding actuator distribution function. The following typical values are given to the process parameters: $\beta_T = 50.0$, $\beta_U = 2.0$, $\gamma = 4.0$. For these values, the operating steady state $x(z,t) = 0$ is an unstable one, as can be seen from Fig.2. The control objective is to stabilize the reactor temperature profile at this

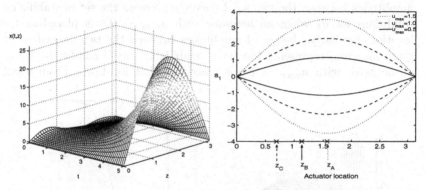

Fig. 2. (Left) Open-loop temperature profile showing the instability of the $x(t,z) = 0$ steady-state. (Right) Stability regions as a function of actuator location for $u_{max} = 1.5$ (dotted), $u_{max} = 1.0$ (dashed), and $u_{max} = 0.5$ (solid).

unstable steady state by manipulating the temperature of the cooling medium, subject to hard constraints. The eigenvalue problem for the spatial differential operator of the process can be solved analytically and its solution is

$$\lambda_j = 1.66 - j^2, \quad \phi_j(z) = \sqrt{\frac{2}{\pi}}sin(j\,z), \quad j = 1,\ldots,\infty$$

(23)

For this system, we consider the first eigenvalue as the dominant one and use standard modal decomposition to derive an ODE that describes the temporal evolution of the amplitude, $a_1(t)$, of the first eigenmode, where $x_s(t) = a_1(t)\phi_1(z)$. This ODE is used for the synthesis of the controller, using Eq.18-19, which is then implemented on a 30-th order Galerkin discretization of the parabolic PDE of Eq.22 (higher order discretizations led to identical results).

In order to demonstrate the utility of the switching scheme proposed in Theorem 1 for dealing with actuator failures, we consider the following problem where three point control actuators, A, B, and C, located at $z_A = 0.5\pi$, $z_B = 0.36\pi$, and $z_C = 0.22\pi$, respectively, are available for stabilization. In practice, this can be realized through multiple cooling systems, distributed along the length of the reactor (similar to the idea of having multiple heating zones discussed in [16]). The three actuators have different constraints of $u_{max_A} = 1.5$ $u_{max_B} = 0.5$ and $u_{max_C} = 1.0$. Only one actuator can be active at any given moment while the other two remain dormant. The question is how to choose the alternative or "backup" actuator, in order to maintain closed-loop stability, in the event that the operating actuator fails.

Using Eq.20 with $\rho = 0.02$, the stability region for $u_{max} = 1.5$ (dotted line), the stability region for $u_{max} = 0.5$ (solid line) and the stability region for $u_{max} = 1.0$ (dashed line) are computed as functions of actuator location and shown in Fig.2 (right plot). To simplify the presentation of our results, we plot in Fig.2 (right) the variation of the set of admissible initial conditions for the amplitude of the first eigenmode, $a_1(0)$, with actuator location (note that $x_s(0) = a_1(0)\phi_1(z)$). For example, for a given actuator location, the set of amplitudes between the two solid curves represents the set of stabilizing initial conditions for a_1 when an actuator with $u_{max} = 0.5$ is placed at the given location. Similarly, the set of amplitudes between the two dashed curves, at a given location, represents the set of stabilizing initial conditions for a_1 when an actuator with $u_{max} = 1.0$ is placed at that location. From Fig.2 (right

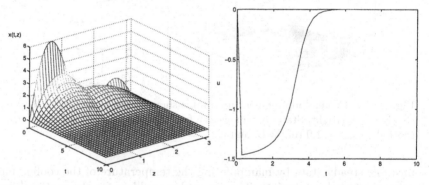

Fig. 3. Closed-loop temperature profile (top) and manipulated input profile (bottom) when actuator A ($z = 0.5\pi$, $u_{max} = 1.5$) is used, starting at $a_1(0) = 3.0$.

plot), it is easy to see that for an initial condition $a_1(0) = 3.0$, only actuator A ($z_A = 0.5\pi$, $u_{max} = 1.5$) can be used initially since the initial condition lies outside the stability regions for both actuator B and actuator C. Fig.3 depicts the corresponding closed-loop state (top) and manipulated input (bottom) profiles when actuator A is used (with no actuator failures). As expected the bounded controller stabilizes the closed-loop system at the zero steady state. Now, suppose that sometime after startup, say at $t = 2.4$, a fault occurs in actuator A and it becomes necessary to switch to an alternative actuator to maintain closed-loop stability. Without using the switching logic of Theorem 1, it is not clear whether actuator B or C should be activated at this time. Fig.4 depicts the resulting closed-loop state (top) and manipulated input (bottom) profiles when actuator B is switched in at the time of the failure of actuator A. It is clear in this case that the controller is unable to stabilize the closed-loop system at the desired steady-state. Note that the control action stays saturated at the lower

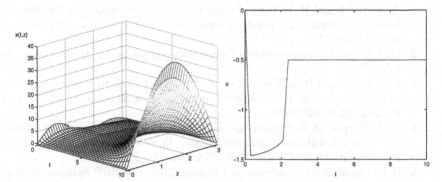

Fig. 4. Closed-loop temperature profile (top) and manipulated input profile (bottom) when actuator A ($u_{max} = 1.5$, $z_A = 0.5\pi$) fails at $t = 2.4$ and actuator B ($u_{max} = 0.5$, $z_B = 0.36\pi$) is activated in its place.

constraint for actuator C. In contrast, when the switching law of Theorem 1 is implemented, we track the evolution of $a_1(t)$ over time and find that, at the time of the failure of actuator A, we have $a_1(2.4) = 1.4$, i.e. the state is inside the stability region of actuator C and outside the stability region of actuator B. Based on this, we decide to switch to actuator B. Fig.5 depicts the resulting closed-loop state (top) and manipulated input (bottom) profiles when actuator C is switched in at $t = 2.4$. As expected, activation of actuator C preserves closed-loop stability at the desired steady-state.

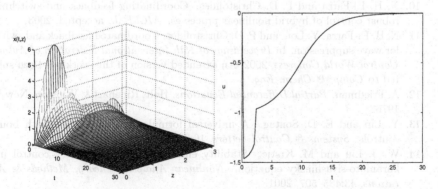

Fig. 5. Closed-loop temperature profile (left) and manipulated input profile (right) when actuator A fails at $t = 2.4$ and actuator C ($u_{max} = 1.0$, $z_C = 0.22\pi$) is activated in its place.

Acknowledgements. Financial support from the Air Force Office of Scientific Research and the National Science Foundation is gratefully acknowledged.

References

1. J. A. Atwell and B. B. King. Proper orthogonal decomposition for reduced basis feedback controllers for parabolic equations. *Mathematical and Computer Modeling*, 33:1–19, 2001.
2. M. J. Balas. Feedback control of linear diffusion processes. *Int. J. Contr.*, 29:523–533, 1979.
3. J. A. Burns and B. B. King. A reduced basis approach to the design of low-order feedback controllers for nonlinear continuous systems. *Journal of Vibration and Control*, 4:297–323, 1998.
4. C. A. Byrnes, D. S. Gilliam, and V. I. Shubov. Global lyapunov stabilization of a nonlinear distributed parameter system. In *Proc. of 33rd IEEE Conference on Decision and Control*, pages 1769–1774, Orlando, FL, 1994.
5. P. D. Christofides. *Nonlinear and Robust Control of PDE Systems: Methods and Applications to Transport-Reaction Processes*. Birkhäuser, Boston, 2001.
6. R. F. Curtain. Finite-dimensional compensator design for parabolic distributed systems with point sensors and boundary input. *IEEE Trans. Automat. Contr.*, 27:98–104, 1982.
7. N. H. El-Farra, A. Armaou, and P. D. Christofides. Analysis and control of palabolic PDE systems with input constraints. *Automatica, to appear*, 2003.
8. N. H. El-Farra and P. D. Christofides. Hybrid control of parabolic PDE systems. In *Proceedings of 41st IEEE Conference on Decision and Control*, pages 216–222, Las Vegas, NV, 2002. An extended version of this work has been submitted to *Comp. & Chem. Eng.*
9. N. H. El-Farra and P. D. Christofides. Switching and feedback laws for control of constrained switched nonlinear systems. In *Lecture Notes in Computer Science, Proc. of 5th Intr. Workshop on Hybrid Systems: Computation and Control*, volume 2289, pages 164–178, Tomlin, C. J. and M. R. Greenstreet Eds., Berlin, Germany: Springer-Verlag, 2002.
10. N. H. El-Farra and P. D. Christofides. Coordinating feedback and switching for robust control of hybrid nonlinear processes. *AIChE J., accepted*, 2003.
11. N. H. El-Farra, Y. Lou, and P. D. Christofides. Coordinated feedback and switching for wave suppression. In *Proceedings of 15th International Federation of Automatic Control World Congress*, 2002. An extended version of this work has been submitted to *Comp. & Chem. Eng.*
12. A. Friedman. *Partial Differential Equations*. Holt, Rinehart & Winston, New York, 1976.
13. Y. Lin and E. D. Sontag. A universal formula for stabilization with bounded controls. *Systems & Control Letters*, 16:393–397, 1991.
14. W. J. Liu and M. Krstic. Stability enhancement by boundary control in the kuramoto-sivashinsky equation. *Nonlinear Analysis: Theory, Methods & Applications*, 43:485–507, 2001.
15. A. Palazoglu and A. Karakas. Control of nonlinear distributed parameter systems using generalized invariants. *Automatica*, 36:697–703, 2000.
16. W. H. Ray. *Advanced Process Control*. McGraw-Hill, New York, 1981.

17. P. K. C. Wang. Asymptotic stability of distributed parameter systems with feedback controls. *IEEE Trans. Automat. Contr.*, 11:46–54, 1966.
18. E. B. Ydstie and A. A. Alonso. Process systems and passivity via the Clausius-Planck inequality. *Syst. & Contr. Lett.*, 30:253–264, 1997.

5   Appendix

Proof (of Theorem 1).
Part 1: Consider the finite-dimensional closed-loop system of Eqs.16-18-19. Using a standard Lyapunov argument, one can show that, for each actuator configuration, the time-derivative of the Lyapunov function satisfies

$$\dot{V} \leq \frac{-\rho|a_s|^2}{\left[1 + \sqrt{1 + (u_{max}^k|(L_G V(\bar{z}_k))^T|)^2}\right]} \equiv -\alpha(\bar{z}_k) < 0, \ \forall \ a_s \neq 0 \tag{24}$$

$k = 1, \cdots, N$, whenever Eq.20 is satisfied. Since the set $\Omega(u_{max}^k, \bar{z}_k)$ is, by definition, the largest invariant set within the region described by Eq.20, then starting from any initial condition $a_s(0) \in \Omega(u_{max}^k, \bar{z}_k)$, the closed-loop state satisfies Eq.20 for all time, and consequently, V decreases monotonically according to $\dot{V} \leq -\alpha(\bar{z}_k) < 0$, which implies that, for each actuator configuration, $\bar{z}_k$, the origin of the closed-loop system of Eqs.16-18-19 (without switching) is asymptotically stable.

Without loss of generality, assume that $a_s(0) \in \Omega(u_{max}^1, \bar{z}_1)$. Since the set $\Omega(u_{max}^1, \bar{z}_1)$ is invariant, then for all times that the configuration $\bar{z}_k = \bar{z}_1$ is active, the closed-loop state satisfies Eq.20 with $\bar{z}_k = \bar{z}_1$ and V decreases monotonically according to the dissipation inequality $\dot{V} \leq -\alpha(\bar{z}_1) < 0$. Now if, at any time T where $a_s(T) \in \Omega(u_{max}^j, \bar{z}_j)$ for some $j \in \{1, \cdots, N\}$, configuration $\bar{z}_j$ is switched in (and $\bar{z}_1$ switched out), then it is clear from the invariance of the set $\Omega(u_{max}^j, \bar{z}_j)$ that for all times that the configuration $\bar{z}_k = \bar{z}_j$ remains active, the closed-loop state will satisfy Eq.20 with $\bar{z}_k = \bar{z}_j$, and, consequently (from Eq.24) V will continue to decrease monotonically, albeit with a (possibly) different dissipation rate $\dot{V} \leq -\alpha(\bar{z}_j) < 0$. From this analysis, we conclude that as long as the k-th configuration is switched in at a time T, where $a_s(T) \in \Omega(u_{max}^k, \bar{z}_k)$, the time-derivative of the Lyapunov function (for the switched closed-loop system) will always satisfy the following worst-case dissipation inequality for all $t \geq 0$

$$\dot{V} \leq \max_{k=1,\cdots,N}\{-\alpha(\bar{z}_k)\} < 0 \tag{25}$$

which implies that the origin of the finite-dimensional switched closed-loop system of Eq.16-18-19 is asymptotically stable. Hence, there exists a function β of class KL such that

$$|a_s(t)| \leq \beta(|a_s(0)|, t) \ \forall \ t \geq 0 \tag{26}$$

which implies that $a_s(t) \to 0$ as $t \to \infty$.

Using the fact that $x_s = \sum\limits_{j=1}^{m} a_j(t)\phi_j(z)$, and the definition of the L_2 norm defined for the Hilbert space $\mathcal{H}_s$, we have

$$|x_s|_2 = \int_0^\pi \left(\sqrt{a_1^2(t)\phi_1^2(z) + \cdots + a_m^2(t)\phi_m^2(z)} \right) dz \qquad (27)$$

From Eq.12, we have $\phi_j^2(z) = \dfrac{2}{\pi} sin^2(j\,z) \leq \dfrac{2}{\pi}$ which yields

$$|x_s|_2 \leq \int_0^\pi \left(\sqrt{\frac{2}{\pi}} \sqrt{a_1^2(t) + \cdots + a_m^2(t)} \right) dz$$
$$\qquad (28)$$
$$= \int_0^\pi \left(\sqrt{\frac{2}{\pi}} |a_s(t)| \right) dz \leq \sqrt{2\pi}\, \beta(|a_s(0)|, t)$$

which implies that the state x_s is bounded and $|x_s|_2 \to 0$ as $t \to \infty$. Therefore the origin of the switched closed-loop slow subsystem of Eq.15-18-19-21 is asymptotically stable.

Part 2: Substituting the controller of Eq.18 into Eq.15, the infinite-dimensional closed-loop system takes the form

$$\dot{x}_s = \mathcal{A}_s x_s + \mathcal{B}_s u(a_s, u_{max}^k, \bar{z}_k)$$
$$\dot{x}_f = \mathcal{A}_f x_f + \mathcal{B}_f u(a_s, u_{max}^k, \bar{z}_k) \qquad (29)$$

We have already established, in part 1 above, asymptotic stability of the x_s-closed-loop subsystem under the switching law of Eq.21. In this part, we show that the fast, x_f-subsystem, under the control law of Eq.18-19 and the switching law of 21, is also asymptotically stable, for any $x_f(0)$ (provided that $a_s(0) \in \Omega(u_{max}^k, \bar{z}_k)$ or, equivalently, $x_s(0) \in \Theta_k$, for any k), and that, therefore, the infinite-dimensional closed-loop system of Eq.29 (and hence the PDE of Eq.1), under the switching rule of Eq.21, is asymptotically stable. To this end, we first note that, from exponential stability of the operator $\mathcal{A}_f$ and boundedness of the control input (recall that $|u(a_s, u_{max}^k, \bar{z}_k)| \leq u_{max}^k \; \forall \, a_s \in \Omega(u_{max}^k, \bar{z}_k)$), the x_f-subsystem can be treated as an exponentially stable system with a bounded (and decaying) input. Specifically, from the exponential stability of $\mathcal{A}$ (which follows from the fact that $\lambda_{m+1} < 0$ and the selection of $\mathcal{H}_s, \mathcal{H}_f$), and using the converse Lyapunov theorem for infinite-dimensional systems [17], we have that there exists a Lyapunov functional $W : \mathcal{H}_f \to \mathbb{R}_{\geq 0}$ and a set of positive real numbers (b_1, b_2, b_3, b_4) such that for all $x_f \in \mathcal{H}_f$, the following conditions hold

$$b_1 \|x_f\|_2^2 \leq W(x_f) \leq b_2 \|x_f\|_2^2$$
$$\frac{\partial W}{\partial x_f} \mathcal{A}_f x_f \leq -b_3 \|x_f\|_2^2$$
$$\left\| \frac{\partial W}{\partial x_f} \right\|_2 \leq b_4 \|x_f\|_2 \qquad (30)$$

Evaluating the time derivative of the Lyapunov functional, W, along the trajectories of the closed-loop fast subsystem in Eq.29, we obtain

$$\dot{W}(x_f) = \frac{\partial W}{\partial x_f}\left[A_f x_f + B_f u(a_s, u_{max}^k, \bar{z}_k)\right]$$

$$\leq -b_3\|x_f\|_2^2 + \sigma\left\|\frac{\partial W}{\partial x_f}\right\|_2 |u(a_s, u_{max}^k, \bar{z}_k)| \tag{31}$$

for some $\sigma > 0$ which bounds the bounded input operator B_f. Note that the control input $u(a_s, u_{max}^k, \bar{z}_k)$ is a continuous bounded function, for all $a_s \in \Omega_k$, $k \in \{1, \cdots, N\}$, that converges to zero as $a_s \to 0$. Therefore, given that we have only a finite number of actuator configurations to switch between, the following bounds hold irrespective of which configuration is active, whenever switching is carried according to the rule of Eq.21

$$\dot{W}(x_f) \leq -b_3\|x_f\|_2^2 + \sigma b_4\|x_f\|_2 \max_{k=1,\cdots,N}\left(|u(a_s, u_{max}^k, \bar{z}_k)|\right)$$

$$\leq -\frac{b_3}{2}\|x_f\|_2^2 \quad \forall \ \|x_f\|_2 \geq \frac{2\sigma b_4}{b_3} \max_{k=1,\cdots,N}\left(|u(a_s, u_{max}^k, \bar{z}_k)|\right) \equiv \mu(|a_s|) \tag{32}$$

Note that $\mu(|a_s|) \to 0$ as $|a_s| \to 0$. The above inequality implies that $\dot{W}_f$ is negative outside some residual set whose size depends on a_s. This, in turn, implies that, for any $x_f(0)$, there exists a finite time, t_1, such that the state of the closed-loop switched fast subsystem satisfies

$$\|x_f(t)\|_2 \leq \varphi\|x_f(0)\|_2 e^{-\alpha t} \quad \forall \ 0 \leq t < t_1$$

$$\|x_f(t)\|_2 \leq \gamma(\mu(|a_s|)) \quad \forall \ t \geq t_1 \tag{33}$$

for some $\varphi > 1, \alpha > 0$, where $\gamma(\cdot)$ is a class $\mathcal{K}$ function of its argument ($\gamma(\mu(\cdot)) = \sqrt{\frac{b_2}{b_1}}\mu(\cdot)$). This implies that $\|x_f(t)\|_2$ is ultimately bounded with an ultimate bound that depends on a_s. We have already shown in part 1 that, starting from any $a_s(0) \in \Omega_k$, for any $k \in \{1, \cdots, N\}$, the state a_s (under the control law of Eq.18-19 and the switching law of Eq.21) is bounded and converges to zero as $t \to \infty$. Therefore, by taking the limit of both sides of the second inequality in Eq.33, we have

$$\lim_{t\to\infty}\|x_f(t)\|_2 \leq \lim_{t\to\infty}\gamma(\mu(|a_s(t)|)) = 0 \tag{34}$$

which implies that $\|x_f\|_2 \to 0$ as $t \to \infty$. To summarize, we have that, starting from any $x_s(0) \in \Theta_k$ (or equivalently $a_s(0) \in \Omega(u_{max}^k, \bar{z}_k)$ for any $k \in \{1, \cdots, N\}$), and for any $x_f(0)$, the states of the slow and fast switched closed-loop subsystems are bounded and converge to the origin as $t \to \infty$ which implies that origin of the switched infinite dimensional closed-loop system of Eq.29 is asymptotically stable. This completes the proof of the theorem.

Conditions of Optimal Classification for Piecewise Affine Regression

Giancarlo Ferrari-Trecate[1]* and Michael Schinkel[2]

[1] INRIA, Domaine de Voluceau
Rocquencourt - B.P.105, 78153 Le Chesnay Cedex, France
Giancarlo.Ferrari-Trecate@inria.fr
[2] Department of Mechanical Engineering
Center for Systems and Control, University of Glasgow,
University Avenue, Glasgow, G12 8QQ, Scotland,
m.schinkel@mech.gla.ac.uk

Abstract. We consider regression problems with piecewise affine maps. In particular, we focus on the sub-problem of classifying the datapoints, i.e. correctly attributing a datapoint to the affine submodel that most likely generated it. Then, we analyze the regression algorithm proposed in [4,3] and show that, under suitable assumptions on the dataset and the weights of the classification procedure, optimal classification can be guaranteed in presence of bounded noise. We also relax such assumptions by introducing and characterizing the property of weakly optimal classification. Finally, by elaborating on these concepts, we propose a procedure for detecting, a posteriori, misclassified datapoints.

1 Introduction

In this paper we consider the problem of reconstructing a Piece-Wise Affine (PWA) map from a finite number of noisy datapoints. A PWA map $f : \mathbb{X} \mapsto \mathbb{R}$ is defined by the equations

$$f(x) = f_q(k) \quad \text{if} \quad x \in \bar{\mathcal{X}}_q \tag{1}$$

$$f_q(x) = \begin{bmatrix} x^T & 1 \end{bmatrix} \bar{\theta}_q \tag{2}$$

where $\mathbb{X} \subset \mathbb{R}^n$ is a bounded polyhedron, $\{\bar{\mathcal{X}}_q\}_{q=1}^s$ is a polyhedral partition of $\mathbb{X}$ in s regions and $\bar{\theta}_q \in \mathbb{R}^{n+1}$ are Parameter Vectors (PVs). Therefore, a PWA map is composed of s affine submodels defined by the pairs $(\bar{\theta}_q, \bar{\mathcal{X}}_q)$. The dataset $\mathcal{N}$ collects the samples $(x(k), y(k))$, $k = 1, \dots, N$ generated by the model

$$y(k) = f(x(k)) + \eta(k) \tag{3}$$

where $\eta(k)$ are Gaussian, independent, identically distributed random variables. For sake of simplicity, we assume that all the PVs are different and that the

---

* Corresponding author.

O. Maler and A. Pnueli (Eds.): HSCC 2003, LNCS 2623, pp. 188–202, 2003.

number s of submodels is known. Then, the aim of PWA regression is to estimate both the PVs and the regions by using the information provided by $\mathcal{N}$.

When considering hybrid systems, an input/output description of a PWA system (see [11] for a definition) with inputs $u(k) \in \mathbb{R}^m$ and outputs $y(k) \in \mathbb{R}$ is provided by Piece-Wise ARX models that are defined by equation (3) where k is now the time index and the vector of regressors $x(k)$ is given by

$$ x(k) = \left[y(k-1) \, y(k-2) \, \ldots \, y(k-n_a) \, u^T(k-1) \, u^T(k-2) \ldots \, u^T(k-n_b) \right]^T . $$

It is apparent that, if the orders n_a and n_b are known, the identification of a Piece-Wise ARX model amounts to a PWA regression problem.

In order to highlight the main difficulties of PWA regression, consider the partition $\{\bar{\mathcal{F}}_q\}_{q=1}^s$ of the dataset defined by the rule: $(x(k), y(k)) \in \bar{\mathcal{F}}_q$ if the datapoint is *associated* to the q-th submodel (i.e. if $x(k) \in \bar{\mathcal{X}}_q$). If the sets $\bar{\mathcal{F}}_q$ are known, the identification problem can be easily solved. In fact, the PVs can be estimated by solving a linear regression problem for each dataset $\bar{\mathcal{F}}_q$. Moreover, the regions can be reconstructed by finding the hyperplanes separating pairwise the sets $\{x : (x, y) \in \bar{\mathcal{F}}_q\}$, $\{x : (x, y) \in \bar{\mathcal{F}}_{q'}\}$ for all indices $q \neq q'$.

It is important to realize that, independently of the algorithms used for estimating the submodels, the sets $\{\bar{\mathcal{F}}_q\}_{q=1}^s$ partition the dataset in the optimal way. A key problem in PWA regression is that such sets are not known a priori because the regions are unknown. Then, it is apparent that any PWA regression method aims at providing, implicitly or explicitly, estimates $\mathcal{F}_q$ of the sets $\bar{\mathcal{F}}_q$. We say that an algorithm achieves *optimal classification* if it gives $\mathcal{F}_q = \bar{\mathcal{F}}_q$. We point out that the classification task is also the most challenging step in PWA regression, because, in absence of further information about the submodels, it cannot be decoupled from the estimation of the PVs.

Various methods have been proposed in literature for circumventing the problems associated with classification by exploiting some a priori information about the model structure. For instance, in [6], only monodimensional PWA functions are considered. In [9] and [8] a gridding procedure is used to find the regions, that are constrained to have rectangular shape. More classical techniques, like Hinging Hyperplanes [2] or neural networks with PWA activation functions [7] focus on the estimation of continuous PWA models (that can represent only a limited number of logic features, in the case of hybrid behaviors). Analogously, in [1], the attention is restricted to special subclasses of PWA systems.

In this paper we consider the PWA regression algorithm proposed in [4,3] and summarized in Section 2. Its main feature is the capability of reconstructing general PWA maps without using any a priori knowledge on the PVs and/or the regions. Moreover, it allows to reduce the classification problem to a clustering problem, that ultimately amounts to the minimization of a suitably defined cost functional J. Note that, independently of the optimization algorithm used, the minimization of J can be viewed as an inference principle for finding the sets $\mathcal{F}_q$. Then, the question arises of assessing the soundness of this principle, or, in other words, to study the assumptions guaranteeing optimal classification. This analysis is carried out in Section 3 and 4.

The main result of Section 3 is that if the dataset c−separates the true regions, if the weights characterizing J have an homogeneous magnitude and if the noise samples satisfy suitable bounds, then optimal classification can be achieved. The c-separability property means that for each point $x(k) \in \bar{\mathcal{X}}_q$ its first $c-1$ neighboring points in the dataset belong to the same region. Since c-separability, although conceptually important, cannot be verified a priori, we also analyze the quality of the sets $\mathcal{F}_q$ when it does not hold. In Section 4 it is proven that there still exist suitable bounds on the noise samples and the weights of J guaranteeing optimality of the estimates $\mathcal{F}_q$ in a weaker sense.

Moreover, in Section 5 we provide an algorithm, based on the weak optimality property, for improving a posteriori the estimated sets $\mathcal{F}_q$. Its effectiveness is demonstrated in Section 6 through an illustrative example.

2   The PWA Regression Algorithm

In this section we describe a slightly simplified version of the PWA regression method proposed in [4,3]. The simplifications follow from the fact that all the true PVs are different (further details on the problems arising from having identical PVs on different regions can be found in [4,3]). The algorithm is structured in three steps.

1. Local Regression. For $j = 1, \dots, N$ we build a Local Dataset (LD) $\mathcal{C}_j$ collecting $(x(j), y(j))$ and its $c-1$ distinct neighboring datapoints, i.e. the pairs $(\tilde{x}, \tilde{y}) \in \mathcal{N}$ that satisfy

$$\|x(j) - \tilde{x}\|^2 \leq \|x(j) - \hat{x}\|^2, \quad \forall (\hat{x}, \hat{y}) \in \mathcal{N} \backslash \mathcal{C}_j. \tag{4}$$

The cardinality c of an LD is a parameter of the algorithm, and we assume $c > n+1$. We refer to $\mathcal{C}_j$ as a *pure LD* if it collects only datapoints associated to a single submodel (and we say that $\mathcal{C}_j$ is *associated* to this submodel). Otherwise the LD is termed *mixed*. Note that the distinction between pure and mixed LDs is conceptual and cannot be done, in practice, at this stage of the algorithm because the true regions are unknown. Nevertheless, the following definition can be introduced.

Definition 1. *The dataset $\mathcal{N}$ c-separates the regions $\{\bar{\mathcal{X}}_q\}_{q=1}^s$ if all the LDs of size c are pure.*

For each LD $\mathcal{C}_j$ we compute a Local Parameter Vector (LPV) θ_j through least squares

$$\theta_j = Q_j Y_j, \quad Q_j = (\Phi_j^T \Phi_j)^{-1} \Phi_j^T \tag{5}$$

$$\Phi_j = \begin{bmatrix} x_1 \cdots x_c \\ 1 \cdots 1 \end{bmatrix}^T, \quad Y_j = \begin{bmatrix} y_1 \cdots y_c \end{bmatrix}^T$$

where x_i and y_i, $i = 1, \ldots, c$ satisfy $(x_i, y_i) \in C_j$. For every LPV, its covariance matrix is also estimated through the formulae

$$V_j = \frac{SSR_j}{c - (n+1)}(\Phi_j^T \Phi_j)^{-1}, \quad SSR_j = Y_j^T \left(I - \Phi_j(\Phi_j^T \Phi_j)^{-1}\Phi_j^T\right) Y_j. \quad (6)$$

$\square$

2. Clustering. This steps aims to find s clusters $\{\mathcal{D}_q\}_{q=1}^s$ that partition the set Θ of all LPVs. As usual in clustering theory, we compute the clusters by minimizing a suitable cost functional. We choose the following cost

$$J\left(\{\mathcal{D}_q\}_{q=1}^s, \{\mu_q\}_{q=1}^s\right) = \sum_{q=1}^s \sum_{j \in \Im \mathcal{D}_q} \|\theta_j - \mu_q\|_{V_j^{-1}}^2. \quad (7)$$

where μ_q are the centers of the clusters and the operator $\Im$, acting on the set $\mathcal{D}_q$, gives the collection of indices of the elements in $\mathcal{D}_q$. For instance, if $\mathcal{D}_1 = \{\theta_1, \theta_3, \theta_8\}$, we have $\Im\mathcal{D}_1 = \{1, 3, 8\}$. The minimizers of J will be denoted as $\mathcal{D}_q^*$ and μ_q^*, respectively.

$\square$

3. Estimation of the submodels. By using the bijective maps

$$(x(j), y(j)) \longleftrightarrow C_j \longleftrightarrow \theta_j \quad (8)$$

we can build the sets $\{\mathcal{F}_i\}_{q=1}^s$ according to the rule: $(x(j), y(j)) \in \mathcal{F}_q \Leftrightarrow \theta_j \in \mathcal{D}_q^*$. The points in each final set $\mathcal{F}_q$ can be used for estimating the PVs of each submodel (for instance through least squares). Also the regions $\{\mathcal{X}_q\}_{q=1}^s$ can be found on the basis of the final sets by resorting to multicategory pattern recognition algorithms. For further details on the implementation aspects, we defer the reader to [4,3].

$\square$

Steps 2 and 3 deserve some comments. Consider the sets $\bar{\mathcal{D}}_q$, each one collecting only the pure LPVs associated to the same submodel. If the dataset c-separates the true regions, we have that $\{\bar{\mathcal{D}}_q\}_{q=1}^s$ partition $\mathcal{N}$ and the best result we can obtain from clustering is $\mathcal{D}_q^* = \bar{\mathcal{D}}_q$. Indeed, one would obtain, from step 3, $\mathcal{F}_q = \bar{\mathcal{F}}_q$, so achieving optimal classification. On the other hand, if mixed LPVs are present, one gets $\Theta = \cup_{q=1}^s \bar{\mathcal{D}}_q \cup \mathcal{D}_{mix}$, where $\mathcal{D}_{mix}$ collects all mixed LPVs. Since $\{\bar{\mathcal{D}}_q\}_{q=1}^s$ do not partition Θ, the best result we can expect from clustering is $\mathcal{D}_q^* \supset \bar{\mathcal{D}}_q$. This means that the presence of mixed LPVs does not spoil the accuracy in clustering the pure LPVs. This leads to the following definition.

Definition 2. *The clusters $\{\mathcal{D}_q^*\}_{q=1}^s$ are weakly optimal if $\mathcal{D}_q^* \supset \bar{\mathcal{D}}_q$, $q = 1, \ldots, s$. If, in addition, the dataset c-separates the true regions, the clusters are optimal.*

Remark 1. An intuitive way of understanding the expected performance of the algorithm is the following (a more thorough description is provided in [4]). The LD C_j collects the datapoints characterizing the behavior of the PWA map in a neighborhood of $x(j)$. Then, if C_j is pure and associated to the q-th submodel, θ_j is an estimate of $\bar{\theta}_q$. Moreover, if the noise level is "low", then V_j is "small". On the other hand, if C_j is mixed, then θ_j is likely to be different from all the pure LPVs and V_j is "big". This follows from the fact that both θ_j and V_j account for the model mismatch (they result from fitting, with an affine model, datapoints generated by at least two different submodels). As a consequence, we expect that, in the LPV space, all pure LPVs are concentrated in s dense clouds, whereas the mixed LPVs form a pattern of isolated points. The primary goal of clustering is to find such clouds of LPVs. The secondary goal is to attribute also the mixed LPVs to the clusters, possibly without spoiling the accuracy in achieving the primary goal. This second aim is achieved through the use of the matrices V_j^{-1} for weighting the distances in (7). In fact, it is expected that mixed LPVs are poorly weighted with respect to pure LPVs. We point out that the accuracy in clustering can be also spoiled by an "high" noise level that makes the clouds scattered and possibly overlapping (examples are reported in [4]). The only countermeasure against noise is to increase the size c of the LDs, thus reducing the covariance of pure LPVs but also possibly increasing the number of mixed LPVs. We conclude by observing that if the ratio r between the number of mixed and pure LPVs is small and if the noise level is sufficiently small, we expect that the algorithm correctly classify the largest part of the datapoints. We also highlight that, under mild assumption on the sampling of the domain $\mathbb{X}$, the ratio r tends to zero as N increases (see Theorem 1 in [4]). □

Remark 2. For the practical implementation of the algorithm, one should note that step 1 is computationally cheap. In order to give an idea of the computational burden, when considering a bi-dimensional domain $\mathbb{X}$, a dataset of $N = 1000$ points and $c = 10$, step 1 takes 28.4 sec. by running a Matlab code on a $1Ghz$ Pentium III laptop. For step 2, the common practice is to resort to suboptimal but efficient algorithms like K-means [10] (a discussion of our K-means implementation is provided in [4,3]). In the above example, by identifying $s = 10$ submodels, step 2 takes 12.9 sec. to be executed. □

In the following Sections, we give a sound mathematical foundation to Remark 1 by clarifying the conditions that guarantee optimal and weakly optimal classification.

3   Optimal Classification

The main theorem of this Section applies to the case of datasets that c-separate the true regions. Nevertheless, we prove some general results that are useful also for deriving weak-optimality conditions (see Section 4). In the proofs, we shall use the vectors

$$\bar{Y}_j = \left[f(x_1) \cdots f(x_c) \right]^T, \quad \bar{\varepsilon}_j = \left[\eta_1 \cdots \eta_c \right]^T$$

that collects the noise-free outputs and the noise samples, respectively contributing to the output samples in $\{y : (x, y) \in C_j\}$.

We start showing that all pure LPVs associated to the same submodel fall within a ball centered in the true PV whose radius depends on the noise level.

Lemma 1. *For each* $\theta_j \in \bar{\mathcal{D}}_q$ *it holds* $\theta_j \in B(\bar{\theta}_q, \rho_q)$, *where* $\rho_q = \max_{j \in \Im \bar{\mathcal{D}}_q} \|$ $Q_j \bar{\varepsilon}_j \|$.

Proof. The proof follows directly from the fact that, $\forall j \in \Im \bar{\mathcal{D}}_q$,

$$\theta_j = Q_j Y_j = Q_j \bar{Y}_j + Q_j \bar{\varepsilon}_j = \bar{\theta}_q + Q_j \bar{\varepsilon}_j. \tag{9}$$

In view of the definition of ρ_q the thesis follows. $\square$

Before proceeding we need to introduce some further notation. For a set $\bar{\mathcal{D}}_q$, let $\bar{\lambda}_q = \max_{j \in \Im \bar{\mathcal{D}}_q} \lambda_{max}(V_j^{-1})$, where, for a square symmetric matrix A, $\lambda_{max}(A)$ denotes its maximum eigenvalue. Analogously, define $\underline{\lambda}_q = \min_{j \in \Im \bar{\mathcal{D}}_q} \lambda_{min}(V_j^{-1})$. Since V_j^{-1} is positive definite, both $\bar{\lambda}_q$ and $\underline{\lambda}_q$ are positive. In the next Lemma we derive an upper bound to the optimal clustering cost when $\mathcal{D}_q^* = \bar{\mathcal{D}}_q$.

Lemma 2. *If the dataset c-separates the true regions, the following upper bound holds*

$$\tilde{J} = \min_{\{\mu_q\}_{q=1}^s} J(\{\bar{\mathcal{D}}_q\}_{q=1}^s, \quad \{\mu_q\}_{q=1}^s) \leq \sum_{q=1}^s n_q \bar{\lambda}_q \rho_q^2 \tag{10}$$

where n_q *denotes the cardinality of* $\bar{\mathcal{D}}_q$.

Proof. By using the fact that $\| \theta_j - \mu_q \|_{V_j^{-1}}^2 \leq \bar{\lambda}_q \| \theta_j - \mu_q \|^2$, we get

$$\tilde{J} \leq \min_{\{\mu_q\}_{q=1}^s} \sum_{q=1}^s \sum_{j \in \Im \bar{\mathcal{D}}_q} \bar{\lambda}_q \| \theta_j - \mu_q \|^2 \tag{11}$$

From optimality we have

$$\min_{\{\mu_q\}_{q=1}^s} \sum_{q=1}^s \sum_{j \in \Im \bar{\mathcal{D}}_q} \bar{\lambda}_q \| \theta_j - \mu_q \|^2 \leq \sum_{q=1}^s \sum_{j \in \Im \bar{\mathcal{D}}_q} \bar{\lambda}_q \| \theta_j - \bar{\theta}_q \|^2 \tag{12}$$

where the last inequality follows from the choice of $\mu_q = \bar{\theta}_q$. Lemma 1 implies that if $\theta_j \in \bar{\mathcal{D}}_q$, we have $\| \theta_j - \bar{\theta}_q \|^2 \leq \rho_q^2$. Hence,

$$\tilde{J} \leq \sum_{q=1}^s \sum_{j \in \Im \bar{\mathcal{D}}_q} \bar{\lambda}_q \| \theta_j - \bar{\theta}_q \|^2 \leq \sum_{q=1}^s n_q \bar{\lambda}_q \rho_q^2. \tag{13}$$

$\square$

The next goal is to derive a lower bound to the optimal clustering cost if at least one clustering error is committed. A clustering error arises when two parameter vectors, say $\theta_{\bar{k}} \in \bar{\mathcal{D}}_k$ and $\theta_{\bar{h}} \in \bar{\mathcal{D}}_h$, $k \neq h$, are grouped together in the same cluster. Such errors can be represented through the pairs of indices $(\bar{k}, \bar{h})$ meaning that $\theta_{\bar{k}}$ and $\theta_{\bar{h}}$ fall within the same cluster. The set of possible errors is then given by

$$\mathcal{E} = \left\{ (\bar{k}, \bar{h}) : \forall \bar{k} \in \Im \bar{\mathcal{D}}_k, \ \forall \bar{h} \in \Im \bar{\mathcal{D}}_h, \ \forall k, h \in \{1, \dots, N\}, k \neq h \right\} \tag{14}$$

Lemma 3. *Consider the clusters $\{\mathcal{D}_q\}_{q=1}^s$ and assume that at least the clustering error $(\bar{k}, \bar{h})$ is committed, where $\theta_{\bar{k}} \in \bar{\mathcal{D}}_k$ and $\theta_{\bar{h}} \in \bar{\mathcal{D}}_h$. Then, there exists $\beta_{\bar{k}, \bar{h}} > 0$ such that if $|\eta(j)| < \beta_{\bar{k}, \bar{h}}, \ \forall j \in \{1, \dots, N\}$, the following inequality holds*

$$J(\{\mathcal{D}_q\}_{q=1}^s, \ \{\mu_q^*\}_{q=1}^s) \geq \frac{\underline{\lambda}_k \underline{\lambda}_h}{\underline{\lambda}_k + \underline{\lambda}_h} \mid T_{\bar{\theta}_k, \bar{\theta}_m} - (\rho_k + \rho_m) \mid^2 \tag{15}$$

where $T_{\bar{\theta}_k, \bar{\theta}_m} = \| \bar{\theta}_k - \bar{\theta}_m \|$ and ρ_k, ρ_m are defined as in Lemma 1.

Proof. Without loss of generality, assume that $\theta_{\bar{k}}$ and $\theta_{\bar{h}}$, are grouped together in the cluster $\mathcal{D}_{\bar{q}}$. Then, we have

$$\min_{\{\mu_q\}_{q=1}^s} J(\{\mathcal{D}_q\}_{q=1}^s, \ \{\mu_q\}_{q=1}^s) \geq \min_{\mu_{\bar{q}}} \sum_{j \in \Im \mathcal{D}_{\bar{q}}} \| \theta_j - \mu_{\bar{q}} \|_{V_j^{-1}}^2 \geq \tag{16}$$

$$\geq \min_{\mu_{\bar{q}}} \| \theta_{\bar{k}} - \mu_{\bar{q}} \|_{V_{\bar{k}}^{-1}}^2 + \| \theta_{\bar{h}} - \mu_{\bar{q}} \|_{V_{\bar{h}}^{-1}}^2 \tag{17}$$

By using the fact that $\| \theta_{\bar{k}} - \mu_{\bar{q}} \|_{V_{\bar{k}}^{-1}}^2 \geq \underline{\lambda}_k \| \theta_{\bar{k}} - \mu_{\bar{q}} \|^2$ and $\| \theta_{\bar{h}} - \mu_{\bar{q}} \|_{V_{\bar{h}}^{-1}}^2 \geq \underline{\lambda}_h \| \theta_{\bar{h}} - \mu_{\bar{q}} \|^2$, we obtain

$$\min_{\mu_{\bar{q}}} \left[\| \theta_{\bar{k}} - \mu_{\bar{q}} \|_{V_{\bar{k}}^{-1}}^2 + \| \theta_{\bar{h}} - \mu_{\bar{q}} \|_{V_{\bar{h}}^{-1}}^2 \right] \geq \min_{\mu_{\bar{q}}} \underline{J}(\mu_{\bar{q}}) \tag{18}$$

where

$$\underline{J}(\mu_{\bar{q}}) = \left[\underline{\lambda}_k \| \theta_{\bar{k}} - \mu_{\bar{q}} \|^2 + \underline{\lambda}_h \| \theta_{\bar{h}} - \mu_{\bar{q}} \|^2 \right] \tag{19}$$

We proceed by computing the minimum of $\underline{J}(\mu_{\bar{q}})$. The functional $\underline{J}(\mu_{\bar{q}})$ is convex and the minimizer $\mu_{\bar{q}}^*$ satisfies $\nabla_{\mu_{\bar{q}}} \underline{J}(\mu_{\bar{q}}^*) = 0$. Hence, the minimum is given by

$$\underline{J}(\mu_{\bar{q}}^*) = \frac{\underline{\lambda}_k \underline{\lambda}_h}{\underline{\lambda}_k + \underline{\lambda}_h} \| \theta_{\bar{k}} - \theta_{\bar{h}} \|^2 \tag{20}$$

From Lemma 1 we have that $\theta_{\bar{k}} \in B(\bar{\theta}_k, \rho_k)$ and $\theta_{\bar{h}} \in B(\bar{\theta}_h, \rho_h)$. Moreover, $T_{\bar{\theta}_k, \bar{\theta}_h} = \| \bar{\theta}_k - \bar{\theta}_h \|$ is strictly positive in view of the assumption that all the true PVs are different. Then, if it holds

$$T_{\bar{\theta}_k, \bar{\theta}_h} - (\rho_k + \rho_h) > 0 \tag{21}$$

we get the inequality, $\| \theta_{\bar{k}} - \theta_{\bar{h}} \|^2 \geq | T_{\bar{\theta}_k, \bar{\theta}_h} - (\rho_k + \rho_h) |^2$ from which (15) follows. The condition (21) represents the fact that the balls $B(\bar{\theta}_k, \rho_k)$ and $B(\bar{\theta}_h, \rho_h)$ do not intersect. Since both ρ_k and ρ_h tend to zero if the bound to the noise $\beta_{\bar{k}, \bar{h}}$ goes to zero, we conclude that there exists a positive $\beta_{\bar{k}, \bar{h}}$ for which condition (21) holds. $\square$

We are now in a position to state the main result.

Theorem 1. *Let $H_j = (I - \Phi_j Q_j)$ and $\bar{\gamma} = \max_{j \in \{1, \dots, N\}} \lambda_{max}(H_j)$. If the dataset c-separates the true regions, then, for all $\phi \in \mathbb{R}$ verifying $0 < \phi < \min\{1, \bar{\gamma}\}$, there exists $\beta > 0$ such that if $\beta > \|\eta(k)\|^2$ and $SSR_k > \phi\beta$, $\forall k \in \{1, 2, \dots, N\}$, the clusters $\{\mathcal{D}_q^*\}_{q=1}^s$ are optimal.*

Proof. From Lemma 2 we get an upper bound to the cost by considering optimal clusters and from Lemma 3 we get a lower bound to the cost when an error $(\bar{k}, \bar{h})$ $\theta_{\bar{k}} \in \bar{\mathcal{D}}_k$, $\theta_{\bar{h}} \in \bar{\mathcal{D}}_h$ is committed. Therefore, the global minimum is attained for optimal clusters if the following inequality holds

$$\sum_{q=1}^{s} n_q \bar{\lambda}_q \rho_q^2 \leq \min_{(\bar{k}, \bar{h}) \in \mathcal{E}} \frac{\lambda_k \lambda_h}{\lambda_k + \lambda_h} | T_{\bar{\theta}_k, \bar{\theta}_h} - (\rho_k + \rho_h) |^2 \tag{22}$$

where, without loss of generality, we assumed that $\theta_{\bar{k}} \in \bar{\mathcal{D}}_k$ and $\theta_{\bar{h}} \in \bar{\mathcal{D}}_h$. The next goal is to get an explicit dependence of (22) on β. This is done in four steps.

Step 1. Prove that, $\forall \phi > 0$, $\phi < \min\{1, \bar{\gamma}\}$, if $\beta > \|\eta(j)\|^2$ and $SSR_j > \phi\beta$, then it holds

$$\phi\beta < SSR_j \leq \bar{\gamma}\beta. \tag{23}$$

By direct calculation it is easy to verify that $H_j \bar{Y}_j = 0$. Therefore, by recalling that $Y_j = \bar{Y}_j + \bar{\varepsilon}_j$, we have $SSR_j = Y_j^T H_j Y_j = \bar{\varepsilon}_j^T H_j \bar{\varepsilon}_j$ from which inequality (23) directly follows.

Step 2. Prove that, $\forall \phi > 0$, $\phi < \min\{1, \bar{\gamma}\}$, if $\beta > \|\eta(j)\|^2$ and $SSR_j > \phi\beta$, we have, $\forall q \in 1, \dots, N$

$$\bar{\delta}_q (\phi\beta)^{-1} \geq \bar{\lambda}_q \geq \underline{\delta}_q \beta^{-1}, \tag{24}$$

$$\bar{\nu}_q (\phi\beta)^{-1} \geq \bar{\lambda}_q \geq \underline{\nu}_q \beta^{-1} \tag{25}$$

where $\underline{\delta}_q > 0$, $\bar{\delta}_q > 0$, $\underline{\nu}_q > 0$ and $\bar{\nu}_q > 0$ are suitable constants. Consider the matrix V_j. Then

$$\lambda_{min}(V_j^{-1}) = \lambda_{min}(\Phi_j^T \Phi_j) \frac{c - (n+1)}{SSR_j} \tag{26}$$

and, from step 1, we get

$$\lambda_{min}(\Phi_j^T \Phi_j) \frac{c - (n+1)}{\phi\beta} \geq \lambda_{min}(V_j^{-1}) \geq \lambda_{min}(\Phi_j^T \Phi_j) \frac{c - (n+1)}{\bar{\gamma}\beta} \tag{27}$$

Since, by definition, $\underline{\lambda}_q = \min_{j \in \mathfrak{I} \mathcal{D}_q} \lambda_{min}(V_j^{-1})$, we have

$$\min_{j \in \mathfrak{I} \mathcal{D}_q} \lambda_{min}(\Phi_j^T \Phi_j) \frac{c - (n+1)}{\phi \beta} \geq \underline{\lambda}_q \geq \min_{j \in \mathfrak{I} \mathcal{D}_q} \lambda_{min}(\Phi_j^T \Phi_j) \frac{c - (n+1)}{\bar{\gamma} \beta} \quad (28)$$

from which the inequality (24) follows. Inequality (25), can be proven by using a similar argument.

Step 3. Prove that, $\forall \beta > 0$, if $|\eta(j)| < \beta$, $\forall j \in \{1, \dots, N\}$, then

$$\rho_q \leq \kappa_q \sqrt{\beta} \quad (29)$$

where $\kappa_q > 0$ is a suitable constant. This inequality immediately follows from the definition of ρ_q

$$\rho_q = \max_{j \in \mathfrak{I} \mathcal{D}_q} \| Q_j \bar{e}_j \| \leq \max_{j \in \mathfrak{I} \mathcal{D}_q} \| Q_j \| \| \bar{e}_j \| \leq \max_{j \in \mathfrak{I} \mathcal{D}_q} \| Q_j \| \sqrt{\beta} \quad (30)$$

Step 4. We now analyze both sides of (22) by combining the results of the previous steps. Consider the term $\bar{\zeta}_{\bar{k}, \bar{h}}$ associated with the error $(\bar{k}, \bar{h})$ and defined as

$$\bar{\zeta}_{\bar{k}, \bar{h}} = \frac{\underline{\lambda}_k \underline{\lambda}_h}{\underline{\lambda}_k + \underline{\lambda}_h} \, | \, T_{\bar{\theta}_k, \bar{\theta}_h} - (\rho_k + \rho_h) \, |^2 \quad (31)$$

Since the PVs are all different, we have $T_{\bar{\theta}_k, \bar{\theta}_h} > 0$. Then, it holds

$$\lim_{\beta \to 0} \bar{\zeta}_{\bar{k}, \bar{h}} = +\infty \quad (32)$$

In fact, for $q \in \{\bar{k}, \bar{h}\}$, we have $\underline{\lambda}_q \geq \underline{\delta}_q \beta$ (from step 2) and $\rho_q \leq \kappa_q \sqrt{\beta}$ (from step 3). Then, $\forall U > 0$ it is possible to choose β small enough such that $\min_{(\bar{k}, \bar{h}) \in \mathcal{E}} \bar{\zeta}_{\bar{k}, \bar{h}} > U$. Consider now the term

$$\underline{\zeta}_q = n_q \bar{\lambda}_q \rho_q^2 \quad (33)$$

From the fact that $\bar{\nu}_q(\phi \beta)^{-1} \geq \bar{\lambda}_q$ (step 2) and $\rho_q \leq \kappa_q \sqrt{\beta}$ (step 3) we can conclude that $\underline{\zeta}_q$ remains bounded for $\beta \to 0$. Then, the l.h.s. of (22) is bounded because it can be written as $\sum_{q=1}^s \underline{\zeta}_q$. Therefore, for $\beta > 0$ sufficiently small, inequality (22) can be verified since, for $\beta \to 0$ the l.h.s is bounded while the r.h.s. diverges. $\square$

Note that, in Theorem 1, the bounds on $\eta(k)$ and SSR_k are not in contradiction with the assumption that the noise samples are a random variables with a Gaussian distribution. Indeed, the bounds must hold only for a finite number of noise realizations. The magnitude of the parameter β depends mainly on how much the models are different. In fact, in view of Lemma 1, if $\bar{\theta}_q \approx \bar{\theta}_{q'}$ for $q \neq q'$, the LPVs associated to the submodels q and q' lie in disjoint balls only if the noise is sufficiently small. The second key assumption in Theorem 1 is that the sums of the squared residuals SSR_j are within the same order of magnitude. Note that this property does not follow from the fact that the noise samples are identically distributed. In fact, there exists nonnull noise realizations giving $SSR_j = 0$. Although this case in unlikely too happen, on average, we must explicitly exclude it for the following reason. Assume that the SSR is "almost zero" just for the datapoints in s local datasets C_j associated with a single submodel. Then, the corresponding matrices V_j^{-1} are "almost infinite". In this case the LPVs θ_j jeopardize all the cluster centers, meaning that, in order to minimize J, all centers must be placed almost at θ_j, independently of all the other LPVs. In Theorem 1, this scenario is ruled out because it is required that $\bar{\gamma}\beta \geq SSR_j \geq \phi\beta$ (see (23)). Moreover, β depends on the choice of ϕ, and, if ϕ is small, also β will be small, so reducing the permitted range for SSR_j.

4   Weakly Optimal Classification

In this section we remove the assumption of c-separability and give conditions that guarantee weak-optimality. As described in Remark 1, mixed LPVs are expected to account for the model mismatch. However, in principle there may exist mixed LDs containing collinear points. In this case, if noise is absent, the corresponding LPVs would perfectly fit the data so preventing the detection of mixed LDs from the analysis of the SSR. This limit case, that seldom happens if the samples $x(k)$ are randomly distributed and c is not too small, is excluded by the following definition.

Definition 3. *An LD C_j is strongly mixed if it is mixed and there is no $\theta \in \mathbb{R}^{n+1}$ such that $\bar{Y}_j = \Phi_j\theta$.*

The relation between a strongly mixed LDs C_j and the corresponding SSR_j is clarified by the following Lemma.

Lemma 4. *Let C_j be a strongly-mixed LD and assume that, for $\beta > 0$ it holds $\beta > \|\eta(k)\|$, $\forall k \in \{1, \ldots, N\}$. Then, $\lim_{\beta \to 0} SSR_j = \ell > 0$.*

Proof. Consider the symmetric positive semidefinite matrix $H_j = I - \Phi_j Q_j$ having the property that $\ker(H_j) = \mathrm{range}(\Phi_j)$. By direct calculation one obtains the decomposition $SSR_j = t_{j,1} + t_{j,2} + t_{j,3}$ where

$$t_{j,1} = (\bar{Y}_j - \Phi_j\theta_j)^T H_j (\bar{Y}_j - \Phi_j\theta_j)$$
$$t_{j,2} = 2(\bar{Y}_j - \Phi_j\theta_j)^T H_j (\Phi_j\theta_j + \bar{\varepsilon}_j)$$
$$t_{j,3} = (\Phi_j\theta_j + \bar{\varepsilon}_j)^T H_j (\Phi_j\theta_j + \bar{\varepsilon}_j)$$

Since C_j is strongly mixed, we have $(\bar{Y}_j - \Phi_j\theta_j) \in \ker(H_j)^\perp$. By setting $\ell = t_{j,1}$, it follows that $\ell > 0$. Moreover it holds $t_{j,2} = 2\bar{Y}_j^T H_j \bar{\varepsilon}_j$, from which we have $t_{j,2} \to 0$ for $\beta \to 0$. In a similar way, one obtains $t_{j,3} = \bar{\varepsilon}_j^T H \bar{\varepsilon}_j \to 0$ for $\beta \to 0$. $\square$

Theorem 2. *Assume that $\forall q \in \{1, \ldots, s\}$, $\bar{D}_q \neq \emptyset$ and that all mixed LDs are strongly mixed. Define also $H_j = (I - \Phi_j Q_j)$ and $\bar{\gamma} = max_{j \in \{1, \ldots, N\}} \lambda_{max}(H_j)$. Then, for all $\phi > 0$, $\phi < max\{\bar{\gamma}, 1\}$ there exists $\beta > 0$ such that if $\beta > \|\eta(k)\|^2$, $\forall k \in \{1, \ldots, N\}$ and $SSR_k > \phi\beta$, $\forall k \in \Im\left(\bigcup_{q=1}^{s} \bar{D}_q\right)$, the clusters $\{D_q^*\}_{q=1}^{s}$ are weakly optimal.*

Proof. Consider the clusters $\{\mathcal{D}_q\}_{q=1}^s$ and assume that at least the clustering error $(\bar{k}, \bar{h})$, $\theta_{\bar{k}} \in \bar{\mathcal{D}}_k$, $\theta_{\bar{h}} \in \bar{\mathcal{D}}_h$ has been committed. Then, Lemma 3 provides a lower bound to the clustering cost.

As an upper bound to the cost, in the case of weakly optimal clusters $\{\mathcal{D}_q^*\}_{q=1}^s$, by using the same rationale employed for proving Lemma 2, we get

$$\min_{\{\mu_q\}_{q=1}^s} J(\{\mathcal{D}_q^*\}_{q=1}^s, \{\mu_q\}_{q=1}^s) \leq \sum_{q=1}^s n_q \bar{\lambda}_q \rho_q^2 + \tag{34}$$

$$+ \sum_{q=1}^s \sum_{j \in \Im\{\mathcal{D}_q^* \cap \mathcal{D}_{mix}\}} \| \theta_j - \bar{\theta}_q \|_{V_j^{-1}}^2$$

where n_q denotes the cardinality of $\mathcal{D}_q^* \cap \bar{\mathcal{D}}_q$. The global minimum of the clustering cost is then attained for weakly optimal clusters, if the following inequality holds

$$\sum_{q=1}^s n_q \bar{\lambda}_q \rho_q^2 + \sum_{q=1}^s \sum_{j \in \Im\{\mathcal{D}_q^* \cap \mathcal{D}_{mix}\}} \| \theta_j - \bar{\theta}_q \|_{V_j^{-1}}^2 < \tag{35}$$

$$< \min_{(\bar{k}, \bar{h}) \in \mathcal{E}} \frac{\lambda_k \lambda_h}{\lambda_k + \lambda_h} \mid T_{\bar{\theta}_k, \bar{\theta}_h} - (\rho_k + \rho_h) \mid^2$$

In the proof of Theorem 1 we have shown that the r.h.s of (35) goes to infinity as β decreases (and this property is independent of the presence of mixed LPVs). Moreover, we proved that, for a given ϕ, the term

$$\sum_{q=1}^s n_q \bar{\lambda}_q \rho_q^2$$

remains bounded, for $\beta \to 0$. Therefore, if we show that the term

$$\sum_{q=1}^s \sum_{j \in \Im\{\mathcal{D}_q^* \cap \mathcal{D}_{mix}\}} \| \theta_j - \bar{\theta}_q \|_{V_j^{-1}}^2 \tag{36}$$

remains bounded, as β decreases, the thesis follows. Note that

$$\| \theta_j - \bar{\theta}_q \|_{V_j^{-1}}^2 = (\theta_j - \bar{\theta}_q)^T \Phi_j^T \Phi_j \frac{c - (n+1)}{SSR_j} (\theta_j - \bar{\theta}_q) \tag{37}$$

From Lemma 4 we have that, for strongly mixed LPVs, the sum of the squared residuals SSR_j is strictly positive if β is small enough. Moreover,

$$\|\theta_j - \bar{\theta}_q\| = \|Q_j \bar{Y}_j + Q_j \bar{\varepsilon}_j - \bar{\theta}_q\| \leq$$

$$\leq \|Q_j \bar{Y}_j - \bar{\theta}_q\| + \|Q_j \bar{\varepsilon}_j\| \leq \|Q_j \bar{Y}_j - \bar{\theta}_q\| + \|Q_j\| \sqrt{c\beta} \tag{38}$$

thus proving that the quantity (36) is bounded, for $\beta \to 0$. $\square$

As for Theorem 1, the parameters ϕ and β cannot be computed in practice, since they depend on the "true" (and unknown) models. However, the results suggest also to check the SSR_j. In a good scenario, one should have few "high" SSR_j many "low" SSR_j corresponding to mixed and pure LDs, respectively. Moreover the latter ones should have the same order of magnitude and one should be warned against some SSR_j close to zero that may compromising the clustering accuracy.

5 A Posteriori Detection of Mixed LDs

We will now show that under certain conditions it is possible to detect mixed LDs a posteriori. For this purpose we define the following operators.

Definition 4. *The projection operator* P_x *acting on an LD returns the collection of all input datapoints in LD, $P_x(\mathcal{C}_j) = \{x : (x,y) \in \mathcal{C}_j\}$. The operator $class(\mathcal{C}_j)$ returns the index of the cluster which collects the LPV θ_j, i.e. $class(\mathcal{C}_j) = l$ if $\theta_j \in \mathcal{D}_l^*$.*

Lemma 5. *Assume that the clusters $\{\mathcal{D}_q^*\}_{q=1}^s$ are weakly optimal. If there is a set of indices $I \subset \{1, \ldots, s\}$, $\#I \geq 2$, such that $\exists\ x(k) \in \bigcap_{j \in I} P_x(\mathcal{C}_j)$ with $class(\mathcal{C}_w) \neq class(\mathcal{C}_p)$, for at least two indices $w, p \in I$, then at least one $\mathcal{C}_j$, $j \in I$, is mixed.*

Proof. By contradiction, assume that all $\mathcal{C}_j$, $j \in I$ are pure. Under the assumptions of weak optimality all pure LPVs are correctly classified. Consider the indices $w, p \in I$ as defined above. Then, both θ_w, θ_p are pure and the fact that $x(k) \in \cap_{j \in I} P_x(\mathcal{C}_j)$ implies $class(\theta_w) = class(\theta_p)$. But this contradicts the assumption that $class(\mathcal{C}_w) \neq class(\mathcal{C}_p)$. Therefore, at least one $\mathcal{C}_j$, $j \in I$, is mixed. □

Lemma 5 uses only pieces of information that depend on the regression results but not on knowledge of the true PWA model. Therefore, it defines an algorithm that allows to detect, a posteriori, a number of LDs among which one is surely mixed. It follows that all the datapoints in $\bigcup_{j \in I} P_x(\mathcal{C}_j)$ are suspected of having been misclassified. In practice, even if the clusters are not weakly optimal, it is still wise to build and analyze such set of suspected datapoints.

Usually, it is possible isolate the misclassified points because they cause big errors between the true and predicted outputs. However, the detection of the misclassified datapoints is not strictly necessary and different strategies, involving only the set of suspected points, can be used in order to improve the quality of the identified affine maps. Apparently, the simplest one is to neglect such points. It is obvious that this will improve the quality of the of the estimated PVs. However, for reconstructing the regions, the points $x(k)$ belonging to mixed LDs contain useful information. In fact, if $\mathcal{C}_j$ is mixed, then $P_x(\mathcal{C}_j)$ contains input data points belonging to different sub-models. Therefore, it is expected that $x(k)$ is close to the true boundary between different regions. Thus, it makes sense to remove the suspected points from the sets $\{\mathcal{F}_q\}_{q=1}^s$, compute the estimates

$\{\hat{\theta}_q\}_{q=1}^s$ of the true PVs and re-attribute the suspected points to the models that most likely generated them, before reconstructing the regions. For the re-attribution, one can use, for instance, the Maximum Likelihood criterion, that, in the case of Gaussian noise, amounts to assign the point $(x(k), y(k))$ to the q^*-th submodel verifying $q^* = \min_{q=1,\dots,s} \|x(k)'\hat{\theta}_q - y(k)\|$.

6 Example

The example demonstrates the outlier detection procedure through the identification of two affine maps. The true PVs of the maps are $\bar{\theta}_1 = [0.6, 0.6, 5]$ and $\bar{\theta}_2 = [-0.6, -0.6, 0]$. The noise variance is $\sigma^2 = 0.04$. We collected 25 datapoints and created LDs of size $c = 12$. The LPVs are obtained for each LD by using least squares. Then, the LPVs are clustered into the sets $\mathcal{D}_1^*$ and $\mathcal{D}_2^*$ and the PVs of the submodels are reconstructed. Figure 1(a) shows the clustering results and the LPVs suspected of being mixed and detected by using the procedure described in Lemma 5. The knowledge of the true model allows us to indicate, in Figure 1(a), the mixed LPV. We point out that, obviously, this information is not available to the outlier detection algorithm. The comparison of the distances between the predicted and collected output samples revealed the misclassified datapoints. Figure 1(b) gives the clustering results obtained by removing such points. Note that the corresponding mixed LPV also disappeared. The identified parameters of the affine map are $\theta_1 = [0.6, 0.55, 5.0]$ and $\theta_2 = [-1.3, -0.4, 0.7]$, when the whole dataset is used, and $\theta_1 = [0.6, 0.55, 5.0]$ and $\theta_2 = [-0.7, -0.45, 0]$, when the misclassified datapoints has been removed. By comparing the parameters, we can see that neglecting the the misclassified datapoints improves considerably the identification results.

7 Conclusions

PWA regression is significantly different from linear regression, due to the fact that regions and parameters of the submodels must be jointly estimated. In this paper we focused on the most challenging step in PWA regression, namely the task of classifying the datapoints. In fact, any PWA regression algorithms faces this problem and the performance of various methods can be objectively assessed by characterizing the conditions guaranteeing optimal (or sub-optimal but still "good") classification. Theoretical results of this kind provide also a precise mathematical basis for comparing merits and drawbacks of different strategies.

The classification capabilities of the method proposed in [4,3] have been investigated. In particular, it has been shown that, for bounded noise, and homogeneous weights in the clustering cost, optimal and weakly optimal classification can be achieved. These results gives also ideas about possible improvements of the algorithm. For instance, the presence of the parameter ϕ in the lower bounds to the sums of squared residuals could be avoided by reconsidering the use of the matrices V_j^{-1} as weights in the clustering cost. This would provide a

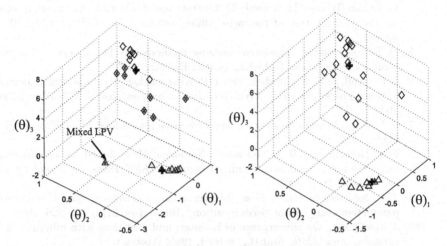

(a) Clusters of originals LPVs: The
LPVs suspected of being mixed are
filled with a gray square

(b) Clusteing results after removing
the misclassified datapoint

Fig. 1. Clusters of LPVs. Diamonds: LPVs in $\mathcal{D}_1^*$. Triangles: LPVs in $\mathcal{D}_2^*$. Bold crosses: centers of the clusters.

new algorithm enjoying better classification capabilities. Moreover, it would be interesting to derive optimal classification conditions when using unsupervised clustering algorithms (like Growing Neural Gas [5]) that estimate also the number of clusters needed. In this case, the corresponding PWA regression algorithm would be capable to tune automatically also the number s of submodels.

Acknowledgments. We are indebted to Dr. Marco Muselli for all the useful discussions about the paper. We also thank an anonymous reviewer for her/his valuable comments about Theorem 1 and Lemma 4.

References

1. A. Bemporad, J. Roll, and L. Ljung. Identification of hybrid systems via mixed-integer programming. *Proc. IEEE Conference on Decision and Control*, pages 786–792, 2001.
2. L. Breiman. Hinging hyperplanes for regression, classification, and function approximation. *IEEE Trans. Inform. Theory*, 39(3):999–1013, 1993.
3. G. Ferrari-Trecate, M. Muselli, D. Liberati, and M. Morari. A clustering technique for the identification of piecewise affine systems. In M. Di Benedetto and A. Sangiovanni-Vincentelli, editors, *Proc. 4th International Workshop on Hybrid Systems: Computation and Control*, volume 2034 of *Lecture Notes in Computer Science*, pages 218–231. Springer-Verlag, 2001.

4. G. Ferrari-Trecate, M. Muselli, D. Liberati, and M. Morari. A clustering technique for the identification of piecewise affine systems. *Automatica*, 39(2), 2002. To appear.
5. B. Fritzke. Some competitive learning methods. Technical report, Institute for Neural Computation. Ruhr-Universit at Bochum, 1997.
6. R.E. Groff, D.E. Koditschek, and P.P. Khargonekar. Piecewise linear homeomorphisms: The scalar case. *Proc. Int. Joint Conf. on Neural Networks*, 3:259–264, 2000.
7. S. Haykin. *Neural networks - a comprehensive foundation*. Macmillan, Englewood Cliffs, 1994.
8. E.A. Heredia and R.A. Gonzalo. Nonlinear filters based on combinations of piecewise polynomials with compact support. *IEEE Trans. on Signal Processing*, 48(10):2850–2863, 2000.
9. T.A. Johansen and B.A. Foss. Identification of non-linear system structure and parameters using regime decomposition. *Automatica*, 31(2):321–326, 1995.
10. J. MacQueen. On convergence of K-means and partitions with minimum average variance. *Ann. Math. Statist.*, 36:1084, 1965. Abstract.
11. E. D. Sontag. Nonlinear regulation: The piecewise linear approach. *IEEE Trans. Automatic Control*, 26(2):346–358, April 1981.

Approximate Stabilisation of Uncertain Hybrid Systems

Yan Gao[1], John Lygeros[1], Marc Quincampoix[2], and Nicolas Seube[3]

[1] Department of Engineering,
University of Cambridge, Cambridge, CB2 1PZ, U.K.
{yg221, jl290}@eng.cam.ac.uk
[2] Département de Mathematiques, Université de Bretagne Occidentale,
6 Avenue Le Gorgeu, B. P. 809, 29285 Brest Cedex, France
Marc.Quincampoix@univ-brest.fr
[3] ENSIETA, 2 Rue Francois Verny, 29806 Brest Cedex 9, France
Nicolas.Seube@ensieta.fr

Abstract. The problem of stabilisation of a class of uncertain hybrid systems is considered. Uncertainty enters in the form of a disturbance input that can affect both the continuous and the discrete dynamics. A method for designing piecewise constant feedback controllers is developed. The controllers achieve approximate exponential convergence of the runs of the closed loop system to the zero level set of a Lyapunov function.

1 Introduction

Stability conditions for hybrid systems have been the topic of intense research for many years. Many of the proposed methods involve the use of Lyapunov functions [1,2,3,4]. These methods are especially useful for certain classes of systems (for example, switched linear systems) for which computationally efficient methods such as LMI's can be used to construct Lyapunov functions automatically [5]. An overview of the different issues and approaches in this area can be found in [6].

The topic of stabilisation has been somewhat less extensively studied. Much of the work in this area deals with switched systems (usually linear and/or planar). The proposed stabilisation schemes typically involve selecting appropriate times for switching between a set of given systems [7,8,9,10,11]. In some cases this approach has been extended to robust stabilisation schemes for systems that involve certain types of uncertainty [12,13].

In this paper we concentrate on this last issue of robust stabilisation. We consider a fairly wide class of hybrid systems, with non-linear continuous dynamics and nonlinear transition functions. Uncertainty enters both the continuous evolution and discrete transitions, in the form of an uncontrollable disturbance input. The only "certain" aspect of the dynamics is the occurrence of the discrete transitions, which is determined exclusively by the state. Motivated by the work of [14] we use viability theory techniques to establish conditions under

O. Maler and A. Pnueli (Eds.): HSCC 2003, LNCS 2623, pp. 203–215, 2003.
© Springer-Verlag Berlin Heidelberg 2003

which a controller that approximately stabilises the system exponentially can be designed. The controller signal is piecewise constant and involves feedback whenever a discrete transition takes place and at regular sampling times along continuous evolution. The advantage of such a controller from a practical point of view is that it is easy to implement, using an interrupt driven sampled data system and a zero order hold.

2   Stabilisation Problem

2.1   Notation

The development of the stabilisation scheme makes use of a few concepts from non-smooth analysis and viability theory. We briefly review the necessary material below; for a more thorough treatment the reader is referred to [15,16, 17].

Let $\langle \cdot, \cdot \rangle$ denote the standard inner product in $\mathbb{R}^n$ and let $| \cdot |$ denote the corresponding metric. Let B denote the closed unit ball in $\mathbb{R}^n$ centred at the origin. For $x \in \mathbb{R}^n$ and $K \subseteq \mathbb{R}^n$ let $d(x, K)$ denote the distance of the point x to the set K defined by

$$d_K(x) = \inf_{y \in K} |x - y|.$$

The set of *proximal normals* to the set $K \subseteq \mathbb{R}^n$ at the point $x \in K$ is defined by

$$NP_K(x) = \{y \in \mathbb{R}^n \mid d_K(y + x) = |y|\}.$$

For $y \notin K$, we denote by $\Pi_K(y)$ the *projection* of y onto K, i.e. the set

$$\Pi_K(y) = \{x \in K \mid d_K(y) = |x - y|\}.$$

Given a real valued function $V : \mathbb{R}^n \to \mathbb{R}$, the *epigraph* of V is defined as

$$\text{Epi}(V) = \{(x, y) \in \mathbb{R}^{n+1} \mid V(x) \le y\}.$$

We say that V is *l-Lipschitz* if there exists a constant $l \ge 0$ such that for all $x, y \in \mathbb{R}^n$, $|V(x) - V(y)| \le l|x - y|$.

A set valued map $F(\cdot) : \mathbb{R}^n \to 2^{\mathbb{R}^n}$ is called *upper-semicontinuous* if for all $x \in \mathbb{R}^n$ and all $\epsilon > 0$ there exists $\delta > 0$ such that for all x' with $|x - x'| < \delta$, $F(x') \subseteq F(x) + \epsilon B$. F is called *Marchaud* if

1. F is upper-semicontinuous;
2. for all $x \in \mathbb{R}^n$, $F(x)$ is convex, compact and nonempty; and,
3. the growth of F is linear, i.e. there exists $\alpha > 0$ such that for all $x \in \mathbb{R}^n$

$$\sup\{|v| \mid v \in F(x)\} \le \alpha(|x| + 1).$$

We say F is *k-Lipschitz* if there exists a constant $k > 0$ such that for all $x, x' \in \mathbb{R}^n$

$$F(x) \subseteq F(x') + k|x - x'|B.$$

2.2 Dynamics

We consider a dynamical system defined by the following elements: $x \in \mathbb{R}^n$ state, $u \in U \subset \mathbb{R}^m$ control, $d \in D \subset \mathbb{R}^p$ disturbance, $f : \mathbb{R}^n \times U \times D \to \mathbb{R}^n$ vector field, $r : \mathbb{R}^n \times U \times D \to \mathbb{R}^n$ transition map, $J \subseteq \mathbb{R}^n$ transition set. To eliminate technical difficulties, we impose the following assumptions throughout.

Assumption 1 *1.* $f : \mathbb{R}^n \times U \times D \to \mathbb{R}^n$ *is continuous.*
2. f *has linear growth with respect to* x, *i.e. there exists an* $\alpha \geq 0$ *such that* $|f(x, u, d)| \leq \alpha(1 + |x|)$ *for all* $(x, u, d) \in \mathbb{R}^n \times U \times D$.
3. f *is bounded, i.e. there exists* $M \geq 0$ *such that* $|f(x, u, d)| \leq M$ *for all* $(x, u, d) \in \mathbb{R}^n \times U \times D$.
4. For all $u \in U$ *the set valued map* $x \to \{f(x, u, d) \mid d \in D\}$ *is Marchaud and* k-*Lipschitz.*
5. The sets U *is compact.*
6. The set J *is closed.*

Some of these assumptions can be relaxed, or replaced by others. We will not pursue such refinements of the results here.

Based on this collection of elements we define a fairly wide class of hybrid dynamics. Informally, the continuous dynamics are given by

$$\dot{x} = f(x, u, d)$$

where $x \in \mathbb{R}^n$ is the state, $u \in U$ are the control inputs and $d \in D$ are the disturbance inputs. Continuous evolution is interrupted by discrete transitions. The occurrence of the discrete transitions depends on the current state: transitions take place if and only if $x \in J$. The destination of a discrete transition depends on the state, control and disturbance and is given by

$$x \to r(x, u, d)$$

We write this system as

$$\left. \begin{array}{c} \dot{x} = f(x, u, d) \\ x \to r(x, u, d) \end{array} \right\} \tag{1}$$

The purpose of the present paper is to develop a method for designing a controller to select u so that the solutions of the system (1) converge to the zero level set of a Lyapunov function for all d.

To formally define the solutions of this class of hybrid systems, we recall the following notion from [4].

Definition 1 (Hybrid Time Set). *A hybrid time set* $\tau = \{I_i\}_{i=0}^N$ *is a finite or infinite sequence of intervals of the real line, such that*

- *for all* $i < N$, $I_i = [\tau_i, \tau_i']$;
- *if* $N < \infty$, *then either* $I_N = [\tau_N, \tau_N']$, *or* $I_N = [\tau_N, \tau_N'[$, *possibly with* $\tau_N' = \infty$;
- *for all* i, $\tau_i \leq \tau_i' = \tau_{i+1}$.

Without loss of generality we assume that $\tau_0 = 0$. For a hybrid time set $\tau = \{I_i\}_{i=0}^N$ define the continuous duration, $|\tau|$, by

$$|\tau| = \sum_{i=0}^N (\tau_i' - \tau_i) \tag{2}$$

and the discrete duration $\langle \tau \rangle$ by

$$\langle \tau \rangle = N \tag{3}$$

(possibly $\langle \tau \rangle = \infty$).

Definition 2 (Run). *A run of system* (1) *is a collection* (τ, x, u, d) *with* $\tau = \{I_i\}_{i=0}^N$ *a hybrid time set,* $x = \{x_i(\cdot)\}_{i=0}^N$ *a sequence of functions* $x_i(\cdot) : I_i \to X$, $u = \{u_i(\cdot)\}_{i=0}^N$ *a sequence of functions* $u_i(\cdot) : I_i \to U$ *and* $d = \{d_i(\cdot)\}_{i=0}^N$ *a sequence of functions* $d_i(\cdot) : I_i \to D$, *that satisfies*

- Discrete Evolution: *for* $i < N$, $x_i(\tau_i') \in J$ *and* $x_{i+1}(\tau_{i+1}) = r(x_i(\tau_i'), u_i(\tau_i'), d_i(\tau_i'))$.
- Continuous Evolution: *for all* i *with* $\tau_i < \tau_i'$
  1. $u_i(\cdot)$ *and* $d_i(\cdot)$ *are Lebesgue measurable;*
  2. $x_i(\cdot)$ *is the solution of the differential equation*

$$\dot{x}_i(t) = f(x_i(t), u_i(t), d_i(t))$$

  over the interval I_i *starting at* $x_i(\tau_i)$; *and,*
  3. $x_i(t) \notin J$, *for all* $t \in [\tau_i, \tau_i')$.

A run (τ, x, u, d) is called *finite* if τ is a finite sequence of compact intervals and *infinite* if either $|\tau| = \infty$, or $\langle \tau \rangle = \infty$. It is called *Zeno* if $\langle \tau \rangle = \infty$ but $|\tau| < \infty$.

2.3   Lyapunov Functions

Our aim is to design a controller that ensures that all runs of the closed loop system converge to a given set. We will encode this target set as the zero level set, $\{x \in \mathbb{R}^n \mid V(x) = 0\}$ of a Lyapunov function $V(\cdot) : \mathbb{R}^n \to \mathbb{R}$. In fact, the design will be such that V will not only converge to zero, but will do so exponentially (the meaning of this statement will be made precise shortly). In this section we briefly discuss the properties that the Lyapunov function should satisfy and the types of controller that will be used for the stabilisation.

A function $V(\cdot) : \mathbb{R}^n \to \mathbb{R}$ is said to satisfy condition (4) for $c \in [0, 1)$ at a point $x \in \mathbb{R}^n$ if

$$\inf_{u \in U} \sup_{d \in D} V(r(x, u, d)) - cV(x) \le 0. \tag{4}$$

Roughly speaking, condition (4) implies that if a discrete transition takes place from x, a $u \in U$ can be chosen so that V decreases by at least a factor of c as a result of the transition. Similarly, V is said to satisfy condition (5) for $a \in (0, \infty)$ at a point $x \in \mathbb{R}^n$ if for all $(p, q) \in NP_{Epi(V)}(x, V(x))$,

$$\inf_{u \in U} \sup_{d \in D} \langle p, f(x, u, d) \rangle - aqV(x) \le 0. \tag{5}$$

Roughly speaking, condition (5) implies that if continuous evolution takes place from x, a $u \in U$ can be chosen so that V decays initially at an instantaneous rate of at least a.

Definition 3 (Lyapunov Function). *A function* $V(\cdot) : \mathbb{R}^n \to \mathbb{R}$ *is called an* (l, c, a) *Lyapunov function for the system* (1) *if*

1. *it is* l*-Lipschitz continuous;*
2. *satisfies condition* (4) *for* $c \in [0, 1)$ *for all* $x \in J$;
3. *satisfies condition* (5) *for* $a \in (0, \infty)$ *for all* $x \in \mathbb{R}^n \setminus J$.

Notice that, the Lyapunov function is required to be Lipschitz but not necessarily differentiable.

What types of controller can be used to satisfy the requirement that the Lyapunov function converges to zero? The presence of the disturbance term d complicates this question even for continuous systems [18,19,20]. It is possible, for example, to construct counter examples to demonstrate that exact stabilisation may be possible using a discontinuous feedback controller, but impossible with continuous (even time varying) feedback [14]. Continuity of the controller is clearly desirable in our case, since only classical solutions are allowed for the differential equations. To allow discontinuous feedback controllers one may have to resort to relaxed (and technically more challenging) solution concepts [21,22].

Another alternative is to approach the problem in the context of differential games, by considering for example controllers in the class of non-anticipative strategies (see for example [23]). Besides being theoretically more complicated, non-anticipative strategies are also more difficult to interpret in practice, since they require instantaneous knowledge of the action of the disturbance by the controller.

To avoid such problems the authors of [14] propose to relax the exponential stabilisation requirement to allow approximate exponential stabilisation. Roughly speaking, the requirement in this case is that for any $\eta > 0$ we should be able to design the controller such that the Lyapunov function decreases exponentially to within η of zero for all actions of the disturbance. In [14] it is shown that this type of requirement can be met by feedback controllers that are piecewise constant in time and update the value of u only at regular intervals. Besides resolving a number of technical difficulties, controllers of this type are also attractive from a practical point of view, since they can be implemented by a sampled data system and a zero order hold.

Here we extend this approach to the class of hybrid systems introduced above. The controller can no longer be purely time driven (generate new inputs at regular sampling intervals) since it will also have to account for the discrete transitions. The controllers we consider will be dynamic, with internal state $y \in \mathbb{R}$. They can be specified by a sampling interval, $h > 0$, and two feedback functions, $g_1(\cdot, \cdot) : \mathbb{R}^n \times \mathbb{R} \to U$ and $g_2(\cdot, \cdot) : \mathbb{R}^n \times \mathbb{R} \to U$. Whenever a discrete transition is about to take place ($x \in J$) the controller sets u according to the feedback map $g_1(x, y)$. The controller sets u according to the feedback map $g_2(x, y)$ either after a discrete transition, or if h time units elapse since the last time that u was set (provided in both cases that $x \notin J$). Otherwise, u is kept constant to the value it was last set. Notice that the value of u is again piecewise constant: the value changes if either enough time elapses, or if a discrete transition takes place. From a practical point of view, one can think of implementing such a controller using a sample data system (with sampling period h), an interrupt that is set whenever $x \in J$ and a zero order hold.

Given an (l, c, a) Lyapunov function V, a time horizon $T > 0$ and an accuracy parameter $\eta > 0$, the discussion in the next section will show how to choose h, g_1 and g_2 to ensure that all runs (τ, x, u, d) of the closed loop system with $|\tau| \leq T$ satisfy

$$V(x_i(t)) \leq c^i e^{-a(t-\tau_0)} V(x_0(\tau_0)) + \eta, \qquad (6)$$

for all $I_i \in \tau$ and all $t \in I_i$. We will not define formally what is meant by the "runs of the closed loop system"; we hope that the meaning is clear from the above discussion. The formal statement would require one to define the controller as a hybrid system and define the composition of the controller with the plant using appropriate operators. While this is possible (for example, using the language of Hybrid Input/Output Automata [24]) we will not pursue this direction here.

Notice also that Zeno runs are not treated specially. A run of the closed loop systems may be Zeno and still satisfy the stabilisation requirement of equation (6). In fact, because each time a discrete transition takes place V decreases by a factor of c, there is an incentive for the controller to cause as many transitions as possible. In an extreme case, if the controller succeeds in making the run Zeno it can ensure that V converges to zero in finite time! We will not impose any requirement on the controller to avoid this strategy. We assume that if Zeno solutions are undesirable, the system model (1) should be constructed in such a way that it does not allow the controller this freedom (for example, imposes a minimum time between discrete transitions).

3   Stabilising Controller

The following discrete time version of the well known Bellman-Gronwall Lemma will be useful in the proofs. The two facts can be established by induction.

Lemma 1. *Suppose that for all* $i = 0, 1, \cdots$, $a_i, b_i, r_i \geq 0$ *and* $r_{i+1} \leq a_i r_i + b_i$. *Then,*

$$r_{N+1} \leq \max_{0 \leq i \leq N} \{r_0, b_i\} \{ \sum_{i=0}^{N} (\prod_{j=i}^{N} a_j) + 1 \} \qquad (7)$$

and

$$r_{N+1} \leq r_0 \prod_{i=0}^{N} a_i + \max_{0 \leq i \leq N} \{b_i\} \{ \sum_{i=1}^{N} (\prod_{j=i}^{N} a_j) + 1 \}. \qquad (8)$$

The construction of the stabilising controller makes use of some basic concepts from viability theory. Viability theory provides a systematic way of dealing with questions of reachability for a wide class of dynamical systems. Roughly speaking a subset, K, of the state space of a dynamical system is called viable if for every initial condition in K a solution of the system that stays in K exists. Viability theory has been studied extensively for continuous dynamical systems [16]. More recently, the approach has been extended to a wide class of hybrid systems known as impulse differential inclusions [25].

The class of hybrid systems considered here can also be thought of as a type of impulse differential inclusion. However, because of the presence of both a control u and a disturbance d extending the results of [25] to this class of systems is not entirely straightforward; viability would have to be interpreted in the context of differential games, with all the technical complications this implies [23,26]. To avoid these problems we instead consider a somewhat weaker definition of viability. We require that for every $\eta > 0$ and every initial condition in K a solution that stays η close to K (but not necessarily in K) exists. The main result in this direction is summarised in the following theorem.

Theorem 1. *Consider a nonempty closed set $K \subset \mathbb{R}^n$, a time horizon $T \geq 0$ and an accuracy parameter $\epsilon > 0$. Assume that, in addition to Assumption 1, we have the following.*

1. *$\inf_{u \in U} \sup_{d \in D} d_K(r(x, u, d)) \leq c d_K(x)$, for all $x \in J$.*
2. *$\inf_{u \in U} \sup_{d \in D} \langle f(x, u, d), p \rangle \leq 0$, for all $x \in K \setminus J$ and all $p \in NP_K(x)$.*

Then for any $x_0 \in K$, there exist a piecewise constant controller such that all finite runs (τ, x, u, d) starting at x_0 with $|\tau| \leq T$ satisfy

$$x_i(t) \in K + \epsilon B, \quad \forall I_i \in \tau, \forall t \in I_i. \tag{9}$$

Proof. As discussed above, the piecewise constant controller will be specified by three elements:

1. A sampling time $h > 0$.
2. A feedback map $\hat{g}_1(\cdot) : J \to U$, which is used to set u before a discrete transition (i.e. whenever $x \in J$).
3. A feedback map $\hat{g}_2(\cdot) : \mathbb{R}^n \setminus J \to U$, which is used to set u either after a discrete transition, or whenever h time units elapse from the last time u was set (provided in both cases $x \notin J$).

Notice that in this case the controller is assumed to be static (no internal state). Also $\hat{g}_1$ and $\hat{g}_2$ do not need to be defined on the whole of the state space. We start by defining the maps $\hat{g}_1$ and $\hat{g}_2$. We then show how h can be selected to ensure the desired approximate viability property.

$\hat{g}_1(x)$ for $x \in J$ is chosen using condition 1 of Theorem 1. The condition, together with the fact that U is compact, implies that for all $x \in J$ there exists $\tilde{u}(x) \in U$ such that

$$\sup_{d \in D} d_K(r(x, \tilde{u}(x), d)) \leq c d_K(x).$$

For $x \in J$ we set $\hat{g}_1(x) = \tilde{u}(x)$.

For $\hat{g}_2(x)$ we distinguish two cases. If $x \in K \setminus J$ pick an arbitrary $u \in U$ and set $\hat{g}_2(x) = u$. If $x \in \mathbb{R}^n \setminus (K \cup J)$, pick an arbitrary $y \in \Pi_K(x)$. Notice that

$x - y \in NP_K(y)$. By condition 2 of Theorem 1 and the compactness of U, there exists a $\tilde{u}(x) \in U$ such that

$$\sup_{d \in D} \langle f(x, \tilde{u}(x), d), x - y \rangle \leq 0.$$

We define $\hat{g}_2(x) = \tilde{u}(x)$. This method for determining the feedback for the continuous evolution (which is also used in [14]) is sometimes referred to as "proximal aiming" [17].

Assume the sampling time satisfies $h \leq \frac{1}{2k}$. Let (τ, x, u, d) be an arbitrary finite run of the closed loop system with $\tau = \{[\tau_i, \tau'_i]\}_{i=0}^N$ and $|\tau| \leq T$, starting at some $x_0(\tau_0) \in K$. For each $I_i = [\tau_i, \tau'_i]$ let $\{t_{ij}\}_{j=0}^{N_i}$ denote the set of times at which u is set by the controller. Clearly, $N_i < \infty$ (recall that $|\tau| \leq T$ and $h > 0$), $t_{i0} = \tau_i$, $t_{iN_i} = \tau'_i$ and for all $0 \leq j < N_i$, $t_{i(j+1)} - t_{ij} \leq h$. In particular, $t_{i(j+1)} - t_{ij} = h$ for all $0 \leq j < N_i - 1$.

Because of the proximal aiming construction used to define $\hat{g}_2(x)$, a result from [14] (Lemma 5.2, see also [27]) shows that for all $t \in [t_{ij}, t_{i(j+1)}]$,

$$d_K(x_i(t))^2 \leq eM^2(t - t_{ij})^2 + e^{2k(t - t_{ij})}d_K(x_i(t_{ij}))^2.$$

for the k and M defined in Assumption 1. In particular,

$$d_K(x_i(t_{i(j+1)}))^2 \leq eM^2h^2 + e^{2k(t_{i(j+1)} - t_{ij})}d_K(x_i(t_{ij}))^2.$$

By (8) of Lemma 1, for all $t \in [t_{ij}, t_{i(j+1)}]$

$$d_K(x_i(t))^2 \leq d_K(x_i(t_{i0}))^2 e^{2k(t - t_{ij})} \prod_{\alpha=0}^{j-1} e^{2k(t_{i(j+1)} - t_{ij})}$$

$$+ eM^2h^2 \left(e^{2k(t - t_{ij})} + \sum_{\alpha=1}^{j-1} e^{2k(t - t_{ij})} \prod_{\beta=\alpha}^{j-1} e^{2k(t_{i(j+1)} - t_{ij})} + 1 \right)$$

$$= d_K(x_i(\tau_i))^2 e^{2k(t - \tau_i)} + eM^2h^2 \left(e^{2k(t - t_{ij})} + e^{2k(t - t_{ij})} \sum_{\alpha=1}^{j-1} \prod_{\beta=\alpha}^{j-1} e^{2kh} + 1 \right)$$

$$\leq d_K(x_i(\tau_i))^2 e^{2k(t - \tau_i)} + eM^2h^2 \left(e^{2kh} \sum_{\alpha=0}^{j-1} e^{2kh\alpha} + 1 \right)$$

$$= d_K(x_i(\tau_i))^2 e^{2k(t - \tau_i)} + eM^2h^2 e^{2kh} \left(\frac{e^{2khj} - 1}{e^{2kh} - 1} + 1 \right)$$

$$= d_K(x_i(\tau_i))^2 e^{2k(t - \tau_i)} + e^{2kh+1}M^2h \left(\frac{2kh}{e^{2kh} - 1} \frac{e^{2khj} - 1}{2k} + h \right)$$

$$\leq d_K(x_i(\tau_i))^2 e^{2k(t - \tau_i)} + e^{2kh+1}M^2h \left(\frac{e^{2khj} - 1}{2k} + h \right)$$

$$\leq d_K(x_i(\tau_i))^2 e^{2k(t - \tau_i)} + e^{2kh+1}M^2h \left(\frac{e^{2kT} - 1}{2k} + h \right)$$

The last term decreases to zero as h decreases. Therefore, for any $\delta > 0$ we can choose $h \leq 1/2k$ small enough to ensure that for all $t \in [\tau_i, \tau'_i]$

$$d_K(x_i(t))^2 \leq \delta + d_K(x_i(\tau_i))^2 e^{2k(t - \tau_i)}.$$

By the construction of $\hat{g}_1(x)$,

$$d_K(x_{i+1}(\tau_{i+1}))^2 = d_K(r(x_i(\tau_i'), g(x_i(\tau_i')), d(\tau_i')))^2 \le c^2 d_K(x_i(\tau_i'))^2.$$

Therefore,

$$d_K(x_{i+1}(\tau_{i+1}))^2 \le \left(c^2 e^{2k(\tau_i' - \tau_i)}\right) d_K(x_i(\tau_i))^2 + c^2\delta.$$

Recall that $x_0(\tau_0) \in K$, therefore $d_K(x_0(\tau_0)) = 0$. By (7) of Lemma 1 we have that

$$d_K(x_N(\tau_N))^2 \le \delta c^2 \left(\sum_{i=0}^{N-1} \prod_{j=i}^{N-1} c^2 e^{2k(\tau_j' - \tau_j)} + 1\right)$$

$$= \delta c^2 \left(\sum_{i=0}^{N-1} \prod_{j=i}^{N-1} e^{2k(\tau_j' - \tau_j)} \prod_{j=i}^{N-1} c^2 + 1\right)$$

$$= \delta c^2 \left(\sum_{i=0}^{N-1} e^{2k(\tau_{N-1}' - \tau_i)} \prod_{j=i}^{N-1} c^2 + 1\right)$$

$$\le \delta c^2 e^{2kT} \left(\sum_{i=1}^{N} c^{2i} + 1\right)$$

$$\le \delta c^2 e^{2kT} \left(\sum_{i=0}^{\infty} c^{2i} + 1\right)$$

$$= \delta c^2 e^{2kT} \frac{2 - c^2}{1 - c^2}.$$

Choosing h small enough to give

$$\delta \le \frac{\epsilon^2(1 - c^2)}{c^2 e^{2kT}(2 - c^2)}$$

we have that

$$x_N(\tau_N) \in K + \epsilon B.$$

The claim of the theorem follows, since this holds for an arbitrary finite run with $|\tau| \le T$.

Notice that the sampling time, h, depends on the parameters of the continuous system (k and M) the desired stabilization horizon (T) and the desired accuracy (ϵ).

Theorem 1 will be used to provide the required stabilisation conditions. Roughly speaking, given a Lyapunov function V we show that the epigraph of the function satisfies the conditions of Theorem 1 for an appropriate choice of extended dynamics (in $\mathbb{R}^{n+1}$). The choice of dynamics is such that the approximate viability result implies the approximate convergence of the value of the Lyapunov function to 0.

Theorem 2. *Assume that $V(\cdot)$ is an (l, c, a) Lyapunov function and fix a time horizon $T \geq 0$ and an accuracy parameter $\eta > 0$. There exists a piecewise constant controller such that all runs of the closed loop system with $|\tau| \leq T$ satisfy*

$$V(x_i(t)) \leq c^i e^{-a(t-\tau_0)} V(x_0(\tau_0)) + \eta$$

for all $I_i \in \tau$, $t \in I_i$.

Proof. Consider the extended system with state $\hat{x} = (x, y) \in \mathbb{R}^{n+1}$, control $u \in U$, disturbance $d \in D$, continuous evolution given by

$$\hat{f}(\hat{x}, u, d) = \begin{bmatrix} f(x, u, d) \\ -ay \end{bmatrix}$$

discrete evolution given by

$$\hat{r}(\hat{x}, u, d) = \begin{bmatrix} r(x, u, d) \\ cy \end{bmatrix}$$

and transition set

$$\hat{J} = J \times \mathbb{R} \subseteq \mathbb{R}^{n+1}.$$

It is easy to see that since the original system fulfils Assumption 1, so does the augmented system (notice that the additional y dynamics are linear).

Let $K = \mathrm{Epi}(V) \subseteq \mathbb{R}^{n+1}$. Since V is an (l, c, a) Lyapunov function, it satisfies condition (5) for all $x \in \mathbb{R}^n \setminus J$. Therefore, the augmented system satisfies condition 2 of Theorem 1 for all $\hat{x} \in \mathbb{R}^n \setminus \hat{J}$. Here we prove that the augmented system satisfies condition 1 of Theorem 1 for all $\hat{x} \in \hat{J}$. Given $\hat{x} = (x, y) \in \hat{J}$, suppose that $d_{\mathrm{Epi}(V)}(\hat{x}) = \gamma$. Then $(x, y) \in \mathrm{Epi}(V) + \gamma B$. Therefore, $V(x) \leq y + \gamma$. By condition (4) there exists $u \in U$ such that

$$V(r(x, u, d)) \leq cV(x) \leq cy + c\gamma, \forall d \in D.$$

This yields $(r(x, u, d), cy) \in \mathrm{Epi}(V) + c\gamma B$ for all $d \in D$. Thus $d_{\mathrm{Epi}(V)}(r(x, u, d), cy) \leq c\gamma, \forall d \in D$, i.e. $\sup_{d \in D} d_{\mathrm{Epi}(V)}(\hat{x}) \leq c d_{\mathrm{Epi}(V)}(\hat{x})$. Thus it is proved that the augmented system satisfies condition 1 of Theorem 1 for all $\hat{x} \in \hat{J}$.

Select an accuracy parameter $\epsilon > 0$. By Theorem 1 we can choose $h > 0$, $\hat{g}_1 : \mathbb{R}^{n+1} \to U$ and $\hat{g}_2 : \mathbb{R}^{n+1} \to U$ to form a static piecewise constant controller such that all runs $(\tau, \hat{x}, u, d)$ of the closed loop system with $|\tau| \leq T$ that start in K satisfy

$$\hat{x}_i(t) \in K + \epsilon B, \text{ for all } I_i \in \tau, t \in I_i. \tag{10}$$

For an arbitrary $x_0(\tau_0) \in \mathbb{R}^n$ initialise the internal state of the controller to $y_0(\tau_0) = V(x_0(\tau_0))$ and consider the runs of the extended system starting at $(x_0(\tau_0), y(\tau_0))$. By construction, $(x_0(\tau_0), y(\tau_0)) \in \mathrm{Epi}(V)$. Moreover, the values of the internal state y are not affected directly by x. In particular, for all $I_i \in \tau$ and all $t \in I_i$

$$y_i(t) = c^i e^{-a(t-\tau_0)} y_0(\tau_0) = c^i e^{-a(t-\tau_0)} V(x_0(\tau_0)).$$

By equation (10),

$$d_{\mathrm{Epi}(V)}\left(x_i(t), c^i e^{-a(t-\tau_0)} V(x_0(\tau_0))\right) \leq \epsilon.$$

Therefore, there exists x' with $|x_i(t) - x'| \leq \epsilon$ such that

$$\left(V(x') - c^i e^{-a(t-\tau_0)} V(x_0(\tau_0))\right)^2 + |x_i(t) - x'|^2 \leq \epsilon^2.$$

In particular,

$$V(x') \leq c^i e^{-a(t-\tau_0)} V(x_0(\tau_0)) + \epsilon.$$

Since V is l-Lipschitz, $V(x') \geq V(x_i(t)) - l\epsilon$. Hence,

$$V(x_i(t)) \leq c^i e^{-a(t-\tau_0)} V(x_0(\tau_0)) + \epsilon(1 + l).$$

Choosing

$$\epsilon \leq \frac{\eta}{1+l}$$

concludes the proof.

Theorem 2 implies that the sampling interval h also depends on the Lipschitz constant of the Lyapunov function l (in addition to the parameters listed above).

Summarising, the internal state of the controller is initialised to $y(\tau_0) = V(x_0(\tau_0))$ and subsequently evolves according to the dynamics

$$\left.\begin{array}{c} \dot{y} = -ay \\ y \to cy \end{array}\right\} \tag{11}$$

The two feedback maps $g_1 : \mathbb{R}^n \times \mathbb{R} \to U$ and $g_2 : \mathbb{R}^n \times \mathbb{R} \to U$ are simply given by $g_1(x, y) = \hat{g}_1(x, y)$ and $g_2(x, y) = \hat{g}_2(x, y)$ for $\hat{g}_1$, $\hat{g}_2$ as in the proof of Theorem 2. The sampling time h is chosen as in the proof of Theorem 1.

4   Concluding Remarks

We presented a first step towards a general method for the stabilization of uncertain hybrid systems based on non-smooth analysis and viability theory techniques. The advantage of the proposed control scheme is that it only involves feedback at the transition times and at regular sampling instants along continuous evolution. It is therefore easy to implement using sample data systems and interrupts.

The work is currently being extended to allow systems with controllable transitions (notice that in this paper all transitions are forced). The extension seems procedural if transitions are controlled by u. The case where transitions can also be forced by d is more challenging however.

Acknowledgement. The work of Y. Gao and J. Lygeros was supported by the EPSRC under grant GR/R51575/01.

References

1. Ye, H., Michel, A., Hou, L.: Stability Theory for Hybrid dynamical Systems, IEEE Trans. Automatic Control **43** (1998) 461–474
2. Branicky, M.S.: Multiple Lyapunov Functions and Other Analysis Tools for Switched and Hybrid Systems. IEEE Trans. Automatic Control **43** (1998) 475–482
3. Michel, A.N., Hu, B.: Towards a Stability Theory for Hybrid Dynamical Systems. Automatica **35** (1999) 371–384
4. Lygeros, J., Johansson, K.H., Simić, S.N., Zhang, J., Sastry, S.: Dynamical Properties of Hybrid Automata. IEEE Trans. Automatic Control (2002) (to appear)
5. Johansson, M., Rantzer, A.: Computation of Piecewise Quadratic Lyapunov Functions for Hybrid Systems. IEEE Trans. Automatic Control **43** (1998) 555–559
6. De Carlo, R., Branicky, M., Pettersson, S., Lennarston, B.: Perspectives and Results on the Stability and Stabilizability of Hybrid Systems. Proceedings of the IEEE **88** (2000) 1069–1082
7. Morse, A.S.: Control Using Logic Based Switching. In: Isidori, A. (ed.): Trends in Control. Springer-Verlag Berlin Heidelberg (1995) 69–114
8. Wicks, M., Peleties, P., De Carlo, R.: Switched Controller Synthesis for the Quadratic Stabilization of a Pair of Unstable Linear Systems. European J. Control **4** (1998) 140–147
9. Liberzon, D., Morse, A.S.: Basic Problems in Stability and Design of Sswitched Systems. IEEE Control Systems Magazine **19** (1999) 59–70
10. Liberzon, D., Hespanha, J.P., Morse, A.S.: Stability of Switched Systems: A Lie Algebraic Approach. Systems & Control Letters **37** (1999) 117–122
11. Xu X., Antsaklis, P.J.: Stabilization of Second Order LTI Switched Systems. International J. Control **73** (2000) 1261–1279
12. Savkin, A.V., Skafidas, E., Evans, R.J.: Robust Output Feedback Stabilizability via Controller Switching. Automatica **35** (1999) 69–74
13. Hu, B., Xu, X., Michel, A.N., Antsaklis, P.J.: Robust Stabilizing Control Laws for a Class of Second Order Switched Systems. Systems & Control Letters **38** (1999) 197–207
14. Quincampoix, M., Seube, N.: Stabilization of Uncertain Control Systems Through Piecewise Constant Feedback. J. Math. Analysis and Applications **218** (1998) 240–255
15. Aubin, J.-P., Frankowska, H.: Set Valued Analysis. Birkhäuser Boston (1990)
16. Aubin, J.-P.: Viability Theory. Birkhäuser Boston (1991)
17. Clarke, F.H., Ledyaev, Yu.S., Stern, R.J., Wolenski, P.R.: Nonsmooth Analysis and Control Theory. Springer-Verlag New York (1998)
18. Gutman, S.: A Lyapunov Min-Max Approach. IEEE Trans. Automatic Control **24** (1979) 437–443
19. Corless, M.J., Leitmann, G.: Continuous State Feedback Guaranteeing Uniform Uultimate Boundedness for Uncertain Dynamic Systems. IEEE Trans. Automatic Control **26** (1981) 1139–1144
20. Kokotovic, P.K., Freeman, R.A.: Robust Nonlinear Control Design. Birkhauser Basel (1996)

21. Filippov, A.F.: Differential Equations with Discontinuous Righthand Sides. Kluwer Academic Publishers (1988)
22. Krasovskii, N.N., Subottin, A.I.: Game Theoretical Control Problems. Springer-Verlag New York (1988).
23. Cardaliaguet, P.: A Differential Game with Two Players and One Target. SIAM J. Control and Optimization **34** (1996) 1441–1460
24. Lynch, N., Segala, R., Vaandrager, F., Weinberg, H.B.: Hybrid I/O Automata. In: Hybrid Systems III. Lecture Notes in Computer Science, Vol. 1066. Springer-Verlag Berlin Heidelberg (1996) 496–510
25. Aubin, J.-P., Lygeros, J., Quincampoix, M., Sastry, S., Seube, N.: Impulse Differential Inclusions: A Viability Approach to Hybrid Systems. IEEE Trans. Automatic Control **47** (2002) 2–20
26. Cardaliaguet, P., Quincampoix, M., Saint-Pierre, P.: Pursuit Differential Games with State Constraints. SIAM J. Control and Optimization, **39** (2001) 1615–1632
27. Cardaliaguet, P.: Domaines Discriminants et Jeux Différentieles. PhD Thesis, Université Paris IX Dauphine (1993)

Efficient Mode Enumeration of Compositional Hybrid Systems

Tobias Geyer, Fabio Danilo Torrisi, and Manfred Morari

Automatic Control Laboratory, Swiss Federal Institute of Technology (ETH)
CH-8092 Zurich, Switzerland, {geyer,torrisi,morari}@aut.ee.ethz.ch

Abstract. A hyperplane arrangement is a polyhedral cell complex where the relative position of each cell of the arrangement and the composing hyperplanes are summarized by a sign vector computable in polynomial time. This tool from computational geometry enables the development of a fast and efficient algorithm that translates the composition of hybrid systems into a piecewise affine model. The tool provides also information on the real combinatorial degree of the system which can be used to reduce the size of the search tree and the computation time of the optimization algorithms underlying optimal and model predictive control.

1 Introduction

A *hybrid system* is a collection of digital programs interacting among each other and with an analog environment. Each *logic state* of the digital part of the hybrid system acts on the analog part inducing a different operational *mode*. On the other hand, the evolution of the analog part triggers switches in the states of the digital part. The practical relevance of hybrid systems is twofold. Digital controllers embedded in a continuous environment demand for adequate modelling, analysis and design tools. Moreover, many physical phenomena admit a natural hybrid description, like circuits integrating relays or diodes, biomolecular networks and TCP/IP networks.

Hybrid systems can be composed to form *compositional hybrid systems* [2,21, 22,24]. The resulting system is in general very complex, as the number of different operational modes depends exponentially on the number of component systems. The explosion of the size of the logic state leads to computational difficulties as the time and space complexity of many algorithms depends on the number of operational modes.

In some cases, the composition induces a structure that can be exploited, like in hierarchical hybrid systems [1]. This allows one to break the problem down into pieces and to apply the assume-guarantee approach [2,19]. Recognizing that a system can be modelled as a hierarchical hybrid system is part of the "art" of model building. In many cases it may not be possible at all, because the cross interactions among the components are too tight. However, tight interactions often render many modes infeasible and the complexity of the system can be reduced

O. Maler and A. Pnueli (Eds.): HSCC 2003, LNCS 2623, pp. 216–232, 2003.

by explicitly computing and taking into account only the feasible modes. This paper presents an efficient technique to enumerate the modes of a compositional hybrid system.

We will focus on *discrete hybrid automata* (DHA) [28]. DHA models are a mathematical abstraction of the features provided by other computation oriented and domain specific hybrid system frameworks: *Mixed logical dynamical* (MLD) *models* [7], *piecewise affine* (PWA) *systems* [25], *linear complementarity* (LC) *systems* [29], *extended linear complementarity* (ELC) *systems* [18], and *max-min-plus-scaling* (MMPS) *systems* [10,18]. In particular, as shown first in [26] and then, with different arguments, in [18,28] all those modelling frameworks are equivalent and it is possible to represent the same system using any of these frameworks.

DHAs are formulated in the discrete-time domain. They generalize many computation oriented models for hybrid systems and therefore represent a universal starting point for solving complex analysis and synthesis problems for hybrid systems. In particular, the enumeration of feasible modes is easily solvable for DHA systems by using algorithms that compute the cells of an arrangement of hyperplanes [16]. This is a classical problem in computational geometry [9] and admits optimal [14] and efficient [3,15,16] algorithms.

The impact of those techniques on applications is threefold. First, at the modelling stage, the enumeration of modes allows the designer to understand the real complexity of the compound model. This is mandatory for performing model reduction by merging modes.

Second, after the modelling stage, the model can be efficiently translated into a PWA model. This operation is trivial once all modes have been enumerated. In this respect, this paper solves a problem similar to [4] where the author computes the PWA model equivalent to an MLD system. The main difference is that the approach in [4] is based on multi-parametric programming and mixed integer linear programming and deals directly with the MLD model, while the approach presented here relies on the computation of the cells of the hyperplane arrangement and is applicable to DHAs. Note that, as shown in [28], DHAs can be automatically translated into MLD models using the tool HYSDEL and most of the MLD models that have been presented in the literature were derived from DHA descriptions using HYSDEL [5,8,13].

Third, during the computational stage (i.e. analysis and control), the explicit computation of the set of feasible modes of the compound system allows to prune unnecessary modes from the resulting system and to reduce the combinatorial explosion of related algorithms. This is of particular importance for *model predictive control* (MPC) of hybrid models [7], where the aim is to compute the next N inputs that optimize a performance index defined on the variables of a hybrid *prediction model*. The prediction model is the series-connection of N identical single-step prediction models where each model uses the state predicted by the previous model. The mode enumeration allows one to introduce cuts on the modes of the complete prediction model.

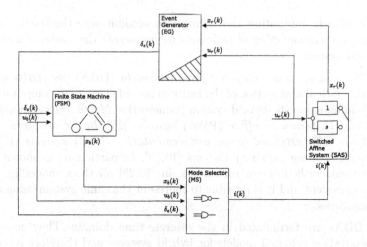

Fig. 1. A discrete hybrid automaton (DHA) is the connection of a finite state machine (FSM) and a switched affine system (SAS) through a mode selector (MS) and an event generator (EG). The output signals are omitted for clarity.

The paper is organized as follows: In Sect. 2, we introduce the class of DHA. Section 3 presents the problem of cell enumeration in hyperplane arrangements and in Sect. 4, the equivalence between the class of DHA and PWA systems is proved. Section 5 details how these results can be applied in the hybrid domain. Finally, Sect. 6 contains experimental results where we enumerate the modes of a hybrid model built using the HYSDEL [28] modelling language. The information collected during this mode enumeration allows one to either build efficiently an equivalent PWA model or to speed up the computation of the hybrid MPC feedback law by automatically adding cuts to the optimization problem. Section 7 summarizes the results and points out directions for future research.

2   Discrete Hybrid Automata

Discrete hybrid automata [28] are the interconnection of a finite state machine and a switched affine system through a mode selector and an event generator (see Fig. 1).

Switched Affine System (SAS). A switched affine system is a collection of affine systems:

$$x_r(k+1) = A_{i(k)}x_r(k) + B_{i(k)}u_r(k) + f_{i(k)} \qquad (1a)$$

$$y_r(k) = C_{i(k)}x_r(k) + D_{i(k)}u_r(k) + g_{i(k)}, \qquad (1b)$$

where $k \in \mathbb{N}$ is the time indicator, $x_r \in \mathcal{X}_r \subseteq \mathbb{R}^{n_r}$ is the continuous state vector, $u_r \in \mathcal{U}_r \subseteq \mathbb{R}^{m_r}$ is the exogenous continuous input vector, $y_r \in \mathcal{Y}_r \subseteq \mathbb{R}^{p_r}$ is the continuous output vector, $\{A_i, B_i, f_i, C_i, D_i, g_i\}_{i \in \mathcal{I}}$ is a collection of matrices of appropriate dimensions and the mode $i(k) \in \mathcal{I} \subset \mathbb{N}$ is an input signal selecting the affine state-update dynamics and the affine output function[1].

Event Generator (EG). An event generator is a mathematical object that generates a logic signal according to the fulfillment of a constraint:

$$\delta_e(k) = f_H(x_r(k), u_r(k)), \tag{2}$$

where $f_H : \mathbb{R}^{n_r} \times \mathbb{R}^{m_r} \to \mathcal{D} \subseteq \{0,1\}^{n_e}$ is a vector of descriptive functions of a set of linear constraints. In particular, *threshold events* are modelled as $[\delta_e^i(k) = 1] \leftrightarrow [f_H^i(x_r(k), u_r(k)) \leq 0]$, and *time events* are modelled by adding a clock variable $t(k)$ in the switched affine system with dynamics $t(k+1) = t(k)+T_s$ and setting $[\delta_e^i(k) = 1] \leftrightarrow [t(k) \geq t_0]$, where the superscript i denotes the i-th component of a vector and T_s is the sampling time.

Finite State Machine (FSM). A finite state machine (or automaton) is a discrete dynamic process that evolves according to a logic state-update function:

$$x_b(k + 1) = f_B(x_b(k), u_b(k), \delta_e(k)) \tag{3a}$$

$$y_b(k) = g_B(x_b(k), u_b(k), \delta_e(k)), \tag{3b}$$

where $x_b \in \mathcal{X}_b \subseteq \{0,1\}^{n_b}$ is the binary state, $u_b \in \mathcal{U}_b \subseteq \{0,1\}^{m_b}$ the exogenous binary input, $y_b \in \mathcal{Y}_b \subseteq \{0,1\}^{p_b}$ the output, $\delta_e(k)$ the logic signal defined by the EG and $f_B : \mathcal{X}_b \times \mathcal{U}_b \times \mathcal{D} \to \mathcal{X}_b$, $g_B : \mathcal{X}_b \times \mathcal{U}_b \times \mathcal{D} \to \mathcal{Y}_b$ are deterministic logic functions.

Mode Selector (MS). The logic state $x_b(k)$, the binary input $u_b(k)$, and the event $\delta_e(k)$ select the dynamic mode $i(k)$ of the SAS through a Boolean function $f_M : \mathcal{X}_b \times \mathcal{U}_b \times \mathcal{D} \to \mathcal{I}$, which is therefore called *mode selector*. The output of this function

$$i(k) = f_M(x_b(k), u_b(k), \delta_e(k)) \tag{4}$$

is called *active mode*. We say that a *mode switch* occurs at time k if $i(k-1) \neq i(k)$. Note that one may associate with a state $x_b(k)$ of the FSM more than one mode $i(k)$ according to the event $\delta_e(k)$.

Definition 1. *A DHA is well-posed on* $\mathcal{X}_r \times \mathcal{X}_b$, $\mathcal{U}_r \times \mathcal{U}_b$, $\mathcal{Y}_r \times \mathcal{Y}_b$, *if for all initial conditions* $x(0) = \begin{bmatrix} x_r(0) \\ x_b(0) \end{bmatrix} \in \mathcal{X}_r \times \mathcal{X}_b$ *and for all inputs* $u(k) = \begin{bmatrix} u_r(k) \\ u_b(k) \end{bmatrix} \in \mathcal{U}_r \times \mathcal{U}_b$, *for all* $k \in \mathbb{N}$, *the state trajectory* $x(k) \in \mathcal{X}_r \times \mathcal{X}_b$ *and output trajectory* $y(k) = \begin{bmatrix} y_r(k) \\ y_b(k) \end{bmatrix} \in \mathcal{Y}_r \times \mathcal{Y}_b$ *are uniquely defined.*

3   Cell Enumeration in Hyperplane Arrangement

In this section, we recall the notation and the solution approach to the problem of enumerating the cells of a hyperplane arrangement using reverse search [3].

---

[1] A SAS of the form (1) preserves the value of the state when a switch occurs, however it is possible to implement reset maps on a DHA as shown in [28, Proposition 1].

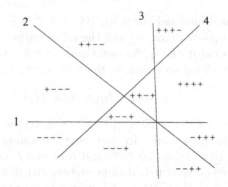

Fig. 2. Arrangement of four hyperplanes (lines) in $\mathbb{R}^2$ with the markings.

Let $\mathcal{A}$ be a collection of n distinct hyperplanes $\{H_i\}_{i=1,\ldots,n}$ in $\mathbb{R}^d$, where each hyperplane is given by a linear equality $H_i = \{x : a_i x = b_i\}$. Let $SV : \mathbb{R}^d \to \{-, 0, +\}^n$ be the sign vector defined as

$$SV_i(x) = \begin{cases} - & \text{if } a_i x < b_i \\ 0 & \text{if } a_i x = b_i \quad i \in \{1, 2, \ldots, n\} \\ + & \text{if } a_i x > b_i \end{cases} \tag{5}$$

Consider the set $\mathcal{P}_m = \{x : SV(x) = m\}$ for a given sign vector m. This set is called *cell* of the arrangement and is a polyhedron as it is defined by equalities and inequalities. Note, that each 0 element of m is associated with an equality constraint in (5) and reduces the dimension of $\mathcal{P}_m$ by one. We will refer to m as the *marking* of the polyhedron or the cell $\mathcal{P}_m$ in the *hyperplane arrangement* $\mathcal{A}$ (see Fig. 2). Let $M(\mathcal{R})$ be the image of the function $SV(x)$ for $x \in \mathcal{R} \subseteq \mathbb{R}^d$, namely the collection of all the possible markings of all the points in $\mathcal{R}$.

The problem of enumerating the cells of an arrangement amounts to enumerate all the elements of the set $M(\mathcal{R})$. Clearly, it is enough to enumerate the sign vectors that have all nonzero entries, as any lower dimensional cell is a face of a full dimensional cell [30, Theorem 7.16].

We say that n hyperplanes $\{H_i\}_{i=1,\ldots,n}$ in $\mathbb{R}^d$ are in *general position*, if there are no two parallel hyperplanes and if any point of $\mathbb{R}^d$ belongs at most to d hyperplanes. Let $\#M(\mathcal{R})$ be the number of full dimensional cells identified by $M(\mathcal{R})$. Buck's formula defines the following upper bound: $\#M \le \sum_{i=0}^{d} \binom{n}{i} = O(n^d)$ [9], with the equality satisfied when the hyperplanes are in general position and $\mathcal{R} = \mathbb{R}^d$.

The cell enumeration problem admits an optimal solution with time and space complexity $O(n^d)$ [14]. An alternative approach based on reverse search was presented in [3], improved in [16] and implemented in [15]. Reverse search is an exhaustive search technique which can be considered as a special graph search. This search technique has been used to design efficient algorithms for various enumeration problems such as enumeration of all spanning trees and cells in hyperplane arrangements. Before evaluating the complexity of the algorithm based on reverse search, let $\mathrm{lp}(n,d)$ denote the complexity of solving a linear program (LP) with n constraints in d variables.

Proposition 1. *[16, Theorem 4.1] There is a reverse search algorithm for enumeration of hyperplane arrangements that runs in $O(n\mathrm{lp}(n,d)\#M)$ time and $O(n,d)$ space.*

Note that in many cases of interest, the hyperplanes are not in general position and $\#M$ can be considerably smaller than the theoretical upper bound.
   The following proposition follows directly from the definition of $\mathcal{P}_m$ and (5).

Proposition 2. *The collection of polyhedral sets $\{\mathcal{P}_m\}_{m\in M(\mathcal{R})}$ satisfies:*

$$(i) \ \bigcup_{m\in M(\mathcal{R})} \mathcal{P}_m = \mathcal{R}, \qquad (ii) \ (\mathcal{P}_i)\cap(\mathcal{P}_j) = \emptyset, \forall i \neq j.$$

A collection of polyhedral sets that satisfies points *(i)* and *(ii)* in Proposition 2 is a *polyhedral partition* of a polyhedral set $\mathcal{R}$.

4   Discrete Hybrid Automata and Piecewise Affine Systems

PWA systems [18,25] are defined by partitioning the state space into polyhedral regions and associating with each region a different linear state-update function

$$x(k+1) = A_{j(k)}x(k) + B_{j(k)}u(k) + f_{j(k)} \tag{6a}$$
$$y(k) = C_{j(k)}x(k) + D_{j(k)}u(k) + g_{j(k)} \tag{6b}$$
$$j(k) \text{ such that } \quad H_{j(k)}x(k) + J_{j(k)}u(k) \leq K_{j(k)} \tag{6c}$$
$$\tilde{H}_{j(k)}x(k) + \tilde{J}_{j(k)}u(k) < \tilde{K}_{j(k)}, \tag{6d}$$

where $x \in \mathcal{X} \subseteq \mathbb{R}^n$, $u \in \mathcal{U} \subseteq \mathbb{R}^m$, $y \in \mathcal{Y} \subseteq \mathbb{R}^p$, the matrices $A_{j(k)}$, $B_{j(k)}$, $f_{j(k)}$, $C_{j(k)}$, $D_{j(k)}$, $g_{j(k)}$, $H_{j(k)}$, $J_{j(k)}$, $K_{j(k)}$, $\tilde{H}_{j(k)}$, $\tilde{J}_{j(k)}$, $\tilde{K}_{j(k)}$, $j(k) \in \mathcal{J}$, $\mathcal{J}$ finite, are constant and have suitable dimensions, the inequalities in (6c) and (6d) should be interpreted componentwise and the constraints (6c) and (6d) define a polyhedral partition $\{\mathcal{P}_j\}_{j\in\mathcal{J}}$ of the set $\mathcal{X} \times \mathcal{U}$.[2]

Definition 2. *Let Σ_1, Σ_2 be hybrid models with inputs $u_1(k), u_2(k) \in \mathcal{U}$, states $x_1(k), x_2(k) \in \mathcal{X}$ and outputs $y_1(k), y_2(k) \in \mathcal{Y}$, $k \in \mathbb{N}$. The hybrid models Σ_1 and Σ_2 are equivalent on $\mathcal{X}, \mathcal{U}, \mathcal{Y}$ if for all $u_1(k) = u_2(k) = u(k) \in \mathcal{U}$ the output trajectories $y_1(k)$ and $y_2(k)$ coincide and $x_1(k) = x_2(k)$ for all time-instants $k \in \mathbb{N}$.*

---

[2] Note that (6d) ensures the single definition of the functions (6a) and (6b) on borders of the cells of the partition.

Lemma 1. *[28, Lemma 1] Let Σ_{PWA} be a well-posed[3] PWA model defined on a set of states $\mathcal{X} \subseteq \mathbb{R}^n$, a set of inputs $\mathcal{U} \subseteq \mathbb{R}^m$ and a set of outputs $\mathcal{Y} \subseteq \mathbb{R}^p$. Then there exists a well-posed DHA model Σ_{DHA} such that Σ_{DHA} and Σ_{PWA} are equivalent.*

The equivalence of the previous lemma allows us to call $\mathcal{J}$ modes of the PWA system (6a)-(6d).

Lemma 2. *Let Σ_{DHA} be a well-posed DHA model defined on a set of states $\mathcal{X} \subseteq \mathbb{R}^n$, a set of inputs $\mathcal{U} \subseteq \mathbb{R}^m$ and a set of outputs $\mathcal{Y} \subseteq \mathbb{R}^p$. Then there exists a well-posed PWA model Σ_{PWA} such that Σ_{PWA} and Σ_{DHA} are equivalent.*

Proof. Consider the arrangement of a set of hyperplanes defining the linear constraints of the EG. By Proposition 2 this defines a polyhedral partition. Let $\mathcal{P}_m$ be a polyhedron of that partition. By construction, $\delta_e = \bar{\delta}_e(m) = f_{\text{H}}(x_r, u_r)$ for any point $[x_r^T, u_r^T]^T \in \mathcal{P}_m$, namely all the points in $\mathcal{P}_m$ trigger the same event vector $\bar{\delta}_e(m)$. Given a marking m, the associated event $\bar{\delta}_e(m)$, a binary state $\bar{x}_b \in \mathcal{X}_b$ and a binary input $\bar{u}_b \in \mathcal{U}_b$, the MS determines the mode $\bar{i}$ using the Boolean function (4). The $\bar{i}$-th dynamic in the SAS given by (1a) and (1b) is the corresponding affine dynamic. The FSM yields the binary state-update $x_b(k+1)$ as well as the binary output $y_b(k)$ according to (3a) and (3b). Therefore, for each $m \in M$, $\bar{x}_b \in \mathcal{X}_b$ and $\bar{u}_b \in \mathcal{U}_b$, the system

$$x_r(k+1) = A_{f_{\text{M}}(\bar{x}_b, \bar{u}_b, \bar{\delta}_e(m))} x_r(k) + B_{f_{\text{M}}(\bar{x}_b, \bar{u}_b, \bar{\delta}_e(m))} u_r(k) + f_{f_{\text{M}}(\bar{x}_b, \bar{u}_b, \bar{\delta}_e(m))}, \quad (7a)$$

$$x_b(k+1) = f_{\text{B}}(\bar{x}_b, \bar{u}_b, \bar{\delta}_e(m)), \quad (7b)$$

$$y_r(k) = C_{f_{\text{M}}(\bar{x}_b, \bar{u}_b, \bar{\delta}_e(m))} x_r(k) + D_{f_{\text{M}}(\bar{x}_b, \bar{u}_b, \bar{\delta}_e(m))} u_r(k) + g_{f_{\text{M}}(\bar{x}_b, \bar{u}_b, \bar{\delta}_e(m))}, \quad (7c)$$

$$y_b(k) = g_{\text{B}}(\bar{x}_b, \bar{u}_b, \bar{\delta}_e(m)), \quad (7d)$$

$$\text{if } x_b(k) = \bar{x}_b, \quad u_b(k) = \bar{u}_b, \quad [x_r^T(k), u_r^T(k)]^T \in \mathcal{P}_m, \quad (7e)$$

defines a PWA system. In fact, by collecting $x = \left[\begin{smallmatrix} x_r \\ x_b \end{smallmatrix}\right]$ and $y = \left[\begin{smallmatrix} y_r \\ y_b \end{smallmatrix}\right]$, (7a)–(7d) are formally equivalent to (6a)–(6b) and (7e) is formally equivalent to (6c)–(6d). $\square$

5   Algorithm

The following section presents an algorithm based on the cell enumeration summarized in Sect. 3 that efficiently enumerates the feasible modes of a composition of DHAs and derives an equivalent PWA model.

5.1   Single DHA

Consider the DHA Σ as in Sect. 2 and let $\mathcal{U}_r \times \mathcal{U}_b \times \mathcal{X}_r \times \mathcal{X}_b$ denote the input-state space of the DHA, for which we want to solve the following problem. Find the set of feasible modes $\mathcal{J} \subseteq \mathcal{I}^4$, the polyhedral partition $\{\mathcal{P}_j\}_{j \in \mathcal{J}}$ and the corresponding PWA dynamics $\{\mathcal{S}_j\}_{j \in \mathcal{J}}$, where $\mathcal{S}_j = \{A_j, B_j, f_j, C_j, D_j, g_j\}$. As this is

---

[3] For PWA systems, well-posedness is defined similarly to Definition 1.
[4] $\mathcal{J} = \mathcal{I}$ holds, if all the modes $\mathcal{I}$ of the SAS are feasible.

the same problem as in Lemma 2, we derive an algorithm from the constructive proof of the lemma. Note, that $\mathcal{I}$ is the image of the MS and can be computed once the set $M(\mathcal{U}_r \times \mathcal{X}_r)$ has been enumerated.

Algorithm 1

function SingleDHA(Σ, $\mathcal{U}_r$, $\mathcal{X}_r$, $u_b(k)$, $x_b(k)$)
for $m \in M(\mathcal{U}_r \times \mathcal{X}_r)$
  get $\mathcal{P}_m$ defined by m and $\mathcal{A}$, get $\delta_e(k)$ based on m
  $i(k) = f_M(x_b(k), u_b(k), \delta_e(k))$
  $x_r(k+1) = A_{i(k)} x_r(k) + B_{i(k)} u_r(k) + f_{i(k)}$, $x_b(k+1) = f_B(x_b(k), u_b(k), \delta_e(k))$
  $y_r(k) = C_{i(k)} x_r(k) + D_{i(k)} u_r(k) + g_{i(k)}$, $y_b(k) = g_B(x_b(k), u_b(k), \delta_e(k))$
  push { $\mathcal{P}_m$, $S_{i(k)}$, $u_b(k)$, $x_b(k)$, $x_b(k+1)$, $y_b(k)$ } on STACK

Algorithm 1 enumerates the feasible modes and leads to a set of PWA models defined on $\mathcal{U}_r \times \mathcal{X}_r$, where each model is associated with a feasible combination of binary states and inputs $x_b \in \mathcal{X}_b$, $u_b \in \mathcal{U}_b$. This representation is advantageous if determining the state-update and the outputs for a given state and input is the main purpose, as choosing the respective PWA model can be done by binary search. The model can be transformed easily into a PWA model defined over $\mathcal{U}_r \times \mathcal{U}_b \times \mathcal{X}_r \times \mathcal{X}_b$ by associating additional hyperplanes with the binary inputs and states.

5.2 Composition of DHAs

The algorithm proposed above can be extended in a natural way to deal with a composition of DHAs. Consider s DHAs denoted as Σ_i, $i = 1, \ldots, s$ with inputs $u_i = \begin{bmatrix} u_r^i \\ u_b^i \end{bmatrix} \in \mathcal{U}_r^i \times \mathcal{U}_b^i$, states $x_i = \begin{bmatrix} x_r^i \\ x_b^i \end{bmatrix} \in \mathcal{X}_r^i \times \mathcal{X}_b^i$, and outputs $y_i = \begin{bmatrix} y_r^i \\ y_b^i \end{bmatrix} \in \mathcal{Y}_r^i \times \mathcal{Y}_b^i$, $i = 1, \ldots, s$. Let $\mathcal{I}_i$ be the set of feasible modes of the DHA Σ_i. The composition has the exogenous input $u_e = \begin{bmatrix} u_r^e \\ u_b^e \end{bmatrix} \in \mathcal{U}_r^e \times \mathcal{U}_b^e$ and the exogenous output $y_e = \begin{bmatrix} y_r^e \\ y_b^e \end{bmatrix} \in \mathcal{Y}_r^e \times \mathcal{Y}_b^e$. Let the compound vector $x_b = [(x_b^1)^T, \ldots, (x_b^s)^T]^T \in \mathcal{X}_b^1 \times \ldots \times \mathcal{X}_b^s$ be the sorted aggregation of the binary states of the s DHAs. The time index k has been omitted for brevity.

Before describing the algorithm, we recall some definitions and results from graph theory [11] to describe the topology of the composition.

Definition 3. *A* directed graph *or* digraph *is an ordered pair of sets* $G = (V, E)$, *where V is a set of* vertices *and E is a set of ordered pairs of vertices of V called* edges. *A* directed closed walk *is defined as an alternating sequence of vertices and edges, beginning and ending with the same vertex, such that each edge is oriented from the vertex preceding it to the vertex following it. If additionally, no vertices except the initial and terminal one appear more than once, the directed closed walk is called a* directed circuit. *A digraph, that has no directed circuits is called* acyclic.

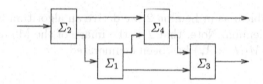

Fig. 3. Example composition of DHAs.

The definitions above can be applied directly to the composition of DHAs by defining DHA Σ_i, $i = 1, \ldots, s$ as vertex v_i and the connections from outputs to inputs as directed edges. In general one edge can represent several connections. Note that directed circuits correspond to loops and the lack of loops is equivalent to having an acyclic directed graph. We define the connections among the DHAs by an adjacency matrix.

Definition 4. *Let G be a digraph with s vertices containing no parallel edges. Then the adjacency matrix $W = [w_{ij}]$ of the digraph G is a $s \times s$ $(0, 1)$-matrix with $w_{ij} = 1$ if there is an edge directed from the i-th vertex to the j-th vertex and $w_{ij} = 0$ otherwise.*

Given a composition of DHAs, the adjacency matrix W can be easily determined based on the connections.

Theorem 1. *[11, Theorem 9.17] Digraph G is acyclic if and only if $\det(I - W)$ is not equal to zero, where I is the identity matrix of the same size as W.*

Theorem 2. *[11, Theorem 9.16] If digraph G is acyclic, then its vertices can be ordered such that the adjacency matrix W is an upper (or lower) triangular matrix.*

Definition 5. *Given an acyclic graph, the computational order $\mathcal{O}$ is the sequence of indices of W.*

Example 1. Figure 3 depicts four DHAs and the connections among them. DHA 2 has an exogenous input, DHA 3 and 4 have exogenous outputs. The adjacency matrix W follows to

$$W = \begin{bmatrix} 0 & 0 & 1 & 1 \\ 1 & 0 & 0 & 1 \\ 0 & 0 & 0 & 0 \\ 0 & 0 & 1 & 0 \end{bmatrix} \begin{matrix} 1 \\ 2 \\ 3 \\ 4, \end{matrix}$$

where the indices of the corresponding DHAs are shown on the right side. As the condition $\det(I - W) \neq 0$ holds, the digraph is acyclic and we can reorder W as

$$W' = \begin{bmatrix} 0 & 1 & 1 & 0 \\ 0 & 0 & 1 & 1 \\ 0 & 0 & 0 & 1 \\ 0 & 0 & 0 & 0 \end{bmatrix} \begin{matrix} 2 \\ 1 \\ 4 \\ 3, \end{matrix}$$

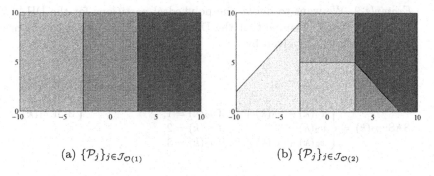

(a) $\{\mathcal{P}_j\}_{j \in \mathcal{J}_{\mathcal{O}(1)}}$ (b) $\{\mathcal{P}_j\}_{j \in \mathcal{J}_{\mathcal{O}(2)}}$

Fig. 4. Polyhedral partitions for the first two DHAs of Example 5.

where the rows refer to Σ_2, Σ_1, Σ_4, Σ_3 and the associated sequence of indices is $\{2, 1, 4, 3\}$ which is also the computational order. This implies for example, that the inputs of Σ_1 do not depend on the outputs of Σ_4 because $\mathcal{O}(1) = 2 <$ $\mathcal{O}(4) = 3$.

Compositions without Loops. In a first step, we assume that the connections do not form loops and that the digraph is therefore acyclic. This can be easily determined by Theorem 1. From Theorem 2 follows, that W can be transformed into an upper triangular matrix employing for example topological sorting [11]. The computational order $\mathcal{O}$ follows from Definition 5.

According to the single DHA case, our aim is to determine for the composition of DHAs $\{\Sigma_i\}_{i=1,\ldots,s}$ with the corresponding adjacency matrix W the set of feasible modes $\mathcal{J} \subseteq \mathcal{I}_1 \times \ldots \times \mathcal{I}_s$, the polyhedral partition $\{\mathcal{P}_j\}_{j \in \mathcal{J}}$ and the corresponding PWA dynamics $\{\mathcal{S}_j\}_{j \in \mathcal{J}}$, where $\mathcal{S}_j = \{A_j, B_j, f_j, C_j, D_j, g_j\}$. For a given binary compound state $x_b \in \mathcal{X}_b$ and a given exogenous binary input $u_b^e \in \mathcal{U}_b^e$, the Algorithm 2 is the following.

Let $\Sigma_{\mathcal{O}(1)}$ denote the DHA with computational order 1. Its real input-state space is given by $\mathcal{R}_{\mathcal{O}(1)} = \mathcal{U}_r^{\mathcal{O}(1)} \times \mathcal{X}_r^{\mathcal{O}(1)}$, where $\mathcal{U}_r^{\mathcal{O}(1)} \subseteq \mathcal{U}_r^e$ and $\mathcal{X}_r^{\mathcal{O}(1)}$ is a property of $\Sigma_{\mathcal{O}(1)}$. Therefore, Algorithm 1 can be used to determine the polyhedral partition $\{\mathcal{P}_j\}_{j \in \mathcal{J}_{\mathcal{O}(1)}}$ and the corresponding PWA dynamics $\{\mathcal{S}_j\}_{j \in \mathcal{J}_{\mathcal{O}(1)}}$ of $\Sigma_{\mathcal{O}(1)}$. Every polyhedron $\mathcal{P}_j$, $j \in \mathcal{J}_{\mathcal{O}(1)}$ defines via the connections a real input set $\mathcal{U}_r^{\mathcal{O}(2)}$ for the DHA $\Sigma_{\mathcal{O}(2)}$ with computational order 2. Thus, for a given $j \in \mathcal{J}_{\mathcal{O}(1)}$, Algorithm 1 can be used again to compute the polyhedral partition $\{\mathcal{P}_j\}_{j \in \mathcal{J}_{\mathcal{O}(2)}}$ and the corresponding PWA dynamics $\{\mathcal{S}_j\}_{j \in \mathcal{J}_{\mathcal{O}(2)}}$ of $\Sigma_{\mathcal{O}(2)}$. This is repeated for all the remaining $j \in \mathcal{J}_{\mathcal{O}(1)}$.

The algorithm introduced above is repeated until the DHA $\Sigma_{\mathcal{O}(k)}$ with the highest computational order is reached. The polyhedral partition of this DHA is part of the overall polyhedral partition $\{\mathcal{P}_j\}_{j \in \mathcal{J}}$ of the compound DHA system and is therefore added to it. Stepping recursively through the composition of DHAs according to their computational order leads to the polyhedral partition $\{\mathcal{P}_j\}_{j \in \mathcal{J}}$ and the corresponding PWA dynamics $\{\mathcal{S}_j\}_{j \in \mathcal{J}}$.

Example 2. We want to derive the polyhedral partitions for the DHAs Σ_1 and Σ_2 of Example 1. Assume that the DHA Σ_1 yields as output the 1-norm of its input and that Σ_2 is given by[5]

$$\text{EG:} \begin{cases} \delta_1(k) = [x_2(k) \geq -3], \\ \delta_2(k) = [x_2(k) \geq 3] \end{cases}$$

$$\text{MS:} \; i_2(k) = \begin{cases} 1 & \text{if } \bar{\delta}_1(k) \wedge \bar{\delta}_2(k), \\ 2 & \text{if } \delta_1(k) \wedge \bar{\delta}_2(k), \\ 3 & \text{if } \delta_1(k) \wedge \delta_2(k) \end{cases}$$

$$\text{SAS:} \; y_2(k) = \begin{cases} x_2(k) - u_2(k) + 12 & \text{if } i_2(k) = 1, \\ u_2(k) - 5 & \text{if } i_2(k) = 2, \\ x_2(k) + u_2(k) - 8 & \text{if } i_2(k) = 3. \end{cases}$$

Let the input-state space of Σ_2 be $\mathcal{R}_2 = \mathcal{U}_r^2 \times \mathcal{X}_r^2 = \{0, 10\} \times \{-10, 10\}$. Remembering that Σ_2 has computational order 1 and using Algorithm 2 leads to the polyhedral partition $\{\mathcal{P}_j\}_{j \in \mathcal{J}_{\mathcal{O}(1)}}$ shown in Fig. 4(a). The PWA dynamics are defined on the polyhedral partition and are omitted due to space limitations. DHA Σ_1 with computational order 2 further divides the polyhedral partition $\{\mathcal{P}_j\}_{j \in \mathcal{J}_{\mathcal{O}(1)}}$ depending on the PWA dynamics of its predecessor Σ_2 as shown in Fig. 4(b).

Compositions with Loops. The algorithm is now generalized to compositions of DHAs $\{\Sigma_i\}_{i=1,\dots,s}$ containing loops. Having identified the adjacency matrix W and verified that the digraph is not acyclic, we first have to find the feedback arc set.

Definition 6. *Let $G = (V, E)$ be a digraph. A set $F \subseteq E$ is a feedback arc set (FAS) for G, if $G' = (V, E - F)$ is acyclic. The set F is a minimum FAS if the number of edges in F is minimum.*

Finding the minimum FAS is NP-hard. However, for a given digraph $G = (V, E)$ a fast and effective heuristic exist [12] yielding an FAS F with upper bounded cardinality $\#F \leq \#E/2 - \#V/6$ and time complexity $O(\#E)$. This algorithm yields a vertex sequence inducing a rearranged adjacency matrix W' and an FAS. Letting the feedback arc be a directed edge from vertex v_i to vertex v_j, every feedback arc $f \in F$ is replaced by a directed edge v_i from a newly created auxiliary input vertex v_u to v_j. The auxiliary input is real if v_i corresponds to a real variable and binary if v_i relates to a binary variable. This yields a composition of DHAs with an acyclic digraph and an augmented exogenous input space $\mathcal{U}_r^e \times \bar{\mathcal{U}}_r^e \times \mathcal{U}_b^e \times \bar{\mathcal{U}}_b^e$, where $\bar{\mathcal{U}}_r^e$ and $\bar{\mathcal{U}}_b^e$ denote the auxiliary real and binary input spaces, respectively. As connections between DHAs are equivalent to equality constraints of the respective inputs and outputs, the removed connections corresponding to the FAS are added as equality constraints to a separate constraint list $\mathcal{C}$.

Using the computational order given by the sequence of indices of W' allows us to use Algorithm 2 to derive the set of feasible modes $\mathcal{J}$, the polyhedral

---

[5] In general, the state-update function does not influence the polyhedral partition and is therefore omitted for brevity.

partition $\{\mathcal{P}_j\}_{j\in\mathcal{J}}$ and the corresponding PWA dynamics $\{\mathcal{S}_j\}_{j\in\mathcal{J}}$. Adding the equality constraints in $\mathcal{C}$ removes the auxiliary inputs as well as infeasible modes together with the corresponding polyhedra and PWA dynamics.

For further details and examples on loops in compositions of DHAs, refer to the extended version of this paper [17].

6   Examples and Applications

This final section presents two examples showing how the mode enumeration algorithm can be used to efficiently derive the PWA representation of a given hybrid system and in which way it can be exploited to speed up MPC.

Car Example. In [27], the authors proposed a hybrid model of a car with robotized gear shift. This example was adopted in [4] where the author computes the MLD model using HYSDEL and the PWA system equivalent to the MLD model using multi-parametric programming. As the model is given in HYSDEL, the algorithm in Sect. 5 starts from this description to translate the car example into a PWA model. The resulting PWA model encompasses 30 polyhedra and 6 modes and is computed in 7.5 s in Matlab 5.3 on a Pentium III 650 MHz machine. This is ten times faster than the algorithm reported in [4] on a similar machine.

The reason for this is twofold. First, the algorithm presented here exploits the structure of the DHA models, while the algorithm presented in [4] deals with MLD models concealing that structural information. Second, the approach in [4] needs to remove redundant inequalities at each iteration of the exploration algorithm. This operation may dominate the total computation time in [4].

Paperboy Example. A paperboy delivers by bike two heavy and bulky mail items to two different houses within a neighborhood consisting of four properties and one road. The properties and the road have different slopes and different friction coefficients.

The input of the system at time instant k is given by the force $F_b(k) \in \mathcal{U} \subset \mathbb{R}^2$, $\mathcal{U} = \{-F_{max}, F_{max}\}^2$, $F_{max} = 162\,\mathrm{N}$ that the paperboy applies to his bike in order to accelerate and brake. Driven by F_b, the paperboy cycles in the 2-dimensional neighborhood $\mathcal{X} = \{-s_n, s_n\}^2$ with $s_n = 1000\,\mathrm{m}$. His position is given by $x(k) = [x_1(k), x_2(k)]^T \in \mathcal{X} \subset \mathbb{R}^2$ and his speed $v(k) \in \mathcal{V} \subset \mathbb{R}^2$ is limited by $\mathcal{V} = \{-v_{max}, v_{max}\}^2$, where $v_{max} = 15\,\mathrm{m/s} = 54\,\mathrm{km/h}$. Two binary states $d_1(k), d_2(k) \in \{0,1\}$ denote the status of the mail delivery. The outputs of the model are the position $x(k)$ and the number of delivered mail items $n(k) \in \{0,1,2\}$.

As depicted in Fig. 5, the paperboy problem can be decomposed in three DHAs. Each DHA is described in the following.

Topology of Neighborhood. A road of width $w_r = 4\,\mathrm{m}$ divides the neighborhood into two parts which are further partitioned into two properties yielding a total of four properties and one road. These five regions are each characterized by

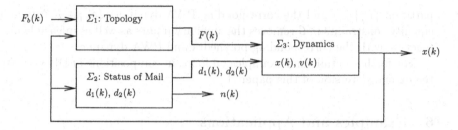

Fig. 5. Paperboy example consisting of three DHAs with the respective states.

different slopes and friction coefficients. Given the force $F_b(k) \in \mathbb{R}^2$ that the paperboy applies, the effective force $F(k) \in \mathbb{R}^2$ acting on the bike thus depends on the partition $i(k) \in \{1, \dots, 5\}$: $F(k) = F_b(k) - \mu_{i(k)} - \nu_{i(k)}v(k)$, where $\mu_{i(k)}$ is the grade resistance corresponding to the slope and $\nu_{i(k)}$ is a friction coefficient. The parameters are given by $\mu_1 = [\begin{smallmatrix} 2 \\ 0 \end{smallmatrix}]$, $\mu_2 = [\begin{smallmatrix} 1.5 \\ 0 \end{smallmatrix}]$, $\mu_3 = [\begin{smallmatrix} -0.5 \\ 0 \end{smallmatrix}]$, $\mu_4 = [\begin{smallmatrix} -1 \\ 0 \end{smallmatrix}]$, $\mu_5 = [\begin{smallmatrix} 0 \\ 0 \end{smallmatrix}]$ and $\nu_1 = [\begin{smallmatrix} 2 & 0 \\ 0 & 2 \end{smallmatrix}]$, $\nu_2 = [\begin{smallmatrix} 0.5 & 0 \\ 0 & 0.5 \end{smallmatrix}]$, $\nu_3 = [\begin{smallmatrix} 1 & 0 \\ 0 & 1 \end{smallmatrix}]$, $\nu_4 = [\begin{smallmatrix} 1.5 & 0 \\ 0 & 1.5 \end{smallmatrix}]$, $\nu_5 = [\begin{smallmatrix} 0.05 & 0 \\ 0 & 0.05 \end{smallmatrix}]$.

Therefore, the first DHA is static and has the real inputs $x(k)$, $v(k)$ and $F_b(k)$. The real output is $F(k)$.

$$\text{EG}_1: \begin{cases} \delta_{x1}(k) = [x_1(k) \le -0.5w_r], \\ \delta_{x2}(k) = [x_1(k) \ge 0.5w_r], \\ \delta_y(k) = [x_2(k) \ge 0] \end{cases} \qquad \text{MS}_1: i(k) = \begin{cases} 1 & \text{if } \delta_{x1}(k) \wedge \delta_y(k), \\ 2 & \text{if } \delta_{x2}(k) \wedge \delta_y(k), \\ 3 & \text{if } \delta_{x1}(k) \wedge \bar{\delta}_y(k), \\ 4 & \text{if } \delta_{x2}(k) \wedge \bar{\delta}_y(k), \\ 5 & \text{if } \delta_{x1}(k) \wedge \bar{\delta}_{x2}(k) \end{cases}$$

$$\text{SAS}_1: F(k) = F_b(k) - \mu_{i(k)} - \nu_{i(k)}v(k),$$
$$i(k) = 1, \dots, 5$$

Status of Mail Delivery. The houses are squares of size $s_h = 10\,\text{m}$ centered at $x_{h1} = [-p_h, -p_h]$ and $x_{h2} = [p_h, p_h]$, $p_h = 40\,\text{m}$. The four walls of a house can be modelled by four hyperplanes with corresponding binary variables equal to 1, if the paperboy is 'within' the respective wall. The respective flag $\delta_{hi}(k)$, $i = 1, 2$ denoting that the paperboy has reached House i and delivered the mail, is the logic *and* of these four binary variables. Finally, a FSM stores the mail delivery status using the binary states $d_1(k)$, $d_2(k)$.

This leads to the following DHA with the real input $x(k)$, the binary states $d_1(k)$ and $d_2(k)$, which are also outputs and a third output $n(k) = d_1(k) + d_2(k)$ denoting the number of delivered mail items.

$$\text{EG}_2: \begin{cases} \delta_{h1}(k) = |x(k) - x_{h1}|_\infty \le 0.5s_h, \\ \delta_{h2}(k) = |x(k) - x_{h2}|_\infty \le 0.5s_h \end{cases} \qquad \text{FSM}_2: \begin{cases} d_1(k+1) = d_1(k) \vee \delta_{h1}(k), \\ d_2(k+1) = d_2(k) \vee \delta_{h2}(k) \end{cases}$$

Dynamics of Paperboy. The weight $m(k)$ is the weight of the paperboy and his bike ($M_b = 90\,\text{kg}$) plus the weight of the undelivered mail items (each mail item weighs $M_m = 10\,\text{kg}$). Therefore, the total weight is time-dependent and decreasing as the paperboy delivers the mail. By Newton's law, the effective force $F(k)$ divided by the total weight is the acceleration and by integrating this, the velocity and the position of the paperboy are obtained. The integral is approximated by two discrete-time dynamical systems with sampling time $T_s = 1$ s.

The third DHA has the real input $F(k) \in \mathbb{R}^2$, the two binary inputs $d_1(k)$, $d_2(k)$ denoting the status of the mail delivery and the real states $x(k)$ and $v(k)$ characterizing the position and the velocity, respectively. The outputs are the position $x(k)$ and the velocity $v(k)$.

$$\text{MS}_3: \quad i(k) = \begin{cases} 1 & \text{if } \bar{d}_1(k) \wedge \bar{d}_2(k), \\ 2 & \text{if } (d_1(k) \wedge \bar{d}_2(k)) \vee (\bar{d}_1(k) \wedge d_2(k)), \\ 3 & \text{if } d_1(k) \wedge d_2(k) \end{cases}$$

$$\text{SAS}_3: \quad \begin{bmatrix} v(k+1) \\ x(k+1) \end{bmatrix} = \begin{bmatrix} v(k) \\ x(k) \end{bmatrix} + \begin{bmatrix} F(k)/m(k) \\ v(k) \end{bmatrix} T_s, \quad \text{where } m(k) = \begin{cases} M_b + 2M_m & \text{if } i(k) = 1, \\ M_b + M_m & \text{if } i(k) = 2, \\ M_b & \text{if } i(k) = 3 \end{cases}$$

The paperboy starts the mail delivery at a random position $x(0)$ with speed $v(0) = 0$. His objective is to first deliver one mail item to House 1 centered around x_{h1} and then to move on to House 2 at position x_{h2} to deliver the second mail item. This can be expressed by the objective function

$$J(t) = \sum_{k=0}^{N-1} \|x(t+k|t) - x_{ref}(t)\|_1 \tag{8}$$

defined over the horizon N using the 1-norm. The reference $x_{ref}(t)$ is switched from x_{h1} to x_{h2} once the paperboy has reached House 1.

In the next section, we will use the paperboy example to evaluate the potential of the mode enumeration algorithm to reduce the computation time of MPC. The MPC control problem amounts to minimizing the objective function (8) subject to the evolution of the paperboy model over the prediction horizon and subject to constraints on F_b, x and v as given above. The solution of this optimization problem which is a *Mixed-Integer Linear Program* (MILP) yields the force F_b.

6.1   Model Predictive Control

When translating a composition of DHAs into an MLD model, information about the structure of the hybrid model is lost. However, the explicit computation of the set of feasible modes of the composition of DHAs allows one to add structural information and to prune infeasible modes from the resulting system. This is of particular importance for MPC of hybrid models [7], where MPC computes the next N inputs optimizing a performance index which is defined on the variables of a hybrid prediction model. The prediction model (see Fig. 6) is the series-connection of N identical single-step prediction models, where each model uses the state predicted by the previous one as initial state. The mode enumeration allows to introduce cuts on the modes of the complete prediction model.

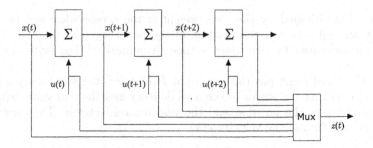

Fig. 6. Conceptual scheme of the 3-steps ahead prediction model.

This information can be formulated in terms of additional logic constraints. According to [23], two methods can be used to transform logic constraints into mixed integer inequalities which can be added to the MLD model. The *Symbolical Method* converts the constraints into a canonical normal form, which is then translated into integer inequalities, whereas the *Geometrical Method* computes the convex hull of the integer points for which the constraints are fulfilled. In general, the second method is superior to the first one because the convex hull is the smallest set containing all the integer feasible points and because it introduces less additional inequalities.

We used HYSDEL to transform the paperboy example of the previous section into an MLD model. The algorithm in Sect. 5 computed the set of feasible modes which were added as additional constraints to the MLD model using the symbolical method as well as the geometrical method. We solved MPC with the objective function (8) and various prediction horizons. Using CPLEX [20] as MILP solver, Fig. 7 reports the average computation times for MPC on the two improved models normalized to the plain model produced by HYSDEL.

Note that both methods add non-trivial cuts reducing the computation time of CPLEX up to a factor of 2. This improvement is more evident when using less advanced solvers like [6], where for a prediction horizon of 3 for example, the additional information reduces the computation time by a factor of 210. Figure 7 shows clearly, that the cuts introduced by the geometrical method are more effective than the ones of the symbolical method. This is mainly due to the fact that the symbolical method needs much more constraints to define the feasible modes. For the paperboy example, the symbolical method introduces 239 additional constraints, whereas the geometrical method only adds 42. The third conclusion is, that both methods become more effective as the prediction horizon is increased, as the benefit of additional cuts grows with the number of binary variables.

7   Conclusions

We have presented an effective method to enumerate the set of feasible modes for a given composition of DHAs. The same procedure transforms the compound model into a PWA model. The mode enumeration can be exploited in order to

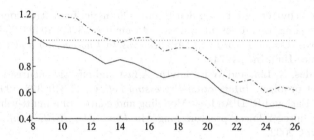

Fig. 7. Normalized average computation time vs. prediction horizon N, $N=8, \ldots, 26$, when using prediction models with additional constraints generated by either the symbolical method (dash-dotted line) or the geometrical method (straight line).

reduce the computation time of MPC by adding additional cuts. We have also an optimal algorithm to build an equivalent PWA model minimal in the number of polyhedra of the partition that has been omitted for space limitations. Future research will be devoted to develop fast and suboptimal algorithms.

Acknowledgements. This work was partially supported by the EU project *Control and Computation.* The authors would like to thank Prof. Alberto Bemporad and Prof. Komei Fukuda for inspiring discussions and Mato Baotic and Prof. Komei Fukuda for sharing their tools.

References

1. R. Alur, T. Dang, J. Esposito, R. Fierro, Y. Hur, F. Ivančić, V. Kumar, I. Lee, P. Mishra, G. Pappas, and O. Sokolsky. Hierarchical hybrid modeling of embedded systems. Volume 2211 of *Lecture Notes in Computer Science*, pages 14–31. Springer Verlag, 2001.
2. R. Alur and T. A. Henzinger. Modularity for timed and hybrid systems. Volume 1243 of *Lecture Notes in Computer Science*, pages 74–88, Springer Verlag, 1997.
3. D. Avis and K. Fukuda. Reverse search for enumeration. *Discrete Applied Mathematics*, 65:21–46, 1996.
4. A. Bemporad. An efficient technique for translating mixed logical dynamical systems into piecewise affine systems. In *Proc. 41st IEEE Conf. on Decision and Control*, 2002.
5. A. Bemporad, N. Giorgetti, I.V. Kolmanovsky, and D. Hrovat. A hybrid systems approach to modeling and optimal control of disc engines. In *Proc. 41st IEEE Conf. on Decision and Control*, 2002.
6. A. Bemporad and D. Mignone. *MIQP.M: A Matlab function for solving mixed integer quadratic programs.* ETH Zurich, 2000.
7. A. Bemporad and M. Morari. Control of systems integrating logic, dynamics, and constraints. *Automatica*, 35(3):407–427, March 1999.
8. F. Borrelli, A. Bemporad, M. Fodor, and D. Hrovat. A hybrid approach to traction control. Volume 2034 of *Lecture Notes in Computer Science*, pages 162–174. Springer Verlag, 2001.
9. R.C. Buck. Partition of space. *Amer. Math. Monthly*, 50:541–544, 1943.

10. B. De Schutter and T. van den Boom. On model predictive control for max-min-plus-scaling discrete event systems. *Automatica*, 37(7):1049–1056, 2001.
11. N. Deo. *Graph Theory with Applications to Engineering and Computer Science*. Prentice-Hall, Inc., 1974.
12. P. Eades, X. Lin, and W.F. Smyth. A fast and effective heuristic for the feedback arc set problem. *Information Processing Letters*, 47:319–323, 1993.
13. M.G. Earl and R. D'Andrea. Modeling and control of a multi-vehicle system using mixed integer linear programming. In *Proc. 41st IEEE Conf. on Decision and Control*, 2002.
14. H. Edelsbrunner. *Algorithms in Combinatorial Geometry*. 1987.
15. J.A. Ferrez and K. Fukuda. Implementations of LP-based reverse search algorithms for the zonotope construction and the fixed-rank convex quadratic maximization in binary variables using the ZRAM and the cddlib libraries. Technical report, July 2002. http://www.cs.mcgill.ca/~fukuda/download/mink.
16. J.A. Ferrez, K. Fukuda, and Th.M. Liebling. Cuts, zonotopes and arrangements. Technical report, EPF Lausanne, November 2001.
17. T. Geyer, F.D. Torrisi, and M. Morari. Efficient Mode Enumeration of Compositional Hybrid Systems. Technical Report AUT03-01, ETH Zurich, 2003.
18. W.P.M.H. Heemels, B. De Schutter, and A. Bemporad. Equivalence of hybrid dynamical models. *Automatica*, 37(7):1085–1091, July 2001.
19. T.A. Henzinger, M. Minea, and V. Prabhu. Assume-guarantee reasoning for hierarchical hybrid systems. Volume 2034 of *Lecture Notes in Computer Science*, pages 275–290. Springer Verlag, March 2001.
20. ILOG, Inc. *CPLEX 8.0 User Manual*. Gentilly Cedex, France, 2002.
21. K.H. Johansson. Hybrid systems:modeling, analysis and control – composition of hybrid automata. Lecture notes of the class EECS 291e, Lecture 5, University of California at Berkley, 2000.
22. N. Lynch, R. Segala, and F. Vaandrager. Hybrid I/O automata revisited. Volume 2034 of *Lecture Notes in Computer Science*, pages 403–417. Springer Verlag, 2001.
23. D. Mignone. *Control and Estimation of Hybrid Systems with Mathematical Optimization*. Diss. ETH No. 14520, ETH Zurich, 2002.
24. S. Rashid and J. Lygeros. Hybrid systems:modeling, analysis and control – open hybrid automata and composition. Lecture notes of the class EECS 291e, Lecture 8, University of California at Berkley, 1999.
25. E.D. Sontag. Nonlinear regulation: The piecewise linear approach. *IEEE Trans. on Aut. Control*, 26(2):346–358, April 1981.
26. E.D. Sontag. Interconnected automata and linear systems: A theoretical framework in discrete-time. Volume 1066 of *Lecture Notes in Computer Science*, pages 436–448. Springer-Verlag, 1996.
27. F.D. Torrisi and A. Bemporad. Discrete-time hybrid modeling and verification. In *Proc. 40th IEEE Conf. on Decision and Control*, pages 2899–2904, 2001.
28. F.D. Torrisi and A. Bemporad. Hysdel — a tool for generating computational hybrid models for analysis and synthesis problems. Technical Report AUT02-03, ETH Zurich, http://control.ethz.ch/~hybrid/hysdel, March 2002.
29. A.J. van der Schaft and J.M. Schumacher. Complementarity modelling of hybrid systems. *IEEE Trans. on Aut. Control*, 43:483–490, 1998.
30. G.M. Ziegler. *Lectures on Polytopes*, volume 152 of *Graduate Texts in Mathematics*. Springer, New York, 1994.

Automated Symbolic Reachability Analysis; with Application to Delta-Notch Signaling Automata[*]

Ronojoy Ghosh[1], Ashish Tiwari[2], and Claire Tomlin[1]

[1] Stanford University, Stanford, CA, USA
{ronojoy,tomlin}@stanford.edu
[2] Computer Science Laboratory, SRI International, Menlo Park, CA, USA
tiwari@csl.sri.com

Abstract. This paper describes the implementation of predicate abstraction techniques to automatically compute symbolic backward reachable sets of high dimensional piecewise affine hybrid automata, used to model Delta-Notch biological cell signaling networks. These automata are analyzed by creating an abstraction of the hybrid model, which is a finite state discrete transition system, and then performing the computation on the abstracted system. All the steps, from model generation to the simplification of the reachable set, have been automated using a variety of decision procedure and theorem-proving tools. The concluding example computes the reach set for a four cell network with 8 continuous and 256 discrete states. This demonstrates the feasibility of using these tools to compute on high dimensional hybrid automata, to provide deeper insight into realistic biological systems.

1 Introduction

Reachability analysis may be used to gain insight into the behavior of the physical system modeled by a hybrid automaton. In the context of hybrid automaton models of biological networks, the backward reachable sets from the equilibria of the automaton are of considerable interest, because they contain the initial conditions from which a particular biologically significant steady state is attainable. If the reachability analysis is performed on a model with symbolic parameters and rate constants, the computed reachable sets will not depend on numerical instantiations of those parameters. This is particularly important in biological systems, where the exact values of switching thresholds and chemical reaction rates might be unknown, but a range of possible values, usually expressed in terms of other symbolic constants, can be inferred. This in turn may be used to "reverse engineer" parts of a biological circuit model, by attaining through analysis parameters which are difficult or impossible to obtain experimentally.

The goal of this paper is to present our work in *automated symbolic backward reachable set computations for high-dimensional (in both continuous and discrete variables) hybrid automata with multiple equilibria*. The motivating example is the Delta-Notch cell signaling system described and analyzed in [10]. The

[*] This research is supported by the DARPA Bio:Info:Micro program, grant MDA972-00-1-0032, and the DARPA BioSpice program under contract DE-AC03-765F00098.

O. Maler and A. Pnueli (Eds.): HSCC 2003, LNCS 2623, pp. 233–248, 2003.
© Springer-Verlag Berlin Heidelberg 2003

hybrid automaton is suitably high-dimensional, with $2n$ continuous variables and 4^n modes, for an n cell network. The continuous dynamics are governed by piecewise affine differential equations and mode switching occurs only through the continuous state variables crossing switching hyperplanes. Both the single ($n = 1$) and the two cell ($n = 2$) hybrid automata were analyzed in [10], to obtain constraints on the range of the protein kinetic parameters and switching thresholds for biologically feasible equilibria to exist. The two cell automaton was also shown to have a Zeno state with a particular Zeno execution. These results were validated through extensive simulations, but a formal backward reachable set computation of even the two cell system was lacking, due to the difficulty of computing and keeping track of the 4 dimensional reachable set across switching boundaries.

Computing reachable sets for hybrid systems is in general difficult, due to the difficulty of representing and propagating sets in high dimensional continuous spaces. There has been a recent research focus on techniques which use approximations of various types to make the problem of computing reachable sets tractable; these include the use of linear hybrid automata [12,20], polyhedral representations [3,7], piecewise affine systems [4], ellipsoidal approximations [6], and projections of convergent approximations [18,19]. Recently, qualitative simulation models [14,15] have been proposed to abstract continuous phase portraits of hybrid automata to simpler transition graphs, on which reachability analysis can be performed. Predicate abstraction [1,11] and quantifier elimination [24] have been proposed for computing discrete abstractions of hybrid automata. Predicate abstraction provides a means for combining theorem proving and model checking techniques by automatically mapping an infinite state system to a finite state system (called the abstract system), in which the states correspond to truth assignments to a set of user-supplied predicates. Most existing tools suffer from two disadvantages from our point of view: (a) the complexity of the computations on the hybrid automaton restricts its dimensionality, and (b) symbolic computations are not possible. The last two computation methods mentioned above circumvent these restrictions by performing the formal verification on a discrete abstraction.

In this paper, we demonstrate the application of these predicate abstraction methods to automated reachable set computation. We use quantifier elimination based decision procedures, implemented using the Symbolic Analysis Laboratory (SAL) [24], which is a framework for combining different tools for abstraction, program analysis, theorem proving, and model checking of transition systems, to abstract the hybrid automaton to a discrete finite-state automaton. The reachable set computations are then performed on the discrete abstraction. The entire process, from generating the SAL model for an arbitrarily large cell network, to obtaining the final reachable sets, is completely automated using MATLAB code written by us, the SAL tool set, and QEPCAD [13] (Quantifier Elimination by Partial Cylindrical Algebraic Decomposition), which is used to simplify the formula defining the reachable set. However, some analysis necessary to generate the parameter constraints for equilibrium existence was done manually. Techniques to automate those analysis procedures is a current research topic. We apply this automatic computation to the reachability analysis of the Delta-Notch four cell signaling system: an affine hybrid automaton with eight continuous variables and 256 discrete states. The computation time for this is about eight hours on a Pentium III 500MHz machine, and there are good prospects to go to higher dimensions.

The reachable set computation follows the procedure (Fig. 1): (i) automated generation of the SAL code specifying the hybrid automaton for an arbitrarily large cell network, (ii) automated abstraction of the hybrid automaton into a discrete finite state automaton (FSA), (iii) automated computation of the backward reachable set using the reachability tool, and (iv) simplification of the reachable set definition using QEPCAD. In this paper, we start by briefly describing the Delta-Notch signaling pathway in cells, the hybrid automaton model of that process (for more details, see [10]), and the relevant analytical results that are used in the abstraction. We then describe the tool as outlined above, followed by results for large hybrid automata for two and four cell networks. Each step in the process is explained using the automaton for a single cell as an illustrative example.

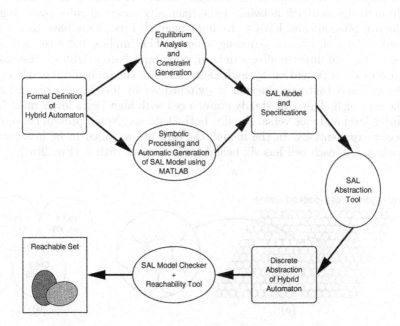

Fig. 1. Computation process for reach set construction

2   Delta-Notch Protein Signaling

2.1   Biological Background

Delta and Notch are both transmembrane proteins that actively signal only when cells are in direct contact, in a densely packed epidermal layer. Delta is a ligand that binds and activates its receptor Notch in neighboring cells. The activation of Notch in a cell affects the production of Notch ligands (i.e. Delta) both in itself and its neighbors, thus forming a feedback control loop. In the case of lateral inhibition, high Notch levels suppress ligand production in the cell and thus a cell producing more ligands forces its neighboring cells to produce less. The Delta-Notch signaling mechanism has been found to cause pattern formation in many different biological systems, such as the South African claw-toed frog (*Xenopus laevis*) embryonic skin [16] studied here. An example of the distinctive "salt-and-pepper" pattern formed due to lateral inhibition is in the *Xenopus* epidermal layer where a regular set of ciliated cells form within a matrix of smooth epidermal cells.

2.2 Hybrid Automaton Model

To model the regulation of intracellular Delta and Notch protein concentrations through the feedback network, experimentally observed rules governing the biological phenomenon have to be implemented. First, cells have to be in direct contact for Delta-Notch signaling to occur. This implies that a cell is directly affected by, and directly affects in turn, only immediate neighbors. Second, Notch production is turned on by high Delta levels in the immediate neighborhood of the cell and Delta production is switched on by low Notch concentrations in the same cell. Third, at steady state, a cell with high Delta levels must have low Notch level and vice versa. Finally, both Delta and Notch protein concentrations decay exponentially. In the model, the cells are assumed to be hexagonal close packed, i. e. each cell has six neighbors in contact with it (Fig. 2(a)).

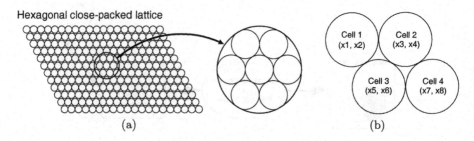

Fig. 2. (a) Hexagonal close-packed layout scheme for cells in two dimensional arrays. (b) Layout and variable associations of a four cell Delta-Notch signaling network

Each biological cell is modeled as a four state piecewise affine hybrid automaton. The four states capture the property that Notch and Delta protein production can be individually switched on or off at any given time. It is assumed that there is no command-actuation delay in the mode switching. The formal definition of the hybrid automaton is given by:

$$H_1 = (Q_1, X_1, \Sigma_1, V_1, Init_1, f_1, Inv_1, R_1)$$

$$Q_1 = \{q_1, q_2, q_3, q_4\}$$

$$X_1 = (x_1, x_2)^T \in \Re^2$$

$$\Sigma_1 = \left\{ u_D, u_N : u_D = -x_2, u_N = \sum_{i=1}^{6} x_{1,i} \right\}$$

$$V_1 = \emptyset$$

$$Init_1 = Q_1 \times \left\{ X_1 \in \Re^2 : x_1, x_2 > 0 \right\}$$

$$f_1(q, x) = \begin{cases} [-\lambda_D x_1; -\lambda_N x_2]^T & \text{if } q = q_1 \\ [R_D - \lambda_D x_1; -\lambda_N x_2]^T & \text{if } q = q_2 \\ [-\lambda_D x_1; R_N - \lambda_N x_2]^T & \text{if } q = q_3 \\ [R_D - \lambda_D x_1; R_N - \lambda_N x_2]^T & \text{if } q = q_4 \end{cases}$$

$$Inv_1 = \{q_1, \{u_D < h_D, u_N < h_N\}\} \cup \{q_2, \{u_D \geq h_D, u_N < h_N\}\}$$
$$\cup \{q_3, \{u_D < h_D, u_N \geq h_N\}\} \cup \{q_4, \{u_D \geq h_D, u_N \geq h_N\}\}$$

$$R_1 : \begin{bmatrix} R_1(q_1, \{u_D \geq h_D \wedge u_N < h_N\}) \in q_2 \times \Re^2 \\ R_1(q_1, \{u_D < h_D \wedge u_N \geq h_N\}) \in q_3 \times \Re^2 \\ \vdots \\ R_1(q_4, \{u_D < h_D \wedge u_N \geq h_N\}) \in q_3 \times \Re^2 \end{bmatrix}$$

where, x_1 and x_2: Delta and Notch protein concentrations, respectively, in a cell; $x_{1,i}$: Delta protein concentration in i^{th} neighboring cell; λ_D and λ_N: Delta and Notch protein decay constants respectively; R_D and R_N: constant Delta and Notch protein production rates, respectively; h_D and h_N: switching thresholds for Delta and Notch protein production, respectively. The switching thresholds h_D and h_N are unknown and possible ranges for them are derived in [10].

In the single cell, $x_{1,i} = 0, \forall i \in \{1, \ldots 6\}$. The inputs u_D and u_N are the physical realization of the protein regulatory properties in the model outlined before. The two cell hybrid automaton H_2 is the composition of two single cell automata, to form a model with four continuous states $(x_1, \ldots, x_4)$ and sixteen discrete modes. Here, $u_N \neq 0$ for each of the two cells, and thus the Delta level of each cell is communicated to its neighbor to control Notch production. Modeling the full two dimensional layer of cells involves composing $M \times N$ single cell hybrid automata, with the coupling through the input functions as described above.

2.3   Equilibrium Analysis

Both the single and two cell hybrid automata were analyzed in [10], to obtain constraints on the ranges of the protein kinetic parameters and switching thresholds for biologically feasible equilibria to exist:

$$h_D, h_N : -\frac{R_N}{\lambda_N} < h_N \leq 0 \wedge 0 < h_N \leq \frac{R_D}{\lambda_D}$$

The two cell automaton was also shown to have a Zeno state with a particular Zeno execution that is an invariant: $x_1 = x_3 \wedge x_2 = x_4$, where x_3 and x_4 are the Delta and Notch protein concentrations, respectively, in the second cell. In the discrete abstraction procedure, it is essential to include the parameter constraints and the Zeno execution as "polynomials of interest" (explained in the following section), to produce an abstraction with sufficient resolution. Hence, the analysis is an indispensable part of any formal verification done on the discrete abstraction in general.

3   SAL Model

The first step of the procedure is to generate the SAL language description of the hybrid model and the necessary user-defined predicates (for example, constraints derived from analysis). This task is non-trivial because the size of the model (and the number of lines of code) increase exponentially with the number of cells, since each one of the 4^n distinct modes has to be encoded. Hence, we have automated the generation of the SAL specification file using MATLAB, for an arbitrarily large network. The equilibrium existence conditions and consequent parameter constraints described in the previous section are included in the SAL model.

3.1   The SAL Modeling Language

Hybrid systems described in terms of interacting hybrid automata can be specified using the SAL modeling language [5,9]. Here we shall only describe those features of the SAL modeling language that will be used in the specification of the Delta-Notch signaling mechanism.

A SAL specification consists of *module* definitions. A special kind of module, called *basemodule*, corresponds to a hybrid automaton. It consists of definitions of the *variables*, the *initial states*, and the discrete and continuous *transitions* of the hybrid automaton. The variables are classified as *input, output, local,* and *global.* Variables are typed, discrete variables are usually of type BOOLEAN and continuous variables are of type REAL. The initial states of the hybrid automaton can be specified either directly, or by specifying a formula. In the latter case, the set of initial states consists of all those valuations of variables that make the formula true.

The discrete and continuous transitions are specified using a set of *guarded commands*. A guarded command is written as:

$$guard \longrightarrow x'_1 = e_1; x'_2 = e_2; x'_3 = e_3; \ldots$$

where *guard* is a formula over the variables, x_i are variables, and e_i are expressions over the variables. Semantically, the above command means that if the formula in the guard is true for some state (a state is a valuation of all the variables), then the transition can be taken. Note that the new value of a variable, say x_1, is denoted by priming it, x'_1. In case of a discrete transition, the variables x_i are updated to the new values given by expressions e_i. In a continuous transition, the variables x_i on the left-hand sides of the assignment are special variables, whose names end with the suffix "dot". They specify the time-derivative of the corresponding continuous variable. For example, the automatically generated SAL module specifying the single cell Delta-Notch hybrid automaton H_1 is given below.

```
one_cell : CONTEXT =
BEGIN
system[u, hD, hN, RD, RN, 1D, 1N : REAL] : MODULE =
BEGIN
        GLOBAL x1, x2 : REAL
        GLOBAL x1dot, x2dot : REAL
        INVARIANT
            x1 > 0 AND 1D*x1 < RD AND x2 > 0 AND 1N*x2 < RN AND
            u < hN AND 1N* hD > -RN AND hD < 0 AND hN > 0 AND
            1D*hN < RD AND RN > 0 AND RD > 0 AND 1N > 0 AND 1D > 0
        INITFORMULA
            u < hN AND x2 < -hD
        TRANSITION
            [
                -x2 < hD AND u < hN -->
                        x1dot' = -(-1D*x1);
                        x2dot' = -(-1N*x2)
                []
                -x2 < hD AND u >= hN -->
                        x1dot' = -(-1D*x1);
                        x2dot' = -(RN-1N*x2)
                []
                -x2 >= hD AND u < hN -->
                        x1dot' = -(RD-1D*x1);
                        x2dot' = -(-1N*x2)
                []
                -x2 >= hD AND u >= hN -->
                        x1dot' = -(RD-1D*x1);
                        x2dot' = -(RN-1N*x2)
            ]
        END;
END
```

Note that the parameter constraints are explicitly included as invariant polynomials, and the initial state, defined using the INITFORMULA declaration, is q_2,
which has an equilibrium that implies high Delta level and low Notch level and
is biologically consistent. Here, the backward reachable set from the equilibrium
in q_2 is desired, hence the dynamics in each mode are reversed, by negating
the right-hand-sides of the governing equations. In the SAL model, λ has been
replaced by l for brevity, λ_N is written as lN for example. Also note that the
input $u = u_N$ for the system has been fixed to $u_N < h_N$ for this example.

4 Discrete Abstraction

The second step of the reachable set computation procedure is the automatic
generation of the discrete abstraction of the hybrid automaton. An abstract
model is usually obtained from a given hybrid model by partitioning the state-
space of the original model into a finite set and mapping the dynamics of the
original model onto this finite set. In the case of a model described using n real-
variables (representing, say, the concentrations of n different protein complexes),
the state-space is the n-dimensional real space $\Re^n$. We partition this space into
a finite number of zones using a finite set P of polynomials over the n variables.
Each zone corresponds to a subset of $\Re^n$ that is sign-invariant for all polynomials
in the set P. Increasing the number of polynomials in the set P results in more
zones, and consequently, a finer abstraction. This basic idea, although in a much

simplified form, is also at the core of qualitative reasoning techniques developed in the AI community (see, for example [21]).

The process of construction of the abstract system requires logical reasoning in the theory of reals. The first-order theory of real closed fields is known to be decidable [23] and the first practical algorithm, based on cylindrical algebraic decomposition, was given in [8], which has gone through several improvements [13, 17]. We use the first-order theory of reals to represent sets of continuous states and use reasoning over this theory for creating the abstract transition system.

4.1   Abstraction Process

The abstraction technique is completely automatic and is described in [24]. The abstraction algorithm works in two phases: In the first phase, the algorithm computes a set of polynomials (over the continuous variables), which is used to partition the continuous state-space. This is achieved by starting with a finite set of polynomials which appear in the vector field of the continuous dynamics, in the conditions of discrete transitions, initialization expressions, and property to be proved. This set is saturated under the derivative operator, that is, the time derivative of a polynomial in this set is also added to this set. Note that computation of the derivative of a polynomial can be symbolically performed using the derivatives of individual variables. This saturation process may not terminate, but for our purposes can be stopped at any time. The termination condition is specified by giving the bound on the order of the derivatives that is computed.

In the second phase, the discrete and continuous transitions are abstracted. The abstract state-space is given as a cross-product of the discrete-state space and the regions of the original continuous state-space where the polynomials computed in the saturation phase are sign-invariant. This requires the use of decision procedures for the real-closed fields, intermingled with theorem-proving strategies.

For scalability of the abstraction technique, it is necessary that the formulas that arise in proof obligations while constructing an abstraction and when checking for feasibility of abstract states, do not grow in size. We have achieved this by partitioning the set of variables into classes such that variables that interact with each other (occur in the same polynomial) are put into the same class. Furthermore, when proving a proof obligation, atomic formulas that are not "relevant" to the succedent (that is, atomic formulas that do not contain any variables that occur in the polynomials in the succedent) are removed from the formula. This optimization simplifies the formulas to be proved. Furthermore, it also reduces the number of proof obligations that arise in the construction of the feasible abstract state space. An unique feature of the abstraction algorithm (and its implementation) is that it allows to abstract parameterized systems, without instantiating the parameters. Following our one cell Delta-Notch example, the abstraction procedure maps six abstract variables, $g_0, g_1, \ldots, g_5$, to polynomials in the original hybrid system:

```
g0 --> 1N*x2 - RN      g2 --> u - hN      g4 --> 1D*x1 - RD
g1 --> 1N*x2           g3 --> x1          g5 --> x2 + hD
```

The polynomials are either related to the continuous evolution of the model, for example g_0, g_1, g_3, g_4, or are the switching planes defining mode transitions, for example g_2 and g_5. The transitions in the abstract model arise from the discrete mode change transitions of the original model, or from the continuous dynamics. For example, the continuous evolution in mode q_1 is abstracted to the following SAL transition:

```
g2 = neg AND g5 = pos
      -->
        g5' IN IF g5 = pos
              THEN IF g1 = pos OR g1 = zero THEN {pos} ELSE {pos, zero} ENDIF
              ELSIF g5 = neg
              THEN IF g1 = neg OR g1 = zero
                   THEN {neg}
                   ELSE {neg, zero}
                   ENDIF
              ELSE IF g1 = pos
                   THEN {pos}
                   ELSIF g1 = neg THEN {neg} ELSE {zero}
                   ENDIF
           ENDIF;
        g4' = g4; g3' = g3; g2' = g2;
        g1' IN IF g1 = pos
              THEN IF FALSE THEN {pos} ELSE {pos, zero} ENDIF
              ELSIF g1 = neg
              THEN IF FALSE THEN {neg} ELSE {neg, zero} ENDIF
              ELSE IF FALSE
                   THEN {zero}
                   ELSIF FALSE
                        THEN {pos}
                        ELSIF FALSE THEN {neg} ELSE {pos, zero, neg}
                   ENDIF
           ENDIF;
        g0' = g0
```

The invariant $-x_2 < h_D \wedge u < h_N$ has been abstracted to ($g_2 = neg$ AND $g_5 = pos$). The binary "IN" operator denotes that the (new) value of the left-hand side variable is non-deterministically chosen from the set of values specified on the right-hand side (in contrast, the "=" operator sets the value of the left-hand side variable to a deterministic value). The new value of the variable is determined by the sign of its derivative. For example, the new value of g_5 depends on g_1, which is the derivative of g_5 in mode q_1.

5   Reachability Computation

The next step is the automatic computation of the backward reachable set using the SAL model-checker coupled with the reachability tool, written by us. The result is in the form of a vector that gives the reachable set of states. This is the input to another MATLAB script which reads the vector, and uses the polynomial invariants defining each set in that vector to construct the reachable set as a union of those invariants. This is then passed to QEPCAD which returns a compact, human-understandable form of the reachable set.

The reachability computation takes advantage of the fact that the SAL model- checker is an explicit-state model checker, i. e. it traces all possible executions of the FSA explicitly by firing all valid transitions from all reachable states, and checks each state against a linear temporal logic (LTL) formula. By giving the model checker a trivial formula to check, for example G(TRUE), we can ensure that the model-checker will search the entire reachable state space without coming up with a counter-example. The reachability tool is a LISP program which runs concurrently with the model-checker and stores each valid state that the model-checker visits during its state space exploration. The model checker is initialized from the hybrid automaton mode (which may be equivalent to several discrete states of the abstract FSA) containing the equilibrium whose backward reachable set we want to compute. Initializing the model-checker with the equilibrium-containing mode is valid for our example, because simple eigenvalue analysis of the equations show that the dynamics in that mode are exponentially stable, therefore the entire mode is backward reachable from the equilibrium point. After the model-checker terminates, it returns a vector of backward reachable sets. In our example, for the single cell automaton H_1 after simplification, the backward reachable set is given by: $x_1 > 0 \land x_2 > 0 \land \lambda_d x_1 < R_D \land \lambda_N x_2 < R_N \land u_N < h_N$. This means that the entire state space of interest is reachable from the equilibrium provided the input condition is satisfied. For larger systems, the simplification of the reachable set vector is non-trivial because we have to compute conjunctions of a large number of inequalities defining the invariants of states. This is done using QEPCAD, which can return a reasonably compact equivalent formula.

6   Results

6.1   Two Cell System

The two cell hybrid automaton H_2 is constructed by composing two single cell hybrid automata. It has four continuous state variables $x_1, \ldots, x_4$ and sixteen discrete modes $q_1, \ldots, q_{16}$. x_1 and x_2 represent the Delta and Notch protein concentration in the first cell, and x_3 and x_4 represent the Delta and Notch protein concentration in the second cell. From previous analysis [10], it was determined that only two biologically feasible equilibria exist for this system: (i) $x_1^* = 0, x_2^* = \frac{R_N}{\lambda_N}, x_3^* = \frac{R_D}{\lambda_D}, x_4^* = 0$, which means the Delta protein level in the second cell is high and that in the first cell is low, and the Notch protein level is high in the first cell and low in the second, and (ii) $x_1^* = \frac{R_D}{\lambda_D}, x_2^* = 0, x_3^* = 0, x_4^* = \frac{R_N}{\lambda_N}$, which is the symmetric result. We are interested in finding the set of initial conditions which converge to either one or the other equilibrium. Therefore the backward reachable set computation is performed for both the equilibria. The time required for the model construction and abstraction is around 25 minutes and another 40 minutes for the reachability computation using the model checker, on a Pentium III 500MHz computer running Linux. The computed sets are given below:

Eq 1: (0,RN/1N,RD/1D,0)

```
x3 - x1 >= 0 /\ x4 - x2 <= 0 /\ [
[ x3 - x1 > 0 /\ hN - x3 > 0 ] \/
[ x3 - x1 > 0 /\ hN - x1 < 0 ] \/
[ x4 - x2 < 0 /\ hN - x3 > 0 ] \/
[ x3 - x1 > 0 /\ hN - x1 < 0 ] \/
[ x3 - x1 > 0 /\ hD + x4 > 0 ] \/
[ x3 - x1 > 0 /\ hD + x2 < 0 ] \/
[ x4 - x2 < 0 /\ hD + x4 > 0 ] \/
[ x4 - x2 < 0 /\ hD + x2 < 0 ] \/
[ hN - x3 <= 0 /\ hN - x1 > 0 /\ hD + x2 > 0 ]]
```

Eq 2: (RD/1D,0,0,RN/1N)

```
x3 - x1 <= 0 /\ x4 - x2 >= 0 /\ [
[ x3 - x1 < 0 /\ hN - x1 > 0 ] \/
[ x3 - x1 < 0 /\ hN - x3 < 0 ] \/
[ x4 - x2 > 0 /\ hN - x1 > 0 ] \/
[ x4 - x2 > 0 /\ hN - x3 < 0 ] \/
[ x3 - x1 < 0 /\ hD + x2 > 0 ] \/
[ x3 - x1 < 0 /\ hD + x4 < 0 ] \/
[ x4 - x2 > 0 /\ hD + x2 > 0 ] \/
[ x4 - x2 > 0 /\ hD + x4 < 0 ] \/
[ hN - x3 > 0 /\ hN - x1 <= 0 /\
                hD + x4 > 0 ] ]
```

The reachable set for equilibrium 1 implies that all initial conditions that satisfy $x_3 > x_1 \wedge x_4 < x_2$ converge to that equilibrium and the reachable set for equilibrium 2 implies that all initial conditions that satisfy $x_3 < x_1 \wedge x_4 > x_2$ converge to that equilibrium. The four dimensional reachable sets can be better visualized by looking at their projections in lower dimensional space, examples of which are shown in Fig. 3.

In Fig. 3(a), both reachable sets are projected onto a three dimensional space with $x_3 - x_1$, $x_4 - x_2$ and x_3 as the axes. In this projection, the reachable sets are disjoint cubes with the respective equilibria at the corners. Note that the edge $x_3 = x_1 \wedge x_4 = x_2$ separates the two reach sets. Neither of the two equilibria are reachable from this edge: this separatrix defines the Zeno trajectory previously identified [10]. The two dimensional projection onto the x_1, x_3 plane shown in Fig. 3(b) makes the role of the separatrix clearer. It divides the plane into two half-planes, each of which is reachable from exactly one equilibrium point. These results are significant because, first, they involve symbolic computations over relatively high dimensional hybrid automata, and, second, they predict conditions that are biologically significant but not obvious from either the model or the biological system.

6.2   Four Cell System

Currently, the largest network we have performed the reach set computation for, is a four cell network. The hybrid automaton for a four cell network is constructed by composing four single cell automata as shown in Fig. 2(b). The sum of the Delta protein levels of neighboring cells is used to control Notch protein production in a cell. For example, cell 1 reads the Delta protein levels from cells 2 and 3, x_3 and x_5 respectively, and uses the sum $x_3 + x_5$ to regulate its Notch protein concentration, x_2. The set of parameter constraints from the two cell hybrid automaton is used for abstraction. The four cell automaton has eight continuous state variables (two proteins for each of the four cells), and 256 discrete states. There are three biologically feasible equilibria for this network: (i) cells 1 and 4 have high Delta levels and low Notch levels, and cells 2 and 3 have high Notch levels and low Delta levels, (ii) cell 2 has high Delta levels and low Notch levels at steady state, and all the other cells have low Delta levels and high Notch levels, and (iii) cell 3 has high Delta concentration and low Notch concentration at steady state and the other three cells have low Delta levels and high Notch

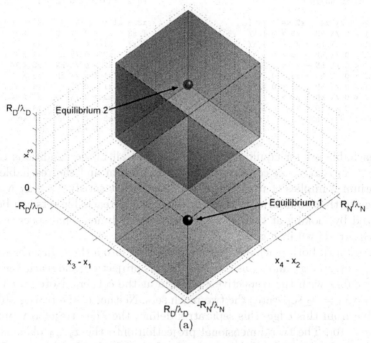

(a)

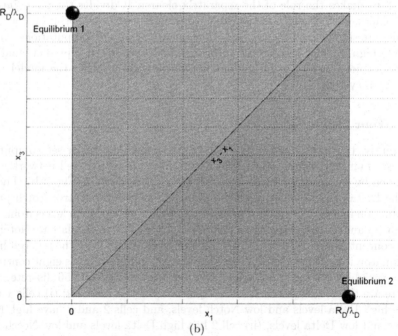

(b)

Fig. 3. Projections of reach set for two cell hybrid automaton

levels. It is important to identify the backward reachable sets for each of these three equilibria and we have investigated the reach set computation for the first equilibrium mentioned above. The model generation and reach set computation time required for that is 8 hours, on a Pentium III 500MHz computer running Linux. The resultant reach set generated by the SAL model checker is rather large, it comprises the union of 1576 states of the abstracted discrete automaton defined in terms of the abstraction polynomials. Computation of a simplified formula equivalent to the union of those 1576 states is non-trivial. QEPCAD has memory and dimensionality limitations which precludes the simplification computation of all 1576 states at once. To circumvent these limitations, we analyzed the polynomials defining the abstracted states and reduced the dimensionality of the problem by appropriate projections, as explained next. The state space of the hybrid automaton is abstracted by mapping it to the following set of polynomials:

```
g0 --> -x2-hD    g3 --> -x8-hD       g6 --> x5+x3-hN       g9 --> x5+x3-RD/lD
g1 --> -x4-hD    g4 --> x7+x3+x1-hN  g7 --> x7+x5+x1-RD/lD g10 --> x7+x5+x1-2*RD/lD
g2 --> -x6-hD    g5 --> x7+x5+x1-hN  g8 --> x7+x3+x1-RD/lD g11 --> x7+x3+x1-2*RD/lD
g12 --> x7+x3+x1-3*RD/lD
```

Each state of the abstracted FSA is defined by assigning a sign to the above polynomials and computing their conjunction. For example, (g0 = 0 $\wedge$ g1 = 0 $\wedge$ g2 = 0 $\wedge$ g3 > 0 $\wedge$ g4 = 0 $\wedge$ g5 = 0 $\wedge$ g6 > 0 $\wedge$ g7 < 0 $\wedge$ g8 < 0 $\wedge$ g9 > 0 $\wedge$ g10 < 0 $\wedge$ g11 < 0 $\wedge$ g12 < 0) is a mode of the abstracted FSA. The polynomials involve twelve symbolic variables, eight variables $x_1, \ldots, x_8$ denoting the protein concentrations in the cells and four parameters associated with the dynamics. Note that the variables x_2, x_4, x_6, x_8 only appear in conjunction with the parameter h_D and nowhere else. Hence, we can map those five into the following four variables: p1 = -x2-hD, p2 = -x4-hD, p3 = - x6-hD, p4 = -x8-hD. This reduces the dimensionality by one. Also, note that x_7 and x_1 always occur together as the sum $x_7 + x_1$, hence we can map it into a single variable p5 = x7 + x1 enabling us to reduce the dimensionality by one more. Similarly, the ratio R_D/l_D can be mapped to a single variable p6 = RD/lD, which reduces the dimensionality by another order. Therefore, instead of twelve symbolic variables to simplify over, we now have only nine. This is a substantial savings as the complexity of the problem grows exponentially with the dimensionality.

The simplified reach set thus computed turns out to be the union of 1192 states, which is still too large to interpret as a whole. Instead of trying to find meaning in a large non-convex set, we then partition the reach set using the definitions of the hybrid states from the four cell hybrid automaton, and compute the intersections of the invariants defining each of the 256 hybrid states, with the simplified reach set. This enables us to determine the hybrid states that are completely or partially backward reachable from the equilibrium. The natural structure of the state space is thus used to divide the reach set into smaller parts that are easier to interpret. It is observed that out of the 256 hybrid states, only 90 states are backward reachable from the equilibrium, completely or partially. The hybrid states are defined in terms of the signs of the switching functions governing Delta and Notch production, which are: p1, p2, p3, p4, x3+x5-hN, p5+x3-hN and p5+x5-hN. For example, the mode in which neither Delta nor Notch is produced in any of the four cells is defined as:

```
p1 < 0 /\ p2 < 0 /\ p3 < 0 /\ p4 < 0 /\ x3+x5-hN < 0 /\ p5+x3-hN < 0 /\ p5+x5-hN < 0
```

To simplify the representation of the states, we define the following expressions:

```
e1  = p1 < 0 /\ p2 < 0 /\ p3 < 0 /\ p4 < 0
e2  = p1 < 0 /\ p2 < 0 /\ p3 < 0 /\ p4 >= 0
e3  = p1 < 0 /\ p2 < 0 /\ p3 >= 0 /\ p4 < 0
e4  = p1 < 0 /\ p2 < 0 /\ p3 >= 0 /\ p4 >= 0
e5  = p1 < 0 /\ p2 >= 0 /\ p3 < 0 /\ p4 < 0
e6  = p1 < 0 /\ p2 >= 0 /\ p3 < 0 /\ p4 >= 0
e7  = p1 < 0 /\ p2 >= 0 /\ p3 >= 0 /\ p4 < 0
e8  = p1 < 0 /\ p2 >= 0 /\ p3 >= 0 /\ p4 >= 0
e9  = p1 >= 0 /\ p2 < 0 /\ p3 < 0 /\ p4 < 0
e10 = p1 >= 0 /\ p2 < 0 /\ p3 < 0 /\ p4 >= 0
e11 = p1 >= 0 /\ p2 < 0 /\ p3 >= 0 /\ p4 < 0
e12 = p1 >= 0 /\ p2 < 0 /\ p3 >= 0 /\ p4 >= 0
e13 = p1 >= 0 /\ p2 >= 0 /\ p3 < 0 /\ p4 < 0
e14 = p1 >= 0 /\ p2 >= 0 /\ p3 < 0 /\ p4 >= 0
e15 = p1 >= 0 /\ p2 >= 0 /\ p3 >= 0 /\ p4 < 0
e16 = p1 >= 0 /\ p2 >= 0 /\ p3 >= 0 /\ p4 >= 0
f1 = x3+x5-hN < 0 /\ p5+x3-hN < 0 /\ p5+x5-hN < 0
f2 = x3+x5-hN < 0 /\ p5+x3-hN < 0 /\ p5+x5-hN >= 0
f3 = x3+x5-hN < 0 /\ p5+x3-hN >= 0 /\ p5+x5-hN < 0
f4 = x3+x5-hN < 0 /\ p5+x3-hN >= 0 /\ p5+x5-hN >= 0
f5 = x3+x5-hN >= 0 /\ p5+x3-hN < 0 /\ p5+x5-hN < 0
f6 = x3+x5-hN >= 0 /\ p5+x3-hN < 0 /\ p5+x5-hN >= 0
f7 = x3+x5-hN >= 0 /\ p5+x3-hN >= 0 /\ p5+x5-hN < 0
f8 = x3+x5-hN >= 0 /\ p5+x3-hN >= 0 /\ p5+x5-hN >= 0
```

Using the above expressions, the reachable hybrid states can be listed:

```
Completely reachable        Partially reachable
e1 /\ [f1 \/ f5]            e1 /\ [f2 \/ f6 \/ f7 \/ f8]
e2 /\ [f1 \/ f5]            e2 /\ [f6 \/ f7 \/ f8]
e3 /\ f1                    e3 /\ [f5 \/ f6 \/ f8]
e4 /\ f1                    e4 /\ [f5 \/ f6 \/ f7]
e5 /\ f1                    e5 /\ [f2 \/ f6 \/ f8]
e6 /\ f1                    e6 /\ [f2 \/ f5 \/ f6 \/ f7]
e7 /\ f1                    e7 /\ [f2 \/ f6 \/ f8]
e8 /\ f1                    e8 /\ [f2 \/ f5 \/ f6 \/ f7 \/ f8]
e9 /\ f1                    e9 /\ [f3 \/ f5 \/ f6 \/ f7]
e10 /\ [f1 \/ f4]           e10 /\ [f3 \/ f5 \/ f6 \/ f7 \/ f8]
e11 /\ f1                   e11 /\ [f3 \/ f5 \/ f6 \/ f7]
e12 /\ f1                   e12 /\ [f3 \/ f5 \/ f6 \/ f7 \/ f8]
e13 /\ f1                   e13 /\ [f2 \/ f3 \/ f4 \/ f6]
e14 /\ f1                   e14 /\ [f2 \/ f3 \/ f4 \/ f5 \/ f6 \/ f7 \/ f8]
                           e15 /\ [f1 \/ f2 \/ f3 \/ f4 \/ f5 \/ f6 \/ f7 \/ f8]
                           e16 /\ [f1 \/ f2 \/ f3 \/ f4 \/ f5 \/ f6 \/ f7 \/ f8]
```

We are currently in the process of analyzing the reach set results for biologically significant information, but a few interesting properties of this equilibrium can be mentioned:

— Among the hybrid states that are completely reachable, fourteen states satisfy the constraint f1, i.e. $x_7 + x_3 + x_1 - h_N < 0 \wedge x_7 + x_5 + x_1 - h_N < 0 \wedge x_5 + x_3 - h_N < 0$. This implies that for all Notch protein levels except $-h_D \geq x_2 \wedge -h_D \geq x_4 \wedge -h_D \geq x_6$, if the Delta levels satisfy the constraint f1, then the equilibrium will be attained.

- It is observed that all hybrid states with $-h_D < x_2 \wedge x_5 + x_3 < h_N \wedge x_7 + x_3 + x_1 \geq h_N$ are completely unreachable. This implies that regardless of the Notch protein levels of cells 2, 3 and 4 (Fig. 2(b)), if the Notch protein concentration of cell 1 and the Delta protein levels of all four cells satisfy the above constraints, then the equilibrium will be unreachable.

7 Conclusion

We have described, in this paper, the automatic computation of backward reachable sets for high dimensional piecewise affine hybrid automata. The reachability procedure combines previously developed code in SRI's SAL with automation steps written by us. We have achieved results for a hybrid automaton with 8 continuous dimensions and 256 discrete modes. The concrete example that we have used, that of a Delta-Notch signaling network, is one of many physical systems that can be modeled using this class of hybrid automata. The ability to do symbolic computations makes our hybrid automaton-based modeling and analysis framework ideal for a wide range of cell biological regulatory and signaling processes. One of our current research projects focuses on applying the reachability tools that we have developed to analyze planar cell polarity signaling in *Drosophila* (fruit fly) pupal wing epithelium [2].

References

1. R. Alur, T. Dang, and F. Ivancic. Reachability analysis of hybrid systems via predicate abstraction. In C. J. Tomlin and M. Greenstreet, editors, *Hybrid Systems: Computation and Control*, LNCS 2289, pages 35–48. Springer Verlag, 2002.
2. K. Amonlirdviman, R. Ghosh, J. Axelrod and C. Tomlin. A hybrid systems approach to modeling and analyzing planar cell polarity. In *International Conference on Systems Biology*, Stockholm, 2002.
3. E. Asarin, T. Dang, and O. Maler. d/dt: A verification tool for hybrid systems. In *Proc. of the IEEE Conf. on Decision and Control*, pages 2893–2898, Orlando, 2001.
4. A. Bemporad, F. D. Torrisi, and M. Morari. Optimization-based verification and stability characterization of piecewise affine and hybrid systems. In B. Krogh and N. Lynch, editors, *Hybrid Systems: Computation and Control*, LNCS 1790, pages 45–59. Springer Verlag, 2000.
5. S. Bensalem, V. Ganesh, Y. Lakhnech, C. Muñoz, S. Owre, H. Rueß, J. Rushby, V. Rusu, H. Saïdi, N. Shankar, E. Singerman, and A. Tiwari. An overview of SAL. In C. M. Holloway, editor, *LFM 2000: Fifth NASA Langley Formal Methods Workshop*, pages 187–196, Hampton, VA, June 2000. NASA Langley Research Center.
6. O. Botchkarev and S. Tripakis. Verification of hybrid systems with linear differential inclusions using ellipsoidal approximations. In B. Krogh and N. Lynch, editors, *Hybrid Systems: Computation and Control*, LNCS 1790, pages 73–88. Springer Verlag, 2000.
7. A. Chutinan and B. H. Krogh. Verification of infinite-state dynamic systems using approximate quotient transition systems. *IEEE Trans. on Automatic Control*, 46(9):1401–1410, 2001.

8. G. E. Collins. Quantifier elimination for the elementary theory of real closed fields by cylindrical algebraic decomposition. In *Proc. Second GI Conf. Automata Theory and Formal Languages*, LNCS 33, pages 134–183. Springer Verlag, 1975.

9. Computer Science Laboratory, SRI International, Menlo Park , California. SAL: Symbolic Analysis Laboratory. http://www.csl.sri.com/projects/sal/.

10. R. Ghosh and C. J. Tomlin. Lateral inhibition through delta-notch signaling: a piecewise affine hybrid model. In M. D. D. Benedetto and A. Sangiovanni-Vincentelli, editors, *Hybrid Systems: Computation and Control*, LNCS 2034, pages 232–246. Springer Verlag, 2001.

11. S. Graf and H. Saïdi. Construction of abstract state graphs with PVS. In O. Grumberg, editor, *Proc. 9th International Conference on Computer Aided Verification (CAV'97)*, volume 1254, pages 72–83. Springer Verlag, 1997.

12. T. A. Henzinger, P. H. Ho, and H. Wong-Toi. Hytech: A model checker for hybrid systems. *Software Tools for Technology Transfer*, 1:110–122, 1997.

13. H. Hong. An improvement of the projection operator in cylindrical algebraic decomposition. In *Proc. ISAAC 90*, pages 261–264, 1990.

14. H. de Jong. Modeling and simulation of genetic regulatory systems: A literature review. *J. Computational Biology*, 9(1):69–105, 2002.

15. B. Kuipers and S. Ramamoorthy. Qualitative modeling and heterogeneous control of global systems behavior. In C. J. Tomlin and M. Greenstreet, editors, *Hybrid Systems: Computation and Control*, LNCS 2289, pages 294–307. Springer Verlag, 2002.

16. G. Marnellos, G. A. Deblandre, E. Mjolsness, and C. Kintner. Delta-notch lateral inhibitory patterning in the emergence of ciliated cells in *Xenopus*: experimental observations and a gene network model. In *Pacific Symposium on Biocomputing*, pages 326–337, 2000.

17. S. McCallum. An improved projection operator for cylindrical algebraic decomposition of three dimensional space. *J. Symbolic Computation*, 5:141–161, 1988.

18. I. Mitchell. *Application of level set methods to control and reachability problems in continuous and hybrid systems*. PhD thesis, Stanford University, August 2002.

19. I. Mitchell and C. J. Tomlin. Overapproximating reachable sets by Hamilton-Jacobi projections. *J. Symbolic Computation*, 2003.

20. J. Preußig and H. Wong-Toi. A procedure for reachability analysis of rectangular automata. In *Proc. of the American Control Conference*, pages 1674–1678, Chicago, 2000.

21. B. Shults and B. J. Kuipers. Proving properties of continuous systems: qualitative simulation and temporal logic. *AI Journal*, 92:91–129, 1997.

22. O. Sokolsky and H. S. Hong. Qualitative modeling of hybrid systems. In *Proc. of the Montreal Workshop*, 2001. Available from http://www.cis.upenn.edu/~rtg/rtg_papers.htm.

23. A. Tarski. *A Decision Method for Elementary Algebra and Geometry*. University of California Press, second edition, 1948.

24. A. Tiwari and G. Khanna. Series of abstractions for hybrid automata. In C. J. Tomlin and M. Greenstreet, editors, *Hybrid Systems: Computation and Control*, LNCS 2289, pages 465–478. Springer Verlag, 2002.

Modelling, Well-Posedness, and Stability of Switched Electrical Networks*

W.P.M.H. Heemels[1], M.K. Çamlıbel[1,2,3], A.J. van der Schaft[4], and
J.M. Schumacher[2]

[1] Dept. of Electrical Engineering, Eindhoven University of Technology, P.O. Box 513,
5600 MB Eindhoven, The Netherlands, m.heemels@tue.nl
[2] Dept. of Econometrics and Operations Research, Tilburg University, P.O. Box
90153, 5000 LE Tilburg, The Netherlands, {k.camlibel,jms}@uvt.nl
[3] Dept. of Electronics and Communication Eng., Dogus University, Acibadem 81010,
Kadikoy-Istanbul, Turkey
[4] Faculty of Mathematical Sciences, University of Twente, P.O. Box 217, 7500 AE
Enschede, The Netherlands, twarjan@math.utwente.nl

Abstract. A modeling framework is proposed for circuits that are subject to both time and state events. The framework applies to switched
networks with linear and piecewise linear elements including diodes and
switches. We show that the linear complementarity formulation, which
already has proved effective for piecewise linear networks, can be extended in a natural way to cover also switching circuits. We show that
the proposed framework is sound in the sense that existence and uniqueness of solutions is guaranteed under a passivity assumption. We prove
that only first-order impulses occur and characterize all situations that
give rise to a state jump; moreover, we provide rules that determine the
jump. Finally, we derive a stability result. Hence, for a subclass of hybrid
dynamical systems, the issues of well-posedness, regularity of trajectories, jump rules, consistent states and stability are resolved.

1 Introduction

In the field of power converters one is often confronted with systems that are
most easily modelled as going through a succession of periods of smooth evolution separated by instantaneous events that mark transitions of one set of
laws of evolution to another. Events may be externally induced (as in the case of
switches) or internally induced (as in the case of diodes). From this point of view
switched networks form one of the most natural and broadly applied instances
of *hybrid dynamical systems*.

It is the main purpose of the present paper to propose a modelling framework
for systems with events, designed in particular for switched piecewise linear networks. By an example of a boost circuit we illustrate that the well-known hybrid
automaton model is not suitable as it becomes very complex and the physical

---

* Sponsored by the EU project "SICONOS" (IST-2001-37172) and STW grant EES
5173

O. Maler and A. Pnueli (Eds.): HSCC 2003, LNCS 2623, pp. 249–266, 2003.

structure of the underlying system is lost. Our approach is based on the complementarity modelling that was used in [11] for dynamic networks with diodes. Here we extend the framework of [11] to include also external switches and sources (external inputs). It turns out that the extension can be carried out in a very natural way. Instead of working with the cone of componentwise nonnegative vectors as in [11], we use here cones of a more general type. This corresponds to the generalization of the linear complementarity problem of mathematical programming to a "cone complementarity problem" (cf. for instance [7, p. 31]). This generalization brings a more geometric flavor to the setting of [11] and may be useful as well in the modelling of mode-switching elements other than diodes. Essentially, we describe switched piecewise linear networks as cone complementarity systems that are switched in time between several different cones from a given family. In addition to the notion of cone complementarity, the concept of passivity is central to the development of this paper.

One of the main problems in setting up a rigorous framework for continuous-time switched systems is to take into account the possibility of state jumps. We need a sufficiently rich solution space that allows discontinuities in state trajectories and consequently even impulses in input trajectories. In this paper we choose a distributional framework in combination with a hybrid perspective. Although this choice effectively limits us to considering only (piecewise) linear networks, an advantage of using distributions is that we do not need to impose *a priori* a restriction on the nature of the jumps; rather we can *prove* that only first-order impulses arise, even though our setting in principle allows distributional solutions of arbitrarily high order. The framework is exploited further to characterize the states from which impulses / state jumps occur and moreover, the jump rules are specified in various forms ranging from cone complementarity problems to quadratic optimization problems, which have nice physical interpretations. These jump rules are used to access the stability of this class of hybrid systems. The proofs of the results can be found in the report [6], which form an extension of [5] that deals with the diode case only.

2   Notation

For any set S, 2^S denotes the power set, i.e. the collection of all subsets of S. The set of real numbers is denoted by $\mathbb{R}$. $\mathbb{R}_+$ stands for the set of nonnegative real numbers. $\mathbb{C}$ denotes the set of complex numbers. For a complex number z, $\bar{z}$ and $\operatorname{Re} z$ stand for the complex conjugate and the real part of z, respectively. The notations v^T and v^* denote the transpose and conjugate transpose of a vector v. When two vectors v and w are orthogonal, i.e. $v^T w = 0$, we write $v \perp w$. Inequalities for real vectors must be understood componentwise. The notation $\mathbb{R}^{n \times m}$ denotes the set of $n \times m$ matrices with real elements. The transpose of A is denoted by A^T. The matrix M (not necessarily symmetric) is said to be *nonnegative definite* ($M \geqslant 0$) if $v^T M v \geqslant 0$ for all vectors v. We say that M is *positive definite* ($M > 0$) if M is nonnegative definite and $v^T M v = 0$ implies $v = 0$. Similarly, *nonpositive definite* and *negative definite* matrices are defined. For two matrices M and N with the same number of columns, $\mathrm{col}(M,N)$ will denote the matrix obtained by stacking M over N. The identity matrix will be denoted by I, the zero matrix by 0. A triple of matrices $(A,B,C) \in \mathbb{R}^{n \times n} \times \mathbb{R}^{n \times m} \times \mathbb{R}^{m \times n}$ is said to be minimal if $\mathrm{rank}(B, AB, \dots, A^{n-1}B) = n$ and $\mathrm{rank}(\mathrm{col}(C, CA, \dots, CA^{n-1})) = n$.

A rational matrix $G(s)$ is said to be *proper* if $\lim_{s \uparrow \infty} G(s)$ exists and is finite. It is said to be *strictly proper* if it is proper and the limit above is zero.

Let f be a function. We write $f|_{\Omega}$ for the restriction of f to the set Ω. The notation $f(\tau+)$ $(f(\tau-))$ will denote the limit $\lim_{t \uparrow \tau} f(t)$ $(\lim_{t \downarrow \tau} f(t))$ whenever it is well-defined. The set of all Lebesgue measurable, square integrable functions $f : \Omega \to \mathbb{R}$ will be denoted $\mathcal{L}_2(\Omega)$. In case, $\Omega = \mathbb{R}_+$, we write only $\mathcal{L}_2$. The notation $\mathcal{L}_2^{loc}$ denotes locally $\mathcal{L}_2$-functions, i.e., the set $\{f \mid f|_{[t,T]} \in \mathcal{L}_2 \text{ for all } 0 \leqslant t < T\}$. The Dirac distribution supported at θ will be denoted by δ_θ and its k-th derivative by $\delta_\theta^{(k)}$. When it is supported at zero, we usually write δ and $\delta^{(k)}$.

A set $\mathcal{C} \subseteq \mathbb{R}^\ell$ is said to be a *cone* if $v \in \mathcal{C}$ implies that $\alpha v \in \mathcal{C}$ for all $\alpha \geqslant 0$. For any nonempty set $\mathcal{Q} \subseteq \mathbb{R}^\ell$, we define the *dual cone* as the set $\mathcal{Q}^* := \{w \in \mathbb{R}^\ell \mid w^T v \geqslant 0 \text{ for all } v \in \mathcal{Q}\}$.

2.1 Complementarity Problems

The linear complementarity problem plays an important role in the sequel.

Definition 1. $LCP(q, M)$: *Given an m-vector q and an $m \times m$ matrix M find an m-vector z such that*

$$z \geqslant 0; \ q + Mz \geqslant 0; z^T(q + Mz) = 0. \tag{1}$$

One interesting generalization of the LCP, that will be of interest in the context of switched circuits, can be obtained as follows.

Definition 2. $LCP_\mathcal{C}(q, M)$: *Let $\mathcal{C}$ be a cone. Given an m-vector q and an $m \times m$ matrix M find an m-vector z such that*

$$z \in \mathcal{C}; \ q + Mz \in \mathcal{C}^*; \ z^T(q + Mz) = 0. \tag{2}$$

We say that the $LCP_\mathcal{C}(q, M)$ is *solvable* if such a z exists. In this case, we also say that z *solves (is a solution of)* $LCP_\mathcal{C}(q, M)$. The set of all solutions of $LCP_\mathcal{C}(q, M)$ is denoted by $\mathrm{SOL}_\mathcal{C}(q, M)$. If $\mathcal{C} = \mathbb{R}^m_+$ then $LCP_\mathcal{C}(q, M)$ becomes the ordinary LCP defined in Definition 1.

3 Modelling Switched Electrical Circuits

In this paper we consider electrical circuits that can be realized by using linear resistors, capacitors, inductors, gyrators, transformers, current and voltage sources, ideal diodes and pure switches. Many switching circuits already fall directly in the class of networks considered in the paper like the well-known Čuk,

Boost and Flyback circuits [9]. Moreover, surprisingly many other piecewise linear networks, which do not seem to fit the framework at first sight, can be built from these elements as well (see e.g. [11] for an example). As a running example we consider the Boost circuit as in Figure 1.

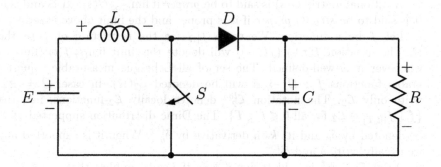

Fig. 1. Boost circuit with clamping diode

Example 1. The Boost circuit (see e.g. [9]) consists of a capacitor C with electric charge q, an ideal diode D, a battery (voltage source) E, an inductor L with magnetic flux ϕ, a resistor R, and an ideal switch S. The voltage-current characteristics of the ideal diode and switch are depicted in Figure 2. These type of circuits, usually called *step-up* converters, are used to obtain a voltage at the resistance load that is higher than the voltage E of the input source.

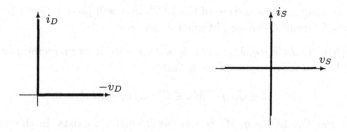

Fig. 2. Voltage-current characteristic of an ideal diode and ideal switch

The presence of switching elements (D and S) introduces hybrid dynamics. Depending on the (discrete) state of the diode and the switch, one can distinguish four modes (locations): $\{(v_S = 0, v_D = 0), (v_S = 0, i_D = 0), (i_S = 0, v_D = 0), (i_S = 0, i_D = 0)\}$. A hybrid automaton representation can be obtained by analyzing these four modes. For instance, mode 1 in which the switch S is open ($i_S = 0$ or $S = 0$ – note that $S = 1$ complies with $v_S = 0$) and the diode is conducting (see Figure 3) is governed by the following network equations

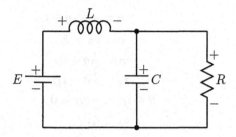

Fig. 3. Mode 1 complying with $i_S = 0$ and $v_D = 0$.

$\dot{q} = -\frac{1}{RC}q + \frac{1}{L}\phi$ and $\dot{\phi} = -\frac{1}{C}q + E$. This mode is active as long as $i_D \geqslant 0$, i.e., $\phi \geqslant 0$ since $i_D = i_L = \frac{1}{L}\phi$. Stated differently, $\phi \geqslant 0$ determines the invariant set of this mode. A mode transition occurs if either the current through the diode tends to be negative or the switch is closed. The former is an autonomous event whereas the latter is a controlled event. A similar (tedious) analysis of each mode yields a hybrid automaton model as depicted in Figure 4. The mode transitions and the corresponding guards and reset maps are summarized in the following table.

transition	guard	reset
mode 1→mode 2	$S = 1$ and $q \geqslant 0$	
mode 1→mode 3	$\phi = 0$ and $q > CE$	
mode 1--→mode 3	$\phi < 0$	$\phi^+ = 0$
mode 1→mode 4	$S = 1$ and $q \leqslant 0$	$q^+ = 0$
mode 2→mode 1	$S = 0$ and $\phi \geqslant 0$	
mode 2→mode 3	$S = 0$ and $\phi \leqslant 0$	$\phi^+ = 0$
mode 2→mode 4	$q = 0$	
mode 2--→mode 4	$q < 0$	$q^+ = 0$
mode 3→mode 1	$q = CE$	
mode 3→mode 2	$S = 1$ and $q \geqslant 0$	
mode 3→mode 4	$S = 1$ and $q \leqslant 0$	$q^+ = 0$
mode 4→mode 1	$S = 0$ and $\phi \geqslant 0$	
mode 4→mode 3	$S = 0$ and $\phi \leqslant 0$	$\phi^+ = 0$
mode 4--→mode 4	$q < 0$	$q^+ = 0$

It is obvious that the hybrid automaton model is very involved (even its derivation) and does not maintain the structure of the system at hand. Therefore, we propose to use for these types of systems the more compact model:

$$\dot{q} = -\frac{1}{RC}q + i_D \tag{3a}$$

$$\dot{\phi} = v_S + E \tag{3b}$$

$$-v_D = \frac{1}{C}q + v_S \tag{3c}$$

$$i_s = \frac{1}{L}\phi - i_D \tag{3d}$$

$$0 \leqslant i_D \perp -v_D \geqslant 0 \tag{3e}$$

$$v_s \perp i_s. \tag{3f}$$

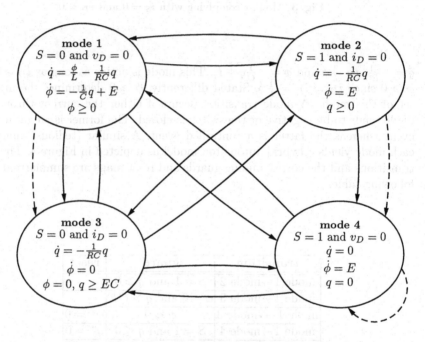

Fig. 4. A hybrid automaton model of the Boost circuit.

All the networks consisting of an RLCTG part together with sources, diodes and switches lead to a structure as in the example of the Boost circuit. Indeed, the linear (RLCGT)-part can be described by the state space model

$$\dot{x}(t) = Ax(t) + Bu(t) \tag{4a}$$

$$y(t) = Cx(t) + Du(t) \tag{4b}$$

under suitable conditions (the network does not contain all-capacitor/voltage sources loops or nodes with the only elements incident being inductors/current sources, see [1, Ch. 4] for more details). In (4) x denotes the state variable of the network (typically consisting of linear combinations of the fluxes through the inductors and charges at the capacitors). The pair (u_i, y_i) denotes the voltage-current variables at the terminals of the linear part of the circuit. The variables

(u_i, y_i) are connected to the diodes, switches and sources, which leads to additional equations as will be introduced in Section 5. Note that in case of the Boost circuit, we have the conditions for the ideal diode (3e) and for the pure switch (3f). The source is modelled by specifying a function of time for the voltage E. The complete model will be given in (7)-(8). First we will focus on the properties of (4) representing the linear (RLCGT) part of the circuit.

4 Linear Network Models

Since (4) is a model for a linear circuit, (A, B, C, D) is passive.

Definition 3. [15] *A system* (A, B, C, D) *given by (4) is called* passive, *or* dissipative *with respect to the supply rate* $u^T y$, *if there exists a nonnegative-valued function* $V : \mathbb{R}^n \to \mathbb{R}_+$, *(a storage function), such that for all* $t_0 \leqslant t_1$ *and all time functions* $(u, x, y) \in \mathcal{L}_2^{k+n+k}(t_0, t_1)$ *satisfying (4) it holds that:*

$$V(x(t_0)) + \int_{t_0}^{t_1} u^T(t)y(t)dt \geqslant V(x(t_1)). \tag{5}$$

The above inequality is called the *dissipation inequality*. The storage function represents a notion of "stored energy" in the network.

Proposition 1. [15] *Consider a system* (A, B, C, D) *in which* (A, B, C) *is a minimal representation. The following statements are equivalent.*

- *(A, B, C, D) is passive.*
- *The following matrix inequalities have a solution K:*

$$\begin{pmatrix} -A^T K - KA & -KB + C^T \\ -B^T K + C & D + D^T \end{pmatrix} \geqslant 0 \text{ and } K = K^T \geqslant 0 \tag{6}$$

Moreover, in case (A, B, C, D) *is passive, all solutions to the linear matrix inequalities (6) are positive definite and a symmetric K is a solution to (6) if and only if* $V(x) = \frac{1}{2}x^T K x$ *defines a storage function of the system* (A, B, C, D).

A technical assumption that we will often use is the following.

Assumption 1 $\mathrm{col}(B, D + D^T)$ has full column rank and (A, B, C) is minimal.

5 Switched Network Models

In the previous section we concentrated on the linear part (4) of the circuit. Adding the switches, diodes and sources will lead to the class of circuits (including the example in (3)) that form the object of study of the paper.

5.1 Adding Diodes, Switches, and Sources

The equations that are added to (4), if the terminals are terminated by diodes, switches and sources are given as follows:

- If the i-th port is connected to a *diode*, we obtain $(u_i = -V_i \wedge y_i = I_i) \vee (u_i = I_i \wedge y_i = -V_i)$, where V_i and I_i are the voltage across and current through the i-th diode, respectively, and $\vee$ denotes the Boolean (nonexclusive) "or" and $\wedge$ the Boolean "and"-operator. The ideal diode characteristics are described by the relations $V_i \leqslant 0 \wedge I_i \geqslant 0 \wedge (V_i = 0 \vee I_i = 0)$ as shown in Figure 2. Putting the above equations together leads to $0 \leqslant u_i \perp y_i \geqslant 0$ where $u_i \perp y_i$ means that either $u_i = 0$ or $y_i = 0$.
- If the i-th port is connected to a *switch*, we have $u_i = 0 \vee y_i = 0$ or stated differently, $u_i \perp y_i$ as shown in Figure 2.
- If the i-th port is connected to a *source*: u_i is being described by a suitable function w_i of time, which reflects the applied voltage or current to the port.

Based on the previous discussion, we obtain network models of the form (note that we replaced the variable u_i related to the source ports (u_i, y_i) by the variable w_i as external input and omitted the corresponding variable y_i as it is irrelevant to the remainder of the discussion):

$$\dot{x}(t) = Ax(t) + Bu(t) + Ew(t) \tag{7a}$$
$$y(t) = Cx(t) + Du(t) + Fw(t) \tag{7b}$$
$$0 \leqslant y_i(t) \perp u_i(t) \geqslant 0, \ i = 1, 2, \ldots, m \tag{7c}$$
$$y_i(t) \perp u_i(t), \ i = m+1, m+2, \ldots, k, \tag{7d}$$

where we assumed that the first m ports are terminated with diodes and the last $k - m$ ports by pure switches. Note that $w_i(t)$ denotes the current or voltage of the sources (depending if the corresponding port is voltage or current controlled). We will use the terminology *switched complementarity systems* for systems of the form (7) together with the notation SCS(A, B, C, D, E, F).

Note that for the example of the Boost circuit we have $x = (q, \phi)^T$, $y = (-v_D, i_S)^T$, $u = (i_D, v_S)$ and the matrices in (7) are given as (by taking $R = 1\Omega$ and $C = 1F$ and $L = 1H$):

$$A = \begin{pmatrix} -1 & 0 \\ 0 & 0 \end{pmatrix}; \ B = C = \begin{pmatrix} 1 & 0 \\ 0 & 1 \end{pmatrix}; \ E = (0 \ 1)^T; \ D = \begin{pmatrix} -1 & 0 \\ 0 & 1 \end{pmatrix}; \ F = (0 \ 0)^T. \tag{8}$$

5.2 Cone Complementarity Systems

A certain similarity between diodes and switches can be made apparent by using a formulation in terms of *cones*. The constitutive equations for a k-tuple of diodes may be written in the form

$$u \in \mathcal{C}, \quad y \in \mathcal{C}^*, \quad y \perp u \tag{9}$$

where $\mathcal{C}$ denotes the nonnegative cone $\mathbb{R}_+^k$ in $\mathbb{R}^k$, i.e. the set of k-vectors with nonnegative entries. The conditions (9) however become the specification of a set of switches in a particular configuration if we let $\mathcal{C}$ denote a set of the form $\Pi_{i=1}^k \mathcal{C}_i$ where each $\mathcal{C}_i$ is either $\mathbb{R}$ or $\{0\}$. This set is a subspace and so in particular it is a cone. The cones corresponding to diodes and to switches may be taken together in a product cone. Consequently, linear RCLTG networks with diodes and switches can always be written in the form

$$\dot{x}(t) = Ax(t) + Bu(t) + Ew(t) \tag{10a}$$
$$y(t) = Cx(t) + Du(t) + Fw(t) \tag{10b}$$
$$\mathcal{C}_{\pi(t)}^* \ni y(t) \perp u(t) \in \mathcal{C}_{\pi(t)} \tag{10c}$$

where $\pi(\cdot)$ is a switching sequence taking values in a finite set $\{\pi_1, \ldots, \pi_N\}$, and for each i the set $\mathcal{C}_{\pi_i}$ is a closed convex cone in $\mathbb{R}^k$.

6 Dynamics in a Given Mode

At this point, we start studying the properties of solution trajectories to (7). Note that (7c)-(7d) implies that for all $i \in \{1, 2, \ldots, k\}$ either $y_i(t) = 0$ or $u_i(t) = 0$ must be satisfied. In other words, each diode is either conducting or blocking, and each switch is either open or closed. This results in a multimodal system with 2^k modes, where each mode is characterized by a subset $\mathcal{I}$ of $\{1, 2, \ldots, k\}$, indicating that $y_i(t) = 0$ if $i \in \mathcal{I}$ and $u_i(t) = 0$ if $i \in \mathcal{I}^c$ with $\mathcal{I}^c := \{1, 2, \ldots, k\} \setminus \mathcal{I}$. We split $\mathcal{I}$ as $\mathcal{I} = \mathcal{D} \cup \mathcal{S}$ with $\mathcal{D} \subseteq \{1, 2, \ldots, m\}$ and $\mathcal{S} \subseteq \{m+1, m+2, \ldots, k\}$, where $\mathcal{D}$ denotes the status of the diodes and $\mathcal{S}$ of the switches[1].

For each mode $\mathcal{I}$ the laws of motion are given by the differential and algebraic equations (DAEs)

$$\dot{x}(t) = Ax(t) + Bu(t) + Ew(t) \tag{11a}$$
$$y(t) = Cx(t) + Du(t) + Fw(t) \tag{11b}$$
$$y_i(t) = 0, \; i \in \mathcal{I} \tag{11c}$$
$$u_i(t) = 0, \; i \in \mathcal{I}^c. \tag{11d}$$

During the time evolution of the system, the mode will vary whenever some of the diodes and/or switches change their state (i.e. diodes go from conducting to blocking or vice versa and/or switches from open to close or vice versa). The switches induce *time events* since an external device triggers the mode change, while the mode transitions of the diodes are due to *state events*: the current mode remains active as long as the inequalities in (7c) are satisfied.

---

[1] In the sequel of the paper when we write $\mathcal{D}$ or $\mathcal{S}$, we always mean a subset of $\{1, 2, \ldots, m\}$ or $\{m+1, m+2, \ldots, k\}$, respectively. By $\mathcal{D}^c$ and $\mathcal{S}^c$, we will denote the sets $\{1, 2, \ldots, m\} \setminus \mathcal{D}$ and $\{m+1, m+2, \ldots, k\} \setminus \mathcal{S}$, respectively.

7   Solution Concept

During the smooth continuation phases, the system trajectories satisfy the DAEs (11) for some mode $\mathcal{I}$ in the classical sense. For the moment, we restrict ourselves to so-called Bohl functions (sines, cosines, polynomials, exponentials and their sums and products) as inputs w, which leads to Bohl functions as solutions to (11) (see [10]). More precisely, a function f is called a *Bohl function* (or *Bohl type*) if $f(t) = He^{Ft}G$ for some matrices F, G, and H of appropriate sizes. We denote the set of all Bohl function by $\mathcal{B}$.

At the event of a mode transition, the system may in principle display jumps in the state variable x. Jumping phenomena are well-known in the theory of unilaterally constrained mechanical systems [4], where at impacts the change of velocity of the colliding bodies is often modelled as being instantaneous. These discontinuous and impulsive motions are also observed in electrical networks.

To obtain a mathematically precise solution concept, we will use a distributional framework in which Dirac distributions play a key role.

Definition 4. *A Bohl distribution is a distribution* $\mathbf{u}$ *of the form* $\mathbf{u} = \mathbf{u}_{imp} + \mathbf{u}_{reg}$, *where* $\mathbf{u}_{imp}$ *is a linear combination of* δ *and its derivatives, i.e.,*

$$\mathbf{u}_{imp} = \sum_{i=0}^{l} u^{-i} \delta^{(i)}$$

for real numbers u^{-i}, $i = 0, \dots, l$ *and* $\mathbf{u}_{reg}$ *is a Bohl function on* $[0, \infty)$. *The class of Bohl distributions is denoted by* $\mathcal{B}_{imp}$. *For a distribution* $\mathbf{u} \in \mathcal{B}_{imp}$, $\mathbf{u}_{imp}$ *is called the impulsive part and* $\mathbf{u}_{reg}$ *is called the regular or smooth part. In case* $\mathbf{u}_{imp} = 0$ *we call* $\mathbf{u}$ *a* regular *or* smooth *distribution.*

Note that the Laplace transform of a Bohl distribution is a rational function. It can be easily verified that a Bohl distribution is regular if and only if its Laplace transform is strictly proper. In what follows, Bohl distributions having a proper Laplace transform will play an important role. We call them *first order* Bohl distributions. Note that a Bohl distribution is of first order if and only if its impulsive part does not contain derivatives of the Dirac distribution.

With this machinery we can now introduce the concept of an initial solution given an initial state $x(0) = x_0$ and a switch configuration $\mathcal{S}$ for the pure switches. In view of (10) with $\pi(t) = \mathcal{S}$ this actually implies that $u(t)$ is contained in the cone

$$\mathcal{C}_{\mathcal{S}} := \{v \in \mathbb{R}^k \mid v_i \in \mathbb{R}_+, \ i = 1, \dots, m, \ \text{and} \ v_i = 0, \ i \in \mathcal{S}^c\} \tag{12}$$

and $y(t)$ should be in the dual cone $\mathcal{C}_{\mathcal{S}}^*$. Note that

$$\mathcal{C}_{\mathcal{S}}^* = \{v \in \mathbb{R}^k \mid v_i \in \mathbb{R}_+, \ i = 1, \dots, m, \ \text{and} \ v_i = 0, \ i \in \mathcal{S}\} \tag{13}$$

Hence, that means that given $\mathcal{S}$ the governing equations (7) are reduced to

$$\dot{x}(t) = Ax(t) + Bu(t) + Ew(t) \tag{14a}$$

$$y(t) = Cx(t) + Du(t) + Fw(t) \tag{14b}$$

$$\mathcal{C}_{\mathcal{S}} \ni u(t) \perp y(t) \in \mathcal{C}_{\mathcal{S}}^* \tag{14c}$$

for some Bohl input w. Note that this system can be considered as an extension of the standard linear complementarity system (LCS) in [13] as it uses general positive cones C_S. The equations (14) become an ordinary LCS when $C_S = \mathbb{R}_+^k$.

Note that the "modes" $\mathcal{D}$ of the diodes are not specified by the formulation (14), i.e. $\mathcal{I} = \mathcal{D} \cup \mathcal{S}$ in (11) is not completely known. Hence, a solution in a mode $\mathcal{I}$ being governed by (11) is valid as long as $\mathcal{D}$ does not change. This means that mode $\mathcal{I}$ will only be valid for a limited amount of time in general, since a change of mode (diode going from conducting to blocking or vice versa) may be triggered by the inequality constraints. Therefore, we would like to express some kind of "local satisfaction of the constraints."

We call a (smooth) Bohl function v *initially in the cone* C if there exists an $\varepsilon > 0$ such that $v(t) \in C$ for all $t \in [0, \varepsilon)$. We know from the initial value theorem (see e.g. [8]) that there is a connection between small time values of time functions and large values of the indeterminate s in the Laplace transform. In fact, one can show that v is initially in the cone C if and only if there exists a $\sigma_0 \in \mathbb{R}$ such that its Laplace transform $\hat{v}(\sigma) \in C$ for all $\sigma \geqslant \sigma_0$.

The definition of being initially in the cone C for Bohl distributions will be based on this observation (see also [13, 12]).

Definition 5. *We call a Bohl distribution* v *initially in the cone* C *if its Laplace transform* $\hat{v}(s)$ *satisfies* $\hat{v}(\sigma) \in C$ *for all sufficiently large real* σ.

Remark 1. To relate the definition to the time domain, note that a scalar-valued[2] first order Bohl distribution v (i.e., $v_{imp} = v^0 \delta$ for some $v^0 \in \mathbb{R}$) is initially in the cone C if and only if

1. $v^0 \in C$, or
2. $v^0 = 0$ and there exists an $\varepsilon > 0$ such that $v_{reg}(t) \in C$ for all $t \in [0, \varepsilon)$.

Now, we are in a position to define a local solution concept.

Definition 6. *We call a Bohl distribution* $(\mathrm{u}, \mathrm{x}, \mathrm{y}) \in \mathcal{B}_{imp}^{k+n+k}$ *an initial solution to (7) with initial state* x_0 *and pure switch configuration* $\mathcal{S}$ *if*

1. *there is a diode configuration* $\mathcal{D}$ *such that* $(\mathrm{u}, \mathrm{x}, \mathrm{y})$ *satisfies (11) for mode* $\mathcal{I} = \mathcal{D} \cup \mathcal{S}$ *and initial state* x_0 *in the distributional sense, i.e. satisfies*

$$\dot{\mathrm{x}} = A\mathrm{x} + B\mathrm{u} + E w + x_0 \delta \tag{15a}$$
$$\mathrm{y} = C\mathrm{x} + D\mathrm{u} + Fw \tag{15b}$$
$$\mathrm{y}_i = 0, \ i \in \mathcal{I} \tag{15c}$$
$$\mathrm{u}_i = 0, \ i \notin \mathcal{I} \tag{15d}$$

as equalities of distributions, and
2. (u, y) *are initially in the cone* $(C_S \times C_S^*)$.

---

[2] In this case the cone C can only be equal to $\mathbb{R}, \mathbb{R}_+, -\mathbb{R}_+$ or $\{0\}$.

Note that the condition 2, together with real-analiticity of Bohl functions, already implies that (15c) and (15d) hold for $i \in \mathcal{S}$ and $i \in \mathcal{S}^*$, respectively.

Theorem 2. *Consider an SCS given by (7) such that Assumption 1 is satisfied and (A, B, C, D) represents a passive system. Let a pure switch configuration $\mathcal{S}$ be given and let $\mathcal{Q}_{\mathcal{S}}$ be the solution set of $LCP_{C_{\mathcal{S}}}(0, D)$, i.e., $\mathcal{Q}_{\mathcal{S}} = \{v \in \mathbb{R}^k \mid v \in C_{\mathcal{S}}, Dv \in C_{\mathcal{S}}^* \text{ and } v \perp Dv\}$. Then, the following statements hold.*

1. *For each initial state $x_0 \in \mathbb{R}^n$ and input $w \in \mathcal{B}^p$, there exists exactly one initial solution to SCS.*
2. *This solution is of first order. Stated differently, its impulsive part is of the form $(u^0 \delta, 0, Du^0 \delta)$ for some $u^0 \in \mathcal{Q}_{\mathcal{S}}$.*
3. *This impulsive part results in a re-initialization (jump) -if applicable- of the state from x_0 to $x_0 + Bu^0$.*
4. *For all $x_0 \in \mathbb{R}^n$, $Cx_0 + Fw(0) + CBu^0 \in \mathcal{Q}_{\mathcal{S}}^*$.*
5. *The initial solution is smooth (i.e., $u^0 = 0$) if and only if $Cx_0 + Fw(0) \in \mathcal{Q}_{\mathcal{S}}^*$.*

The fact that solutions of linear passive networks with ideal diodes and pure switches do not contain derivatives of Dirac impulses is widely believed true on "intuitive" grounds, but the authors are not aware of any previous rigorous proof. The framework proposed here makes it possible to prove the intuition. Only for the diode-case it was proven in [11].

A direct implication of the statements 3, 4, and 5 in Theorem 2 is that if smooth continuation is not possible for x_0, it is possible after one re-initialization. Indeed, by 3 the state after the re-initialization is equal to $x_0 + Bu^0$ where u^0 as in 2. Since $C(x_0 + Bu^0) + Fw(0) \in \mathcal{Q}_{\mathcal{S}}^*$ due to 4, it follows from statement 5 that from $x_0 + Bu^0$ there exists a smooth initial solution with input w and switch configuration $\mathcal{S}$. This yields a local existence result on an interval of the form $[0, \varepsilon)$ for some $\varepsilon > 0$. This can be generalized to *global* existence by concatenation of initial solutions as outlined in [13,12]. To allow changes in switch configuration $\mathcal{S}$, we have to describe the allowed switching sequences and moreover, we have to define the class of functions that the sources are allowed to produce.

Definition 7. *A function $\pi : \mathbb{R}_+ \to 2^{\{m+1, m+2, \dots, k\}}$ is said to be an* admissible *switching function if it is piecewise constant and it changes value at most finitely many times on every finite length interval. The set of point at which π changes value will be denoted by Γ_π.*

Note that Γ_π is a set of isolated points due to the fact that there are finitely many points at which π changes value on every interval of finite length.

Definition 8. *A function $w : \mathbb{R}_+ \to \mathbb{R}$ is called* piecewise Bohl,[3] *(denoted as $w \in \mathcal{PB}$), if w is right-continuous[4] and there exists a collection $\Gamma_w = \{\tau_i\} \subset \mathbb{R}_+$ such that*

---

[3] Strictly speaking, we define a subspace of the class of piecewise Bohl functions. For reasons of brevity we will refer to this subspace as the space of piecewise Bohl functions.

[4] This means that $\lim_{t \downarrow \tau} w(t) = w(\tau)$ for all $\tau \in \mathbb{R}_+$, which is just a normalization.

– Γ_w is a set of isolated points, and
– for every i there exists a $v \in \mathcal{B}$ such that $w(t) = v(t)$ for all $t \in (\tau_i, \tau_{i+1})$.

We call the collection Γ_w the set of *transition points* associated with w. The subset of Γ_w at which w is not continuous is called the collection of *discontinuity points* of w and is denoted by Γ_w^d.

Definition 9. *The distribution space $\mathcal{L}_{2,\delta}$ is defined as the set of all* $\mathbf{u} = \mathbf{u}_{imp} + \mathbf{u}_{reg}$, *where* $\mathbf{u}_{imp} = \sum_{\theta \in \Gamma} u^\theta \delta_\theta$ *for* $u^\theta \in \mathbb{R}$ *with* $\Gamma \subset \mathbb{R}_+$ *a set of isolated points, and* $\mathbf{u}_{reg} \in \mathcal{L}_2^{loc}$.

The isolatedness of the points of the set Γ is required to prevent the occurrence of an accumulation of Dirac impulses in the solution trajectories (a kind of Zeno behavior). One could relax this requirement, but we prefer to keep the exposition simple at this point.

Definition 10. *Let the impulsive part of the distribution* $(\mathbf{u}, \mathbf{x}, \mathbf{y}) \in \mathcal{L}_{2,\delta}^{m+n+m}$ *be supported on a set of isolated points Γ, i.e.,*

$$(\mathbf{u}_{imp}, \mathbf{x}_{imp}, \mathbf{y}_{imp}) = \sum_{\theta \in \Gamma} (u^\theta, x^\theta, y^\theta) \delta_\theta$$

for $(u^\theta, x^\theta, y^\theta) \in \mathbb{R}^{k+n+k}$. Then we call $(\mathbf{u}, \mathbf{x}, \mathbf{y})$ a (global) solution to SCS (7) for the initial state x_0, $w \in \mathcal{PB}$ and the admissible switching function π if the following properties hold.

1. *For any interval (a, b) such that $(a, b) \cap \Gamma = \varnothing$ the restriction $\mathbf{x}_{reg}|_{(a,b)}$ is absolutely continuous and satisfies for almost all $t \in (a, b)$*

$$\dot{\mathbf{x}}_{reg}(t) = A\mathbf{x}_{reg}(t) + B\mathbf{u}_{reg}(t) + Ew(t)$$
$$\mathbf{y}_{reg}(t) = C\mathbf{x}_{reg}(t) + D\mathbf{u}_{reg}(t) + Fw(t)$$
$$\mathcal{C}_{\pi(t)} \ni \mathbf{u}_{reg}(t) \perp \mathbf{y}_{reg}(t) \in \mathcal{C}^*_{\pi(t)}.$$

2. *For each $\theta \in \Gamma$ the corresponding impulse $(u^\theta \delta_\theta, x^\theta \delta_\theta, y^\theta \delta_\theta)$ is equal to the impulsive part of the unique initial solution to (7) with initial state $\mathbf{x}_{reg}(\theta-) := \lim_{t \uparrow \theta} \mathbf{x}_{reg}(t)$ (taken equal to x_0 for $\theta = 0$), input[5] $t \mapsto w(t + \theta)$ and switch configuration $S = \pi(\theta+)$.*

3. *For times $\theta \in \Gamma$ it holds that $\mathbf{x}_{reg}(\theta+) = \mathbf{x}_{reg}(\theta-) + Bu^\theta$.*

Note that the solution in the above sense satisfies the equations $\dot{\mathbf{x}} = A\mathbf{x} + B\mathbf{u} + Ew$ and $\mathbf{y} = C\mathbf{x} + D\mathbf{u} + Fw$ in the distributional sense.

Theorem 3. *Consider an SCS given by (7) such that Assumption 1 is satisfied and (A, B, C, D) represents a passive system. The SCS (7) has a unique (global) solution $(\mathbf{u}, \mathbf{x}, \mathbf{y}) \in \mathcal{L}_{2,\delta}^{m+n+m}$ for any initial state x_0, input $w \in \mathcal{PB}$ and admissible switching function π. Moreover, $\mathbf{x}_{imp} = 0$ and impulses in $(\mathbf{u}, \mathbf{y})$ only show up at the initial time, at times for which π changes value and for which the piecewise Bohl function Fw has discontinuities (i.e. Γ in Definition 10 can be taken as a subset of $\{0\} \cup \Gamma_\pi \cup \Gamma_{Fw}^d$).*

---

[5] Note that initial solutions are only defined for Bohl inputs so strictly speaking we have to extract the Bohl part from w that starts at time θ.

8   Regular States

Another consequence of Theorem 2 is the characterization of so-called *regular states* (sometimes also called *consistent states*) as introduced next.

Definition 11. *A state x_0 is called* regular *for SCS(A, B, C, D, E, F) with respect to a pure switch configuration and input $w \in \mathcal{B}$ if the corresponding initial solution for the same pure switch configuration is smooth. The collection of regular states for a given quadruple (A, B, C, D, E, F) with respect to the pure switch configuration S and input w is denoted by $\mathcal{R}_{S,w}$.*

Theorem 4. *Consider an SCS given by (7) such that Assumption 1 is satisfied and (A, B, C, D) represents a passive system. Let a pure switch configuration S be given and let $\mathcal{Q}_S$ be the solution set of $LCP_{C_S}(0, D)$, i.e., $\mathcal{Q}_S = \{v \in \mathbb{R}^k \mid v \in C_S, Dv \in C_S^* \text{ and } v \perp Dv\}$. The following statements are equivalent.*

1. *x_0 is a regular state for (7) with respect to the pure switch configuration S and input w.*
2. *$Cx_0 + Fw(0) \in \mathcal{Q}_S^*$.*
3. *$LCP_{C_S}(Cx_0 + Fw(0), D)$ has a solution.*
4. *There exist two vectors $v_1 \in C_S^*$ and $v_2 \in C_S$ such that $Cx_0 + Fw(0) = v_1 - Dv_2$.[6]*

Hence, several tests are available for deciding the regularity of an initial state x_0. In [2] it is stated that a well-designed circuit does not exhibit impulsive behavior. As a consequence, the characterization of regular states forms a verification of the synthesis of the network.

9   Jump Rules

If a state jump occurs at time $t = 0$, the new state is given by $x(0+) = x_0 + Bu^0$, see Theorem 2 item 3. We now give a characterization of this jump multiplier u^0 for SCS.

Theorem 5. *Let a switch configuration S, an initial state x_0 and an input $w \in \mathcal{B}$ be given. The following characterizations can be obtained for u^0.*

1. *The jump multiplier u^0 is the unique solution to the cone complementarity problem*

$$\mathcal{Q}_S \ni v \perp C(x_0 + Bv) + Fw(0) \in \mathcal{Q}_S^* \tag{16}$$

2. *The cone $\mathcal{Q}_S$ is equal to pos $N := \{N\lambda \mid \lambda \geqslant 0\}$ and $\mathcal{Q}_S^* = \{v \mid N^T v \geqslant 0\}$ for some real matrix N. The re-initialized state $x_{reg}(0+)$ is equal to $x_0 + BN\lambda^0$ and $u^0 = N\lambda^0$ where λ^0 is a solution of the following ordinary LCP.*

$$0 \leqslant \lambda \perp (N^T Cx_0 + N^T Fw(0) + N^T CBN\lambda) \geqslant 0. \tag{17}$$

---

[6] When $\mathcal{Q}_S$ is the usual positive cone (i.e. equals to $\mathbb{R}_+^k$), this comes down to saying that $Cx_0 + Fw(0)$ is a positive linear combination of the columns of $(I - D)$.

3. *The re-initialized state* $x_{reg}(0+)$ *is the unique minimum of*

$$\text{minimize } \tfrac{1}{2}(x-x_0)^T K(x-x_0) \tag{18a}$$

$$\text{subject to } Cx + Fw(0) \in \mathcal{Q}_S^* \tag{18b}$$

and the multiplier $u^0 \in \mathcal{Q}_S$ *is uniquely determined by* $x_{reg}(0+) = x_0 + Bu^0$.

4. *The jump multiplier* u^0 *is the unique minimizer of*

$$\text{minimize } \tfrac{1}{2}(x_0+Bv)^T K(x_0+Bv) + v^T Fw(0) \tag{19}$$

$$\text{subject to } v \in \mathcal{Q}_S \tag{20}$$

The optimization problems have nice physical interpretations. Indeed, we can see that (18) states that the re-initialized state $x_{reg}(0+)$ is the regular initial state for the given switch configuration S and input w, such that the distance in the metric defined by the storage function $\tfrac{1}{2}x^T Kx$ (energy of the system) is minimal. In case $Fw(0) = 0$, the minimization problem (19) states that the u^0 is selected in the cone $\mathcal{Q}_S$ such that the state after the re-initialization has minimal energy expressed by the storage function $\tfrac{1}{2}x^T Kx$.

10   The Example of the Boost Circuit

To return to Example 1 of the boost circuit, we reconsider the system equations (14) with the matrices given by (8). A first thing that we can say is that on the basis of Theorem 4 and the fact that $F = 0$ it follows that jumps in the state are only triggered by the switch and not by the source. Discontinuities in w will not cause discontinuities in x. To demonstrate the results of the regular states and the jump rules, we consider the switch configuration $S = \{1\}$ (which means that we consider the open circuit $i_S = 0$). Since the diode can be both discrete states (conducting or blocking), this means that we are dealing with mode 1 or mode 3 in the hybrid automaton as in Figure 4.

Computing $\mathcal{Q}_S$ gives the cone $\{v \in \mathbb{R}^2 \mid v_1 = 0, \ v_2 \geqslant 0\}$ and the dual cone $\mathcal{Q}_S^*$ is then equal to $\{z \in \mathbb{R}^2 \mid z_2 \geqslant 0\}$. Since $F = 0$, the regular states are independent of the input w (being the voltage across the battery) and given by $Cx_0 \in \mathcal{Q}_S^*$, which yields that a state $x_0 = (q_0 \ \phi_0)^T$ is regular if and only if the flux through the inductor $\phi_0 \geqslant 0$. So, if $\phi_0 < 0$, we will have a reset of the state variable characterized by the minimization problems (18) and (19). To use these results, we first note that the identity matrix satisfies (6) and thus $V(x) = \tfrac{1}{2}q^2 + \tfrac{1}{2}\phi^2$ is a storage function. The re-initialized state (q^+, ϕ^+) is then given by the minimum of $(q^+-q_0)^2 + (\phi^+-\phi_0)^2$ subject to $\phi^+ \geqslant 0$. Since $\phi_0 < 0$, this gives $q^+ = q_0$ and $\phi^+ = 0$. Note that this complies with the transition (both guards and reset) in the automaton from mode 1 to mode 3. This jump only takes place at the initial time $t = 0$. Also the minimization problem (19) can be used, which yields the minimization of $\|(q_0+v_1, \phi_0+v_2)^T\|^2$ subject to $v_1 = 0$ and $v_2 \geqslant 0$. The solution is given by $u^0 = (0, -\phi_0)^T$ and consequently, the re-initialized state $(q^+, \phi^+)^T = x_0 + Bu^0 = (q_0, 0)^T$. These results follow in a direct and structured manner, while deriving the jump rules by hand (to come up with the hybrid automaton model) is tedious.

11   Stability

In this section we discuss the stability of Switched Complementarity Systems (SCS) under a passivity assumption without inputs (take w equal to 0):

$$\dot{x}(t) = Ax(t) + Bu(t) \tag{21a}$$

$$y(t) = Cx(t) + Du(t) \tag{21b}$$

$$0 \leqslant y_i(t) \perp u_i(t) \geqslant 0, \ i = 1, 2, \ldots, m \tag{21c}$$

$$y_i(t) \perp u_i(t), \ i = m+1, m+2, \ldots, k, \tag{21d}$$

The Lyapunov stability of hybrid and switched systems in general has already received considerable attention [14, 3]. We have narrowed down the definitions and theorems on the stability of general hybrid systems from and to apply to SCS. From now on, we denote the unique global trajectory for a given switch function π and initial state x_0 of an SCS by $(u^{\pi, x_0}, x^{\pi, x_0}, y^{\pi, x_0})$. For the study of stability we consider the source-free case.

Definition 12 (Equilibrium point). *A state $\bar{x}$ is an equilibrium point of the SCS (21), if for all admissible switching functions π $x_{reg}^{\pi, \bar{x}}(t) = \bar{x}$ for almost all $t \geqslant 0$ and all π, i.e. for all solutions starting in $\bar{x}$ the state stays in $\bar{x}$.*

Note that in an equilibrium point $\dot{x} = 0$, which leads in a simple way to the following characterization of equilibria of an SCS.

Lemma 1. *A state $\bar{x}$ is an equilibrium point of the SCS (21), if and only if for all $S \subset \{m+1, \ldots, k\}$ there exist $u^S \in \mathbb{R}^k$ and $y^S \in \mathbb{R}^k$ satisfying*

$$0 = A\bar{x} + Bu^S \tag{22a}$$

$$y^S = C\bar{x} + Du^S \tag{22b}$$

$$\mathcal{C}_S \ni u^S \perp y^S \in \mathcal{C}_S^*. \tag{22c}$$

Moreover, this means that $\bar{x} \in \mathcal{R}_S$ for all S, i.e. $\bar{x}$ is a regular state for all switch configurations.

From this lemma it follows that $\bar{x} = 0$ is an equilibrium. Note that if A is invertible we get $\bar{x} = -A^{-1}Bu^S$ and $\mathcal{C}_S \ni u^S \perp [-CA^{-1}B + D]u^S \in \mathcal{C}_S^*$, which is a homogeneous LCP over a cone.

Definition 13. *Let $\bar{x}$ be an equilibrium point of the SCS (21) and let d denote a metric on $\mathbb{R}^n$.*

1. *$\bar{x}$ is called stable, if for every $\varepsilon > 0$ there exists a $\delta > 0$ such that $d(x_{reg}^{\pi, x_0}(t), \bar{x}) < \varepsilon$ for almost all $t \geqslant 0$ whenever $d(x_0, \bar{x}) < \delta$ and π being an admissible switching function.*
2. *$\bar{x}$ is called asymptotically stable if $\bar{x}$ is stable and there exists an $\eta > 0$ such that $\lim_{t \to \infty} d(x_{reg}^{\pi, x_0}(t), \bar{x}) = 0$ whenever $d(x_0, \bar{x}) < \delta$ and π being an admissible switching function. By $\lim_{t \to \infty} d(x_{reg}^{\pi, x_0}(t), \bar{x}) = 0$ we mean that for every $\varepsilon > 0$ there exists a t_ε such that $d(x_{reg}^{\pi, x_0}(t), \sigma), \bar{x}) < \varepsilon$ whenever $t \geqslant t_\varepsilon$.*

Theorem 6. *Consider an SCS given by* (21) *such that Assumption 1 is satisfied and* (A, B, C, D) *represents a passive system. This SCS has only stable equilibrium points* $\bar{x}$. *Moreover, if* $A^T K + K A < 0$ *holds with strict inequality, then* $\bar{x} = 0$ *is the only equilibrium point, which is asymptotically stable.*

12   Conclusions

Our aim in this paper has been to demonstrate that a suitable framework for switched piecewise linear networks is provided by the notion of cone complementarity systems. The dynamics described by cone complementarity systems can be very complicated but nevertheless is given by two simple components, to wit a linear system and a closed convex cone. Switching may be described within this context in a conceptually straightforward way as switching between cones, while the underlying linear system remains the same.

Making use of impulsive-smooth distributions to define a sufficiently flexible notion of solution, we have shown that the framework of cone complementarity systems is sound in the sense that, under the passivity assumption, it produces unique solutions for any given initial state. Moreover, the framework allows formal proofs for intuitive properties concerning jumps and stability. We have obtained a characterization of the situations in which jumps occur as well as of the extend of the jump in these cases; this information should be useful both for theoretical and for simulation purposes of this class of hybrid systems.

The cones that we have considered are in fact of a special type in which each component is either unconstrained, constrained to be zero, or constrained to be nonnegative. The formulation of cone complementarity systems however invites a less coordinate-based and more geometric perspective, which helps to achieve a focus on basic issues. Some of the results that we have obtained in this paper still make use of the special properties of cones obtained from diodes and switches; it is a natural question to ask whether these results can be obtained at a more general level, and we intend to return to this in future work.

The notion of passivity has been crucial in this paper. In fact it is remarkable that this energy-related concept turns out to play an important role even in establishing existence and uniqueness of solutions in a context that involves switching.

References

1. B.D.O. Anderson and S. Vongpanitlerd. *Network Analysis and Synthesis. A Modern Systems Theory Approach.* Pentice-Hall, Englewood Cliffs, New Jersey, 1973.
2. D. Bedrosian and J. Vlach. Time-domain analysis of networks with internally controlled switches. *IEEE Trans. Circuits and Systems-I*, 39(3):199–212, 1992.
3. M. S. Branicky. Multiple Lyapunov functions and other analysis tools for switched and hybrid systems. *IEEE Transactions on Automatic Control*, 43(4):475–482, 1998.

4. B. Brogliato. *Nonsmooth Impact Mechanics. Models, Dynamics and Control*, volume 220 of *Lecture Notes in Control and Information Sciences*. Springer, London, 1996.
5. M.K. Çamlıbel, W.P.M.H. Heemels, and J.M. Schumacher. On linear passive complementarity systems. *European Journal of Control. Special issue on "Dissipativity of dynamical systems: applications in control"*, 8(3):220–237, 2002.
6. M.K. Çamlıbel, W.P.M.H. Heemels, A.J. van der Schaft, and J.M. Schumacher. Modelling, well-posedness and stability of switched electrical networks. Technical Report 02I/01, Eindhoven University of Technolgy, Dept. of Electrical Engineering, Control Systems.
7. R.W. Cottle, J.-S. Pang, and R.E. Stone. *The Linear Complementarity Problem*. Academic Press, Inc., Boston, 1992.
8. J.J. DiStefano, A.R. Stubberud, and I.J. Williams. *Theory and problems of feedback and control systems*. Schaum's outline series. McGraw-Hill, 1967.
9. G. Escobar, A. J. van der Schaft, and R. Ortega. A Hamiltonian viewpoint in the modeling of switching power converters. *Automatica*, 35(3):445–452, 1999.
10. M.L.J. Hautus and L.M. Silverman. System structure and singular control. *Linear Algebra and its Applications*, 50:369–402, 1983.
11. W.P.M.H. Heemels, M.K. Çamlıbel, and J.M. Schumacher. On the dynamic analysis of piecewise-linear networks. *IEEE Transactions on Circuits and Systems – I*, 49(3):315–327, 2002.
12. W.P.M.H. Heemels, J.M. Schumacher, and S. Weiland. The rational complementarity problem. *Linear Algebra and its Applications*, 294:93–135, 1999.
13. W.P.M.H. Heemels, J.M. Schumacher, and S. Weiland. Linear complementarity systems. *SIAM Journal on Applied Mathematics*, 60(4):1234–1269, 2000.
14. D. Liberzon and A. S. Morse. Basic problems in stability and design of switched systems. *IEEE Control Systems Magazine*, 19(5):59–70, 1999.
15. J.C. Willems. Dissipative dynamical systems. *Archive for Rational Mechanics and Analysis*, 45:321–393, 1972.

Hybrid Modeling and Simulation of Genetic Regulatory Networks: A Qualitative Approach

Hidde de Jong[1], Jean-Luc Gouzé[2], Céline Hernandez[3], Michel Page[1,4],
Tewfik Sari[5], and Johannes Geiselmann[6]

[1] Institut National de Recherche en Informatique et en Automatique (INRIA), Unité
de recherche Rhône-Alpes, 655 avenue de l'Europe, Montbonnot, 38334 Saint Ismier
Cedex, France,
{Hidde.de-Jong,Michel.Page}@inrialpes.fr,
[2] Institut National de Recherche en Informatique et en Automatique (INRIA), Unité
de recherche Sophia Antipolis, France,
Jean-Luc.Gouze@sophia.inria.fr,
[3] Swiss Institute of Bioinformatics (SIB), Geneva, Switzerland,
Celine.Hernandez@isb-sib.ch,
[4] École Supérieure des Affaires, Université Pierre Mendès France, Grenoble, France,
[5] Laboratoire de Mathématiques, Université de Haute Alsace, Mulhouse, France,
T.Sari@uha.fr,
[6] Laboratoire Plasticité et Expression des Génomes Microbiens, Université Joseph
Fourier, Grenoble, France,
Hans.Geiselmann@ujf-grenoble.fr.

Abstract. The study of genetic regulatory networks has received a major impetus from the recent development of experimental techniques allowing the measurement of patterns of gene expression in a massively
parallel way. This experimental progress calls for the development of
appropriate computer tools for the modeling and simulation of gene regulation processes. We present a method for the hybrid modeling and
simulation of genetic regulatory networks, based on a class of piecewise-
linear (PL) differential equations that has been well-studied in mathematical biology. Distinguishing characteristics of the method are that it
makes qualitative predictions of the behavior of regulatory systems and
that it deals with discontinuities in the right-hand side of the differential
equations. The simulation method has been implemented in Java in the
computer tool Genetic Network Analyzer (GNA). The method and the
tool have been used to analyze several networks of biological interest, including the network underlying the initiation of sporulation in *Bacillus
subtilis*.

1 Introduction

The study of *genetic regulatory networks* has received a major impetus from
the recent development of experimental techniques allowing the measurement
of patterns of gene expression in a massively parallel way. This experimental
progress calls for the development of appropriate computer tools for the modeling

O. Maler and A. Pnueli (Eds.): HSCC 2003, LNCS 2623, pp. 267–282, 2003.
© Springer-Verlag Berlin Heidelberg 2003

and simulation of gene regulation processes. A variety of approaches for the modeling and simulation of genetic regulatory networks has been proposed in the past three decades [4,17,21,25].

A particularly interesting approach towards the computational analysis of genetic regulatory networks, well-adapted to state-of-the-art measurement techniques in genomics, is based on a class of *piecewise-linear (PL)* differential equations originally proposed by Glass and Kauffman [10,14]. The state variables in the PL models correspond to the concentrations of proteins encoded by genes in the network, while the differential equations represent the interactions arising from the regulatory influence of some proteins on the synthesis and degradation of others. The regulatory interactions are modeled by means of step functions, which gives rise to the piecewise-linear structure of the system. More precisely, the use of step functions divides the phase space into hyperrectangular regions, in each of which the system evolves according to a set of linear, uncoupled differential equations. On the boundaries between these regions, the system description switches from one set of linear, uncoupled equations to another.

The dual, continuous and discrete, nature of the PL models of genetic regulatory networks has attracted the interest of researchers in hybrid systems [1, 13]. In this paper, we present a modeling and simulation method [7,8,9] that extends the above work in two respects. First, the PL models being used are *qualitative*, in the sense that numerical values for parameters and initial conditions, which are usually not available, need not be specified. Instead, the models are supplemented by qualitative constraints in the form of algebraic inequalities. Second, the method is able to deal with discontinuities in the right-hand side of the differential equations, resulting from the use of step functions. The discontinuities give rise to non-trivial mathematical problems that are solved through the use of a Filippov generalization of the PL models [12,15]. On a formal level, the PL models are related to a class of asynchronous logical models proposed by Thomas and colleagues [28].

The qualitative simulation method is supported by the publicly-available computer tool *GNA (Genetic Network Analyzer)* [6], which has been used to analyze several genetic regulatory networks of biological interest. We will illustrate the use of GNA by summarizing the results obtained in the modeling and simulation of the large and complex network underlying the initiation of sporulation in *Bacillus subtilis* [5].

2   PL Models of Genetic Regulatory Networks

The dynamics of genetic regulatory networks can be modeled by a class of piecewise-linear differential equations of the following general form [14,22,26]:

$$\dot{x} = f(x) - g(x)\,x, \quad x \geq 0, \tag{1}$$

where $x = (x_1, \ldots, x_n)'$ is a vector of cellular protein concentrations, and $f = (f_1, \ldots, f_n)'$, $g = \mathrm{diag}(g_1, \ldots, g_n)$. The rate of change of each concentration x_i,

$1 \leq i \leq n$, is defined as the difference of the rate of synthesis $f_i(x)$ and the rate of degradation $g_i(x) x_i$ of the protein.

The function $f_i : \mathbb{R}^n_{\geq 0} \to \mathbb{R}_{\geq 0}$ is defined as

$$f_i(x) = \sum_{l \in L} \kappa_{il}\, b_{il}(x), \tag{2}$$

where $\kappa_{il} > 0$ is a rate parameter, $b_{il} : \mathbb{R}^n_{\geq 0} \to \{0, 1\}$ a *regulation function*, and L a possibly empty set of indices of regulation functions. A regulation function b_{il} is the arithmetic equivalent of a Boolean function expressing the logic of gene regulation [22,28]. The function g_i expresses the regulation of protein degradation. It is defined analogously to f_i, except that we demand that $g_i(x)$ is strictly positive. In addition, in order to formally distinguish degradation rates from synthesis rates, we will denote the former by γ instead of κ.

Fig. 1 gives an example of a simple genetic regulatory network. Genes a and b, transcribed from separate promoters, encode proteins A and B, each of which controls the expression of both genes. More specifically, proteins A and B repress gene a as well as gene b at different concentrations. Repression of the genes is achieved by binding of the proteins to regulatory sites overlapping with the promoters.

The network in Fig. 1 can be described by means of the following pair of state equations:

$$\dot{x}_a = \kappa_a\, s^-(x_a, \theta_a^2)\, s^-(x_b, \theta_b^1) - \gamma_a\, x_a \tag{3}$$

$$\dot{x}_b = \kappa_b\, s^-(x_a, \theta_a^1)\, s^-(x_b, \theta_b^2) - \gamma_b\, x_b. \tag{4}$$

Gene a is expressed at a rate $\kappa_a > 0$, if the concentration of protein A is below its threshold θ_a^2 and the concentration of protein B below its threshold θ_b^1, that is, if $s^-(x_a, \theta_a^2)\, s^-(x_b, \theta_b^1) = 1$. Recall that $s^-(x, \theta)$ is a step function evaluating to 1, if $x < \theta$, and to 0, if $x > \theta$. Protein A is spontaneously degraded at a rate proportional to its own concentration ($\gamma_a > 0$ is a rate constant). The state equation of gene b is interpreted analogously.

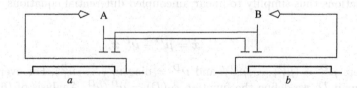

Fig. 1. Example of a genetic regulatory network of two genes (a and b), each coding for a regulatory protein (A and B).

3 Properties of PL Models

The dynamical properties of PL models of the form (1) can be analyzed in the n-dimensional phase space box $\Omega = \Omega_1 \times \ldots \times \Omega_n$, where $\Omega_i = \{x_i \in \mathbb{R}_{\geq 0} \mid 0 \leq x_i \leq max_i\}$, $1 \leq i \leq n$, and max_i is a parameter denoting a maximum concentration for the protein.

In general, a protein encoded by a gene is involved in different interactions at different threshold concentrations, which after ordering are denoted by $\theta_i^1, \ldots, \theta_i^{p_i}$. The $n-1$-dimensional hyperplanes $x_i = \theta_i^{k_i}$, $1 \leq k_i \leq p_i$, divide Ω into regions that are called *domains*. More precisely, a domain $D \subseteq \Omega$ is defined by $D = D_1 \times \ldots \times D_n$, where every D_i, $1 \leq i \leq n$, is defined by one of the equations below:

$$
\begin{aligned}
D_i &= \{x_i \mid 0 \leq x_i < \theta_i^1\}, \\
D_i &= \{x_i \mid x_i = \theta_i^1\}, \\
D_i &= \{x_i \mid \theta_i^1 < x_i < \theta_i^2\}, \\
&\ldots \\
D_i &= \{x_i \mid \theta_i^{p_i} < x_i \leq max_i\}.
\end{aligned}
\tag{5}
$$

If for a domain D, there are some i, j, $1 \leq i \leq n$, $1 \leq j \leq p_i$, such that $D_i = \{x_i \mid x_i = \theta_i^j\}$, then D is called a *switching* domain. The *order* of a switching domain is a number between 1 and n, equal to the number of switching variables. A domain that is not a switching domain is called a *regulatory* domain.

In Fig. 2(a) the two-dimensional phase space box Ω for the example network is shown. As proteins A and B each have two thresholds, the phase space box is partitioned into 9 regulatory and 16 switching domains. For example, $D^1 = \{(x_a, x_b) \in \mathbb{R}^2 \mid 0 \leq x_a < \theta_a^1, \ 0 \leq x_b < \theta_b^1\}$ is a regulatory domain, whereas $D^4 = \{(x_a, x_b) \in \mathbb{R}^2 \mid 0 \leq x_a < \theta_a^1, \ x_b = \theta_b^2\}$ is a (first-order) switching domain.

When evaluating the step function expressions in (1) in a regulatory domain, f_i and g_i reduce to sums of rate constants. More precisely, in a regulatory domain D, f_i reduces to some $\mu_i^D \in M_i \equiv \{f_i(\boldsymbol{x}) \mid \boldsymbol{0} \leq \boldsymbol{x} \leq \boldsymbol{max}\}$, and g_i to some $\nu_i^D \in N_i \equiv \{g_i(\boldsymbol{x}) \mid \boldsymbol{0} \leq \boldsymbol{x} \leq \boldsymbol{max}\}$. M_i and N_i collect the synthesis and degradation rates of the protein in different domains of Ω. Inside D, the state equations thus simplify to linear, uncoupled differential equations

$$
\dot{\boldsymbol{x}} = \boldsymbol{\mu}^D - \boldsymbol{\nu}^D \boldsymbol{x},
\tag{6}
$$

where $\boldsymbol{\mu}^D = (\mu_1^D, \ldots, \mu_n^D)'$ and $\boldsymbol{\nu}^D = \mathrm{diag}(\nu_1^D, \ldots, \nu_n^D)$. For every regulatory domain D, we define the function $\phi_i(D) = \mu_i^D / \nu_i^D$. Analysis of (6) shows that all solution trajectories in D monotonically tend towards a *target equilibrium*, a stable equilibrium given by $\boldsymbol{x} = \boldsymbol{\phi}(D)$, with $\boldsymbol{\phi} = (\phi_1, \ldots, \phi_n)'$ [14,22,26]. The target equilibrium level μ_i^D / ν_i^D of the protein concentration x_i gives an indication of the strength of gene expression in D. Call $\Phi(D) = \{\boldsymbol{\phi}(D)\}$ the *target equilibrium set* of D. If $\Phi(D) \cap D \neq \{\}$, then all trajectories will remain in D. If not, they will leave D at some point.

In the example, we have $M_a = \{0, \kappa_a\}$, $N_a = \{\gamma_a\}$ for protein A, and $M_b = \{0, \kappa_b\}$, $N_b = \{\gamma_b\}$ for protein B. In regulatory domain D^1 in Fig. 2(a), the trajectories tend towards the target equilibrium $\phi(D^1) = (\kappa_a/\gamma_a, \kappa_b/\gamma_b)$. Since $\Phi(D_1) \cap D_1 = \{\}$, the trajectories starting in D will leave this domain at some point. Different regulatory domains generally have different target equilibria. For instance, in regulatory domain D^3, the target equilibrium is given by $(0, \kappa_b/\gamma_b)$.

The global solution of (1) could be obtained by piecing together the local solutions in regulatory domains, in such a way as to guarantee continuity of the global solution across the threshold hyperplanes [10,26]. This works fine as long as trajectories arriving at a threshold hyperplane can be continued in another regulatory domain, e.g., trajectories arriving at the switching domain D^2 from the regulatory domain D^1 (Fig. 2(a)). However, when the trajectories on both sides of a threshold hyperplane evolve towards this plane, as in the case of trajectories arriving from D^3 and D^5 at D^4, mathematical perplexities arise. There is no indication on how the local solutions in D^3 and D^5 can be continued.

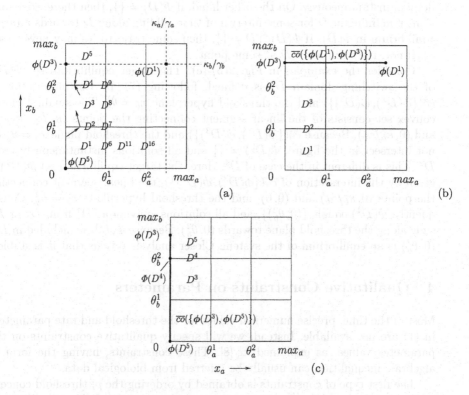

Fig. 2. (a) Phase space box for the example network in Fig. 1. $\phi(D^1)$, $\phi(D^3)$, $\phi(D^5)$ denote the target equilibria of the regulatory domains D^1, D^3, D^5. In addition, the figure shows the discontinuities at the switching domains D^2 and D^4. (b)-(c) Determination of the target equilibrium sets $\Phi(D^2)$ and $\Phi(D^4)$.

The troubles at the threshold hyperplanes are caused by discontinuities in the right-hand side of (1), due to the use of step functions. In order to deal with these discontinuities, we will use a method originally proposed by Filippov [12]. This method, recently applied by Gouzé and Sari [15] to PL systems of the form (1), consists of extending a system of differential equations with discontinuous right-hand sides into a system of differential inclusions. Using this generalization, it can be shown that, in the case of a switching domain D, the trajectories either traverse D instantaneously or tend towards a target equilibrium set $\Phi(D)$. As a summary of the analysis in [7,8], consider a switching domain D of order k, contained in the $n-k$-dimensional hyperplane C. Moreover, let $R(D)$ be the set of regulatory domains that have D in their boundary. Then

$$\Phi(D) = C \cap \{\overline{co}\,(\{\phi(D') \mid D' \in R(D)\}). \tag{7}$$

That is, $\Phi(D)$ is the smallest closed convex set of the target equilibria of regulatory domains D' having D in their boundary, intersected with the hyperplane containing D. If $\Phi(D) = \{\}$, the solutions arriving at D will cross the switching domain instantaneously. On the other hand, if $\Phi(D) \neq \{\}$, then there exist solutions remaining in D for some interval of time, sliding along D towards a target equilibrium in $\Phi(D)$. If $\Phi(D) \cap D \neq \{\}$, then some trajectories may never leave D. If not, they will leave D at some point.

Consider the examples in Fig. 2(b)-(c). The target equilibrium set $\Phi(D^2)$ of the switching domain D^2 is defined, following (7), by the intersection of $\overline{co}(\{\phi(D^1), \phi(D^3)\})$ and the threshold hyperplane $x_b = \theta_b^1$. The smallest closed convex set consists of the linear segment connecting the points $(\kappa_a/\gamma_a, \kappa_b/\gamma_b)$ and $(0, \kappa_b/\gamma_b)$. Because $\overline{co}(\{\phi(D^1), \phi(D^3)\})$ and the threshold plane $x_b = \theta_b^1$ do not intersect in the figure, $\Phi(D^2) = \{\}$ and all solutions instantaneously cross D^2. This is different in the case of D^4. Here, the target equilibrium set $\Phi(D^4)$ is given by the intersection of $\overline{co}(\{\phi(D^3), \phi(D^5)\})$, the linear segment connecting the points $(0, \kappa_b/\gamma_b)$ and $(0, 0)$, and the threshold hyperplane $x_b = \theta_b^2$. Consequently, $\Phi(D^4)$ equals $\{(0, \theta_b^2)\}$, and all solutions arriving at D^4 from D^3 or D^5 slide along the threshold plane towards $(0, \theta_b^2)$. Because $\Phi(D^4)$ is included in D^4, $(0, \theta_b^2)$ is an equilibrium of the system. Closer analysis reveals that it is stable.

4   Qualitative Constraints on Parameters

Most of the time, precise numerical values for the threshold and rate parameters in (1) are not available. Instead, we will specify qualitative constraints on the parameter values, as explained in [8]. These constraints, having the form of algebraic inequalities, can usually be inferred from biological data.

The first type of constraints is obtained by ordering the p_i threshold concentrations of the protein encoded by gene i, yielding the *threshold inequalities*:

$$0 < \theta_i^1 < \ldots < \theta_i^{p_i} < max_i, \tag{8}$$

The threshold inequalities determine the partitioning of Ω into regulatory and switching domains.

In the case of protein A, there are two threshold concentrations: θ_a^1 and θ_a^2. Assuming the first to be lower than the second, we obtain the threshold inequalities $0 < \theta_a^1 < \theta_a^2 < max_a$. The ordering of the thresholds of protein B give rise to $0 < \theta_b^1 < \theta_b^2 < max_b$.

Second, the possible target equilibrium levels μ_i^D/ν_i^D of x_i in different regulatory domains $D \subseteq \Omega$ can be ordered with respect to the threshold concentrations. The resulting *equilibrium inequalities* define the strength of gene expression in the domain in a qualitative way, on the scale of ordered threshold concentrations. More precisely, for every $\mu_i \in M_i$, $\nu_i \in N_i$, and $\mu_i, \nu_i \neq 0$, we specify one of the following pairs of inequalities:

$$0 < \mu_i/\nu_i < \theta_i^1,$$
$$\theta_i^1 < \mu_i/\nu_i < \theta_i^2,$$
$$\ldots$$
$$\theta_i^{p_i} < \mu_i/\nu_i < max_i. \tag{9}$$

The equilibrium inequalities constrain the relative position of D and its target equilibrium set $\Phi(D)$.

The equilibrium inequalities for x_a in the example are $\theta_a^2 < \kappa_a/\gamma_a < max_a$. In the absence of protein B, while protein A has not yet reached its highest level, gene a is expressed at a rate κ_a. The corresponding target equilibrium value κ_a/γ_a of x_a must be above the second threshold θ_a^2, otherwise the concentration of the protein would not be able to reach or maintain a level at which the observed negative autoregulation of gene a occurs. In a similar way, we set $\theta_b^2 < \kappa_b/\gamma_b < max_b$ for x_b.

A *quantitative* PL model of a genetic regulatory network consists of state equations (1) and numerical parameter values θ, κ, γ. In a *qualitative* PL model, on the other hand, the state equations are supplemented by threshold and equilibrium inequalities. Every quantitative PL model can be uniquely abstracted into a qualitative PL model.

5   Qualitative Simulation of Genetic Regulatory Networks

Let x, defined on some time-interval $[0, \tau[$, be a solution of a quantitative PL model describing a genetic regulatory network. Furthermore, at some time-point t, $0 \leq t < \tau$, $x(t) \in D$. A qualitative description of x at t consists of the domain D, supplemented by the relative position of D and $\Phi(D)$. We call this the *qualitative state* of the system. On $[0, \tau[$ the solution traverses a sequence of domains $D^0, \ldots, D^m$ in Ω. Whenever x enters a new domain, the system makes a transition to a new qualitative state. The sequence of qualitative states corresponding to the sequence of domains is called the *qualitative behavior* of the system on the time-interval. Every solution of a quantitative PL model can be uniquely abstracted into a qualitative behavior [8].

Given a qualitative PL model and initial conditions in a domain D^0, the aim of *qualitative simulation* is to determine the possible qualitative behaviors of the system [20]. More precisely, denoting by X the set of solutions $x(t)$ of all quantitative PL models corresponding to the qualitative model, such that $x(0) = x_0 \in D^0$, the aim of qualitative simulation is to find the set of qualitative behaviors abstracting from some $x \in X$.

In [8] a simulation algorithm is described that generates a set of qualitative behaviors by recursively determining qualitative states and transitions from qualitative states, starting at the qualitative state associated with the initial domain D^0. Instead of performing extensive numerical calculations, the simulator reaches its goal through symbolic computation, by exploiting the parameter inequalities (8)-(9). The simulation results in a *transition graph*, a directed graph of qualitative states and transitions between qualitative states. The transition graph contains *qualitative equilibrium states* or *qualitative cycles*. These may correspond to equilibrium points or limit cycles reached by solutions in X, and hence indicate functional modes of the regulatory system.

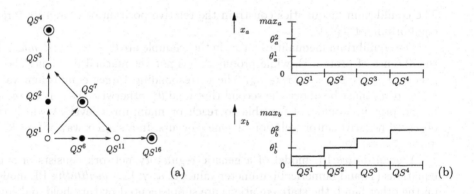

Fig. 3. (a) Transition graph resulting from a simulation of the example system starting in the domain D^1. Qualitative states associated with regulatory domains and switching domains are indicated by unfilled and filled dots, respectively. Qualitative states associated with domains containing an equilibrium point are circled [8]. (b) Detailed description of the qualitative behavior $\langle QS^1, QS^2, QS^3, QS^4 \rangle$.

Fig. 3(a) shows the transition graph for a qualitative simulation of the example system, starting in the regulatory domain D^1, where both x_a and x_b lie below their first threshold. As can be seen, the simulation results in five qualitative behaviors leading to different qualitative equilibrium states. In QS^{16}, associated with the switching domain D^{16} in Fig. 2(a), protein A is present at a high concentration ($x_a = \theta_a^2$), whereas protein B is present at a low concentration ($0 \leq x_b < \theta_b^1$). In QS^4, associated with D^4, protein A is present at a low concentration ($0 \leq x_a < \theta_a^1$) and protein B at a high concentration ($x_b = \theta_b^2$). In QS^7, associated with D^7, protein A and protein B are present at intermediate concentrations ($x_a = \theta_a^1$ and $x_b = \theta_b^1$). The qualitative equilibrium states QS^4 and QS^{16} correspond to stable equilibria of the system, whereas QS^7 corresponds to an unstable equilibrium.

A sequence of qualitative states in the transition graph represents a predicted qualitative behavior of the system. Fig. 3(b) gives a detailed description of one qualitative behavior, $\langle QS^1, QS^2, QS^3, QS^4 \rangle$. It shows for each qualitative state the corresponding domain, by indicating the (threshold) bounds for the concentration variables. In QS^1, for instance, x_a lies between 0 and θ_a^1, while x_b lies between 0 and θ_b^1. In the (instantaneous) state QS^2, x_b equals θ_b^1.

It has been demonstrated that the transition graph generated by the simulation algorithm covers all qualitative behaviors abstracting from some $x \in X$ [8]. That is, whatever the exact numerical values for the parameters be, if these values are consistent with the threshold and equilibrium inequalities specified in the qualitative PL model, the qualitative shape of the solution is described by a sequence of states in the transition graph.

The qualitative simulation method has been implemented in Java 1.3 in the program *Genetic Network Analyzer (GNA)* [6]. GNA is available for non-profit academic research purposes at http://www-helix.inrialpes.fr/gna. The core of the system is formed by the simulator, which generates a transition graph from a qualitative PL model and initial conditions. The input of the simulator is obtained by reading and parsing text files specified by the user. A graphical user interface (GUI), named *VisualGNA*, assists the user in specifying the model of a genetic regulatory network as well as in interpreting the simulation results. Fig. 4 shows a screen capture of GNA for the example network.

6   Application: Initiation of Sporulation in *Bacillus subtilis*

Under conditions of nutrient deprivation, the Gram positive soil bacterium *Bacillus subtilis* can abandon vegetative growth and form a dormant, environmentally-resistant spore instead [3,16,19,27]. During vegetative growth, the cell divides symmetrically and generates two identical cells. During sporulation, on the other hand, cell division is asymmetric and results in two different cell types: the smaller cell (the *forespore*) develops into the spore, whereas the larger cell (the *mother cell*) helps to deposit a resistant coat around the spore and then disintegrates. The decision to abandon vegetative growth and initiate sporulation involves a radical change in the genetic program, the pattern of gene expression, of the cell. The switch of genetic programme is controlled by a complex genetic regulatory network integrating various environmental, cell-cycle, and metabolic signals. Due to the ease of genetic manipulation of *B. subtilis*, it has been possible to identify and characterize a large number of the genes, proteins, and interactions making up this network. Currently, more than 125 genes are known to be involved [11].

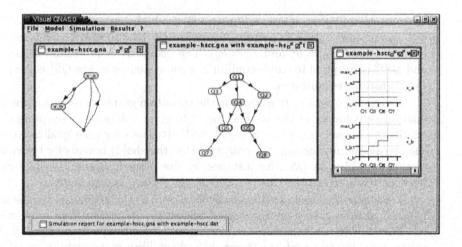

Fig. 4. Modeling and simulation of the genetic regulatory network of Fig. 1 by means of GNA. The window on the left shows the proteins and interactions of the sporulation network, the window in the middle part of the state transition graph resulting from simulation of the network under initial conditions inducing sporulation, and the window on the right the temporal sequence of qualitative states in one selected path in the state transition graph.

The qualitative simulation method based on PL models will be illustrated by analyzing the genetic regulatory network underlying the initiation of sporulation in *B. subtilis*. A graphical representation of the regulatory network controlling the initiation of sporulation is shown in Fig. 5, displaying key genes and their promoters, proteins encoded by the genes, and the regulatory action of the proteins. References to the experimental literature having been used to compile the network are given in [5].

The network is centered around a *phosphorelay*, which integrates a variety of environmental, cell-cycle, and metabolic signals. Under conditions appropriate for sporulation, the phosphorelay transfers a phosphate to the Spo0A regulator, a process modulated by kinases and phosphatases. The phosphorelay has been simplified in this paper by ignoring intermediate steps in the transfer of phosphate to Spo0A. However, this simplification does not affect the essential function of the phosphorelay: modulating the phosphate flux as a function of the competing action of kinases and phosphatases (here KinA and Spo0E). Under conditions conducive to sporulation, such as nutrient deprivation or high population density, the concentration of phosphorylated Spo0A (Spo0A~P) may reach a threshold value above which it activates various genes that commit the bacterium to sporulation. The choice between vegetative growth and sporulation in response to adverse environmental conditions is the outcome of competing positive and negative feedback loops, controlling the accumulation of Spo0A~P [16,19].

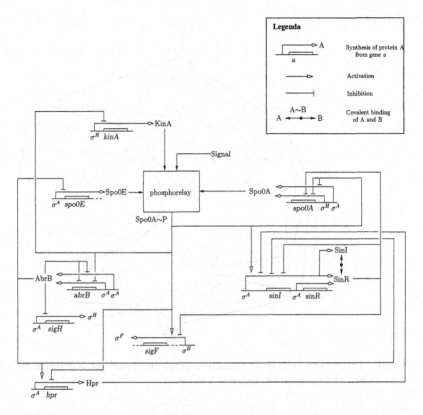

Fig. 5. Key genes, proteins, and regulatory interactions making up the network involved in *B. subtilis* sporulation. In order to improve the legibility of the figure, the control of transcription by the sigma factors σ^A and σ^H has been represented implicitly, by annotating the promoter with the corresponding sigma factor.

Notwithstanding the enormous amount of work devoted to the elucidation of the network of interactions underlying the sporulation process, very little quantitative data on kinetic parameters and molecular concentrations are available. The aim of the example is to show that GNA is able to reproduce the observed qualitative behavior of wild-type and mutant bacteria from a model that is a synthesis of available data in the literature. To this end, the graphical representation of the network has been translated into a PL model supplemented by qualitative constraints on the parameters. The resulting model consists of nine state variables and two input variables. The 49 parameters are constrained by 58 parameter inequalities, the choice of which is largely determined by biological data [5].

GNA has been used to simulate the response of a wild-type *B. subtilis* cell to nutrient depletion and high population density. Starting from initial conditions representing vegetative growth, the system is perturbed by a sporulation signal that causes KinA to autophosphorylate. Simulation of the network takes

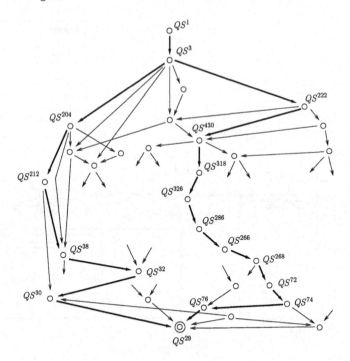

Fig. 6. Fragment of the state transition graph produced for vegetative growth conditions, when the sporulation signal is present.

less than a few seconds to complete on a PC (500 MHz, 128 MB of RAM), and gives rise to a transition graph of 465 qualitative states. Many of these states are associated with switching domains that the system traverses instantaneously. Since the biological relevance of the latter states is limited, they can be eliminated from the transition graph. This leads to a reduced transition graph with 82 qualitative states, part of which is shown in Fig. 6.

The transition graph faithfully represents the two possible responses to nutrient depletion that are observed for *B. subtilis*: either the bacterium continues vegetative growth or it enters sporulation. A typical qualitative behavior for sporulation as well as for vegetative growth are shown in Fig. 7. The initiation of sporulation is determined by positive feedback loops acting through Spo0A and KinA, and a negative feedback loop involving Spo0E. When the rate of accumulation of the kinase KinA outpaces the rate of accumulation of the phosphatase Spo0E, we observe transient expression of *sigF*, *i.e.* a *spo*⁺ phenotype (Fig. 7(a)). If the kinetics of these processes are inversed, *sigF* is never activated and we observe a *spo*⁻ phenotype (Fig. 7(b)). Deletion or overexpression of genes in the network of Fig. 5 may disable a feedback circuit, leading to specific changes in the observed sporulation phenotype. The results of the simulation of a dozen examples of sporulation mutants are discussed in [5].

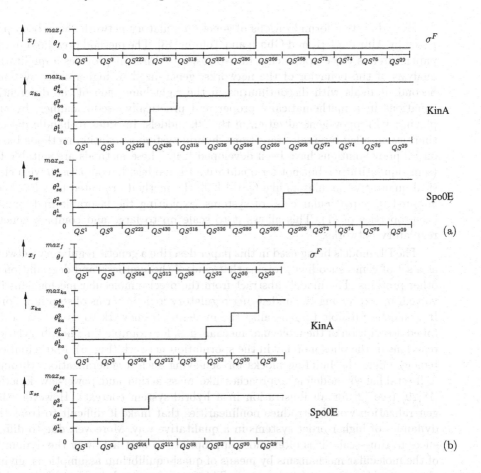

Fig. 7. (a) Temporal evolution of selected protein concentrations in a typical qualitative behavior corresponding to the *spo*[+] phenotype. (b) Idem, but for a typical qualitative behavior corresponding to the *spo*[−] phenotype.

7 Discussion

We have presented a method for the modeling and simulation of genetic regulatory networks. The method is based on a class of piecewise-linear (PL) differential equations that has been well-studied in mathematical biology. The PL models constitute a hybrid description of genetic regulatory networks, in the sense that they distinguish modes in which the system evolves continuously and discrete transitions between these modes. In the terminology of Mosterman and Biswas [23], the transitions are of one of two types. For example, *pinnacle mode transitions* occur when, upon reaching a switching domain D, the domain is traversed instantaneously ($\Phi(D) = \{\}$). On the other hand, *continuous mode transitions* occur when the system remains in D for an interval of time ($\Phi(D) \neq \{\}$).

Hybrid-system formalizations of genetic regulatory networks have been proposed by Alur *et al.* [1] and Ghosh and Tomlin [13]. The method presented in this paper extends these approaches in two respects. First, it provides a qualitative analysis of the behavior of the networks, generalized to higher-order systems. Second, it deals with discontinuities in the right-hand side of the differential equations in a mathematically proper and practically useful manner, by employing a Filippov generalization of the PL models. In order to handle discontinuities entailed by mode transitions, hybrid-system simulation methods based on Filippov solutions have been developed [24]. These methods are suitable for (semi-)quantitative, but not for qualitative PL models. In comparison with classical qualitative simulators like QSIM [20], the method presented here has been adapted to a particular class of systems, exploiting the favorable mathematical properties of (1). This allows it to scale up to large and complex genetic regulatory networks.

The PL models being used in this paper describe a genetic regulatory network as a set of genes encoding proteins that control the synthesis and degradation of other proteins. The models abstract from the precise molecular mechanisms involved, by expressing the underlying regulatory logic in terms of step functions. It would be possible to generalize the modeling framework so as to give a detailed description of the molecular mechanisms, for example the phosphorylation reactions in the phosphorelay in the sporulation network (Fig. 5). Mathematical biology offers the building blocks for achieving such a generalization, through well-established modeling approaches like mass-action and power-law kinetics [18,29] (see [2] for an illustration in a hybrid-system context). However, this generalization would introduce nonlinearities that make it difficult to treat the dynamics of higher-order systems in a qualitative way. Moreover, due to differences in time-scale, it is often more appropriate to abstract away the dynamics of the molecular mechanisms by means of quasi-equilibrium assumptions, giving rise to step function approximations. This latter approach has been followed in the case of the phosphorelay (see [5] for details).

The simulation method has been implemented in Java in the computer tool Genetic Network Analyzer (GNA). The implementation has been used to study the network underlying the initiation of sporulation in *B. subtilis*. GNA is able to reproduce the observed qualitative behavior of wild-type and mutant bacteria from a model that is a synthesis of available data in the literature. Because sporulation in *B. subtilis* is one of the best-studied prokaryotic model systems, it is an excellent case study for the validation of the simulation tool. However, the real interest of tools like GNA comes from the simulation of genetic regulatory networks that are less understood and the use of the predictions thus obtained for guiding further experimental work. We are currently applying GNA in the context of studies of the global regulation of transcription in *E. coli* and *Synechocystis*.

Acknowledgments. The authors would like to thank Grégory Batt for contributions to this paper.

References

1. R. Alur, C. Belta, F. Ivančíc, V. Kumar, M. Mintz, G.J. Pappas, H. Rubin, and J. Schlug. Hybrid modeling and simulation of biomolecular networks. In M.D. Di Benedetto and A. Sangiovanni-Vincentelli, editors, *Hybrid Systems: Computation and Control (HSCC 2001)*, volume 2034 of *LNCS*, pages 19–32. Springer-Verlag, 2001.

2. C. Belta, L.C.G.J.M. Habets, and V. Kumar. Control of multi-affine systems on rectangles with an application to gene transcription control. In *Proc. IEEE 2002 Conf. Decision and Control, CDC 2002*, Las Vegas, NV, 2002.

3. W.F. Burkholder and A.D. Grossman. Regulation of the initiation of endospore formation in *Bacillus subtilis*. In Y.V. Brun and L.J. Shimkets, editors, *Prokaryotic Development*, chapter 7, pages 151–166. ASM, 2000.

4. H. de Jong. Modeling and simulation of genetic regulatory systems: A literature review. *J. Comput. Biol.*, 9(1):69–105, 2002.

5. H. de Jong, J. Geiselmann, G. Batt, C. Hernandez, and M. Page. Qualitative simulation of the initiation of sporulation in *B. subtilis*. Technical Report RR-4527, INRIA, 2002.

6. H. de Jong, J. Geiselmann, C. Hernandez, and M. Page. Genetic Network Analyzer: Qualitative simulation of genetic regulatory networks. *Bioinformatics*, 2003. In press.

7. H. de Jong, J.-L. Gouzé, C. Hernandez, M. Page, T. Sari, and H. Geiselmann. Dealing with discontinuities in the qualitative simulation of genetic regulatory networks. In F. van Harmelen, editor, *Proc. Fifteenth Europ. Conf. Artif. Intell., ECAI 2002*, pages 412–416. IOS Press, 2002.

8. H. de Jong, J.-L. Gouzé, C. Hernandez, M. Page, T. Sari, and H. Geiselmann. Qualitative simulation of genetic regulatory networks using piecewise-linear models. Technical Report RR-4407, INRIA, 2002.

9. H. de Jong, M. Page, C. Hernandez, and J. Geiselmann. Qualitative simulation of genetic regulatory networks: Method and application. In B. Nebel, editor, *Proc. Seventeenth Int. Joint Conf. Artif. Intell., IJCAI-01*, pages 67–73. Morgan Kaufmann, 2001.

10. R. Edwards, H.T. Siegelmann, K. Aziza, and L. Glass. Symbolic dynamics and computation in model gene networks. *Chaos*, 11(1):160–169, 2001.

11. P. Fawcett, P. Eichenberger, R. Losick, and P. Youngman. The trancriptional profile of early to middle sporulation in *Bacillus subtilis*. *Proc. Natl. Acad. Sci. USA*, 97(14):8063–8068, 2000.

12. A.F. Filippov. *Differential Equations with Discontinuous Righthand Sides*. Kluwer Academic Publishers, 1988.

13. R. Ghosh and C.J. Tomlin. Lateral inhibition through Delta-Notch signaling: A piecewise affine hybrid model. In M.D. Di Benedetto and A. Sangiovanni-Vincentelli, editors, *Hybrid Systems: Computation and Control (HSCC 2001)*, volume 2034 of *LNCS*, pages 232–246. Springer-Verlag, Berlin, 2001.

14. L. Glass and S.A. Kauffman. The logical analysis of continuous non-linear biochemical control networks. *J. Theor. Biol.*, 39:103–129, 1973.

15. J.-L. Gouzé and T. Sari. A class of piecewise linear differential equations arising in biological models. *Dynam. Syst.*, 2003. To appear.

16. A.D. Grossman. Genetic networks controlling the initiation of sporulation and the development of genetic competence in *Bacillus subtilis*. *Ann. Rev. Genet.*, 29:477–508, 1995.

17. J. Hasty, D. McMillen, F. Isaacs, and J.J. Collins. Computational studies of gene regulatory networks: *in numero* molecular biology. *Nat. Rev. Genet.*, 2(4):268–279, 2001.
18. R. Heinrich and S. Schuster. *The Regulation of Cellular Systems*. Chapman & Hall, New York, 1996.
19. J.A. Hoch. Regulation of the phosphorelay and the initiation of sporulation in *Bacillus subtilis*. *Ann. Rev. Microbiol.*, 47:441–465, 1993.
20. B. Kuipers. *Qualitative Reasoning: Modeling and Simulation with Incomplete Knowledge*. MIT Press, 1994.
21. H.H. McAdams and A. Arkin. Simulation of prokaryotic genetic circuits. *Ann. Rev. Biophys. Biomol. Struct.*, 27:199–224, 1998.
22. T. Mestl, E. Plahte, and S.W. Omholt. A mathematical framework for describing and analysing gene regulatory networks. *J. Theor. Biol.*, 176:291–300, 1995.
23. P.J. Mosterman and G. Biswas. A comprehensive methodology for building hybrid models of physical systems. *Artif. Intell.*, 121:171–209, 2000.
24. P.J. Mosterman, F. Zhao, and G. Biswas. Sliding mode model semantics and simulation for hybrid systems. In P.J. Antsaklis, W. Kohn, M. Lemmon, A. Nerode, and S. Sastry, editors, *Hybrid Systems V*, pages 19–32. Springer-Verlag, Berlin, 1999.
25. P. Smolen, D.A. Baxter, and J.H. Byrne. Modeling transcriptional control in gene networks: Methods, recent results, and future directions. *Bull. Math. Biol.*, 62:247–292, 2000.
26. E.H. Snoussi. Qualitative dynamics of piecewise-linear differential equations: A discrete mapping approach. *Dyn. Stabil. Syst.*, 4(3-4):189–207, 1989.
27. P. Stragier and R. Losick. Molecular genetics of sporulation in *Bacillus subtilis*. *Ann. Rev. Genet.*, 30:297–341, 1996.
28. R. Thomas, D. Thieffry, and M. Kaufman. Dynamical behaviour of biological regulatory networks: I. Biological role of feedback loops and practical use of the concept of the loop-characteristic state. *Bull. Math. Biol.*, 57(2):247–276, 1995.
29. E.O. Voit. *Computational Analysis of Biochemical Systems: A Practical Guide for Biochemists and Molecular Biologists*. Cambridge University Press, Cambridge, 2000.

On Systematic Simulation of Open Continuous Systems

Jim Kapinski[1], Bruce H. Krogh[1], Oded Maler[2], and Olaf Stursberg[3]

[1] Dept. of Electrical and Computer Engineering
Carnegie Mellon University, 5000 Forbes Avenue
Pittsburgh, PA 15213-3890 USA
krogh@ece.cmu.edu jpk3@andrew.cmu.edu
[2] VERIMAG
Centre Equation, 2, av. de Vignate
38610 Gières, France
Oded.Maler@imag.fr
[3] Process Control Lab (CT-AST)
University of Dortmund
44221 Dortmund, Germany
olaf.stursberg@uni-dortmund.de

Abstract. In this paper we investigate a new technique to determine whether an open continuous system behaves correctly for all admissible input signals. This technique is based on a discretization of the set of possible input signals, and on storing neighborhoods of points reachable by trajectories induced by those signals. Alternatively, this technique, inspired by automata theory, can be seen as an attempt to make simulation a more systematic activity by finding a small set of input signals such that the behaviors they induce "cover" the whole reachable state space.

1 Introduction

Practitioners in control and in other domains use numerical simulations in order to convince themselves that their systems behave correctly. It is a trivial observation that the level of confidence for analysis results from simulations of continuous dynamic systems is much lower than what can be obtained for discrete finite-state systems [M98,M01]. Consider first a closed continuous system over $\mathbb{R}^n$ defined by a differential equation $\dot{\mathbf{x}} = f(\mathbf{x})$ and the following question: does the trajectory ξ of that system starting from a point $\mathbf{x}_0$ ever reach a set P? Even if the differential equation admits a closed form solution, this solution is not of much help for answering the reachability problem. For example, in linear systems the problem

$$\exists t \; e^{At}\mathbf{x}_0 \in P$$

is not known to be solvable except for some very special cases [PLY99].

Numerical simulation is based on selecting a discrete set of time points $\bar{T} \subset \mathbb{R}_+$, a discrete but very large subset of the state space $\bar{X} \subset X$ (the floating

O. Maler and A. Pnueli (Eds.): HSCC 2003, LNCS 2623, pp. 283–297, 2003.

point numbers), and on successive generation, via numerical integration, of a discretized approximation of ξ of the form $\xi' : \bar{T} \to \bar{X}$ such that for every $t \in \bar{T}$ there is some bound on the distance between $\xi[t]$ and $\xi'[t]$. The user looks at the image of ξ' (with sufficiently fine discretization and graphical resolution it looks continuous to the human eye) and draws conclusions about ξ. The fact that the time domain of ξ' is restricted to $\bar{T}$ (and, even there, its value only approximates ξ) can be overcome by replacing the condition $\xi'[t] \in P$ with a weaker condition on the distance between ξ' and P, or equivalently by over-approximating P by P' to compensate for the approximation error (see Figure 1). This way one can guarantee that if $\xi[t] \in P$ for some $t \in [0,r]$ then there is some $t' \in \bar{T} \cap [0,r]$ such that $\xi'[t'] \in P'$.

The more challenging problem is when the simulated trajectory *does not* reach P and the question is when to stop the simulation. In deterministic finite-state systems every trajectory is ultimately-periodic and the simulation can be stopped once $\xi[t] = \xi[t']$ for some $t' < t$. This is rarely the case in numerical simulation of continuous systems, including those that admit limit cycles.[1] Nevertheless, an intelligent user observing the evolution of ξ', and having a strong intuition regarding the behavior of continuous systems, can become convinced in the non-reachability of P by ξ after performing the simulation for a *finite* amount of time. Given the undecidability of most reachability problems for continuous systems this is the best we can hope for, excluding, of course, techniques of a different nature such as those based on Lyapunov functions. So our starting point is:

Postulate 1 (Simulation is Fine) *An intelligent mortal can solve the reachability problem for a well-behaved closed continuous system using a finite amount of numerical simulation.*

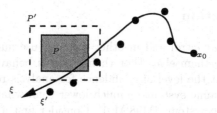

Fig. 1. A continuous behavior ξ and its numerical approximation ξ'.

Consider now *open systems*, that is, systems exposed to input signals, each of which induces a distinct trajectory. When inputs are interpreted as uncontrolled disturbances or parameters, we want to convince ourselves that such a system behaves correctly *for all inputs*. When we interpret input as control, our goal

---

[1] And if such an equality occurs it might be the result of rounding errors.

is to find an input signal that makes the system behave as desired or optimizes some performance index. In both cases we want to lift simulation practice from a single trajectory to many and to this end discretize the space of admissible inputs.

2   The Basic Idea

Let $\mathcal{T} = \mathbb{R}_+$ be the time domain, X be a bounded subset of $\mathbb{R}^n$ (state space) and V be a bounded subset of $\mathbb{R}^m$ (input space). An open dynamical system is a system whose dynamics is defined by

$$\dot{\mathbf{x}} = f(\mathbf{x}, \mathbf{v}).$$

We use $\mathcal{S}(V)$ to denote all V-valued signals, i.e. functions from $\mathcal{T}$ to V, without putting any restrictions on them. Every input signal $\psi \in \mathcal{S}(V)$ and initial state $\mathbf{x} \in X$ induces a behavior $\xi(\mathbf{x}, \psi) : \mathcal{T} \to X$ and we use the notation

$$\mathbf{x} \xrightarrow{\psi, t} \mathbf{x}'$$

to denote the fact that $\xi(\mathbf{x}, \psi)[t] = \mathbf{x}'$, that is, ψ steers the system from $\mathbf{x}$ to $\mathbf{x}'$ at time t. Our goal is to show that for every $\psi \in \mathcal{S}(V)$, the trajectory $\xi(\psi)$ behaves correctly, or, in other words, that the set of states reachable from $\mathbf{x}$,

$$\mathcal{R}(\mathbf{x}) = \{\mathbf{x}' : \exists \psi \in \mathcal{S}(V) \; \exists t \in \mathcal{T} \; \mathbf{x} \xrightarrow{\psi, t} \mathbf{x}'\},$$

does not intersect P.

For each individual input signal the problem can be reduced to a simulation of a closed system. If we could conduct a simulation with each and every such signal, the problem could be solved. However, the set of input signals is very uncountable, consisting of $(2^{\aleph_0})^{2^{\aleph_0}}$ elements, and even if we restrict it to more reasonable sub-classes, such as measurable, piecewise-continuous or even smooth functions from $\mathcal{T}$ to V, its size excludes the possibility of exhaustive simulation.

Our first step is to discretize the set of input signals by discretizing both time and space. To avoid notational complications we assume V to be a hyper-rectangle that fits a uniform discrete grid.[2]

Definition 1 ((δ, ε)-Discretization). *A (δ, ε)-discretization of $\mathcal{S}(V)$ consists of a discrete time domain*

$$\mathcal{T}_\delta = \{n\delta : n \in \mathbb{N}\}$$

and a discrete input space

$$V_\varepsilon = V \cap \{(n_1\varepsilon, \ldots n_m\varepsilon) : (n_1, \ldots n_m) \in \mathbb{Z}^m\}.$$

A discrete input signal is a function $\psi' : \mathcal{T}_\delta \to V_\varepsilon$ which induces naturally a piecewise-constant signal $\bar{\psi} : \mathcal{T} \to V_\varepsilon$ defined for every $r \in \mathbb{R}_+$ as $\bar{\psi}[r \cdot \varepsilon] = \psi'[\lfloor r \rfloor \cdot \varepsilon]$. We denote the set of all such signals by $\mathcal{S}_\delta(V_\varepsilon)$.

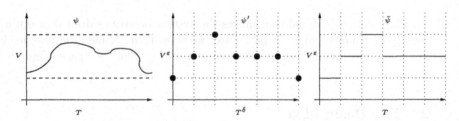

Fig. 2. A signal ψ, its discretization ψ' and the induced piecewise-constant signal $\bar{\psi}$.

The whole situation is illustrated in Figure 2. Since $\mathcal{S}_\delta(V_\varepsilon)$ is a subset of $\mathcal{S}(V)$, the set of states reachable by piecewise-constant signals,

$$\mathcal{R}_{\delta,\varepsilon}(\mathbf{x}) = \{\mathbf{x}' : \exists \psi \in \mathcal{S}_\delta(V_\varepsilon)\ \exists t \in \mathcal{T}\ \mathbf{x} \xrightarrow{\psi,t} \mathbf{x}'\},$$

is a subset of $\mathcal{R}(\mathbf{x})$. However, for most cases of practical interest, we can find for every signal $\psi \in \mathcal{S}(V)$ a (δ, ε)-discretization and a piecewise-constant signal $\bar{\psi} \in \mathcal{S}_\delta(V_\varepsilon)$ as close to ψ as we want (in terms of some appropriate metric), by making δ and ε small enough. For well-behaved systems, this means that for every reachable point in $\mathcal{R}$ we can find a close point in $\mathcal{R}_{\delta,\varepsilon}$. Moreover, we can restrict further the set of reachable states to those that are reached at discrete time points,

$$\bar{\mathcal{R}}_{\delta,\varepsilon}(\mathbf{x}) = \{\mathbf{x}' : \exists \psi \in \mathcal{S}_\delta(V_\varepsilon)\ \exists t \in \mathcal{T}_\delta\ \mathbf{x} \xrightarrow{\psi,t} \mathbf{x}'\},$$

and this set approaches $\mathcal{R}_{\delta,\varepsilon}$ as δ goes to zero. The number of discretized signals of (real-time) length t is $(V/\delta)^{(t/\varepsilon)}$ and one can pose some interesting questions concerning the trade-off between time and space discretization. From now on we consider fixed δ and ε, use $\bar{\mathcal{T}}$ and $\bar{V}$ to denote the discretized domains, and assume:

Postulate 2 (Discretized Signals) *Solving the reachability problem with respect to $\mathcal{S}_\delta(V_\varepsilon)$, that is, computing $\mathcal{R}_{\delta,\varepsilon}$ or even $\bar{\mathcal{R}}_{\delta,\varepsilon}$ instead of $\mathcal{R}$, is interesting.*

The set $\mathcal{S}_\delta(V_\varepsilon)$ is "isomorphic" to one of the most fundamental structures of computer science, namely the set $\bar{V}^*$ of all sequences over a finite alphabet, also known as the free monoid generated by $\bar{V}$. From now on we will use the $\bar{V}^*$ notation for signals, with a sequence like $\mathbf{v}_1\mathbf{v}_2\mathbf{v}_1$ corresponding to a signal of length 3δ whose value is $\mathbf{v}_1$ at $[0, \delta)$, $\mathbf{v}_2$ at $[\delta, 2\delta)$ and $\mathbf{v}_1$ at $[2\delta, 3\delta)$. The juxtaposition of signals corresponds to concatenation of sequences, e.g. $\mathbf{v}_1\mathbf{v}_2\mathbf{v}_1 \cdot \mathbf{v}_1\mathbf{v}_1 = \mathbf{v}_1\mathbf{v}_2\mathbf{v}_1\mathbf{v}_1\mathbf{v}_1$. We denote by $\bar{V}^k$ the set of sequences of length k, with $\bar{V}^0$ being the set consisting of the empty sequence which corresponds to a zero-duration signal, and let $\bar{V}^{\leq k} = \bigcup_{i=1}^{k} \bar{V}^i$. The set $\bar{V}^*$ can be visualized as a tree

---

[2] Grids that are non-uniform inside a dimension or have different scales at each dimension pose no problem for the techniques described in this paper.

rooted in the empty word where every node has $|\bar{V}|$ successors as in Figure 3-(a). The trajectories induced by elements of $\bar{V}^*$ on the state space inherit the same structure as can be seen in Figure 3-(b).

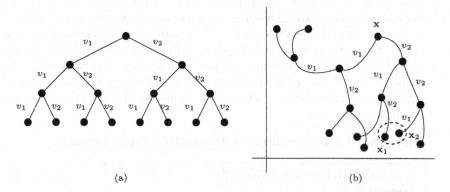

(a)   (b)

Fig. 3. (a) A finite fragment of the $\bar{V}^*$ tree; (b) The trajectories it induces on X starting from point **x**.

Endowing the input space and its induced trajectory space with a tree structure opens new possibilities for state-space exploration techniques inspired from the enormous amount of work on graph searching procedures. The input and state spaces can be explored in breadth-first, depth-first or best-first search regimes, with or without user intervention. Many heuristics developed for test-case generation or for algorithmic debugging can be applied, as well as probabilistic techniques. Moreover, if we interpret V as control rather than disturbances, similar search techniques can be used to synthesize controllers that steer systems into goal states. In the rest of the paper we demonstrate the potential of this approach on the problem of computing reachable states under all disturbance signals. From now on we work in discrete time, i.e. we consider the problem computing $\bar{\mathcal{R}}_{\delta,\varepsilon}$.

3   Simulation-Guided Reachability

In this section we develop a new algorithm for computing an approximation of reachable states of an open system. Unlike "traditional" approaches for solving this problem, e.g. [KV97,V98,ABDM00,CK03], in this approach the exploration of the state space is guided by individual input signals and the trajectories they generate.

A useful algebraic notation that we will employ is to write the "action" of a sequence $\psi \in \bar{V}^*$ on a state **x** as $\mathbf{x} \cdot \psi = \mathbf{x}'$, meaning that the input signal ψ drives the system from **x** to **x'**. This notation can be lifted naturally to sets of states and sets of inputs. The set of points reachable from **x** at time k is $R^k(\mathbf{x}) =$

$\{\mathbf{x} \cdot \psi : \psi \in \bar{V}^k\}$ and those reachable until time k is $R^{\leq k}(\mathbf{x}) = \{\mathbf{x} \cdot \psi : \psi \in \bar{V}^{\leq k}\}$. Clearly, $R^{k+1}(\mathbf{x}) = R^k(\mathbf{x}) \cdot \bar{V}$.

If we are interested only in reachability within a bounded time horizon, we can do with a finite (although exponential) number of simulations. The semigroup property $\mathbf{x} \cdot (\psi \cdot \mathbf{v}) = (\mathbf{x} \cdot \psi) \cdot \mathbf{v}$ allows us to "re-use" partial simulation; that is, instead of running two simulations for $\psi \cdot \mathbf{v}_1$ and $\psi \cdot \mathbf{v}_2$ starting from the initial state, we can simulate with ψ to reach a point $\mathbf{x}'$ and then simulate from $\mathbf{x}'$, once with $\mathbf{v}_1$ and once with $\mathbf{v}_2$. In other words, we can compute $R^{k+1}(\mathbf{x})$ directly from $R^k(\mathbf{x})$ using the following standard breadth-first algorithm, which has the property that at the end of the kth iteration of the main loop the set *Reached* is equal to $R^{\leq k}(\mathbf{x})$ which is exactly the set of points that we will encounter if we run $|\bar{V}|^k$ simulations.

Algorithm 1 (Reachability for Discretized Input Signals)

$Reached{:=}Waiting{:=}\{\mathbf{x}_0\}; New{:=}\emptyset;$
Repeat $k = 0, 1, \ldots$
   For *each* $\mathbf{x} \in Waiting$
     For *each* $\mathbf{v} \in \bar{V}$
       Compute $\mathbf{x}' = \mathbf{x} \cdot \mathbf{v};$
       Insert $\mathbf{x}'$ *into New;*
     Remove $\mathbf{x}$ *from Waiting;*
     $Waiting{:=}New; Reached{:=}Reached \cup New; New{:=}\emptyset;$
Forever

For unbounded time (or just for large k), even Postulate 1 is not going to help us because the number of trajectories to simulate grows indefinitely (and exponentially). We borrow the following observation from automata theory, which is just another instance of the semigroup property: If $\mathbf{x} \cdot \psi_1 = \mathbf{x} \cdot \psi_2$, then for every $\mathbf{v}$ we have $\mathbf{x} \cdot (\psi_1 \cdot \mathbf{v}) = \mathbf{x} \cdot (\psi_2 \cdot \mathbf{v})$ and the simulations with extensions of ψ_2 need not be performed since all of them will be "represented" by extensions of ψ_1. Thus, we could modify the algorithm slightly by not inserting to *New* points that are already in *New* or in *Reached*. For finite automata with n states this usually results in a dramatic decrease of the number of input sequences needed to reach all states from $|\bar{V}|^n$ to $O(n)$.

For continuous systems, however, strict equality is rare and should be replaced by a weaker notion. Looking, for example, at the trajectories of Figure 3-(b) we see that inputs $\mathbf{v}_2\mathbf{v}_1\mathbf{v}_2$ and $\mathbf{v}_2\mathbf{v}_2\mathbf{v}_1$ lead to two neighboring points $\mathbf{x}_1$ and $\mathbf{x}_2$. For certain systems and under certain conditions we can guarantee that for every input ψ, $\mathbf{x}_1 \cdot \psi$ will remain close to $\mathbf{x}_2 \cdot \psi$, and hence the points reachable from $\mathbf{x}_1$ and their neighborhoods can "represent" those reachable from $\mathbf{x}_2$ without the latter being actually computed. This has the potential of slowing down significantly the explosion in the number of explored trajectories.

A naive application of this idea will discard (i.e. not insert into *New*) points that are close to previously-reached points. This will not work, however, as the two following types of counter-examples show. In the simpler one, shown in

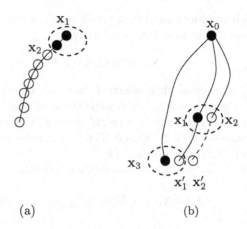

(a)   (b)

Fig. 4. (a) Someone should represent your ancestors; (b) Nearness is not transitive.

Figure 4-(a), we have a slow system such that the successor $\mathbf{x}_2 = \mathbf{x}_1 \cdot \mathbf{v}$ is close to $\mathbf{x}_1$ and the simulation is stopped without any other representative of the trajectory that goes further away from $\mathbf{x}_1$. This problem, which is the same as the problem of deciding when to stop a single simulation, could be easily prevented by not discarding a point just because it is in the neighborhood of its predecessor.

The second counter-example in Figure 4-(b) is more problematic. Suppose that $\mathbf{x}_1$ and $\mathbf{x}_2$ are two close points in $R^k(\mathbf{x}_0)$ for some k and we decide not to explore $\mathbf{x}_2$ further and let it be represented by $\mathbf{x}_1$. At some later time k' a successor $\mathbf{x}_1'$ of $\mathbf{x}_1$ is close to some $\mathbf{x}_3$ and is discarded, but the successor $\mathbf{x}_2'$ of $\mathbf{x}_2$ is not close to $\mathbf{x}_3$ and is not represented by it. In other words, nearness, unlike equality, is not transitive.

To overcome this problem we move from a point-based to a neighborhood-based algorithm, where a neighborhood $N(\mathbf{x})$ is a set consisting of all points close to $\mathbf{x}$ according to some metric (a metric which may change during the system evolution). The problem is then re-formulated as finding $\bar{\mathcal{R}}_{\delta,\varepsilon}(N(\mathbf{x}_0))$, all points reachable from an initial neighborhood. The action of an input $\mathbf{v}$ on a neighborhood $N(\mathbf{x})$, denoted by $N(\mathbf{x}) \cdot \mathbf{v}$ is the result of applying $\mathbf{v}$ to all elements of $N(\mathbf{x})$, yielding a neighborhood $N'(\mathbf{x}')$ of $\mathbf{x}' = \mathbf{x} \cdot \mathbf{v}$. Algorithm 1 when applied to $N(\mathbf{x}_0)$ will produce at each step k a set of neighborhoods whose union is exactly the set of points reachable from $N(\mathbf{x}_0)$ at time k.

Now we can record the fact that a point represents another point by increasing its neighborhood, that is, whenever two close points are "merged" their neighborhoods are merged into a neighborhood that contains both. This way an algorithm for over-approximating $\bar{\mathcal{R}}_{\delta,\varepsilon}(N(\mathbf{x}_0))$ is obtained. We will first describe the exploration technique in abstract terms, without specifying the actual form of neighborhoods and operations. The algorithm needs three operations:

1. *Next* which produces an over-approximation of the action of an input on a neighborhood, that is, a function satisfying

$$Next(N(\mathbf{x}), \mathbf{v}) \supseteq N(\mathbf{x}) \cdot \mathbf{v}.$$

2. *JoinTest*, a function that selects from a set of neighborhoods one which should be merged with a given neighborhood. For example, the result of *JoinTest(Set, N(\mathbf{x}))* may be a neighborhood $N'(\mathbf{x}') \in Set$ which minimizes some distance between $N(\mathbf{x})$ and $N(\mathbf{x}')$. It may return the empty set in case no elements of *Set* is close to $N(\mathbf{x})$.

3. *Join*, merging two neighborhoods into a containing neighborhood, a function satisfying

$$Join(N_1(\mathbf{x}_1), N_2(\mathbf{x}_2)) \supseteq N_1(\mathbf{x}_1) \cup N_2(\mathbf{x}_2).$$

Algorithm 2 (Reachability with Neighborhoods)

```
Reached:=Waiting:={N(x₀)}; New:=∅;
Repeat k = 0, 1, . . .
  For each N(x) ∈ Waiting
    For each v ∈ V̄
      Compute N'(x') = Next(N(x), v);
      N̂(x̂) := JoinTest (Reached∪New, N'(x'));
      If N̂(x̂) ≠ ∅ Then
        If N'(x') ⊄ N̂(x̂) Then
          Remove N̂(x̂) from New and from Reached
          If N̂(x̂) ⊆ N'(x') Then
            Insert N'(x') into New
          Else
            Compute N*(x*) = Join(N'(x'), N̂(x̂));
            Insert N*(x*) into New
      Else
        Insert N'(x') into New;
  Remove N(x) from Waiting;
  Waiting:=New; Reached:=Reached∪New; New:=∅;
Forever
```

The *JoinTest* function for merging neighborhoods can be subject to heuristic considerations related to the trade-off between accuracy (the degree of over-approximation) and complexity (the number of points).

Claim 1 (Coverage) *For every* k

$$R^{\leq k}(N(\mathbf{x}_0)) \subseteq \bigcup_{N(\mathbf{x}) \in Reached} N(\mathbf{x})$$

holds at the end of the kth *iteration of the main loop of Algorithm 2.*

4   Linear Systems in Discrete Time

In this section we describe a concrete version of the algorithm for linear time-invariant (LTI) systems in discrete time, i.e., systems with state equations of the form

$$\mathbf{x}_{k+1} = \varPhi \mathbf{x}_k + \varGamma \mathbf{v}_k,$$

with $\varPhi$ nonsingular.[3] As neighborhoods we use ellipsoids, each parameterized by a positive definite symmetric matrix $Q \in \mathbb{R}^{n \times n}$, i.e.

$$N_Q(\mathbf{x}) = \{\hat{\mathbf{x}} : \|\hat{\mathbf{x}} - \mathbf{x}\|_{Q^{-1}} \leq 1\},$$

where $\|\mathbf{x}\|_Q$ is defined as $\mathbf{x}^T Q \mathbf{x}$. The action of an input $\mathbf{v}$ on a neighborhood is defined as

$$Next(N_Q(\mathbf{x}), \mathbf{v}) = N_{Q'}(\mathbf{x}')$$

with $\mathbf{x}' = \mathbf{x} \cdot \mathbf{v}$ and

$$Q' = \varPhi Q \varPhi^T.$$

The join operation for merging of two ellipsoidal neighborhoods is defined as

$$Join(N_{Q_1}(\mathbf{x}_1), N_{Q_2}(\mathbf{x}_2)) = N_{\tilde{Q}}(\tilde{\mathbf{x}}),$$

where $N_{\tilde{Q}}(\tilde{\mathbf{x}})$ is the minimum volume ellipsoid containing $N_{Q_1}(\mathbf{x}_1)$ and $N_{Q_2}(\mathbf{x}_2)$. Efficient LMI-based numerical routines exist for computing $\tilde{Q}$ and $\tilde{\mathbf{x}}$ [BGFB94]. The function $JoinTest(Set, N(\mathbf{x}))$ returns the ellipsoid in Set whose center minimizes the distance to $\mathbf{x}$, provided that this distance is smaller than a given threshold (a tunable parameter of the algorithm).

It is not hard to see that this concrete version of Algorithm 2 satisfies Claim 1 and computes an over-approximation of the reachable set. It is important to distinguish this technique from other reachability algorithms, for example [CK99, BM99,ABDM00] including those that use ellipsoids for representing reachable sets [KV97,V98,BT00]. Typically such algorithms are inherently "breadth-first" where at every step k there is one object (a polyhedron or an ellipsoid) that represents all reachable points for all inputs at time k. This set is computed by running an optimization over the input domain V to find the input that takes the system mostly "outwards". Our approach is more enumerative in nature and may use several ellipsoids at each time step. Our technique can be tuned by modifying the neighborhood size, the $JoinTest$ definition, and the $Next$ and $Join$ operations. Working with small neighborhoods makes the algorithm closer to exhaustive simulation while larger neighborhoods make it closer to "standard" reachability algorithms. Like those algorithms, ours can be easily adapted to hybrid automata by intersecting the reachable sets with transition guards.

---

[3] We note that the matrix $\varPhi$ is always nonsingular when the discrete-time system is obtained by sampling a continuous LTI dynamic system.

5   Experimental Results

We have implemented the algorithm in MATLAB and we illustrate its behavior
with the following two examples.

5.1   Servo System Example

For the servo system shown in figure 5 we want to show that for all reference
inputs, the distance between the actual value and the reference remains within
a given bound. The system has first-order plant dynamics and a first-order reference signal filter. In the figure, x_1 is the plant output, v is the reference input,
x_2 is the output of the reference signal filter, and $d = x_2 - x_1$ is the error. The
continuous time dynamic equations are given by $\dot{\mathbf{x}} = A\mathbf{x} + Bv$ with

$$A = \begin{bmatrix} -g & g \\ 0 & -\frac{1}{\tau} \end{bmatrix} \qquad B = \begin{bmatrix} 0 \\ \frac{1}{\tau} \end{bmatrix}$$

For piecewise constant inputs with a sampling period of δ, the sampled system
dynamics are

$$\mathbf{x}_{k+1} = \Phi\mathbf{x}_k + \Gamma v_k$$

$$\Phi = e^{A\delta} \qquad \Gamma = A^{-1}(e^{A\delta} - I)B$$

For $g = 10$, $\tau = 0.1$, and $\delta = 0.1$ this yields

$$\Phi = \begin{bmatrix} 0.368 & 0.368 \\ 0.000 & 0.368 \end{bmatrix} \qquad \Gamma = \begin{bmatrix} 0.264 \\ 0.632 \end{bmatrix}$$

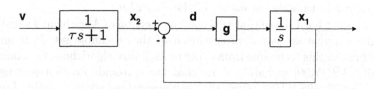

Fig. 5. A simple servo system.

We wish to verify that the system does not reach the set

$$P = \{\mathbf{x} : |x_1 - x_2| > 1\}$$

for all sequences in $\bar{V}^*$, $\bar{V} = \{0.0, 0.5, 1.0\}$. Figure 6-(a) shows one sample 8-
step trajectory of the system and Figure 6-(b) shows the states reached along
the trajectories generated by all elements of $\bar{V}^8$ starting from $\mathbf{x}_0 = [0\ 0]^T$. The
boundaries of P are the diagonal lines in the figure. The number of simulation
points is $\sum_{k=0}^{8} 3^k = 9841$. Figure 6-(c), generated by exhaustive simulation (i.e.,
iterative application of the $Next$ operator), shows the set of states reachable from

all points within $N_{10I}(\mathbf{x}_0)$ (a circle with radius $\sqrt{0.1}$ centered at the origin). Figure 6-(d) shows the result of applying 8 iterations of Algorithm 2 to the example, starting with the same initial set. Only 273 *Next* operations were required and upon completion of the procedure, *Reach* contained only the 21 ellipsoids shown in the figure.

Figure 7 shows a comparison of the computation time for exhaustive simulation versus our algorithm for the servo system. Note that that the computation time of our algorithm grows only linearly with the number of time increments in contrast to the exponential inherent in exhaustive simulation. For small numbers of steps ($k < 8$) exhaustive simulation requires less computation time due to the LMI optimizations in the *Join* operation of our algorithm. We are currently investigating other examples of stable systems hoping to reproduce the phenomenon of sub-exponential growth in the number of computed points.

5.2   A Marginally Stable System

We next consider a four-dimensional system with a four-dimensional input space derived from the continuous-time system $\dot{\mathbf{x}} = A\mathbf{x} + \mathbf{v}$ with

$$
A = \begin{bmatrix} 0 & 1 & 0 & 0 \\ -8 & 0 & 0 & 0 \\ 0 & 0 & 0 & 1 \\ 0 & 0 & -4 & 0 \end{bmatrix}
$$

and

$$
\mathbf{v} \in V = [-1,1] \times [-0.1, 0.1] \times [-1,1] \times [-0.1, 0.1].
$$

This example appeared first in [KV97], p. 279, where it was subject to an ellipsoid-based reachability algorithm and was treated later in [D00], p. 83, using polyhedra. The system is marginally stable, but the inputs can make it diverge.

As a discretized input space for the continuous-time model we use the vertices, i.e.

$$
V' = \{-1,1\} \times \{-0.1, 0.1\} \times \{-1,1\} \times \{-0.1, 0.1\}.
$$

Time-discretization with $\delta = 0.2$ yields

$$
\mathbf{x}_{k+1} = \varPhi \mathbf{x}_k + \mathbf{v}_k,
$$

where $\varPhi = e^{0.2A}$, and $\mathbf{v}_k \in \bar{V}$, where

$$
\bar{V} = \{(\varPhi - I)\mathbf{v} : \mathbf{v} \in V'\}
$$

Figure 8 shows the over approximation of the set of reachable states (projected onto third and fourth dimensions) generated with Algorithm 2, computed for 3 time steps, starting with the top left plot showing the initial ellipsoid, which is a hyper-sphere of radius 0.01. Note that the ellipsoids that appear to be subsets of other ellipsoids are not subsets in the full four-dimensional space.

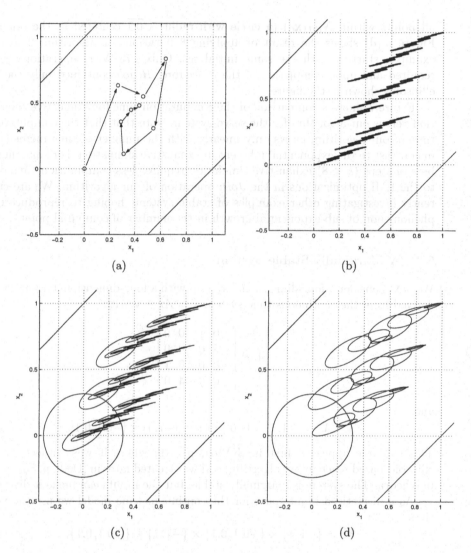

Fig. 6. (a) A sample trajectory of the system under the input $\psi = 1.0 \cdot 0.5 \cdot 1.0 \cdot 0.0 \cdot 0.0 \cdot 0.5 \cdot 0.5 \cdot 0.5$; (b) The states reachable from $(0,0)$ for all 8-step trajectories generated by exhaustive simulation; (c) states reachable from a circle around $(0,0)$ for all these trajectories as computed by exhaustive simulation; (d) The over-approximation of the reachable states as computed by our algorithm.

For each time increment, the set of reachable states grows due to the fact that the system is marginally stable.

Figure 9 shows a comparison of the computation times between exhaustive simulation and systematic simulation. For this system, the time required by systematic simulation is exponential in the number of time increments. For the

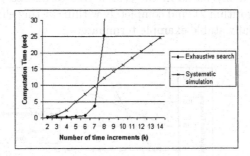

Fig. 7. Computation times for exhaustive simulation and our algorithm for the servo example

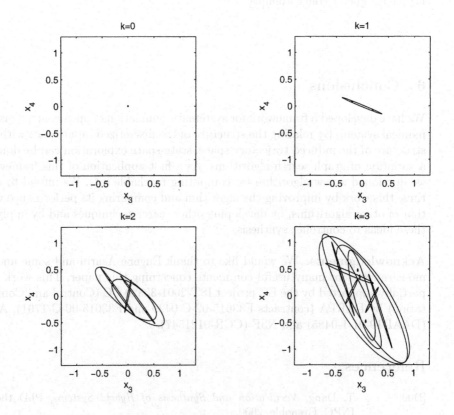

Fig. 8. Reachable set for the marginally stable example from 0 to 3 time increments, projected on the first two variables.

servo system many paths in the search tree terminate because new ellipsoids ($N'(x')$ in Algorithm 2) land completely within existing ellipsoids; only few paths in the marginally stable example terminate.

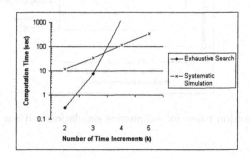

Fig. 9. Computation times for exhaustive simulation method and systematic simulation for the marginally stable example

6   Conclusions

We have developed a framework for systematic simulation of open continuous dynamical system. By relating the structure of the discretized input space with the structure of the induced trajectory space, state-space exploration can be done as a variation of graph search algorithms. As a first application of this framework we developed a new algorithm for computing reachable sets. We intend to continue this work by improving the algorithm and comparing its performance with that of other algorithms, by developing other search techniques and by applying these ideas to controller synthesis.

Acknowledgments. We would like to thank Eugene Asarin and some anonymous referees for many useful comments concerning this paper. This work was partially supported by the EC project IST-2001-33520 CC (Control and Computation) by DARPA (contracts F33615-02-C-0429 and F33615-00-C-1701), ARO (DAAD19-01-1-0485) and NSF (CCR-0121547).

References

[D00]   T. Dang, *Verification and Synthesis of Hybrid Systems*, PhD thesis, INPG, Grenoble, 2000.

[ABDM00]   E. Asarin, O. Bournez, T. Dang and O. Maler, Reachability Analysis of Piecewise-Linear Dynamical Systems, in B. Krogh and N. Lynch (Eds.), *Hybrid Systems: Computation and Control*, 20–31, LNCS 1790, Springer, 2000.

[BM99]   A. Bemporad and M. Morari, Verification of Hybrid Systems via Math-
            ematical Programming, in F.W. Vaandrager and J.H. van Schuppen
            (Eds.), *Hybrid Systems: Computation and Control*, 31–45, LNCS 1569,
            Springer, 1999.

[BT00]   O. Botchkarev and S. Tripakis, Verification of Hybrid Systems with Lin-
            ear Differential Inclusions Using Ellipsoidal Approximations, in B. Krogh
            and N. Lynch (Eds.), *Hybrid Systems: Computation and Control*, 73–88,
            LNCS 1790, Springer, 2000.

[BGFB94]   S. Boyd, L. El Ghaoui, E. Feron, and V. Balakrishnan, *Linear Matrix
            Inequalities in System and Control Theory*, SIAM, 1994.

[CK99]   A. Chutinan and B.H. Krogh, Verification of Polyhedral Invariant Hybrid
            Automata Using Polygonal Flow Pipe Approximations, in F.W. Vaan-
            drager and J.H. van Schuppen (Eds.), *Hybrid Systems: Computation and
            Control*, 76–90, LNCS 1569, Springer, 1999.

[CK03]   A. Chutinan and B.H. Krogh, Computational Techniques for Hybrid Sys-
            tem Verification, *IEEE Transactions On Automatic Control*, 2003.

[KV97]   A. Kurzhanski and I. Valyi, *Ellipsoidal Calculus for Estimation and Con-
            trol*, Birkhauser, 1997.

[M98]   O. Maler, A Unified Approach for Studying Discrete and Continuous
            Dynamical Systems, *Proc. CDC'98*, IEEE, 1998.

[M01]   O. Maler, Control from Computer Science, *IFAC Symposium Nonlinear
            Control (NOLCOS'01)*, Elsevier, 2001.

[PLY99]   G. Pappas, G. Lafferriere and S. Yovine, A New Class of Decidable Hy-
            brid Systems, in F.W. Vaandrager and J.H. van Schuppen (Eds.), *Hybrid
            Systems: Computation and Control*, LNCS 1569, 29–31, Springer, 1999.

[V98]   P. Varaiya, Reach Set Computation using Optimal Control, *Proc. KIT
            Workshop*, Verimag, Grenoble, 1998.

Estimation of Distributed Hybrid Systems Using Particle Filtering Methods

Xenofon Koutsoukos[1], James Kurien[2], and Feng Zhao[2]

[1] Department of Electrical Engineering and Computer Science
Vanderbilt University
Nashville, TN 37235, USA
Xenofon.Koutsoukos@vanderbilt.edu
[2] Palo Alto Research Center
3333 Coyote Hill Rd
Palo Alto, CA 94304, USA
{jkurien,zhao}@parc.com

Abstract. Networked embedded systems are composed of a large number of components that interact with the physical world via a set of sensors and actuators, have their own computational capabilities, and communicate with each other via a wired or wireless network. Such systems are best modeled by distributed hybrid systems that capture the interaction between the physical and computational components. Monitoring and diagnosis of any dynamical system depend crucially on the ability to estimate the system state given the observations. Estimation for distributed hybrid systems is particularly challenging because it requires keeping track of multiple models and the transitions between them. This paper presents a particle filtering based estimation algorithm for a class of distributed hybrid systems. The hybrid estimation methodology is demonstrated on a cryogenic propulsion system.

1 Introduction

The work in this paper is motivated by existing and emerging applications of networked, embedded systems. Such systems contain a large number of distributed nodes, each of which performs a moderate amount of computation, collaborates with other nodes via a wired or wireless network, and is embedded in the physical world via a set of sensors and actuators. Examples include complex electro-mechanical systems with embedded controllers [13] and smart matter systems [6]. State estimation from the available measurements in such systems presents a number of interesting new challenges. The system dynamics are best described by hybrid models of computation and hybrid estimation techniques are required. The complexity that arises from the distribution of both the physical and computing components must be also addressed. A large amount of computation is potentially available, but it may be partitioned into relatively small, embedded chunks. Communication between nodes is available, but may involve unreliable delivery, power-constrained wireless networks, or large, complex topologies requiring multiple hops to connect two arbitrary nodes.

O. Maler and A. Pnueli (Eds.): HSCC 2003, LNCS 2623, pp. 298–313, 2003.

Estimation of hybrid systems is particularly challenging because keeping track of multiple models and the autonomous transitions between them is computationally very expensive. Simple extension of conventional estimation techniques, like the Kalman filter, leads to algorithms that require tracking of all possible trajectories, and therefore, are exponential in the number of time steps. Approximation by Gaussians is often used to collapse the distributions for each trajectory resulting in poor performance. A related approach to our work based on banks of extended Kalman filters has been presented in [4] where only trajectories with high confidence probability are traced. A methodology using both discrete and continuous observers based on finite state machines and linear systems has been proposed in [1]. Sequential Monte Carlo (or particle filtering) methods can support process densities that contain both continuous and discrete dynamics and have been explored for hybrid diagnosis in [11]. However, autonomous transitions between modes triggered by the continuous dynamics have not been considered. Particle filtering has been applied also for a class of hybrid systems modeled by dynamic Bayesian networks in [7] where the autonomous transitions between discrete states are defined using the so-called softmax conditional probability distributions. A fault modeling and diagnosis approach for hybrid systems based on qualitative representation of the fault hypotheses has been presented in [8]. A Bayesian approach for mode estimation of hybrid systems has been presented in [13] and has been demonstrated for monitoring and diagnosis of electro-mechanical systems. This approach uses continuous measurements and prior from a temporal discrete event model to compute the likelihood functions for the mode transitions.

In this paper, we present a particle filter based estimation algorithm that addresses the challenge of the double-sided interaction between continuous and discrete dynamics in hybrid systems. The algorithm is applicable to a large class of hybrid systems, where the continuous dynamics and the guard conditions can be nonlinear, and the noise can be represented by arbitrary multi-modal distributions. We show how we can estimate autonomous transitions based on complex guard conditions. We also describe how we can improve the performance and robustness of the algorithm by using guard conditions that cover the state space of the system. In particle filters, complex integrals are computed efficiently by approximating the belief state by finitely many samples. General process densities that can represent the interaction between discrete and continuous dynamics in hybrid systems can be used in an efficient manner. Detailed descriptions of particle filtering methods for estimation of dynamical systems can be found in [3]. Our approach is similar to algorithms with mixed-state and automatic model switching that have been successfully applied for tracking of motion boundaries in video images [5,2]. The centralized estimation algorithm and its application to a two-tank system can be found in [9]. In this paper, we demonstrate the algorithm for the estimation and fault detection of the rocket propulsion example of an experimental NASA vehicle (X34) using simulation results. The hybrid estimation approach presented in this paper is part of a distributed, hybrid diagnostic system that has been developed for the cryogenic propulsion system; details can be found in [10].

The remainder of the paper is organized as follows. The class of distributed models and hybrid estimation problems considered in this paper are presented in Section 2. Section 3 presents the cryogenic propulsion system used to illustrate the approach. Our approach for distributed hybrid system estimation is described in Section 4. The particle filtering algorithm is presented in Section 5. Simulation results for the cryogenic propulsion system are presented in Section 6. Finally, conclusions and future work are discussed in Section 7.

2   Problem Statement

Hybrid systems contain interacting discrete and continuous dynamics. The discrete dynamics are usually described by discrete event models with a finite state space Q. Every discrete state (or mode) q corresponds to a unique differential (difference) equation $\dot{x} = f(q, x)$ that governs the continuous dynamics. The state of the hybrid system is described by $s = (q, x)$. The state can change either by time delay as described by the differential/difference equation or by a transition. Mode transitions $e = (q_1, q_2)$ may occur either upon receiving an external control command or when the continuous state satisfies a guard $x \in G(e)$ that labels the transition. The state may be reset after the occurrence of such a transition according to the reset map $x' = R(e, x)$. Mode transitions that depend on the continuous behavior of the system are called autonomous.

In the hybrid system literature, it is often assumed that the state is directly observable. However, in real-world applications, the state has to be reconstructed from the observations. In this paper, we follow a Bayesian state estimation approach using a discrete-time representation of the system dynamics. The continuous dynamics of the system can be described, using zero-order hold sampling for example, by the discrete-time model

$$x_{t+1} = f_q(x_t, u_t) + \nu_t$$
$$y_t = g_q(x_t) + \xi_t$$

and ν_t and ξ_t denote process and measurement noise respectively. The evolution of the discrete state can be described by the transition function

$$q_{t+1} = \delta(q_t, \sigma_t, x_t)$$

where σ_t denotes events corresponding to the control commands. A discrete transition occurs when either the controller issues an appropriate command or when the continuous state satisfies the guard of the transition. The hybrid estimation problem is to compute the most likely hybrid state $s_t = (q_t, x_t)$ given the observation sequence $Y_t = (y_0, y_1, \ldots, y_t)$, the sequence of continuous control inputs $U_t = (u_0, u_1, \ldots, u_t)$, and the history of control events $(\sigma_1, \sigma_2, \ldots)$ up to time t.

A distributed embedded system consists of multiple components that can be described by interacting hybrid systems. In this paper, we consider a class of distributed hybrid systems where the coupling occurs only through the guards that govern the mode transitions. We model such systems by a collection of subsystems $\{H_n\}, n = 1, \ldots, N$. The state of the nth subsystem is $s^{(n)} = (q^{(n)}, x^{(n)})$. We assume that if there exists coupling between H_n and H_m, it can be described by a guard condition of the form $G(e^{(n)}, x^{(m)})$. Thus, a mode transition $e^{(n)}$ in H_n can be triggered by a condition on the state $x^{(m)}$ of H_m. A cryogenic propulsion system that is modeled by such a distributed hybrid system is presented in Section 3.

In distributed hybrid systems, the state s_t is the aggregate state of all the subsystems $\{s_t^{(1)}, s_t^{(2)}, \ldots, s_t^{(N)}\}$. Centralized estimation algorithms are computationally very expensive because they are based on high-dimensional models. They also require high-bandwidth networks since all the remote measurements must be communicated to a centralized location at every time step. Distributed estimation algorithms offer significant computational advantages, especially, because they can exploit the computation that is embedded in several components of the system. The local hybrid estimation problem at subsystem H_n is to compute the most likely state $s_t^{(n)} = (q_t^{(n)}, x_t^{(n)})$ using local or remote observations and control inputs. For the class of systems considered in this paper, estimating the local state $s_t^{(n)} = (q_t^{(n)}, x_t^{(n)})$ only requires knowledge of remote guard conditions $G(e^{(n)}, x^{(m)})$ that affect the local behavior.

3   The Propulsion System Domain

Space launch vehicles that reach Earth orbit do so by carrying large quantities of oxygen which is combined with a fuel and burned to produce thrust. The oxygen is stored in the form of liquid oxygen (LOX) at a temperature several hundred degrees below that of the launch environment. Figure 1 illustrates the LOX venting system for the X-34, an experimental, rocket-powered vehicle designed for NASA. During flight, the tank absorbs heat and the LOX temperature and pressure are increasing. A digital controller is responsible for keeping the LOX pressure in a safe region. When the pneumatic valve is open, the LOX tank can vent to the atmosphere. The vehicle's control system does not directly actuate the pneumatic valve. Instead, the pneumatic valve opens when it is pressurized by the pneumatic system to its left. The pneumatic tank and regulators provide high pressure gas to the solenoid valve. When the control system opens the solenoid valve, the pneumatic valve is pressurized and opens.

The cryogenic propulsion system can be best modeled as a distributed hybrid system consisting of the LOX tank subsystem and the pneumatic subsystem. The dynamics of the LOX tank follow a multi-modal behavior that represents if LOX is boiling to gas oxygen (GOX) or not and if GOX is venting in the atmosphere or not. The continuous dynamics are governed by mass and energy conservation laws. The discrete dynamics include the behavior of the solenoid valve which is controlled by a digital controller that monitors the output pressure of the LOX tank. In the following, we present a dynamical model of the system. The notation including units and constants can be found in Table 1.

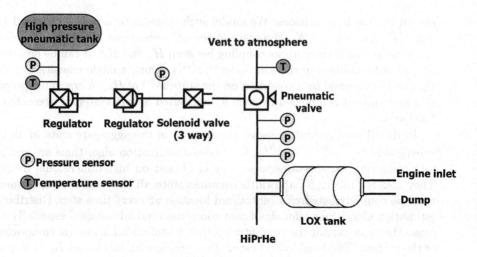

Fig. 1. LOX Tank System

The dynamics of the LOX tank are described by the following set of nonlinear differential equations:

$$\dot{m}_{lox} = -B$$
$$\dot{m}_{gox} = B - r_{vent}$$
$$\dot{T}_{lox} = \frac{q_{lox} - h_v B}{c_p m_{lox}}$$
$$\dot{u}_{gox} = \frac{1}{m_{gox}}(Bh_{gox_{in}} - r_{vent}h_{gox_{out}} + q_{gox} + Bu_{gox})$$

Liquid oxygen is boiling if its saturation pressure is larger than the pressure of the GOX inside the tank according to

$$B = \begin{cases} 0, & \text{if } P_{gox} > P_{sat} \\ r_{vent} + \frac{r_{vent}}{2}(P_{sat} - P_{gox}) - 0.001, & \text{if } P_{sat} \geq P_{gox} \end{cases}$$

where the saturation pressure is a function of the LOX temperature approximated by

$$P_{sat}(T_{lox}) = 272.968 - 9.83445T_{lox} + 0.139169T_{lox}^2 - 9.4813 \times 10^{-4}T_{lox}^3$$
$$+2.9745 \times 10^{-6}T_{lox}^4 - 3.00628 \times 10^{-9}T_{lox}^5$$

and the GOX pressure is given using the ideal gas law

$$P_{gox} = \frac{m_{gox}}{w_{gox}}R\frac{T_{gox}}{V_{gox}}.$$

Table 1. Nomenclature

PARAMETER	DESCRIPTION	VALUE (for constants)	UNITS
m_{lox}	mass of LOX		lbm
m_{gox}	mass of GOX		lbm
T_{lox}	temperature of LOX		deg R
T_{lox}	temperature of LOX		deg R
u_{gox}	internal energy of GOX		BTU/lbm
B	boil rate		lbm/s
r_{vent}	venting mass rate		lbm/s
q_{gox}	heat dissipation of GOX		BTU/s
q_{lox}	heat dissipation of LOX		BTU/s
q_{total}	total heat dissipation		BTU/s
h_v	heat of vaporization of LOX	91.5	BTU/lbm
C_p	specific heat of LOX	0.4	BTU/deg R
$h_{gox_{in}}$	input enthalpy of GOX		BTU/lbm
$h_{gox_{out}}$	output enthalpy of GOX		BTU/lbm
P_{lox}	pressure of LOX		psi
P_{gox}	pressure of GOX		psi
P_{sat}	saturation pressure of LOX		psi
w_{gox}	molecular weight of GOX	0.0705	lbm/mol
V_{lox}	volume of LOX		ft^3
V_{gox}	volume of GOX		ft^3
V_{tank}	volume of LOX tank	16800	ft^3
d_{lox}	density of LOX	71.5	lbm/ft^3
d_{gox}	density of GOX		lbm/ft^3
m_{PVT}	mass of He in PVT		lbm
T_{PVT}	temperature of He in PVT		deg R
P_{PVT}	pressure of PVT		psi
r_{in}	PVT input mass rate		lbm/s
h_{PVT}	input enthalpy of He in PVT		BTU/lbm
V_{PVT}	volume of PVT	0.04	ft^3
d	diameter of the pneumatic valve	0.065	ft
α	loss coefficient	2	
w_{he}	molecular weight of He	0.00882	lbm/mol
R	gas constant	2.365×10^{-2}	$\dfrac{\text{psi ft}^3}{\text{mol mol}}$

The GOX temperature is computed using the internal energy as $T_{gox} = (u_{gox} - 54.503)/0.1606$. The GOX volume is computed by $V_{gox} = V_{tank} - V_{lox}$ where $V_{lox} = m_{lox}/d_{lox}$. The input and output enthalpy are given by

$$h_{gox_{in}} = 0.2184 T_{lox} + 56.906$$
$$h_{gox_{out}} = 0.2184 T_{gox} + 56.906$$

and the GOX and LOX head dissipation are defined by

$$q_{gox} = 1.75 \times 10^{-5} (550 - T_{gox}) q_{total}$$

$$q_{lox} = q_{total} - q_{gox}.$$

The pneumatic subsystem consists of a pneumatic tank with high pressure helium (He), two pressure regulators, a three-way solenoid valve, and a pneumatic valve as shown in Figure 1. When the solenoid valve is open, high pressure He flows from the pneumatic tank and pressurizes the pneumatic valve. We omit the dynamical model of the pneumatic subsystem due to space limitations and we focus on the pneumatic valve that directly affects the behavior of the LOX tank subsystem.

The pneumatic valve includes a tank called pneumatic valve tank (PVT) whose dynamics are

$$\dot{m}_{PVT} = r_{in}$$

$$\dot{T}_{PVT} = \frac{r_{in}h_{PVT}}{13.2 + 3.125m_{PVT}}$$

where $h_{PVT} = 5.2T_{PVT} + 30.2$ is the input enthalpy. The pressure in the PVT is

$$P_{PVT} = \frac{m_{PVT}}{w_{he}}R\frac{T_{PVT}}{V_{PVT}}.$$

The behavior of the pneumatic valve is described using the pressure P_{PVT} as follows:

$$\text{pneumatic valve} = \begin{cases} \text{open,} & \text{if } P_{PVT} < 410 \\ \text{closed,} & \text{if } P_{PVT} \geq 410 \end{cases}$$

The above guard conditions on the pressure P_{PVT} define the coupling between the pneumatic system and the LOX tank. If $P_{PVT} < 410$ then the valve is open and LOX is venting in the atmosphere. The venting mass rate is given by

$$r_{vent} = \frac{\pi d^2 \sqrt{\frac{2(P_{gox}-P_{atm})4636.8}{\alpha d_{gox}}}}{4}d_{gox}.$$

If the valve is closed then there is no venting. We also assume that the flow goes only in one direction through the valve.

The venting of GOX is monitored by pressure and temperature sensors. A digital controller is used to actuate the solenoid valve based on the GOX pressure measurements using the following rule: if the pressure P_{gox} falls below 12.2, the controller closes the solenoid valve and if the pressure exceeds 18, then the controller opens the solenoid valve. The overall system can be modeled as a distributed hybrid system composed of the LOX tank and the pneumatic subsystem coupled by the guards that define the operation of the pneumatic valve and the controller. The hybrid system model for the LOX tank is shown in Figure 2. The hybrid estimation problem is to compute the most likely state including the LOX mass and temperature from the pressure and temperature measurements and the commands of the controller.

4   Hybrid System Estimation

The most challenging aspect of every hybrid estimation algorithm is monitoring the autonomous mode transitions and using the appropriate mode q for updating the estimate of the continuous state x. The probability of mode transitions triggered by control commands can be usually computed by discrete estimation techniques based, for example, on hidden Markov models. Our estimation algorithm is based on the following decomposition of the process density

$$p(q_t, x_t | q_{t-1}, x_{t-1}) = p(x_t | q_t, q_{t-1}, x_{t-1})P(q_t | q_{t-1}, x_{t-1})$$

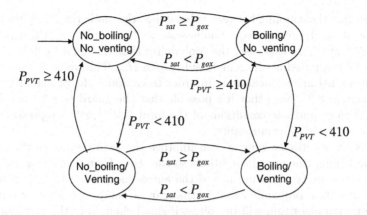

Fig. 2. Hybrid system model for the LOX tank

where the density $p(x_t|q_t, q_{t-1}, x_{t-1})$ describes the evolution of the continuous state conditioned on the mode and the distribution $P(q_t|q_{t-1}, x_{t-1})$ describes the mode transition probability conditioned on the continuous state.

We define the mode transition probability matrix with elements

$$T_{ij}(t) = p(q_t = j|x_{t-1}, q_{t-1} = i), \ i, j = 1, \ldots, |Q|.$$

Let G_{ij} be the guard corresponding to the transition from mode i to mode j. Assuming that the system is at mode q_i and that the probability of the transition $q_i \rightarrow q_j$ is equal to the probability the guard G_{ij} is satisfied, the mode transition probability matrix can be computed as

$$T_{ij}(t) = \int_{G_{ij}} p(x_{t-1}|Y_{t-1}, U_{t-1}, q_{t-1} = i)dx_{t-1} \qquad (1)$$

where $p(x_{t-1}|Y_{t-1}, U_{t-1}, q_{t-1} = i)$ is the conditional density of the continuous state at time $t-1$.

The above integral represents the probability of switching from mode q_i to mode q_j. The general idea of our estimation algorithm is that at every time step we evaluate the transition probability matrix based on the estimate of the continuous state. Then, we focus on the most likely modes and we update the continuous estimate by conditioning our belief on the new measurements. Our current implementation is based on a particle filtering approach described in Section 5. This approach allows the efficient computation of the transition probabilities using Monte Carlo methods. The transition probabilities are then used to dynamically assign particles to the discrete modes, thus focusing on the most likely transitions.

In the distributed algorithm proposed in this paper, local estimators communicate with each other by messages that contain the probability values of the guard conditions that define the coupling between the subsystems. Consider a local mode transition $e^{(n)}$ of the nth subsystem H_n. Based on our assumptions regarding the coupling between subsystems, the mode transition probability may depend on the remote continuous state $x^{(m)}$ according to the guard condition $G(e^{(n)}, x^{(m)})$. In this case, the probability that this guard condition is satisfied can be computed at the remote subsystem H_m. This value is the only information needed at the local node in order to compute the probability of the mode transition $e^{(n)}$. Note that it's possible that the guard $G(e^{(n)})$ is a logical combination of multiple conditions of the form $G(e^{(n)}, x^{(m)})$ representing coupling between multiple components.

Next, we discuss how we can improve the performance of the algorithm by transforming the guard conditions so that they form a cover of the state space. The probability of occurrence of the autonomous transitions is represented by the transition probability matrix that can be computed at every time step. The estimation algorithm will be robust if small changes in the continuous state do not result in large changes in the probabilities T_{ij}. Practically, it is desirable to (1) avoid chattering phenomena, where the probability mass oscillates between modes at every time step, and (2) allow enough time after a mode change for the transient to converge to the steady state behavior for that particular mode. These aspects of the algorithm can be considerably improved by transforming the guard conditions so that they form a cover of the continuous state space as explained in the following.

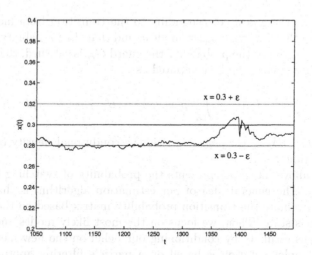

Fig. 3. Guard conditions that cover the state space

Figure 3 shows a simple example of a continuous state trajectory and a guard condition. The system switches from q_1 to q_2 if $x(t) > .3$ and from q_2 to q_1 if $x(t) < .3$. Our estimation algorithm returns a probability distribution over possible continuous states that approximates the actual state $x(t)$ at every time step. If the transition probability matrix T is computed using the original guard conditions, the performance of the algorithm is degraded by the fast switching around $t = 1380$ and leads to chattering between modes q_1 and q_2. While the most likely discrete state oscillates between q_1 and q_2, the estimation of the continuous state is unreliable.

Hybrid estimation can be considerably improved by transforming the guard conditions to form a cover of the state space as illustrated in Figure 3. The transition $q_1 \rightarrow q_2$ occurs if $x(t) > .3 + \epsilon$. Similarly, the transition $q_2 \rightarrow q_1$ occurs if $x(t) < .3 - \epsilon$. The small variations of the state around $x(t) = .3 - \epsilon$, for example, will not trigger any transitions since the system is not in mode q_2. The design parameter ϵ depends on the process and measurement noise. The transition probability matrix can be represented by the transformed guard conditions by equation (1). This method has been used also for removing Zeno behavior from hybrid system models. The guard transformation is desirable, however, even for non-Zeno hybrid systems in order to improve the robustness of the estimation algorithm in the presence of process and measurement noise. It should be noted that the continuity of analog-to-digital maps based on covers of the state space has been studied using small topologies in [12].

5   Particle Filtering Methods

In the following, we describe the particle filtering algorithm for distributed hybrid estimation. To simplify the notation, first we consider only one subsystem and we assume that there are not any control inputs. Then, we describe the step where communication between subsystems is required and how the coordination between the local estimators is accomplished. Note that detailed descriptions of particle filtering methods for estimation of dynamical systems can be found in [3].

Let $\{s_{t-1}^{(k)}, w_{t-1}^{(k)}, k = 1, \ldots, N\}$ denote the sample set at time $t - 1$ where $s_{t-1}^{(k)} = (q_{t-1}^{(k)}, x_{t-1}^{(k)})$ is the kth sample of the local hybrid state and $w_{t-1}^{(k)}$ its probability weight. The kth sample of the predicted local state at time t is denoted by $\tilde{s}_t^{(k)} = (\tilde{q}_t^{(k)}, \tilde{x}_t^{(k)})$. The estimation algorithm consists of the following steps:

1. Initialization $t = 0$.
   a. sample $s_0^{(k)} = (q_0^{(k)}, x_0^{(k)}), k = 1, 2, \ldots, N$ from $p(q_0)$ and $p(x_0)$ and set $t = 1$.
2. Prediction
   a. apply $p(s_t | s_{t-1}^{(k)})$ to compute each $\tilde{s}_t^{(k)}$.
      i. compute $T_{ij}(t) = p(q_t = j | x_{t-1}, q_{t-1} = i)$ from $s_{t-1}^{(k)} = (q_{t-1}^{(k)}, x_{t-1}^{(k)})$ and $w_{t-1}^{(k)}$.
      ii. sample $\tilde{q}_t^{(k)}$ from $T_{ij}(t)$.
      iii. apply $p(x_t | x_{t-1}^{(k)}, q_{t-1}^{(k)}, \tilde{q}_t^{(k)})$ to compute $\tilde{x}_t^{(k)}$.
   b. evaluate the importance weights $w_t^{(k)} = p(y_t | \tilde{s}_t^{(k)})$.
   c. normalize the weights.
3. Re-sampling
   a. re-sample N particles $s_t^{(k)}$ from $\tilde{s}_t^{(k)}$.
   b. set $t \leftarrow t + 1$ and go to step 2.

The interaction between the discrete and continuous dynamics is addressed at the prediction step of the algorithm in order to compute the distribution of the predicted state $\tilde{s}_t^{(k)}$. Consider that at time t the prediction $p(q_{t-1}, x_{t-1} | Y_{t-1})$ is represented by the sample set $\{q_{t-1}^{(k)}, x_{t-1}^{(k)}, w_{t-1}^{(k)}, k = 1, \ldots, N\}$. The mode transition probability matrix can be computed by

$$T_{ij}(t) = \begin{cases} \dfrac{\sum_{k \in \hat{G}_{ij}} w_{t-1}^{(k)}}{\sum_{k \in \hat{I}} w_{t-1}^{(k)}}, & i \neq j \\[1.5em] 1 - \sum_{\ell \neq i} T_{i\ell}(t), & i = j \end{cases} \tag{2}$$

where $k \in \hat{G}_{ij} \Leftrightarrow q_{t-1}^{(k)} = i \wedge x_{t-1}^{(k)} \in G_{ij}$ and $k \in \hat{I} \Leftrightarrow q_{t-1}^{(k)} = i$.

The computation of the mode transition probability matrix is the only step of the distributed algorithm that requires communication between subsystems. For the class of distributed hybrid systems studied in this paper, a mode transition $e = (q_i, q_j)$ in subsystem H_n can be triggered by either a guard condition on the local continuous state or a guard condition on the continuous state of another subsystem H_m. In both cases, the probability for each mode transition can be computed locally at each subsystem. In order to proceed with the prediction of its local state, however, each subsystem must assemble the probabilities for all the local mode transitions. Therefore, at every time step each subsystem must receive messages with the probabilities of the local mode transitions that depend on the continuous state of remote subsystems.

Let $(q_{t-1}^{(k)}, x_{t-1}^{(k)}, w_{t-1}^{(k)})$ be the kth particle and assume $q_{t-1}^{(k)} = i$, then we sample from the ith row of the mode transition probability matrix to select the kth sample $\tilde{q}_t^{(k)}$ for the discrete mode. Suppose that $\tilde{q}_t^{(k)} = j$, then we sample from the density $p_{ij}(x_t | x_{t-1}^{(k)}) = p(x_t | x_{t-1}^{(k)}, q_{t-1} = i, q_t = j)$ to compute the kth sample $\tilde{x}_t^{(k)}$ for the continuous state. Next, we compute that importance weights, normalize, reinforce the predicted state using the observations, and re-sample the particles as described in the above algorithm.

At each subsystem, the estimated mode is computed as the most likely mode at every time step and the continuous state is computed using only particles from the most likely mode, that is

$$\hat{q}_t = \arg\max_i \sum_{k \in \hat{Q}_i} w_t^{(k)} \tag{3}$$

and

$$\hat{x}_t = \frac{\sum_{k \in \hat{Q}} w_t^{(k)} x_t^{(k)}}{\sum_{k \in \hat{Q}} w_t^{(k)}} \tag{4}$$

where $\hat{Q}_i = \{k | q_t^{(k)} = i\}$ and $\hat{Q} = \{k | q_t^{(k)} = \hat{q}_t\}$.

Estimation of the hybrid state based on the most likely mode is selected for computational reasons. Our objective is the development of estimation algorithms suitable for the cryogenic propulsion system and applications with real-time requirements. Particle filter methods can also support multiple hypotheses where the continuous state is estimated for every mode. However, keeping track of multiple hypotheses requires a sufficient number of particles to be assigned to each mode at every time step, thus increasing the computational requirements. A possible improvement of the algorithm is to keep multiple hypotheses using the most likely modes if they have sufficient number of particles.

6 Simulation Results

The particle filtering algorithm presented in Section 5 is used for fault detection using an observer-like scheme. The particle filter algorithm plays the role of a hybrid observer which is computing the most likely discrete mode $\hat{q}$ and continuous state $\hat{x}$ and is generating the expected output $\hat{y}$ based on the plant model. The residual signal $r_t = y_t - \hat{y}_t$ is low-pass filtered and thresholded to detect possible failures. Fault detection and isolation is performed by considering both the residual r_t and the mode $\hat{q}_t$. For example, the observer may not be able to perfectly track fast transients after each mode transition and therefore, the residual exceeding the threshold immediately after a mode transition does not necessarily correspond to a fault. Also information about the modes for which the discrepancy is present can be used for fault isolation. A leakage in a pneumatic valve, for example, will cause a discrepancy only if the valve is closed.

The particle filtering algorithm was implemented in C++ and integrated into a distributed fault detection and diagnosis system for the X34. For the purposes of distribution, we considered the LOX tank, its pneumatic valve, and the associated sensors to be one subsystem, and the pneumatic tank and remaining components to be another. The mode of the LOX tank depends upon the mode of the solenoid valve of the pneumatic subsystem. In practice, the task of the particle filter for the LOX subsystem is thus to estimate the state of the LOX tank given the observations from the pressure and temperature sensors attached to the LOX subsystem and a distribution on the current mode of the venting valve provided by the pneumatic subsystem. In the current implementation, the LOX particle filter is provided with the most likely mode of the venting valve at each sampling point, rather than a probability distribution over its mode. In addition, in our experiments the role of the vehicle and its sensors was played by a Matlab simulation developed from a model of the X34 provided by NASA.

Using these observations, the particle filter estimates the most likely state of its subsystem from a model that does not include failures. We next compute the residual between the expected output of that non-failure state and the current observations from the vehicle's sensors. A diagnostic system then detects and diagnoses faults. It uses a feature extraction algorithm and a neuro-fuzzy classifier to compute the probability of its fault hypotheses based on the residual signals. Details are beyond the scope of this paper. These fault hypotheses would then be reported to the vehicle operator or on-board control system.

The simulator, particle filter and diagnosis systems were integrated as a multi-process distributed system using the Open Control Platform, a distributed computing platform developed by Boeing for the DARPA Software Enabled Control program. The simulator and particle filter were separate OCP processes while the diagnosis system was distributed between two OCP processes. The simulation and particle filter processes each ran on a 1.7GHz Pentium 4 processor within a dual-processor PC while the diagnostic processes ran on a second 600MHz PC connected by a a 100Mbit/second Ethernet LAN. The use of OCP made the location of each process reconfigurable and transparent. The observations were sampled in the simulator and fed into the particle filter via OCP, where particle filtering was performed using $N = 100$ particles. The simulated sampling rate was 10Hz (i.e., ten samples per simulated second) but for our experiments the LOX particle filter could be reliably run 10 times faster than real time. In the following, we present simulation results for the LOX hybrid estimation portion of the distributed diagnosis system for two scenarios (1) normal behavior, and (2) leakage in the pneumatic valve.

Normal behavior. We have demonstrated that the algorithm can track the state in the case when there are no faults in the system. The continuous states corresponding to the LOX and GOX masses are shown in figure 4. The system is discretized using a sampling period $T = 100ms$. The outputs are the GOX pressure and temperature and are contaminated with Gaussian noise. Figure 5 shows when the LOX is boiling or not and the expected venting pressure, as computed using the estimated state, plotted versus the actual venting pressure. The expected pressure is tracking closely the actual pressure. The GOX pressure is increasing because the tank absorbs heat from the atmosphere. The LOX starts boiling increasing the GOX pressure above 18 *psi* which triggers the controller to open the venting valve. GOX is venting in the atmosphere and the pressure is decreasing although LOX is still boiling in the tank. When the pressure falls below 12 *psi* the controller closes the solenoid valve.

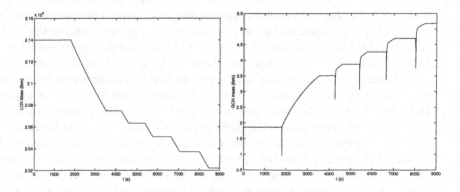

Fig. 4. LOX and GOX mass

Pneumatic valve leakage. The estimation algorithm can be used also to detect continuous faults such as leakage in the pneumatic valve. The valve leakage was

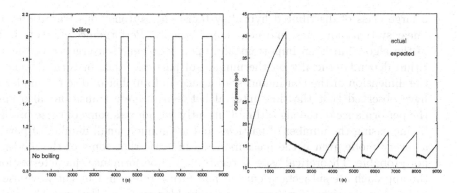

Fig. 5. Discrete mode and venting pressure

simulated by including an additive term in the equation that represents the flow balance when the pneumatic valve is closed. Figure 6 shows the expected and the actual venting pressure. The estimated discrete mode and the residual signal computed as the difference between the actual GOX pressure and the expected are also shown. Whenever there is no boiling then the actual pressure is less than the expected one and a fault is detected.

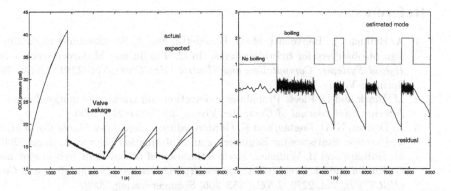

Fig. 6. Expected vs. actual venting pressure, residual, and estimated discrete mode in the case of leakage

7   Discussion and Future Work

Monitoring and diagnosis of embedded systems depends crucially on the ability to estimate the hidden hybrid state from the available measurements. In this paper, we have presented a particle filtering based method and demonstrate the algorithm using a rocket propulsion system. The algorithm can be applied to a large class of distributed hybrid systems with autonomous transitions, non-linear system dynamics, and non-Gaussian noise. Performance characterization of the algorithm is an important and open problem. Convergence of the algorithm depends crucially on the number of particles that, in turn, depends on the dimension of the continuous state space and number of discrete modes. We have observed that the time interval between discrete transitions also affects the performance of the algorithm. Currently, we address some of these problems by increasing the number of particles and assigning a small number of particles at every mode even if the measurements indicate that some of the modes are not probable. Theoretical aspects regarding the performance characterization of the approach are subjects of current and future research. Currently, we use the estimation algorithm for diagnosis of embedded systems. However, the computational performance allows real-time estimation of the state, and therefore, the algorithm can be used for feedback control as well.

Acknowledgments. This work is supported in part by the Defense Advanced Research Projects Agency (DARPA) under contract F33615-99-C3611. Girish Baliga performed much of the implementation on OCP as a PARC summer intern. NASA Ames Research Center provided L2 and collaborated with PARC on HCC, simulation software used for the LOX system. Anupa Bajwa and Adam Sweet of NASA Ames provided expertise on the propulsion system model.

References

1. A. Balluchi, L. Benvenuti, M. D. Benedetto, and A. Sangiovanni-Vincentelli. Design of observers for hybrid systems. In C. Tomlin and M. Greenstreet, editors, *Hybrid Systems: Computation and Control (HSCC'02)*, Vol. 2289, *LNCS*, 76–89. Springer-Verlag, 2002.
2. M. Black and D. Fleet. Probabilistic detection and tracking of motion boundaries. *International Journal of Computer Vision*, 38(3):231–245, 2000.
3. A. Doucet, N. D. Freitas, and N. Gordon, editors. *Sequential Monte Carlo Methods in Practice*. Statistics for Engineering and Information Science. Springer, 2001.
4. M. Hofbaur and B. Williams. Mode estimation of probabilistic hybrid systems. In C. Tomlin and M. Greenstreet, editors, *Hybrid Systems: Computation and Control (HSCC'02)*, Vol. 2289, *LNCS*, 253–266. Springer-Verlag, 2002.
5. M. Isard and A. Blake. A mixed-state condensation tracker with automatic model switching. In *Proc. of the 6th International Conference on Computer Vision*, pages 107–112, 1998.
6. W. Jackson, M. Fromherz, D. Biegelsen, J. Reich, and D. Goldberg. Constrained optimization based control of real time large scale systems: Airjet movement object system. In *Proc. of the 40th IEEE Conference on Decision and Control*, pages 4717–4720, Orlando, FL, December 2001.
7. D. Koller and U. Lerner. Sampling in factored dynamic systems. In Doucet et al. [3], pages 445–464.
8. X. Koutsoukos, F. Zhao, H. Haussecker, J. Reich, and P. Cheung. Fault modeling for monitoring and diagnosis of sensor-rich hybrid systems. In *Proc. of the 40th IEEE Conference on Decision and Control*, pages 793–801, Orlando, FL, December 2001.

9. X. Koutsoukos, J. Kurien, and F. Zhao. Estimation of Hybrid Systems Using Particle Filtering Methods. In *Proc. of MTNS 2002*, Notre Dame, IN, August 2002.

10. J. Kurien, X. Koutsoukos, and F. Zhao. Distributed diagnosis of networked hybrid systems. In *AAAI Spring Symposium on Information Refinement and Revision for Decision Making: Modeling for Diagnostics, Prognostics, and Prediction*, pages 37–44, Stanford, CA, March 2002.

11. S. McIlraith, G. Biswas, D. Clancy, and V. Gupta. Hybrid systems diagnosis. In N. Lynch and B. Krogh, editors, *Hybrid Systems: Computation and Control*, Vol. 1790, *LNCS*, 282–295. Springer, 2000.

12. A. Nerode and W. Kohn. Models for hybrid systems: Automata, topologies, controllability, observability. In R. L. Grossman, A. Nerode, A. P. Ravn, and H. Rischel, editors, *Hybrid Systems*, Vol. 736, *LNCS*, 317–356. Springer-Verlag, 1993.

13. F. Zhao, X. Koutsoukos, H. Haussecker, J. Reich, P. Cheung, and C. Picardi. Distributed monitoring of hybrid systems: A model-directed approach. In *Proc. IJCAI'2001*, pages 557–564, Seattle, WA, 2001.

Event Prediction for Switching Linear Systems with Time Varying Thresholds Using Orthogonal Functions

Andreas Kwiatkowski, Gerwald Lichtenberg, and Axel Schild

Department of Control Engineering,
Technische Universität Hamburg–Harburg, Germany
{kwiatkowski, lichtenberg, a.schild}@tuhh.de

Abstract. This paper concerns the prediction of switching times for switching linear systems. The instance when a state trajectory exceeds a predefined threshold signal can be determined for input signals and time-varying thresholds without calculating the state-trajectories explicitly. This is obtained by transforming the switching conditions in the Orthogonal Function Domain of the Legendre polynomials. The problem of predicting the event time can be transposed into the problem of finding the minimal, positive and real root of a polynomial. In general, the event time can not be determined exactly, but approximated with sufficient accuracy.

Keywords: Event prediction, switching linear systems, orthogonal functions

1 Introduction

In many disciplines, like in process engineering, systems need to hold several time variable contraints. For example, the temperature of a combustion plant or a concentration in a chemical process have to fulfill several time dependent boundaries due to mechanical stress or product quality. Exceeding these contraints leads to transitions or 'autonomous jumps' between different phases, such as changes of control parameter or some emergency actions. On the other hand, transitions can also be triggered externally, causing 'controlled jumps'. In both cases these systems are called hybrid. A typical property of hybrid systems is thus discontinuous jumps in the state trajectories, as illustrated in figure 1.

It is shown in [1] that the initial value problem can be solved for linear switching systems, by means of orthogonal functions if the event times, i.e. the times a transition occurs, can be predetermined. For predetermined event times, the series of the phases of the hybrid system can be divided into a sequence of time intervals which is specified by a series of generalised spectra of orthogonal functions. This sequence can be determined in the domain of orthogonal functions by the means of the GHOF matrix of integration. This can be achieved easily for

O. Maler and A. Pnueli (Eds.): HSCC 2003, LNCS 2623, pp. 314–327, 2003.

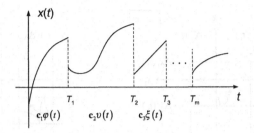

Fig. 1. Discontinuous jumps in a state trajectory

systems which can be described by controlled jumps, but leads to considerable problems if the dynamics of the hybrid system is defined by autonomous jumps. This paper presents an approach to predict these event times using the means of orthogonal functions. This approach does not only provide a way to simulate hybrid systems, but generates a symbolic representation of the event times.

According to [2], a *hybrid dynamical system (HDS)* can be formally described by the set $H = [\,\mathcal{Q},\, \Sigma,\, \mathcal{J},\, \mathcal{G}\,]$, where

- $\mathcal{Q} \subset \mathbb{N}$ is the set of index
- $\Sigma = \{\Sigma_q\}_{q \in \mathcal{Q}}$ is the collection of subsystems $\Sigma_q = [X_q,\, \mathbb{R}_+,\, f_q,\, U_q,\, Y_q]$
- $\mathcal{J} = \{J_q\}_{q \in \mathcal{Q}},\ J_q \subset X_q$ is the collection of autonomous jump sets
- $\mathcal{G} = \{G_q\}_{q \in \mathcal{Q}}$, where $G_q : J_q \to S$ is the autonomous jump transition map.

We consider switching linear systems, which change their modes when a state trajectory $x_{q,i}(t)$ exceeds a given threshold $\Delta x_{q,i}(t)$. Thus, the general HDS can be restricted to systems with linear transition functions and simple jump sets :

$$
\left.
\begin{array}{ll}
\text{dyn. subsystems } \Sigma_q : & \dot{x}_q(t) \;=\; A_q x_q(t) + B_q u_q(t), \quad x_{q,i}(t) \notin J_q(t), \\
\text{index transitions} \quad : & q(t^+) = G_q(x_q(t), q(t)) \\
\text{autonomous jumps} : & x_q(t^+) = G_x(x_q(t), q(t)) \\
\text{time variable jump sets} : & J_q(t) := \{\, x_q(t) \mid \exists i \,:\, x_{q,i}(t) = \Delta x_{q,i}(t)\},
\end{array}
\right\}, \quad x_{q,i}(t) \in J_q(t),
\tag{1}
$$

where G_q describes the transitions between the subsystems and G_x indicates how to determine the initial state of the next phase. The time variable jump sets describe thresholds $\Delta x_{q,i}(t)$ for each state. Defining lower bounds $\Delta \underline{x}_{q,i}(t)$ and upper bounds $\Delta \overline{x}_{q,i}(t)$ for each state, the jump sets define a time variable rectangular space in $\mathbb{R}^n$, illustrated for $n{=}2$ in figure 2. The left figure shows the bounds for $x_1(t)$ and $x_2(t)$ for $t = t_1$, the right one shows the bounded region for another time $t = t_2$. In the following, there is no need to distinguish between lower and upper bounds. Thus, only one symbol $\Delta x_{q,i}(t)$ is used.

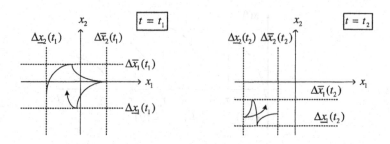

Fig. 2. Phase portrait with time variable bounds

One of the major problems in simulating and analysing these linear switching systems is the determination of the switching times T_e. Because the instant when a state exceeds a threshold can be seen as a *state event*, we call this determination *event prediction*. We present an approach which predicts these event times for each phase of the hybrid system. By determining the events successively, one is able to generate a sequence of events without calculating the state-trajectories. We use the domain of orthogonal polynomials, because [1] demonstrated that a domain which is restricted to a finite time interval can be a natural domain for the handling of hybrid systems.

The Event Prediction Problem

We make the assumption that the system's behaviour has no Zeno effects. Therefore, the event prediction problem can be solved sequentially for each subsystem, neglecting the index q:

Given: - linear Model (A, B, C, D) of a MIMO-System
   - Input-vector $u(t)$
   - Initial state $x_0 = [x_{0,1} \ x_{0,2} \ \cdots \ x_{0,n}]^T$
   - Threshold signals $\Delta x(t) = [\Delta x_1(t) \ \Delta x_2(t) \ \cdots \ \Delta x_n(t)]^T$
   - Switching condition $\exists i \in \{1, 2, \ldots, n\}$ with $\Delta x_i(t) = x_i(t)$

Find: Event time $T_{e,i}$, with $\Delta x_i(T_{e,i}) = x_i(T_{e,i})$.

Describing the state trajectories by

$$x(t) = e^{At} x_0 + \int_0^t e^{A(t-\tau)} B u(\tau) \, d\tau \qquad (2)$$

one needs to find symbolic descriptions for the states $x_i(t)$ that hold $\Delta x_i(T_{e,i}) = x_i(T_{e,i})$. In general, a symbolic solution for $x_i(t)$ can only be determined for $n < 3$ and constant inputs u. For time variable inputs $u(t)$ and thresholds $\Delta x(t)$, the event times can only be identified by numerical simulation, using numerical integration methods and suitable methods of event detection [3,4,5,6].

In contrast to [7,8] the new approach does not require a qualitative model of the hybrid system. The initial value problem is first solved in the domain of orthogonal functions. The standard items of signal approximation and integration are stated in the appendix as they can be found in [1,9]. We expand this method, using *time dependent basis functions* and *time dependent spectra*. Using this generalised spectra and the properties of the Legendre polynomials, we obtain the characteristic polynomials. The minimal, real and positive root of these polynomials is an approximation of the desired event time T_e.

2   Time Variable Approximation of Signals

Determining the generalized spectra of a function leads to a representation of the signal in the domain of orthogonal functions. In contrast to the Laplace domain, the spectra describe the signal within a finite time interval $[0, T]$. The following section derives time dependent spectra, i.e. the representation can be evaluated for a variabel end time T.

2.1   Time Variable Basis Functions

It is shown in appendix A.3 how to transform the time interval with a fixed upper bound T using the transformation matrix $\boldsymbol{\Gamma}_T$. To achieve time variable descriptions of Legendre polynomials, $\boldsymbol{\Gamma}_T$ can be expressed with a symbolic variable T. In this instance, the elements of $\boldsymbol{\Gamma}_T = (t_{i,j})$ are rational functions of the end time T and the transformation matrix is marked as $\boldsymbol{\Gamma}_T(T)$. By using $\boldsymbol{\Gamma}_T(T)$, a set of basis functions $\varphi_{N,T}(t,T)$, that depends on the time t and the variable end time T can be calculated from the matrix $\boldsymbol{P}_T(T)$ of time variable Legendre coefficients and the vector $\boldsymbol{\theta}_N(t)$ of monomials

$$\boldsymbol{\varphi}_{N,T}(t,T) = \boldsymbol{P}_T(T)\,\boldsymbol{\theta}_N(t), \quad \text{with} \quad \boldsymbol{P}_T(T) = \boldsymbol{P}_N\,\boldsymbol{\Gamma}_T(T), \tag{3}$$

where $\boldsymbol{P}_N$ denotes the matrix of time invariable Legendre coefficients (31). Thus, a time dependent polynomial basis function of i-th order, defined over the interval $t \in [0, T]$ can be written as

$$\varphi_{i,T}(t,T) = \boldsymbol{p}_{i,T}(T)\,\boldsymbol{\theta}_N(t) = \boldsymbol{\theta}_N'(t)\,\boldsymbol{p}_{i,T}'(T), \tag{4}$$

with $\boldsymbol{p}_{i,T}(T)$ being the i-th row-vector of $\boldsymbol{P}_T(T)$. The final value of all basis functions is equal to 1 (cf. eqn.(32)), and this holds true, if the basis functions are defined with variable end time T

$$\varphi_{i,T}(T,T) = 1, \quad \forall i \quad \Rightarrow \quad \boldsymbol{\varphi}_{N,T}(T,T) = [\,1\,1\,1\,\cdots\,1\,]^T. \tag{5}$$

2.2   Time Variable Approximations of Inputs and Thresholds

To predict the switching time T_e for arbitrary input signals $u(t)$ and thresholds $\Delta x(t)$, one needs suitable descriptions of the signals. It is shown in A.4 how to approximate a signal by its spectra, for a given time interval $[0, T]$ with a fixed end time T. We do now derive an approximation of signals with a variable end time T. The idea is to approximate the original signal first in a time-interval $[0, \bar{T}]$, with $\bar{T} \geq T$, and afterwards use this first approximation to determine a second approximation with variable time interval. The result is a generalized spectra of $u(t)$, with coefficients that depend on the interval time. First, one defines an interval $[0, \bar{T}]$ that holds $0 \leq T \leq \bar{T}$ and derives the spectra for the i-th input signal $u_i(t)$:

$$u_{i,\bar{T}}(t) \approx \hat{u}_{i,\bar{T}}(t) = \sum_{j=0}^{N_u} u_{c,i_j}\, \varphi_{j,\bar{T}}(t) = \boldsymbol{u}_{c,i}\, \boldsymbol{\varphi}_{N_u,\bar{T}}(t), \tag{6}$$

with $N_u \leq N$ being the maximum required order of approximation. Because the approximation $\hat{u}_{i,\bar{T}}(t)$ is valid in the whole interval $[0, \bar{T}]$, one is able to insert $\hat{u}_{i,\bar{T}}(t)$ as a signal representation in the calculation of a second approximation. Now, using the interval time dependent description of the basis functions (4) and combining equations (6) and (37) leads to the instruction to determine the j-th coefficient of the i-th input

$$\hat{u}_{c,i_j}(T) = \gamma_{j,T} \int_0^T \hat{u}_{i,\bar{T}}(t)\varphi_{j,T}(t,T)\, dt = \gamma_{j,T} \int_0^T \sum_{k=0}^{N_u} u_{c,i_k}\, \varphi_{k,\bar{T}}(t)\, \varphi_{j,T}(t,T)\, dt$$

$$= \gamma_{j,T} \int_0^T \boldsymbol{u}_c\, \boldsymbol{P}_{\bar{T}}\boldsymbol{\theta}_{N_u}(t)\boldsymbol{\theta}'_N(t)\boldsymbol{p}'_{k,T}(T)\, dt$$

$$= \boldsymbol{u}_c\, \boldsymbol{P}_{\bar{T}}\left(\gamma_{j,T} \int_0^T \boldsymbol{\psi}(t)\, dt\right) \boldsymbol{p}'_{k,T}(T) = \boldsymbol{u}_c\, \boldsymbol{P}_{\bar{T}}\boldsymbol{\Psi}(T)\boldsymbol{p}'_{k,T}(T). \tag{7}$$

The elements of the matrix $\boldsymbol{\psi}(t) = \boldsymbol{\theta}_{N_u}(t)\, \boldsymbol{\theta}'_N(t)$ are monomials. Therefore, $\boldsymbol{\Psi}(T)$ can be determined easily and (7) results in a *coefficient polynomial* $\hat{u}_{c,i_j}(T)$. That is, the coefficients of the generalized spectra $\boldsymbol{u}_{c,i}(T)$ are again polynomials in T

$$u_{i,\bar{T}}(t,T) \approx \hat{u}_{i,\bar{T}}(t,T) = \boldsymbol{u}_{c,i}(T)\, \boldsymbol{\varphi}_{N,T}(t,T) \quad \text{with} \tag{8}$$

$$\boldsymbol{u}_{c,i}(T) = [\,\hat{u}_{c,i_0}(T)\ \ \hat{u}_{c,i_1}(T)\ \ \cdots\ \ \hat{u}_{c,i_N}(T)\,] \quad \text{and} \quad \hat{u}_{c,i_j}(T) = \sum_{l=0}^{N_u} v_{i,j,l}\, T^l. \tag{9}$$

In the same way, the input-signals $u_i(t)$ are expressed as coefficient polynomials $\boldsymbol{u}_{c,i}(T)$, the threshold functions can be approximated by their time-dependent spectra $\Delta x_{c,i}(T)$ and coefficient polynomials $\Delta x_{c,i_j}(T)$ up to order N_Δ

$$\Delta \hat{x}_{i,\bar{T}}(t,T) = \Delta x_{c,i}(T)\, \boldsymbol{\varphi}_{N,T}(t,T) \quad \text{and} \quad \Delta x_{c,i_j}(T) = \sum_{l=0}^{N_\Delta} \chi_{i,j,l}\, T^l. \tag{10}$$

3 Solution of the Initial Value Problem

Consider a state equation of a MIMO system

$$\dot{x}(t) = Ax(t) + Bu(t), \qquad x(0) = x_0 = [x_{0,1} \; x_{0,2} \; \cdots \; x_{0,n}]' \tag{11}$$

where $x(t)$ and $u(t)$ are n states and m inputs respectively.
As [1] shows, the initial value problem (IVP)

given: x_0, $u(t)$,
find: $x(t)$ holding (11)

can be approximately solved in the interval $t \in [0, T]$, using orthogonal functions. We are interested in the trajectories in an interval $[0, T]$ and use the upper interval bound T with $T \leq \bar{T}$ as a free variable. The solution of the IVP, calculated by means of orthogonal functions can be expressed by their time dependent generalized spectra

$$\begin{aligned} \dot{x}(t) &: \check{\ddot{x}}_{\bar{T}}(t,T) = \check{V}_c(T)\, \varphi_{N,T}(t,T), \\ x(t) &: \check{\tilde{x}}_{\bar{T}}(t,T) = \check{X}_c(T)\, \varphi_{N,T}(t,T), \end{aligned} \tag{12}$$

subject to the time dependent approximations of $u(t)$ and x_0:

$$\begin{aligned} u(t) &\approx \hat{u}_{\bar{T}}(t,T) = U_c(T)\, \varphi_{N,T}(t,T), \quad \text{for } 0 \leq t \leq T \\ x_0 &= X_0 \varphi_{N,T}(t,T), \end{aligned} \tag{13}$$

with $X_0 = (x_{0,c,i_j})$ and $x_{0,c,i_0} = x_{0,i}\; \forall i$, $x_{0,c,i_j} = 0\; \forall j \neq 0$. Inserting the spectra into the state-equation and cancelling the vectors of basis functions $\varphi_{N,T}(t,T)$, we obtain

$$\check{V}_c(T) = A\check{X}_c(T) + BU_c(T), \quad X_0 = [\,x_0 \; O\,]\,\varphi_{N,T}(t,T). \tag{14}$$

To substitute the coefficient-matrix $\check{X}_c$ in the state-equation (14), we make use of the relation between $x(t)$ and $\dot{x}(t)$ and approximate the integration by the operational matrix of integration E given in the appendix A.5

$$x(t) = \int_0^t \dot{x}(\tau)d\tau + x_0 \quad \longleftrightarrow \quad \check{X}_c(T) = \check{V}_c(T)\,E(T) + X_0. \tag{15}$$

Combining the terms (14) and (15) results in

$$\check{V}_c(T) = A\,\check{V}_c(T)\,E(T) + S_c(T), \quad \text{where} \quad S_c(T) = AX_0 + BU_c(T), \tag{16}$$

and

$$\check{V}_c(T) = \begin{bmatrix} \check{v}_{c,1_0}(T)\check{v}_{c,1_1}(T) \cdots \check{v}_{c,1_N}(T) \\ \check{v}_{c,2_0}(T)\check{v}_{c,2_1}(T) \cdots \check{v}_{c,2_N}(T) \\ \vdots \quad \vdots \quad \ddots \quad \vdots \\ \check{v}_{c,n_0}(T)\check{v}_{c,n_1}(T) \cdots \check{v}_{c,n_N}(T) \end{bmatrix}, \; S_c(T) = \begin{bmatrix} s_{c,1_0}(T)s_{c,1_1}(T) \cdots s_{c,1_N}(T) \\ s_{c,2_0}(T)s_{c,2_1}(T) \cdots s_{c,2_N}(T) \\ \vdots \quad \vdots \quad \ddots \quad \vdots \\ s_{c,n_0}(T)s_{c,n_1}(T) \cdots s_{c,n_N}(T) \end{bmatrix}.$$

The exact solution of equation (16) is given by

$$\check{V}_c^*(T) = (I - E'(T) \otimes A)^{-1} S_c^*(T), \tag{17}$$

with $\otimes$ denoting the *Kronecker product* and

$$\check{V}_c^*(T) = [\, \check{v}_{c,1_0}(T)\, \check{v}_{c,2_0}(T)\, \cdots\, \check{v}_{c,n_0}(T)\, |\, \cdots\cdots\, |\, \check{v}_{c,1_N}(T)\, \check{v}_{c,2_N}(T)\, \cdots\, \check{v}_{c,n_N}(T)\,]^T$$
$$S_c^*(T) = [\, s_{c,1_0}(T)\, s_{c,2_0}(T)\, \cdots\, s_{c,n_0}(T)\, |\, \cdots\cdots\, |\, s_{c,1_N}(T)\, s_{c,2_N}(T)\, \cdots\, s_{c,n_N}(T)\,]^T$$

being the expanded coefficient matrices of $\check{V}_c$ and S_c, [1]. It is important to note, that all elements of $\check{V}_c^*(T)$, $\check{V}_c(T)$ are rational functions in T and the elements of $S_c^*(T)$, $S_c(T)$ are polynomials in T. Finally, the coefficient matrix $\check{V}_c(T)$ is used to determine

$$\check{X}_c(T) = \check{V}_c(T)\, E(T) + X_0 = \begin{bmatrix} \check{x}_{c,1_0}(T)\check{x}_{c,1_1}(T) \cdots \check{x}_{c,1_N}(T) \\ \check{x}_{c,2_0}(T)\check{x}_{c,2_1}(T) \cdots \check{x}_{c,2_N}(T) \\ \vdots \qquad \vdots \quad \ddots \quad \vdots \\ \check{x}_{c,n_0}(T)\check{x}_{c,n_1}(T) \cdots \check{x}_{c,n_N}(T) \end{bmatrix} = \begin{bmatrix} \check{x}_{c,1}(T) \\ \check{x}_{c,2}(T) \\ \vdots \\ \check{x}_{c,n}(T) \end{bmatrix} \tag{18}$$

and the desired trajectories $\check{x}_{\bar{T}}(t,T) = \check{X}_c(T)\,\varphi_{N,T}(t,T)$. Thus, a time dependent solution for the state $x_i(t)$ in the interval $[0, T]$, with $T < \bar{T}$ is given by

$$\check{x}_{i,\bar{T}}(t,T) = \check{x}_{c,i}(T)\,\varphi_{N,T}(t,T). \tag{19}$$

The reasons for this time dependent approach are less errors in the solutions $\check{x}_{i,\bar{T}}(t,T)$, and thus, better approximations for event the time T_e, for $T_e \ll \bar{T}$. To predict the event times, the solutions $\check{x}_{i,\bar{T}}(t,T)$ are *not* computed explicitly, but one needs the matrix (18) of polynomial coefficients, where each element $\check{x}_{c,ij}(T)$ is a rational functions in T with a maximum polynomial order $N_x < n{\cdot}N + N_u + 1$. In general, the solutions $\check{x}_{\bar{T}}(t,T)$ are *not* equal to the signal approximations $\hat{x}_{\bar{T}}(t,T)$ of the exact solutions $x(t)$, with $t \in [0, T]$.

4 Method of Event Prediction

The task to predict the event time $T_{e,i}$, when one of the states $x_i(t)$ exceeds the corresponding time varying threshold $\Delta x_i(t)$ is equivalent to solving the equation below:

$$x_i(T_{e,i}) - \Delta x_i(T_{e,i}) \overset{!}{=} 0. \tag{20}$$

Substituting the terms of (20) by the solution of the IVP (19) and the approximation (10), one is able to determine an approximation $\hat{T}_{e,i}$ of the event-time $T_{e,i}$

$$\check{x}_{i,T}(\hat{T}_{e,i}, T) - \Delta\hat{x}_{i,T}(\hat{T}_{e,i}, T) = 0 \tag{21}$$

$$\check{x}_c(T)\,\varphi_{N,T}(\hat{T}_{e,i}, T) - \Delta x_c(T)\,\varphi_{N,T}(\hat{T}_{e,i}, T) = 0\,. \tag{22}$$

The above equation can not be solved easily, because both terms describe a superposition of functions in $\hat{T}_{e,i}$ and T. Equation (22) simplifies considerably, if (21) has to hold for the end of the variable interval bound $T = \hat{T}_{e,i}$

$$\check{x}_{i,T}(\hat{T}_{e,i}, \hat{T}_{e,i}) - \Delta\hat{x}_{i,T}(\hat{T}_{e,i}, \hat{T}_{e,i}) = 0 \tag{23}$$

$$\check{x}_c(\hat{T}_{e,i})\,\varphi_{N,\hat{T}_{e,i}}(\hat{T}_{e,i}, \hat{T}_{e,i}) - \Delta x_c(\hat{T}_{e,i})\,\varphi_{N,\hat{T}_{e,i}}(\hat{T}_{e,i}, \hat{T}_{e,i}) = 0\,. \tag{24}$$

On the one hand, this choice simplifies the solution, on the other hand, we assume, the approximation (19) is better with respect to the event times than the not time variable solution. Concerning the relation (5) for the upper interval bound, and inserting it into (24), leads to

$$\sum_{j=0}^{N} \check{x}_{c,i_j}(\hat{T}_{e,i}) - \sum_{j=0}^{N} \Delta x_{c,i_j}(\hat{T}_{e,i}) = 0\,,. \tag{25}$$

Determining the sums over the rational functions $\check{x}_{c,i_j}(\hat{T}_{e,i})$ and the polynomials $\Delta x_{c,i_j}(\hat{T}_{e,i})$ results in

$$\frac{\sum_{\iota=0}^{N_x} \xi_{\Sigma,i,\iota}^{nom}\, \hat{T}_{e,i}^{\iota}}{\sum_{\kappa=0}^{N_x} \xi_{\Sigma,i,\kappa}^{den}\, \hat{T}_{e,i}^{\kappa}} - \sum_{\mu=0}^{N_\Delta} \Delta\xi_{\Sigma,i,\mu}\, \hat{T}_{e,i}^{\mu} = 0 \tag{26}$$

assuming, the denominator to be unequal zero. The elements $\xi_{\Sigma,i}^{nom}$, $\xi_{\Sigma,i}^{den}$ denote the real coefficients of the rational function that describes the final value of the the i-th state. The coefficients $\Delta\xi_{\Sigma,i}$ form the polynomial that approximates the value of the i-th threshold signal. Using the polynomial descriptions, the task of predicting the event-time $T_{e,i}$ can be formulated into the task of finding the roots of the *characteristic polynomial*

$$P_{char,i}(\hat{T}_{e,i}) = \sum_{\iota=0}^{N_x} \xi_{\Sigma,i,\iota}^{nom}\, \hat{T}_{e,i}^{\iota} - \sum_{\mu=0}^{N_\Delta} \Delta\xi_{\Sigma,i,\mu}\, \hat{T}_{e,i}^{\mu} \cdot \sum_{\kappa=0}^{N_x} \xi_{\Sigma,i,\kappa}^{den}\, \hat{T}_{e,i}^{\kappa} = 0\,. \tag{27}$$

The maximum order of $P_{char,i}(\hat{T}_{e,i})$ is $N_P < nN + N_u + N_\Delta + 1$, therefore, the characteristic polynomial has N_P roots, at most. We are looking for the first instance, a state trajectory $x_i(t)$ exceeds the threshold $\Delta x_i(t)$, that is, the smallest, positive and real root of $P_{char,i}$. The approach of event prediction can be resumed as follows:

Algorithm:

1. Predetermine an upper bound $\bar{T}$ for the estimated event-time, $T_e < \bar{T}$.

2. Calculate time variable approximations of the inputs $\hat{u}_{i,\bar{T}}(t,T) = U_c(T)\varphi_{N,T}(t,T)$ and the thresholds $\Delta\hat{x}_{\bar{T}}(t,T) = \Delta X_c(T)\varphi_{N,T}(t,T)$.

3. Determine the coefficient matrix $S_c(T)$ and X_0 by (13) and (16); expand it to $S_c^*(T)$.

4. Solve equation (17) and derive $\check{V}_c(T)$ from $\check{V}_c^*(T)$.

5. Calculate the matrix of coefficient polynomials $\check{X}_c(T) = \check{V}_c(T)E(T) + X_0$.

6. Determine the characteristic polynomials $P_{char,i}$.

7. Compute the smallest, real and positive root $\hat{T}_e$ of all characteristic polynomials.

Result: Approximation $\hat{T}_e$ of the next switching time T_e.

5 Examples

Ball in a Box
A simple example for a switching linear system with time variable bounds can be given by a ball in a box, illustrated in figure 3. The right figure shows the scheme of the system. The ball is embedded in a box with three fixed walls. The lower wall is moved with a periodic triangular signal and accelerates the ball if it hits, thus, it can be interpreted as a time varying threshold, triggering the state event e_2. Each time, the ball hits a wall, one of the state events e_1, e_2, e_3, e_4 takes place, causing a jump of the velocity of the ball. The state-space model of the ball in 'uninterrupted' phase is of order $n=5$. Using an approximation order $N=2$, the event times can be determined exactly, due to the properties of the plant and the inputs and thresholds, respectively. The result of the successive calculations of the state events is shown in the right figure. The sequence of events is given by the marked integers and the corresponding time values.

Second Order Dynamical System
For other examples, like second order dynamical systems, the predicted event time $\hat{T}_e$ is an approximation of the exact event time. For a lightly damped system

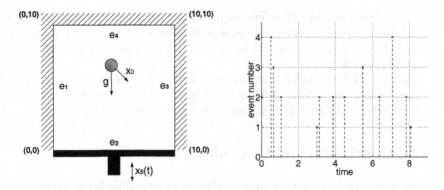

Fig. 3. Ball in a box and sequence of state events

the event times have been computed for a series of approximation up to order N and for 10 equidistant constant thresholds of the state $x_2(t)$.

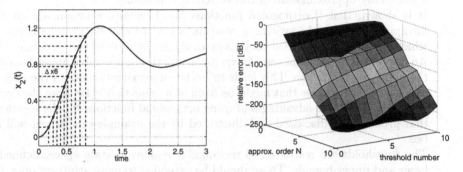

Fig. 4. State trajectory and events of a 2nd order system and relative error

In the left plot of figure 4 the state trajectory, the equidistant thresholds Δx_i and their corresponding event times for the second state are shown. The thresholds are numbered with increasing threshold values. For instance, the state trajectory crosses the threshold Δx_6 at approximately 0.51s. To compare the event times $\hat{T}_e$ of the proposed approach with the results T_e of classical numerical simulation methods, the relative error

$$e_{rel} = \left| \frac{T_e - \hat{T}_e}{T_e} \right| \qquad (28)$$

is displayed in the right graph of figure 4. It is plotted over approximation order N and threshold number Δx_i. It is clearly visible that for increasing approximation order N and for decreasing threshold number the relative error decreases. For higher order polynomials a more accurate approximation of a state trajectory can be achieved and therefore an increasing accuracy of event times. Likewise the approximation accuracy in general decreases if a trajectory is approximated within a larger time interval for a fixed N and therefore the accuracy of the event times drops.

Thus it has been shown for systems of first and second order, that the relative error of approximation can be reduced by increasing the order of approximation N, which is well suited for engineering applications.

6   Conclusion and Outlook

An approach to switching time prediction of switching linear systems was presented. In the case of time varying thresholds as switching regions, the problem of determining the time when the system hits one of the thresholds is in general not solvable explicitly. An implicit equation can be derived by using hitting conditions for the trajectory with the thresholds. Inserting a symbolic solution of the initial value problem as trajectory leads to nonlinear and nonpolynomial equations. The idea is to use an approximation of the trajectory and then derive a more easy approximation of the switching conditions.

It is shown, that if orthogonal functions like Legendre Polynomials are used for approximation, the switching conditions lead to characteristic polynomials, which smallest positive real root gives an approximation of the switching time. An important detail is the use of a symbolic and thus, adjustable upper bound for the approximation time. This leads to better approximations than the only use of constant boundaries that might be fixed at a value that is far from the desired switching time. The advantages of using orthogonal functions for the solution of that problem are discussed and illustrated by the example of a driven ball in a box.

The thresholds are restricted to rectangular regions in state space, defined by lower and upper bounds. These should be extended to more arbitrary ones. One of the strengths of the approach is the possibility to include symbolic parameters into the characteristic polynomials for the event times. In the future, this can be used for further analysis of hybrid behaviour.

References

1. A. Patra and G. P. Rao, *General Hybrid Orthogonal Functions and their Applications in Systems and Control.* Lecture Notes in Control and Information Sciences, Springer Verlag London, 1996.
2. M. Branicky and S. Mattsson, *Simulation of Hybrid Systems*, pp. 31–56. Lecture Notes in Computer Sciences 1273, HSCC97, Springer-Verlag, Berlin, 1997.
3. A. Back, J. Guckenheimer, and M. Myers, *A Dynamical Simulation Facility for Hybrid Systems*, pp. 255–267. Lecture Notes in Computer Sciences 736, HSCC93, Springer-Verlag, Berlin, 1993.
4. J. Esposito, V. Kumar, and G. Pappas, *Accurate Event Detection for Simulating Hybrid Systems*, pp. 204–217. Lecture Notes in Computer Sciences 2034, HSCC2001, Springer-Verlag, Berlin, 2001.

5. P. Mosterman, *An Overview of hybrid simulation phenomena and their support by simulation packages*, pp. 163–177. Lecture Notes in Computer Sciences 1569, HSCC99, Spinger-Verlag, Berlin, 1999.

6. M. Morari, A. Bemporad, and D. Mignone, "A framework for control, state estimation, fault detection, and verification of hybrid systems," *Scientific Computing in Chemical Engineering II*, vol. 2 (Simulation, Image Processing, Optimization and Control), pp. 46–61, 1999.

7. J. Lunze, "A timed discrete-event abstraction of continuous-variable systems," *International Journal of Control*, vol. 72, no. 13, pp. 1147–1164, 1999.

8. J. Raisch and S. O'Young, *A totally ordered set of discrete abstractions for a given hybrid or continuous system*, vol. 1273, pp. 342–360. Berlin Springer–Verlag, 1997. Lecture Notes in Computer Science, Hybrid System IV.

9. K. Henneberger, *Regelung nichtlinearer Systeme auf der Basis bilinearer Approximationsmodelle*. PhD thesis, Erlangen, 1996.

A   Appendix

A.1   Orthogonal Functions

Definition 1 (Orthogonal Functions). *A set of functions $\varphi_N(\tau)$, $N \in \mathbb{N}_0$, is said to be orthogonal in the interval (a, b) with weighting function $\varrho(\tau)$ if*

$$\langle \varphi_i(\tau), \varphi_j(\tau) \rangle = \int_a^b \varrho(\tau)\, \varphi_i(\tau)\, \varphi_j(\tau)\, d\tau = \begin{cases} \sigma^2 \text{ for } i = j \\ 0 \text{ for } i \neq j \end{cases}. \qquad (29)$$

A.2   Legendre Polynomials

Legendre polynomials

$$L_i(\tau) = \varphi_i(\tau) = \frac{1}{2^i\, i!} \frac{d^i}{d\tau^i} \left(\tau^2 - 1 \right)^i, \quad \tau \in [-1, 1]. \qquad (30)$$

are a special case of Jacobi polynomials and form a set of orthogonal functions, defined over the interval $[-1, 1]$.

To describe the orthogonal functions in a compact way, the *vector $\boldsymbol{\theta}(\tau)$ of monomials* and the *vector $\boldsymbol{\varphi}(\tau)$ of basis functions* are defined:

$$\boldsymbol{\varphi}_N(\tau) = \begin{bmatrix} \varphi_0(\tau) \\ \varphi_1(\tau) \\ \vdots \\ \varphi_N(\tau) \end{bmatrix}, \quad \boldsymbol{\theta}_N(\tau) = \begin{bmatrix} \theta_0(\tau) \\ \theta_1(\tau) \\ \vdots \\ \theta_N(\tau) \end{bmatrix} = \begin{bmatrix} 1 \\ \tau \\ \vdots \\ \tau^N \end{bmatrix}.$$

Using $\boldsymbol{\theta}(\tau)$ and $\boldsymbol{\varphi}(\tau)$, the set of basis functions of order N kann be written shortly as

$$\boldsymbol{\varphi}_N(\tau) = \boldsymbol{P}_N \cdot \boldsymbol{\theta}_N(\tau), \qquad (31)$$

with P_N being the matrix of Legendre coefficients $P_N = (p_{i,j})$. For example, the set of Legendre polynomials with order $N = 4$ can be noticed as $\varphi_4(\tau) = P_4 \cdot \theta_4(\tau)$

$$
\begin{bmatrix} \varphi_0(\tau) \\ \varphi_1(\tau) \\ \varphi_2(\tau) \\ \varphi_3(\tau) \\ \varphi_4(\tau) \end{bmatrix} = \begin{bmatrix} 1 & 0 & 0 & 0 & 0 \\ 0 & 1 & 0 & 0 & 0 \\ -\frac{1}{2} & 0 & \frac{3}{2} & 0 & 0 \\ 0 & -\frac{3}{2} & 0 & \frac{5}{2} & 0 \\ \frac{3}{8} & 0 & -\frac{15}{4} & 0 & \frac{35}{8} \end{bmatrix} \cdot \begin{bmatrix} 1 \\ \tau \\ \tau^2 \\ \tau^3 \\ \tau^4 \end{bmatrix} .
$$

The Legendre-polynomials equal 1, if evaluated at the upper bound of the definition interval

$$
\varphi_i(1) = 1, \quad \forall i \quad \text{with} \quad \tau \in [-1, 1]. \tag{32}
$$

A.3 Transformation of Time-Interval

For the purpose of event prediction, signals $f(t)$ of dynamical systems, will not be defined for the time interval $[-1, 1]$ but for $f(t)$, with $0 \le t \le T$ and a finite time T. Therefore, one needs to transform the Legendre polynomials to fit the time-interval $[0, T]$. This can be achieved by a linear operation, using a transformation matrix $\boldsymbol{\Gamma}_T$ that combines the vectors $\boldsymbol{\theta}(\tau)$ and $\boldsymbol{\theta}(t)$ of monomials

$$
\boldsymbol{\theta}(\tau) = \boldsymbol{\Gamma}_T \cdot \boldsymbol{\theta}(t) \quad \text{with} \quad \tau \in [-1, 1], \ t \in [0, T]. \tag{33}
$$

Inserting equation (33) into (31) leads to the representation of a set of Legendre-polynomials $\varphi_T(t)$ that are orthogonal for the interval $[0, T]$, where the index T denotes the transformed interval

$$
\varphi_T(t) = \boldsymbol{P}_T \cdot \boldsymbol{\theta}(t) \quad \text{with} \quad \boldsymbol{P}_T = \boldsymbol{P} \cdot \boldsymbol{\Gamma}_T. \tag{34}
$$

A.4 Approximation of Signals by Orthogonal Functions

Let $f(t)$ be a function, that satisfies the Dirichlet conditions, defined over a finite time interval $t \in [0, T]$. Then, $f(t)$ can be formally expanded as

$$
f(t) = \sum_{i=0}^{\infty} f_{c,i} \, \varphi_{i,T}(t) = \sum_{i=0}^{N} f_{c,i} \, \varphi_{i,T}(t) + e_{sa,f}(t) \tag{35}
$$

with basis functions $\varphi_{i,T}(t)$ and their corresponding coefficients $f_{c,i}$. Neglecting the higher order terms and with it, the error of approximation $e_{sa,f}(t)$, we obtain an approximation

$$
\hat{f}(t) = \sum_{i=0}^{N} f_{c,i} \, \varphi_{i,T}(t) = \boldsymbol{f}_c \, \varphi_{N,T}(t) \approx f(t). \tag{36}
$$

The coefficient vector f_c can be seen as a *generalized spectra* of $f(t)$. For vectors $f(t) = [f_1(t) \ f_2(t) \ \cdots \ f_n(t)]^T$ of functions, the row vectors $f_{c,i}$ form a matrix of coefficients:

$$\hat{f}(t) = F_c \, \varphi_{N,T}(t) = \begin{bmatrix} f_{c,1_0} & f_{c,1_1} & \cdots & f_{c,1_N} \\ f_{c,2_0} & f_{c,2_1} & \cdots & f_{c,2_N} \\ \vdots & \vdots & \ddots & \vdots \\ f_{c,n_0} & f_{c,n_1} & \cdots & f_{c,n_N} \end{bmatrix} \begin{bmatrix} \varphi_{0,T}(t) \\ \varphi_{1,T}(t) \\ \vdots \\ \varphi_{N,T}(t) \end{bmatrix} = \begin{bmatrix} f_{c,1} \\ f_{c,2} \\ \vdots \\ f_{c,n} \end{bmatrix} \varphi_{N,T}(t) .$$

The spectral coefficients can be determined by calculating the inner product between $f_i(t)$ and the basis functions

$$f_{c,i_j} = \frac{2j+1}{T} \int_0^T f_i(t) \, \varphi_{j,T}(t) \ dt = \gamma_{j,T} \int_0^T f_i(t) \, \varphi_{j,T}(t) \ dt . \tag{37}$$

A.5   Approximation of the Integration Operator

Similar to the Laplace transformation, the functional operation of integration can be substituted by a linear operation in the domain of orthogonal functions. The task to integrate a function $f(t)$ can be solved by describing $f(t)$ by $\hat{f}(t)$ of equation (36) and approximating the integration by multiplying the vector of basis functions by the *operational matrix* $E(T)$ *of integration*

$$\int_0^t \hat{f}(\vartheta) d\vartheta = f_c \int_0^t \varphi_{N,T}(\vartheta) \ d\vartheta \approx f_c \, E(T) \, \varphi_{N,T}(t) \quad \text{with} \tag{38}$$

$$E(T) = \frac{T}{2} E_0. \tag{39}$$

On the Causality of Mixed-Signal and Hybrid Models

Jie Liu[1] and Edward A. Lee[2]

[1] Palo Alto Research Center,
Palo Alto, CA 94304
jieliu@parc.com
[2] Department of EECS, University of California
Berkeley, CA 94720
eal@eecs.berkeley.edu

Abstract. This paper extends the application of the Cantor metric as a mathematical tool for defining causalities from pure discrete models to mixed-signal and hybrid models. Using the Cantor metric, which maps timed signals, continuous or discrete, into a metric space, we define causality as contractive properties of processes operating on these signals. Thus, the Banach fixed point theorem can be applies to establish conditions for the existence, uniqueness, and liveness of the behaviors for mixed-signal and hybrid systems. The results also provide theoretical foundations for the simulation technologies for such systems, including the time-marching strategy, evaluation of feedback loops, and the necessity of supporting rollback.

1 Introduction

Engineering systems that exhibit both continuous and discrete dynamics have obtained great attention from many perspectives, such as modeling, simulation, control, and verification. Although continuous-time models and various discrete models themselves are relatively well-understood, the integration of different models imposes new questions on system properties such as definability (existence of behaviors), determinism (uniqueness of the behavior) and liveness (the behavior extends to time ∞). In the context of hybrid automata (e.g. [1], [2]), these questions have been analyzed from a state trajectory point of view [3], [4], [5]. However, due to the explicit representation of continuous and discrete states, the compositions (I/O composition in particular) of hybrid automata can be quite involved, which makes state based analysis techniques not quite scalable to complex systems [6].

Mixed-signal models, on the other hand, characterize that the signals connecting different components of a system may be continuous or discrete. Hybrid automata can be examples for such components. Mixed-signal models hide the implementation detail of each component, thus are widely used as a coordination model in modeling languages and simulation tools, such as VHDL-AMS [7] and Simulink [8].

O. Maler and A. Pnueli (Eds.): HSCC 2003, LNCS 2623, pp. 328–342, 2003.
© Springer-Verlag Berlin Heidelberg 2003

This paper takes a denotational approach and studies the existence, uniqueness, and liveness properties of mixed-signal models in a tagged-signal semantic framework [9], under notions of various causalities defined using the Cantor metric. This framework allows us to apply the Banach fixed point theorem to define the denotational behavior for mixed-signal systems. The strength of this approach is its generality: causalities are defined based on the input and output signals rather than on the implementation of the components, which makes the analysis applicable to a wide variety of models, including pure discrete event models [10], pure continuous-time models, hybrid automata, and practically all timed systems.

A practical implication of the discussion on causalities is the simulation strategies of mixed-signal and hybrid systems. By introducing a notion of ideal ODE solvers, we abstract the simulation of continuous-time systems into a sequence of discrete operations. This discrete abstraction allow us to apply the Banach fixed point iteration to show that the commonly used time-marching simulation strategy is compatible with the denotational semantics, and it yields a correct behavior if there exists one.

The rest of the paper is organized as the following. Section 2 gives an overview of the tagged-signal model, with a focus on a formal definition of mixed-signal processes. Section 3 defines three kinds of causalities and analyzes some typical mixed-signal processes in terms of their causality properties. It gives a sufficient condition for the existence, uniqueness, and liveness of the behaviors of mixed-signal systems using the Banach fixed-point theorem. Section 4 applies the causality concepts in the simulation of mixed-signal and hybrid systems, and shows the rationale of the common simulation strategies.

2   Tagged-Signal Model

The tagged-signal model is a denotational semantics framework for a variety of models of computation [9]. The model looks at the *signals* communicating among a set of components (called *processes*), and defines the behaviors of the processes as the set of signals they constrain.

2.1   Tags and Signals

In the tagged-signal model, an *event* $e = (t, v)$ is a tag-value pair. That is, e is a member of the set $E = T \times V$, where T is a set of tags, and V is a set of values. The set T can be finite, countably infinite, or uncountable; it may also be partially ordered or totally ordered. Here, the *ordering relation* is a reflexive, transitive, and antisymmetric relation, denoted by $\leq$. The order defined on T also defines the order of events in E.

A *signal* s is a set of events. That is, $s \in \wp(E)$, where $\wp(E)$ is the power set (i.e. the set of all subsets) of E. We denote by $S = \wp(E)$ the set of all signals, and by S^N a N tuple of signals. A signal s is called *functional* or *proper* if it is a (possibly partial[1]) function from T to V. That is, if $e_1 = (t, v_1) \in s$ and

---

[1]   A partial function is a function defined only on a subset of its domain.

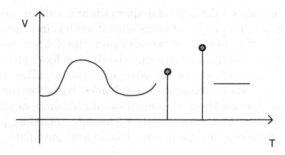

Fig. 1. This is neither a continuous-time signal nor a discrete-event signal.

$e_2 = (t, v_2) \in s$, then $v_1 = v_2$. A proper signal can be written as a function $s : T \to V$, such that if $e = (t, v) \in s$, then $s(t) = v$. A signal s is called *totally ordered* or *ordinary* if it is totally ordered with respect to the ordering relation defined on E. In this paper, we only consider ordinary proper signals.

In the context of mixed-signal and hybrid system modeling, T represents time. More precisely, $T \subseteq R_0^+$, where R_0^+ is the set of all positive real numbers and zero, and T inherits the total ordering and metric from R_0^+. For $T_1 \subseteq T_2 \subseteq T$, T_1 is called the *prefix* of T_2, if for all $t \in T_1$ and for all $t' \in T_2$ but $t' \notin T_1$, the relation $t \leq t'$ holds. If $s_1 : T_1 \to V, s_2 : T_2 \to V$ and $s_1(t) = s_2(t), \forall t \in T_1$, then s_1 is called the prefix of s_2, written as $s_1 \sqsubseteq s_2$. In addition, we introduce an empty value λ to the value set, i.e. $V = R \cup \{\lambda\}$. A metric is not required for the value set. We denote by Λ a signal that contains only empty events, and Λ_N a N-tuple of such signals.

Under these definitions, the difference between various kinds of signals is captured in the topologies of the tag and value sets. A *continuous-time signal* has the entire R_0^+ as its tags and the real numbers R as the value set. A *partial continuous-time signal* is a function defined only on a *connected* prefix of R_0^+. The prefix may be open or closed. In a degenerate case, an event defined on a single point $\{0\}$ is a partial continuous-time signal.

Intuitively, a discrete-event signal only takes non-empty values at a "discrete" subset of T. Formally, a set $T_d \subset T$ is *discrete* if it is *order isomorphic* to a subset of integers [10]. That is, there exists a bijective map between the tags and a subset of integers that preserves the order. By introducing the empty value, a discrete-event signal is defined on the entire tag set R_0^+. A signal s is a *discrete-event signal* if there exists a discrete subset $T_d \subset R_0^+$ such that $\forall t \notin T_d, s(t) = \lambda$. Note that the signal shown in Figure1 is neither a continuous-time signal nor a discrete-event signal.

A continuous-time signal is not necessarily a *continuous signal*, which, in addition to having a connected tag set, is also a *continuous function* from T to R. A signal s on T is *piecewise continuous*, if there exist a discrete set $T_d \subset T$, such that s is continuous on $T - T_d$ and right continuous on T_d.

2.2 Continuous, Discrete, and Mixed-Signal Processes

From a denotational point of view, a *process* P is a subset of S^N for some N. A particular signal tuple $s \in S^N$ is said to *satisfy* the process if $s \in P$. Thus, a process is a set of possible behaviors. Intuitively, the implementation of a process P has N *ports* and S^N are all possible signals on these ports. It is useful in the context of this paper to have the notions of inputs and outputs of processes, depending on whether the process constrains the signal. An input to a process $P \subseteq S^N$ is an external constraint $A \subseteq S^N$ such that $A \cap P$ is the total set of acceptable behaviors under that input. A process is *functional* if the output signals are given as a function of the input signals.

Viewing processes as sets of signal is a powerful concept, such that the composition of processes are simply reordering and projections of signal tuples, and the composed behaviors are the intersection of component process behaviors. A composition of processes is *definable* if the behavior intersection is not empty; and it is *deterministic* if the behavior intersection has exactly zero or one element. Figure 2 shows the serial, serial/parallel, parallel, and feedback compositions of two processes P_1 and P_2. Connecting the output of one process to the input of another imposes a constraint that the two signal to be the same. A full discussion of process composition is out of the scope of this paper, and can be found in [9].

We further distinguish the types of processes by the signals they contain. A process $P \subseteq S^N$ is *piecewise-continuous* (or a *continuous process*, in short) if all S in S^N are (possibly partial) piecewise-continuous signals. Similarly, P is a *discrete-event process* (or, a *discrete process*, in short) if all S in the tuple are discrete-event signals. Some processes may contain both piecewise-continuous and discrete-event signals in their behavior. Such processes are called *mixed-signal processes*. A mixed-signal system is a composition of processes in S^N, such that there exists N_C, N_D, and $S^N = S^{N_C} \times S^{N_D}$, where S^{N_C} is a tuple of piecewise-continuous signals and S^{N_D} is a tuple of discrete-event signals.

For example, an integrator is a continuous process. It takes an integrable signal as input and produces an integrable output signal whose derivative is the input signal almost everywhere. An ordinary differential system (ODS),

$$\dot{x} = f(x, u, t) \tag{1}$$
$$y = g(x, u, t) \tag{2}$$
$$x(0) = x_0 \tag{3}$$

is also a continuous process, where u is the input signal, y is the output signal, and x is the state variable. There are many examples of discrete processes. A time delay process delays all events in the input signal with a specific amount of time. An I/O automaton can be viewed as a discrete process that does not introduce delays from input events to output events. Timed I/O automata, however, are discrete processes that manipulate both values and tags in the signals.

Event generators are processes that have at least one continuous-time input signal and discrete-event output signals. Waveform generators converts discrete-event input signals to (usually piecewise) continuous output signals. They are examples of mixed-signal processes. Hybrid automata, in their most general forms,

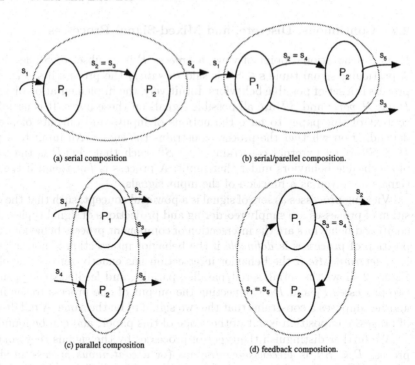

(a) serial composition

(b) serial/parellel composition.

(c) parallel composition

(d) feedback composition.

Fig. 2. Two processes P_1, P_2 and their compositions. I/O composition imposes additional constraints on the possible behaviors of the processes, in the sense that the signals on the connected arcs have to be the same.

can have both piecewise-continuous and discrete-event inputs and outputs, thus are mixed-signal processes.

Notice that these definitions classify continuous and discrete processes by the signals they exhibit, rather than their internal implementation. A discrete process may be implemented internally by continuous-time differential equations with event detection and waveform generation mechanisms. A hybrid automata may only expose piecewise-continuous signals at its interface, in which case, it is a continuous process.

3   Causality

Using the tagged-signal model allows us to study system behaviors as signals in a signal space, in particular, a signal space with metric.

3.1   Cantor Metric and Causality

The Cantor metric is a metric that compares the distance among timed signals. Consider a N tuple of (mixed) signals S^N defined on the tag set $T \subseteq R_0^+$. For

$\mathbf{s}, \mathbf{s}' \in S^N$, $\mathbf{s}(t) = [(t, v_1), ..., (t, v_N)]^\top$ and $\mathbf{s}'(t) = [(t, v_1'), ..., (t, v_N')]^\top$, we say that $\mathbf{s}(t) \neq \mathbf{s}'(t)$ if $\exists i \in \{1, ...N\}$, s.t., $v_i \neq v_i'$.

Definition 1. *For two signals* $\mathbf{s}, \mathbf{s}' \in S^N$, *the* Cantor metric *defines the distance between* $\mathbf{s}, \mathbf{s}'$ *as:*

$$d(\mathbf{s}, \mathbf{s}') = \sup\{\frac{1}{2^t}|\mathbf{s}(t) \neq \mathbf{s}'(t)\} \tag{4}$$

It is easy to check that this is indeed a metric, satisfying $d(\mathbf{s}, \mathbf{s}') \geq 0$, $d(\mathbf{s}, \mathbf{s}) = 0$, $d(\mathbf{s}, \mathbf{s}') = d(\mathbf{s}', \mathbf{s})$, and the triangle inequality. In fact, it is an *ultrametric*, satisfying a stronger form of the triangle inequality:

$$d(\mathbf{s}, \mathbf{s}'') \leq \max(d(\mathbf{s}, \mathbf{s}'), d(\mathbf{s}', \mathbf{s}'')). \tag{5}$$

Under this metric, two signals are *close* if they agree over a great amount of time. It is also easy to verify that under the Cantor metric, the space of mixed signals is *complete*, *i.e.* all Cauchy sequences of mixed signals converge to a mixed signal.

We use the Cantor metric to define three increasingly stronger notions of causality on functional processes:

Definition 2. *A functional process* $P : S^I \to S^O$ *is* causal *if for all* $\mathbf{s}, \mathbf{s}' \in S^I$,

$$d(P(\mathbf{s}), P(\mathbf{s}')) \leq d(\mathbf{s}, \mathbf{s}'). \tag{6}$$

Definition 3. *A functional process* $P : S^I \to S^O$ *is* strictly causal *if for all* $\mathbf{s}, \mathbf{s}' \in S^I$,

$$d(P(\mathbf{s}), P(\mathbf{s}')) < d(\mathbf{s}, \mathbf{s}'). \tag{7}$$

Definition 4. *A functional process* $P : S^I \to S^O$ *is* δ-causal *if for all* $\mathbf{s}, \mathbf{s}' \in S^I$, *there exists* $0 \leq \delta < 1$, *s.t.*

$$d(P(\mathbf{s}), P(\mathbf{s}')) \leq \delta \cdot d(\mathbf{s}, \mathbf{s}'). \tag{8}$$

Note that these definitions are compatible with but more precise than the common understanding of causality, which is usually stated as "the output of a process at time t should not depend on inputs that are later than t."

3.2 Causality of Continuous, Discrete, and Mixed-Signal Processes

In this section, we give some examples of continuous, discrete, and mixed-signal processes, and analyze their causality properties. Unless otherwise stated, throughout this section, we assume that P is a functional process $P : S^I \to S^O$ and $\mathbf{s}, \mathbf{s}' \in S^I$.

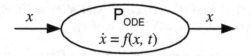

Fig. 3. An ordinary differential equation as a process P_{ODE}.

Memoryless Processes. Memoryless processes are point-wise operators on input signals. That is, if P is memoryless and $\mathbf{s}(t) = \mathbf{s}'(t)$, then $P(\mathbf{s}(t)) = P(\mathbf{s}'(t))$, regardless of the other events in $\mathbf{s}$ and $\mathbf{s}'$. Thus, a memoryless process is causal but usually not strictly causal or δ-causal.

Integrators. An integrator is a continuous process that takes integrable piecewise-continuous signals as input and produces a continuous signal as output. Let u be an input signal and x be the corresponding output signal, then an integrator implements:

$$x(t) = x(0) + \int_0^t u(\tau)d\tau \qquad (9)$$

In the theory of Lebesgue integration (see e.g. [11]), for any $t \in T$, $u(t)$ has measure 0, thus, $x(t)$ depends only on $u[0,t)$ but not on $u(t)$. For two inputs u and u', satisfying $u(\tau) = u'(\tau), \forall \tau \in [0,t)$, the outputs of the integrator satisfies $x(\tau) = x'(\tau), \forall \tau \in [0,t]$, even when $u(\tau) \neq u'(\tau)$. However, this useful insight does not directly improve the causality of the integrator. In fact, an integrator is not strictly causal, since $d(x,x') = d(u,u')$.

Ordinary Differential Equations. An ordinary differential equation (ODE)

$$\dot{x} = f(x,t), \; x(0) = x_0 \qquad (10)$$

can be viewed as a process P_{ODE} mapping X, the set of all partial and complete solutions of (10), to X, as shown in Figure 3. Formally, $X = \{x[0,t_f]|t_f \in T$, and x satisfies the ODE in interval $[0,t_f]\}$. We define that the degenerate partial continuous-time signal $(0,x_0) \in X$. So, X is never empty.

Let M be the dimension of x, and $x, x' \in X$ be two inputs to P_{ODE} with $d(x,x') = 1/2^\tau$, then, by continuity, $x(\tau) = x'(\tau)$. The local existence and uniqueness theorem of ODE (see, e.g. [12]) states that if there exists $\sigma > \tau$ and $L, r > 0$, such that $f(x,t)$ satisfies the local Lipschitz condition:

$$\|f(u,t) - f(v,t)\| \leq L\|u-v\|, \qquad (11)$$

for all $u, v \in \{z \in R^M|\; \|z - x(\tau)\| \leq r\}$ and for all $t \in [\tau,\sigma]$, then, there exists $\tau < \omega \leq \sigma$ such that the ODE (10) has a unique solution on $[\tau,\omega]$. That is, P_{ODE} extends the agreement of the partial solution by $\omega - \tau$ amount, $i.e.$ P_{ODE} is strictly causal under the local Lipschitz condition with $d(P_{ODE}(x), P_{ODE}(x')) = 1/2^\omega < d(x,x')$.

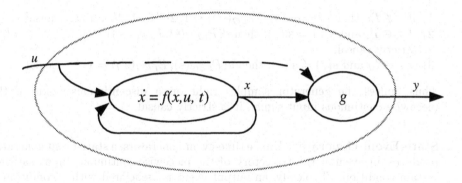

Fig. 4. An ordinary differential system.

In addition, if the ODE satisfies global Lipschitz condition, such that there is a smallest $\Delta > 0$ and P_{ODE} extends the solution for at least Δ amount in time for any inputs, then P_{ODE} is δ-causal, with $\delta = 1/2^{\Delta}$. The extension from the local solution to the global solution will be further discussed in section 3.3.

An ODS (1)-(3) can be viewed as a composition of an ODE process with input and a memoryless output map process, g, as shown in Figure 4.

If u is piecewise continuous and f is globally Lipschitz on its first argument, the existence and uniqueness theorem of ODE guarantees that the ODE (1) and (3) has a unique solution. It is causal from u to x. Similar to the integrator case, $x(t)$ does not depend on $u(t)$, for any $t \in R_0^+$. But this does not directly improve the causality. The memoryless output map (2) is also causal. Thus, an ordinary differential system is causal under the global Lipschitz condition. Note that if the output map g does not have u as its direct input, then $y(t)$ does not directly depend on $u(t)$.

Time-Event Generators. Time-event generators take piecewise-continuous input signals and generate discrete events at a *predefined* set of discrete time instants. Given a discrete set of time points $T_d = \{t_1, t_2, ...\} \subset T$, a time-event generator $P_{TEG} : S^I \to S^O$ is a process that for a piecewise-continuous input $s \in S^I$,

$$P_{TEG}(s)(t) = \begin{cases} G(s[0, T_d]) & \text{if } t \in T_d \\ \lambda & \text{otherwise} \end{cases} \tag{12}$$

where $G(s[0, T_d])$ is a function of the input signal up to time T_d.

Typically, a time-event generator omits some values in the input signal, and replace them with the empty value λ. Take a periodic sampler as an example, where T_d contains a set of equidistance points. Let ts be the sampling period. Suppose that for two inputs $s, s' \in S^I$, $d(s, s') = 1/2^\tau$, we examine the distance of the output signals. Let $\lceil \tau \rceil$ be the smallest element in T_d that is greater than or equal to τ. There are three cases:

1) if $\tau \notin T_d$, then $d(P_{TEG}(\mathbf{s}), P_{TEG}(\mathbf{s}')) \leq 1/2^{\lceil \tau \rceil} < 1/2^{\tau}$, strictly causal.
2) if $\tau \in T_d$ and $\mathbf{s}(\tau) = \mathbf{s}'(\tau)$, then $d(P_{TEG}(\mathbf{s}), P_{TEG}(\mathbf{s}')) \leq 1/2^{(\tau+ts)} < 1/2^{\tau}$, strictly causal.
3) if $\tau \in T_d$ and $\mathbf{s}(\tau) \neq \mathbf{s}'(\tau)$, then $d(P_{TEG}(\mathbf{s}), P_{TEG}(\mathbf{s}')) = 1/2^{\tau}$, causal.

Thus, unless the generator samples right on a discontinuous point of the piecewise-continuous input signal, it is strictly causal.

State-Event Generator. Unlike time-event generators, a state-event generator produces an event if the trajectory of the piecewise-continuous input satisfies certain conditions. Typically, an output event is associated with a condition h and a value assignment rule r. For an input signal $\mathbf{s} \in S^I$, a condition $h(\mathbf{s}) = 0$ defines a surface in the value space R^I. A discrete event $e = (\tau, v)$ is in the output of a state-event generator if $h(\mathbf{s}(\tau)) = 0$ and there exists a nonempty open interval (τ', τ) such that $h(\mathbf{s}(t)) \neq 0$, for $t \in (\tau', \tau)$. The assignment r defines the value of e, *i.e.* $v = r(\mathbf{s}[0, \tau])$. We call this type of event *zero-reaching event*. Similar to time-event generators, if at the event occurrence time the input signal $\mathbf{s}$ is continuous, the process is strictly causal. Otherwise, the process is simply causal.

Sometimes, it is useful to specify an event condition that also takes the future trajectory into account. For example, a *transverse event* requires that the input not stay on the surface $h(\mathbf{s}) = 0$ after reaching the surface [13]. That is, there also exists an open interval (τ, τ''), s.t. $h(\mathbf{s}(t)) \neq 0$, for $t \in (\tau, \tau'')$. This includes *zero-crossing events* which require that the signal $\mathbf{s}$ be on two different sides of the surface before and after the event occurrence. It also includes *zero-touching events* which require that the signal $\mathbf{s}$ be on the same side of the surface before and after the event occurrence. Although transverse events may seem non-causal under this description, there are ways to define them using zero-reaching condition and the Lie derivatives if at the event occurrence point the input signal and the event surface are analytic [13].

Zero-Order Hold. A zero-order hold (ZOH) process is one of the most primitive type of waveform generators. Given a discrete-event signal $s_d = \{(t_1, v_1), (t_2, v_2), ...\}$, and an initial value v_0, a zero-order hold process outputs a unique continuous-time extension of s_d, denoted by $zoh\langle s_d, v_0 \rangle$, such that $zoh\langle s_d, v_0 \rangle(t) = v_i$, for $t_i \leq t < t_{i+1}$ and $t_0 = 0$. Obviously, $zoh\langle s_d, v_0 \rangle$ is a piecewise-continuous signal, and a zero-order hold process is causal but not strictly causal.

Sampled Differential Systems. A sampled differential system, as studied in discrete-time systems, is a composition of ZOH processes, ordinary differential systems, and periodic samplers, as shown in Figure 5. Here we assume that the input v and the output z have the same set of tags T_d, and that u does not feed directly into the output map g.

Let t_s be the sampling period, and $0 \in T_d$. We order the elements in $T_d = \{t_0, t_1, ...\}$ such that $t_0 = 0$ and $t_{k+1} - t_k = t_s$ for $k \geq 0$. Let $v, v' \in S^I$ be two

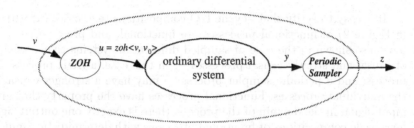

Fig. 5. A sampled differential system provides a discrete interface at input v and output z. The ordinary differential system process may be internally implemented by processes shown in Figure 4.

input signals to the sampled differential system, and assume $d(v, v') = 1/2^\tau \neq 0$. Then, there must exist some index k such that $\tau = t_k \in T_d$. Since the ZOH process is causal, $d(u, u') = 1/2^\tau$. However, for a differential system, $x(\tau) = x'(\tau)$ and $y(\tau) = y'(\tau)$, even though $u(\tau) \neq u'(\tau)$. As the periodic sampler samples at τ, the output $z(\tau) = z'(\tau)$. This equality will hold until the next sampling time t_{k+1}, i.e. $d(z, z') = 1/2^{t_{k+1}}$. Thus, from the input/output point of view, a sampled differential system is δ-causal, with $\delta = 1/2^{t_s}$.

Hybrid Automata. In the formalism of hybrid automata [1], there is a set of discrete states, Σ, a set of continuous state variables X. At each discrete state in Σ, the automaton is refined into an ordinary differential system on some state variables in X. There are transitions among the discrete states. A hybrid automaton may have both continuous and discrete inputs and outputs. A discrete state σ may have *invariants* that specify the condition that the system can stay in σ. If a invariant is violated, a discrete transition must be taken. A transition may have *guards* and *actions*. The guards may depend on the discrete and continuous input signal values and specify the conditions that the transition may be taken. The actions is performed when the transition is taken, and may include producing discrete events and resetting the values of the continuous state variables in the destination discrete state.

Notice that in a hybrid automaton model, there is no mechanism to directly specify time delays from input events to output events. A transition is instantaneous. If a reachable transition is triggered by an input event, and the corresponding action produces an output event, then the hybrid automaton is causal. The only way to introduce strict causality in a hybrid automaton is to ensure that the automaton stays in a discrete state for some of time, so that the differential system that refines the discrete state becomes effective, similarly for δ-causality.

3.3   Existence, Uniqueness, and Liveness

Causality plays a central role in the existence, uniqueness, and liveness of behaviors of mixed-signal systems.

It is easy to verify that acyclic I/O compositions (e.g. cases (a), (b), and (c) in Figure 2) of functional processes are functional, and preserve causality. We have also shown in the case of sampled differential systems that a composition of causal and strictly causal processes — in this case, a ZOH process, an ODS process, and a periodic sampler process — may have a stronger causality than the individual processes. Functional processes have the property that given any input signal in the domain of the process, there is exactly one output signal. So, for acyclic compositions of functional processes with deterministic input signals, a behavior exists and is unique.

Feedback compositions are more complicated. Through sorting and projection of signals in the signal tuples S^N, a mixed-signal system with feedback can be viewed as a function $F : S^N \to S^N$. It is not obvious whether there exists any $s \in S^N$, such that $F(s) = s$ (*existence*); if such s exists, whether it is unique (*uniqueness*); and whether the signal is defined on the entire R_0^+ (*liveness*). One example of mixed-signal systems lacking the liveness property is the *Zeno phenomena* where in a finite time interval there can be an infinite number of discrete events.

From the definitions, the forms of causality are "contraction" relations among input and output signals in a metric space, thus the Banach fixed point theorem may ensure that a system with feedback loops has a unique behavior under certain conditions. The Banach fixed point theorem states that for S^N complete, (which is true for mixed-signal systems), if F is δ-causal, then there is exactly one $s \in S^N$ such that $F(s) = s$. This signal is called a *fixed point*. Moreover, the theorem also gives a constructive algorithm to find the fixed point. Given s_0 in the domain of F, s is the limit of the sequence:

$$s_1 = F(s_0), s_2 = F(s_1), s_3 = F(s_2), ... \tag{13}$$

Thus, the theorem gives a sufficient condition for existence and uniqueness of the behavior of a mixed-signal system.

A direct application of the theorem to ordinary differential equations is the obtainment of global unique solution under the global Lipschitz condition. Starting with $s_0 = \{(0, x_0)\}$, a partial continuous signal in the solution space, each application of the Banach fixed-point iteration corresponds to extending the local solution for at least Δ amount of time into the future:

$$s_0 \sqsubseteq s_1 \sqsubseteq s_2 \sqsubseteq ... \tag{14}$$

Since the sequence of solutions converges, it must embeds a Cauchy sequence, *i.e.* $d(s_M, s_K) \to 0$ as $M > K \to \infty$. Thus, the solution is unique on $[0, \infty)$. Similar analysis can be applied to mixed-signal systems, where the initial signal is $\Lambda_{N_D} \times \{(0, x_0)\}$, i.e. empty discrete events and the initial values for continuous state variables.

The δ-causality requirement is fairly strong. A closely related theorem (see e.g. [14], chapter 4) states that if F is strictly causal and S^N is complete, then there is at most one fixed point for F. Thus, strict causality guarantees determinism, but does not ensure that a feedback system has a behavior, nor is it enough to prevent Zeno phenomena. When we weaken the condition further, the simple causality does not even provide determinism.

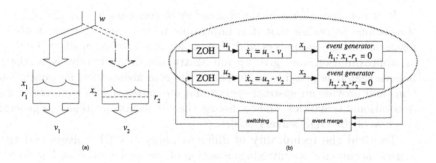

Fig. 6. The two-tank problem and its mixed-signal model.

The δ-causality requirement is also tight, in the sense that violation of this condition may introduce Zeno phenomena or non-determinism. For example, the two-tank problem is a classical hybrid system with a Zeno execution [15]. As shown in Figure 6 (a), x_i denotes the water level in tank $i \in \{1, 2\}$, and $v_i > 0$ is the constant flow of water out of tank i. Let w be the constant flow of water into the system, delegated exclusively to either tank 1 or tank 2, controlled by a switch. Let r_i be the reference level of tank i, such that if $x_i = v_i$, an alarm will be generated requesting the in-flow water to be switched to tank i. The switching logic is that whenever it receives an alarm, the in-flow water is directed to the requested water tank instantaneously. We further assume that $x_i(0) > r_i$, for $i = 1, 2$, that the in-flow water rate satisfies $v_i < w < v_1 + v_2$, and that it is initially directed to tank 1. A mixed-signal model of this system is shown in Figure 6(b).

Applying similar analysis as in section 3.2, the composition of the ZOH, the ordinary differential system modeling the water tank, and the zero-reaching event generator is a strictly causal process. The merge of discrete events is also a causal process [10]. Thus, if the switching process does not introduce any time delay, then the entire system is a feedback composition of a strictly causal process. In fact, the system exhibits Zeno behavior that the in-flow water will switch between the two water tanks infinitely many times within a finite time interval. This Zeno phenomenon will not appear if the composition is δ-causal: for example, if the switching of in-flow water from one tank to another always takes at least Δ amount of time, or if the water tank part of the system (processes within the circle in Figure 6) is implemented as a sampled differential system instead of using state-event detections.

4   Simulation Strategies

Existence and uniqueness theorems give a denotation of a system behavior. It is of practical importance to compute the behavior operationally, and to answer questions such as whether the operational semantics is a precise establishment of the denotational semantics (a.k.a. the *full abstraction* problem), and if not, how close they are.

It is not uncommon in the discussion of continuous-time and mixed-signal simulations to realize that it is impossible to represent continuous-time waveforms in digital computers and that a numerical solution of an ODE is only an approximation, and give up full abstraction immediately. Nevertheless, we believe that it is possible to develop a discrete abstraction for continuous systems and provide an *abstract operational semantics* that is compatible with the denotational semantics, and to discuss the simulation strategies in general, irrespective of the ODE solvers used.

To avoid the technicality of different kinds of ODE solvers and their numerical accuracies, we introduce a notion of ideal ODE solvers. For an ordinary differential system (1), given a known point $x(t)$ on the trajectory, a time instant $t' > t$, such that the ODE satisfies the Lipschitz condition in $[t, t']$, and known input $u[t, t')$, an *ideal ODE solver* gives the exact value of $x(t')$. So, an ideal ODE solver operates discretely. Instead of trying to represent the waveform on the entire time interval, it only computes the solution at the end point of that interval. The notion of ideal ODE solvers is not completely unrealistic. Certain kinds of ODEs can be solved analytically, such that an exact solution can be obtained on any given time instant, as long as we ignore the error of representing a real number by a floating point number, say, in double precision. A degenerate form of this concept, applying to the ODE, $\dot{x} = 1$, has been shown useful in the verification of timed automata [1]. Practical numerical ODE solvers can only give an approximation of $x(t')$, but they operate in the same discrete way as an ideal ODE solver.

Under this abstraction, the continuous-time simulation problem becomes how to find the sequence of time points, such that conditions for the uniqueness of solution are not violated in each interval. This is by no means a trivial problem, especially when the continuous dynamics interacts with discrete-event processes. The causality properties of mixed-signal processes contributes to the understanding of this abstract operational semantics through the following observations.

Observation 1 *For causal functional processes, if the input is the prefix of the potentially infinite-length input signal up to time t, then the output is the prefix of the final output signal up to at least time t.*

In most mixed-signal and hybrid system modeling environments, the processes are implemented as components with states and firings, where the state of a component at time t summaries all the inputs before time t, and the firing of a component at time t computes the new state and the output of the component at some $t' \geq t$. Causality makes "state" a well-define notion. Applying Observation 1 iteratively implies that a mixed-signal system can be simulated by computing partial behaviors chronologically, a *time-marching* strategy adopted by most mixed-signal and hybrid system simulators. That is, the simulator maintains a global, monotonically increasing notion of time, and computes the behavior of the system "step-by-step." This strategy essentially implements the constructive procedure in the Banach fixed point theorem, and will converge, in the sense of the Cantor metric, to the denotational behavior if there is one. Thus, by using an ideal ODE solver, we still obtain full abstraction.

Observation 2 *For ODS* (1) - (3) *satisfying the Lipschitz condition in* $[t, t']$, *if the values* $x(t)$ *of the state variables at time t are known, and the input* $u[t, t')$ *is known, then an ideal ODE solver can compute* $x(t')$.

The increase of the global notion of time from one Banach fixed point iteration to the next corresponds to the step sizes in simulations. A key issue of simulating continuous parts of a mixed-signal system is find the right t'. Under the assumption of an ideal ODE solver, for a continuous-time system, it is essential that the ODE satisfies the local Lipschitz condition in every such step. So, each simulation step size should be within the value implied by the Lipschitz condition. In numerical ODE solvers, this may be approximated by monitoring local errors or the numerical convergence of integration methods. When the system also contains discrete dynamics, discrete events may effect the local Lipschitz conditions. In practice, breakpoints can be introduced to explicitly represent the time instants when the local Lipschitz conditions are violated, and require that no ODE solving steps go across break points [16].

The operation of an ideal ODE solver also requires it to know the input $u[t, t')$ when it starts computing at time t. In the interaction of continuous and discrete dynamics, $u[t, t')$ may be generated from future discrete events, which may not be all known at time t. A practical solution for this problem is to perform optimistic execution [16], where the simulator assumes that the inputs are fully predictable and runs ahead of the global time. If the prediction is wrong, the simulator rolls back to a previous state and recomputes.

Observation 3 *For* δ-*causal processes, strictly causal processes, and indirect causal processes (i.e. causal processes with no direct I/O dependencies, for example, continuous or mixed-signal processes that have at least one differential equation type of relation from the input to the output), the output at time t does not directly depend on the input at t.*

This implies that we can schedule the execution order for feedback loops. That is, at time t, we can evaluate a feedback loop by first letting the δ-causal, strictly causal, and indirect causal processes to produce their outputs at t. (These outputs can be empty events.) Then, evaluate other processes in their I/O dependency order.

As a summary, even with ideal ODE solvers, a correct mixed-signal simulator still needs to support breakpoint, rollback, and proper managing of time progression. Once a full abstraction is established through ideal ODE solvers, further approximation are required when using numerical ODE solvers.

5   Conclusion

In this paper, the causality issues in mixed-signal and hybrid systems are studied as part of their denotational semantics. Using the Cantor metric, we give precise definitions of causality, strictly causality, and δ-causality in mixed-signal systems. With these definitions, we apply the Banach fixed point theorem to define the denotational behavior for these systems. These causality results validate the common mixed-signal and hybrid system simulation techniques, including the time-marching strategy, evaluation of feedback loops, step size control, and the necessity of supporting rollback.

Acknowledgments. This research is supported in part by the Ptolemy project, which is supported by DARPA/ITO, the State of California MICRO program, and the following companies: Agilent, Cadence Design Systems, Hitachi, and Philips.

References

1. Henzinger, T.A.: The theory of hybrid automata. In: Proceedings of the 11th Annual Symposium on Logic in Computer Science (LICS). IEEE Computer Society Press (1996) 278–292
2. Bornot, S., Sifakis, J.: On the composition of hybrid systems. In: Hybrid Systems: Computation and Control, HSCC'98, Berkeley, CA, April, 1998. Volume 1386 of Lecture Notes in Computer Science. Springer (1998) 49–63
3. Lygeros, J., Johansson, K.H., Simic, S.N., Zhang, J., Sastry, S.: Dynamical properties of hybrid automata. IEEE Transactions on Automatic Control **48** (2003) ,to appear.
4. van der Schaft, A., Schumacher, J.: Complementarity modeling of hybrid systems. IEEE Transactions on Automatic Control **43** (1998) 483–490
5. Lemmon, M.: On the existence of solutions to controlled hybrid automata. In: Hybrid Systems: Computation and Control, HSCC'00, Pittsburgh, PA, USA, March, 2000. Volume 1790 of Lecture Notes in Computer Science. Springer (2000) 229–242
6. Benveniste, A.: Compositional and uniform modeling of hybrid systems. IEEE Transactions on Automatic Control **43** (1998) 579–584
7. IEEE 1076.1 Working Group: VHDL 1076.1-1999: Analog and mixed-signal extensions to VHDL (1999)
8. Harman, T.L., Dabney, J.B.: Mastering Simulink 4. Prentice Hall (2001)
9. Lee, E.A., Sangiovanni-Vincentelli, A.: A framework for comparing models of computation. IEEE Transactions on CAD **17** (1998) 1217–1229
10. Lee, E.A.: Modeling concurrent real-time processes using discrete events. Annals of Software Engineering **7** (1999) 25–45
11. Royden, H.: Real Analysis. 3rd edn. Prentice Hall, Englewood Cliffs, NJ (1988)
12. Sastry, S.: Nonlinear Systems, Analysis, Stability and Control. Springer-Verlag (1999)
13. Zhang, J., Johansson, K.H., Lygeros, J., Sastry, S.: Dynamical systems revisited: Hybrid systems with Zeno executions. In Krogh, B., Lynch, N., eds.: Hybrid Systems: Computation and Control, LNCS 1790. Springer-Verlag (2000)
14. Bryant, V.: Metric Spaces. Cambridge University Press (1985)
15. Johansson, K., Egerstedt, M., Lygeros, J., Sastry, S.: On the regularization of Zeno hybrid automata. Systems and Control Letters **38** (1999) 141–150
16. Liu, J., Lee, E.A.: Component-based hierarchical modeling of systems with continuous and discrete dynamics,. In: IEEE Symposium on Computer-Aided Control System Design (CACSD'00), Anchorage, Alaska, USA. (2000) 95–100

Safety Verification of Model Helicopter Controller Using Hybrid Input/Output Automata*

Sayan Mitra[1], Yong Wang[2], Nancy Lynch[1], and Eric Feron[2]

[1] MIT Laboratory for Computer Science,
200 Technology Square, Cambridge, MA 02139
{mitras,lynch}@theory.lcs.mit.edu,
[2] MIT Laboratory for Information and Decision Systems,
77 Massachusetts Avenue, Cambridge, MA 02139
{y_wang,feron}@mit.edu

Abstract. This paper presents an application of the Hybrid I/O Automaton (HIOA) framework [12] in verifying a realistic hybrid system. A supervisory pitch controller for a model helicopter system is designed and then verified. The design of the supervisor is limited by the actuator bandwidth, the sensor inaccuracies, and the sampling rates. Verification is carried out by induction over the length of an execution of the composed system automaton. The HIOA model makes the inductive proofs tractable by decomposing them into independent discrete and continuous parts. The paper also presents a set of language constructs for specifying hybrid I/O automata.

1 Introduction

Formal verification of hybrid systems is a hard problem. It has been shown that checking reachability for even a simple class of hybrid automata is undecidable [7]. Algorithmic verification techniques have been developed for smaller subclasses of hybrid automata [1], but these subclasses are too weak to model realistic hybrid systems. Languages and tools [6] developed for algorithmic verification are also inadequate for describing general hybrid systems. More recently, algorithms for overapproximating the unsafe sets of general hybrid systems have been developed [3], but applying these algorithms to systems with high dimensionality remain a challenging problem.

An alternative to algorithmic verification is to derive the desired properties of an automaton by induction over the length of its executions. The Hybrid Input/Output Automaton (HIOA) model [13,14,12] model has been developed for this purpose; see [8,19,11] for related earlier works. Being more expressive, HIOA can model a larger class of hybrid systems. The inductive proofs are tractable in this model because they are decomposed into independent discrete

---

* Funding for this research has been provided by AFRL contract F33615-01-C-1850 and DARPA/AFOSR MURI Award F49620-02-1-0325

O. Maler and A. Pnueli (Eds.): HSCC 2003, LNCS 2623, pp. 343–358, 2003.

and continuous parts. Further, owing to the assertional style of proving the invariants, it will be possible to partially automate the proofs using mechanical theorem provers.

This paper presents the verification of a supervisory controller of a model helicopter system using the HIOA framework. The helicopter system (Figure 1), manufactured by Quanser [17], is driven by two rotors mounted at the two ends of its frame. The frame is suspended from an instrumented joint mounted at the end of a long arm. The arm is gimbaled on another instrumented joint and is free to pitch and yaw, giving the helicopter three degrees of freedom. The rotor inputs are either controlled by the user with a joystick, or by controllers designed by the user. Students of Aeronautics and Astronautics at MIT experiment with these systems by writing different controllers which often tend to damage the equipment by pitching the helicopter too high or too low. This is also a hazard for the users, and therefore the safety of the system is important.

The supervisory controller is designed to prevent the helicopter from reaching unsafe states. It periodically observes the position and the velocity of the helicopter and overrides the user controller by conservatively estimating the worst that might happen if the latter is allowed to remain in control. The design of the supervisor is limited by the actuator bandwidth, the sampling rate, and sensor inaccuracies. Safety of the supervisor is verified by modeling each component of the system as a hybrid I/O automaton, and proving a set of invariants for the composed system automaton.

This paper also describes a specification language for HIOA. In this language discrete transitions of hybrid I/O automata are specified in the usual precondition-effect style, and the continuous evolution is written in terms of constrained "state-space" models called activities. At present we have tool support for IOA [5], a formal language for distributed systems, which is similar to HIOA without the continuous part. We intend to extend the IOA Toolkit for checking HIOA code, by adding the language constructs for the continuous part. We are also working on building a theorem prover interface for HIOA.

Fig. 1. Helicopter model with three degrees of freedom.

The contributions of this paper are: (1) demonstration of a realistic application of the hybrid I/O automata based verification methodology, (2) design of the supervisory controller which ensures safety of the Quanser helicopter system along the pitch axis, and (3) a set of language constructs for specifying hybrid I/O automata.

In Section 2 we review the hybrid I/O automata model and describe the specification language. We present the HIOA models of the system components and the supervisor in Sections 3 and 4 respectively. Due to limited space we present brief proof sketches for the important invariants required for proving safety of the system in Section 5. The full version of the paper with complete proofs appears as a technical report [16]. Concluding remarks and future directions for research are discussed in Section 6.

2   Hybrid I/O Automata

A brief review of the HIOA model is presented in this section. For a complete discussion refer to [12]. Earlier versions of the model appeared in [13] and [14].

We introduce some notations used in the rest of the paper. If f is a function and S is a set then we write $f \lceil S$ for the function g with $dom(g) = dom(f) \cap S$ such that for every $c \in dom(g)$, $g(c) = f(c)$. If also the range of f is a set of functions then we write $f \downarrow S$ for the function g with $dom(g) = dom(f)$ such that $g(c) = f(c) \lceil S$ for every $c \in dom(g)$.

2.1   The HIOA Model

A hybrid I/O automaton captures the hybrid behavior of a system in terms of discrete transitions and continuous evolution of its state variables. Let V be the set of variables of automaton $\mathcal{A}$. Each $v \in V$ is associated with a *(static) type* defining the set of values v can assume. A *valuation* **v** for V is a function that associates each variable $v \in V$ to a value in $type(v)$. A trajectory τ of V is defined as a mapping $\tau : J \to val(V)$ where J is a left closed interval of time. If J is right closed then τ is said to be *closed* and its *limit time* is the supremum of the domain of τ, also written as $\tau.ltime$. Each variable $v \in V$ is also associated with a *dynamic type* (or *dtype*) which is the set of trajectories that v may follow.

A hybrid I/O automaton $\mathcal{A}$ consists of : (1) a set V of variables, partitioned into *internal* X, *input* U, and *output variables* Y. The internal variables are also called state variables. $Z \triangleq X \cup Y$ is the set of *locally controlled or local variables*. (2) a set A of actions , partitioned into *internal* H, *input* I, and *output actions* O. (3) a set of states $Q \subseteq val(X)$, (4) a non-empty set of *start states* $\Theta \subseteq Q$, (5) a set of *discrete transitions* $\mathcal{D} \subseteq Q \times A \times Q$. A transition $(\mathbf{x}, a, \mathbf{x}') \in \mathcal{D}$ is written in short as $\mathbf{x} \xrightarrow{a}_\mathcal{A} \mathbf{x}'$. (6) a set of *trajectories* $\mathcal{T}$ for V, such that for every trajectory τ in $\mathcal{T}$, and for every $t \in \tau.dom$, $\tau(t).X \in Q$. It is required that $\mathcal{T}$ is closed under prefix, suffix, and concatenation. The first state $\tau(0).X$ of trajectory is denoted by $\tau.fstate$. If $\tau.dom$ is finite then $\tau.lstate = \tau(\tau.ltime).X$.

In addition, a hybrid I/O automaton also satisfies: (1) the input action enabling property, which prevents it from blocking any input action and (2) the input trajectory enabling property, which ensures that it is able to accept any trajectory of the input variables either by allowing time to progress for the entire length of the trajectory or by reacting with some internal action before that.

An *execution* of $\mathcal{A}$ is a finite or infinite sequence of actions and trajectories $\zeta = \tau_0, a_1, \tau_1, a_2 \ldots$, where (1) each $\tau_i \in \mathcal{T}$, (2) $\tau_0.fstate \in \Theta$ and (3) if τ_i is not the last trajectory in ζ then τ_i is finite and $\tau_i.lstate \overset{a_{i+1}}{\to} \tau_{i+1}.fstate$. An execution is *closed* if the sequence is finite and the domain of the final trajectory is a finite closed interval. The length of an execution is the number of elements (actions and trajectories) in the sequence.

An invariant $\mathcal{I}$ of $\mathcal{A}$ is either derived from other invariants or proved by induction on the length of a closed execution of $\mathcal{A}$. The induction consists of a base case, and an induction step. The base case tests that $\mathcal{I}(s)$ is satisfied for all $s \in \Theta$. The induction step consists of : (1) A discrete part—which tests that for every discrete step $s \overset{\pi}{\to} s' \in \mathcal{D}$, $\mathcal{I}(s)$ implies $\mathcal{I}(s')$. (2) A continuous part—which tests that for any closed trajectory $\tau \in \mathcal{T}$, with $\tau.fstate = s$ and $\tau.lstate = s'$, $\mathcal{I}(s)$ implies $\mathcal{I}(s')$. We shall use s and s' to denote the pre and the post states of discrete transitions, and also the $fstate$ and the $lstate$ of closed trajectories, as will be clear from the context.

2.2   New Addition to HIOA Structure: *Activities*

In the earlier works [8,19,11] using the HIOA model, trajectories of automata were specified using an ad hoc mixture of integral, algebraic equations and English. This form of specification cannot be analyzed easily, and it does not enforce a consistent style in writing specifications. The specification language [15] used in this paper uses "state space" representation [9] of the trajectories. To make this representation work, the following extra structure has been introduced into the basic HIOA model of [12].

The time domain is assumed to be the set of reals R. A variable v is *discrete* if its dynamic type is the pasting closure of the set of constant functions from left closed intervals of time to $type(v)$. A variable is *continuous* if its dynamic type is the pasting closure of the set of continuous functions from left closed intervals of time to R. For any set S of variables, S_d and S_a refer to the discrete and continuous subsets of S respectively.

Let e be a real valued algebraic expression involving the variables in $X \cup U$. For a given trajectory τ, $\tau.e$ denotes the function with domain $\tau.dom$ that gives the value of the expression e at all times over τ. Given that v is a local continuous variable, a trajectory τ *satisfies* the algebraic equation $v = e$, if for every $t \in \tau.dom$, $(\tau \downarrow v)(t) = \tau.e(t)$. If an algebraic equation involves a nondeterministic choice such as $v \in [e_1, e_2]$, then τ satisfies the equation if for every $t \in \tau.dom$, $(\tau \downarrow v)(t) \in [\tau.e_1(t), \tau.e_2(t)]$. If the expression e is integrable when viewed as a function, then τ satisfies the differential equation $\dot{v} = e$, if for every $t \in \tau.dom$, $(\tau \downarrow v)(t) = (\tau \downarrow v)(0) + \int_0^t \tau.e(t') \, dt'$.

A *state model* of HIOA $\mathcal{A}$ consists of $|Z_a|$ number of independent algebraic and/or differential equations with exactly one equation having v or $d(v)$ as its left hand side. The right hand sides of the equations are algebraic expressions involving the variables in $X \cup U$. A state model specifies[1] the evolution of every variable v in Z_a from some initial valuation. A trajectory τ satisfies a state model E if at all times over τ, all the variables in Z_a satisfy the differential and algebraic equations in E with $\tau(0)$ defining the initial valuations.

An *activity* α of HIOA $\mathcal{A}$ consists of three components: (1) an *operating condition* $P \subseteq Q$, (2) a *stopping condition* $P^+ \subseteq Q$, and (3) a state model E. The set of trajectories defined by activity α is denoted by $[\alpha]$. A trajectory τ belongs to the set $[\alpha]$ if the following conditions hold:

1. τ satisfies the state model E.
2. For all $t \in \tau.dom$, $(\tau \downarrow X)(t) \in P$.
3. If $(\tau \downarrow X)(t) \in P^+$ for $t \in dom(\tau)$ then τ is closed and $t = \tau.ltime$.

We impose the following restrictions on hybrid I/O automata model in order to specify the trajectories of an automaton as the union of the sets of trajectories specified by its activities.

R1. Every variable is either discrete or continuous.
R2. Discrete variables are constant over trajectories, i.e.,
$\forall \tau \in \mathcal{T}, \tau.lval \lceil Z_d = \tau.fval \lceil Z_d$.
R3. Operating conditions are disjoint,i.e., $P_i \cap P_j = \emptyset$ if $i \neq j$.

It is proved in [16] that a set of trajectories specified by a set of activities, satisfy the prefix, suffix, and concatenation closure properties.

2.3 Language Constructs

In the HIOA specification language variables are declared by their names and types. Varibales declared with the **analog** keyword are continuous, else they are discrete. Actions are declared by their names, types, and optional list of parameters. Algebraic expressions are written using the operators $+, -, *,$ and $\backslash$. A nondeterministic assignment, such as $v \in [e_1, e_2]$, is written as $v := \textbf{choose}[e_1, e_2]$. The derivative of a continuous variable x is written as $d(x)$. The discrete transitions are written in the precondition—effect style of the IOA language [5]. An activity $\alpha : (P, P^+, E)$ is written as:

activity α **when** P **evolve** E **stop at** P^+.

For automata with a single activity, if either P or P^+ are not specified, then they are assumed to be equal to Q and $\emptyset$ respectively.

3   Specification of System Components

This section describes the HIOA models for the components of the helicopter system, except for the supervisory controller, which is in Section 4. Discrete

---

[1] By *specifies* we mean restricts rather than uniquely determines. Due to possible nondeterminism in the state model, unique determination might not be possible.

and continuous communication among the components are shown in Figure 3. We consider the pitch dynamics of the helicopter, which are critical for safety. A complete dynamical model of the helicopter with three degrees of rotational freedom can be found in [18]. In practice the roll and yaw effects are eliminated by making the initial conditions along these axes to be zero and giving identical input to the two rotors. The pitch dynamics is described by $\ddot{\theta} + \Omega^2 \cos\theta = U(t)$, where Ω is the characteristic frequency of the system and U is the net input for the pitch axis ranging over U_{min} and U_{max}.

```
type RAD = Real  suchthat (i : RAD, |i| ≤ Θ)             % Θ max abs val for angles
type RADPS = Real  suchthat (i : RADPS, |i| ≤ Θ̇)         % Θ̇ max abs val for ang velocity
type UTYPE = Real  suchthat (i : UTYPE | Umin ≤ i ≤ Umax)
hybridautomaton Plant(Ω : Real )
variables                                                 trajectories
  input analog U : UTYPE,                                 activity pitch_dynamics
  internal analog θ_p^0 : RAD, θ_p^1 : RADPS, initially (θ_p^0, θ_p^1) ∈ U,    evolve d(θ_p^0) = θ_p^1;
  output analog θ_e^0 : RAD, θ_e^1 : RADPS                 d(θ_p^1) = −Ω^2 cos θ_p^0 + U;
                                                          θ_e^0 = θ_p^0; θ_e^1 = θ_p^1
```

Fig. 2. HIOA specification of the plant

The `Plant` automaton (Figure 2) specifies the evolution of the pitch angle θ_p^0 and the velocity θ_p^1 with U as input. The global types RAD, RADPS, and UTYPE define the domains for variables representing angle, angular velocity and actuator output respectively. The state variables θ_p^0 and θ_p^1 are initialized to some value from the set $\mathbf{U}$, which is defined in equation (4). A `Plant` state s is *safe* if the pitch angle $s.\theta_p^0$ is within θ_{min} and θ_{max}, which are the lower and the upper safety bounds corresponding to the helicopter hitting the ground and a fragile mechanical stop. The set of safe states is defined as:

$$\mathbf{S} \triangleq \{s \mid \theta_{min} \leq s.\theta_p^0 \leq \theta_{max}\}. \tag{1}$$

The `Sensor` automaton (Figure 4) periodically conveys the state of `Plant` to the controllers as observed by the physical sensors. It is parameterized by the sampling period Δ, the sensor errors for pitch angle ϵ_0, and velocity ϵ_1. The variable *now* serves as a clock. The stopping condition of the *read* activity ensures that a *sample* action occurs after every Δ interval of time. The value of θ_d^0 (and θ_d^1) is nondeterministically chosen to be within $\pm\epsilon_0$ of θ_a^0 ($\pm\epsilon_1$ of θ_a^1 resp.) to model the noise or the uncertainties in the sensing devices.

The `UsrCtrl` automaton (Figure 5) models an arbitrary user controller. It reads the *sample* action and triggers an output *control(u_d)* action, which communicates the user's output U_u to the supervisor. The output U_u is modeled as a

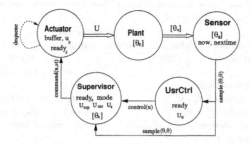

Fig. 3. Components of Helicopter system. Continuous and discrete communication among components are shown by wide and thin arrows respectively. The internal variables are marked inside the circles and internal actions are shown by a dashed self loop.

---

hybridautomaton Sensor($\epsilon_0, \epsilon_1, \Delta$: Real)
actions
    output *sample* (θ_d^0 : RAD , θ_d^1: RADPS)

discrete transitions
    output *sample* (θ_d^0 , θ_d^1)
    pre *now* = *next_time* $\wedge$
        $\theta_d^0 \in [\theta_a^0 - \epsilon_0, \theta_a^0 + \epsilon_0] \wedge$
        $\theta_d^1 \in [\theta_a^1 - \epsilon_1, \theta_a^1 + \epsilon_1]$
    eff *next_time* := *now* + Δ

trajectories
    activity *read*
        evolve d(*now*) =1; $\theta_a^0 = \theta_e^0$; $\theta_a^1 = \theta_e^1$;
        stop at *now* = *next_time*

variables
    input analog θ_e^0 : RAD, θ_e^1 : RADPS,
    internal analog θ_a^0 : RAD := 0, θ_a^1 : RADPS := 0,
        now: Real   := 0,
    internal *next_time* : Real   := Δ

    derived variable
        $s.time\_left \stackrel{\Delta}{=} s.next\_time - s.now.$

Fig. 4. HIOA specification of the sensor and A/D conversion circuit

---

nondeterministic choice over the entire range U_{min} to U_{max}. This captures our assumption that the user is capable of issuing arbitrarily bad control inputs to the plant. The design of a safe supervisor for UsrCtrl ensures that the system would be safe for *any* user controller because every controller must implement this specification of UsrCtrl.

The Actuator automaton (Figure 6) models the actuator and the D/A converter. The delay in the actuator response is modeled by a FIFO *buffer* of (u, st) pairs, where u is a command issued from Supervisor, and the scheduled time st is the time at which u is to be delivered to the plant. A *command(u, m)* action appends $(u, timer + \tau_{act})$ to *buffer* and a *dequeue* action copies *buffer*.head.u to u_o and removes *buffer*.head.

```
hybridautomaton UsrCtrl
actions                                    variables
   input sample ( θ_d^0 : RAD , θ_d^1 : RADPS ),    internal θ_u^0: RAD := 0 , θ_u^1 : RADPS := 0,
   output control ( u_d : UTYPE)                        U_u : UTYPE := 0,
                                                        ready : Bool := false
discrete transitions
   input sample ( θ_d^0 , θ_d^1 )          output control ( u_d )
   eff θ_u^0 := θ_d^0; θ_u^1 = θ_d^1        pre (u_d = U_u) ∧ ready
       U_u := choose [U_min, U_max];        eff ready := false
       ready := true


trajectories
   activity void
      evolve stop at ready
```

Fig. 5. Specification of User's Controller

The following invariant for `Actuator` can be proved by a simple induction.

Invariant 1 *In any reachable state s of* `Actuator`,
for all $0 \le i < s.buffer.\texttt{size} - 1$,
$s.now \le s.buffer[\texttt{i}].\texttt{st} \le s.buffer[\texttt{i+1}].\texttt{st} \le s.now + \tau_{\text{act}}$.

```
type MODES = { usr, sup }
hybridautomaton Actuator(τ_act)
actions                         variables
   input command ( u : UTYPE )     internal u_o : UTYPE := 0, ready_d : Bool := false,
   internal dequeue                   buffer : seq of (u:UTYPE, st:Real, m:MODE) := {}
                                   output analog U : UTYPE := 0,
                                   input analog now : Real
discrete transitions
   input command ( u )
   eff buffer + := (u, now + τ_act);   internal dequeue
       ready_d := true                 pre buffer.head.st = now ∧ ready_d
                                        eff u_o := buffer.head.v;
trajectories                            buffer := buffer.tail;
   activity d2a                         ready_d := false
   evolve U = u_o
   stop at buffer.head.st = now
```

Fig. 6. Actuator and D/A conversion

4   Supervisory Controller

The goal of the supervisory controller is to ensure safety of the plant while interfering as little as possible with the user controller. There are well known algorithms [4,2,10] for synthesizing controllers for linear hybrid systems. Our design of the supervisory controller, however, is based on finding a *safe operating region* **U**, from where , if the supervisor takes over control then it is guaranteed to restore the plant to a safe state. In order to satisfy the minimal interference requirement it is also desirable to make **U** as large as possible.

4.1 Switching Regions

Consider a region **C** ⊆ **S**, from which all the reachable states are contained in **S**, provided that the input U to the plant is *correct*. By correct we mean that the input to the plant is $U = U_{min}$ (or U_{max}) if the pitch angle θ_p^0 is in the danger of reaching θ_{min} (θ_{max} resp.). As there is a τ_{act} delay in **Actuator** *buffer*, the supervisor cannot change U instantaneously, and therefore the region **C** is not a safe operating region. We define another region **R** ⊆ **C** as the set of states from which all reachable states over a period of τ_{act} are within **C**. Even **R** is not a safe operating region because the supervisor *cannot* observe the plant state accurately, and relies on the periodic updates from the inaccurate sensors. Finally, we define the safe operating region **U** as follows: An *observed* state s' is in **U** if starting from any actual plant state s corresponding to s', all the reachable states over a Δ interval of time are in **R**.

Switching back to the user controller from the supervisor is performed at the boundary of an *inner* region **I** ⊆ **U**. This asymmetry in switching prevents high frequency chattering between the user and the supervisory controllers.

The regions **C**, **R**, **U**, and **I** are defined as follows. $U_{mag} = U_{max} - U_{min}$.

$$\mathbf{C} \triangleq \{s \mid s.\theta_p^0 \in [\theta_{min}, \theta_{max}] \land s.\theta_p^1 \in [\Gamma^-(s.\theta_p^0, 0), \Gamma^+(s.\theta_p^0, 0)]\}, \tag{2}$$

$$\mathbf{R} \triangleq \{s \mid \theta_{min} \leq s.\theta_p^0 \leq \theta_{max} \land \Gamma^-(s.\theta_p^0, \tau_{act}) \leq s.\theta_p^1 \leq \Gamma^+(s.\theta_p^0, \tau_{act})\}, \tag{3}$$

$$\mathbf{U} \triangleq \{s \mid \theta_{min} + \epsilon_0 \leq s.\theta_s^0 \leq \theta_{max} - \epsilon_0 \land U^-(s.\theta_s^0) \leq s.\theta_s^1 \leq U^+(s.\theta_s^0)\}, \tag{4}$$

$$\mathbf{I} \triangleq \{s \mid \theta_{min} + \epsilon_0 \leq s.\theta_s^0 \leq \theta_{max} - \epsilon_0 \land I^-(s.\theta_s^0) \leq s.\theta_s^1 \leq I^+(s.\theta_s^0)\}. \tag{5}$$

$$\Gamma^+(\theta, \mathcal{T}) = -U_{mag}\mathcal{T} + \sqrt{2(\Omega^2 \cos\theta_{max} - U_{min})(\theta_{max} - \theta + \frac{1}{2}U_{mag}\mathcal{T}^2)}, \tag{6}$$

$$\Gamma^-(\theta, \mathcal{T}) = U_{mag}\mathcal{T} - \sqrt{2(U_{max} - \Omega^2)(\theta - \theta_{min} + \frac{1}{2}U_{mag}\mathcal{T}^2)}, \tag{7}$$

$$U^+(\theta) = -\epsilon_1 + \Gamma^+(\theta + \epsilon_0, \tau_{act} + \Delta) \qquad U^-(\theta) = +\epsilon_1 + \Gamma^-(\theta - \epsilon_0, \tau_{act} + \Delta)$$

$$I^+(\theta) = -2\epsilon_1 + \Gamma^+(\theta + 2\epsilon_0, \tau_{act} + \Delta) \qquad I^-(\theta) = +2\epsilon_1 + \Gamma^-(\theta - 2\epsilon_0, \tau_{act} + \Delta).$$

From the above definitions the following properties are derived.

Property 1 *Over the interval* $-\frac{\pi}{2} \leq \theta \leq \frac{\pi}{2}$ *the following hold:*

1. *$\Gamma^+(\theta, \mathcal{T})$ and $\Gamma^-(\theta, \mathcal{T})$ are monotonically decreasing with respect to θ.*
2. *$\Gamma^+(\theta, \mathcal{T})$ is monotonically decreasing with respect to $\mathcal{T}$. ($\mathcal{T} \geq 0$).*
3. *$\Gamma^-(\theta, \mathcal{T})$ is monotonically increasing with respect to $\mathcal{T}$. ($\mathcal{T} \geq 0$).*
4. *$\Gamma^+(\theta_{max}, \mathcal{T}) < 0$ and $\Gamma^-(\theta_{min}, \mathcal{T}) > 0$ for $\mathcal{T} > 0$.*

Property 2 **I** ⊆ **U** ⊆ **R** ⊆ **C** ⊆ **S**

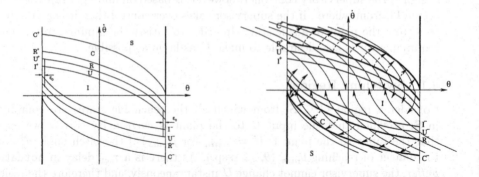

Fig. 7. (a) Regions in the statespace. (b) Trajectories in the settling (dashed lines) and recovery(solid lines) periods.

4.2 Supervisor Automaton

The Supervisor automaton (Figure 8) copies the observed plant state into internal variables θ_s^0 and θ_s^1 when the *sample* action occurs. Based on this state information the tentative output U_{sup} to the actuator is decided. When the *control* action occurs, the supervisor copies the user's command into another internal variable U_{usr}, and sets the values of U_s and *mode* for the next Δ interval based on (θ_s^0, θ_s^1) and the current value of *mode*. If *mode* is usr and the observed state is in **U** then *mode* remains unchanged and U_s is set to U_{usr}. If the present state is not in **U** then *mode* is changed to sup and the U_s is set to U_{sup}. If *mode* = sup then U_s is copied from U_{sup} and the mode changes only when (θ_s^0, θ_s^1) is in **I**.

5   Analysis of Helicopter System

In this section we present the safety verification of the composed system. Let $\mathcal{A}$ denote the composition of the **Plant**, **Sensor**, **UsrCtrl**, **Actuator**, and the **Supervisor** automata. Safety is preserved if all the reachable states of $\mathcal{A}$ are contained within the region **S**. It is assumed that: (1) $\theta_{min} < 0 < |\theta_{min}| < \theta_{max}$, (2) $U_{max} > \Omega^2$, $U_{min} \leq 0$, and (3) For any *sample* action $s \xrightarrow{\pi} s'$, if $s.\theta_s^1 > I^+(s.\theta_s^0)$ then, $s'.\theta_s^1 \geq I^-(s'.\theta_s^0)$, and if $s.\theta_s^1 < I^-(s.\theta_s^0)$ then, $s'.\theta_s^1 \leq I^+(s'.\theta_s^0)$. Assumptions (1) and (2) are derived from the dimensions of the physical system. Assumption (3) is a requirement which limits the speed of the plant and the sampling period so that it is not possible for the plant to jump across **I** without the sensors detecting it.

In the next section, first we present some preliminary properties of $\mathcal{A}$, then we state the invariants of $\mathcal{A}$, and prove some of the more important ones. The details of all the invariant proofs can be found in [16].

hybridautomaton Supervisor

actions

    input *sample* $(\theta_d^0$: RAD θ_d^1: RADPS),

    input *control* $(u_d$: UTYPE),

    output *command* $(u_d$: UTYPE, m : MODES)

variables

    internal θ_s^0 : RAD := 0, θ_s^1 : RADPS := 0,

        U_{sup}, U_{usr}, U_s : UTYPE := 0,

    internal $ready_c$: Bool   := false, $mode$: MODES := usr

    internal analog rt : Real := 0;

discrete transitions

    input *sample* (θ_d^0, θ_d^1)

    eff $\theta_s^0 := \theta_d^0; \theta_s^1 := \theta_d^1;$

        if $\theta_s^1 \geq I^+(\theta_s^0)$ then $U_{sup} := U_{min}$

        elseif $\theta_s^1 \leq I^-(\theta_s^0)$ then $U_{sup} := U_{max}$ **fi**

    output *command* (u_d, m)

    pre $ready_c \wedge (u_d = U_s) \wedge m = mode$

    eff $ready_c :=$ false

    input *control* (u_d)

    eff $U_{usr} := u_d; ready_c :=$ true

        if $mode =$ usr then

          if $(\theta_s^0, \theta_s^1) \in$ **U** then $U_s := U_{usr}$

          else $U_s := U_{sup}; mode :=$ sup **fi**

        elseif $mode =$ sup then

          if $(\theta_s^0, \theta_s^1) \in$ **I** then $U_s := U_{usr}; mode :=$ usr

          else $U_s := U_{sup}$ **fi fi**

trajectories

    activity *supervisor*

        when $mode =$ sup

        evolve $d(rt) = 1$ stop at $ready_c$

    activity *user*

        when $mode =$ usr

        evolve $rt = 0$ stop at $ready_c$

Fig. 8. HIOA specification of supervisor automaton

5.1   Some Preliminary Properties of A

The specification of the components of $\mathcal{A}$ satisfy restrictions **R2**, **R2** and **R3** and the plant state variables θ_p^0 and θ_p^1 are not modified by any discrete action. The next two properties follow from these facts:

Property 3 *Discrete variables of $\mathcal{A}$ are unaltered over all closed trajectories.*

Property 4 *For any discrete step $s \xrightarrow{\pi} s'$ of $\mathcal{A}$, $s'.\theta_p^0 = s.\theta_p^0$ and $s'.\theta_p^1 = s.\theta_p^1$.*

Invariant 2 follows from the code by a straightforward induction. Lemma 1 follows from Invariant 2 and indicates the times at which the different actions of $\mathcal{A}$ occur. Invariant 3 limits the size of the *buffer* and it is a consequence of Invariant 1 and Lemma 1.

Invariant 2 *In every reachable state s of $\mathcal{A}$, $0 \leq s.time\_left \leq \Delta$.*

Lemma 1 *In any execution of $\mathcal{A}$, sample, control, and command actions occur when $now = n\Delta$, and dequeue actions occur when $timer = \tau_{act} + n\Delta$ for some integer $n > 0$.*

Invariant 3 *In every reachable state s, for all $0 \leq i < s.buffer.size - 1$, $s.buffer[\text{i+1}].st = s.buffer[\text{i}].st + \Delta$, and $s.buffer.size \leq \lceil \frac{\tau_{act}}{\Delta} \rceil$.*

5.2   User Mode

In this section we prove that $\mathcal{A}$ is safe in the user mode. We define a set of regions $\mathbf{A}_t$ for $0 \leq t \leq \Delta$, and Lemma 2 states the properties of the $\mathbf{A}_t$ regions.
$\mathbf{A}_t \triangleq \{s \mid s.\theta_p^0 \in [\theta_{min}, \theta_{max}] \wedge s.\theta_p^1 \in [\Gamma^-(s.\theta_p^0, \tau_{\texttt{eff}} + t), \Gamma^+(s.\theta_p^0, \tau_{\texttt{eff}} + t)]\}$.

Lemma 2 *The regions* $\mathbf{A}_t$ *satisfy:*   1. $\mathbf{A}_0 = \mathbf{R}$,   2. $\mathbf{U} \subseteq \mathbf{A}_\Delta$, *and*
3. *If* $0 \leq t \leq t' \leq \Delta$ *then* $\mathbf{A}_{t'} \subseteq \mathbf{A}_t$.

The next lemma bounds the reachable sates over a singe trajectory and is used to prove safety when a tarjectory starts from the safe operating region $\mathbf{U}$. Invariant 4 makes use of Lemma 3. The safety of the system in the user mode is established by Invariant 5.

Lemma 3 *For any closed trajectory* τ *of* $\mathcal{A}$,
if $\tau.fstate \in \mathbf{A}_t$ *then* $\tau.lstate \in \mathbf{A}_{t - ltime(\tau)}$.

Proof: Consider a closed trajectory τ. Assume that $s \in \mathbf{A}_t$. From the definition of $\mathbf{A}_t$ it follows that, $\theta_{min} \leq s.\theta_p^0 \leq \theta_{max}$ and $\Gamma^-(s.\theta_p^0, \tau_{\texttt{eff}} + t) \leq s.\theta_p^1 \leq \Gamma^+(s.\theta_p^0, \tau_{\texttt{eff}} + t)$. We conservatively estimate s' by considering the maximum and the minimum input U to $\texttt{Plant}$. First considering the maximum positive input, $U = U_{max}$, from the state model of $\texttt{Plant}$ we get the upper bound on the acceleration at any state s'' in $\tau : d(s''.\theta_p^1) \leq -\Omega^2 \cos\theta_{max} + U_{max}$. Integrating from t to t', it follows that $s'.\theta_p^1 \leq (U_{max} - \Omega^2 \cos\theta_{max})t' + s.\theta_p^1$, and $s'.\theta_p^0 \leq \frac{1}{2}(U_{max} - \Omega^2 \cos\theta_{max})t'^2 + s.\theta_p^1 t' + s.\theta_p^0$. Simplifying and using the definition of Γ^+ we get the following bounds on $s'.\theta_p^0$ and $s'.\theta_p^1$: $s'.\theta_p^0 \leq \theta_{max}$, and $s'.\theta_p^1 \leq \Gamma^+(s'.\theta_p^0, \tau_{\texttt{eff}} + t - t')$. Similarly considering maximum negative output, $U = U_{min}$, we get the lower bounds on $s'.\theta_s^0$ and $s'.\theta_s^1$. $s'.\theta_p^0 \geq \theta_{min}$, and $s'.\theta_p^1 \geq \Gamma^-(s'.\theta_p^0, \tau_{\texttt{eff}} + t - t')$. Combining equations all the above bounds on s' it follows that $s' \in \mathbf{A}_{t - t'}$. $\square$

Invariant 4 *In any reachable state* s,
if $s.mode = \texttt{usr}$ *and* $\neg s.ready$ *then* $s \in \mathbf{A}_{s.time\_left}$.

Invariant 5 *In any reachable state* s, *if* $s.mode = \texttt{usr}$ *then* $s \in \mathbf{R}$.

Proof: The base case holds because all initial states are in $\mathbf{U}$ and $\mathbf{U} \subseteq \mathbf{R}$. Consider any discrete transition $s \xrightarrow{\pi} s'$, with $s'.mode = \texttt{usr}$. We split the proof into two cases: If $\neg s'.ready$, then using Invariant 4, $s' \in \mathbf{A}_{s'.time\_left} \subseteq \mathbf{R}$. On the other hand, if $s'.ready$, then $\pi \neq control$, and $s.mode = \texttt{usr}$ since only the *control* action can change *mode*. So from the inductive hypothesis $s \in \mathbf{R}$. It follows that $s' \in \mathbf{R}$ from the Property 4.

     For the continuous part consider a closed trajectory τ with $\tau.fstate = s$, $\tau.lstate = s'$, and $s'.mode = \texttt{usr}$. Once again there are two cases, if $\neg s'.ready$ then $s' \in \mathbf{R}$ by Invariant 4. Else if $s'.ready$, then $s.ready$ and $s.mode = \texttt{usr}$ because *ready* and *mode* does not change over the trajectories. Since s satisfies the stopping condition for activity *void* in $\texttt{UsrCtrl}$, therefore τ is a point trajectory, that is, $s' = s$. From the inductive hypothesis, $s \in \mathbf{R}$. Therefore $s' \in \mathbf{R}$. $\square$

5.3 Supervisor Mode: Settling Phase

For proving safety in the supervisor mode, we first state some of the simple invariants. Invariant 6 states that, in all reachable with *ready* set to false, if the sensed plant state is within I^+ and I^-, then the system is in the user mode. Invariant 7 follows from the code of the *sample* action. And Invariant 8 is proved by a simple induction.

Invariant 6 *In any reachable state s,*
$I^-(s.\theta_s^0) \le s.\theta_s^1 \le I^+(s.\theta_s^0) \ \wedge \ \neg s.ready \Rightarrow s.mode = \mathsf{usr}.$

Invariant 7 *In any reachable state s,*
if $s.\theta_s^1 > I^+(s.\theta_s^0)$ then $s.U_{sup} = U_{min}$, and
if $s.\theta_s^1 < I^+(s.\theta_s^0)$ then $s.U_{sup} = U_{max}$.

Invariant 8 *In any reachable state s,*
$s.rt = n\Delta - s.time\_left$, for some integer $n \ge 1$.

We define two predicates $\mathcal{Q}_k^+$ and $\mathcal{Q}_k^-$ that capture the progress made by the system while the actuator delays the delivery of commands issued by the supervisor. A state s satisfies $\mathcal{Q}_k^+$ (or $\mathcal{Q}_k^-$), if the last k commands in $s.buffer$ are equal to U_{min} (or U_{max} respectively). More formally, for any $k \ge 0$,

$\mathcal{Q}_k^+(s) \triangleq \forall i, \ max(0, s.buffer.\texttt{size} - k) \le i < s.buffer.\texttt{size}, \ s.buffer[i].u = U_{min},$
$\mathcal{Q}_k^-(s) \triangleq \forall i, \ max(0, s.buffer.\texttt{size} - k) \le i < s.buffer.\texttt{size}, \ s.buffer[i].u = U_{max}.$

Clearly, for all $k > 0$, $\mathcal{Q}_k^+(s)$ implies $\mathcal{Q}_{k-1}^+(s)$, and therefore for any $k \ge s.buffer.\texttt{size}$, $\mathcal{Q}_k^+(s)$ implies that $\mathcal{Q}_j^+(s)$ holds for all $j < s.buffer.\texttt{size}$. Similar results hold for $\mathcal{Q}_k^-$. The next invariant states that every reachable state s in the supervisor mode, satisfies either $\mathcal{Q}_{\lceil \frac{s.rt}{\Delta} \rceil}^+(s)$ or $\mathcal{Q}_{\lceil \frac{s.rt}{\Delta} \rceil}^-(s)$, depending on whether s is above I^+ or below I^- respectively. In addition if $s.ready_d$ is true, that is, s is in between a *command* action and a *dequeue* action, then $\mathcal{Q}_{\lceil \frac{s.rt}{\Delta} \rceil+1}^+(s)$ or $\mathcal{Q}_{\lceil \frac{s.rt}{\Delta} \rceil+1}^-(s)$ holds, depending on the location of s with respect to I^+ and I^-.

Invariant 9 *In any reachable state s, such that $s.mode = \mathsf{sup}$:*
If $s.\theta_s^1 > I^+(s.\theta_s^0)$ then (a) $\mathcal{Q}_{\lceil \frac{s.rt}{\Delta} \rceil}^+(s)$, (b) If $ready_d$ then $\mathcal{Q}_{\lceil \frac{s.rt}{\Delta} \rceil+1}^+(s)$,
If $s.\theta_s^1 < I^-(s.\theta_s^0)$ then (a) $\mathcal{Q}_{\lceil \frac{s.rt}{\Delta} \rceil}^-(s)$, (b) If $ready_d$ then $\mathcal{Q}_{\lceil \frac{s.rt}{\Delta} \rceil+1}^-(s)$

The next invariant formalizes the notion that after a certain τ_{act} period of time in the supervisor mode the input to the plant is correct.

Invariant 10 *In any reachable state s, such that $s.mode = \mathsf{sup}$ and $s.rt > \tau_{act}$*
1. If $s.\theta_s^1 > I^+(s.\theta_s^0)$ then $s.U = U_{min}$, and 2. If $s.\theta_s^1 < I^-(s.\theta_s^0)$ then $s.U = U_{max}$,

We split the execution of $\mathcal{A}$ in the supervisor mode (Figure 7(b)) into (a) a *settling phase* of length τ_{act} in which the input U to the plant is arbitrary, and (b) a variable length *recovery phase* during which $rt > \tau_{\mathrm{act}}$ and the input to the plant is correct, that is, in accordance with Invariant 10.

Next we define a set of regions $\mathbf{B}_t$, for $0 \leq t \leq \tau_{\mathrm{act}}$, which are analogous to the $\mathbf{A}_t$ regions: $\mathbf{B}_t \triangleq \{s \mid s.\theta_p^0 \in [\theta_{min}, \theta_{max}] \wedge s.\theta_p^1 \in [\Gamma^-(s.\theta_p^0, \tau_{\mathrm{act}} - t), \Gamma^+(s.\theta_p^0, \tau_{\mathrm{act}} - t)]\}$. Lemma 4 states the relationship between the $\mathbf{B}_t$ regions. Invariant 11 bounds the location of a state s in terms of the $\mathbf{B}_t$ regions, when $s.rt \leq \tau_{\mathrm{act}}$. This implies the safety of the system in the settling phase.

Lemma 4 *The regions* $\mathbf{B}_t$ *satisfy:* 1. $\mathbf{B}_0 = \mathbf{R}$, 2. $\mathbf{B}_{\tau_{\mathrm{act}}} = \mathbf{C}$, 3. *If* $0 \leq t \leq t' \leq \tau_{\mathrm{act}}$ *then* $\mathbf{B}_t \subseteq \mathbf{B}_{t'}$.

Invariant 11 *For any reachable state s,* *if* $s.mode = \mathrm{sup} \wedge s.rt \leq \tau_{\mathrm{act}}$ *then* $s \in \mathbf{B}_{s.rt}$.

5.4   Supervisor Mode: Recovery Phase

Invariant 12 states that $\mathbf{C}$ is an invariant set for the system in the recovery phase. A sketch of the proof is given here, the complete proof can be found in [16].

Invariant 12 *In any reachable states s,* *if* $s.mode = \mathrm{sup}$ *and* $s.rt \geq \tau_{\mathrm{act}}$ *then* $s \in \mathbf{C}$.

proof sketch: The base case is trivially satisfied. The discrete part of the induction is also straightforward, the *control* action alters the *mode*. If $s.mode = \mathrm{sup}$ then using the inductive hypothesis, $s' \in \mathbf{C}$. Otherwise $s.mode = \mathrm{usr}$ and $s'.rt = 0$ and the invariant holds vacuously. For all other discrete actions the invariant is preserved. For the continuous part of the induction, consider closed trajectory τ with $s'.mode = \mathrm{sup}$ and $s'.rt \geq \tau_{\mathrm{act}}$. We claim that $s \in \mathbf{C}$. From Property 3 it is known that $s.mode = \mathrm{sup}$, (1) If $s.rt < \tau_{\mathrm{act}}$ then from Invariant 11 it follows that $s \in \mathbf{C}$. Otherwise (2) $s.rt \geq \tau_{\mathrm{act}}$ and from the inductive hypothesis it follows that $s \in \mathbf{C}$. If $s \in \mathbf{U}$, then from Lemma 3 it follows that $s' \in \mathbf{R} \subseteq \mathbf{C}$. So it remains to show that if $s \in \mathbf{C} \setminus \mathbf{U}$ then $s' \in \mathbf{C}$. This is proved by contradiction, suppose $s' \notin \mathbf{C}$, then there must exist $t' \in \tau.dom$ such that τ leaves the $\mathbf{C}$ at $\tau(t')$. Then it must be the case that the trajectory τ and the outer-normal of boundary of $\mathbf{C}$ should form an acute angle. It is known from Lemma 10 that at any intermediate state $\tau(t')$, the input U to the plant is correct. A contradiction is reached by showing that if $\tau(t')$ is on the boundary of $\mathbf{C}$, then the angle between the above-mentioned vectors is obtuse. Finally, combining the Invariants proved above the safety property of the composed system can be proved.

Theorem 1 *All reachable states of $\mathcal{A}$ are contained in $\mathbf{C}$.*

Proof: For any reachable state s, if $s.mode = \mathsf{usr}$ then $s \in \mathbf{R} \subseteq \mathbf{C}$ by Invariant 5. Otherwise $s.mode = \mathsf{sup}$, and there are two possibilities: if $s.rt < \tau_{\mathsf{act}}$ then, by Invariant 11, $s \in \mathbf{B}_{s.rt} \subseteq \mathbf{C}$. Else $s.rt \geq \tau_{\mathsf{act}}$ and it follows from Invariant 12 that $s \in \mathbf{C}$.

6 Conclusions

In this paper we have presented an advanced application of the HIOA framework for verifying hybrid systems. The safety of the designed supervisory controller was established by proving a set of invariants. The proof techniques demonstrate two properties that we believe are important for reasoning about complex hybrid systems: (1) the proofs are decomposed into discrete and continuous parts, which are independent of each other, and (2) the reasoning style is purely assertional, that is, based on the current state of the system, rather than complete executions.

The design of the supervisory controller uses a safe operating region of the plant, beyond which the supervisor overrides the user controller, performs appropriate recovery, and returns control to the user. The duration of the recovery period has not been discussed here, but it has been shown in [18] to be bounded. The size of the safe operating region, depends on the plant dynamics, sensor errors, sampling period, actuator bandwidth, and saturation. An implementation of the supervisory controller in the actual system is in progress. In the future we intend to design and verify a class of supervisory controllers that reduce unnecessary interferences by utilizing additional information about particular user controllers.

The specification language used is based on the hybrid I/O automaton model of [12] with the addition of certain extra structures to specify the trajectories using activities. We intend to incorporate the language extensions into a toolkit for automatically checking HIOA programs. At present we are also working on building a theorem prover interface for HIOA that will partially automate the verification process.

References

1. Rajeev Alur, Costas Courcoubetis, Nicolas Halbwachs, Thomas A. Henzinger, P.-H. Ho, Xavier Nicollin, Alfredo Olivero, Joseph Sifakis, and Sergio Yovine. The algorithmic analysis of hybrid systems. *Theoretical Computer Science*, 138(1):3–34, 1995.
2. Eugene Asarin, Olivier Bournez, Thao Dang, Amir Pnueli, and Oded Maler. Effective synthesis of switching controllers for linear systems. In *Proceedings of IEEE*, volume 88, pages 1011–1025, July 2000.
3. Alexandre M. Bayen, Eva Cruck, and Claire Tomlin. Guaranteed overapproximations of unsafe sets for continuous and hybrid systems: solving the hamilton-jacobi equation using viability techniques. In *Hybrid Systems: Computation and Control 2002*, volume 2289 of *LNCS*, pages 90–104. Springer, March 2002.
4. Enrique D. Ferreira and Bruce H. Krogh. Switching controllers based on neural network: Estimates of stability regions and controller performance. In *Hybrid Systems: Computation and Control 1998*, pages 126–142, 1998.

5. Stephen Garland, Nancy Lynch, and Mandana Vaziri. IOA: A language for specifying, programming and validating distributed systems. Technical report, Laboratory for Computer Science, Massachusetts Institute of Technology, Cambridge, MA, October 1999.
6. Thomas A. Henzinger, Pei-Hsin Ho, and Howard Wong-Toi. Hytech: A model checker for hybrid systems. In *Computer Aided Verification (CAV '97)*, volume 1254 of *Lecture Notes in Computer Science*, pages 460–483, 1997.
7. Thomas A. Henzinger, Peter W. Kopke, Anuj Puri, and Pravin Varaiya. What's decidable about hybrid automata? In *ACM Symposium on Theory of Computing*, pages 373–382, 1995.
8. Carolos Livadas, John Lygeros, and Nancy A. Lynch. High-level modeling and analysis of TCAS. In *Proceedings of the 20th IEEE Real-Time Systems Symposium (RTSS'99),Phoenix, Arizona*, pages 115–125, December 1999.
9. David G. Luenberger. *Introduction to Dynamic Systems: Theory, Models, and Applications*. John Wiley and Sons, Inc., New York, 1979.
10. John Lygeros, Claire Tomlin, and Shankar Sastry. Controllers for reachability specifications for hybrid systems. In *Automatica*, volume 35, March 1999.
11. Nancy Lynch. A three-level analysis of a simple acceleration maneuver, with uncertainties. In *Proceedings of the Third AMAST Workshop on Real-Time Systems*, pages 1–22, Salt Lake City, Utah, March 1996. World Scientific Publishing Company.
12. Nancy Lynch, Roberto Segala, and Frits Vaandraager. Hybrid I/O automata. To appear in *Information and Computation*. Also, Technical Report MIT-LCS-TR-827d, MIT Laboratory for Computer Science Technical Report, Cambridge, MA 02139, January 13, 2003.
    theory.lcs.mit.edu/tds/papers/Lynch/HIOA-final.ps.
13. Nancy Lynch, Roberto Segala, Frits Vaandrager, and H. B. Weinberg. Hybrid I/O automata. In T. Henzinger R. Alur and E. Sontag, editors, *Hybrid Systems III*, volume 1066 of *Lecture Notes in Computer Science*, New Brunswick, New Jersey, October 1995. Springer-Verlag.
14. Nancy A. Lynch, Roberto Segala, and Frits W. Vaandrager. Hybrid I/O automata revisited. In M.D. Di Benedetto and A.L. Sangiovanni-Vincentelli, editors, *Proceedings Fourth International Workshop on Hybrid Systems: Computation and Control (HSCC'01)*, Rome, Italy, volume 2034 of *lncs*. springer, March 2001.
15. Sayan Mitra. Language for Hybrid Input/Output Automata, 2002. Work in progress. http://theory.lcs.mit.edu/mitras/research/composing_activities.ps.
16. Sayan Mitra, Yong Wang, Nancy Lynch, and Eric Feron. Application of hybrid I/O automata in safety verification of pitch controller for model helicopter system. Technical Report MIT-LCS-TR-880, MIT Laboratory for Computer Science, Cambridge, MA 02139, January 2003.
    http://theory.lcs.mit.edu/~mitras/research/QuanTR02.ps
17. URL:. http://www.quanser.com/english/html/products/fs_product_challenge.asp?, lang_code=english&pcat_code=exp-spe&prod_code=S1-3dofheli.
18. Yong Wang, Masha Ishutkina, Sayan Mitra, Nancy A. Lynch, Eric Feron. Design of Supervisory Safety Control for 3DOF Helicopter using Hybrid I/O Automata, 2002. pre-print http://gewurtz.mit.edu/ishut/darpa_sec_mit/papers/quanser.ps.
19. H. B. Weinberg, Nancy Lynch, and Norman Delisle. Verification of automated vehicle protection systems. In T. Henzinger R. Alur and E. Sontag, editors, *Hybrid Systems III: Verification and Control (DIMACS/SYCON Workshop on Verification and Control of Hybrid Systems)*, volume 1066 of *Lecture Notes in Computer Science*, pages 101–113, New Brunswick, New Jersey, October 1995. Springer-Verlag.

Multi-object Adaptive Cruise Control

Rainer Möbus[1,2], Mato Baotic[2], and Manfred Morari[2]

[1] DaimlerChrysler Research and Technology Assisting Systems, (RIC/AA)
70546 Stuttgart, Germany, rainer.moebus@daimlerchrysler.com
[2] Automatic Control Laboratory, ETH Zentrum - ETL, CH-8092 Zürich, Switzerland,
tel: +41-1-632 5290, fax: +41-1-632 1211, {rainer,baotic,morari}@aut.ee.ethz.ch

Abstract. In this paper we propose an algorithm for solving a Multi-Object Adaptive Cruise Control problem. In a multi-object traffic scene the optimal acceleration is to be found respecting traffic rules, safety distances and driver intentions. The objective function is modelled as a quadratic cost function for the discrete time piecewise affine system. We find the optimal state-feedback control law by solving the underlying constrained finite time optimal control problem via dynamic programming.

1 Introduction

Cruise control is a common and well known automotive driver assistance system. The driver sets a reference speed and the engine is controlled so that this reference speed is maintained regardless of external loads such as wind, road slope or changing vehicle parameters. Further development led to the so called Adaptive Cruise Control (ACC) that takes into account the traffic in front of the car. Good acceleration and deceleration control is essential for the ACC systems and over the last decades it has been subject of extensive research. The reader is referred to [5,6,7] for an overview.

To obtain information about the distance between vehicles the ACC system uses infrared or radar sensors.[1] If another car crosses into the driver's lane, and the distance is less than a certain safety distance (a separation interval of 1 to 2 seconds), the control system slows down the car by reducing the throttle or applying the brakes. If the leading car speeds up or goes out of the driver's lane the controller accelerates the vehicle to the cruising speed. In all those maneuvers the ACC system has to deal with the constraints imposed on acceleration and deceleration. Acceleration limitation increases comfort, while with deceleration limitation we avoid unnecessary emergency brakes that can be caused by sensor noise, limited sensor range, or the imperfections of the traffic scene modelling. However, limiting deceleration has its drawbacks, since, in rare but dangerous situations, an accident could be avoided if higher deceleration is used. Additionally, the ACC system should respect traffic rules (e.g. overtaking only on the left) and lane changers have to be considered early to avoid dangerous situations. To fulfill all those requirements, sensors and processing systems should be

---

[1] Radar sensors at the same time provide distance *and* relative speed measurement.

O. Maler and A. Pnueli (Eds.): HSCC 2003, LNCS 2623, pp. 359–374, 2003.
© Springer-Verlag Berlin Heidelberg 2003

used, that can detect and represent the complete traffic scene ahead of the car. In that way we can achieve a better prediction and design a better controller in a multi-object scenario.

In this paper we present a way to model and estimate a complex traffic scene sensed by radar, infrared laser and video sensors and compute the optimal acceleration as a state-feedback control law by using hybrid system theory. Estimation and representation of the traffic scene were implemented and tested. Simulation and experimental results of the designed controller are reported.

2   Modelling and Estimation

2.1   Sensors

To get a good representation of the actual traffic scene radar, infrared and stereo vision systems are mounted on a research car. With these external sensors, the road ahead, as well as position and velocity of the neighboring cars, can be estimated. Internal sensors deliver information about speed, acceleration and yaw rate of the driver's vehicle (*ego*-car).[2] Figure 1 shows the ranges of sight of the different external sensors.

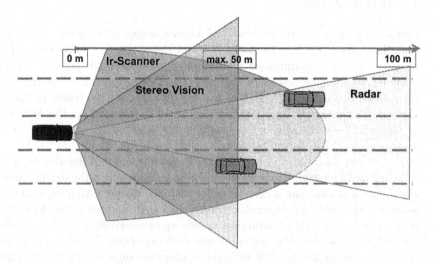

Fig. 1. Range of sight of different sensors.

The radar sensor measures distance and relative speed independently based on different physical principles. The sensor's range is up to 150 m with an aperture angle of 7° but a rather poor angular resolution. The infrared sensors scans

---

[2] Throughout this paper with the word/subscript *ego* we refer to the driver's vehicle, while with the word/subscript *obj* we refer to the vehicle(s) that is in the driver's range of sight.

nearly 180° up to about 50 m. The stereo vision system has the best lateral resolution but the object recognition based on disparity detection and clustering is sensitive to noise. The idea is to use all these sensors and to benefit from the best of each one of them.

2.2   Lane Recognition

For an accurate ACC system it is not enough to know the relative positions and velocities of the neighboring cars. Only with additional information about the road curvature good ACC performance can be achieved. For this reason a vision-based lane recognition system is implemented in the car. Optical lane recognition was introduced in the 1980s [2] and has often been implemented and refined since. The system is thoroughly described in many publications [2, 3,4], but the modelling shall be repeated here briefly. According to recommendations for highway construction [1], highways are built with the constraint of slowly changing curvature. Therefore the lane recognition system is based on a clothoidal lane model, that is given by

$$c(L) = c_0 + c_1 L. \tag{1}$$

where $c(L)$ describes the curvature at arclength L of the clothoid, c_0 the initial curvature and c_1 the curvature rate or clothoid parameter. The clothoide is defined as $c = R^{-1}$, with R the radius of the curve. With this road model and assuming only small angles and curvatures (which is true for highways and highway-like roads) a simple model of the vehicle in the lane can be stated as

$$\dot{x}_L = A_L x_L + B_L u_L \tag{2}$$

where

$$x_L = \begin{bmatrix} x_{off} \\ \Delta\Psi \\ c_0 \\ c_1 \end{bmatrix}, \quad A_L = \begin{bmatrix} 0 & v_{ego} & 0 & 0 \\ 0 & 0 & -v_{ego} & 0 \\ 0 & 0 & 0 & v_{ego} \\ 0 & 0 & 0 & 0 \end{bmatrix}, \quad B_L = \begin{bmatrix} 1 & 0 \\ 0 & 1 \\ 0 & 0 \\ 0 & 0 \end{bmatrix}, \quad u_L = \begin{bmatrix} v_{lat} \\ \dot{\Psi} \end{bmatrix}. \tag{3}$$

Here x_{off} denotes the lateral offset of the car in the lane, $\Delta\Psi$ the yaw angle, i.e. the angle between road direction and vehicle direction, $\dot{\Psi}$ the yaw rate i.e. the rotational speed of the car, v_{ego} the longitudinal and v_{lat} the lateral speed of the car. To determine the offset of the car from the middle of the lane, the width of the lane w is needed as well. To estimate x_L (for illustration see Figure 2), image processing algorithms detect the white lane markings. With these lane markings and internal sensor data the states from (2) can be estimated via Kalman filtering. The lane width w is treated as a disturbance variable.

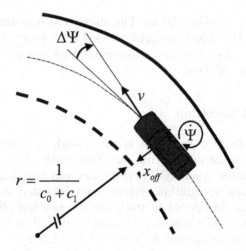

Fig. 2. Model of car in the lane.

2.3   Object Recognition

With all sensors having different ranges, measuring principles and accuracies, various algorithms are needed to process collected sensor data. Therefore, we set up the following model of longitudinal and lateral dynamics of the *ego*-vehicle and the *obj*-vehicle

$$\dot{x}_M = A_M x_M \tag{4}$$

where

$$x_M = \begin{bmatrix} d_i \\ v_{ego} \\ a_{ego} \\ v_{obj_i} \\ a_{obj_i} \\ d_{lat_i} \\ v_{lat_i} \end{bmatrix}, \quad A_M = \begin{bmatrix} 0 & -1 & 0 & 1 & 0 & 0 & 0 \\ 0 & 0 & 1 & 0 & 0 & 0 & 0 \\ 0 & 0 & 0 & 0 & 0 & 0 & 0 \\ 0 & 0 & 0 & 0 & 1 & 0 & 0 \\ 0 & 0 & 0 & 0 & 0 & 0 & 0 \\ 0 & 0 & 0 & 0 & 0 & 0 & 1 \\ 0 & 0 & 0 & 0 & 0 & 0 & 0 \end{bmatrix}. \tag{5}$$

Here v_{ego}, a_{ego} and v_{obj_i}, a_{obj_i} refer to velocity and acceleration of the *ego*-vehicle and the ith neighboring car respectively, d_i denotes the longitudinal distance between the *ego*-vehicle and the ith neighboring car, d_{lat_i} and v_{lat_i} describe relative lateral distance and speed of the ith neighboring car.

The dimension of system (5) varies with the number of neighboring cars that are taken into account. This model is then used for the Kalman filter based estimators. With measurements for d_i, v_{ego}, a_{ego}, $v_{rel_i} = v_{obj_i} - v_{ego}$ and d_{lat_i} system (5) is observable. The measurement noise parameter of the Kalman filter is used to weight measurements of the three sensor types differently. Distance measurements from more trustworthy sensors are respected with smaller measurement noise than measurements from less trustworthy sensors. To achieve good data association and tracking behavior in the presence of noise, probabilistic data association filters (PDAF) with gating techniques are used [8,9,10]. Further, it was observed that most of the time a neighboring car's motion can be described well either with zero acceleration or with a rather strong acceleration. For this reason multiple model filters are used in the estimation process [11,12]. For longitudinal modelling one filter assumes constant speed and another filter constant acceleration; for lateral dynamics one filter runs with a zero velocity and one with a constant velocity model. The two filters then interact according to their likelihood ratio.

2.4 Control Model

For control a model is needed to predict the future system behavior, given the actual states. With small changes, system (5) can be used. In system (5) the relative lateral distance d_{lat_i} was introduced. In the ACC control problem, however, the *difference in lane offset* is important rather than d_{lat_i}. In exaggerated form this can be seen in Figure 3. Here d_{lat_i} is zero since the advancing car is exactly in the direction of the *ego*-vehicle. The difference in lane offset, δ_i, however, is clearly not zero. The states that are needed to calculate δ_i and its derivative ν_i are all known from lane recognition and object recognition. The calculation is as follows (see Figure 4):

$$\delta_i = x_{off} - x_{off_i} = -d_{lat_i} - \Delta\Psi d_i + \frac{1}{2}c_0 d_i^2 + \frac{1}{6}c_1 d_i^3, \tag{6}$$

$$\nu_i = \frac{\partial}{\partial t}\delta_i = -v_{lat_i} + \frac{1}{2}c_1 v_{ego} d_i^2 - (\dot{\Psi} - c_0 v_{ego})d_i. \tag{7}$$

In (7) we assume d_i to be constant. As control variable, the reference acceleration, a_{ref}, of the *ego*-vehicle is introduced. We will assume that a low level acceleration controller, which manipulates the vehicle engine, gear shift and brakes, can be described as a first order lag with time constant τ.

Introducing the control variable a_{ref} and substituting d_{lat_i} and v_{lat_i} with δ_i and ν_i, respectively, we obtain the continuous model of the system

$$\dot{x} = A_c x + B_c u \tag{8}$$

where

$$x = \begin{bmatrix} d_i \\ v_{ego} \\ a_{ego} \\ v_{obj_i} \\ a_{obj_i} \\ \delta_i \\ \nu_i \end{bmatrix}, \quad u = [a_{ref}], \quad A_c = \begin{bmatrix} 0 & -1 & 0 & 1 & 0 & 0 & 0 \\ 0 & 0 & 1 & 0 & 0 & 0 & 0 \\ 0 & 0 & -\frac{1}{\tau} & 0 & 0 & 0 & 0 \\ 0 & 0 & 0 & 0 & 1 & 0 & 0 \\ 0 & 0 & 0 & 0 & 0 & 0 & 0 \\ 0 & 0 & 0 & 0 & 0 & 0 & 1 \\ 0 & 0 & 0 & 0 & 0 & 0 & 0 \end{bmatrix}, \quad B_c = \begin{bmatrix} 0 \\ 0 \\ \frac{1}{\tau} \\ 0 \\ 0 \\ 0 \\ 0 \end{bmatrix}. \tag{9}$$

For control purpose we are interested in the discrete representation

$$x(k+1) = A_d x(k) + B_d u(k) \tag{10}$$

that is obtained by sampling system (8) with the Zero Order Hold (ZOH).

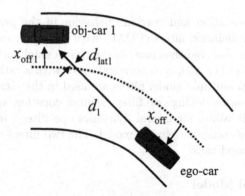

Fig. 3. Illustration of a difference in the lane offset.

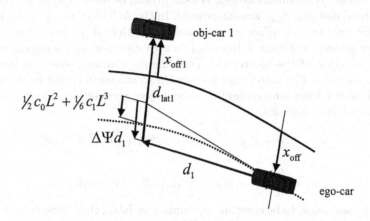

Fig. 4. Computation of the difference in the lane offset δ.

3 Problem Formulation

Control objectives for a traffic scene depicted in Figure 5 are the following

- track reference speed v_{ref} if possible
- respect safety distance d_{min} if neighboring car is in the same lane
- do not overtake on the right side of a neighboring car

while constraining

- maximal acceleration
- changes in acceleration
- changes in deceleration

Loosely speaking we would like to maintain a comfortable drive for the *ego*-car and prevent any *obj*-car from entering the shaded area in Figure 5. By inspection of the above mentioned objectives - inherent logic (traffic rules and lane

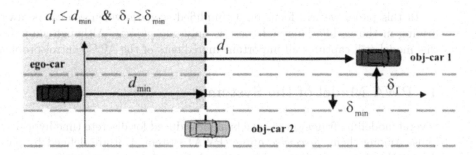

Fig. 5. Hybrid problem formulation.

assignment) and constraints on system states and input - it is straightforward to see that we are dealing with a constrained hybrid optimal control problem.

Whenever *obj*-car is outside of the shaded area (Figure 5), only the reference speed should enter the cost function

$$J = (v_{ego}(k) - v_{ref})^2 Q_v,$$

but if *obj*-car is closer than a certain d_{min} and it is in the same lane or on the left of the *ego*-car, the safety distance violation should enter the cost

$$J = (v_{ego}(k) - v_{ref})^2 Q_v + (d_{min} - d(k))^2 Q_d,$$

where Q_v and Q_d are appropriately chosen weights.

Note that the problem has two different cost functions defined over two regions, one of which is a non-convex polyhedron. Hence, to formulate one overall objective function we have to introduce some binary information.[3] For this purpose two new states are introduced. One of those states corresponds to the past manipulated variable $u(k-1) = a_{ref}(k-1)$, and is needed if changes in acceleration and deceleration are to be constrained. The second additional state incorporates the above mentioned *logic* condition

$$h_i(k) = \begin{cases} d_{min} - d_i(k) & \text{if} \quad d_i(k) \leqslant d_{min} \ \& \ \delta_i(k) \geqslant \delta_{min} \\ 0 & \text{if} \qquad\qquad \text{otherwise} \end{cases} \qquad (11)$$

so that the overall cost can be expressed simply as

$$J = (v_{ego}(k) - v_{ref})^2 Q_v + \sum_{i=1}^{\#obj} (h_i(k))^2 Q_d \qquad (12)$$

where δ_{min} is lateral distance for which *obj*-car is considered to be in the same lane as *ego*-car, and $\#obj$ is a total number of *obj*-cars.

---

[3] If lateral dynamics of the *obj*-car is neglected, or, equivalently, if *ego*-car is driving in the rightmost lane, the problem can be simplified even further. In such a case, using argumentation from [14], the problem can be reformulated as a multi-parametric Quadratic Program (mp-QP).

In this paper we will focus on a simplified scenario when *ego*-car is always driving in the middle lane and there is only one *obj*-car. Although simplified, this model still captures all important ingredients of the ACC control problem.

4   PWA Model of the System

Several modelling frameworks have been introduced for discrete time hybrid systems. Among them, *piecewise affine* (PWA) systems [13] are defined by partitioning the state space into polyhedral regions, and associating with each region a different linear state-update equation

$$x(t+1) = A_i x(t) + B_i u(t) + f_i$$
$$\text{if } \begin{bmatrix} x(t) \\ u(t) \end{bmatrix} \in \mathcal{P}_i \qquad (13)$$
$$i = 1, \dots, s$$

where $x \in \mathbb{R}^{n_c} \times \{0,1\}^{n_\ell}$, $u \in \mathbb{R}^{m_c} \times \{0,1\}^{m_\ell}$, $\{\mathcal{P}_i\}_{i=1}^{s}$ is a polyhedral partition of the sets of state+input space $\mathbb{R}^{n+m}$, $n \triangleq n_c + n_\ell$, $m \triangleq m_c + m_\ell$.

After incorporating additional states $u(k-1)$ and $h(k)$, we derive an equivalent PWA model from the continuous model (8). For simplicity, constant safety distance d_{min}, constant lateral distance δ_{min} and a constant reference speed v_{ref} are assumed. The maximum acceleration and deceleration are constrained to $\pm a_{ref_{max}}$ and the change in acceleration is constrained to $\pm \Delta a_{ref_{max}}$. Assuming that a time constant τ of the low level acceleration controller is known, by sampling the system (8) with Zero Order Hold (ZOH) with the sampling time T_s we get the following discrete time PWA model

$$x(t+1) = A_i x(t) + B_i u(t) + f_i$$
$$\text{if } \begin{bmatrix} x(t) \\ u(t) \end{bmatrix} \in \mathcal{P}_i \triangleq \{ [\begin{smallmatrix} x \\ u \end{smallmatrix}] : H_i x + L_i u \le K_i \} \qquad (14)$$
$$i = 1, 2, 3$$

where the state vector is

$$x(k) = [d(k), v_{ego}(k), a_{ego}(k), v_{obj}(k), a_{obj}(k), \delta(k), \nu(k), a_{ref}(k-1), h(k)]^T$$

and input is defined as $u(k) = a_{ref}(k)$. Having in mind that there are two cost functions we are trying to define, it seems natural to use *only* 2 regions in the PWA model. However, in the PWA model (14) we have 3 regions. The reason for such a choice is illustrated in Figure 6. Note that the region where contribution of distance d_i to the overall cost (12) is zero has a non-convex shape. Hence, it has to be sliced into two convex polyhedra. Numerical values of the parameters and system matrices A_i, B_i, f_i, H_i, L_i and K_i are given in the Appendix. Note that although original system has only one dynamics we had to introduce some logic condition to describe overall objective. In our example logic is incorporated in the auxiliary state $h(k)$ and in the state+input space partition. As a consequence we obtain a PWA model of the system.

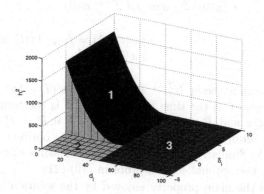

Fig. 6. Contribution of the distance d_i to the overall cost (12). Region where contribution is equal to zero has a non-convex shape, and thus it has to be partitioned into two polyhedra, marked with numbers 2 and 3.

5   Optimal State Feedback Control Law for PWA Systems

Consider the PWA system (13) subject to input and state constraints

$$E_c x(t) + L_c u(t) \le M_c \tag{15}$$

for $t \ge 0$. Matrices E_c, L_c and M_c are easily derived from general constraints

$$-a_{ref_{max}} \le u(k) \le a_{ref_{max}},$$
$$-\Delta a_{ref_{max}} \le u(k) - x_8(k) \le \Delta a_{ref_{max}}. \tag{16}$$

Denote by constrained PWA system (CPWA) the restriction of the PWA system (13) over the set of states and inputs defined by (15),

$$x(t+1) = A_i x(t) + B_i u(t) + f_i$$
$$\text{if } \begin{bmatrix} x(t) \\ u(t) \end{bmatrix} \in \tilde{\mathcal{P}}_i \tag{17}$$

where $\{\tilde{\mathcal{P}}_i\}_{i=1}^s$ is the new polyhedral partition of the sets of state+input space $\mathbb{R}^{n+m}$ obtained by intersecting the polyhedrons $\mathcal{P}_i$ in (13) with the polyhedron described by (15). Let $\tilde{\mathcal{P}} \triangleq \cup_{i=1}^s \{\tilde{\mathcal{P}}_i\}$. In the following we will denote the CPWA system equations (17) with the shorter form

$$x(k+1) = \tilde{f}_{PWA}(x(k), u(k)) \tag{18}$$

where $\tilde{f}_{PWA} : \tilde{\mathcal{P}} \to \mathbb{R}^n$ and $\tilde{f}_{PWA}(x, u) = A_i x + B_i u + f_i$ if $\begin{bmatrix} x \\ u \end{bmatrix} \in \tilde{\mathcal{P}}_i$, $i = 1, \dots, s$. Define the following cost function

$$J(U_0^{T-1}, x(0)) \triangleq \|P(x(T) - x_e)\|_2 + \sum_{k=0}^{T-1} \|Q(x(k) - x_e)\|_2 + \|R(u(k) - u_e)\|_2 \tag{19}$$

and consider the finite-time constrained optimal control problem (FTCOC)

$$J^*(x(0)) \triangleq \min_{U_0^{T-1}} J(U_0^{T-1}, x(0)) \qquad (20)$$

$$\text{s.t.} \quad \begin{cases} x(t+1) = \tilde{f}_{PWA}(x(t), u(t)) \\ x(T) \in \mathcal{X}^f \end{cases} \qquad (21)$$

where the column vector $U_0^{T-1} \triangleq [u'(0), \ldots, u'(T-1)]' \in \mathbb{R}^{mT}$, is the optimization vector, T is the time horizon and $\mathcal{X}^f$ is the terminal region. In (19), $\|Qx\|_2 = x'Qx$ and $R = R' \succ 0$, $Q = Q' \succeq 0, P = P' \succeq 0$. We denote by $\mathcal{X}^0 \subseteq \mathbb{R}^n$ the set of initial states $x(0)$ for which the optimal control problem (19)-(21) is feasible. Similarly, $\mathcal{X}^k$ denotes the set of feasible states $x(k)$, $k = 1, \ldots, T$ at time k for the optimal control problem (19)-(21).

We recall the main property enjoyed by the solution of problem (19)-(21). For more details see [14,16].

Theorem 1. *The solution to the optimal control problem (19)-(21) is a PWA state feedback control law of the form*

$$u^*(x(k)) = F_i^k x(k) + G_i^k \; if \; x(k) \in \mathcal{R}_i^k \qquad (22)$$

where $\mathcal{R}_i^k$, $i = 1, \ldots, N_i$ is a partition of the set $\mathcal{X}^k$ of feasible states $x(k)$ and the closure $\bar{\mathcal{R}}_i^k$ of the sets $\mathcal{R}_i^k$ has the following form:

$$\bar{\mathcal{R}}_i^k \triangleq \left\{ x : \; x'(k) L(j)_i^k x(k) + M(j)_i^k x(k) \leq N(j)_i^k, \; j = 1, \ldots, n_i^k \right\},$$

with $k = 0, \ldots, T - 1$.

As shown in [14], the problem (19)-(21) can be solved via dynamic programming

$$J_j^*(x(j)) \triangleq \min_{u(j)} \left\{ \|Q(x(j) - x_e)\|_2 + \|R(u(j) - u_e)\|_2 + J_{j+1}^*(\tilde{f}_{PWA}(x(j), u(j))) \right\}$$

$$\text{s.t.} \; \tilde{f}_{PWA}(x(j), u(j)) \in \mathcal{X}^{j+1} \qquad (23)$$

for $j = T - 1, \ldots, 0$, with boundary conditions

$$\mathcal{X}^T = \mathcal{X}^f \qquad (24)$$

$$J_T^*(x) = \|Px\|_2 \qquad (25)$$

where $\mathcal{X}^j$ is the set of all initial states for which problem (23) is feasible:

$$\mathcal{X}^j = \{x \in \mathbb{R}^n | \; \exists u, \; \tilde{f}_{PWA}(x, u) \in \mathcal{X}^{j+1}\} \qquad (26)$$

The dynamic program (23)-(25) can be solved backwards in time by using a multiparametric quadratic programming solver [15] combined with some basic polyhedral manipulations.

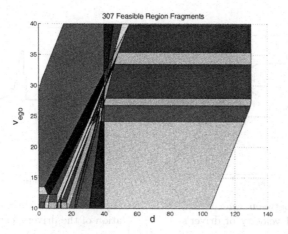

Fig. 7. Partition of the state space corresponding to the optimal control law, for $a_{ego} = 0$, $v_{obj} = 30\frac{m}{s}$, $a_{obj} = 0\frac{m}{s^2}$, $a_{ref}(k-1) = 0\frac{m}{s^2}$.

6   Simulation Results

We design a receding horizon controller based on the optimization problem (19)–(21) for a system (14)–(16), with $T_s = 0.5$, $T = 3$, $Q = diag([0\ 1\ 0\ 0\ 0\ 0\ 10])$, $R = 1$, $P = Q$, and desired velocity $v_{ref} = 30\frac{m}{s}$. The corresponding optimal solution is composed of 2740 polyhedra in $\mathbb{R}^9$ (the dimension of the state space is 9). In Figure 7 we show one slice of the optimal state feedback control law partition for the fixed states $a_{ego} = 0\frac{m}{s^2}$, $v_{obj} = 28\frac{m}{s}$, $a_{obj} = 0\frac{m}{s^2}$, $a_{ref}(k-1) = 0\frac{m}{s^2}$, $\delta = 2m$, $\nu = 0\frac{m}{s}$. In Figure 8, starting with initial state $x(0) = [45\ 30\ 0\ 28\ 0\ 2\ -0.1\ 0\ 0]^T$, we report the following traffic scenario. An *ego*-car and an *obj*-car are driving in the middle lane (see Figure 5). *obj*-car has a constant speed $v_{obj} = 28\frac{m}{s}$ and it is moving to the right lane with the constant lateral velocity $\nu = -0.1$. Since $v_{obj} < v_{ref} = 30$ we notice that at $t = 3s$ *obj*-car reaches the safety distance and from that point onward it is maintaining the same speed as the *obj*-car. At $t = 20s$ *obj*-car leaves the middle lane and *ego*-car speeds up to the reference cruising speed v_{ref}.

7   Experimental Results

For the experiment we simplify problem (19)–(21) for a system (14)–(16) by neglecting the lateral dynamics of the *obj*-car. We design a receding horizon with $T = 3$, $Q = diag([0\ 1\ 0\ 0\ 0\ 0\ 10])$, $R = 1$, $P = Q$, $v_{ref} = 30\frac{m}{s}$ and $d_{min} = 40m$. The corresponding optimal solution is composed of 753 polyhedra in $\mathbb{R}^7$ (dimension of the state space is 7). In Figure 9 we report the response of the system starting from $x(0) = [45\ 23\ 0\ 20\ 0\ 0\ 0]^T$ when the optimal state-feedback control law is used. Similarly to Figure 8, we see that *ego*-car reaches and keeps a safety distance $d_{min} = 40m$ while tracking the speed of *obj*-car. The

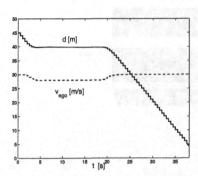

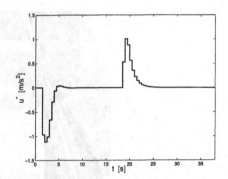

(a) Distance between *ego*-car and *obj*-car d, and velocity of driver's car v_{ego}.

(b) Manipulated variable - acceleration of the driver's car a_{ref}.

Fig. 8. Simulation of the ACC system with implemented optimal state-feedback controller for initial state $x(0) = [45\ 30\ 0\ 28\ 0\ 2\ -0.1\ 0\ 0]^T$ and with *obj*-car slowly moving out of *ego*-car's lane.

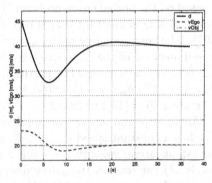

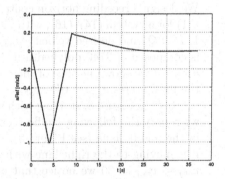

(a) Distance between *ego*-car and *obj*-car d, and velocities v_{ego} and v_{obj}.

(b) Acceleration of the driver's car a_{ref}.

Fig. 9. Simulation of the ACC system with implemented optimal state-feedback controller for initial state $x(0) = [45\ 23\ 0\ 20\ 0\ 0\ 0]^T$. Lateral dynamics is neglected and the *obj*-car has a constant speed $v_{obj} = 20$.

optimal state-feedback control law was tested on a research car Mercedes E430 (Figure 10). Special interfaces to throttle and brakes, sensor fusion, visualization and the ACC controller were running in a real-time environment with an 80 ms cycle time on an Intel Pentium4 1.4GHz machine with 500 MByte RAM. In Figure 11 experimental data from a test drive are shown. The plots start with

(a) Mercedes E430.   (b) Look from the cockpit.

Fig. 10. Experimental setup.

initial states approximately $x(0) = [28\ 26\ -0.5\ 23.5\ 0\ -0.7\ 12]^T$. As time increases, the distance between *ego*-car and *obj*-car approaches $d_{min} = 40$m and v_{ego} approaches v_{obj}, as can be seen in Figure 11(a). The corresponding accelerations a_{ego} and a_{obj} and controller action a_{ref} are shown in Figure 11(b).

In Section 3 and Section 4 the piecewise affine problem formulation was introduced to incorporate the lane assignment into the controller design. In this approach the controller decides implicitly whether an *obj*-car is relevant for the controller or not. In a second experiment lane assignment is calculated every cycle by an external logic before the controller is called. If the *obj*-car changes its lane to the right it is declared *not relevant* and thus it is not taken into account by the controller. In Figure 12 results of this strategy are shown. The scenario starts with $v_{ego} > v_{obj}$ and $d > d_{min}$. In the sequel the distance between *ego*-car and *obj*-car approaches $d_{min} = 40$m and v_{ego} approaches v_{obj}. At time instant $t = 6$s the *obj*-car changes its lane to the right and is thus declared *not relevant*. As time goes on v_{ego} approaches $v_{ref} = 30\frac{m}{s}$. Note that although from $t = 6$s the *obj*-car is in the right lane (and neglected by the controller) it is still seen by the sensors until $t = 12.7$s, when it completely moves out of the sight. This can be seen as a drop of the distance d to the zero value in Figure 12(a).

8 Conclusion

We have shown that the Multi-Object Adaptive Cruise Control problem can be solved via hybrid system theory. The objective function is modelled as a quadratic cost function for the discrete time piecewise affine system. The optimal state-feedback control law is found by solving the underlying constrained finite time optimal control problem via dynamic programming. Experimental results were presented for the car-following scenario.

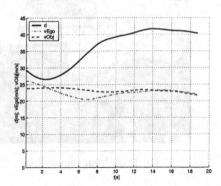

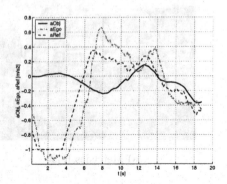

(a) Measured distance between *ego*-car and *obj*-car d, and velocities v_{ego} and v_{obj}.

(b) Manipulated variable a_{ref} and measured/estimated accelerations a_{ego} and a_{obj}.

Fig. 11. Experimental results of the ACC system with implemented optimal state-feedback controller. Initial state is approximately $x(0) = [28 \ 26 \ -0.5 \ 23.5 \ 0 \ -0.7 \ 12]^T$. After a transient *ego*-car manages to track speed of *obj*-car while maintaining the safety distance.

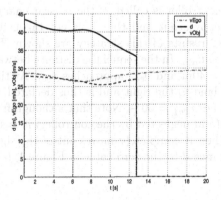

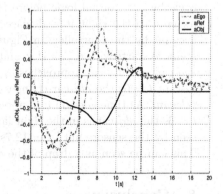

(a) Measured distance d between *ego*-car and *obj*-car, and velocities v_{ego} and v_{obj}.

(b) Manipulated variable a_{ref} and measured/estimated accelerations a_{ego} and a_{obj}.

Fig. 12. Experimental results of the ACC system with implemented optimal state-feedback controller. Until $t = 7$s *obj*-car is in the same lane as *ego*-car, but then it goes into the right lane. From that point controller has only reference speed as an objective. At $t = 12.7$s *obj*-car leaves the road completely.

References

1. Richtlinien für die Anlage von Strassen (RAS-L-1), *Forschungsgesellschaft für Strassen- und Verkehrswesen*, Köln, (1984)
2. Zapp, A., Dickmanns, E.D.: A curvature-based scheme for improved road vehicle guidance by computer vision. *SPIE conference on mobile robots*, (1986)
3. Franke, U., Gavrila, D., Gern, A., Goerzig, S., Janssen, R., Paetzold, F., Woehle,r C.: From Door to Door - Principles and Applications of Computer Vision for Driver Assistance Systems. *Intelligent Vehicles Technologies: Theory and Applications*, Arnold, (2000)
4. Franke, U., Gavrila, D., Goerzig, S., Lindner, F., Paetzold, F., Woehler, C.: Autonomous Driving Goes Downtown. *IEEE Intelligent Systems*, Vol. 13(6):40–48, (1998)
5. Liubakka, M.K., Rhode, D.S., Winkelman, J.R., Kokotovic, P.V.: Adaptive Automotive Speed Control. *IEEE Transactions on Automatic Control*, Vol. 38(7):1011–1020, (1993)
6. Ha, I., Tugcu, A.K., Boustany, N.M.: Feedback Linearizing Control of Vehicle Longitudinal Acceleration. *IEEE Transactions on Automatic Control*, Vol. 34(7):689–698, (1989)
7. Won, M. Hedrick, J.K.: Disturbance Adaptive Discrete-Time Sliding Control With Application to Engine Speed Control. *Journal of Dynamic Systems, Measurement and Control*, Vol. 123(1):1–9, (2001)
8. Bar-Shalom, Y., Fortmann, T.E.: *Tracking and Data Association*. Academic Press INC, San Diego, New York (1988)
9. Bar-Shalom, Y., Dale Blair, W.: *Multitarget-Multisensor Tracking: Applications and Advances Volume III*. Artech House, Boston, London, (2000)
10. Blackman, S.S.: *Multiple Target Tracking with Radar Applications*. Artech House, (1986)
11. Magill, D.T.: Optimal Adaptive Estimation of Sampled Stochastic Processes. *IEEE Transactions on Automatic Control*, Vol. 10(4):434–439, (1965)
12. Blom, A.P., Bar-Shalom, Y.: The Interacting Multiple Model Algorithm for Systems with Markovian Switching Coefficients. *IEEE Transactions on Automatic Control*, Vol. 33(8):780–783, (1988)
13. Sontag, E.D.: Nonlinear regulation: The piecewise linear approach. *IEEE Trans. Automatic Control*, 26(2):346–358, (1981)
14. Borrelli, F., Baotic, M., Bemporad, A., Morari, M.: An efficient algorithm for computing the state feedback optimal control law for discrete time hybrid systems. Technical Report AUT02-04, ETH Zurich, http://control.ethz.ch/~hybrid/hysdel, (2002)
15. Bemporad, A., Morari, M., Dua, V., Pistikopoulos, E.N.: The explicit linear quadratic regulator for constrained systems. *Automatica*, 38(1):3–20, (2002)
16. Borrelli, F.: Discrete Time Constrained Optimal Control. *Dr.sc.tech. thesis*, Swiss Federal Institute of Technology (ETH), Zürich, Switzerland, (2002)

Appendix

In the following we report numerical values for the PWA model (14):

$$d_{min} = 40\text{m}, \quad \delta_{min} = 3\text{m}, \quad v_{ref} = 30\frac{\text{m}}{\text{s}},$$

$$a_{ref_{max}} = 1.5\frac{\text{m}}{\text{s}^2}, \quad \Delta a_{ref_{max}} = 0.02\frac{\text{m}}{\text{s}^3},$$

$$\tau = 0.1\text{s}, \quad T_s = 2.7\text{s}.$$

$$
A_1 = \begin{bmatrix}
1 & -2.7 & -0.26 & 2.7 & 3.645 & 0 & 0 & 0 & 0 \\
0 & 1 & 0.1 & 0 & 0 & 0 & 0 & 0 & 0 \\
0 & 0 & 0 & 0 & 0 & 0 & 0 & 0 & 0 \\
0 & 0 & 0 & 1 & 2.7 & 0 & 0 & 0 & 0 \\
0 & 0 & 0 & 0 & 1 & 0 & 0 & 0 & 0 \\
0 & 0 & 0 & 0 & 0 & 1 & 2.7 & 0 & 0 \\
0 & 0 & 0 & 0 & 0 & 0 & 1 & 0 & 0 \\
0 & 0 & 0 & 0 & 0 & 0 & 0 & 0 & 0 \\
-1 & 0 & 0 & 0 & 0 & 0 & 0 & 0 & 0
\end{bmatrix}, \quad
B_1 = \begin{bmatrix}
-3.385 \\ 2.6 \\ 1 \\ 0 \\ 0 \\ 0 \\ 0 \\ 1 \\ 0
\end{bmatrix}, \quad
f_1 = \begin{bmatrix}
0 \\ 0 \\ 0 \\ 0 \\ 0 \\ 0 \\ 0 \\ 0 \\ d_{min}
\end{bmatrix},
$$

$$
H_1 = \begin{bmatrix}
1 & 0 & 0 & 0 & 0 & 0 & 0 & 0 & 0 \\
0 & 0 & 0 & 0 & 0 & -1 & 0 & 0 & 0
\end{bmatrix}, \quad
L_1 = \begin{bmatrix} 0 \\ 0 \end{bmatrix}, \quad
K_1 = \begin{bmatrix} d_{min} \\ -\delta_{min} \end{bmatrix}.
$$

$$
A_2 = \begin{bmatrix}
1 & -2.7 & -0.26 & 2.7 & 3.645 & 0 & 0 & 0 & 0 \\
0 & 1 & 0.1 & 0 & 0 & 0 & 0 & 0 & 0 \\
0 & 0 & 0 & 0 & 0 & 0 & 0 & 0 & 0 \\
0 & 0 & 0 & 1 & 2.7 & 0 & 0 & 0 & 0 \\
0 & 0 & 0 & 0 & 1 & 0 & 0 & 0 & 0 \\
0 & 0 & 0 & 0 & 0 & 1 & 2.7 & 0 & 0 \\
0 & 0 & 0 & 0 & 0 & 0 & 1 & 0 & 0 \\
0 & 0 & 0 & 0 & 0 & 0 & 0 & 0 & 0 \\
0 & 0 & 0 & 0 & 0 & 0 & 0 & 0 & 0
\end{bmatrix}, \quad
B_2 = \begin{bmatrix}
-3.385 \\ 2.6 \\ 1 \\ 0 \\ 0 \\ 0 \\ 0 \\ 1 \\ 0
\end{bmatrix}, \quad
f_2 = \begin{bmatrix}
0 \\ 0 \\ 0 \\ 0 \\ 0 \\ 0 \\ 0 \\ 0 \\ 0
\end{bmatrix},
$$

$$
H_2 = \begin{bmatrix}
1 & 0 & 0 & 0 & 0 & 0 & 0 & 0 & 0 \\
0 & 0 & 0 & 0 & 0 & 1 & 0 & 0 & 0
\end{bmatrix}, \quad
L_2 = \begin{bmatrix} 0 \\ 0 \end{bmatrix}, \quad
K_2 = \begin{bmatrix} d_{min} \\ \delta_{min} \end{bmatrix}.
$$

$$A_3 = A_2, \quad B_3 = B_2,$$

$$f_3 = f_2, \quad H_3 = \begin{bmatrix} -1 & 0 & 0 & 0 & 0 & 0 & 0 & 0 & 0 \end{bmatrix}, \quad L_3 = \begin{bmatrix} 0 \end{bmatrix}, \quad K_3 = \begin{bmatrix} -d_{min} \end{bmatrix}.$$

Universality and Language Inclusion for Open and Closed Timed Automata*

Joël Ouaknine[1] and James Worrell[2]

[1] Computer Science Department, Carnegie Mellon University,
5000 Forbes Ave., Pittsburgh PA 15213, USA
joelo@andrew.cmu.edu

[2] Department of Mathematics, Tulane University,
New Orleans LA 70118, USA
jbw@math.tulane.edu

Abstract. The algorithmic analysis of timed automata is fundamentally limited by the undecidability of the universality problem. For this reason and others, there has been considerable interest in restricted classes of timed automata. In this paper we study the universality problem for two prominent such subclasses: *open* and *closed* timed automata. This problem is described as open in [6,8] in the case of open timed automata. We show here that the problem is undecidable for open timed automata over *strongly monotonic* time (no two events are allowed to occur at the same time), and decidable over *weakly monotonic* time. For closed timed automata, we show that the problem is undecidable regardless of the monotonicity assumptions on time. As a corollary, we settle the various language inclusion problems over these classes of timed automata.

1 Introduction

Timed automata were introduced by Alur and Dill [1] and have since become a standard modelling paradigm for real-time systems. Unfortunately, the algorithmic analysis of timed automata is limited by the undecidability of the universality problem (can a given timed automaton perform every timed trace?) [1]. It has also been argued that timed automata provide unrealistic and too powerful expressive power to the system designer. In attempting to address these difficulties, a number of researchers have studied restricted classes of timed automata [6,2,4,5].

---

* The first author was supported by the Defense Advanced Research Project Agency (DARPA) and the Army Research Office (ARO) under contract no. DAAD19-01-1-0485, and the Office of Naval Research (ONR) under contract no. N00014-95-1-0520. The second author was supported by ONR and NSF. The views and conclusions contained in this document are those of the authors and should not be interpreted as representing the official policies, either expressed or implied, of DARPA, ARO, ONR, NSF, the U.S. Government or any other entity.

O. Maler and A. Pnueli (Eds.): HSCC 2003, LNCS 2623, pp. 375–388, 2003.

Two prominent such subclasses are *open* timed automata (all clock constraints must be strict, as in $x < 3$ as opposed to $x \leqslant 3$) and *closed* timed automata (clock constraints are non-strict). Open timed automata have the desirable property of being 'acceptance-robust': whenever they accept a timed trace, they also accept all neighbouring traces that are sufficiently 'close' to the trace in question. Closed timed automata, on the other hand, are 'rejection-robust', in that rejected traces are stable under small temporal perturbations. Closed timed automata also precisely correspond to the finite-state fragment of Timed CSP [10], and can conservatively approximate mixed timed automata with infinitesimal 'precision' [6,9]. For this reason, they are very often used in practice [4,3]. In addition, open and closed timed automata have certain complementary 'digitization' properties which can prove extremely valuable to the efficient algorithmic analysis of their behaviour [7,3,4].

In this paper, we study the universality problem for both these important classes of timed automata. This problem is described as open in [6,8] in the case of open timed automata. We show here that it is undecidable if the underlying dense-time domain is *strongly monotonic* (no two events can occur at the same time), and decidable (for open timed automata) if the dense-time domain is *weakly monotonic* (several events are allowed to occur simultaneously). This is a rather surprising result as most researchers usually regard the monotonicity assumptions on time as unimportant, and indeed often pick one and never look back. In the case of closed timed automata, we show that the universality problem is undecidable regardless of the dense-time domain used.

Alur and Dill's original proof of the undecidability of the universality problem for timed automata encodes the halting computations of a Turing-complete machine M as a set of timed traces $L_{\text{AD}}(M)$, and then shows that the complement of this language can be captured by some timed automaton [1]. As noted in [5,8], this encoding is quite fragile, and requires the timed automaton to differentiate points in time with infinite precision. This, of course, can be difficult to achieve with either exclusively open or exclusively closed clock constraints. Nonetheless, we show here that, by at most doubling the number of clocks used, open timed automata are still powerful enough to capture the required undecidable language, under the semantic assumption of strongly monotonic time.

The reason this device breaks down over weakly monotonic time is that it is impossible to construct an open timed automaton which captures precisely all timed traces that fail to be strongly monotonic, in other words all timed traces that have at least two events occurring at the same time. And indeed, digitization techniques [7] can be used to show that the universality problem is decidable in that case.

Alur and Dill's construction is unfortunately not directly applicable when it comes to closed timed automata. The reason is that closed timed automata only accept languages that are closed in the 'd-topology' [6], whereas the language meant to be captured (the complement of $L_{\text{AD}}(M)$) is not d-closed. A similar problem was noticed by Henzinger and Raskin in the context of robust timed automata. In particular they established the undecidability of the universality problem for robust timed automata and tube languages using a variant of $L_{AD}(M)$ stable under small temporal perturbations [8]. Unfortunately, when interpreted over mere timed traces, the language complement they define again fails to be d-closed. Nonetheless, we were able to utilize their ideas to define a suitable language having d-closed complement and which can be captured by a closed timed automaton. The basic trick is to alter the definition of $L_{AD}(M)$ so that events have strictly positive durations; this is achieved by having separate signals explicitly denote the beginning and end of a previously instantaneous event. These delimiters are then required to lie in certain iteratively defined open sets, yielding a language with d-closed complement. This establishes that the universality problem for closed timed automata is indeed undecidable.

These results enable us to settle the various language inclusion problems (does a timed automaton accept all the timed traces of another one?) over these classes of timed automata. It turns out that the only decidable instance is whether the language of a closed timed automaton is a subset of that of an open timed automaton, when interpreted over weakly monotonic time.

2   Timed Automata and Timed Traces

Let C be a finite set of clocks, denoted x, y, z, etc. We define the set Φ_C of clock constraints over C via the following grammar (here $k \in \mathbb{N}$ is a non-negative integer).

$$\phi ::= \textbf{true} \mid x < k \mid x \leqslant k \mid x > k \mid x \geqslant k \mid \phi \wedge \phi \mid \phi \vee \phi .$$

Definition 1. *A (mixed) timed automaton is a tuple $(\Sigma, S, S_0, S_f, C, E)$, where*

- *Σ is a finite alphabet of events,*
- *S is a finite set of locations,*
- *$S_0 \subseteq S$ is a set of start locations,*
- *$S_f \subseteq S$ is a set of final locations,*
- *C is a finite set of clocks, and*
- *$E \subseteq S \times S \times \Phi_C \times \Sigma \times \mathcal{P}(C) \times \Phi_C$ is a finite set of transitions. A transition $(s, s', \phi, a, R, \phi')$ allows a jump from location s to s', communicating event $a \in \Sigma$ in the process, provided the precondition ϕ on clocks is met. Afterwards, the clocks in R are nondeterministically reset to values satisfying the postcondition ϕ', and all other clocks remain unchanged. We assume that all clocks appearing in ϕ' are in R, and that ϕ' is satisfiable.*

An open timed automaton is a timed automaton in which all pre- and postconditions $\phi, \phi' \in \Phi_C$ on edges are open, i.e., are generated by the grammar

$$\phi ::= \textbf{true} \mid x < k \mid x > k \mid \phi \wedge \phi \mid \phi \vee \phi .$$

A closed timed automaton is a timed automaton in which all pre- and postconditions on edges are closed, i.e., are generated by the grammar

$$\phi ::= \textbf{true} \mid x \leqslant k \mid x \geqslant k \mid \phi \wedge \phi \mid \phi \vee \phi .$$

Remark 2. Our definitions of mixed, open, and closed timed automata follow [6, 8]. One however finds many variants in the literature: allowing direct comparisons between clocks, e.g., $x - y > k$; allowing rational, rather than integral, bounds in constraints; including invariant clock constraints on locations; allowing clocks to be reset to zero only; considering infinite trace semantics with Büchi or Muller acceptance conditions, rather than finite traces as we do in this paper. It is however not difficult to verify that all the results presented here extend straightforwardly to any combination of these variants.

A *clock interpretation* is a function $\nu : C \longrightarrow \mathbb{R}^+$, where $\mathbb{R}^+$ stands for the non-negative real numbers. If $t \in \mathbb{R}^+$, we let $\nu + t$ be the clock interpretation such that $(\nu + t)(x) = \nu(x) + t$ for all $x \in C$.

A *state* is a triple (s, t, ν), where $s \in S$ is a location, $t \in \mathbb{R}^+$ is the global time elapsed since the automaton was switched on, and ν is a clock interpretation.

A *run* of a timed automaton $A = (\Sigma, S, S_0, S_f, C, E)$ is a finite alternating sequence of states and transitions $e = (s_0, t_0, \nu_0) \xrightarrow{\alpha_1} (s_1, t_1, \nu_1) \xrightarrow{\alpha_2} \ldots \xrightarrow{\alpha_n} (s_n, t_n, \nu_n)$, with the t_i's non-decreasing, and each state (s_i, t_i, ν_i) recording the data immediately following the previous transition $\alpha_i = (s_{i-1}, s_i, \phi_i, a_i, R_i, \phi_i') \in E$. In addition,

1. $s_0 \in S_0$ and $t_0 = 0$.
2. For all $0 \leqslant i \leqslant n-1$: $\nu_i + (t_{i+1} - t_i)$ satisfies ϕ_{i+1}, $\nu_{i+1}(x) = \nu_i(x) + (t_{i+1} - t_i)$ for all $x \in C \setminus R_{i+1}$, and ν_{i+1} satisfies ϕ_{i+1}'.
3. $s_n \in S_f$.

A *timed event* is a pair (t, a), where $t \in \mathbb{R}^+$ is called the *timestamp* of the *event* $a \in \Sigma$. A *timed trace* is a finite sequence of timed events with non-decreasing timestamps. The set of all timed traces is denoted **WMTT**, which stands for 'Weakly Monotonic Timed Traces'. The set of all timed traces in which all timestamps are strictly positive and no two timed events have the same timestamp is denoted **SMTT** (the 'S' stands for 'Strongly').

If $u = \langle (t_1, a_1), (t_2, a_2), \ldots, (t_n, a_n) \rangle$ is a timed trace, we define an operator $\text{untime}(u) \mathbin{\widehat{=}} a_1 a_2 \ldots a_n$ which removes all timestamps from u, retaining only the relative order of events. This operator extends to sets of timed traces in the obvious way.

Given a run $e = (s_0, t_0, \nu_0) \xrightarrow{\alpha_1} (s_1, t_1, \nu_1) \xrightarrow{\alpha_2} \ldots \xrightarrow{\alpha_n} (s_n, t_n, \nu_n)$, we produce an associated timed trace $\text{tt}(e) = \langle (t_1, a_1), (t_2, a_2), \ldots, (t_n, a_n) \rangle$, where each a_i is the event component of the transition α_i.

Finally, we define the following two trace semantics for timed automata: $\mathcal{W}[\![A]\!] \mathbin{\widehat{=}} \{\text{tt}(e) \mid e \text{ is a run of } A\}$ represents the set of dense-time weakly monotonic timed traces of A, whereas $\mathcal{S}[\![A]\!] \mathbin{\widehat{=}} \mathcal{W}[\![A]\!] \cap \textbf{SMTT}$ denotes the set of dense-time strongly monotonic timed traces of A.

3   Regions, Digitization, and Topology

In this section we review the region automaton construction of Alur and Dill [1], the digitization results of Henzinger, Manna, and Pnueli [7], and the d-topology of Jagadeesan, Henzinger, and Gupta [6].

3.1   Region Automata

Let $A = (\Sigma, S, S_0, S_f, C, E)$ be a timed automaton. Let k be the largest integer constant appearing in any of the clock constraints associated with the transitions of A. We define an equivalence relation $\sim$ on the set of clock interpretations as follows: $\nu \sim \nu'$ if

1. For all clocks $x \in C$, either $\lfloor \nu(x) \rfloor = \lfloor \nu'(x) \rfloor$, or both $\nu(x)$ and $\nu'(x)$ are greater than k.
2. For all $x, y \in C$ with $\nu(x), \nu(y) \leqslant k$, we have $fract(\nu(x)) \leqslant fract(\nu(y)) \Leftrightarrow fract(\nu'(x)) \leqslant fract(\nu'(y))$.
3. For all $x \in C$ with $\nu(x) \leqslant k$, $fract(\nu(x)) = 0 \Leftrightarrow fract(\nu'(x)) = 0$.

It is easy to check that $\sim$ partitions the set of clock interpretations into finitely many equivalence classes, termed *clock regions*.

We define a partial order $\preccurlyeq$ on clock regions as follows: $r \preccurlyeq r'$ if, for any $\nu \in r$, there exists a non-negative real $t \in \mathbb{R}^+$ such that $\nu + t \in r'$. We also define a transitive and antisymmetric relation $\prec$ on clock regions in the same way except that t is required to be strictly positive. Note that $r \prec r$ for some, but not all, clock regions r.

We now define the *(weakly monotonic) region automaton* $WREG(A)$ of A as follows. Its alphabet is the same as that of A, Σ. The states of $WREG(A)$ consist of all pairs (s, r), where $s \in S$ is a location of A and r is a clock region of A. The start states of $WREG(A)$ consist of all states of the form (s_0, r), where $s_0 \in S_0$, and its accepting states consist of all states of the form (s_f, r), where $s_f \in S_f$. $WREG(A)$ has a transition $(s, r) \xrightarrow{a} (s', r')$ provided there exist a clock region $r'' \succcurlyeq r$ and an A-transition $(s, s', \phi, a, R, \phi') \in E$ such that all clock interpretations in r'' satisfy ϕ, r'' and r' agree when restricted to clocks not belonging to R, and all clock interpretations in r' meet ϕ'.

We also define the *(strongly monotonic) region automaton* $SREG(A)$ in exactly the same way except that we replace the relation $\preccurlyeq$ with $\prec$.

The (untimed) languages accepted by $WREG(A)$ and $SREG(A)$ are denoted $[\![WREG(A)]\!]$ and $[\![SREG(A)]\!]$ respectively.

We now have:

Theorem 3 (Alur and Dill [1]). *For any timed automaton A,* $[\![WREG(A)]\!] = \mathsf{untime}(\mathcal{W}[\![A]\!])$ *and* $[\![SREG(A)]\!] = \mathsf{untime}(\mathcal{S}[\![A]\!])$.

We refer the reader to [1] for the proof.

The *emptiness problem* is to decide whether the set of timed traces of a timed automaton is empty. As an immediate consequence of Theorem 3, the emptiness problem for timed automata over either weakly or strongly monotonic time is decidable.

The *reachability problem* is to decide, given an arbitrary fixed event, whether a timed automaton has at least one trace in which this event occurs. This problem is equivalent to the emptiness problem, and is thus always decidable.

3.2   Digitization

Let $t \in \mathbb{R}^+$ and let $0 \leqslant \varepsilon \leqslant 1$ be real numbers. If $fract(t) < \varepsilon$, let $[t]_\varepsilon \cong \lfloor t \rfloor$, otherwise let $[t]_\varepsilon \cong \lceil t \rceil$.

We can then extend $[\cdot]_\varepsilon$ to timed traces by pointwise application to the timestamps of the trace's events. We then further extend $[\cdot]_\varepsilon$ to sets of timed traces in the usual way.

Definition 4. *Let T be a set of timed traces.*

*T is closed under digitization if, for any $0 \leqslant \varepsilon \leqslant 1$, $[T]_\varepsilon \subseteq T$. T is closed under inverse digitization if, whenever a timed trace $u \in$ **WMTT** is such that $[u]_\varepsilon \in T$ for all $0 \leqslant \varepsilon \leqslant 1$, then $u \in T$.*

For A a timed automaton, the above definitions apply to $\mathcal{W}[\![A]\!]$.

For $T \subseteq$ **WMTT** a set of timed traces, let $\mathbb{Z}(T)$ be the set of all integral timed traces of T, i.e., those timed traces in T all of whose events have integral timestamps.

The main digitization result is as follows:

Theorem 5 (Henzinger, Manna, and Pnueli [7]). *Let T be a set of timed traces closed under digitization, and let T' be a set of timed traces closed under inverse digitization. Then $T \subseteq T'$ if and only if $\mathbb{Z}(T) \subseteq \mathbb{Z}(T')$.*

The right-to-left implication is trivial. For the positive direction, let $u \in T$. Since T is closed under digitization, $[u]_\varepsilon \in T$ for any ε. However $\mathbb{Z}(T) \subseteq \mathbb{Z}(T')$, thus $[u]_\varepsilon \in T'$ for any ε. Since T' is closed under inverse digitization, $u \in T'$ as required.

Observe that integral timed traces over alphabet Σ are in natural one-to-one correspondence with untimed traces over alphabet $\Sigma \cup \{\checkmark\}$, where the event $\checkmark \notin \Sigma$ represents the passage of one time unit. For T a set of integral timed traces, we write $T^\checkmark$ for the corresponding unique set of untimed $\checkmark$-traces.

Proposition 6. *Let A be a timed automaton. Then $(\mathbb{Z}(\mathcal{W}[\![A]\!]))^\checkmark$ is a regular language. In other words, the integral timed traces of A can essentially be generated by an untimed finite automaton.*

The required untimed automaton can be obtained by a straightforward modification of the region automaton $WREG(A)$. The construction is identical but for transitions. Postulate a transition $(s, r) \xrightarrow{a} (s', r')$ of the untimed automaton if there is a transition $(s, s', \phi, a, R, \phi')$ of A such that all clock interpretations in r satisfy ϕ, r and r' agree when restricted to clocks not belonging to R, and all clock interpretations in r' meet ϕ'. In addition, postulate a transition $(s, r) \xrightarrow{\checkmark} (s, r')$ of the untimed automaton if, for all clock interpretations $\nu \in r$, $\nu + 1 \in r'$. It is easily checked that this untimed automaton accepts precisely $(\mathbb{Z}(\mathcal{W}[\![A]\!]))^\checkmark$, as required.

Corollary 7. *Let A and B be timed automata with A closed under digitization and B closed under inverse digitization. Then the timed language inclusion problem of whether $\mathcal{W}[\![A]\!] \subseteq \mathcal{W}[\![B]\!]$ is decidable.*

We will also make use of the following result:

Proposition 8. *Closed timed automata are closed under digitization, and open timed automata are closed under inverse digitization.*

Our proof follows that presented in [7].

Let us first consider the case in which A is a closed timed automaton. Let $e = (s_0, t_0, \nu_0) \xrightarrow{\alpha_1} (s_1, t_1, \nu_1) \xrightarrow{\alpha_2} \ldots \xrightarrow{\alpha_n} (s_n, t_n, \nu_n)$ be a run of A, with $\alpha_j = (s_{j-1}, s_j, \phi_j, a_j, R_j, \phi'_j)$. Observe that, for any clock x and index j, $\nu_j(x) = t_j - t_i + r_i(x)$, where $i \leqslant j$ is the index of the last transition which reset clock x (or is 0 if x was never reset), and $r_i(x)$ is the nondeterministic value that x was reset to. For $i \geqslant 1$, $r_i(x)$ must satisfy the closed postcondition $\phi'_i(x)$.

To show that A is closed under digitization, it suffices to show, given $0 \leqslant \varepsilon \leqslant 1$, that the prospective run $e' = (s_0, [t_0]_\varepsilon, \nu'_0) \xrightarrow{\alpha_1} (s_1, [t_1]_\varepsilon, \nu'_1) \xrightarrow{\alpha_2} \ldots \xrightarrow{\alpha_n} (s_n, [t_n]_\varepsilon, \nu'_n)$ is a valid run of A. Here $\nu'_j(x) = [t_j]_\varepsilon - [t_i]_\varepsilon + r'_i(x)$, where the indices j and i are obtained from e as explained above, and the $r'_i(x)$'s are carefully chosen as we now explain. For e' to be a valid run of A, each reset value $r'_i(x)$ and clock interpretation ν'_i must meet the relevant closed pre- and postconditions. Since by assumption the r_i's and ν_i's do meet these constraints, it suffices to show that one can choose each $r'_i(x)$ subject to: (i) $r_i(x) \leqslant k \Rightarrow r'_i(x) \leqslant k$ and $r_i(x) \geqslant k \Rightarrow r'_i(x) \geqslant k$, for any integer k, and (ii) $\nu_j(x) \leqslant k \Rightarrow \nu'_j(x) \leqslant k$ and $\nu_j(x) \geqslant k \Rightarrow \nu'_j(x) \geqslant k$, again for any integer k.

First observe that, for any integer k, any real numbers p and q, and any ε, $p - q \leqslant k \Rightarrow [p]_\varepsilon - [q]_\varepsilon \leqslant k$, and $p - q \geqslant k \Rightarrow [p]_\varepsilon - [q]_\varepsilon \geqslant k$.

Now choose $r'_i(x) = [t_i]_\varepsilon - [t_i - r_i(x)]_\varepsilon$. By the above, $r'_i(x)$ clearly satisfies (i). For any index j, we also have $\nu'_j(x) = [t_j]_\varepsilon - [t_i]_\varepsilon + r'_i(x) = [t_j]_\varepsilon - [t_i - r_i(x)]_\varepsilon$ by definition of $r'_i(x)$. Since $\nu_j(x) = t_j - (t_i - r_i(x))$, our earlier observation implies that (ii) must too be satisfied, as required.

We now tackle the case in which A is an open timed automaton. We establish the stronger claim that whenever $u \in \mathbf{WMTT}$ is a timed trace such that $[u]_0 \in \mathcal{W}[\![A]\!]$, then $u \in \mathcal{W}[\![A]\!]$. Thus consider $u = \langle (t_1, a_1), (t_2, a_2), \ldots, (t_n, a_n) \rangle \in \mathbf{WMTT}$ such that $[u]_0 = \lceil u \rceil \in \mathcal{W}[\![A]\!]$. $\lceil u \rceil$ must originate from a run $e = (s_0, \lceil t_0 \rceil, \nu_0) \xrightarrow{\alpha_1} (s_1, \lceil t_1 \rceil, \nu_1) \xrightarrow{\alpha_2} \ldots \xrightarrow{\alpha_n} (s_n, \lceil t_n \rceil, \nu_n)$ of A. For each clock x, let $\nu_j(x) = \lceil t_j \rceil - \lceil t_i \rceil + r_i(x)$ as above. We must show that the prospective run $e' = (s_0, t_0, \nu'_0) \xrightarrow{\alpha_1} (s_1, t_1, \nu'_1) \xrightarrow{\alpha_2} \ldots \xrightarrow{\alpha_n} (s_n, t_n, \nu'_n)$ is a valid run of A, where $\nu'_j(x) = t_j - t_i + r'_i(x)$, for suitable values of $r'_i(x)$.

Choose δ a strictly positive real number such that $\delta < fract(t_j)$ for every non-integral t_j. Let $r'_i(x) = fract(t_i) + \lfloor r_i(x) \rfloor - \delta$ if t_i is not integral, and let $r'_i(x) = \lceil r_i(x) \rceil - \delta$ otherwise. A simple case analysis (considering integral and non-integral cases for t_i, t_j, and $r_i(x)$ as needed) establishes the following facts: (i) $r_i(x) < k \Rightarrow r'_i(x) < k$ and $r_i(x) > k \Rightarrow r'_i(x) > k$, for any integer k, and (ii) $\nu_j(x) < k \Rightarrow \nu'_j(x) < k$ and $\nu_j(x) > k \Rightarrow \nu'_j(x) > k$, again for any integer k. This shows that e' is a valid run of A and completes the proof.

3.3   The d-Topology

Define a metric d on **WMTT** as follows. For $u = \langle(t_1, a_1), \dots, (t_n, a_n)\rangle$ and $u' = \langle(t'_1, a'_1), \dots, (t'_m, a'_m)\rangle$ two timed traces, if $\mathsf{untime}(u) \neq \mathsf{untime}(u')$, then $d(u, u') \stackrel{\scriptscriptstyle\wedge}{=} \infty$. Otherwise, $d(u, u') \stackrel{\scriptscriptstyle\wedge}{=} \max\{|t_i - t'_i| : 1 \leqslant i \leqslant n\}$.

Proposition 9. *The semantic mapping $\mathcal{W}[\![\cdot]\!]$ takes open timed automata to d-open sets of timed traces, and closed timed automata to d-closed sets of timed traces.*

The assertion concerning open timed automata appears in [6], with the following proof. Let A be an open timed automaton, and consider a run $e = (s_0, t_0, \nu_0) \xrightarrow{\alpha_1} \cdots \xrightarrow{\alpha_n} (s_n, t_n, \nu_n)$ that accepts the timed trace u. Since all clock constraints are open, for each $0 \leqslant i \leqslant n$, there is an $\varepsilon_i > 0$ such that substituting $\nu_i - \varepsilon_i$ or $\nu_i + \varepsilon_i$ (or any clock interpretation in between) for ν_i in e still gives a valid run of A. Let $\varepsilon = \min\{\varepsilon_i / 2 \mid 0 \leqslant i \leqslant n\}$. It is clear that any timed trace within ε of u can be accepted by A.

Let us now consider the case of a closed timed automaton A. Let u be any timed trace, and let $\langle u_i \rangle_{i \geqslant 1}$ be a sequence of timed traces in $\mathcal{W}[\![A]\!]$ converging to u. Without loss of generality, since A has only finitely many transitions, we can assume that the runs e_i corresponding to these timed traces share the same transitions, in the same order. The reset sets associated with these transitions are required to be closed; we may assume that they are bounded as well (if they are not, pick an artificial bound that is large enough not to disrupt anything). The sequence of e_i's therefore essentially lies in a compact subset of $\mathbb{R}^n$ (for some finite n) and must therefore have an accumulation point e. The run e is clearly a valid run of A, since its clock interpretations are limits of clock interpretations of the e_i's, and the constraints these must satisfy are all closed. It is also plain that the run e gives rise to the timed trace u, so that $u \in \mathcal{W}[\![A]\!]$ as required.

4   Universality

The *universality problem* is to decide whether a timed automaton can perform all possible timed traces. In our framework, this problem gives rise to six subcases, which depend on the class of automata considered (mixed, open, or closed), as well as on the semantic assumptions on the dense-time domain (weakly or strongly monotonic time). In the case of mixed timed automata and either weakly or strongly monotonic dense time, this problem was shown to be undecidable in [1]. We now address the remaining cases.

A *two-counter machine* M is a triple $(\{b_0, b_1, \dots, b_k\}, C, D)$, where the b_i's are instructions and C and D are two counters ranging over the non-negative integers. Both counters are initially empty, and the first instruction M executes is b_0. Each instruction b_i, for $i < k$, either: (i) increments or decrements (if non-zero) one of the counters, and subsequently jumps to the next instruction, or (ii) tests one of the counters for emptiness and conditionally jumps to the next instruction. The instruction b_k represents successful termination. A *configuration* of M is a triple (b_i, c, d), where c and d are the respective values of the counters C and D. A *halting computation* of M is a finite sequence of configurations starting with $(b_0, 0, 0)$ and ending with a b_k-configuration, subject to the constraint that each successive configuration be a valid successor of the previous one. The problem of deciding whether a two-counter machine has a halting computation is undecidable.

Let M be a two-counter machine. Following [1], we define a set of timed traces $L_{AD}(M)$ as follows. Given any halting computation $\langle (b_{i_0}, c_0, d_0), (b_{i_1}, c_1, d_1), \dots ,$ $(b_{i_n}, c_n, d_n) \rangle$ of M, we include in $L_{AD}(M)$ the following timed trace u over the alphabet $\Sigma = \{b_0, b_1, \dots, b_k, c, d\}$: $\mathrm{untime}(u) = b_{i_0} c^{c_0} d^{d_0} b_{i_1} c^{c_1} d^{d_1} \dots b_{i_n} c^{c_n} d^{d_n}$; u is strongly monotonic (no two events occur at the same time); the timestamp of b_{i_j} is $j + t_0$, where t_0 is the timestamp of b_{i_0}; for all $0 \leqslant j \leqslant n - 1$: (i) if $c_{j+1} = c_j$, then for each timed event (t, c) in the time interval $(j, j+1) + t_0$, there is a timed event $(t+1, c)$ in the time interval $(j+1, j+2) + t_0$; (ii) if $c_{j+1} = c_j + 1$, then for every (t, c) in the time interval $(j+1, j+2) + t_0$, except the last one, there is a timed event $(t-1, c)$; (iii) if $c_{j+1} = c_j - 1$, then for every (t, c) in the time interval $(j, j+1) + t_0$, except the last one, there is a timed event $(t+1, c)$; (iv) the same requirements hold of the d's.

By construction, M has a halting computation if and only if $L_{AD}(M) \neq \emptyset$, which is equivalent to $\mathbf{SMTT} \setminus L_{AD}(M) \neq \mathbf{SMTT}$. We now show that there exists an open timed automaton A such that $S[\![A]\!] = \mathbf{SMTT} \setminus L_{AD}(M)$. The following theorem then immediately follows.

Theorem 10. *The universality problem for open timed automata over strongly monotonic dense time is undecidable. In other words, given an open timed automaton A, it is undecidable whether $S[\![A]\!] = \mathbf{SMTT}$.*

It remains to exhibit said open automaton A. The construction we sketch is similar to that of [1]; even though the automaton they construct is not open, with a little care and a few additional clocks it is possible to produce an open automaton A such that $S[\![A]\!] = \mathbf{SMTT} \setminus L_{AD}(M)$.

Since open automata are trivially closed under finite unions, it is sufficient to exhibit a collection of open automata, each of which accepts timed traces not in $L_{AD}(M)$, and the sum total of which accepts all such traces. We illustrate two cases; the remainder are left to the reader.

The automaton below accepts exactly those timed traces u of the form $\mathrm{untime}(u) = (\Sigma \setminus \{b_i\})^* b_{i_0} (\Sigma \setminus \{b_i\})^* b_{i_1} (\Sigma \setminus \{b_i\})^* \dots b_{i_n} (\Sigma \setminus \{b_i\})^*$ with the property that some b_{i_j} fails to occur j time units after the occurrence of b_{i_0}. In what follows, start locations are depicted with an incoming arrow not originating from any other location, and final locations are doubly circled. Preconditions are decorated with a question mark (?), and postconditions with an exclamation mark (!). An edge labelled with a set of events stands for a collection of edges with the same source and target, one for each of the events in the set. The rest of the notation is self-explanatory.

We claim that this automaton accepts exactly the required timed traces. Let u be such a trace, with b_{i_0} occurring at time t_0. There must be some m such that b_{i_j} occurred at time $j + t_0$ for all $j < m$, but b_{i_m} occurred at some time other than $m+t_0$. If the occurrence of b_{i_m} was too early, that can be captured with the clock y reset to 0. If, on the other hand, b_{i_m} occurred too late, then by resetting x sufficiently close to 1 the trace will also be accepted. Of course, if each b_{i_j} did occur exactly one time unit after the previous one, then no assignments of values to x or y can make the automaton accept the trace.

As a second example, suppose that instruction b_1 is meant to leave the value of counter C unchanged. The automaton below accepts precisely those timed traces u in which some instance of b_1 is followed, within one time unit, by a list of c's which cannot be put in one-to-one unit-duration-delayed correspondence with the list of c's in the following unit-duration time interval.

Our claim can be justified as follows. We are asserting one of two things: either there is a c in the unit-duration time interval immediately following b_1 which has no counterpart one time unit later, or vice-versa. The former is captured by the top component, whereas the latter is captured by the bottom component. For simplicity, we are assuming that only traces in which the b_{i_j}'s happen exactly at unit-duration time intervals need be considered (cf. previous automaton). In the bottom automaton, this forces all transitions up to that resetting y to occur within one time unit of the occurrence of b_1.

The other cases are left to the reader. We remark that, while these constructions produce an open automaton A with $\mathcal{S}[\![A]\!] = \mathbf{SMTT} \setminus L_{AD}(M)$, it is in general not possible to exhibit an open automaton A such that $\mathcal{W}[\![A]\!] = \mathbf{WMTT} \setminus L_{AD}(M)$. Intuitively, this is because we would need in addition to provide A with the ability to accept any timed trace in which at least two events occurred at the same time. However, no open timed automaton can capture precisely this requirement, since it does not correspond to a d-open set of timed traces. This difficulty turns out to be insuperable, as the following result demonstrates.

Theorem 11. *The universality problem for open timed automata over weakly monotonic dense time is decidable. In other words, there is an algorithm which, given an open timed automaton A, decides whether $\mathcal{W}[\![A]\!] = \textbf{WMTT}$.*

Indeed, let A be an open timed automaton. Note that deciding whether $\mathcal{W}[\![A]\!] = \textbf{WMTT}$ is clearly equivalent to deciding whether $\textbf{WMTT} \subseteq \mathcal{W}[\![A]\!]$. But A is closed under inverse digitization (Proposition 8), and $\textbf{WMTT}$ is obviously closed under digitization. By Corollary 7, the inclusion $\textbf{WMTT} \subseteq \mathcal{W}[\![A]\!]$ can therefore be decided.

We now move on to closed timed automata. We begin by stating the chief undecidability result:

Theorem 12. *The universality problem for closed timed automata over either weakly or strongly monotonic dense time is undecidable. In other words, given a closed timed automaton A, whether $\mathcal{W}[\![A]\!] = \textbf{WMTT}$ and whether $\mathcal{S}[\![A]\!] = \textbf{SMTT}$ are undecidable.*

Unfortunately, we cannot employ the above method to establish this result, since the complement of $L_{\text{AD}}(M)$ is clearly not a d-closed set; indeed, $L_{\text{AD}}(M)$ is in general not d-open since we require certain events to occur exactly one time unit apart, etc.

Instead, we draw upon a construction of Henzinger and Raskin [8] to manufacture a suitable language.[1] The basic idea is to alter the definition of $L_{\text{AD}}(M)$ so that events have strictly positive durations; this is achieved by having separate signals explicitly denote the beginning and end of a previously instantaneous event. These delimiters are then required to lie in certain iteratively defined open sets. As a result, the complement of this language is then d-closed.

To this end, define a *slot* to be a non-empty open interval of the non-negative real numbers of length less than one. Given $t_1 < t_2 < t_1 + 1$, the slot *between* t_1 and t_2 is the open interval (t_1, t_2), and the slot *generated* by t_1 and t_2 is the open interval $(t_1 + 1, t_2 + 1)$.

Let $M = (\{b_0, b_1, \ldots, b_k\}, C, D)$ be a two-counter machine. We define a set of strongly monotonic timed traces $L_{\text{HR}}(M)$. The untimed traces of $L_{\text{HR}}(M)$ are the same as those of $L_{\text{AD}}(M)$ except that every event p in $L_{\text{AD}}(M)$ is replaced by a pair of consecutive events pp' in $L_{\text{HR}}(M)$. Configurations are encoded in successive slots. Moreover, whenever there was a requirement in $L_{\text{AD}}(M)$ that some event q should occur exactly one time unit after some event p, this translates

---

[1] The undecidable language defined by Henzinger and Raskin was also meant to be stable under small temporal perturbations. However, the primary purpose of their construction was to establish the undecidability of universality for robust timed automata and tube languages. When interpreted over mere timed traces, the language complement they define unfortunately fails to be d-closed.

for $L_{HR}(M)$ into a requirement that the pair qq' appear in the slot generated by the pair pp'. Likewise, $L_{AD}(M)$ requirements that some event q appear between events p and r translate into $L_{HR}(M)$ requirements that qq' lie in some slot between pp' and rr'.

It is clear that $L_{HR}(M)$ is a d-open strongly monotonic subset of **WMTT**, and that M has a halting computation if and only if $L_{HR}(M) \neq \emptyset$. The latter is equivalent to both $\textbf{WMTT} \setminus L_{HR}(M) \neq \textbf{WMTT}$ and $\textbf{SMTT} \setminus L_{HR}(M) \neq \textbf{SMTT}$. One can now adapt the constructions appearing in the proof of Theorem 10 (or simpler yet the constructions of [1] or [8]) to manufacture a closed timed automaton A such that $\mathcal{W}[\![A]\!] = \textbf{WMTT} \setminus L_{HR}(M)$ (from which it also follows that $\mathcal{S}[\![A]\!] = \textbf{SMTT} \setminus L_{HR}(M)$). Taken together, these facts establish Theorem 12.

We illustrate two cases of the automaton construction. Let Σ stand for the set $\{b_0, b'_0, b_1, b'_1, \dots, b_k, b'_k, c, c', d, d'\}$. The automaton below accepts any trace which is not strongly monotonic.

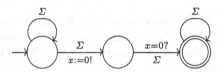

Suppose now that instruction b_1 is meant to leave the value of counter C unchanged. A possible timed trace violating this requirement is one in which the event b_1 is eventually followed, prior to the next instruction, by a pair of events $\langle (t,c), (t',c') \rangle$, with no pair of consecutive events cc' appearing in the slot $(t+1, t'+1)$. (This, of course, handles only one half of the required bijection.) The automaton below accepts all such timed traces.

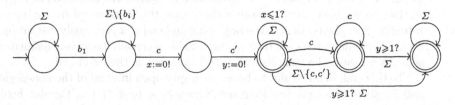

We justify our claim as follows. A pair of consecutive events cc' fails to appear in a slot $(t+1, t'+1)$ precisely when every occurrence of c (if any) after time $t+1$ fails to be immediately followed by a c' before time $t'+1$.

5   Language Inclusion

Theorem 13. *Let A and B be timed automata drawn independently from the classes of mixed, open, or closed timed automata. The language inclusion problem over weakly monotonic dense time as to whether $\mathcal{W}[\![A]\!] \subseteq \mathcal{W}[\![B]\!]$ is only decidable when A is drawn from the class of closed timed automata and B is drawn from the class of open timed automata. The language inclusion problem over strongly monotonic dense time as to whether $\mathcal{S}[\![A]\!] \subseteq \mathcal{S}[\![B]\!]$ is undecidable in all instances.*

Let us first consider the case of weakly monotonic time. The single decidable instance (A closed and B open) follows directly from Proposition 8 and Corollary 7. On the other hand, by choosing A such that $\mathcal{W}[\![A]\!] = \mathbf{WMTT}$ (so that the question $\mathcal{W}[\![A]\!] \subseteq \mathcal{W}[\![B]\!]$ reduces to the universality problem for B), we can dispose of all cases in which B is either mixed or closed (Theorem 12).

For the remaining two cases (B open and A either mixed or open), let A be the following timed automaton:

$$x>1?\ x<1!$$
$$\Sigma$$

Notice that A accepts exactly the strongly monotonic timed traces—in other words, $\mathcal{W}[\![A]\!] = \mathbf{SMTT}$. The question $\mathcal{W}[\![A]\!] \subseteq \mathcal{W}[\![B]\!]$ therefore reduces to the universality problem for B over strongly monotonic time, and is therefore undecidable (Theorem 10).

The case of strongly monotonic time is dealt with in similar fashion.

6 Summary

The two tables below summarize the universality and language inclusion results discussed in this paper.

Class of	Universality	
Timed Automata	Weakly Monotonic Time	Strongly Monotonic Time
Mixed	Undecidable	Undecidable
Open	Decidable	Undecidable
Closed	Undecidable	Undecidable

A	B	$\mathcal{W}[\![A]\!] \subseteq \mathcal{W}[\![B]\!]$?	$\mathcal{S}[\![A]\!] \subseteq \mathcal{S}[\![B]\!]$?
Mixed	Mixed	Undecidable	Undecidable
Open	Mixed	Undecidable	Undecidable
Closed	Mixed	Undecidable	Undecidable
Mixed	Open	Undecidable	Undecidable
Open	Open	Undecidable	Undecidable
Closed	Open	Decidable	Undecidable
Mixed	Closed	Undecidable	Undecidable
Open	Closed	Undecidable	Undecidable
Closed	Closed	Undecidable	Undecidable

References

[1] R. Alur and D. Dill. A theory of timed automata. *Theoretical Computer Science*, 126:183–235, 1994.

[2] R. Alur, L. Fix, and T. A. Henzinger. Event-clock automata: A determinizable class of timed automata. *Theoretical Computer Science*, 211:253–273, 1999.

[3] E. Asarin, O. Maler, and A. Pnueli. On discretization of delays in timed automata and digital circuits. In *Proceedings of CONCUR 98*, volume 1466, pages 470–484. Springer LNCS, 1998.

[4] D. Bošnački. Digitization of timed automata. In *Proceedings of FMICS 99*, 1999.

[5] M. Fränzle. Analysis of Hybrid Systems: An ounce of realism can save an infinity of states. In *Proceedings of CSL 99*, volume 1683, pages 126–140. Springer LNCS, 1999.

[6] V. Gupta, T. A. Henzinger, and R. Jagadeesan. Robust timed automata. In *Proceedings of HART 97*, volume 1201, pages 331–345. Springer LNCS, 1997.

[7] T. A. Henzinger, Z. Manna, and A. Pnueli. What good are digital clocks? In *Proceedings of ICALP 92*, volume 623, pages 545–558. Springer LNCS, 1992.

[8] T. A. Henzinger and J.-F. Raskin. Robust undecidability of timed and hybrid systems. In *Proceedings of HSCC 00*, volume 1790, pages 145–159. Springer LNCS, 2000.

[9] J. Ouaknine and J. B. Worrell. Revisiting digitization, robustness, and decidability for timed automata. Submitted, 2003. Available from www.andrew.cmu.edu/~joelo.

[10] J. Ouaknine and J. B. Worrell. Timed CSP = closed timed ε-automata. Submitted, 2003. Available from www.andrew.cmu.edu/~joelo.

On the Application of Hybrid Control to CPU Reservations

Luigi Palopoli, Luca Abeni, and Giuseppe Lipari*

ReTiS Laboratory – Scuola Superiore S. Anna, Pisa, Italy
{palopoli, luca, lipari}@sssup.it

Abstract. An important class of soft real-time applications require dynamic allocation of computational resources in order to comply with their quality of service (QoS) requirements. These applications are characterised by large fluctuations in their computation time requirements. One of the biggest problems in such systems is how to assign the bandwidths to the software tasks so that every task meets its QoS requirements and computational resources are not wasted.

In this paper, we present a novel feedback scheduling controller based on a scheduling strategy called resource reservation. First, we model the scheduler as a discrete time switching system; then, we present hybrid control techniques for the design of the feedback scheduler; finally, we report simulation results that show the effectiveness of our approach.

1 Introduction

An emerging class of real-time systems requires the dynamic allocation of computational resources to time-sensitive applications realised by software tasks. Important examples are multimedia streaming programs video/audio players, software sound mixers, etc. Other examples are embedded systems used in data-intensive contexts, where relatively high volumes of sensor data are flowing and must be processed and analysed in real time (i.e. radar systems).

The amount of computation time, and more generally of hardware/software resources, required by this class of applications presents large fluctuations. Design approaches based on classical hard real-time techniques, being based on worst case assumption, can be overly conservative. Moreover, occasional failures in respecting the timing constraints attached to a task do not necessarily lead to catastrophic consequences. However, if failures are too frequent the Quality of Service (QoS) provided by the application degrades beyond acceptable limits. As an example, for a multimedia application it is not necessary to decode every frame within a fixed interval as long as fluctuations in the decoding rate do not overcome the threshold of human perception. Constraints of this type are referred to as QoS constraints.

When multiple real-time tasks of this type share the same CPU, guaranteeing simultaneous compliance with their QoS constraints is a challenging goal, for

---

* Partial support from E.C. Project OCERA, IST-2001-35102

O. Maler and A. Pnueli (Eds.): HSCC 2003, LNCS 2623, pp. 389–404, 2003.

which a properly designed CPU scheduler can provide considerably better results than schedulers/resource allocators used in conventional operating systems. In this context, a fundamental requirement is the enforcement of *temporal protection*: i.e. each task has to be guaranteed a certain bandwidth independently of the fluctuations of CPU requirements of the other tasks in the system. If this property is respected, each task executes as if it were on a dedicated slower processor. The so called *resource reservation techniques*, first proposed in [12] for the CPU, proved to be very effective in providing temporal isolation, and have been implemented in a number of different systems using different scheduling algorithms [14,1,7,15].

One of the biggest problems of CPU reservation systems is the selection of the fraction (or bandwidth) of the CPU assigned to each task. In presence of wide variations of the required computation time, one could either give the task too low or too high a bandwidth. In the former case the system experiences unacceptable degradations in the offered QoS, whereas in the latter case system resources are wasted. To cope with this problem, many authors proposed the use of feedback control mechanism inside the operating system. A first proposal of this kind for time sharing systems dates back to 1962 [5]. More recently, feedback control techniques have been applied to real-time scheduling [13,16,9, 11] and multimedia systems [17,2]. However, little theoretical analysis of such mechanisms has been provided. One of the main problems that hinders this type of analysis is the lack of a realistic and analytically tractable model for "the plant", i.e. for a real-time scheduler. In [3], this gap has been filled in for CPU reservation schedulers: the authors proved that a CPU reservation scheduler for a task can realistically be modelled as a switching and parametric dynamic system (the varying parameter being the computation time of each activation of the task).

In this paper the problem of analytical design for the controller is tackled. As a first step toward a more general theory, and for the sake of simplicity, we consider here the case of a single periodically activated task with varying computation time. Also, we assume that the internal state of the scheduler is measurable. Under these assumptions, the resulting system is piecewise affine. The control design has to be carried out taking into account QoS requirements for the task and physical limitation of the control action (the assigned bandwidth cannot exceed the total power of the processor). As a solution to this problem, we propose a switching dynamic controller and offer techniques for synthesising its parameters and analysing its performance.

The QoS requirements and the physical constraints (input saturation) can be captured defining a polyhedral region in the state space of the closed loop system. The proposed analysis problem is aimed at the construction of an invariant set for the closed loop system that is entirely contained in the polyhedral "safe" set. The solution that we advocate is based on ellipsoidal reachability analysis. As far as the synthesis problem is concerned, we show that the problem is one of robust static output feedback synthesis. The application of the devised methodology to a general situation where multiple feedback control loops operate on the same CPU and the internal state of the scheduler is not accessible are discussed throughout the paper.

Notation. In the sequel, symbol $\succ$ ($\succeq$) denotes that a matrix is positive definite (semidefinite). Similarly, symbol $\prec$ ($\preceq$) denotes that a matrix is negative definite (semidefinite). Let $Q = Q^T \succ 0$, by $\mathcal{E}(Q, \hat{x})$ we will denote the ellipsoid $(x - \hat{x})^T Q^{-1}(x - \hat{x}) \leq 1$. We recall that given a set of matrices $\mathcal{A}_0, \mathcal{A}_1, \ldots, \mathcal{A}_m$ with $\mathcal{A}_i = \mathcal{A}_i^T$ and a vector of parameters $x = [x_1, \ldots, x_m]^T$, the expression

$$\mathcal{A}_0 + x_1 \mathcal{A}_1 + \ldots + x_m \mathcal{A}_m \preceq 0$$

is called a linear matrix inequality (LMI). Finding a feasible solution vector to a LMI is a problem that can be solved in polynomial time by means of convex optimisation [4]. In this paper, we will make frequent use of LMI based analysis techniques.

2   Problem Presentation

Definitions. Before developing a formal model for a reservation-based system, we need to introduce some definitions. In particular, we use the *real-time task model*, which associates a temporal constaint, called *deadline*, to each execution of a task. If these temporal constraints are violated, it means that the amount of resource associated with the task is insufficient, and the size of the reservation should be increased.

According to the real-time task model, a task $\mathcal{T}_i$ is a stream of jobs $J_i(k)$. Each job $J_i(k)$ arrives (becomes executable) at time $r_i(k)$, and finishes at time $f_i(k)$ after executing for a time $c_i(k)$. Moreover, $J_i(k)$ is characterised by a deadline $d_i(k)$, that is respected if $f_i(k) \leq d_i(k)$, and is missed if $f_i(k) > d_i(k)$.

For the sake of simplicity, we will only consider *periodic tasks*, in which $r_i(k + 1) = r_i(k) + T_i$, where T_i is the *task period*. Moreover, we will assume that $d_i(k) = r_i(k) + T_i$; hence, $r_i(k + 1) = d_i(k)$.

Our goal is to provide support for time-sensitive application in which a deadline miss can degrade the QoS of the task but does not have any catastrophic consequence. Therefore, we will consider *soft deadlines*, as opposed to *hard deadlines*: the goal of a soft real-time system is to control the number of deadline misses, whereas in a hard real-time system even a single deadline miss is not acceptable.

Reservation-Based Scheduling. A reservation is a pair (B_i, T_i^s), where B_i is the fraction of resource utilisation dedicated to task $\mathcal{T}_i$, and T_i^s is the *period* of the reservation: task $\mathcal{T}_i$ will be allowed to use the resource for $Q_i = B_i T_i^s$ units every period T_i^s. Q_i is also called *budget* or *capacity* of the reservation. It is important not to confuse the reservation period T_i^s with the task period T_i. Intuitively, the reservation period T_i^s can be seen as the *temporal granularity* of the reservation: the smaller is T_i^s, the more precise is the allocation of the resource to task $\mathcal{T}_i$

in the system. It is possible to define a reservation for all kind of resources. In this paper we will consider only CPU reservations: however, most of the results presented can easily be extended to other kind of resources (network, disk, etc.).

A reservation mechanism is often implemented on the top of a "host" scheduler enforcing a real-time policy (such as Rate monotonic or Earliest Deadline First [10]). If $\sum_i B_i \leq U_l$, with $U_l \leq 1$ depending on the "host" scheduling algorithm, then each task $\mathcal{T}_i$ attached to a reservation (B_i, T_i^s) is guaranteed to receive its reserved amount of time (i.e., Q_i time units over T_i^s).

Every reservation-based scheduler provides the *temporal isolation property*: the ability of a task to meet its deadline depends only on the reservation (B_i, T_i^s), and not on the presence of other tasks in the system. It can be easily proved [7] that, thanks to the isolation property, each task executes as it were on a dedicated processor of speed B_i.

For any reservation based system, we can define the *virtual finishing time* $\text{VFT}_i(k) = \frac{c_i(k-1)}{B_i}$ of job $J_i(k-1)$ as the time it would finish in a dedicated processor of speed B_i. Intuitively, if $\text{VFT}_i(k) > T_i$, then we need to allocate a larger reservation to task $\mathcal{T}_i$, (i.e. we need to speed-up the dedicated processor) in order to fulfil its requirements.

The quantity thus defined takes continuous values and it can be computed if the internal state of the scheduler is accessible (which is possible only for certain classes of scheduling algorithms and implementations). For other classes of systems it is useful to define the concept of *latest possible finishing time* for a job. The latest possible finishing time $\text{LFT}_i(k)$ for job $J_i(k-1)$ is the end of the latest reservation period used by the job, minus the job arrival time: for example, if $J_i(k-1)$ has execution time $c_i(k-1) = 5$, it has been reserved a bandwidth $B_i = 0.5$, and the reservation period is $T_i^s = 4$, then it uses $\lceil \frac{5}{0.5 \cdot 4} \rceil = 3$ reservation periods, and its latest possible finishing time is 12, whereas its VFT is given by $5/0.5 = 10$. This quantity clearly carries a somewhat quantised information but it can easily be measured on any CPU reservation scheduler.

Dynamic Model of a Single Reservation. The reservation mechanism presented in the previous section can be modelled as a discrete time dynamic system. It is to stress that, due to the temporal isolation property, the model can be built for a single task regardless of other tasks present in the system. More precisely, the only coupling between the different dynamics is the constraint $\sum B_i \leq U_l$, which will be briefly discussed by the end of the section. Henceforth, we simplify the notation by removing the task index from all the quantities (e.g. we will use Q instead of Q_i and so for the other quantities). In this context we merely summarise results that are reported in detail in [3].

The evolution of the system is evaluated at the termination $f(k)$ of each job. We distinguish between two different situations: 1) the internal state of the scheduler is accessible, 2) the internal state of the scheduler is not accessible.

For the first case the most natural quantity that can be used as output variable is the scheduling error defined as the difference between VFT and relative deadline T: $\epsilon(k) = \text{VFT}(k) - T$. If the scheduling error at the previous instance is less than 0, the virtual time can be easily calculated as:

$\text{VFT}(k) = \frac{c(k-1)}{B(k-1)}$. However, if the previous scheduling error is greater than 0, the virtual time at step k depends on the value of the previous virtual time: $\text{VFT}(k) = V(k-1) - T + \frac{c(k-1)}{B(k-1)}$. By substituting, we can express the dynamic equation of the system as follows:

$$\epsilon(k+1) = \begin{cases} \epsilon(k) + \frac{c(k)}{B(k)} - T & \epsilon(k) \geq 0 \\ \frac{c(k)}{B(k)} - T & \epsilon(k) < 0 \end{cases} \quad (1)$$

When the internal state is not accessible, the scheduling error is more conveniently defined using the difference between the *latest possible finishing time* and the task period: $\epsilon(k) = \text{LFT}(k) - T$. In this case, the scheduling error is a discrete variable and it is multiple of T^s. As shown in the cited paper, it is possible to write the dynamic of a conservative approximation $\tilde{\epsilon}(k)$ of the scheduling error as follows:

$$\tilde{\epsilon}(k+1) = \begin{cases} \tilde{\epsilon}(k) + \frac{c(k)}{B(k)} - T + q(k) & \tilde{\epsilon}(k) \geq T_s \\ \frac{c(k)}{B(k)} - T + q(k) & \tilde{\epsilon}_k < T_s \end{cases} \quad (2)$$

where: $q(k) = \lceil \frac{c(k)}{B(k)T_s} \rceil - \frac{c(k)}{B(k)T_s}$. Equations (1) and (2) are similar, except for the switching point (which is 0 for Equation (1) and T^s for Equation (2)) and for the addition of a quantisation error term $q(k)$.

Feedback scheduling. It is now possible to formally define the problem of feedback control. The variable we want to control is the QoS provided by each task, which is represented by the $\epsilon(k)$ scheduling error. This variable, as we said, can be measured for each task upon the termination of a job and a feedback controller can adjust the bandwidth $B(k)$ reserved to the task. The purpose of the controller is to maintain this quantity below a specified level: $\epsilon(k) \leq E$. Moreover, if the computation time $c(k) = \bar{c}$ is constant or slowly varying, we require that the scheduling error be reduced exactly to zero and the bandwidth exactly to the value $\frac{\bar{c}}{T}$.

Considering the general situation of multiple tasks sharing the processor, a problem to cope with is that the termination of the jobs are asynchronous events. Therefore, designing a global controller for the entire task set is not a viable solution. However, the temporal isolation property allows us to adopt a decentralised strategy designing a separate controller for each task. The only global constraint is $\sum B_i \leq U_l$, which has to be enforced upon every control decision lest the correctness of the reservation algorithm be jeopardised. A possible way for handling this situation, which gave good results in real situations, is the adoption of a compression mechanism. Each decentralised controller can decide a bandwidth $B_i(k)$ constrained by $B_i(k) \leq B_0$. To achieve efficiency in handling the CPU, in the worst case the sum of all bandwidth is allowed to exceed the bound U_l: i.e. $nB_0 \geq U_l$. However, whenever a controller decides a bandwidth such that $\sum B_i$ would exceed the U_l bound, a compression mechanism comes into play that reduces the bandwidth within the bound: The compression function is given by:

$$B_i = \begin{cases} B_i & \text{if } \sum_i B_i \le U_l \\ B_i w_i \frac{U_l}{\sum_j B_j w_j} & \text{otherwise} \end{cases}$$

where w_i are weights assigned to the different tasks. Effects of the compression mechanism can be considered as an additive disturbance ΔB_i on the bandwidths assigned to the tasks. It is not difficult to show that the maximum absolute value of ΔB_i is upper-bounded by $|\Delta B_i| \le \frac{1-w_i U_l}{W}$ where $W = \sum w_i$.

Summarising the discussion above, a control design methodology that applies to the case of *a single task with accessible internal state* dealing with possible additive noise is instrumental to the solution of the overall problem. A first contribution in this direction is offered in the next section. Constraints and requirements can be formally expressed as follows:

R.1 the maximum available bandwidth is upper bounded: $B(k) \le B_0$; we'll find it convenient as command variable $u(k) = \frac{1}{B(k)}$ that has to be lower bounded by $u(k) \ge u_0 = \frac{1}{B_0}$.

R.2 the scheduling error $\epsilon(k)$ has to be upper bounded: $\epsilon(k) \le E$

R.3 if the computation time is unknown but constant, it is required that $\epsilon(k) \to 0$ and the assigned bandwidth $B(k)$ tends to the equilibrium value $\frac{\bar{c}}{T}$. Moreover we require a guaranteed exponential rate of convergence, i.e.the existence of a real number $\gamma \in]0,1[$ such that $|\epsilon(k)| \le M\gamma^k|\epsilon_0|$ for some $M \in \mathbb{R}$.

3   Controller Design

In order to comply with requirement R.3 in case of constant computation time, we use a switching proportional integral (PI) policy:

$$u(k) = \begin{cases} u(k-1) + \alpha_1 \epsilon(k) + \beta_1 \epsilon(k-1) & \text{if } \epsilon(k) > 0 \\ u(k-1) + \alpha_2 \epsilon(k) + \beta_2 \epsilon(k-1) & \text{if } \epsilon(k) \le 0 \end{cases} \tag{3}$$

The use of a two degrees of freedom controller for each mode might seem exaggerate for a first order system. However, as the synthesis procedure shown below is based on sufficient conditions, enlarging the design space enables an easier convergence.

The closed loop dynamics can be derived considering the two conditions $\epsilon_k \ge 0$ and $\epsilon_k \le 0$. Let us introduce the state vector $x(k) = [x_1(k), x_2(k), x_3(k)]^T$ where $x_1(k) = \epsilon(k)$, $x_2(k) = \epsilon(k-1)$ and $x_3(k) = u(k-1) - \frac{T}{c(k-1)}$. The closed loop equations can be written as follows:

$$x(k+1) = \begin{cases} A_1(c(k))x + w(k) & \text{if } x_1(k) > 0 \\ A_2(c(k))x + w(k) & \text{if } x_1(k) \le 0, \end{cases} \tag{4}$$

where

$$A_1(c(k)) = \begin{bmatrix} 1 + \alpha_1 c(k) & c(k)\beta_1 & c(k) \\ 1 & 0 & 0 \\ \alpha_1 & \beta_1 & 1 \end{bmatrix}, \ A_2(c(k)) = \begin{bmatrix} \alpha_2 c(k) & c(k)\beta_2 & c(k) \\ 1 & 0 & 0 \\ \alpha_2 & \beta_2 & 1 \end{bmatrix},$$

$$w(k) = \begin{bmatrix} 0 \\ 0 \\ \frac{T}{c(k-1)} - \frac{T}{c(k)} \end{bmatrix}.$$

The resulting system is piecewise affine and time varying. In the sequel, we will deal both with the problems of control analysis (i.e. is a given controller compliant with the requirements?) and with the control synthesis (i.e. find a controller able to stabilise the system). We will first provide results on the simpler case of constant computation times and then the more general case will be analysed.

3.1   Analysis

As a preliminary consideration, observe that requirements R.1 and R.2 are met if the system state evolves in the polyhedral region:

$$\mathcal{P} = \{x \text{ such that } x_1 \le E \text{ and } x_3 \ge u_0 - \frac{T}{H}\} \tag{5}$$

In addition, for the case of constant $c(k)$, attractivity of the origin of the state space is required (requirements R.3). Thereby, the proposed analysis strategy is aimed at finding regions that are contained in $\mathcal{P}$ and that ensure [exponential] attractivity of the state space if $c(k)$ is constant. To this aim, it is useful to introduce the following definitions:

Definition 1. *Consider a time varying discrete time system* $x(k+1) = f_k(x(k)), x_k \in \mathbb{R}^n$ *and a set* $\mathcal{P} \subseteq \mathbb{R}^n$ *regarded as safe for the system's state. A set* $\mathcal{D}$ *is said:*

a $\mathcal{P}$**-safe invariant set:** *if* $\mathcal{D} \subseteq \mathcal{P}$ *and* $x(k) \in \mathcal{D} \forall k \in \mathbb{N}$, *and* $\forall x_0 \in \mathcal{D}$
a $\mathcal{P}$**-safe exponential stability basin with decay rate** γ: *for* $\gamma \in]0,1[$ *if* $\mathcal{D}$ *is a* $\mathcal{P}$*-safe invariant set and if there exist* $M \in \mathbb{R}^+$ *such that* $\forall k \in \mathbb{N}$, *and* $\forall x(0) \in \mathcal{D} it holds ||x(k)|| \le M\gamma^k$.

Using this terminology we can define an analysis scheme in two steps. In the first step, we construct a set $\mathcal{D}$ that is $\mathcal{P}$-safe exponential stability basin in case of constant $c(k)$. This result has been inspired by the approach for dealing with control under input saturations shown in [8]. In the second one, we will provide conditions for $\mathcal{D}$ to be a $\mathcal{P}$-safe invariant set for variable $c(k)$.

Step 1: the case of constant $c(k)$. This step receives as inputs the gains $\alpha_1, \beta_1, \alpha_2, \beta_2$, the minimum and the maximum computation times h and H, the bounds E and u_0 for the scheduling error and for the control commands and the required exponential decay rate γ. The output is an ellipsoid $\mathcal{D}$ that is a $\mathcal{P}$-safe exponential stability basin.

The basic tool for this step is formally expressed by the following:

Theorem 1. *Assume that the following LMIs have a feasible solution:*

$$
\begin{aligned}
i)\quad & \begin{bmatrix} \gamma^2 Q & (A_i(H)Q)^T \\ (A_i(h)Q) & Q \end{bmatrix} \succeq 0 \quad i = 1,\,2 \\
ii)\quad & \begin{bmatrix} \gamma^2 Q & (A_i(h)Q)^T \\ (A_i(h)Q) & Q \end{bmatrix} \succeq 0 \quad i = 1,\,2 \\
iii)\quad & Q_{1,\,1} \le E^2,\, Q_{3,\,3} \le (u_0 - \tfrac{T}{H})^2)
\end{aligned}
\tag{6}
$$

then $\mathcal{E}(\bar{\alpha}^2 Q, 0)$, with $\bar{\alpha} = \min\{E, (u_0 - \tfrac{T}{H})\}$, is a $\mathcal{P}$-safe exponential stability basin with respect to the set $\mathcal{P}$ in Equation (5) and with guaranteed decay rate γ.

In order to prove the above, it is useful to recall some standard results. The following is derived from quadratic lyapunov stability theory:

Lemma 1. *Consider a discrete time linear and time varying system:*

$$
x(k+1) = A(k)x(k),
\tag{7}
$$

where A_k belongs to a set $\mathcal{A}$ for all k and assume that there exists a matrix Q such that:

$$
\begin{aligned}
& Q^{-1} \succeq 0 \\
& \gamma^2 Q^{-1} - A_s^T Q^{-1} A_s \preceq 0,\ \forall A_s \in \mathcal{A}
\end{aligned}
\tag{8}
$$

then $\mathcal{E}(\alpha^2 Q, 0)$ for any $\alpha \in \mathbb{R}$ is an exponential stability basin with a guaranteed decay rate γ.

From easy considerations of convex analysis it is possible to prove the following:

Lemma 2. *Let $V(x) = x^T Q^{-1} x$ with $Q = Q^T \succeq 0$. The minimum of $V(x)$ on the hyperplane $cx = r$ is given by:*

$$
\alpha_r^2 = \frac{r^2}{cQc^T}.
\tag{9}
$$

Proof (Theorem 1). For any instant k, 1) the system's state evolves according to one of the two closed loop dynamics $A_i(c(k))$, 2) matrices A_i depend affinely on $c(k)$, 3) $c(k)$ can be expressed as $\beta h + (1 - \beta)H$ for some $\beta \in [0, 1]$. Thereby, $A_i(c(k)) = \beta A_i(h) + (1 - \beta)A_i(H)$.

If conditions i), ii) hold in Equation (6) then their convex combination with coefficient β yields

$$
\begin{bmatrix} \gamma^2 Q & (A_i(c(k))Q)^T \\ (A_i(c(k))Q) & Q \end{bmatrix} \succeq 0.
$$

Using Schur complements lemma (see [4]) this condition can be written as:

$$Q \succeq 0$$
$$\gamma^2 Q - (A_i(c(k))Q)^T Q^{-1}(A_i(c(k))Q) \geq 0.$$

Pre-multiplying and post-multiplying both sides of the conditions by Q^{-1}, we get exactly the conditions of Lemma 1. In virtue of this result, $\mathcal{E}(\alpha^2 Q, 0)$ is an exponential stability basin. Clearly, $\alpha_1 \leq \alpha_2$ implies $\mathcal{E}(\alpha_1^2 Q, 0) \subseteq \mathcal{E}(\alpha_2^2 Q, 0)$. Therefore $\mathcal{E}(\alpha^2 Q, 0)$ is a subset of $\mathcal{P}$ if and only if lower than or equal to the minimum of $V(x) = x^T Q^{-1} x$ on $z_k = u_0 - \frac{T}{H}$ and $\epsilon_k = E$. Applying Lemma 2 this consideration is easily translated into condition iii), thus proving the claim.

Theorem 1 provides conditions for an ellipsoid to be an $\mathcal{P}$−safe exponential stability basin. Evidently, it is possible to direct the search toward ellipsoids that respect some notion of optimality. To this regard, very intuitive cost functions could be $\max \log det(P)$ or $\max trace(P)$. Both optimisation problems are convex. In the former case, the volume of the ellipsoid is maximised; in the latter maximisation is performed on the sum squared values of the semi-axes of the ellipsoid.

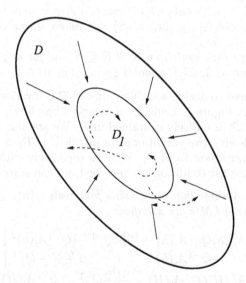

Fig. 1. The basic idea of the analysis for the invariance of $\mathcal{D}$: 1) $\mathcal{D}_1$ is attractive, 2) trajectories starting in $\mathcal{D}_1$ do not leave $\mathcal{D}$.

Step 2: accounting for variations of c(k). Inputs to this step are: 1) the ellipsoid $\mathcal{D} = \mathcal{E}(Q, 0)$ produced at step 1, 2) the maximum and minimum computation times h and H, 3) the task's activation period T, 4) a real m such that $|\frac{T}{c(k)} - \frac{T}{c(k-1)}| \leq m, \forall k$. As an output of this step, if some sufficient conditions are met, we can conclude that $\mathcal{D}$ is an invariant set if the computation time varies as specified in the third input. Clearly, we cannot draw the opposite conclusion if the test fails.

It is interesting to briefly discuss the third input. If the computation time $c(k)$ is allowed to vary, the additive disturbance term $w(k)$ has to be accounted for in the system dynamics described by Equation (4). Both the matrices A_i of the switching systems and the additive disturbance w vary in time depending on the evolution of $c(k)$. However, we will not use this knowledge of the structure of $w(k)$. Namely, we will conduct a worst case study in which $w(k)$ is allowed to evolve freely respecting only the norm constraint $|w(k)| \leq m$. This choice is conservative but it leads to a remarkable simplification in the analysis. A further advantage of this choice is that it provides a tool for handling also other additional noise terms as long as their maximum norm is bounded (and this is the case of the quantisation error for the case of non accessible internal state).

The following definition is useful for our purposes:

Definition 2. *Consider system (4) and two subsets S and R of the state space and let $\xi_{c(.),w(.)}(x_0, k)$ denote the state reached at step k starting from x_0 under the action of sequences $c(.)$ and $w(.)$.*

1. *S is attractive from a R if and only if for any vector $x_0 \in R$ and for any sequence $\tilde{c}(.)$, $\tilde{w}(.)$ either there exists a step $\overline{k}$ such that $\xi_{\tilde{c}(.),\tilde{w}(.)}(x_0, \overline{k}) \in S$ or $\lim_{k \to \infty} dist(\xi_{\tilde{c}(.),\tilde{w}(.)}(x_0, k), S) = 0$, where $dist(x, S)$ denotes the distance of x from the set S.*
2. *S is n-steps invariant from R if $R \subseteq S$ and for any vector $x_0 \in R$ and or any sequence $\tilde{c}(.)$, $\tilde{w}(.)$, it holds $\xi_{\tilde{c}(.),\tilde{w}(.)}(x_0, n) \in S$.*

The idea used to decide whether ellipsoid $\mathcal{D}$ is invariant is very simple and it is illustrated in Figure 1. Consider a second ellipsoid $\mathcal{D}_1 = \mathcal{E}(r^2 Q, 0)$; clearly if $r \in]0, 1[$, then $\mathcal{D}_1$ is entirely contained in $\mathcal{D}$. We are able to conclude invariance of $\mathcal{D}$ if the following two conditions are satisfied: 1) $\mathcal{D}_1$ is attractive from $\mathcal{D} \backslash \mathcal{D}_1$, 2) $\mathcal{D}$ is 1-step invariant from $\mathcal{D}_1$. We deal separately with the two conditions.

As far as the fist condition is concerned, we can state the following:

Theorem 2. *Assume that there exists four reals $\tau_1(h), \tau_2(h), \tau_1(H), \tau_2(H)$ such that the following LMIs are satisfied:*

$$i) \quad \begin{bmatrix} Q^{-1} - A_i^T(h)Q^{-1}A_i(h) - \frac{\tau_i(h)}{r^2}Q^{-1} & -(Q^{-1}A_i(h)^T) \\ -Q^{-1}A_i(h) & I\frac{\tau_i(h)}{m^2} - Q^{-1} \end{bmatrix} \succ 0 \quad i = 1, 2$$

$$ii) \quad \begin{bmatrix} Q^{-1} - A_i^T(H)Q^{-1}A_i(H) - \frac{\tau_i(H)}{r^2}Q^{-1} & -(Q^{-1}A_i(H)^T) \\ -Q^{-1}A_i(H) & I\frac{\tau_i(H)}{m^2} - Q^{-1} \end{bmatrix} \succ 0 \quad i = 1, 2 \tag{10}$$

$$ii) \ \tau_i(h), \tau_i(H) > 0 \qquad\qquad i = 1, 2.$$

Then $\mathcal{D}_1$ is attractive from $\mathcal{D} \backslash \mathcal{D}_1$:

Proof. The claim is true if condition

$$x^T Q^{-1}x - (A_i(c(k))x + w)^T Q^{-1}(A_i(c(k))x + w) > 0, \tag{11}$$

holds whenever

$$x^T Q^{-1} x > r^2 \text{ and } w^T w \leq m^2. \tag{12}$$

Using the $\mathcal{S}$-procedure [18], the above implication is verified if there exist, for all $c(k)$ positive reals $\tau_{i,1}(c(k))$ and $\tau_{i,2}(c(k))$ such that $\forall x \in \mathbb{R}^3$ and $\forall w \in \mathbb{R}^3$:

$$
\begin{aligned}
&x^T Q^{-1} x - (A_i(c(k))x + w)^T Q^{-1} (A_i(c(k))x + w) + \\
&- \tau_{i,1}(c(k))(x^T \tfrac{Q^{-1}}{r^2} x - 1) - \tau_{i,2}(c(k))(1 - \tfrac{w^T w}{m^2}) > 0
\end{aligned}
\tag{13}
$$

Since the above has to be verified also for $x = 0$ and $w = 0$, we derive the condition $\tau_{i,1}(c(k)) \geq \tau_{i,2}(c(k))$. Moreover, it is easy to see that if the inequality is verified for a $\tau_{i,1}^0(c(k)) > \tau_{i,2}(c(k))$ then it is verified also for $\tau_{i,1}(c(k)) = \tau_{i,2}(c(k))$. Hence, it is not restrictive to set $\tau_{i,1}(c(k)) = \tau_{i,2}(c(k)) = \tau_i(c(k))$. The resulting condition can be written as:

$$
[x^T w^T] \begin{bmatrix} Q^{-1} - A_i^T(c(k))Q^{-1}A_i(c(k)) - \tfrac{\tau_i(c(k))}{r^2}Q^{-1} & -(Q^{-1}A_i(c(k)))^T \\ -Q^{-1}A_i(c(k)) & I\tfrac{\tau_i(c(k))}{m^2} - Q^{-1} \end{bmatrix} \begin{bmatrix} x \\ w \end{bmatrix} > 0,
\tag{14}
$$

and it must hold $\forall x \in \mathbb{R}^3, \forall w \in \mathbb{R}^3$. For fixed r, the above is an infinite set of linear matrix inequalities (parametrised by $c(k)$). Following the same line of reasoning as in Theorem 1 it is possible to verify the LMI only at the four "vertexes" $A_i(h)$ and $A_i(H)$ and find by convex combination of $\tau_i(h)$ and $\tau_i(H)$ a a $\tau_i(c(k))$ that satisfies (14) for any $c(k)$.

It is easy to show the following corollary:

Corollary 1. *If condition (10) holds for a real $\bar{r}$ then it also holds for $r \geq \bar{r}$.*

Applying the above it is possible to find the minimum value r_1 in the interval $]0, 1[$ for which attractivity of $\mathcal{D}_1$ is ensured by a simple bi-section scheme.

The second condition can be enforced by the following:

Theorem 3. *Assume that there exists four reals $\tau_1(h), \tau_2(h), \tau_1(H), \tau_2(H)$ such that the following LMIs are satisfied:*

$$
\begin{aligned}
i)\ &\begin{bmatrix} A_i^T(h)Q^{-1}A_i(h) + \tfrac{1-\tau_i(h)}{r^2} & -(Q^{-1}A_i(h)^T) \\ -Q^{-1}A_i(h) & I\tfrac{\tau_i(h)}{m^2} - Q^{-1} \end{bmatrix} \succeq 0, \\
ii)\ &\begin{bmatrix} A_i^T(H)Q^{-1}A_i(H) + \tfrac{1-\tau_i(H)}{r^2} & -(Q^{-1}A_i(H)^T) \\ -Q^{-1}A_i(H) & I\tfrac{\tau_i(H)}{m^2} - Q^{-1} \end{bmatrix} \succeq 0, \\
ii)\ &\tau_i(h), \tau_i(H) > 0 \qquad\qquad\qquad\qquad\qquad\qquad\quad i = 1,\ 2.
\end{aligned}
\tag{15}
$$

Then for $\mathcal{D}$ is 1-step invariant from $\mathcal{D}_1$.

Proof. The claim is satisfied if

$$(A_i(c(k))x + w)^T Q^{-1}(A_i(c(k))x + w) \leq 1, \tag{16}$$

holds whenever

$$x^T Q^{-1} x \leq r^2 \text{ and } w^T w \leq m^2. \tag{17}$$

The proof is completed applying the $\mathcal{S}$-procedure and following the same arguments as in the proof of Theorem 2.

Also in this case, it is immediate to the following:

Corollary 2. *If condition (15) holds for a real $\bar{r}$ then it also holds for $r \leq \bar{r}$.*

A bisection scheme enables one to find, if possible, the maximum value r_2 in the interval for which the 1-step invariance of $\mathcal{D}$ from $\mathcal{D}_1$ is guaranteed.

Summing up, invariance of the set $\mathcal{D}$ can be concluded if $r_1 \leq r_2$ where r_1 and r_2 are found as shown above.

3.2 Synthesis

The analysis algorithms proposed in the previous section can be started if the designer comes up with a set of gains that, at least for constant $c(k) = c$, exponentially stabilise the system. The problem is essentially one of robust static output feedback. Indeed, matrices $A_i(c)$ can be written as:

$$A_i(c) = A_{i,0}(c) + b(c)[\alpha_i, \beta_i]C, \text{ where:}$$

$$A_{1,0}(c) = \begin{bmatrix} 1 & 0 & c \\ 1 & 0 & 0 \\ 0 & 0 & 1 \end{bmatrix}, \quad A_{2,0}(c) = \begin{bmatrix} 0 & 0 & c \\ 1 & 0 & 0 \\ 0 & 0 & 1 \end{bmatrix}, \quad b(c) = \begin{bmatrix} c \\ 0 \\ 1 \end{bmatrix}, \quad C = \begin{bmatrix} 1 & 0 & 0 \\ 0 & 1 & 0 \end{bmatrix}.$$

The problem of finding a stabilising static output feedback is itself regarded as very hard (more precisely it is provably Np-hard if the range of possible values for the gains is limited). The synthesis can be performed requiring a common lyapunov function for the two different modes and for all possible values of the computation time c in the admissible range $[h, H]$. Using Schur complements, a set of sufficient conditions for robust exponential stability (with decay rate γ) are as follows:

$$
\text{i)} \begin{bmatrix} \gamma^2 P & (A_{i,0}(h) + b(h)[\alpha_i, \beta_i]C)^T \\ A_{i,0}(h) + b(h)[\alpha_i, \beta_i]C & Q \end{bmatrix} \succeq 0 \quad i = 1, 2
$$

$$
\text{ii)} \begin{bmatrix} \gamma^2 P & (A_{i,0}(H) + b(H)[\alpha_i, \beta_i]C)^T \\ A_{i,0}(h) + b(H)[\alpha_i, \beta_i]C & Q \end{bmatrix} \succeq 0 \quad i = 1, 2 \quad (18)
$$

iii) $PQ = I.$

Constraint iii) is the most troublesome, since it is nonlinear and non-convex. We attacked this problem using the cone complementarity approach, proposed in [6]. Although based on sufficient conditions, the method behaved acceptably well in our context. For the sake of brevity, we omit further details referring the reader to to the cited paper.

4   Numerical Examples

Extensive simulations were performed to validate the methodology. In this context we report an example consisting of a task with period $T = 20ms$, and computation time varying in the range $[5ms, 15ms]$. The task is quite demanding (the 75% of the processor in the worst case).In order to give enough flexibility to the control action we put the saturation for the bandwidth at $B_0 = 0.92$. The

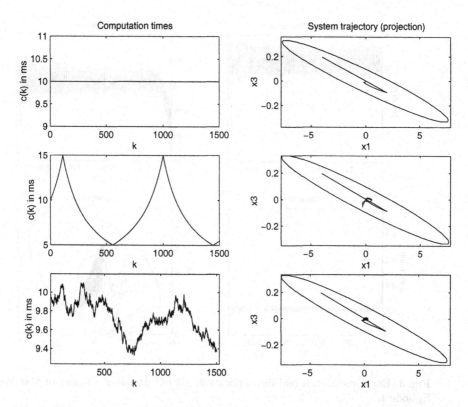

Fig. 2. Numerical example. First row: constant computation time. Second row, deterministically varying computation time. Third row, stochastically varying computation time.

synthesis procedure, requiring a guaranteed convergence rate $\gamma = 0.9$, produced $\alpha_1 = -0.057$, $\beta_1 = 0.044$, $\alpha_2 = -0.065$ and $\beta_2 = 0.0445$. The analysis was performed assuming $|\frac{T}{c(k)} - \frac{T}{c(k-1)}| \leq 0.006$ and it produced a $\mathcal{P}$-safe invariant set that is an exponential stability basin in case of constant $c(k)$. The projection of the ellipsoid onto the x_1-x_3 plane is reported, along with some simulation results in Figure 2. In particular in the first row, we show the results for constant computation time. As it is possible to see trajectories converge to the origin in exponential time. In the second row a simulation is reported for a deterministically varying computation time, where at each step $|\frac{T}{c(k)} - \frac{T}{c(k-1)}| = 0.006$. Finally, at the third row, the computation time was varied stochastically respecting the constraint $|\frac{T}{c(k)} - \frac{T}{c(k-1)}| \leq 0.006$ (random walk). As it is possible to see the safe ellipsoid contains, for both experiments the produced trajectories.

When the application presents sharp variations in computation time, the analysis proposed in Step 2 in the previous section need not produce acceptable results, being based on conservative conditions. This is the case of such real life application as MPEG players. As an example, we considered actual execution traces (profiled on an AMD Athlon 1.8 Ghz computer) for decoding

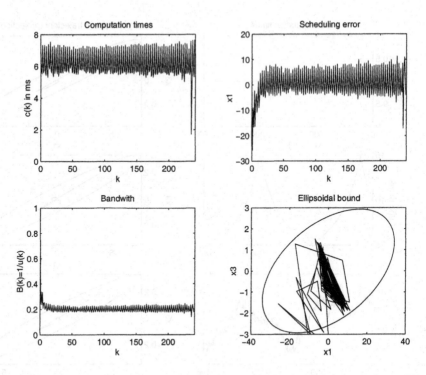

Fig. 3. Experiment on a real life application: MPEG decoding a trailer of Star Wars Episode 1.

a trailer of *Star Wars Episode 1*. Computation times for 250 samples are reported on the upper left plot contained in Figure 3. The maximum and minimum computation times are respectively, in the considered segment, $7.6ms$ and $1.71ms$; the activation period for standard MPEG decoding is $T = 33ms$. For the considered segment we recorded very strong variations in computation time: $\max \frac{|c(k)-c(k+1)|}{\max(c(k))-\min(c(k))} > 0.65$. We applied the synthesis procedure described above requiring $\gamma = 0.85$ and the produced gains were: $\alpha_1 = -0.0972$, $\alpha_2 = -0.1454$m $\beta_1 = \beta_2 = 0.0886$. By Step 1 of the analysis, we produced a $\mathcal{P}$-safe ellipsoid for constant computation time. Due to the strong variations in computation times, Step2 failed. However, as it is possible to see from Figure 3, the controller performs acceptably. Indeed, not only is the scheduling error contained within small bound, but also the assigned bandwidth does not change very much around 0.2 and the evolution in the $[e(k), u(k) - T/c(k)]$ plane lies almost always within the projection of the ellipsoid computed in Step 1.

5   Conclusions and Future Work

In this paper we considered the problem of allocating processor bandwidth to parallel software tasks hosted on a CPU so as to enforce compliance with soft real-time execution constraints. The adoption of resource reservation scheduling allows one to model the scheduler as a discrete-time switching system for which the assigned bandwidth is a control variable, the scheduling error is an output variable and the execution time of each job is a disturbance term. We showed analysis and synthesis techniques for a feedback controller suitable to this kind of application . The control scheme is entirely decentralised whereas occasional interactions between tasks due to the saturation of the total available bandwidth act as disturbance terms on the inputs. We showed the effectiveness of the proposed approach on a laboratory example and on data from a real application.

Many open problems are left for future research. Our first effort will be directed toward reducing conservativeness of the analysis technique for variable computation time, as shown in the MPEG player example above. Moreover, the problem of how to steer the system into the ellipsoidal safe set under the bandwidth saturation constraints is still open. Finally we want to develop mixed centralised/decentralised control to deal with possible interactions between tasks due to the saturation of the total bandwidth.

References

1. Luca Abeni and Giorgio Buttazzo. Integrating multimedia applications in hard real-time systems. In *Proceedings of the IEEE Real-Time Systems Symposium*, Madrid, Spain, December 1998.
2. Luca Abeni and Giorgio Buttazzo. Adaptive bandwidth reservation for multimedia computing. In *Proceedings of the IEEE Real Time Computing Systems and Applications*, Hong Kong, December 1999.
3. Luca Abeni, Luigi Palopoli, Giuseppe Lipari, and Jonathan Walpole. Analysis of a reservation-based feedback scheduler. In *Proc. of the Real-Time Systems Symposium*, Austin, Texas, November 2002.
4. S. Boyd and L.L. Vandenberghe. *Convex optimization*. Course lecture notes - Stanford University, 2002.
5. F. J. Corbato, M. Merwin-Dagget, and R. C. Daley. An experimental time-sharing system. In *Proceedings of the AFIPS Joint Computer Conference*, May 1962.
6. L. El Ghaoui, F. Oustry, and M. Ait Rami. A cone complementary linearization algorithm for static output-feedback and related problems. *IEEE Transaction and Automatic Control*, August 1997.
7. G.Lipari and S.K. Baruah. Greedy reclaimation of unused bandwidth in constant bandwidth servers. In *IEEE Proceedings of the 12th Euromicro Conference on Real-Time Systems*, Stokholm, Sweden, June 2000.
8. Haitham Hindi and Stephen Boyd. Analysis of linear systems with saturation using convex optimization. In *Proc. of the 37th IEEE Conference on decision adn Control (cdc 1998)*, Tampa, Florida, 1998.
9. B. Li and K. Nahrstedt. A control theoretical model for quality of service adaptations. In *Proceedings of Sixth International Workshop on Quality of Service*, 1998.
10. C. L. Liu and J. Layland. Scheduling alghorithms for multiprogramming in a hard real-time environment. *Journal of the ACM*, 20(1), 1973.
11. C. Lu, J. A. Stankovic, T. F. Abdelzaher, G. Tao, S. H. Son, and M. Marley. Performance specifications and metrics for adaptive real-time systems. In *Proceedings of the 21th IEEE Real-Time Systems Symposium*, Orlando, FL, December 2000.

12. Clifford W. Mercer, Stefan Savage, and Hideyuki Tokuda. Processor capacity reserves for multimedia operating systems. Technical Report CMU-CS-93-157, Carnegie Mellon University, Pittsburg, May 1993.
13. Tatsuo Nakajima. Resource reservation for adaptive qos mapping in real-time mach. In *Sixth International Workshop on Parallel and Distributed Real-Time Systems (WPDRTS)*, April 1998.
14. Raj Rajkumar, Kanaka Juvva, Anastasio Molano, and Shuichi Oikawa. Resource kernels: A resource-centric approach to real-time and multimedia systems. In *Proceedings of the SPIE/ACM Conference on Multimedia Computing and Networking*, January 1998.
15. Dickson Reed and Robin Fairbairns (eds.). Nemesis, the kernel – overview, May 1997.
16. John Regehr and John A. Stankovic. Augmented CPU Reservations: Towards predictable execution on general-purpose operating systems. In *Proceedings of the IEEE Real-Time Technology and Applications Symposium (RTAS 2001)*, Taipei, Taiwan, May 2001.
17. David Steere, Ashvin Goel, Joshua Gruenberg, Dylan McNamee, Calton Pu, and Jonathan Walpole. A feedback-driven proportion allocator for real-rate scheduling. In *Proceedings of the Third usenix-osdi*. pub-usenix, feb 1999.
18. V. A. Yakubovich. *Vestnik Leningrad Uiversity*, chapter S-Procedure in nonlinear control theory, pages 66–77. 1971. (English translation in Vestnik Leningrad University 4:73–93,1977).

Stabilization of LTI Systems with Quantized State – Quantized Input Static Feedback[*]

Bruno Picasso[1] and Antonio Bicchi[2]

[1] Scuola Normale Superiore – Pisa & Centro "E. Piaggio", Università di Pisa
picasso@piaggio.ccii.unipi.it
[2] Centro "E. Piaggio", Università di Pisa
Via Diotisalvi 2 – 56126 Pisa, Italy
bicchi@ing.unipi.it

Abstract. This paper is concerned with the stabilizability problem for discrete–time linear systems subject to a uniform quantization of the control set and to a regular state quantization, both fixed a priori. As it is well known, for quantized systems only weak (practical) stability properties can be achieved. Therefore, we focus on the existence and construction of quantized controllers capable of steering a system to within invariant neighborhoods of the equilibrium.

We first consider uniformly quantized, unbounded input sets for which an increasing family of invariant sets is constructed and quantized controllers realizing invariance are characterized. The family contains a minimal set depending only on the quantization resolution.

The analysis is then extended to cases where the control set is bounded: for any given state–space set of the family above, the minimal diameter of the control set which ensures its invariance is found. The finite control set so determined also guarantees that all the states of the set can be controlled in finite time to within the family's minimal set. It is noteworthy that the same property holds for systems without state quantization: hence, to ensure invariance and attractivity properties, the necessary control set diameter is invariant with state quantization; yet the minimal invariant set is larger. An example is finally reported to illustrate the above results.

1 Introduction

Practical applications of control theory reveal some limits of the continuous models in the description of dynamical systems: limited resources or technical constraints, which finally lead to discrete measurements or to a finite number of possible control actions, are typical situations that must be faced. This is part of a broader phenomenon which is referred to as *quantization*.

[*] Support from "European Project Recsys–Ist–2001–37170" and from "Progetto coordinato Agenzia 2000 CNR C00E714"

O. Maler and A. Pnueli (Eds.): HSCC 2003, LNCS 2623, pp. 405–416, 2003.

The example of digitally interconnected systems controlled through finite communication channels (i.e. capable of transmitting only discrete information between the plant and the controller) is usual. Also, many hybrid models (i.e. including the interaction of continuous dynamics and logic) are the result of information quantization.

In the past twenty years the problem of dynamic systems analysis and control synthesis in presence of quantization has developed and is currently growing in interest. It is now consolidated the idea of regarding quantization not as a phenomenon to be neglected and related to the concept of approximation but rather as a useful tool to be studied within proper models (see for instance [1,2, 5,6,7,12,13,14]).
In the last decade many papers addressed the problem of the stabilization of quantized systems (see [4,6,7,8,9,10,11,12,15]): in [6] Delchamps clarifies that the classical concept of stability is not significant in this context, hence "practical" stability properties are introduced for quantized systems. Most of the existing literature on stabilization deals with the problem of looking for the quantized resources necessary to achieve a prefixed stability objective.

We are interested in another kind of question that we think is as much important: the stability problem for systems whose quantized control set is *fixed a priori* is studied in [12] where we found a relevant family of invariant sets. In the present paper this analysis is generalized to the case of a prefixed quantization both in the control and in the state space. This is intended to model situations in which, not only the actuators have a discrete or finite set of possible actions, but also measurements provide a limited (i.e. discrete) information on the state of the system. Such analysis is helpful because it allows to decide a priori whether a desired control objective can be achieved by using a *given* technology (actuators, sensors, communication and computational means).

Our work is focused on the stabilization of single–input discrete–time linear systems; we assume that the control space is uniformly quantized and that a reticular quantization is assigned to the state space.
After some preliminaries, Section 3 is dedicated to the construction of a continuous and increasing family of polyhedral invariant sets: the concept of invariance must be reconsidered because, in the quantized state model, although the states evolve according to a deterministic dynamics, the information on them are limited and the controls are selected on the basis of the quantized results of the measurements. A quantized controller (mapping a quantized state into a quantized input set) capable of steering the states in an invariant neighborhood of the equilibrium is constructed. Our analysis does not rely on classical Lyapunov methods but employs direct geometric considerations, which turn out to be less conservative: we characterize the static controllers (i.e. the control laws based only on the current output) realizing the invariance of the sets we have found. The family contains a minimal set depending only on the quantization resolution, its size is increasing with state–space resolution decreases. In Section 4 the analysis is extended to the finite control set case. For any given state–space set of the family above, the minimal diameter of the control set which ensures its

invariance is found. The finite control set so determined also guarantees that all the states of the set can be controlled in finite time to within the family's minimal set. In particular it is constructed a quantized feedback law which both renders invariant a given set of the family and makes the trajectories converge to the family's minimal element: it turns out that the minimal diameter of the control set needed to complete this task is just the same as in the case in which only the inputs are quantized. Hence the state quantization does not influence the bound on the controls necessary to ensure invariance and attractivity properties; yet the minimal invariant set is larger. In Section 5 an example illustrates the presented theoretical results and shows their applicability.

Notation: $Q_n(\Lambda) := \left[-\frac{\Lambda}{2}; \frac{\Lambda}{2}\right]^n$ is the hypercube of edge length Λ, $\lfloor x \rfloor := \max \{z \in \mathbb{Z} \,|\, z \le x\}$ is the floor function, x^+ is the standard notation for $x(t+1)$, $x_i(t)$ stands for the ith component of the state x at time t, $\|x\|_\infty := \max\limits_{i=1,\dots,n} \{|x_i|\}$ and $\mathbf{0} := (0,\dots,0) \in \mathbb{Z}^n$.

2   Preliminaries

Definition 1. Given a n–tuple $\{w_1,\dots,w_n\} := \mathcal{W}$ of linearly independent vectors of $\mathbb{R}^n$, for any $(z_1,\dots,z_n) := z \in \mathbb{Z}^n$, let the *cell* $\mathcal{C}_z$ be $\{(z_1+a_1)w_1 + \cdots + (z_n+a_n)w_n \,|\, a_i \in \left[-\frac{1}{2},\frac{1}{2}\right)\ \ \forall i = 1,\dots,n\}$.
Consider the quantized set $\mathcal{S} := \left\{\sum_{i=1}^n z_i w_i \,\middle|\, z_i \in \mathbb{Z}\ \ \forall i = 1,\dots,n\right\} \subset \mathbb{R}^n$. The *reticular quantizer* associated to $\mathcal{W}$ is the function $q_{\mathcal{W}} : \mathbb{R}^n \to \mathcal{S}$ defined as follows: $q_{\mathcal{W}}(x) = z_1 w_1 + \cdots + z_n w_n \Leftrightarrow x \in \mathcal{C}_z\ \ \left(z = (z_1,\dots,z_n)\right)$.

We deal with a single–input discrete time–invariant linear system subject to a fixed and uniformly quantized control set and to a reticular state quantization, more precisely:

$$
\begin{cases}
x(t+1) = Ax(t) + bu(t) \\
y(t) = q_{\mathcal{W}}\big(x(t)\big) \\
x \in \mathbb{R}^n, \quad u \in \mathcal{U} \subseteq \epsilon \mathbb{Z}\ (\epsilon > 0), \quad y \in \mathcal{S} \subset \mathbb{R}^n \\
A \in \mathbb{R}^{n \times n}, \quad b \in \mathbb{R}^n.
\end{cases}
\tag{1}
$$

From now on $q_{\mathcal{W}}$ will be simply denoted by q.
A quantizer q models situations where only partial information about the state of the system are available, that is $q(x)$ is known rather than x. More general state–quantizers have been considered in the literature [9]: for the sake of simplicity we restrict to the reticular quantizers, however, as it will be pointed out in Remark 6 at the end of Section 4, the subsequent treatment can be generalized. We associate to system (1) the corresponding system without state quantization, i.e. with q the identity map; it will be denoted by $(A, b, \mathcal{U})$.

We assume that the pair (A, b) is reachable: in this case a change of the coordinates allows us to work with the *controller form* associated to the pair (A, b). Hence, throughout this paper, we will refer to the following hypothesis:

H1) The pair (A, b) is reachable and the system (1) is in controller form. Let $s^n - \alpha_n s^{n-1} - \cdots - \alpha_2 s - \alpha_1$ be the characteristic polynomial of A.

Let us introduce the basic definitions about invariant sets (see also [3]):

Definition 2. The set $D \subseteq \mathbb{R}^n$ is said to be *positively invariant* for a closed–loop system $x^+ = f(x)$ iff $\forall x \in D$, $x^+ \in D$;

Definition 3. The set $D \subseteq \mathbb{R}^n$ is said to be *controlled invariant* for the system $(A, b, \mathcal{U})$ iff $\forall x \in D \; \exists u \in \mathcal{U}$ such that $x^+ = Ax + bu \in D$;

Definition 4. The set $D \subseteq \mathbb{R}^n$ is said to be *q–controlled invariant* for system (1) iff $\forall x \in D \; \exists u \in \mathcal{U}$ such that $\forall \tilde{x} \in q^{-1}(q(x)) \cap D$, $\tilde{x}^+ = A\tilde{x} + bu \in D$.

This means that it must be possible to choose a control action, as a function only of the available measurement $q(x)$, such that $x^+ \in D$.

Remark 1. If D is q–controlled invariant for system (1), then it is controlled invariant for the associated system $(A, b, \mathcal{U})$ without state quantization.

The size of the transformed cell $A\mathcal{C}_z$ along the nth direction is

$$h(A\mathcal{C}_z) := \sup_{(x', x'') \in \mathcal{C}_z^2} \left\{ \left| (Ax')_n - (Ax'')_n \right| \right\};$$

since $h(A\mathcal{C}_z)$ does not depend on $z \in \mathbb{Z}^n$, we determine it for $z = \mathbf{0}$: the set of the vertices of $\mathcal{C}_0$ is $\mathcal{V} := \{a_1 w_1 + \cdots + a_n w_n \,|\, (a_1, \ldots, a_n) \in \{-\frac{1}{2}, \frac{1}{2}\}^n \}$. $\forall v \in \mathcal{V}$, let $h(v) := \left|(Av)_n\right| = \left| \sum_{i=1}^n \alpha_i v_i \right|$. It is easy to see that

$$h(A\mathcal{C}_0) = 2 \cdot \max_{v \in \mathcal{V}} h(v) := H.$$

H, which is defined in the controller form coordinates, depends on the coefficients $(\alpha_1, \ldots, \alpha_n)$ of the characteristic polynomial of A and on the quantizer q.

Let $\delta := \sup_{x \in \mathcal{C}_0} \|x\|_\infty$ be the *state–quantizer resolution*.

3   Construction of q–Controlled Invariant Sets for $\mathcal{U} = \epsilon \mathbb{Z}$

Although invariant sets are very important in control theory, in the current literature few results exist for quantized systems. The input quantization is a severe constraint which often renders unpracticable the classical approaches to the search of controlled invariant sets (see [3]).

In [12] we have found a simple and general technique to construct a family of controlled invariant sets for any uniformly quantized single–input system $(A, b, \mathcal{U})$ such that the pair (A, b) is reachable. The family contains a minimal element which has also good minimality properties with respect to all possible invariant sets.

These results have been derived taking advantage of the controller form coordinates and are summarized in the following

Theorem: If $\mathcal{U} = \epsilon \mathbb{Z}$, then $\forall \Delta \geq \epsilon$, $Q_n(\Delta)$ is controlled invariant.

Owing to Remark 1, it is natural to look for q–controlled invariant sets within the family $\left(Q_n(\Delta) \right)_{\Delta \geq \epsilon}$.

For the unbounded control set case we have the following characterization of the q–controlled invariant hypercubes:

Proposition 1. *Assume that* $\mathcal{U} = \epsilon \mathbb{Z}$.

i) *If* $\frac{\Delta}{2} \geq \delta$, *a necessary condition in order that* $Q_n(\Delta)$ *is* q–*controlled invariant is* $\Delta \geq H$.

ii) *A sufficient condition in order that* $Q_n(\Delta)$ *is* q–*controlled invariant is* $\Delta \geq H + \epsilon$.

Proof. i) $\mathcal{C}_0 \subseteq Q_n(\Delta)$ because $\frac{\Delta}{2} \geq \delta$: hence for the q–controlled invariance of $Q_n(\Delta)$ is necessary that $\exists u \in \mathcal{U}$ such that $A\mathcal{C}_0 + bu \subseteq Q_n(\Delta)$. If $H > \Delta$ then, $\forall v \in \mathbb{R}^n$, $A\mathcal{C}_0 + v \not\subseteq Q_n(\Delta)$.

ii) Let $x \in Q_n(\Delta)$, $y = q(x) = z_1 w_1 + \cdots + z_n w_n$ is the central point of the cell $\mathcal{C}_z \ni x$. The control

$$u(y) := \left(\left\lfloor \frac{-\sum_{i=1}^n \alpha_i y_i + \frac{\epsilon}{2}}{\epsilon} \right\rfloor \right) \epsilon$$

realizes the q–controlled invariance of $Q_n(\Delta)$, that is $\forall \tilde{x} \in \mathcal{C}_z \cap Q_n(\Delta)$, $\tilde{x}^+ = A\tilde{x} + bu(y) \in Q_n(\Delta)$, in fact: since $\tilde{x} \in Q_n(\Delta)$ and A is in controller form (so $\tilde{x}_j^+ = \tilde{x}_{j+1} \ \forall j = 1, \ldots, n-1$), it is sufficient to show that $|\tilde{x}_n^+| \leq \frac{\Delta}{2}$. The central point of the transformed cell $A\mathcal{C}_z$ is $y^+ = Ay + bu(y)$ and is such that $|y_n^+| \leq \frac{\epsilon}{2}$ (see also [12]), $\tilde{x}^+ \in A\mathcal{C}_z + bu(y)$, thus $\tilde{x}^+ = y^+ + v$ with $|v_n| \leq \frac{H}{2}$. Hence $|\tilde{x}_n^+| \leq |y_n^+| + |v_n| \leq \frac{\epsilon}{2} + \frac{H}{2} \leq \frac{\Delta}{2}$ by the hypothesis.   ∎

Corollary 1. *Assume that* $\mathcal{U} = \epsilon \mathbb{Z}$ *and consider the feedback law* $F : \mathbb{R}^n \to \mathcal{U}$

$$F(y) := \left(\left\lfloor \frac{-\sum_{i=1}^n \alpha_i y_i + \frac{\epsilon}{2}}{\epsilon} \right\rfloor \right) \epsilon.$$

The induced closed–loop dynamics

$$x^+ = Ax + bF\big(q(x)\big) \tag{2}$$

for the state–quantized system (1) is such that all $x \in \mathbb{R}^n$ *are steered into* $Q_n(H + \epsilon)$ *in at most* n *steps and* $Q_n(H + \epsilon)$ *is positively invariant.*   □

The function $(F \circ q) : \mathbb{R}^n \to \mathcal{U}$ is a quantized state–quantized input version of the so–called dead–beat controller (whereas F is referred to as the quantized input dead–beat controller).

Remark 2. Note that in Proposition 1.*ii* we do not require that $\frac{\Delta}{2} \geq \delta$ (which is equivalent to the existence of a cell $C_z \subseteq Q_n(\Delta)$): when $H + \epsilon < 2\delta$, for $\Delta \in [H + \epsilon, 2\delta)$ it holds that $\forall x \in Q_n(\Delta)$ the measurement $q(x)$ is not sufficient to guarantee that $x \in Q_n(\Delta)$; in this case Proposition 1.*ii* seems to reduce to a formal assertion. This is not the case: in fact, assume for instance that $H + \epsilon < 2\delta$ and that the system evolves according to the closed–loop dynamics (2), then, even if the measurements $q(x)'s$ are not sufficient to show that $x \in Q_n(H + \epsilon)$, it is known a priori that from the nth step on $x \in Q_n(H + \epsilon)$. Thus it is not unrealistic to investigate the q–controlled invariance for hypercubes of edge length $\Delta < 2\delta$.

In Section 5 we will give an example where this phenomenon occurs.

We conclude this section with the characterization of the quantized controllers which make $Q_n(\Delta)$ positively invariant.

Assume that $\mathcal{U} = \epsilon \mathbb{Z}$, fix $\Delta \geq H + \epsilon$ and consider $Q_n(\Delta)$. Let $\mathcal{S}_{[\Delta]} := \text{Im}(q_{|Q_n(\Delta)}) \subset \mathcal{S}$. $\forall y \in \mathcal{S}_{[\Delta]}$ let $C_{z(y)}$ be the cell containing y and set $H^y := \sum_{i=1}^{n} \alpha_i y_i + \frac{H}{2}$ and $H_y := \sum_{i=1}^{n} \alpha_i y_i - \frac{H}{2}$ which respectively denote the sup and the inf of the nth component of the points of the transformed cell $AC_{z(y)}$. The set

$$\mathcal{U}_{[\Delta, y]} := \left\{ u \in \mathcal{U} \,\middle|\, \forall x \in C_{z(y)} \cap Q_n(\Delta), \ x^+ \in Q_n(\Delta) \right\}$$

consists of the controls which realize the q–controlled invariance of $Q_n(\Delta)$ when the measurement $y = q(x)$ is available. By arguments similar to those used to prove Proposition 1.*ii*, it can be shown that $\mathcal{U}_{[\Delta, y]} \supseteq \mathcal{U}^*_{[\Delta, y]}$, where

$$\mathcal{U}^*_{[\Delta, y]} := \left\{ z \epsilon \,\middle|\, z \in \mathbb{Z} \ \text{and} \ -\left\lfloor \frac{1}{\epsilon}\left(\frac{\Delta}{2} + H_y\right)\right\rfloor \leq z \leq \left\lfloor \frac{1}{\epsilon}\left(\frac{\Delta}{2} - H^y\right)\right\rfloor \right\};$$

if moreover $C_{z(y)} \subseteq Q_n(\Delta)$, then $\mathcal{U}^*_{[\Delta, y]} = \mathcal{U}_{[\Delta, y]}$.

Using the definition of the floor function we calculate $\#\mathcal{U}^*_{[\Delta, y]} = \frac{\Delta - H}{\epsilon} - \theta$ with $\theta \in [-1, 1)$; in particular, for $\Delta = H + \epsilon$, $0 < \#\mathcal{U}^*_{[H + \epsilon, y]} \leq 2$.

Remark 3. Since $\forall y \in \mathcal{S}_{[\Delta]}$, $\#\mathcal{U}_{[\Delta, y]} < +\infty$ and also $\#\mathcal{S}_{[\Delta]} < +\infty$, then there exists a finite number of static quantized controllers defined in $Q_n(\Delta)$ which make it positively invariant, that is

$$\#\left\{ \Phi : \mathcal{S}_{[\Delta]} \to \mathcal{U} \,\middle|\, \forall x \in Q_n(\Delta), \ x^+ = Ax + b\Phi(q(x)) \in Q_n(\Delta) \right\} < +\infty.$$

4   Finite Control Set

We now analyze the q–controlled invariance of the hypercubes $Q_n(\Delta)$'s (with $\Delta \geq H + \epsilon$) in the finite control set case. We consider input sets of the type

$$\mathcal{U}_k := \{-k\epsilon, \ldots, 0, \ldots, +k\epsilon\}$$

and, for a given $\Delta \geq H + \epsilon$, we find the condition on k ensuring the q–controlled invariance of $Q_n(\Delta)$.

We restrict our analysis to systems such that $\sum_{i=1}^{n} |\alpha_i| \geq 1$ which are indeed the interesting ones: in fact in the other case, not only the system is stable, but also $u \equiv 0$ is sufficient for the invariance of any hypercube and for the convergence of the trajectories to the equilibrium. Note that when $\sum_{i=1}^{n} |\alpha_i| \geq 1$, it holds that $\|A\|_\infty = \sum_{i=1}^{n} |\alpha_i|$.

Consider the system $(A, b, \mathcal{U}_k)$ associated to system (1) : in [12] we have proved that

Theorem: $Q_n(\Delta)$ is controlled invariant if and only if

$$k \geq - \left\lfloor \frac{1}{2} \frac{\Delta}{\epsilon} \left(1 - \sum_{i=1}^{n} |\alpha_i| \right) \right\rfloor := \mathcal{K}.$$

By Remark 1 it follows that for the q–controlled invariance of $Q_n(\Delta)$ it is necessary that $k \geq \mathcal{K}$. In next Proposition 2, we construct an explicit quantized feedback law taking values in $\mathcal{U}_\mathcal{K}$ and rendering $Q_n(\Delta)$ positively invariant. Hence the condition $k \geq \mathcal{K}$ is also sufficient: this means that, even if the state space is quantized, it is not necessary to have more control resources to ensure invariance properties.

Proposition 2. *Assume that* $\sum_{i=1}^{n} |\alpha_i| \geq 1$; *let* $\Delta \geq H + \epsilon$ *and* $k := - \left\lfloor \frac{1}{2} \frac{\Delta}{\epsilon} \left(1 - \sum_{i=1}^{n} |\alpha_i| \right) \right\rfloor$. *Consider the feedback law* $\tilde{F} : \mathbb{R}^n \to \mathcal{U}_k$ *defined by*

$$\tilde{F}(y) := \begin{cases} -(k\epsilon) & \text{if} \quad \sum_{i=1}^{n} \alpha_i y_i - k\epsilon \geq \frac{\epsilon}{2}, \\ +(k\epsilon) & \text{if} \quad \sum_{i=1}^{n} \alpha_i y_i + k\epsilon \leq -\frac{\epsilon}{2}, \\ z\epsilon & \text{with} \quad z = \left\lfloor \frac{-\sum_{i=1}^{n} \alpha_i y_i + \frac{\epsilon}{2}}{\epsilon} \right\rfloor & \text{otherwise.} \end{cases} \tag{3}$$

Then $\forall \gamma \in [H + \epsilon, \Delta]$, $Q_n(\gamma)$ *is positively invariant for*

$$x^+ = Ax + b\tilde{F}(q(x)). \tag{4}$$

Proof. Let $\Xi := \{ x \in \mathbb{R}^n \mid \sum_{i=1}^{n} \alpha_i x_i - k\epsilon > \frac{\epsilon}{2} \} \cup \{ x \in \mathbb{R}^n \mid \sum_{i=1}^{n} \alpha_i x_i + k\epsilon < -\frac{\epsilon}{2} \}$ be the region where the quantized input dead–beat controller saturates. Note that $\forall x \notin \Xi$, $v := Ax + b\tilde{F}(x)$ is such that $|v_n| \leq \frac{\epsilon}{2}$.

Since A is in controller form, for $x \in Q_n(\gamma)$ it is sufficient to analyze x_n^+; we divide the analysis in three cases.

I) If $q(x) \notin \Xi$ then, using the same arguments used to prove Proposition 1.ii, $|x_n^+| \leq \frac{H+\epsilon}{2}$.

II) If $q(x) \in \Xi$ and $x \notin \Xi$ then, with $y = q(x)$, $y^+ = Ay + b\tilde{F}(y)$ is such that $|y_n^+| > \frac{\epsilon}{2}$. Suppose that $\sum_{i=1}^{n} \alpha_i y_i > 0$, then $y_n^+ = \sum_{i=1}^{n} \alpha_i y_i - k\epsilon > \frac{\epsilon}{2}$. By Equation (4), $x_n^+ = \sum_{i=1}^{n} \alpha_i x_i - k\epsilon \leq \sum_{i=1}^{n} \alpha_i x_i + \tilde{F}(x) \leq \frac{\epsilon}{2}$ because $x \notin \Xi$; moreover $x_n^+ \geq y_n^+ - \frac{H}{2} > \frac{\epsilon}{2} - \frac{H}{2} > -\frac{H+\epsilon}{2}$: thus $|x_n^+| \leq \frac{H+\epsilon}{2}$. The case $\sum_{i=1}^{n} \alpha_i y_i < 0$ is similar.

III) If $q(x) \in \Xi$ and $x \in \Xi$ then $x^+ = Ax + b\tilde{F}(q(x)) = Ax + b\tilde{F}(x)$. If $\sum_{i=1}^n \alpha_i x_i > 0$, since $x \in \Xi$, then $\sum_{i=1}^n \alpha_i x_i - k\epsilon > \frac{\epsilon}{2} > 0$. Hence $|x_n^+| = \sum_{i=1}^n \alpha_i x_i - k\epsilon \leq \sum_{i=1}^n |\alpha_i| |x_i| - k\epsilon \leq \|x\|_\infty \cdot \sum_{i=1}^n |\alpha_i| - k\epsilon$: in this case the proof of the statement is achieved by showing that $\|x\|_\infty \cdot \sum_{i=1}^n |\alpha_i| - k\epsilon \leq \|x\|_\infty$. By the definition of k it holds that $k\epsilon \geq \frac{\Delta}{2}\left(\sum_{i=1}^n |\alpha_i| - 1\right) \geq \|x\|_\infty \left(\sum_{i=1}^n |\alpha_i| - 1\right)$ because $\frac{\Delta}{2} \geq \|x\|_\infty$ and $\sum_{i=1}^n |\alpha_i| \geq 1$. Thus $k\epsilon \geq \|x\|_\infty \left(\sum_{i=1}^n |\alpha_i| - 1\right)$ which is what we wanted to show.
The case $\sum_{i=1}^n \alpha_i x_i < 0$ is similar.   ∎

Corollary 2. *Consider the system (1) and assume that $\mathcal{U} = \mathcal{U}_k$, let $\Delta \geq H + \epsilon$. $Q_n(\Delta)$ is q-controlled invariant if and only if*

$$k \geq -\left\lfloor \frac{1}{2}\frac{\Delta}{\epsilon}\left(1 - \sum_{i=1}^n |\alpha_i|\right)\right\rfloor.$$

In particular, for $\Delta \geq H + \epsilon$, $Q_n(\Delta)$ is q-controlled invariant for system (1) if and only if it is controlled invariant for the associated system $(A, b, \mathcal{U}_k)$ without state quantization.   □

Note that the closed–loop dynamics in Equation (4) is such that if $\frac{H+\epsilon}{2} \leq \|x\|_\infty \leq \frac{\Delta}{2}$, then $\|x^+\|_\infty \leq \|x\|_\infty$: in next Proposition 3 we will show that a mild supplementary hypothesis is sufficient to ensure that any trajectory starting from $x(0) \in Q_n(\Delta)$ enters $Q_n(H + \epsilon)$ in a finite number of steps.

Proposition 3. *Assume that $\sum_{i=1}^n |\alpha_i| \geq 1$; let $\Delta \geq H + \epsilon$ and $k := -\left\lfloor \frac{1}{2}\frac{\Delta}{\epsilon}\left(1 - \sum_{i=1}^n |\alpha_i|\right)\right\rfloor$. If $\frac{1}{2}\frac{\Delta}{\epsilon}\left(1 - \sum_{i=1}^n |\alpha_i|\right) \notin \mathbb{Z}$, then the closed–loop dynamics*

$$x^+ = Ax + b\tilde{F}(q(x)),$$

induced by the feedback law $\tilde{F} : \mathbb{R}^n \to \mathcal{U}_k$ defined in Equation (3), is such that $Q_n(\Delta)$ is positively invariant, all $x(0) \in Q_n(\Delta)$ are steered into $Q_n(H + \epsilon)$ in a finite number of steps and $Q_n(H + \epsilon)$ is positively invariant. For $x(0) \in Q_n(\Delta)\backslash Q_n(H+\epsilon)$, an upper bound on the number of steps necessary to enter $Q_n(H + \epsilon)$ is given by

$$\mathcal{B} := -n \cdot \left\lfloor \frac{1}{\varphi}\left(\frac{H+\epsilon}{2} - \left(\|q(x(0))\|_\infty + \delta\right)\right)\right\rfloor,$$

where $\varphi := k\epsilon - \frac{\Delta}{2}\left(\sum_{i=1}^n |\alpha_i| - 1\right)$ and δ is the state-quantizer resolution.

Proof. The positive invariance of $Q_n(\Delta)$ and $Q_n(H + \epsilon)$ has been proved in Proposition 2. From $\frac{1}{2}\frac{\Delta}{\epsilon}\left(1 - \sum_{i=1}^n |\alpha_i|\right) \notin \mathbb{Z}$ it follows immediately that $\varphi > 0$. We claim that $\forall x \in Q_n(\Delta)\backslash Q_n(H+\epsilon)$, x^+ is such that $|x_n^+| \leq \frac{H+\epsilon}{2}$ or $|x_n^+| \leq \|x\|_\infty - \varphi$. The claim implies the thesis, in fact: since A is in controller form, after n steps it holds that $|x_j(n)| \leq \max\left\{\|x(0)\|_\infty - \varphi; \frac{H+\epsilon}{2}\right\} \ \forall j = 1, \ldots, n$; thus

$\|x(n)\|_\infty \le \max\left\{\|x(0)\|_\infty - \varphi; \frac{H+\epsilon}{2}\right\}$. Since φ is a strictly positive constant, the thesis follows.

The bound on the number of steps necessary to enter $Q_n(H+\epsilon)$ is obtained by looking for the smallest $m \in n\mathbb{N}$ such that $\|x(0)\|_\infty - \frac{m}{n}\varphi \le \frac{H+\epsilon}{2}$: by simple calculations we get $m = -n \cdot \left\lfloor \frac{1}{\varphi}\left(\frac{H+\epsilon}{2} - \|x(0)\|_\infty\right)\right\rfloor \le \mathcal{B}$ because $\|x(0)\|_\infty \le \|q(x(0))\|_\infty + \delta$.

Let us prove the claim: if $x \notin \Xi$ or $q(x) \notin \Xi$ then in the proof of Proposition 2 we have shown that $|x_n^+| \le \frac{H+\epsilon}{2}$. If $x \in \Xi$ and $q(x) \in \Xi$, for $\sum_{i=1}^n \alpha_i x_i > 0$ it holds that $|x_n^+| \le \|x\|_\infty \cdot \sum_{i=1}^n |\alpha_i| - k\epsilon$, as shown in part III of the proof of Proposition 2; by the definition of φ, $\|x\|_\infty \cdot \sum_{i=1}^n |\alpha_i| - k\epsilon = \|x\|_\infty \cdot \sum_{i=1}^n |\alpha_i| - \varphi - \frac{\Delta}{2}\left(\sum_{i=1}^n |\alpha_i| - 1\right) \le \|x\|_\infty - \varphi$.
The case $\sum_{i=1}^n \alpha_i x_i < 0$ is similar. ∎

Note that if $\frac{1}{2}\frac{\Delta}{\epsilon}\left(1 - \sum_{i=1}^n |\alpha_i|\right) \in \mathbb{Z}$ and $\alpha_i \ge 0$ $\forall i = 1,\ldots,n$ (with $\sum_{i=1}^n \alpha_i \ge 1$), then $x = \left(\frac{\Delta}{2},\cdots,\frac{\Delta}{2}\right)$ is such that $\exists! \, u \in \mathcal{U}_k$ ensuring that $x^+ \in Q_n(\Delta)$; in this case $x^+ = x$, therefore x is not attracted by $Q_n(H+\epsilon)$. Anyway, if the condition $\frac{1}{2}\frac{\Delta}{\epsilon}\left(1 - \sum_{i=1}^n |\alpha_i|\right) \notin \mathbb{Z}$ does not hold, then one more level of controls (i.e. $\mathcal{U} = \mathcal{U}_{k+1}$) is sufficient to guarantee the attractivity of $Q_n(H+\epsilon)$.

Remark 4. Exactly as in the case in which only the input are quantized (see [12]), it holds that the minimal diameter of the control set (the saturation level) needed to ensure the invariance of $Q_n(\Delta)$ is also sufficient to guarantee that all the states of $Q_n(\Delta)$ are initial points of trajectories which lie within $Q_n(\Delta)$ and are attracted towards $Q_n(H+\epsilon)$. This property can be profitably exploited to reduce the amount of resources necessary to complete the stabilization task. For instance, when the dead–beat controller is not saturated, the maximal value that it takes within $Q_n(\Delta)$ is approximately $-\left\lfloor \frac{1}{2}\left(1 - \frac{\Delta}{\epsilon}\sum_{i=1}^n |\alpha_i|\right)\right\rfloor$: hence the optimal saturation makes possible to save about $\frac{1}{2}\frac{\Delta}{\epsilon}$ levels.

Remark 5. Even though the bound $\mathcal{B}$ on the number of steps necessary to enter the final set can be updated at each step, it is a very conservative estimate. Basically there are three ways to know that the state has reached the final set:

A- $q(x)$ corresponds to a cell $C_z \subseteq Q_n(H+\epsilon)$;
B- if $q(x) \notin \Xi$ for n consecutive steps then, by the part I of the proof of Proposition 2 and the controller form of A, we deduce that at the successive step $x \in Q_n(H+\epsilon)$;
C- the use of the bound $\mathcal{B}$.

The third case must be considered just as a parachute in case that A and B fail.

Remark 6 (Beyond reticular quantization). The only relevant information about the state–quantizer q_w which have been involved in the foregoing results are the quantities H and δ: this enables us to apply the presented techniques to more general state–quantizers and to get similar results.

5   Example

Consider the system

$$x^+ = \begin{pmatrix} 0 & 1 \\ \frac{5}{4} & \frac{1}{4} \end{pmatrix} x + \begin{pmatrix} 0 \\ 1 \end{pmatrix} u \, ;$$

suppose that $\mathcal{U} \subseteq \frac{1}{4}\mathbb{Z}$, thus $\epsilon = \frac{1}{4}$, and that the reticular state quantization is associated to

$$\mathcal{W} = \left\{ \begin{pmatrix} 2 \\ 0 \end{pmatrix}, \begin{pmatrix} 0 \\ 4 \end{pmatrix} \right\} :$$

in this case $\delta = 2$ and $H = \frac{7}{2}$. It is worth noting that since $H + \epsilon = \frac{15}{4} < 2 \cdot \delta = 4$, the set $Q_2(H + \epsilon)$ does not contain any cell of the state quantization (see the figure), in particular the criterion A of Remark 5 can not be used in this case.

Let us suppose that at time 0 the quantized result of the measurement of the state $x(0)$ is $y(0) = \begin{pmatrix} 8 \\ 12 \end{pmatrix}$: with $\Delta = 28.1$ we ensure that $x(0) \in Q_2(\Delta)$.

According to Proposition 3, it holds that $k = 29$ and $\varphi = \frac{9}{40}$; let $\mathcal{U} = \mathcal{U}_{29} \subset \frac{1}{4}\mathbb{Z}$ and implement the feedback law defined in Equation (3). The observations of the evolution of the system are summarized in the following table:

Step	0	1	2	3	4	5	6	7	8
y	$\begin{pmatrix} 8 \\ 12 \end{pmatrix}$	$\begin{pmatrix} 10 \\ 8 \end{pmatrix}$	$\begin{pmatrix} 6 \\ 8 \end{pmatrix}$	$\begin{pmatrix} 8 \\ 4 \end{pmatrix}$	$\begin{pmatrix} 2 \\ 4 \end{pmatrix}$	$\begin{pmatrix} 2 \\ 0 \end{pmatrix}$	$\begin{pmatrix} 0 \\ 0 \end{pmatrix}$	$\begin{pmatrix} 0 \\ 0 \end{pmatrix}$	$\begin{pmatrix} 0 \\ 0 \end{pmatrix}$
$u(y)$	$-\frac{29}{4}$	$-\frac{29}{4}$	$-\frac{29}{4}$	$-\frac{29}{4}$	$-\frac{14}{4}$	$-\frac{10}{4}$	0	0	0
$\mathcal{B}$	108	90	74	74	38	20			

Step	9	10	11	12	13	14	15	16	17
y	$\begin{pmatrix} 0 \\ 0 \end{pmatrix}$	$\begin{pmatrix} 0 \\ 0 \end{pmatrix}$	$\begin{pmatrix} 0 \\ 0 \end{pmatrix}$	$\begin{pmatrix} 0 \\ 0 \end{pmatrix}$	$\begin{pmatrix} 2 \\ 0 \end{pmatrix}$	$\begin{pmatrix} 0 \\ 0 \end{pmatrix}$	$\begin{pmatrix} -2 \\ 0 \end{pmatrix}$	$\begin{pmatrix} 0 \\ 0 \end{pmatrix}$	
$u(y)$	0	0	0	0	$-\frac{10}{4}$	0	$\frac{10}{4}$	0	
$\mathcal{B}$									

Since at the 4th and 5th step the controller does not saturate then, using the criterion B of Remark 5, we deduce that from the 6th step on the state x is confined within $Q_2(H + \epsilon)$ (hence the computation of $\mathcal{B}$ has been stopped). We also note that, in spite of the state quantization, just three control values are sufficient to make $Q_2(H + \epsilon)$ invariant.

According to Remark 4, the feedback law defined in Equation (3) makes possible to save approximately $\frac{1}{2}\frac{\Delta}{\epsilon} \simeq 56$ levels in the control set.

The observed behavior is generated by $x(0) = \begin{pmatrix} 17/2 \\ 21/2 \end{pmatrix}$: the following figure shows the real evolution of the state (denoted with black circles " $\bullet$ "), the white circles " $\circ$ " are the output $q(x)$'s, that is the central points of the cells visited by the state, the shaded square is $Q_2(H + \epsilon)$.

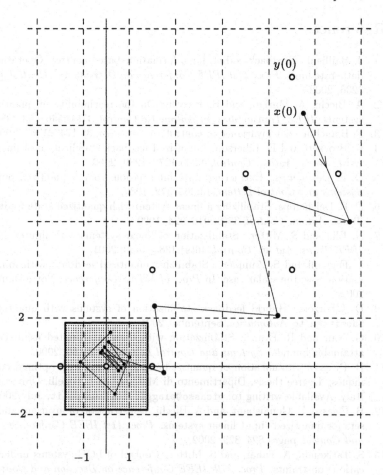

Conclusions

In this paper we have addressed the stabilization analysis for discrete–time linear systems subject to a fixed uniform quantization both in the control and in the state space. We have focused on the study of invariant neighborhoods of the equilibrium and provided quantized controllers steering the system into such sets (i.e. realizing attractivity). Several open problems remain in this field, among which notably is the extension to dynamic feedback of quantized state information, and quantized output feedback. More generally, the combination of quantization with limited communication bandwidths is a most important and challenging area to which further work will be devoted.

References

1. J. Baillieul. Feedback coding for information–based control: Operating near the data–rate limit. *Proc. 41st IEEE Conference on Decision and Control*, pages 3229–3236, 2002.
2. A. Bicchi, A. Marigo, and B. Piccoli. On the reachability of quantized control systems. *IEEE Transactions on Automatic Control*, 47(4):546–563, 2002.
3. F. Blanchini. Set invariance in control. *Automatica*, 35:1747–1767, 1999.
4. R. Brockett and D. Liberzon. Quantized feedback stabilization of linear systems. *IEEE Trans. Autom. Control*, 45(7):1279–1289, 2000.
5. D. F. Delchamps. Extracting state information from a quantized ouput record. *Systems and Control Letters*, 13:365–372, 1989.
6. D. F. Delchamps. Stabilizing a linear system with quantized state feedback. *IEEE Trans. Autom. Control*, 35(8):916–924, 1990.
7. N. Elia and S. Mitter. Stabilization of linear systems with limited information. *IEEE Trans. Autom. Control*, 46(9):1384–1400, 2001.
8. F. Fagnani and S. Zampieri. Stabilizing quantized feedback with minimal information flow: the scalar case. In *Proc. of MTNS Conference*, Notre Dame, Indiana, 2002.
9. D. Liberzon. Hybrid feedback stabilization of systems with quantized signals. Submitted to *Automatica*, September 2001.
10. G. Nair and R. Evans. Stabilization with data rate limited feedback : tightest attainable bounds. *Systems and Control Letters*, 41:49–56, 2000.
11. B. Picasso. Stabilization of quantized–input systems with optimal control techniques. Degree thesis, Dipartimento di Matematica L.Tonelli, University of Pisa, Italy, Available writing to: picasso@piaggio.ccii.unipi.it, July 2002.
12. B. Picasso, F. Gouaisbaut, and A. Bicchi. Construction of invariant and attractive sets for quantized–input linear systems. *Proc. 41st IEEE Conference on Decision and Control*, pages 824–829, 2002.
13. S. Tatikonda, A. Sahai, and S. Mitter. Control of LQG systems under communication constraints. *Proc. 37th IEEE Conference on Decision and Control*, 1998.
14. W. Wong and R. Brockett. Systems with finite communication bandwidth constraints - part I: State estimation problems. *IEEE Transactions on Automatic Control*, 42:1294–1299, 1997.
15. W. Wong and R. Brockett. Systems with finite communication bandwidth constraints - part II: Stabilization with limited information feedback. *IEEE Transactions on Automatic Control*, 44(5):1049–1053, May 1999.

Qualitative Heterogeneous Control of Higher Order Systems[*]

Subramanian Ramamoorthy[1] and Benjamin Kuipers[2]

[1] Electrical and Computer Engineering Department, University of Texas at Austin, Austin, Texas 78712, and National Instruments Corp., Truchard Design Center, 11500 N. Mopac Expwy, Austin, Texas 78759 USA. s.ramamoorthy@ni.com
[2] Computer Science Department, University of Texas at Austin, Austin, Texas 78712 USA. kuipers@cs.utexas.edu

Abstract. This paper presents the qualitative heterogeneous control framework, a methodology for the design of a controlled hybrid system based on attractors and transitions between them. This framework designs a robust controller that can accommodate bounded amounts of parametric and structural uncertainty. This framework provides a number of advantages over other similar techniques. The local models used in the design process are qualitative, allowing the use of partial knowledge about system structure, and nonlinear, allowing regions and transitions to be defined in terms of dynamical attractors. In addition, we define boundaries between local models in a natural manner, appealing to intrinsic properties of the system. We demonstrate the use of this framework by designing a novel control algorithm for the cart-pole system. In addition, we illustrate how traditional algorithms, such as linear quadratic regulators, can be incorporated within this framework. The design is validated by experiments with a physical system.

1 Introduction

Multiple model approaches to control are useful for complex dynamical systems because the local models can be simple and intuitive, and because global behavior can be concisely described as a finite graph of transitions among models. Hybrid systems are often constructed with the local models being linear and their operating regions being polygonal. Qualitative models add the ability to express incomplete knowledge of the dynamical system and of the controller, describing a family of controllers and systems and predicting the behaviors. A qualitative model can often give a completely accurate (though imprecise) description of a nonlinear system over a larger and more naturally defined local region than can be usefully approximated by a local linear model.

---

[*] This work has taken place in the Intelligent Robotics Lab at the Artificial Intelligence Laboratory, The University of Texas at Austin. Research of the Intelligent Robotics lab is supported in part by NSF grants IRI-9504138 and CDA 9617327, and by funding from Tivoli Corporation.

O. Maler and A. Pnueli (Eds.): HSCC 2003, LNCS 2623, pp. 417–434, 2003.
© Springer-Verlag Berlin Heidelberg 2003

Qualitative heterogeneous control (QHC) is an approach to designing controllers for complex nonlinear systems [1,2]. It works by defining a hybrid system consisting of a set of qualitatively described control laws, each with its own operating region. The local controllers and their operating regions are designed so that any fully specified system and controller satisfying the given set of qualitative constraints is guaranteed to exhibit the desired qualitative behavior within each local region and at its boundaries. The local behaviors are designed to abstract to a global transition graph with the desired global behavior. The qualitative constraints are a set of weak sufficient conditions that guarantee the desired global behavior. The remaining degrees of freedom on the way to a concrete design are available to the designer for optimization according to any desired criterion, since the global qualitative behavior is already guaranteed. QHC therefore provides a separation of concerns between qualitative correctness and quantitative optimization.

In recent work [2], we demonstrated the design of a controller for pumping up and balancing a free pendulum, controlling the torque applied at the pivot. The control laws transform the natural dynamics of the pendulum to match different instances of the same generic behavior model: the qualitative damped oscillator, $\ddot{x} + f(\dot{x}) + g(x) = 0$, with positive or negative damping. In the current paper, we extend QHC to a more complex, but still very familiar system. The cart-pole version of the pendulum (Figure 2) has the same goal of pumping the pendulum up and keeping it balanced, but now we must bring the cart to the center of its track and keep it away from the endpoints, and we want it to recover gracefully from large disturbances. We demonstrate a method using time-scale abstraction to decompose the fourth-order cart-pole system into two weakly interacting second-order systems: the pole system that can be controlled by a modified version of the pivot-torque controller, and the cart system that can be controlled in a similar way. The multiple-model structure allows us to handle the interactions between systems effectively at the different model boundaries. We also demonstrate the use of traditional linear controller design methods such as LQR for a local controller for the *Balance* region.

Furthermore, we implement our QHC control law on a physical implementation of the cart-pole system and show that our framework accommodates simple solutions to aspects of the physical dynamics such as static friction that are often omitted or handled in ad hoc ways. The solution to this problem demonstrates the use of a behavior model other than the damped oscillator, the Lienard equation, in order to produce a limit cycle with desired properties.

More generally, QHC exploits the robustness of structurally stable orbits in dynamical systems. From dynamical systems theory, we know that if there exists a connected phase space volume that maps into itself under the forward evolution then the flow is globally contracting onto an attractor [3,4]. In the simplest cases, these attractors will be fixed points. For our purposes, we are interested in implementing controllers that enforce residence of the flow within a finite subset of phase space. In simple systems, fixed points and limit cycles possess this property. Complex systems that exhibit chaotic behavior possess strange attractors that satisfy the same property of residence of the flow in a finite volume in phase space. So we consider stable fixed-points, limit cycles, and chaotic attractors all to be examples of controlled flows. This general notion of viewing the stability question in control design as one of defining an appropriate contraction property or residence of flows in a finite volume has been explored in recent literature, e.g., [4]. The QHC framework makes it possible to utilize stable attractors, periodic orbits, strange attractors and even divergent flows to synthesize global trajectories from appropriately defined local regions and transitions between them. An approach to the composition of global behaviors from such local dynamical models and orbits is seen in [5,6]. The advantage that QHC brings over this existing work is derived from the fact that local models defined in terms of QDEs enable the design of controllers for a *class* of systems, with the guarantee that any numerical instance of the specified QDEs will possess the specified dynamical property.

Similar approaches have been explored in the context of controlling chaotic systems. The idea of chaos control originated with [7], popularly referred to as the OGY technique. The technique consists of waiting for a natural passage of the chaotic orbit close to a desired periodic orbit, and then applying a small perturbation designed to stabilize the periodic dynamics, with flexibility in switching from one behavior to another. [8] contains an extensive review of recent work in this area. These methods have largely focused on algorithms that allow a particular orbit or dynamical state to be achieved due to small control actions. [9] describes the Perfect Moment algorithm that is similar in spirit to the QHC framework. This algorithm autonomously explores and maps the phase space of a chaotic system to identify useful dynamical orbits. Then, utilizing the property of sensitive dependence on initial conditions, it synthesizes a trajectory based on these identified dynamical orbits to achieve a desired dynamical state starting from a specified initial condition. The advantage provided by QHC over these approaches is derived from the use of a variety of *qualitatively* defined dynamical orbits, and a structured synthesis technique with guarantees on behaviors and transitions that apply to classes of systems sharing the specified property.

2   A Qualitative Behavior Model: The Damped Oscillator

To design a local control law, we select a well-understood qualitative behavior model, and define the control law u so that the natural behavior of the system is transformed into that of the model. A model with attractive properties is the linear damped oscillator, $\ddot{x} + a\dot{x} + bx = 0$. It is straight-forward to generalize this to a nonlinear model $\ddot{x} + f(\dot{x}) + g(x) = 0$ where f and g are monotonic functions. As it happens, we can generalize f and g even further to the sign-equality constraints that appear in Lemmas 1 and 2. Lemma 1 tells us that any damped oscillator matching these requirements converges to a stable fixed-point. Lemma 2 tells us that the same oscillator, but with negative damping, necessarily diverges. We will use these models in several different ways.

Definition 1. *Where $[a, b] \subseteq \Re^*$, the function $f : [a, b] \to \Re^*$ is a reasonable function over $[a, b]$ if f is continuous on $[a, b]$, continuously differentiable on (a, b), has only finitely many critical points in any bounded interval, and the one-sided limits $\lim_{t \to a^+} f'(t)$ and $\lim_{t \to b^-} f'(t)$ exist in $\Re^*$. $f'(a)$ and $f'(b)$ are defined to be equal to these limits.*

Notation. M^+ is the set of reasonable functions $f : [a, b] \to \Re^*$ such that $f' > 0$ over (a, b). M_0^+ is the set of $f \in M^+$ such that $f(0) = 0$. $[x]_0 = sign(x) \in \{+, 0, -\}$.

Lemma 1. *Let $A \subseteq \Re^2$ include (0,0) in its interior, and let S be a system governed by the QDE $\ddot{x} + f(\dot{x}) + g(x) = 0$ for every $(x, \dot{x}) \in A$, where f and g are reasonable functions such that $[f(\dot{x})]_0 = [\dot{x}]_0$ and $[g(x)]_0 = [x]_0$. Then for any trajectory $(x(t), \dot{x}(t))$ of S that lies entirely within A, $\lim_{t \to \infty} (x(t), \dot{x}(t)) = (0, 0)$*

Lemma 2. *Let $A \subseteq \Re^2$ include (0,0) in its interior, and let S be a system governed by the QDE $\ddot{x} - f(\dot{x}) + g(x) = 0$ for every $(x, \dot{x}) \in A$, where f and g are reasonable functions such that $[f(\dot{x})]_0 = [\dot{x}]_0$ and $[g(x)]_0 = [x]_0$. Then (0,0) is the only fixed point of S in A, and it is unstable. Furthermore, A cannot contain a limit cycle.*

3   The Pivot-Torque Pendulum Controller

In recent work [2], we demonstrated the design of a controller for pumping up and balancing a free pendulum, controlling the torque applied at the pivot: $\ddot{\theta} + f(\dot{\theta}) + k \cos \theta - u(\theta, \dot{\theta}) = 0$. The resulting QHC controller has three regions: *Pump* (to raise the pendulum upward from its downward position), *Spin* (to slow down a rapidly-spinning pendulum), and *Balance* (to maintain the pendulum in its upward position). All three local controllers were designed by specifying control laws u that would transform the natural dynamics of the pendulum to match different instances of the same generic behavior model: the qualitative damped oscillator, $\ddot{x} + f(\dot{x}) + g(x) = 0$. (In the case of *Pump*, the damping is negative.) The boundary of the *Balance* region is determined by the maximum torque that can be applied, and the boundary separating the *Pump* and *Spin* regions is defined to be a sliding mode controller leading directly into the *Balance* region.

The pivot-torque pendulum controller can be summarized by the following equations. To be able to write each local control law with its fixed point at (0,0), we use $\theta = 0$ to refer to the fixed-point with the pendulum pointing downward, and $\phi = 0 = \theta + \pi$ to refer to the fixed-point with the pendulum pointing upward.

Given a model,

$$\ddot{\phi} + f(\dot{\phi}) - k \sin \phi + u(\phi, \dot{\phi}) = 0 \tag{1}$$

or equivalently, $\ddot{\theta} + f(\dot{\theta}) + k\sin\theta - u(\theta,\dot{\theta}) = 0$, we apply one of the following control laws,

$$Balance: u(\phi,\dot{\phi}) = g(\phi) + h(\dot{\phi}), \text{ such that } [g(\phi) - k\sin\phi]_0 = [\phi]_0, \ [h(\dot{\phi})]_0 = [\dot{\phi}]_0$$
$$Pump: u(\phi,\dot{\phi}) = -h(\dot{\phi}), \text{ such that } [(h-f)(\dot{\phi})]_0 = [\dot{\phi}]_0$$
$$Spin: u(\phi,\dot{\phi}) = f_d(\dot{\phi}), \text{ such that } [f_d(\dot{\phi})]_0 = [\dot{\phi}]_0$$

$$(2)$$

The selection of the control region depends on the values of two parameters:

$$\alpha = \frac{\dot{\phi}^2}{\dot{\phi}_{max}^2} + \frac{\int_0^\phi g(\phi) - k\sin\phi \, d\phi}{\int_0^{\phi_{max}} g(\phi) - k\sin\phi \, d\phi} \text{ and } s(\phi,\dot{\phi}) = \tfrac{1}{2}\dot{\phi}^2 - k(1 - \cos\phi). \quad (3)$$

$\alpha \leq 1$ describes the region of applicability of the *Balance* controller based on physical limitations (ϕ_{max} and $\dot{\phi}_{max}$) and the requirement that the system should not exit the *Balance* region due to control actions, once it has entered it. $s(\phi,\dot{\phi})$ represents the energy of the system, with the *separatrix* of the pendulum (the locus of points where $s(\phi,\dot{\phi}) = 0$) serving as the boundary between the *Pump* and *Spin* regions. The rule for selecting control mode is thus:

$$
\begin{aligned}
&\text{if } \alpha \leq 1 \text{ then } Balance \\
&\text{else if } s < 0 \text{ then } Pump \\
&\text{else } Spin
\end{aligned}
\quad (4)
$$

The operation of the heterogeneous pendulum controller can be summarized in a discrete transition graph, as shown in Figure 1.

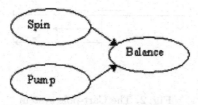

Fig. 1. Transition graph structure of the heterogeneous controller for the pivot-torque pendulum

4   The Cart-Pole System

The cart-pole system is a common benchmark problem in the control systems literature. Early work in linear control and stabilization of unstable systems focused on the basic stabilization problem for this system. The system is still being used in the current literature, e.g., [10] illustrates the idea of energy based control of pendulum swing-up, [11] presents a hybrid control algorithm that globally stabilizes a cart-pole system and [12] presents an approach to the control of a periodic orbit in a nonlinear system using the cart-pole as an example. In a different context, the inverted pendulum model has been used as an abstraction for many physically meaningful phenomena. A hypothesis in the biomechanics community is that a model known as the Spring Loaded Inverted Pendulum is the control target for the musculoskeletal system. This hypothesis has been explored and experimentally supported in [13,14]. Pratt et. al. [15] have implemented successful walking robots based on this principle and suggest that an intuitive control algorithm designed from task specifications would be of value to many communities, such as robotics and biomechanics.

The cart-pole system considered in this paper is seen in Figure 2. It consists of a cart that moves on a horizontal track of finite length. The pole is represented by a point mass attached to the end of a massless thin rod of length l that is attached to the cart at a pivot capable of unconstrained (360°) rotation. The primary control objective is to stabilize the system at $[x, \dot{x}, \phi, \dot{\phi}] = [0, 0, 0, 0]$, starting from $[0, 0, \pi, 0]$.

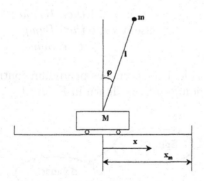

Fig. 2. The Cart-pole system

The cart-pole system is a commonly seen demonstration in many control laboratories. While this system has been stabilized by a wide variety of control algorithms, most of them suffer from a number of failure modes when people interact with these systems. For instance, by hitting the pole with a large velocity, one may cause the control action to become large and the cart may hit the end of the track in an attempt to regain control. We recognize that these sudden disturbances take the form of instantaneous, non-smooth displacement of the system in phase space. Our intent is to map a suitable control action to all regions in the phase space of the physical system in order to improve the robustness of the system.

The dynamic model for the cart-pole system is given by,

$$(M + m)\ddot{x} + ml \cos \phi \ddot{\phi} - ml \sin \phi \dot{\phi}^2 = F - f_c(\dot{x}) \tag{5}$$

$$ml \cos \phi \ddot{x} + ml^2 \ddot{\phi} - mgl \sin \phi = -f_p(\dot{\phi}) \tag{6}$$

where x, ϕ represent the cart position and pole angle respectively. The following simplified equations represent the dynamics of the pole, where we control the state of the system by applying $\ddot{x}$. The dynamics of the cart are defined by the time evolution of $\ddot{x}$. Equation (7) describes the system around the upper fixed-point $\phi = 0$, while equation (8) describes it around the lower fixed-point $\theta = 0$.

$$\ddot{\phi} + f(\dot{\phi}) - k \sin \phi + \ddot{x} \cos \phi = 0 \tag{7}$$

$$\ddot{\theta} + f(\dot{\theta}) + k \sin \theta - \ddot{x} \cos \theta = 0 \tag{8}$$

5   A Qualitative Heterogeneous Controller Based on Time Scale Separation

The cart-pole system as described above includes a pendulum as a sub-system. However, the pivot-torque pendulum is controlled directly by u, while in the cart-actuated version, the effect of the applied acceleration $u = \ddot{x}$ on angular acceleration $\ddot{\phi}$ is scaled by $\cos \phi$. Furthermore, in the cart-pole system, we also have the control objective to stabilize the cart at $x = 0, \dot{x} = 0$ while the pole is stabilized vertically by the pendulum controller.

It is possible to control the position of the cart by a damped spring, similar to the *Balance* control action for the pole (2). The combined control action can be described as,

$$\ddot{x} = varsat \left\{ -\frac{f_1(\dot{x})}{\cos \phi} - \frac{g_1(x)}{\cos \phi} + \frac{u(\phi, \dot{\phi})}{\cos \phi} \right\} \tag{9}$$

where $f_1(\dot{x}), g_1(x)$ represent any reasonable functions satisfying Lemma 1, used to regulate the position and velocity of the cart. The term $u(\phi, \dot{\phi})$ represents the control law (2) for the three control modes of the pole. *varsat* refers to a saturation action whose magnitude depends on the controller mode. This allows the designer to set local control law parameters in such a way that the system never saturates in *Balance* while the *Pump* and *Spin* control actions can be restricted in strength.

$$varsat(x) = \begin{cases} sat(x, x_{\max bal}), controller = Balance \\ sat(x, x_{\max pump}), controller = Pump \\ sat(x, x_{\max spin}), controller = Spin \end{cases}$$

$$sat(x, x_{\max i}) = \begin{cases} -x_{\max i}, x < -x_{\max i} \\ x, -x_{\max i} \leq x \leq x_{\max i} \\ x_{\max i}, x > x_{\max i} \end{cases}$$

There are two independent requirements on the cart controller. When the pole controller is in the *Pump* and *Spin* modes, the addition of the cart stabilizing term to the pole control action should not affect the existence of the sliding mode between the *Pump* and *Spin* regions. On the other hand, when the pole controller is in the *Balance* mode, the sliding mode is not a concern and the primary requirement is that the composite system defined in terms of $[x, \dot{x}, \phi, \dot{\phi}]$ should be stable.

We now derive the constraints on cart control, corresponding to *Pump* and *Spin* modes of the pole controller. Taking the derivative of the expression for s, expressed in terms of variables ϕ and $\dot{\phi}$,

$$\dot{s}(\phi, \dot{\phi}) = -\dot{\phi}f(\dot{\phi}) + \dot{\phi}f_1(\dot{x}) + \dot{\phi}g_1(x) - \dot{\phi}u(\phi, \dot{\phi}) \tag{10}$$

Substitute the *Pump* control law,

$$\dot{s} = \dot{\phi}(h - f)(\dot{\phi}) + \dot{\phi}f_1(\dot{x}) + \dot{\phi}g_1(x) \tag{11}$$

In order to have $\dot{s} \geq 0$,

$$[(h - f)(\dot{\phi}) + f_1(\dot{x}) + g_1(x)]_0 = [\dot{\phi}]_0 \tag{12}$$

If we substitute the *Spin* control law,

$$\dot{s} = -\dot{\phi}(f + f_d)(\dot{\phi}) + \dot{\phi}f_1(\dot{x}) + \dot{\phi}g_1(x) \tag{13}$$

In order to have $\dot{s} \leq 0$

$$[(f + f_d)(\dot{\phi}) - f_1(\dot{x}) - g_1(x)]_0 = [\dot{\phi}]_0 \tag{14}$$

We know that $[(h - f)(\dot{\phi})]_0 = [\dot{\phi}]_0$ and $[(f + f_d)(\dot{\phi})]_0 = [\dot{\phi}]_0$. From equations (12) and (14), we see that $f_1(\dot{x}) + g_1(x)$ need to be sufficiently small with respect to $(h - f)(\dot{\phi}), (f + f_d)(\dot{\phi})$ for the sign equality to be preserved (even if these terms are opposed to each other). It is conceivable that for small values $\dot{\phi} \to 0$, these constraints may be violated for $f_1(\dot{x}) + g_1(x) \neq 0$. Fortunately, the sliding mode constrains the trajectory to be on the separatrix where it is bounded away from $\dot{\phi} = 0$ by the width of the *Balance* region (equation 3). Therefore, it is possible to select f_1 and g_1 to be sufficiently small to satisfy equations (12) and (14). This amounts to requiring a sufficient separation between the time-scales of the pole and the cart controllers.

We then need constraints on cart control, corresponding to the *Balance* mode of the pole controller. The general principle behind this analysis is summarized below.

The uncontrolled cart pole system can be linearized and written as,

$$\dot{\mathbf{x}} = \mathbf{A}\mathbf{x} + \mathbf{B}u = \begin{bmatrix} 0 & 1 & 0 & 0 \\ 0 & 0 & 0 & 0 \\ 0 & 0 & 0 & 1 \\ 0 & 0 & k & -c \end{bmatrix} \begin{bmatrix} x \\ \dot{x} \\ \phi \\ \dot{\phi} \end{bmatrix} + \begin{bmatrix} 0 \\ 1 \\ 0 \\ -1 \end{bmatrix} \ddot{x}, \tag{15}$$

where $\mathbf{x} = \begin{bmatrix} x & \dot{x} & \phi & \dot{\phi} \end{bmatrix}^T$, $\mathbf{u} = [\ddot{x}]$, and $f(\dot{\phi}) = c\dot{\phi}$. It is easy to verify that $(\mathbf{A}, \mathbf{B})$ is controllable (i.e., the controllability matrix has full rank). This implies that there exists some feedback control action that can place the closed loop eigenvalues of the controlled system at any point in the left half of the complex plane.

Now, the controlled, nonlinear equation of the higher order system, $\dot{\mathbf{x}} = \mathbf{f}(\mathbf{x})$, can be similarly linearized to yield the model, $\dot{\mathbf{x}} = \tilde{\mathbf{A}}\mathbf{x}$ where $\tilde{\mathbf{A}}$ refers to the Jacobian linearization of the controlled system, $\tilde{\mathbf{A}} = \partial \mathbf{f} / \partial \mathbf{x}|_{\mathbf{x}=0}$. Applying Lyapunov's Linearization method [16,3], we know that if the linearized system has $\tilde{\mathbf{A}}$ Hurwitz (i.e., if all eigenvalues of $\tilde{\mathbf{A}}$ are strictly in the left-half complex plane), then the equilibrium point of the nonlinear system, $\dot{\mathbf{x}} = \mathbf{f}(\mathbf{x})$, is asymptotically stable. We place the closed loop eigenvalues by appropriate selection of controller parameters to make $\tilde{\mathbf{A}}$ Hurwitz.

Consider an instance of the controller defined by the QDE in equation (9), with a linear pole *Balance* controller,

$$\ddot{x} = -\frac{d_1}{\cos\phi}x - \frac{d_2}{\cos\phi}\dot{x} + \frac{(c_{11}+k)\phi + c_{12}\dot{\phi}}{\cos\phi} \tag{16}$$

The controlled pole equation can be written as,

$$\ddot{\phi} = -c\dot{\phi} + k\sin\phi + d_1 x + d_2\dot{x} - (c_{11}+k)\phi - c_{12}\dot{\phi} \tag{17}$$

From this, the Jacobian linearization $\dot{\mathbf{x}} = \tilde{\mathbf{A}}\mathbf{x}$ becomes,

$$\dot{\mathbf{x}} = \begin{vmatrix} 0 & 1 & 0 & 0 \\ -d_1 & -d_2 & c_{11}+k & c_{12} \\ 0 & 0 & 0 & 1 \\ d_1 & d_2 & -c_{11} & -c-c_{12} \end{vmatrix} \mathbf{x} = \tilde{\mathbf{A}}\mathbf{x} \tag{18}$$

We select parameters that make $\tilde{\mathbf{A}}$ Hurwitz. In many physical systems, the magnitudes and/or direction of x and ϕ may be mismatched. In that case, the appropriate signs and scaling factors would need to be incorporated into the above analysis. The last remaining issue is that of determining the region of attraction for this stable equilibrium. Here one would use a converse Lyapunov argument based on the fact that $\tilde{\mathbf{A}}$ is Hurwitz if and only if, for any given symmetric positive definite $\mathbf{Q}$, there exists a unique symmetric, positive definite $\mathbf{P}$ which is a solution to the Lyapunov equation:

$$\mathbf{PA} + \mathbf{A}^T\mathbf{P} + \mathbf{Q} = 0$$

This matrix $\mathbf{P}$ is the basis for the definition of a Lyapunov function, $\mathbf{V}(\mathbf{x}) = \mathbf{x}^T\mathbf{P}\mathbf{x}$. The boundary of the *Balance* region is defined by a level curve of $\mathbf{V}(\mathbf{x})$. In practice, the Lyapunov equation may be difficult to solve for $\mathbf{P}$, in which case it may be possible to determine the domain of attraction experimentally or by numerical simulations (see [5]).

The above analysis assumed a linear spring model for cart control. One may also use a nonlinear spring controller. The nonlinear spring controller provides the advantage that the cart position can be kept away from the ends of the track, i.e., $|x| < x_m$, by the potential barrier of the spring action. Consider an instance of a nonlinear spring defined by,

$$\ddot{x} = sat \left\{ -\frac{d_1}{\cos\phi} \tanh^{-1} \left(\frac{x}{x_m} \right) - \frac{d_2}{\cos\phi} \dot{x} + \frac{u(\phi, \dot{\phi})}{\cos\phi} \right\} \qquad (19)$$

The first term provides the potential barrier necessary to prevent the cart from hitting the ends of the track. Note that $\tanh^{-1}$ (which is in M_0^+) is very near linear over $[-0.5, +0.5]$ and diverges to $\pm\infty$ at ±1, respectively. As $|x| \to x_m$, the nonlinear cart control action (equation 19) asymptotically approaches infinity and theoretically prevents the cart from reaching the end of the track. In practice, if $\ddot{x}$ saturates, then this potential barrier cannot always prevent the cart from hitting the end of the track. However, by reducing the size of the *Balance* region by reducing ϕ_{max} and hence $\dot{\phi}_{max}$, and by bounding the value of $f_d(\dot{\phi})$ in the *Spin* region, it is possible to constrain the system so that the saturated $\ddot{x}$ is sufficient to keep the cart from hitting the ends of the track.

The controller designed thus far was implemented on a physical system. Figure 3 shows the phase plots of the controlled cart and pole systems. It is seen that the system stabilizes within a very small neighborhood of the point $\phi = 0, \dot{\phi} = 0, x = 0, \dot{x} = 0$. The physical system exhibits a limit cycle about the equilibrium point, due to effects such as static friction that are often omitted from simulations. We address these next.

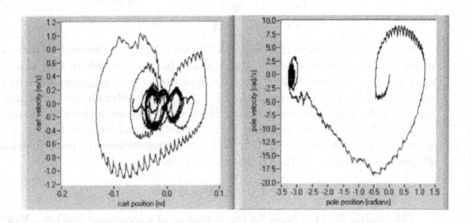

Fig. 3. Phase plots for the cart and pole subsystems. This implementation utilized a qualitative cart-pole controller based on time scale separation.

6   Accommodating Real-World Effects, the Case of Static Friction

Consider the damped oscillator with static, or Coulomb, friction F_c as well as damping friction $f(\dot{x})$. The resistance of static friction is a constant force $F_c = \eta$ opposing the direction of motion, as long as motion is taking place. Once motion stops, a larger frictional resistance $F_c = \eta + \varepsilon$ must be overcome to get it started again. This transforms the damped oscillator model from $\ddot{x} = -g(x) - f(\dot{x}) - F_c$ to

$$
\ddot{x} = \begin{cases} \dot{x} \neq 0 \rightarrow & -g(x) - f(\dot{x}) - [\dot{x}]_0 \eta \\ \dot{x} = 0 \rightarrow -[x]_0 \max(|g(x)| - \eta - \varepsilon, 0) \end{cases} \tag{20}
$$

To avoid being captured by static friction, we require that the system obey the constraint

$$
\dot{x} = 0 \quad \Rightarrow \quad |g(x)| > \eta + \varepsilon \tag{21}
$$

This constraint excludes the stable fixed-point, where $x = \dot{x} = \ddot{x} = 0$. Therefore, we will be required to approach a more complex orbit, such as a limit cycle. This arises under two circumstances.

First, in the *Pump* region, the oscillator with negative damping should diverge from its unstable fixed-point at $(\theta, \dot{\theta}) = (0,0)$, but the initial oscillations in its trajectory are so small as to be absorbed by static friction, so the pendulum never starts pumping. We handle this problem by defining a *Startup* control law, which is only applied when the system state is $[x, \dot{x}, \theta, \dot{\theta}] = [0,0,0,0]$, and which specifies that $\ddot{x}(t) = u_0$ for $t \in [0, \tau]$. The constant cart acceleration $u_0 > \eta + \varepsilon$ and the time interval τ are selected so that the final state $t = \tau$ is contained within the *Pump* region, and is far enough from the origin that an energy argument guarantees that constraint (21) will continue to be satisfied.

Second, in the *Balance* region, as the pendulum approaches the fixed-point at $(\phi, \dot{\phi}) = (0,0)$, static friction can capture it at a small but perceptibly nonzero value of ϕ, leading to a constant non-zero value of $\ddot{x}$, and hence a runaway cart. We handle this problem by modifying the *Balance* controller to approach a limit cycle rather than a fixed-point, and designing the limit cycle to satisfy constraint (21). In order to create a limit cycle, we require a new qualitative behavior model, since the damped oscillator does not include limit cycles in its behavioral repertoire. However, the Lienard equation describes a set of familiar systems that do exhibit limit cycles, and it makes an excellent target for the QHC methodology [16,17].

A Lienard system (e.g., the van der Pol oscillator) is defined in terms of the model $\ddot{x} + f(x)\dot{x} + g(x) = 0$ where, broadly speaking, $f(x)$ is positive when $|x|$ is large and negative when $|x|$ is small, and g is such that, in the absence of the damping term $f(x)\dot{x}$ we expect periodic solutions for small x. The property can be summarized by the following lemma. This lemma is taken from the standard literature, see [16] for the proof.

Lemma 3. *Let $A \subseteq \Re^2$ include (0,0) in its interior, and let S be a system governed by the QDE $\ddot{x} + f(x)\dot{x} + g(x) = 0$ for every $(x, \dot{x}) \in A$, where f and g are reasonable functions. Define the function,*

$$F(x) = \int_0^x f(u)du$$

S has a unique, stable limit cycle surrounding the origin if
$g(x)$ is an odd function and $g(x) > 0$ for $x > 0$ (i.e., $[g(x)]_0 = [x]_0$),
$f(x)$ is an even function,
$F(x)$ is an odd function, which has exactly one positive zero at $x = a$,
$F(x)$ is negative in $0 < x < a$, is positive and nondecreasing in $x > a$, and $F(x) \to \infty$ as $x \to \infty$.

We utilize this lemma and define a switched system inside *Balance*. Starting with the system

$$\ddot{\phi} + c\dot{\phi} - k\sin\phi + \ddot{x}\cos\phi = 0 \qquad (22)$$

In the region, $-a/2 < \phi < a/2$, we define the controller,

$$\ddot{x} = \frac{-(c + p_1)\dot{\phi}}{\cos\phi} + \frac{(k + p_2)\phi}{\cos\phi} \qquad (23)$$

so that the closed loop system takes the form (assume $\cos\phi \approx 1, \sin\phi \approx \phi$),

$$\ddot{\phi} - p_1\dot{\phi} + p_2\phi = 0 \qquad (24)$$

In the region $(-\phi_{\max} < \phi < -a/2) \cup (a/2 < \phi < \phi_{\max})$, the controlled system is,

$$\ddot{\phi} + (c + c_{12})\dot{\phi} + c_{11}\phi = 0 \qquad (25)$$

Setting $(c + c_{12}) = p_1; c_{11} = p_2$ satisfies the conditions in Lemma 3.

Now, Balance was defined such that any trajectory that enters the region will remain inside indefinitely. In order to ensure that the addition of the above controller does not violate this property, the value of a should be chosen such that the energy added in the region $-a/2 < \phi < a/2$ is not greater than what can be dissipated in the region $(-\phi_{\max} < \phi < -a/2) \cup (a/2 < \phi < \phi_{\max})$. This analysis would be identical to that in [2], where energy changes in *Pump* and *Balance* were derived.

The effect of including this region is that the cart-pole system executes a limit cycle as seen in Figure 4. The advantage of this approach lies in the fact that relaxation oscillators retain their structure through a very wide range of parameters p_1, p_2, and overcome practical problems such as static friction [16, 17].

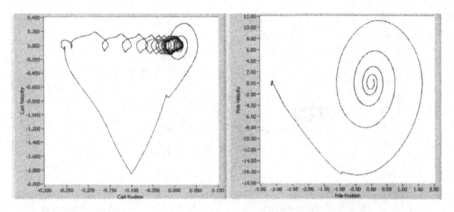

Fig. 4. Phase plots for the cart and pole subsystems, simulation results. These plots illustrate the system executing a limit cycle in both the cart and pole subsystems.

7   A Linear Quadratic Regulator for Balance

A controller is defined by the qualitative constraints it satisfies and its region of applicability. In QHC, it is possible to include local controllers designed by different methodologies, as long as they satisfy the desired qualitative constraints inside the region of applicability. To illustrate this, we designed a linear quadratic regulator (LQR) as the *Balance* controller. The primary requirement on the *Balance* controller is that any trajectory that has entered *Balance* should remain inside until perturbed by an external process. LQR possesses this property, as described in [18]. In addition, ϕ_{max} and $\dot{\phi}_{max}$ can be selected in such a way that the closed loop response of the cart satisfies $-x_m < x < x_m$.

Linear Quadratic Regulators stabilize the plant $\dot{\mathbf{x}} = \mathbf{A}\mathbf{x} + \mathbf{B}\mathbf{u}$, $\mathbf{x} = [x\ \dot{x}\ \phi\ \dot{\phi}]^T$ by applying a control, $\mathbf{u} = -\mathbf{G}\mathbf{x}$ where $\mathbf{G}$ is selected so as to minimize a cost function, $J = \int_0^\infty \mathbf{x}^T\mathbf{Q}\mathbf{x} + \mathbf{u}^T\mathbf{R}\mathbf{u}\,dt$. For our example, we select $\mathbf{Q} = diag(4, 0, 4, 0)$ and $\mathbf{R} = [0.5]$ to penalize cart and pole positions equally, control action to a lesser extent, and cart and pole velocities not at all. Other parameter choices do not affect the substance of our argument.

The operation of this controller is explained by the fact that the controller iteratively minimizes the cost function J which is an 'energy-like' quadratic function. Further, an analysis of the eigenvalues of the closed loop system indicates that all eigenvalues are negative and the system is stable as required.

Figure 5 shows the experimental results of a heterogeneous controller that utilized an LQR *Balance* controller. As expected, a large part of the heterogeneous behavior is identical to the experimental result in Figure 3. The primary observable difference is in the size of the limit cycle in the cart phase portrait, in the *Balance* mode of pole control.

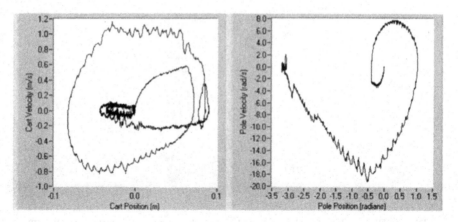

Fig. 5. Phase plots for the cart and pole subsystems. This implementation utilized a qualitative cart-pole controller with LQR in the Balance region.

8   Discussion

8.1   Robustness in Global Behaviors

One of the goals motivating this investigation has been the search for control strategies that are visibly robust in the face of environmental disturbances and user interaction. It is well known that algorithms such as linear quadratic regulators can guarantee asymptotic stability only for initial states that are within a finite region of the origin. Nonlinear control design techniques such as feedback linearization may also suffer from lack of robustness [3,19]. In the QHC methodology, we define local models based on qualitative behavior models. These qualitative behavior models are selected as dynamical systems with stable orbits, such as fixed points and limit cycles that are robust in the face of parametric and structural uncertainties. This makes the global behavior, defined as a composition of these local models, correspondingly robust.

We now present some experimental results to illustrate the results we are able to obtain from the controlled hybrid system. One of our practical goals has been to design a cart-pole controller that can accommodate a large amount of abuse from the user – in terms of state perturbations. The effect of such a perturbation on a traditional control algorithm such as LQR is that the system is pushed outside the region of applicability that results in loss of control or the cart hits the ends of the track, in response to a large control action.

In our design, a large perturbation causes the controller to switch to the *Spin* mode that provides augmented damping until the state variables are within the region of applicability of *Balance*. This behavior is illustrated in Figure 6. It is seen that the system has initially stabilized and then the user imparts a perturbation to the pole velocity, corresponding to an instantaneous change of 30 rads/s. This causes the system to leave *Balance*, to execute *Spin, Spin-Pump Sliding Mode* and eventually to return to *Balance*. In this way, the heterogeneous con-

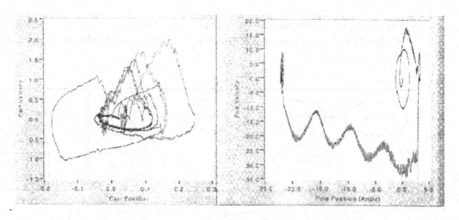

Fig. 6. Phase plots for the cart and pole subsystems. These plots illustrate the system recovering from a hard perturbation in pole velocity.

troller accommodates a wide range of perturbations in state space without losing the global behavior. This is a useful form of robustness for many applications, especially in robotic and biomechanical systems such as those described in [5,6, 13,14,15].

8.2   Transition Graph Structure of the Heterogeneous Controller

The operation of the heterogeneous controller can be described and analyzed in terms of a discrete transition graph, as seen in Figure 7. Some of the more important properties of this graph are summarized below.

1. The graph G1, representing the pole control action, is Figure 1 extended with local regions *Startup* and *Limit Cycle* to handle static friction at very low velocities. The graph G2 represents the cart control action, which has a single mode.
2. The two graphs G1 and G2 execute concurrently. This is the default mode in graph G3. The arguments in this paper provide the basis for stable concurrent operation of G1 and G2.
3. The additional state in G3 provides a way to handle large perturbations. If an excessively high velocity is imparted to the pole, rapidly varying, possibly high amplitude, control signals could be generated by the *Spin* region. To prevent this, the action of the pole controller can be restricted to a subset of the state space, with bounded $\dot{\phi}$. It is clear that this is an invariant set, and any trajectory entering it will converge to the desired setpoint. If the system is perturbed outside this invariant set, the pole controller is turned off (leaving the pole to its natural damping), and damping in the cart controller is augmented. The trajectory must enter the invariant set and stabilize at the desired equilibrium.
4. Energy arguments can be used to determine the residence time of a trajectory in any region, showing that all except *Limit Cycle* have finite residence time.

For example, $\dot{s}$ in equation (10) is the instantaneous rate of change of energy in the *Pump* and *Spin* regions, and $s = 0$ defines their shared boundary.

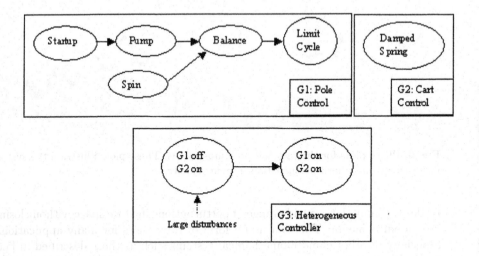

Fig. 7. Transition graph structure of the heterogeneous controller for the cart-pole system

8.3   Conclusions

By applying a control function that transforms the uncontrolled system into one that is an instance of a qualitative behavior model with provable properties, it is possible to design simple, intuitive and robust controllers. QHC applies this concept in a multiple model framework to design global controllers for nonlinear systems. Although the QHC methodology is presented here and in [2] through the simple familiar example of the inverted pendulum, the design method is quite general.

1. Define a transition graph of local regions that guarantees the desired global behavior.
2. For each local region, select a qualitative behavior model (e.g., the damped oscillator) that has the desired qualitative behavior over a region including the intended local region.
3. Select a control policy for each local region that transforms the uncontrolled plant into an instance of the qualitative behavior model over some region containing the intended local model.
4. Define region boundaries with simple reliable descriptions (e.g., energy level curves) such that the local behaviors are guaranteed to cross the region boundaries exactly in the desired ways.

This algorithm is non-deterministic in the sense that earlier choices must be made correctly for later choices to be possible, so backtracking may be necessary. However, if the algorithm terminates, the resulting design is guaranteed to have the desired properties.

Furthermore, since the models are qualitative, the resulting design describes an entire *family* of control laws, all of which are guaranteed to have the desired properties. This allows a useful separation of concerns between qualitative correctness and optimization. Other advantages of QHC include structured handling of real world effects such as static friction, and robustness of global behavior in the face of parametric and structural uncertainty, and in the face of substantial perturbations.

References

1. Kuipers, B.J., Astrom, K.: The composition and validation of heterogeneous control laws. *Automatica* **30** (1994) 223–249
2. Kuipers, B., Ramamoorthy, S.: Qualitative modeling and heterogeneous control of global system behavior. In C. J. Tomlin and M. R. Greenstreet (Eds.), *Hybrid Systems: Computation and Control*, Lecture Notes in Computer Science, Volume 2289, Springer Verlag, 2002
3. Slotine, J.J.E., Li, W.: *Applied Nonlinear Control*. Prentice Hall, Englewood Cliffs NJ (1991)
4. Lohmiller, W., Slotine, J.J.E.: On contraction analysis for nonlinear systems. *Automatica* **34** (1998) 683–696
5. Burridge, R.R., Rizzi, A.A., Koditschek, D.E.: Sequential composition of dynamically dexterous robot behaviors. *International Journal of Robotics Research* **18** (1999) 534–555
6. Klavins, E., Koditschek, D.E.: Phase regulation of decentralized cyclic robotic systems. *International Journal of Robotics Research* **21** (2002) 257–275
7. Ott, E., Grebogi, C., Yorke, J.A.: Controlling chaos. *Physical Review Letters.* **64** (1990) 1196–1199
8. Boccaletti, S., Grebogi, C., Lai, Y.C., Mancini, H., Maza, D.: The control of chaos: Theory and Applications. *Physics Reports* **329** (2000) 103–197
9. Bradley, E.: Autonomous exploration and control of chaotic systems. *Cybernetics and Systems* **26** (1995) 299–319
10. Astrom, K.J., Furuta, K.: Swinging up a pendulum by energy control. *Automatica* **36** (2000) 287–295
11. Zhao, J., Spong, M.W.: Hybrid control for global stabilization of the cart-pendulum system. *Automatica* **37** (2001) 1941–1951
12. Chung, C.C., Hauser, J.: Nonlinear control of a swinging pendulum. *Automatica* **31** (1995) 851–862
13. Full, R., U. Saranli, M. Buehler, Brown. B., N. Moore, D. Koditschek, and H. Komsuoglu. Evidence for Spring Loaded Inverted Pendulum Running in a Hexapod Robot. *Proc. International Symposium on Experimental Robotics*, Honolulu, Hawaii, 2000.
14. Saranli, U., Schwind, W.J., Koditschek, D.E.: Toward the control of a multi-jointed monoped runner. *Proceedings of the IEEE International Conference on Robotics and Automation*, pp 2676–2682, 1998

15. Pratt, J. and Pratt, G.: Intuitive control of a planar bipedal walking robot. *Proceedings of the IEEE International Conference on Robotics and Automation*, 1998
16. Jordan, D.W., Smith, P.: *Nonlinear Ordinary Differential Equations: An Introduction to Dynamical Systems.* 3rd ed. Oxford University Press, Oxford (1999)
17. Guckenheimer, J., Holmes, P.: *Nonlinear Oscillations, Dynamical Systems, and Bifurcations of Vector Fields.* Springer-Verlag, Berlin (1983)
18. Levine, W.E., ed., *The Control Handbook.* CRC Press (1996)
19. Friedland, B.: *Advanced Control System Design.* Prentice-Hall (1996)

The Φ-Calculus: A Language for Distributed Control of Reconfigurable Embedded Systems

William C. Rounds* and Hosung Song

CSE Division, University of Michigan, Ann Arbor, MI 48109, USA
{rounds,hosungs}@eecs.umich.edu

Abstract. The Φ-calculus extends Milner's π-calculus by adding *active environments* which flow continuously over time. This allows us to extend hybrid automata to specify systems of physical agents which can reconfigure themselves. We prove a theorem stating that processes (weakly) bisimilar in the process-algebraic sense, when placed in the same active environment, control it in the same way.

1 Introduction

This paper is an attempt to integrate two research directions. The theory of *process algebras* has been extensively developed within computer science, to the point where control of distributed processes is well-understood, even to the point where these processes are *mobile* (reconfigurable). The field of *hybrid systems* is not as old, but is developing rapidly; integrative work has been extended to proposed programming languages for specifying distributed control of hybrid systems [1,7,5]. Our work is in this latter direction: we propose a simple method for integrating process-algebraic techniques with hybrid automaton-based techniques so that one can use the integrated theory to specify the semantics of real programming languages for *concurrent* and *reconfigurable* embedded systems.

The Φ-calculus is a hybrid extension of Milner's π-*calculus* [13] which allows processes to interact with continuous environments. We choose the π-calculus to extend to the hybrid setting because it has already been shown to be a rich language in which many interesting discrete concurrent phenomena can be expressed: a language for, and theory of, communicating processes which can *reconfigure* themselves; a language in which distributed objects and classes can be defined; and a language and theory capable not only of expressing interaction, but arbitrary computation, in that the λ-calculus of Church can be translated into it. We believe that ours is the first extension of hybrid automata to a process-algebraic language with this much power.

The Φ-calculus has as one of its objectives the study of physical agents, like robots, grouped into clusters at a given time. Agents in each cluster cooperate on a (local) job. When a local job is finished, the agents in a cluster disperse, and are ready to cooperate with agents from other clusters as soon as other

* Research supported by US NSF Grant 0233960.

local jobs are finished and those agents can be freed. Each cluster should be controlled separately, but when the agents disperse and form a new cluster, a controller for that cluster has to be synthesized "on the fly". Such systems are typified, at least informally, by a "square dance", in which partners can change and new configurations form on broadcast signals from a "caller", giving the dance its hybrid character. More mundanely, we may imagine two simultaneously moving conveyor belts as in a baggage recovery area in an airport; the belts are independent but may carry bags as passive agents which are shifted from one belt to another in a simple kind of reconfiguration.

The key idea in the present paper, which allows such system descriptions as well as the ability to extend process-algebraic models to the hybrid setting, involves adding an explicit formal model of the *active* continuous (physical) environment to an algebraic process description, and adding "environmental actions (e-actions)" to processes which allow them to explicitly manipulate their environment. We define an *embedded (hybrid) system* as a pair (E, P), where E is an environment and P is a hybrid process expression (Φ-expression). An embedded system evolves (i) by means of π-actions, which change only the process expression, (ii) by time actions, which change only the environment continuously, or (iii) by e-actions, which change both the environment and a process expression discretely.

The idea of *bisimulation* is fundamental to process-algebraic theory and to the theory of hybrid automata. Most work on bisimulations of hybrid automata has concentrated on bisimulation ideas referring to both the discrete state of a process and to the flow of the environment. Here we define this concept, called *embedded bisimulation*, but we may also study the original bisimulation constructions of the π-calculus, which we call *structural bisimulation*. We may ask how two structurally bisimilar processes will react when embedded (one by one) in the same environment. The answer is that bisimilar processes control the continuous environment in the same way. With the notion of *weak* structural bisimulation this embedding result is not obvious; the expected definition of transitions over time is not correct, and must be replaced with a much subtler one.

1.1 Previous Work

There is already a body of research on the process-algebraic treatment of (some) hybrid phenomena. Timed CSP [15], for example, is a well-known language with a fully compositional semantics based on the extension of "failures" [3] to the timed case. Unfortunately, it is not clear how to extend the expressiveness of this language to the hybrid case, because the timed environment is implicit. Ordinary hybrid automata as in Henzinger [6], on the other do explicitly represent the continuous environment by means of associating a controller (differential equation, differential inclusion) with each state (control mode) of a finite automaton. Events trigger jumps from one control mode to another. There is, moreover, a general "parallel composition" operator for combining these automata, but no syntax is presented for a language which would allow program expressions. There is no provision in these automata for mobile systems. The same remark applies to the *I-O automata* of Lynch and Tuttle [12], and to a process-algebraic version [16] and the hybrid case [11]. The I-O automata do manage continuous variables, but can only combine systems statically, not achieving dynamic reconfiguration.

Two languages which support both hybrid dynamics and algebraic process structuring are CHARON [1] and Masaccio [7]. These languages are both outgrowths of earlier models for reactive discrete systems [2]. At this point they lack reconfigurability, though they do support abstraction (variable hiding). The SHIFT programming language [5] *does* achieve a kind of reconfigurability, in that dynamic networks of hybrid automata can be created over time. The reconfigurability apparatus in the Φ-calculus is, however, more powerful and flexible, because the Φ-calculus does not presume a fixed set of hybrid automaton "types" from which to build networks, and also because code itself can be reconfigured, as in the π-calculus.

Klavins' work [8] on threaded Petri nets (see also Klavins and Koditschek [9] for more detail) was an inspiration for our research. This model of distributed hybrid systems uses the places of a Petri net to hold a set of continuous variables as tokens. This model has interesting applications to robotic assembly problems in factory settings. Moreover, it can be used for large-scale problems without state explosion, since the Petri net keeps interactions local. The model lacks, however, a process-algebraic syntax. Our translation of threaded nets (available in the full paper, [14]) into Φ-calculus provides it.

1.2 Contributions

- A definition of embedded system extending hybrid automata to process algebras;
- Definitions of the behavior of mobile hybrid processes in a continuous environment, via structural operational semantics;
- A method for declaring local environmental variables ("hiding");
- Obtaining recursive definition capabilities by hybridizing Milner's replication operator;
- New definitions of bisimulation for Φ-processes, with an embedding theorem for structural weak bisimulation. This theorem refers to pre-existing ideas of bisimulation in the π-calculus, and extends such bisimulations to hybrid bisimulations. This is the main result in the paper, as it treats the idea of *weak bisimulation.*

1.3 Plan of Paper

In this short paper, we do not have space to present the full definition of the Φ-calculus. Details of the full language, and proofs, can be found in [14]. We present a sub-language Φ_P (Physical Φ), which allows us to define "physically reconfigurable" systems, but not systems in which code fragments can reconfigure themselves. Φ_P is powerful enough to translate threaded Petri nets, and to include systems which can grow, owing to the use of recursion. We illustrate the constructs of the language by example. We then present bisimulation definitions, and state the embedding theorem for weak bisimulation.

2   The Physical Φ-Calculus

2.1   Syntax

Let $\mathcal{N}$ be a countable set of positive actions a, negative actions $\overline{\mathcal{N}} = \{\overline{a} \mid a \in \mathcal{N}\}$ Let $\mathcal{L} = \mathcal{N} \cup \overline{\mathcal{N}}$. These names correspond to the "named actions" of an ordinary finite automaton; the overlined names allow participation in *reactions* (see below). We also have the *silent action* τ, which represents uncontrollable "internal choice."

In the π-calculus, as in most process-algebraic frameworks, finite automata are represented as a system of algebraic equations of the form

$$P ::= a.Q$$

instead of the traditional $P \xrightarrow{a} Q$ notation for changing from state P to state Q under action (event) a. In the Φ-calculus, these events also can range over a set $\mathcal{E}$ of *environmental actions*. These represent events of a process changing its continuous environment, very much like the jumps of hybrid automata. The exact form of these actions is given below (Def. 3.)

Let $\mathcal{X}$ be a countable set of *environment variables* disjoint from $\mathcal{N}$ and let $\dot{\mathcal{X}} = \{\dot{x} \mid x \in \mathcal{X}\}$ be the "dotted versions" (formal variables for differential equations.) These variables are names, which can be "received" or "sent" from one process to another, but which carry real values. In the definition below, receiving actions are of type (i) and sending actions are of type (ii). Note that the names a now are used as "channels" over which variables are sent.

An *action prefix* is an element of $\mathcal{L} \cup \{\tau\}$, or is of the form (i) $a(x_1, \ldots, x_n)$ for $a \in \mathcal{L}$, $x_i \in \mathcal{X}$; (ii) the form $\overline{a}\langle x_1, \ldots, x_n \rangle$ for $a \in \mathcal{L}$ and $x_i \in \mathcal{X}$, or (iii) in the set $\mathcal{E}$. We let μ range over action prefixes.

Definition 1 *The set of Φ-expressions is given by the following syntax:*

$$P ::= M \mid 0 \mid (P_1 \mid P_2) \mid \nu a P \mid \nu x P \mid$$
$$M ::= \mu.P \mid M + M$$

Process expressions (P) can be summations, the null process 0, parallel composition of processes, or restricted processes (νa, νx). Summation expressions (M) represent a choice of actions followed by a process. A notion of *structural congruence* $\equiv$ is employed in the π-calculus; this allows us to claim, for example, that $+$ is associative and commutative. (Finite) sums, then, can be written as $\Sigma \mu_i.P_i$, for example. Further details are omitted here.

2.2   Environments and Environmental Actions

We begin by defining the analogue of "modes" in hybrid automata. Informally, an environment is a triple $\{c; F; I\}$ where $c \in \mathbb{R}^n$, I is a finite set of constraints (predicates) on $\mathbb{R}^n$ (the reason for having a set will be explained later), and F is a dynamic system (typically described by an autonomous differential equation, and typically over $\mathbb{R}^n$). As long as the flow of the differential equation F satisfies the invariant constraints, the system remains in the same "mode".

Definition 2 (Environments) *An environment consists of:*

- *the* state, *an element of* $[\mathcal{V} \to \mathbb{R}]$ *(equivalently* $\mathbb{R}^{\mathcal{V}}$*), the set of all functions (valuations) from a finite subset* $\mathcal{V}$ *of* $\mathcal{X}$ *to* $\mathbb{R}$. *We call* $\mathcal{V}$ *the* domain *of the environment;*
- *the* differential equation*: a valuation from* $\dot{\mathcal{V}}$ *to* $C^1[\mathbb{R}^{\mathcal{U}}]$, *the set of continuously differentiable functions from* $\mathbb{R}^{\mathcal{U}}$ *to* $\mathbb{R}$, *for a finite set* $\mathcal{U} \supseteq \mathcal{V}$;
- *the* invariant*: a finite collection* I *of constraints, where each constraint is a map from* $[\mathcal{W} \to \mathbb{R}]$ *to* $\{0, 1\}$, *for some* $\mathcal{W} \subseteq \mathcal{V}$. *For time-flows to be possible, a system must be in a state satisfying all constraints of the invariant. The reason for postulating a set of constraints instead of just one constraint is that updating the invariant in the presence of parallel processes can then be done "locally" instead of globally.*

Example 1. Here is a sample environment:

$$\left(\begin{array}{c} c = (x : 1.5, y : 0) \\ F = (\dot{x} : x - y - x^3, \ \dot{y} : x + y - y^3) \\ I = \{\{(x, y) \mid (x \geq 0) \wedge (1 \leq \sqrt{x^2 + y^2} \leq \sqrt{2})\}\} \end{array} \right).$$

The state c and the (flow of) the differential equation F are *both* parts of the environment.

We say that a differential equation $F \in [\dot{\mathcal{V}} \to [\mathcal{U} \to \mathbb{R}]]$ is *autonomous* if $\mathcal{U} = \mathcal{V}$. Time-transitions will only be allowed when the equation part of the environment is autonomous.

With regard to the notation for differential equations, all that we are really doing is replacing $\mathbb{R}^n$ with $\mathbb{R}^{\mathcal{U}}$, where $\mathcal{U}$ has n elements, so as to "name" the coordinates of vectors. We allow "free variables" in $\mathcal{U} \setminus \mathcal{V}$ to represent open-loop control.

Environmental actions can be specified many ways. Here we assume a specific syntax for states, differential equations, and predicates. Syntactic "states" will be written, for example, as $d = (x \doteq 0; y \doteq 7; z \doteq 5.3)$. Differential equations can be given in syntactic form like $G = (\dot{y} \doteq y^2 - 5)$. (Notice that these forms denote valuations in an obvious way.) Finally, an invariant predicate ϕ will be a simple open Boolean-valued formula over variables in $\mathcal{X}$. This again denotes a Boolean function over the variables named in the formula.

Definition 3 *An* environmental action *is a syntactic form* $e = [\psi \to d; G; \phi]$, *where the entities* d, G, ϕ *are the syntactic forms above. The predicate form* ψ *is called a* guard. *Any one or more of these entities, including the guard, can be omitted.*

Environmental actions act indivisibly on a semantic environment (c, F, I) when the guard $\psi(c)$ is true. The expressions d, G, ϕ are now interpreted as valuations or Boolean functions, so that we can specify "updating" as in the next definition.

Definition 4 (Effects of environmental actions)

- **"State-update":** Let $c \in [\mathcal{V}_c \to \mathbb{R}]$ and $d \in [\mathcal{V}_d \to \mathbb{R}]$. Then the result of $c \doteq d$ is the valuation s from $\mathcal{V}_c \cup \mathcal{V}_d$ to $\mathbb{R}$ given by

$$s(x) = \begin{cases} c(x) \text{ if } x \in \mathcal{V}_c \setminus \mathcal{V}_d; \\ d(x) \text{ otherwise.} \end{cases}$$

- **"Flow-update":** Let $F \in [\dot{\mathcal{V}}_F \to C^1[\mathbb{R}^{\mathcal{U}_F}]]$ and $G \in [\dot{\mathcal{V}}_G \to C^1[\mathbb{R}^{\mathcal{U}_G}]]$. Then the result of $F \doteq G$ is

$$H(x) = \begin{cases} F(\dot{x}) \text{ if } x \in V_F \setminus \mathcal{V}_G; \\ G(\dot{x}) \text{ otherwise.;} \end{cases}$$

- **"Invariant-update":** Let I be a set of constraints and ϕ be a constraint with domain $dom(\phi) = \mathcal{W}$. Then the result of $I \doteq \phi$ is

$$K = I \setminus \{\phi' \mid dom(\phi') \cap \mathcal{W} \neq \emptyset\} \cup \{\phi\}.$$

This updating of constraint sets with a new constraint reflects the idea that constraints involving variables not in the domain of the new constraint should remain in force; but any constraints some of whose variables are among those of the new constraint are discarded.

Notice that if domains are disjoint in the above definition, and that if differential equations are autonomous, then environmental replacement produces a "decoupled" autonomous equation.

Definition 5 (Embedded system) An embedded system is a pair (E, P) where E is an environment and P is a Φ-expression.

2.3   Transition Relations

We omit discussion of the constructs $\nu x P$ and $!P$ until the next subsection, and turn to the specification of transition relations of Φ_P via structural operational semantics. To express the transition relations correctly, we introduce the notions of *abstractions* and *concretions*. We begin with

Example 2. A process like $a(x).[TRUE \to x \doteq 0; \dot{x} = 1].Q(x)$ may receive an actual variable z along the channel a via a reaction interaction, and will transform itself into the active process $[TRUE \to z \doteq 0; \dot{z} \doteq 1].Q(z)$. The variable x is an abstract variable (formal parameter); it may be instantiated different ways at different times.

To make these abstract variables explicit, we have the following definitions.

Definition 6 *(i) Φ_P-abstractions are of the form $F = (w).P$ (w an ordered list of distinct variables over $\mathcal{X}$). (ii) Φ-concretions are of the form $G = \langle y \rangle.P$, where y is over $\mathcal{X}$. An* agent *is an abstraction or concretion. (iii) The* application *$F@G$ of a ϕ-abstraction and concretion is defined as follows:*

$$((w)P)@\langle y \rangle.Q =_{\text{def}} (\{y \leftarrow w\}P \mid Q)$$

where y and w have the same length.

In (iii), $\{y \leftarrow w\}$ denotes the simultaneous substitution of the variables w_i for the (bound) variables y_i in P. This is a crucial definition, as it allows variables to migrate from one process to another, achieving reconfigurability.

Definition 7 (Transitions in Φ_P) *In the Sum-e rule, e is an environmental action of the form $[\psi \to (d; G; I)]$, E is the environment (c, F, I), and (s, H, K) is the resulting environment. Further, $\alpha \in \mathcal{N} \cup \overline{\mathcal{N}}$, and μ is either an α or an e. Finally, we have elided the symmetric rules $R - par$ and $R - react$.*

$$Sum - pi : (E, \ M + \alpha A + N) \xrightarrow{\alpha} (E, A)$$

$$Sum - e : (E, M + e.P + N) \xrightarrow{e} ((s, H, K), P) \ \textit{if } \psi(c) \textit{ is true;}$$

$$L - React : \frac{(E,P) \xrightarrow{\alpha} (E,G) \qquad (E,Q) \xrightarrow{\overline{\alpha}} (E,C)}{(E, P \mid Q) \xrightarrow{\tau} (E, G@C)}$$

$$L - par : \frac{(E,P) \xrightarrow{\mu} (E',A)}{(E, P \mid Q) \xrightarrow{\mu} (E', A \mid Q)}$$

$$Res - pi : \frac{(E,P) \xrightarrow{\mu} (E',A)}{(E, \nu w P) \xrightarrow{\mu} (E', \nu w A)} \quad \textit{if } \mu \notin \{w, \overline{w}\}$$

An embedded system can evolve over time. This entails a new kind of rule called a *flow transition* rule. In this section we propose provisional rules, which will have to be strengthened in a later section in order to allow weakly bisimilar processes to control an arbitrary continuous environment in the same way.

Definition 8 (Flow transitions - provisional) *Let $c \in [\mathcal{V} \to \mathbb{R}]$, and suppose that the differential equation $F \in [\dot{\mathcal{V}} \to [\mathcal{U} \to \mathbb{R}]]$ is autonomous, i.e., $\mathcal{U} = \mathcal{V}$. Then the flow $\xi(t, c)$ of the equation will be defined in some time-interval $J = [0, u)$ of $\mathbb{R}$. We then have the following flow transitions:*

$$Sum: (\{c, F, I\}, \Sigma_i \mu_i P_i) \xrightarrow{t} (\{\xi(t, c), F, I\}, \Sigma_i \mu_i P_i) \tag{1}$$

provided that for all $0 \le s < t$: (i) $\xi(s, c)$ is defined and satisfies all constraints in I ; and (ii) no μ_i is an environmental action $\psi \to (d; G; \phi)$ with $\psi(s)$ true.

Flow transitions are extended to other Φ-expressions by

$$Par: \frac{(E,P) \xrightarrow{t} (E',P) \qquad (E,Q) \xrightarrow{t} (E',Q)}{(E,P \mid Q) \xrightarrow{t} (E',P \mid Q)} \qquad (2)$$

$$Res: \frac{(E,P) \xrightarrow{t} (E',P)}{(E,\nu aP) \xrightarrow{t} (E',\nu aP)} \qquad (3)$$

We illustrate transitions with a simple example.

Example 3. Consider the embedded system

$$(NULL, [TRUE \to x \doteq 0; \dot{x} \doteq 1; \{(x \le 3)\}].b).$$

This process runs in the environment $NULL = \{\bot, \bot, \emptyset\}$, where the valuations have empty domains, and there are no constraints in the invariant. In this environment, it will have an e-transition to

$$\left(\begin{pmatrix} x:0 \\ \dot{x}:1 \\ \{(x \le 3)\} \end{pmatrix}, b \right),$$

initializing a clock which runs for at most 3 seconds. During any portion of this time, it may do the discrete action b, but must do b within 3 seconds. So, for example,

$$\left(\begin{pmatrix} x:0 \\ \dot{x}:1 \\ \{x \le 3\} \end{pmatrix}, b \right) \xrightarrow{0.5} \left(\begin{pmatrix} x:0.5 \\ \dot{x}:1 \\ x \le 3 \end{pmatrix}, b \right)$$

$$\xrightarrow{b} \left(\begin{pmatrix} x:0.5 \\ \dot{x}:1 \\ \{x \le 3\} \end{pmatrix}, 0 \right)$$

in which the action b happens after one-half second.

In the sequel, if we have an environmental action like $[TRUE \to x \doteq 0; \dot{x} \doteq 1); (x \le 3)]$, we will omit the $TRUE \to$, and write the action as $[x \doteq 0; \dot{x} \doteq 1; (x \le 3)]$.

Remark 1 (Explaining flow transition rules).

1. The Sum rule (provisional) reflects evolution over time in a control mode; the sum represents possible exit transitions from the mode. Note that all parts of the environment must be defined for time to progress here. For later reference we abbreviate (i) by saying the flow is in I during t, and abbreviate condition (ii) by saying that there is no environmental guard enabled in P during time t. The reason for (ii) is to make enabled environmental actions "eager"; see the example below.

2. The rule *Par* (provisional) also needs explanation. One might expect a rule which mirrors the standard notion of direct product, so would involve some "environmental product". Processes, however, can create their own environments via *Sum* environmental action. If we have a parallel composition of two sums, then each sum can manufacture the part of the environment it needs to progress over time. When both parallel sums have contributed their own local environment, then in effect the necessary product environment will have been created, and both processes then can progress simultaneously. Notice also that for parallel composition, no compatibility conditions as in Henzinger [6] need to be assumed.

Example 4 (Eagerness). Why not let any sum evolve over time? Here's an example involving parallel composition. Consider the formation of a closed-loop system given by a plant $\dot{x} = F(x, u)$ and a controller $\dot{u} = G(u)$. Assume initial states x_0 and u_0. We can express this as

$$P \mid Q = ([x \doteq x_0; \dot{x} \doteq F(x, u)].b) \mid ([u \doteq u_0; \dot{u} \doteq G(u)].c).$$

Our intention is that, starting in the null environment, P and Q both initialize their part of the global environment, where the plant and controller are initialized at the same time. If we let any sum evolve over time, then Q can set up its u controller, which can evolve as long as it wants before the plant starts, not what we want. But with the Par and restricted Sum time transition rules, both processes have to use their local environment descriptions to update the actual global environment before any time evolution can happen, so we get the desired simultaneity.

2.4   Recursion and the Environmental Restriction Operator

We have postponed discussion of the operator $!P$, because the π-calculus regards this expression as "structurally equivalent" to the expression $P \mid !P$. That is, $!P$ is always able to spawn a copy of itself to run in parallel with P. Structural equivalence allows us to capture other obviously desirable properties of expressions like $P \mid Q \equiv Q \mid P$ and so on. Details of this equivalence are omitted here. However, the transition rules are simple: When μ is either a π-action or an e-action

$$\frac{(E, P \mid !P) \xrightarrow{\mu} (E', Q)}{(E, !P) \xrightarrow{\mu} (E', Q)}$$

and the flow transition rule is simply

$$\frac{(E, P) \xrightarrow{t} (E', P)}{(E, !P) \xrightarrow{t} (E', !P)}.$$

Notice that this rule dovetails well with the *Par* rule in Definition 8 together with the structural equivalence for recursion above.

We also introduce the *environmental restriction* operator $\nu x P$ for $x \in \mathcal{X}$. The intent of this operator is to make these variables local to the process P. In the literature, this operator is called "variable hiding", and sometimes "abstraction". In Φ-calculus usage, however, it is much more akin to the restriction operator νa.

Definition 9 *For $x \in \mathcal{X}$ the operator $\nu x P$ is called the* environmental restriction *operator. This operator restricts any e-action mentioning the variable x or $\dot{x}$ (we call such actions x-actions). The operator νx binds free occurrences of x in P, and so we may replace occurrences of x in x-actions by a fresh variable not occurring free in P, thus deriving a structurally equivalent expression.*

The hiding effects of this operator are given in the transition rule

$$\frac{(E, P) \xrightarrow{\mu} (E', Q)}{(E, \nu x P) \xrightarrow{\mu} (E', \nu x Q)} \quad \text{if } \mu \text{ is not an } x\text{-action}$$

and the fact that even hidden variables must appear in the global environment by

$$(E, \nu x P) \xrightarrow{\tau} (E, P[x \leftarrow w]) \quad (w \in \mathcal{X}, \ w \text{ not in } E \text{ and not free in } P.)$$

We also add a flow transition rule for the environmental restriction operator; this works in analogy with the *Res* rule in Definition 8.

$$Res - x: \quad \frac{(E, P[x \leftarrow w]) \xrightarrow{t} (E', P[x \leftarrow w])}{(E, \nu x P) \xrightarrow{t} (E', \nu x P)} \quad (w \text{ not in } E, \text{ not free in } P).$$

The reason for the side conditions can be seen from an example:

Example 5. Let $P = \nu x[x \doteq 1]$ and $Q = \nu y[y \doteq 1]$. Then P and Q are structurally equivalent by bound variable conversion. Let E be the environment $\begin{pmatrix} x : 0 \\ \dot{x} : 1 \\ TRUE \end{pmatrix}$. If we did not have the side conditions, then $(E, P) \xrightarrow{t}$ for any t, but (E, Q) cannot flow because y is not defined in the environment. Once again, the νx declaration in P enforces that the local variable x is different from any variable in the environment of P.

Example 6. A *parts feeder* can be modelled using recursion and the ν operator. The task of this feeder is to produce a never-ending stream of different parts in a factory. The feeder operates by proximity; a robot with position r, $0 < r < 2$, is approaching 0 along the x-axis. The parts feeder waits for r to be within some small ϵ of 0, and then produces a new part for the robot. It sends this part out along a channel *feed* to a controller for both the robot r and the part. We call this recursive process PF. It is actually defined using recursion, though we use a familiar syntactic sugaring for this in place of the official replication operator (for details see [13]).

$$PF ::= [r \le \epsilon].\nu p\big(\, [p \doteq \epsilon; \dot{p} \doteq 0].\overline{feed}\langle p \rangle.[r > \epsilon].PF \, \big).$$

The test $r \le \epsilon$ in this process becomes true when the robot gets to exactly ϵ distance of the parts feeder. This triggers a call of the localizing operator νp. This in turn creates a fresh part name, using bound variable conversion to avoid clashes with part names in the environment when the "new" process "decays" at an Env "reaction". The name of the part is sent to the robot along channel pf. A "stop" guard $r > \epsilon$ is set instantaneously to prevent infinite iteration of the call to PF. Parts start with 0 velocity at position ϵ.

The robot moving left along the x-axis is operating under a control law that will slow its velocity to almost zero at $x = \epsilon$. We assume the robot starts at this position. It initializes a (one-dimensional) controller $\dot{r} = f_L(r)$ for this purpose. After picking up the current part, it moves right using another controller which moves it (and the part) back to position $r = 2 - \epsilon$, where it drops the part. The code for these two robot motions is

$$LEFT ::= [\dot{r} \doteq f_L(r); \{2 - \epsilon \ge r > \epsilon\}].RIGHT$$
$$RIGHT ::= feed(p).[(\dot{p}, \dot{r}) \doteq f_R(p,r); \{\epsilon \le r < 2 - \epsilon\}][\dot{p} \doteq 0].LEFT$$

The controller f_L can be specified using a Liapunov-style *navigation function* [10]. We simply find a twice-differentiable function V of x which has the same maximum value at $x = 0$ and $x = 2$, and a minimum at $x = \delta < \epsilon$. If we take the negative gradient (here, just the derivative w.r.t. x) of this function we obtain a one-dimensional vector field which guarantees a stable equilibrium at $x = \delta$. For example, the function

$$V(x) = (x - \delta)^4 / ((x(x - 2))^2 + (x - \delta)^4)$$

has the stated property, so we put $f_L(x) = -dV(x)/dx$. The controller $f_R(p, x)$ similarly has a stable equilibrium at $r = p = 2 - \delta$. The whole system can be started in the environment $E = \begin{pmatrix} r : 0.5 \\ \dot{r} : f_L(r) \\ \{r > \epsilon\} \end{pmatrix}$, and the resulting embedded system is $(E, LEFT \mid PF)$. The system can evolve, e.g., to $(E', LEFT|PF)$, where

$$E' = \begin{pmatrix} (r : 2 - \epsilon : p_1 : 2 - \epsilon; p_2 : 2 - \epsilon) \\ (\dot{p}_1 : 0, \dot{p}_2 : 0, \dot{r} : f_L(r)) \\ \{r > \epsilon\} \end{pmatrix}.$$

3 Bisimulation

This section is devoted to a study of *weak bisimulations* of embedded systems; the terminology comes from Milner's work on CCS and the π-calculus. We start with a simple definition of weak bisimulation on Φ-expressions only, which we call *structural* bisimulation, because it is defined without reference to the continuous environment. We then define full (weak) bisimulation for embedded systems, and state (but do not prove) the main result of the paper, that when structurally bisimilar processes are embedded in the same environment, we obtain systems bisimilar in the embedded sense.

The key to defining structural bisimulation is the notion of *experiment*. These are extended kinds of transitions defined on Φ_P expressions only. We first define the relation $\Rightarrow$ to be the reflexive transitive closure of $\xrightarrow{\tau}$, where we ignore structural equivalence for simplicity.

To proceed further, we must take into account the fact that a process having a binding input prefix cannot actually make a transition which removes this prefix, because the actual variables supplied on the channel may be different at different times. Recalling example 2:

Example 7. A process like $P = a(x).[TRUE \rightarrow x \doteq 0; \dot{x} = 1].Q(x)$ may receive an actual variable z along the channel a via a reaction interaction, and will transform itself into the active process $[TRUE \rightarrow z \doteq 0; \dot{z} \doteq 1].P(z)$.

If z is supplied, then the abstraction $F = (x).[TRUE \rightarrow x \doteq 0; \dot{x} = 1].P(x)$ can combine with the concretion $\langle z \rangle$ to form

$$F@\langle z \rangle = [TRUE \rightarrow z \doteq 0; \dot{z} \doteq 1].P(z).$$

We write

$$Q \xrightarrow{a\langle z \rangle} [TRUE \rightarrow z \doteq 0; \dot{z} \doteq 1].P(z)$$

for this combined operation. In general, we define the relation $P \xrightarrow{a\langle z \rangle} P'$ to hold for processes P and P' if there is an abstraction F and a channel name a such that $P \xrightarrow{a} F$ and $F@\langle z \rangle = P'$. And for outputs along a, we say $P \xrightarrow{\bar{a}\langle z \rangle} P'$ if $P \xrightarrow{\bar{a}} \langle z \rangle.P'$.

Definition 10 (Experiments) *An* input experiment *is an instance of the relation* $\xrightarrow{a\langle y \rangle}$, *defined as*

$$P \xRightarrow{a\langle y \rangle} P' \text{ iff } P \Rightarrow \xrightarrow{a\langle y \rangle} \Rightarrow P'.$$

An output experiment *is an instance of the relation* $\xrightarrow{\bar{a}\langle y \rangle}$, *where*

$$P \xRightarrow{\bar{a}\langle y \rangle} P' \text{ iff } P \Rightarrow \xrightarrow{\bar{a}\langle y \rangle} \Rightarrow P'.$$

An e-experiment *is an instance of the relation* $\xrightarrow{e}$, *where*

$$P \xrightarrow{e} P' \text{ iff } P \Rightarrow \xrightarrow{e} \Rightarrow P'.$$

The following definition of structural simulation and bisimulation corresponds to the usual notion of weak simulation and bisimulation in the π-calculus. This is the only type we consider here, so we omit the adjective "weak."

Definition 11 (Structural simulation) *A binary relation R over Φ- expressions is a simulation if, whenever $P R Q$,*

if $P \Rightarrow P'$ then there is Q' such that $Q \Rightarrow Q'$ and $P' R Q'$;

if $P \overset{a\langle y \rangle}{\Rightarrow} P'$ then there is Q' such that $Q \overset{a\langle y \rangle}{\Rightarrow} Q'$ and $P' R Q'$;

if $P \overset{\bar{a}\langle y \rangle}{\Rightarrow} P'$ then there is Q' such that $Q \overset{\bar{a}\langle y \rangle}{\Rightarrow} Q'$ and $P' R Q'$;

if $P \overset{e}{\Rightarrow} P'$, then there is Q' such that $Q \overset{e}{\Rightarrow} Q'$ and $P' R Q'$.

If both R and its converse are structural simulations, R is a structural bisimulation. Two processes P and Q are structurally bisimilar, written $P \approx Q$, if there is some structural bisimulation relating them.

We want to define the notion of bisimulation now on fully embedded systems, and for this there are many design choices. As a first attempt, we have chosen a very strict kind of embedded bisimulation, because the embedding theorem is not obvious (or even true, without revising flow transition rules) in this simple case.

Definition 12 *Two embedded systems (E, P) and (F, Q) are bisimilar if $E = F$, P and Q are structurally bisimilar, and whenever $(E,P) \overset{t}{\rightarrow} (E',P)$ then $(E,Q) \overset{t}{\rightarrow} (E',Q)$ and conversely.*

We now would like to show that whenever P and Q are structurally bisimilar, then (E, P) and (E, Q) are bisimilar as embedded systems. However, this is not true with the present flow rules.

Example 8. Consider the processes

$$P = \nu a(a.[TRUE \rightarrow x \doteq 1] \mid \bar{a}) \text{ and } Q = [TRUE \rightarrow x \doteq 1].$$

These are structurally bisimilar, but the environment $E = \begin{pmatrix} x : 0 \\ \dot{x} : 1 \\ TRUE \end{pmatrix}$, in the context of process P, can flow for arbitrarily long periods before a reaction happens, while the same E in the context of the process Q is time-blocked because Q's environmental action is enabled.

The way to block this example is not to change the notion of structural bisimulation, but to change the flow rules so that environmental actions enabled by some sequence of τ transition rules, and also reactions, are made eager. Without going into explanations, the new flow rules are as follows:

Definition 13 (Revised flow rules) *We present all of the new flow rules in one display. In the following, E is an environment having an autonomous differential equation with flow $\xi(s,x)$ out of the state x, such that for a given time t, we have that for all $0 \leq s < t$, $\xi(s,x)$ is defined and in the invariant set I. In addition E' is like E but with x changed to $\xi(t,x)$.*

$$Sum: (E, \Sigma_i \mu_i P_i) \xrightarrow{t} (E', \Sigma_i \mu_i P_i)$$

iff no μ_i is an enabled e-action in E,

and for every i such that $\mu_i = \tau$ we have $(E, P_i) \xrightarrow{t} (E', P_i)$

$$Par: \frac{(E, P) \xrightarrow{t} (E', P) \qquad (E, Q) \xrightarrow{t} (E', Q)}{(E, P \mid Q) \xrightarrow{t} (E', P \mid Q)}$$

provided $(\forall S)(P \mid Q \xrightarrow{\tau} S$ implies $(E, S) \xrightarrow{t} (E', S))$.

$$Res\text{-}\pi: \frac{(E, P) \xrightarrow{t} (E', P)}{(E, \nu a P) \xrightarrow{t} (E', \nu a P)}$$

$$Res\text{-}x: \frac{(E, P[x \leftarrow w]) \xrightarrow{t} (E', P[x \leftarrow w])}{(E, \nu x P) \xrightarrow{t} (E', \nu x P)}$$

provided w is not free in P and not mentioned in E.

$$Rep: \frac{(E, P) \xrightarrow{t} (E', P)}{(E, !P) \xrightarrow{t} (E', !P)}.$$

It is understood in these rules that "P" refers to the structural equivalence class of P.

This revision of the flow rules allows us to claim the following.

Theorem 14 (Embedding theorem). *If two structurally bisimilar processes are placed in the same environment, the resulting embedded systems are bisimilar: if $P \approx Q$, then for any E, $(E, P) \xrightarrow{t} (E', P)$ if and only if $(E, Q) \xrightarrow{t} (E', Q)$.*

4   Conclusion

We hope to have demonstrated in this report the feasibility of using process-algebraic techniques in the design of hybrid systems. However, much theoretical work remains to be done.

First, we need to have a deeper understanding of simulations and bisimulations. An important direction is studying the analogue of bisimulations for environments; in the literature these are called *topological equivalences*. We would like to integrate these into a combined definition of bisimulation. It would be nice to give conditions on environments and environmental actions (guarantees that flows will eventually reach the boundary of an invariant, for example), so that a "time-abstract" version of a process could be proven live (deadlock-free) by passing to its discrete version using simulation.

In this preliminary document we have said nothing about possible logics for reasoning about Φ-calculus processes. A possibility is to extend the spatial logic of Caires and Cardelli [4]. Such an extension would incorporate assertions about the continuous state.

References

1. R. Alur, R. Grosu, I. Lee, and O. Sokolsky. Compositional refinement for hierarchical hybrid systems. In Maria Domenica Di Benedetto and Alberto Sangiovanni-Vincentelli, editors, *Hybrid Systems, Computation, and Control*, pages 33–48. Springer-Verlag, 2001. Volume 2034 of Lecture Notes in Computer Science.

2. R. Alur and. T. A. Henzinger. Reactive modules. *Formal methods in System Design*, 15:7–48, 1999.

3. S. D. Brookes, C. A. R. Hoare, and A. W. Roscoe. A theory of communicating sequential processes. *J. Assoc. Comput. Mach.*, 31(3):560–599, 1984.

4. Luis Caires and Luca Cardelli. A spatial logic for concurrency (part i). In *Proceedings, Theoretical Aspects of Computer Software; 4th International Symposium, Sendai, Japan*, 2001. To appear in I & C special issue on TACS'01.

5. A. Deshpande, A. Gollu, and L. Semenzato. The shift programming language and run-time system for dynamic networks of hybrid automata. Technical report, California PATH Research Report UCB-ITS-PRR-97-7, 1997.

6. T. A. Henzinger. The theory of hybrid automata. In *Proc. 11th Annual Symposium on Logic in Computer Science*, pages 278–292, 1996.

7. T. A. Henzinger, M. Minea, and V. Prabhu. Assume-guarantee reasoning for hierarchical hybrid systems. In Maria Domenica Di Benedetto and Alberto Sangiovanni-Vincentelli, editors, *Hybrid Systems, Computation, and Control*, pages 275–290. Springer-Verlag, 2001. Volume 2034 of Lecture Notes in Computer Science.

8. E. Klavins. Automatic compilation of concurrent hybrid factories from product assembly specifications. In *Hybrid Systems: Computation and Control*, LNCS 1790, pages 174–187, Pittsburgh, PA, 2000. Springer-Verlag.

9. Eric Klavins and Daniel Koditschek. A formalism for the composition of loosely coupled robot behaviors. Technical report, University of Michigan CSE Tech Report CSE-TR-12-99, 1999.

10. Daniel E. Koditschek and Elon Rimon. Robot navigation functions on manifolds with boundary. *Advances in Applied Mathematics*, 11:412–442, 1990.

11. Nancy Lynch, Roberto Segala, and Frits Vaandrager. Hybrid i/o automata revisited. In Maria Domenica Di Benedetto and Alberto Sangiovanni-Vincentelli, editors, *Hybrid Systems: Computation and Control. Fourth International Workshop*, pages 403–417. Springer-Verlag, 2001. Volume 2034 of Lecture Notes in Computer Science.

12. Nancy Lynch and Mark Tuttle. Hierarchical correctness proofs for distributed algorithms. In *Proceedings of 6th Annual Symposium on Principles of Distributed Computing*, pages 137–151, 1987.

13. Robin Milner. *Communicating and Mobile Systems: the π-calculus*. Cambridge University Press, 1999.

14. W. C. Rounds and Hosung Song. The ϕ-calculus - a hybrid extension of the π-calculus to embedded systems. Technical report, University of Michigan EECS-CSE Tech Report CSE-TR-458-02, 2002.

15. Steve Schneider. *Concurrent and real-time systems: the CSP approach*. Wiley, 2000.

16. Roberto Segala. A process-algebraic view of i-o automata. Technical report, MIT Tech Memo MIT/LCS/TR557, 1992.

Hybrid Modelling and Control of Power Electronics

Matthew Senesky, Gabriel Eirea, and T. John Koo

EECS Department, University of California, Berkeley
{senesky,geirea,koo}@eecs.berkeley.edu

Abstract. Switched circuits in power electronics by their nature present hybrid behavior. Such circuits can be described by a set of discrete states with associated continuous dynamics. A control objective, usually regulation of the output in the face of disturbances in the continuous system, is accomplished by choosing among discrete states. We describe a hybrid systems perspective of several common tasks in the design and analysis of power electronics. A DC-DC boost converter circuit is presented as an illustrative example, and the extension of this circuit to a multiple output configuration is provided to show the favorable scaling properties and broad utility of the hybrid approach.

1 Introduction

Since their introduction in the 1950's, power semiconductor components have steadily improved in performance, price, and convenience. Modern components like power MOSFETs and IGBTs (Insulated Gate Bipolar Transistors) offer impressive specifications for switching frequency and on-resistance, while eliminating the problems with forced commutation associated with earlier generations of power devices. As these components have become more attractive to designers, the use of switching circuits in power applications has become increasingly common. Such circuits typically employ PWM (Pulse Width Modulation) or similar switching techniques to regulate the voltage or current delivered to a load, and networks of linear circuit elements to filter the switching transients from this output. Switching circuits are found in applications including power supplies, variable–speed machine drives, and DC-DC converters, just to name a few.

As a motivating example, a DC-DC "boost" converter appears in Figure 1. The purpose of the circuit is to draw power from the source V_{in}, and supply power to the load R at a higher voltage V_{out} (hence the name "boost"). This is accomplished by first closing SW1 (with SW2 open) to store energy in the inductor L, and then closing SW2 (with SW1 open) to transfer that energy to the capacitor C, where it is available to the load R. For the circuit to function properly, this switching must occur continually, and its timing must be controlled. In the following, we will refer frequently to this example.

As described in Section 2 below, much of the typical analysis of switching circuits relies on averaging or discretization techniques to make analysis of the

O. Maler and A. Pnueli (Eds.): HSCC 2003, LNCS 2623, pp. 450–465, 2003.

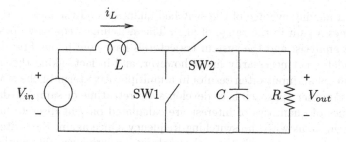

Fig. 1. The DC-DC boost converter.

circuit more tractable. While this approach is adequate in many cases, it is worthwhile and instructive to reconsider the system analysis and controller synthesis in light of hybrid systems literature. This will not only allow the exploration of a larger space of controllers, but also make available a number of hybrid analysis tools.

Switching circuits are a particularly good candidate for such analysis because they are inherently hybrid in structure. Under this hybrid model the system has only discrete inputs, only continuous outputs, and disturbances that are either continuous, as in a changing load or source, or discrete, as in a fault condition for a particular switch. This is the class of systems that will be examined below.

1.1   Outline

The next section explores current practice in the analysis and control of power electronics circuits. Section 3 presents the formal definition of the class of systems we examine, and describes a hybrid systems approach to the analysis of power electronics circuits. In Section 4 we describe a methodology to synthesize guards that guarantee a desired safety property, and illustrate it with an example. In Section 5 we undertake a detailed design exercise by extending the example to a DC-DC converter with two outputs. Finally, we outline some conclusions and future work.

2   State of the Art: Analysis of Power Electronics

Many of the power electronics topologies currently in use predate much of the literature on nonlinear and hybrid systems. In addition, simplicity and low cost often win out over high performance in application. Thus, the most common techniques for analysis, simulation, and control synthesis involve considerable approximation, and produce results that are limited in utility for higher-performance designs.

One approach to simplifying switching circuits is to obtain an averaged, continuous time model (see [1]). Under this method, switching action is replaced by a moving average of the switched quantity, and the switching duty cycle becomes a gain in the range of [0,1]. The switching frequency does not appear in the analysis, and the system trajectories have continuous first derivatives. The model is not necessarily linear however, and in fact taking the continuous duty cycle as an input often results in a multiplicative term in the state equations.

Another approach is to develop a discrete–time or sampled–data model. The values of quantities of interest are calculated only at discrete instants, usually synchronous with the switching frequency. Once again, the switching frequency does not appear explicitly in the analysis. As with averaging methods, discretization does not necessarily result in a linear model.

It is common in either case to perform a small-signal linearization of the model about an operating point of interest by finding the Jacobian of the state–space model. Clearly, models obtained with such methods are limited in their ability to describe system dynamics. Circuit behavior between switching instances is lost, and the ability to predict important nonlinear behaviors is lost.

Control synthesis is often accomplished by applying linear control techniques to a linearized averaged or discretized system as described above. The main drawback to this approach is the fact that controller performance is limited by the accuracy of the model; because the system dynamics are only approximated, the full space of controllers cannot be explored.

There is extensive literature on the use of nonlinear control for power electronics (see for example [2] and its references). Various methods of switching surface control exist, in which switching occurs when a surface in the state space is encountered. Special cases of this are sliding mode control and hysteresis control.

3   Hybrid Modelling and Analysis

Here we more formally define the class of hybrid systems proposed for study, which we refer to as "power electronics circuits". A power electronics circuit can be described as a network of electrical components selected from the following three groups: ideal voltage or current sources, linear elements (e.g. resistors, capacitors, inductors, transformers), and nonlinear elements acting as switches. At this level of abstraction, the behavior of a switch is idealized as having two discrete states: an open circuit and a short circuit.

In a circuit with K switches, there are 2^K possible discrete states. In practice however, not all of these discrete states can be visited. Some of them are not feasible because of the physical characteristics of the switches, while others are banned by the designer because of safety considerations.

Because of the restricted choice of circuit elements, the resulting systems have the desirable property that the continuous dynamics of each discrete state are linear or affine. Note, however, that these dynamics can allow arbitrarily large drift of continuous states, or allow the system to relax to a trivial equilibrium point. It is by exploiting the differences among the dynamics of the various switching configurations that the desired behavior of the circuit is achieved.

Thus under the proposed definition, the only input to the system is the choice of discrete state. Discrete transitions are not necessarily under control. Some are dictated by the physical characteristics of the switching elements and the evolution of currents and voltages in the circuit. This analysis will deal only with continuous disturbances. Hence a disturbance will be considered to be a change in the value of a source or linear element over time. Switching elements are assumed to always function correctly.

3.1   Problem Statement

Let $X \subseteq \mathbb{R}^n$ be a continuous state space and let $Q = \{q_1, \ldots, q_N\}$ be a finite set of discrete states. The continuous state space specifies the possible values of the continuous states for all q, where $q \in Q$ represents the on/off configuration of all the switches in the circuit. As described above, networks are constructed from ideal sources, linear elements and ideal switches; hence for each $q \in Q$ the continuous dynamics can be modelled by differential equations of the form

$$\dot{x}(t) = f_q(x(t)) = A_q x(t) + b_q \tag{3.1}$$

where $x \in X$, $A_q \in \mathbb{R}^{n \times n}$, $b_q \in \mathbb{R}^{n \times 1}$. Furthermore, one can define $I(q) \subseteq X$ as the subset of the continuous state space where the dynamics of f_q can be applied.

How and when to impose discrete transitions is a key problem in the design of power electronics circuits. We propose to address this problem with hybrid automaton theory [3,4]. First, we introduce some useful concepts.

Definition 1 (Mode). *A mode, denoted M_q where $q \in Q$, is the operation of the system (3.1), i.e. $\dot{x}(t) = A_q x(t) + b_q$, while $x \in I(q)$ with $I(q) \subseteq X$.*

From a given discrete state it may not be feasible to visit all other discrete states. Hence, we use $E \subseteq Q \times Q$ to define the collection of feasible discrete transitions. To each edge $e = (q, q') \in E$, the switching condition is defined by $G : E \rightarrow 2^X$ which assigns each edge a guard. Given the collection of modes, edges, and guards, one can form a hybrid automaton which is defined as follows:

Definition 2 (Hybrid Automaton). *A hybrid automaton is a collection $H = (Q, X, f, I, E, G)$ where $Q = \{q_1, \ldots, q_N\}$ is a set of discrete states; $X \subseteq \mathbb{R}^n$ is the continuous state space; $f : Q \rightarrow (X \rightarrow \mathbb{R}^n)$ assigns to every discrete state a Lipschitz continuous vector field on X; $I : Q \rightarrow 2^X$ assigns each $q \in Q$ an invariant set; $E \subseteq Q \times Q$ is a collection of discrete transitions; $G : E \rightarrow 2^X$ assigns each $e = (q, q') \in E$ a guard.*

To simplify the notation, we will use I_q for $I(q)$, f_q for $f(q)$, and $G_{qq'}$ for $G((q, q'))$.

The task of checking if a hybrid automaton satisfies a given system property is called a verification problem. Many tools [5,6,7,8,9] have been developed for verifying different combinations of hybrid automata and system properties. However, we are interested in the synthesis problem, which considers the synthesis of a hybrid automaton that satisfies given system properties. We focus on safety properties of the continuous state, which are typically encoded as subsets of the continuous state space. Let $F \subseteq X$ be the safe set. We use $\Box F$ to denote the safety property on F, i.e., if $\Box F$ is true then $\forall t \; x(t) \in F$.

One can manipulate the evolution of the continuous state by changing the discrete state. A guard can be specified to signal when this change occurs. Once the continuous state reaches the guard condition, a decision can be made whether to jump to one of the next possible discrete states. Since the continuous state x is globally defined, there is no reset in the values of the continuous variables. The design objective for power electronics circuits is to determine the guards between discrete states so that the system trajectories satisfy given performance criteria.

Problem 1 (Synthesis Problem For a Given Safety Property). Given a collection of modes M_q for $q \in Q$, edges defined by $E \subseteq Q \times Q$, and a safety property $\Box F$, determine if there exist guards defined by G for all $e \in E$ such that if $x(t) \in F$ for $t \leq 0$ then $x(t) \in F$ for $t \geq 0$. If so, synthesize the guards and the resulting hybrid automaton H.

Several approaches [9,10] have been proposed to solve the synthesis problem. The idea of these approaches is to obtain a *maximal safe set*, $W \subseteq F$, which satisfies the safety property $\Box W$. If $x(t) \in W \subseteq F$ for $t \leq 0$ then $x(t) \in W \subseteq F$ for $t \geq 0$. If W does exist and can be computed, one can solve the synthesis problem. In [9], an abstract algorithm is proposed to solve the synthesis problem using an iterative computation of reachable states. If the problem is feasible, a fixed point will be reached and a maximal safe set, guards and invariants will be obtained. In [10], the controller synthesis problem is formulated as a game between controller and disturbance. One can then find Hamilton-Jacobi equations whose solutions describe the boundaries of the maximal safe set, and derive an associated least restrictive controller.

We are also interested in the synthesis of guards, as specified in Problem 1. However, there are some distinct characteristics of the application which require that we develop more direct solution methodologies. Using the formal methods presented in [9,10], one can obtain the maximal safe set W inside F if it exists. In general, the safe set W can have an arbitrary shape which depends heavily on the dynamics. However, in order to precisely determine the switching conditions, we seek an explicit form for describing the boundary of the safe set. Furthermore, we require that the switching conditions can be computed effectively. Therefore, we propose to use a closed ball to specify the safe set. A similar consideration has been taken by [11], where an ellipsoid is used to specify the switching conditions. We cast the synthesis problem based on a ball as follows:

Problem 2 (Safety Synthesis Problem For Power Electronics). Given a collection of modes M_q for $q \in Q$, a safety property $\Box F$, and a set point $x_d \in F$, determine if there exists $\delta > 0$ such that $B_{x_d}(\delta) \subseteq F$ and

$$\forall x \in \partial B_{x_d}(\delta) \; \exists q \in Q \text{ s.t. } \langle x - x_d, f_q \rangle \leq 0 \qquad (3.2)$$

where $B_{x_d}(\delta) = \{x \in \mathbb{R}^n : \|x - x_d\|_2 \leq \delta\}$.

Once a "safe ball" is obtained, one can derive the guard by considering the mode that drives the continuous state inside the ball. (Note that in general, the existence of a maximal safe set does not imply the existence of a safe ball.) The ball is made controlled invariant, and thus for every starting point inside the ball the trajectory will stay in F. For points inside the ball, any discrete state is appropriate since the safety property is of concern only at the boundary of the ball. This allows hierarchical organization of a family of controllers to meet different specifications.

4   Control Synthesis

In this section, we address the synthesis problem for power electronics circuits. Our concern is to guarantee the safety property $\Box F$, where F is called the *admissible set*, and represents the specification given by the designer. In a simple formulation, F is a rectangular set given by the minimum and maximum values tolerated for each state variable. It could, however, involve a different shape.

In the remainder of this section, we address the synthesis of a controller in an incremental way. First, we describe the hybrid modelling of a power electronics circuit as suggested by the definitions in Section 3.

4.1   Modelling

It is a straightforward task to formulate the hybrid model for a power electronics circuit as defined in Definition 2. Note that unlike the modelling techniques discussed in Section 2, the hybrid model captures the exact behavior of the circuit, without approximation.

We consider the example of the conventional DC-DC boost converter shown in Figure 1. There are two discrete states ([SW1 on, SW2 off], and [SW1 off, SW2 on]) which we will call q_1 and q_2 respectively. Hence, $Q = \{q_1, q_2\}$ and $E = \{(q_1, q_2), (q_2, q_1)\}$. The state of the system is defined as $x = [i_L \; v_o]^T$, which gives the affine state equations for q_i $(i = 1, 2)$ in the form of Equation 3.1, where

$$A_1 = \begin{bmatrix} 0 & 0 \\ 0 & -\frac{1}{RC} \end{bmatrix}, \quad A_2 = \begin{bmatrix} 0 & -\frac{1}{L} \\ \frac{1}{C} & -\frac{1}{RC} \end{bmatrix}, \quad b_1 = b_2 = b = \begin{bmatrix} \frac{v_{in}}{L} \\ 0 \end{bmatrix}$$

and the numerical values to be used are $v_{in} = 1.5V$, $L = 150\mu H$, $C = 110\mu F$ and $R = 6\Omega$. To further simplify the notation above, we use f_i for f_{q_i}, A_i for A_{q_i} and b_i for b_{q_i}, and we define $\Lambda = \{1, \dots, N\}$ and $I_1 = I_2 = X = \mathbb{R}^2$.

For implementation, in order to decouple the discrete logic with the continuous dynamics, the hybrid automaton H can be decomposed into two hybrid automata H_1 and H_2. H_1 is a finite state machine governing the discrete transition which depends on the continuous signal x from H_2, while H_2 accepts the discrete symbol $\sigma \in \Sigma$ from H_1 and the continuous state x evolves accordingly. The system is shown in Figure 2.

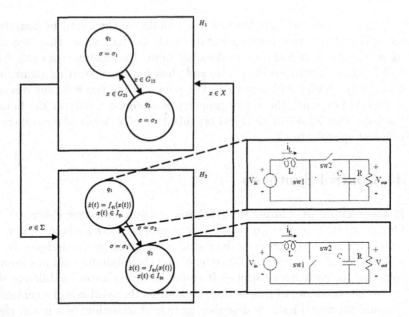

Fig. 2. A power electronics circuit modelled as the parallel composition of two hybrid automata where H_1 governs discrete evolution and H_2 governs continuous evolution.

4.2   Stability

The existence of a safe ball B is directly linked with the notion of stability, at least in a broad sense. If we can find a ball B on whose boundary there always exists an input σ to drive the state into the ball, then we claim that it is possible to stay inside the ball B indefinitely. The only requirement is to choose the appropriate control action when the state reaches the boundary. Here, we propose a strategy for solving Problem 2 by determining the existence of the ball, and constructing the ball if it does indeed exist. The existence of such a safe ball B can be characterized by the following proposition.

Proposition 1. *Given a continuous state space $X \subseteq \mathbb{R}^n$, N continuous vector fields $f_i : X \to \mathbb{R}^n$, $i = 1 \ldots N$, which can be selected at any point in time, a set point $x_d \in X$, an admissible set $F \subseteq X$ s.t. $x_d \in F$, if there exists $\delta > 0$ such that a ball $B_{x_d}(\delta) = \{x \in X : \|x - x_d\| \leq \delta\}$ has the following properties:*

1. *$B_{x_d}(\delta) \subseteq F$;*
2. *$\forall x \in \partial B_{x_d}(\delta), \exists i \in \Lambda$ s.t. $\langle x - x_d, f_i(x) \rangle \leq 0$,*

then, $B_{x_d}(\delta)$ is controlled invariant.

By "controlled invariant" we mean that if $x(0) \in B_{x_d}(\delta)$, then there exists a control input for $t \geq 0$ such that $x(t) \in B_{x_d(\delta)} \ \forall t \geq 0$. The proof is trivial: by construction when the flow reaches the boundary of B, the control can choose a vector field that points into B. As a corollary, the state never leaves the admissible set F.

The set B may not be unique — there could exist a set of balls of different sizes that satisfy our requirement. If we make δ as small as possible, we get a characterization of a controller with the smallest possible deviation from the set point. If we make δ as large as possible, we find a "safety" controller, which protects the system from undesirable states. In between these extremes, it is possible to find a collection of balls that satisfy different control objectives; clearly a trade–off exists between tight regulation and control effort.

```
Algorithm 1: Safe Ball
Initialize δ = 0, largest_good_delta = 0;
While δ < δmax
    δ = δ + Δδ;
    is_good_delta = true;
    For all x ∈ ∂Bxd(δ)
        if min⟨x − xd, fi(x)⟩ > 0
             i∈Λ
            is_good_delta = false; Break;
        End;
    End;
    If is_good_delta
        largest_good_delta = δ;
    End;
End;
```

Fig. 3. An algorithm to find a safe ball B with maximum radius inside F

Figure 3 shows an algorithm to find the safe ball B. The value of $\delta_{\max}$ is computed as the maximum radius of the ball contained in F; when F is rectangular this computation is trivial. The algorithm starts with a ball of radius $\Delta\delta$ and checks if all points in the boundary have at least one element of the vector field pointing inwards, by computing the inner product $\langle x - x_d, f_i(x) \rangle$ for each i. The points in the boundary of B must be parameterized in a grid over ∂B, so it is important to define the size of the grid such that the vector field variation is small between adjacent points. The radius of the ball is increased until $\delta_{\max}$ is reached. The largest δ that satisfies the invariance requirements is chosen; however if at the end of the algorithm largest_good_delta is 0, there is no solution.

The algorithm can be solved in two ways: by setting a grid on the boundary of the ball and solving the problem numerically; or by using symbolic tools [14, 15] to solve it as a Quantifier Elimination problem. The former needs a careful choice of the grid size, while the latter can provide an answer only in limited cases. An additional degree of freedom is the value of $\Delta\delta$, which sets the grid for δ.

Returning to our DC-DC converter example, we choose to parameterize the points in the boundary of the ball as $i_L = i_{L,d} + \delta \cos\theta$ and $v_o = v_{o,d} + \delta \sin\theta$. The inner products are

$$\langle x - x_d, f_1(x) \rangle = \delta \left(\cos\theta \frac{v_{in}}{L} - \sin\theta \frac{v_{o,d}}{RC} \right) - \delta^2 \sin^2\theta \frac{1}{RC}$$

$$\langle x - x_d, f_2(x) \rangle = \delta \left(\cos\theta \left(\frac{v_{in}}{L} - \frac{v_{o,d}}{L} \right) + \sin\theta \left(\frac{i_{L,d}}{C} - \frac{v_{o,d}}{RC} \right) \right) +$$

$$\delta^2 \left(\sin\theta \cos\theta \left(\frac{1}{C} - \frac{1}{L} \right) - \sin^2\theta \frac{1}{RC} \right)$$

The control objective is to regulate the output voltage at $v_{o,d} = 3.3V$ with a tolerance of $\pm 10\%$, while the current in the inductor must remain in the range $[0, 2.5A]$. This implies an admissible set $F = \{x \in \mathbb{R}^2 : 0 \leq x_1 \leq 2.5, 2.97 \leq x_2 \leq 3.63\}$. Steady–state operation requires that $i_{L,ss} = \frac{v_{o,ss}^2}{v_{in} \cdot R}$, where $i_{L,ss}$ and $v_{o,ss}$ are the steady–state inductor current and output voltage respectively. Imposing the condition $v_{o,ss} = v_{o,d}$ we conclude that $i_{L,ss} = 1.21A$, which we will also refer to as $i_{L,d}$. Thus the set point is $(i_{L,d}, v_{o,d}) = (1.21, 3.3)$, which gives $\delta_{\max} = .33$.

A Matlab program using a grid size of .01 on θ and $\Delta\delta = .01$ finds that largest_good_delta $= .33$ (i.e., $\delta_{\max}$). The computation time is $5s$ on a PIII, 800MHz with 256Mb of RAM.

4.3   Regulation

Once a safe set is found, the stability of the system is guaranteed. We can concentrate, then, on the design of controllers for the interior of the safe set. What form these might take depends on the application. In general, it may be useful to formulate controllers that satisfy various performance criteria inside the safe set.

As an example, we present two controllers for the interior of the safe set of the DC-DC converter. The first one, called "minimum ripple control", always chooses the control whose vector field points closer to the set point x_d. The control action minimizes the cosine of the angle between $x - x_d$ and $f_i(x)$ as

$$\sigma_i = \arg\min_{i \in A} \frac{\langle x - x_d, f_i(x) \rangle}{\|f_i(x)\|}$$

where we omit $\|x - x_d\|$ in the denominator because it is independent of i.

The second controller, called "minimum switching control", keeps the control constant until the boundary of the ball is reached. Then a new control driving the state inside the ball is selected and kept constant until the boundary is reached again, and so on. Notice that, by construction, such a control action always exists.

The names chosen for these controllers reveal the purpose of each. In the first case, the state is expected to roam around the set point without moving too far away from it, at the expense of switching continually. It is reasonable to expect that this controller might present Zeno behavior, i.e. try to switch an infinite number of times in a finite time interval; in practice this is avoided by assigning a small fixed minimum time between successive switchings. In the second case the state is allowed to move away from the set point, and switches only when it is necessary for the stability of the system; the average switching is expected to be less than in the previous case, at the expense of a larger ripple of the output variable. Figure 4 shows simulated trajectories for these controllers applied to the example system.

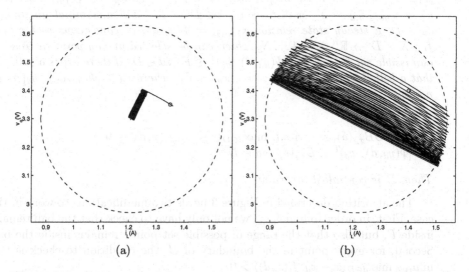

Fig. 4. State trajectories of the example system using (a) the minimum ripple controller, and (b) the minimum switching controller. The circle represents the initial state and the dashed line represents the boundary of the safe set.

4.4 Disturbances

So far in our analysis we have assumed complete knowledge of the dynamics of the system. In practice, there is always uncertainty about the values of the parameters of our model. We consider now the effects of such disturbances on the computation of the safe set, and therefore on the stability of the system. The first natural extension of the previous result is to impose the condition that, while the disturbances d can change arbitrarily in some set D, in the worst case there is always a vector field pointing into the ball. More formally, this requires modification of Proposition 1 to accommodate the condition $\min_{i \in A} \max_{d \in D} \langle x - x_d, f_i(x, d) \rangle \leq 0$, where the vector fields now depend on the disturbances.

However the analysis must be modified further, because the value of the set point is also affected by the disturbances. In this case, it is not possible to specify an arbitrary set point in the state space; one can only specify a range based on the range of the disturbances. This is because the relationship between the average voltages and currents must be maintained in the steady–state, and this relationship depends on the disturbances.

Below we define a function Φ, called a "steady–state relation", such that $v = \Phi(w, d)$ where w are independent state variables, and d are disturbances. The following proposition then formalizes the modifications needed to handle disturbances.

Proposition 2. *Given a continuous state space $X \subseteq \mathbb{R}^n$ with $x = [x_{1:m} \; x_{m+1:n}]^T \in X$, an output space $Y \subseteq \mathbb{R}^{n-m}$ with $y = x_{m+1:n}$, a set point $y_d = x_{m+1:n,d} \in Y$, a disturbance set $D \subseteq \mathbb{R}^p$ with a nominal disturbance $d_0 \in D$, a steady state relation $x_{1:m,ss} = \Phi(y_d, d)$, N continuous vector fields $f_i : X \times D \to \mathbb{R}^n$, $i = 1 \ldots N$, which can be selected at any point in time, an admissible set $F \subseteq X$ s.t. $[\Phi(y_d, d) \; y_d]^T \in F \; \forall d \in D$, if there exists $\delta > 0$ such that a ball $B_{x_d}(\delta) = \{x \in X : \|x - x_d\| \leq \delta\}$, where $x_d = [\Phi(y_d, d_0) \; y_d]$ is the nominal set point, s.t.*

1. $B_{x_d}(\delta) \subseteq F$
2. $\forall x \in \partial B_{x_d}(\delta), \exists i \in \Lambda$ *s.t.* $\max_{d \in D} \langle x - x_d, f_i(x, d) \rangle \leq 0$
3. $[\Phi(y_d, d) \; y_d]^T \in B_{x_d}(\delta) \; \forall d \in D$

Then, B is controlled invariant.

The algorithm described in Figure 3 needs two modifications to work in this case. First, in order to find δ_{max}, we not only have to check that the ball remains inside F, but also that the range of possible set points remains inside the ball. Second, for every point in the boundary of B, the condition to check is that $\min_{i \in \Lambda} \max_{d \in D} \langle x - x_d, f_i(x, d) \rangle > 0$.

Considering our DC-DC converter example, the steady–state relation can be written as $i_{L,ss} = \Phi(x_{o,d}, v_{in}, R) = \frac{v_{od}^2}{v_{in} R}$, where v_{in} and R are the disturbances. Since the control objective is to regulate the output voltage, the current in the inductor has to change to accommodate changes in the disturbances. It is specified that the regulation has to be achieved under changes of $+5\%$ in the load R, and -5% in the input voltage v_{in}. Hence the range of possible values of $i_{L,ss}$ is $[1.15, 1.27]A$, which gives us a minimum value of delta: $\delta_{min} = .06$. We can write the inner products as

$$\langle x - x_d, f_1(x, d) \rangle = \frac{(i_L - i_{L,d})}{L} d_2 - \frac{v_o(v_o - v_{o,d})}{C} d_1$$

$$\langle x - x_d, f_2(x, d) \rangle = \frac{(i_L - i_{L,d})}{L} d_2 - \frac{v_o(v_o - v_{o,d})}{C} d_1 - \frac{v_o(i_L - i_{L,d})}{L} + \frac{i_L(v_o - v_{o,d})}{C}$$

where $d_1 = 1/R$ and $d_2 = v_{in}$. Since the relationship is linear on d, the maximum over all possible $d \in D$ is obtained by substituting d_1 and d_2 by their maximum or minimum value according to the sign of the corresponding coefficient: if $i_L > i_{L,d}$, substitute d_2 by $d_{2,max}$, and else by $d_{2,min}$; if $v_o > v_{o,d}$, substitute d_1 by $d_{1,min}$, and else by $d_{1,max}$. In each one of the four quadrants defined around x_d, the maximum of the inner products is a function with d substituted by a constant, so we can apply the same procedure as before. Instead of having a unique function for $\theta \in [0, 2\pi]$, now we have four functions, one for $\theta \in [0, \pi/2]$, another for $\theta \in [\pi/2, \pi]$, and so on.

We use the same Matlab program described in Section 4.2 with the modifications described above, and we find that $\delta = \delta_{\max} = .33$ still satisfies the conditions in Proposition 2, i.e., the safe ball is robust with respect to the disturbances specified in this problem. The computation time is almost the same, because computing the maximum over the disturbance set adds very little overhead, as described above.

We can also reformulate the controllers described in the previous section to take into account disturbances. In the case of the "minimum ripple control", we select the control by minimizing the cosine of the angle between $x - x_d$ and $f_i(x, d)$ under the worst case for all $d \in D$. The "minimum switching control" can be derived in the same way.

4.5   Sampling Time

The previous results are valid under the assumption that the control action can be taken at any point in continuous time. This is a strong assumption, because in practice switches need a non-zero time to turn on and off. Moreover, the assumption also implies that the controller is able to evaluate the specified functions continuously, while in practice all the evaluations require sampling and finite computation time. Therefore it is necessary to take into account these limitations in our model.

In this section, we describe the system with a sampled data model, i.e., using a global clock of period T, such that the evaluation of the state and the decision about the control action occur at discrete moments in time $t_k = kT$. We assume that the computation time is zero, i.e., both the measurements and the control action occur at the same time.

Under these assumptions, the conditions imposed on the safe set have to be more restrictive. It is not enough to require that a safe control action can be chosen at the points in the boundary; now we must require the same condition on any point that can be reached from inside the safe set in time T.

Given a safe set described by a safe ball B as in Section 4.2, we characterize the set of reachable points from B in time T as included in another ball $\tilde{B}$ of radius $\tilde{\delta}$ larger than that of B. Given any point $x_0 \in \partial B$, let $x_{T,i}$ be the state after flowing for T seconds using the control σ_i. Since the system is affine, then

$$x_{T,i} = e^{A_i T} x_0 + \int_0^T e^{A_i \tau} d\tau b = x_0 + f_i(x_0)T + \cdots$$

And we have

$$\|x_{T,i} - x_d\| = \|x_0 - x_d + f_i(x_0)T + \cdots\|$$
$$\leq \|x_0 - x_d\| + \|f_i(x_0)T + \cdots\| \approx \delta + T\|f_i(x_0)\|$$

where δ is the radius of B, and we have discarded higher order terms. This expression gives an approximation of $\tilde{\delta}$ if we find the worst case for all $x_0 \in \partial B$ and for all i.

Once we have an estimation of $\tilde{\delta}$, we have to verify that the conditions of Proposition 1 are met for all balls with radius between δ and $\tilde{\delta}$. This gives us a sufficient condition for the stability of the sampled–data system. The idea can be extended in the presence of disturbances by computing the worst case for all d, i.e.,

$$\tilde{\delta} = \max_{i \in \Lambda} \max_{d \in D} \max_{x_0 \in \partial B} \|x_{T,i}(x_0, d) - x_d\|$$

To stay inside the admissible set F, we have to impose the condition that $\tilde{\delta} \le \delta_{\max}$. This requires a modification of the algorithm in Figure 3 to compute $\tilde{\delta}$ for each step when is_good_delta is True. In our example, since δ was originally on the edge of the admissible set, the new ball will be naturally smaller. The values computed are $\delta = 0.18$, and $\tilde{\delta} = 0.33$ for a sampling period of $10\mu s$. The time to compute the solution is $6s$. Simulations with these values are shown in Figure 5. The state trajectories are guaranteed to stay inside $\tilde{B}$ in the presence of disturbances.

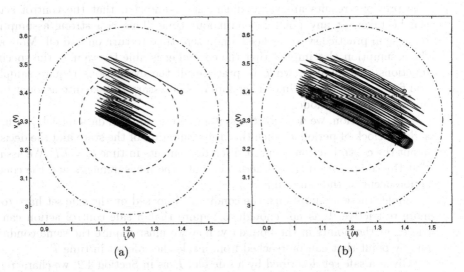

(a)   (b)

Fig. 5. State trajectories of the example system with sampling time $T = 10\mu s$, under the presence of disturbances, using (a) the minimum ripple controller, and (b) the minimum switching controller. The circle represents the initial state, the dashed line represents the boundary of B, and the dash-dotted line represents the boundary of $\tilde{B}$.

5   Design Example: A Double-Output DC-DC Converter

The circuit shown in Figure 6 is an extension of the previous example to a DC-DC converter with two outputs. While such circuits have been proposed (see [13]), traditional methods of analysis have not, to our knowledge, yielded a viable control scheme except for limited special cases. We apply the methodology described above to this example to show the useful scalability properties of our approach. There are now three switches that operate in an exclusive fashion,

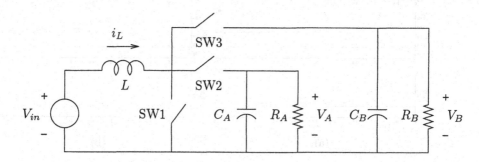

Fig. 6. Double output DC-DC converter

adding another discrete state. The additional capacitor adds another continuous state, and the extra load becomes another disturbance. The task of the controller is now to independently regulate the two output voltages V_A and V_B by switching among three discrete states. If we define the state vector as $x = [i_L \ V_A \ V_B]^T$, the continuous dynamics associated with these states are governed by Equation 3.1 where

$$A_1 = \begin{bmatrix} 0 & 0 & 0 \\ 0 & -\frac{1}{R_A C_A} & 0 \\ 0 & 0 & -\frac{1}{R_B C_B} \end{bmatrix}, \quad A_2 = \begin{bmatrix} 0 & -\frac{1}{L} & 0 \\ \frac{1}{C_A} & -\frac{1}{R_A C_A} & 0 \\ 0 & 0 & -\frac{1}{R_B C_B} \end{bmatrix},$$

$$A_3 = \begin{bmatrix} 0 & 0 & -\frac{1}{L} \\ 0 & -\frac{1}{R_A C_A} & 0 \\ \frac{1}{C_B} & 0 & -\frac{1}{R_B C_B} \end{bmatrix}, \quad b = \begin{bmatrix} \frac{v_{in}}{L} \\ 0 \\ 0 \end{bmatrix}$$

The circuit parameters are $L = 75\mu H$, $R_A = 6.25\Omega$, $R_B = 34.1\Omega$, $C_A = 800\mu F$, $C_B = 146.6\mu F$, and $V_{in} = 1.5V$. The desired output voltages are $V_{A,d} = 1.875V$ and $V_{B,d} = 3.75V$. The steady-state current, computed using an energy balance equation, is $i_{L,d} = 0.65A$. The output voltages are restricted to $\pm 10\%$, and the current limited to the range $[0, 2.5]A$. The load resistors can vary by $+5\%$, and the input voltage by -5%. The range of variation of the steady-state current for the given range of disturbances is $[0.619, 0.684]A$.

Given these specifications, the admissible set is the rectangular set $F = \{x \in \mathbb{R}^3 : 0 \leq x_1 \leq 2.5, 1.6975 \leq x_2 \leq 2.0625, 3.375 \leq x_3 \leq 4.125\}$. The set point is $x = [.65 \ 1.875 \ 3.75]^T$. Then $\delta_{max} = .1875$.

Introducing a sampling time $T = 2.5\mu s$, we compute $\delta = .1$ and $\tilde{\delta} = .18$, using the same algorithm as in the previous section. The computation time is $654s$ on the same computer.

Figure 7 shows simulations of the "minimum ripple" and the "minimum switching" controllers, designed according to the results above.

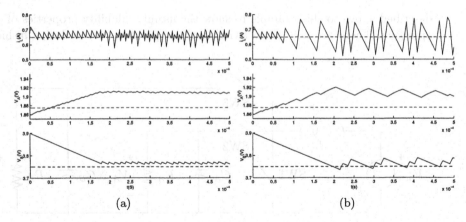

(a)   (b)

Fig. 7. State trajectories of the Single-Input Double-Output DC-DC converter with a sampling time $T = 2.5\mu s$, using (a) the minimum ripple controller, and (b) the minimum switching controller. The dashed line represents the ideal steady-state values.

6   Conclusions and Future Work

We have addressed the study of power electronics circuits using a hybrid systems framework. A general model for power electronics circuits was described. This model is superior to averaged, linearized models in that no approximation is involved, and the controller synthesis is not limited by the model. We developed a simple method for synthesizing the guards that guarantee the safety property, by constructing a ball–shaped safe set. The advantage of this method is that decisions can be made with a small computation effort (just an inner product), making it very convenient for real-time control. Although we restricted our analysis to a ball shape, it is evident that the same methodology can be extended to an ellipsoid shape. The selection of an optimal ellipsoid is an interesting problem left for future research.

Implementation issues such as disturbances and non-zero switching time were addressed. We presented an algorithm to solve the safety synthesis problem for power electronics formulated in Problem 2. However, an important issue exists in the use of sampling in both spatial and temporal domains to validate the safety properties of balls of interest. The safety property is only guaranteed for the sampling points on the boundary of the safe ball at specified times. More research is needed into enhanced algorithms to ensure that the safety property is guaranteed for all points in both domains. One possible research direction is to incorporate the reachability tools developed for hybrid systems to automate the synthesis procedure, even in the presence of finite computation time and disturbances. The techniques presented in this paper may be inefficient for large-dimensional state spaces. However, a large set of problems in power electronics have state spaces of small dimension.

Single–output and double–output DC-DC converters were used as examples to illustrate the favorable properties of our approach. The double–output problem, when considered using hybrid techniques, was shown to be only marginally more difficult to formulate than the single–output problem. The same cannot be said of linear control methods.

We conclude that hybrid systems techniques are a natural choice for power electronics circuits. In the particular case of the double–output DC-DC converter, our approach led to the design of a viable controller; to the best of our knowledge, a solution to this problem has not yet been reported in the literature.

References

1. John G. Kassakian, Marin F. Schlecht and George C. Verghese. *Principles of Power Electronics*, Addison-Wesley, 1991.
2. S. Banerjee and G.C. Verghese. *Nonlinear Phenomena in Power Electronics*. IEEE Press, 2001.
3. R. Alur and D. Dill. A theory of time automata. *Theoretical Computer Science*, 126:183–235, 1994.
4. R. Alur and T.A. Henzinger. Modularity for timed and hybrid systems. In *Proceedings of the Eighth International Conference on Concurrency Theory (CONCUR)*, pages 74–88, 1997.
5. J. Lygeros, C. Tomlin, S. Sastry. Controllers for Reachability Specifications for Hybrid Systems, *Automatica*, Volume 35, Number 3, March 1999.
6. G. Lafferriere, G.J. Pappas, S. Yovine. Reachability Computation for Linear Hybrid Systems. In *Proceedings of the 14th IFAC World Congress*, volume E, pages 7–12, Beijing, 1999.
7. A.B. Kurzhanski, P.Varaiya. Ellipsoidal Techniques for Reachability Analysis, *Hybrid Systems : Computation and Control*, Lecture Notes in Computer Science, 2000.
8. A. Chutinan, B.H. Krogh, Verification of polyhedral-invariant hybrid systems using polygonal flow pipe approximations, *Hybrid Systems : Computation and Control*, Lecture Notes in Computer Science, 1999.
9. E. Asarin, O. Bournez, T. Dang, O. Maler, A. Pnueli. Effective Synthesis of Switching Controllers for Linear Systems, *The Proceedings of IEEE*, Volume 88, Number 7, Pages 1011–1025, July 2000.
10. C. Tomlin, J. Lygeros, S. Sastry. A Game Theoretic Approach to Controller Design for Hybrid Systems, *The Proceedings of IEEE*, Volume 88, Number 7, Pages 949–970, July 2000.
11. C. Altafini, A. Speranzon, K. H. Johansson. Hybrid Control of a Truck and Trailer Vehicle, *Hybrid Systems : Computation and Control*, Lecture Notes in Computer Science, 2002.
12. Ian Mitchell and Claire Tomlin. Level Set Methods for Computation in Hybrid Systems, *Hybrid Systems : Computation and Control*, LCNS series, Volume 1790, Springer-Verlag, 2000.
13. Wing-Hung Ki and Dongsheng Ma. Single-Inductor Multiple-Output Switching Converters, *IEEE Power Electronics Specialists Conference*, pp.226–231, 2001.
14. G. Collins, H. Hong. Partial Cylindrical Algebraic Decomposition for Quantifier Elimination, *J. Symb. Comput.*, 12, 199–328, 1991.
15. A. Dolzman, T. Sturm. REDLOG: Computer Algebra Meets Computer Logic. *ACM SIGSAM Bulletin*, 31, 2–9, 1997.

On the Optimal Control of Hybrid Systems: Optimization of Trajectories, Switching Times, and Location Schedules

M. Shahid Shaikh and Peter E. Caines

Department of Electrical & Computer Engineering,
McGill University, Montréal, Québec, Canada H3A 2A7.
{msshaikh,peterc}@cim.mcgill.ca

Abstract. A class of hybrid optimal control problems is formulated and a set of necessary conditions for hybrid system trajectory optimality is presented. These conditions constitute generalizations of the standard Maximum Principle (MP). Employing these conditions, we propose a class of general Hybrid Maximum Principle (HMP) based algorithms for hybrid systems optimization; these algorithms and the associated theory appear to be significantly simpler than some of the recently proposed algorithms (see [13], [14], for example). Using results from the theory of penalty function methods and Ekeland's variational principle we show the convergence of these algorithms under reasonable assumptions. The efficacy of the proposed algorithms is illustrated via several computational examples.

1 Introduction

In this paper we formulate a class of optimal control problems for general hybrid systems with nonlinear dynamics in each location and with autonomous and controlled switchings. We present a set of necessary conditions for hybrid system optimality related to those in [12], [7], [14]; for simplicity of exposition, the results presented here take control inputs to lie in an open control value set $U \subset \mathbb{R}^u$; in [8], [9] we also establish a more general related result where the controls are subject to box constraint conditions where the control lies in the interior or on the boundary of a closed set U. For hybrid systems in these classes we describe a new class of so-called Hybrid Maximum Principle (HMP) algorithms for the solution of optimal control problems. In [13], Xu and Antsaklis give conditions for the optimality of hybrid systems: a fixed switching schedule and controlled switchings are assumed but no autonomous switchings are permitted. An algorithm is proposed and numerical examples provided which establish the applicability of the proposed methods in the case of linear dynamics with quadratic cost criteria. In [14], Xu and Antsaklis show how their algorithm can be modified for systems with internally forced (autonomous) switchings and nonlinear dynamics. A direct comparison of computational times with those resulting from the methods presented in this paper is not possible since running times are not reported in

O. Maler and A. Pnueli (Eds.): HSCC 2003, LNCS 2623, pp. 466–481, 2003.

[13], [14]; however, it appears that the algorithms presented here are simpler and more efficient than those of [13], [14]. The computational times reported in Examples 1 and 2 in Section 3 are considered to be rapid for the problems under consideration.

In the current paper we provide convergence results for an optimization algorithm (denoted HMP[MAS]) with multiple autonomous switchings (MAS) on guard manifolds. Our convergence proofs are based on results from the theory of the penalty function methods [1] and Ekeland's variational principle [6]. This algorithm extends directly to the case of controlled switchings in a fixed schedule. We present a multiple controlled switching (MCS) times algorithm (denoted HMP[MCS]) which invokes (i.e. calls) HMP[MAS] and computes optimal switching times for a given switching schedule. The efficacy of these algorithms is illustrated via several computational examples.

We further briefly propose combinatoric search algorithms of [8], [9], which generate a list of Hamming distance ($\leq k$) sequences from an initial sequence, executes Algorithm HMP[MCS] on each one of them, and finds the best locally k-optimal sequence from among them.

2 Optimal Control of Hybrid Systems

2.1 Hybrid System

Within the standard overall framework (see e.g. [3], [4]) we define a hybrid control system as follows:

Definition 1. *A hybrid control system* $\mathbb{H}$ *is a 6-tuple*

$$\mathbb{H} \underline{\Delta} \{H \underline{\Delta} Q \times \mathbb{R}^n, I \underline{\Delta} \Sigma \times U, F, \Gamma, \mathcal{M}\}, \tag{1}$$

where
$Q = \{q_1, \cdots, q_k\}$ *is a finite set of* discrete states *(which are called* control locations*);*
H *is the* (hybrid) state space *of* $\mathbb{H}$*;*
$U \subset \mathbb{R}^u$ *is the set of* admissible input control values *lying in an open set in* $\mathbb{R}^u$*. The set of* admissible input control functions *is* $\mathcal{U} \underline{\Delta} L_\infty(U; [0, T_*))$*, the set of all bounded measurable functions on some interval* $[0, T_*)$*,* $T_* \leq \infty$*, taking values in* U*;*
$\Sigma = \Sigma_u \dot{\cup} \Sigma_c \dot{\cup} \{id\}$ *is a finite set of autonomous (uncontrolled) and controlled transition labels extended with the identity element* $\{id\}$*;*
$I \underline{\Delta} \Sigma \times U$ *is the set of system input values;*
$F : Q \times \mathbb{R}^n \times U \to \mathbb{R}^n$ *is an indexed collection of* vector fields $\{f_{q_i}\}_{q_i \in Q}$*, such that* $f_{q_i} : \mathbb{R}^n \times U \to \mathbb{R}^n$ *is a vector field assigned to each control location and* $f_{q_i} \in C^k(\mathbb{R}^n \times U), k \geq 1$*;*
$\Gamma : H \times \Sigma \to H$ *is a time independent (partially defined) discrete transition map;*

$\mathcal{M} = \{M_\alpha : \alpha \in P\}$, where $P \subset Q \times Q$, $M_\alpha : \mathbb{R} \times \mathbb{R}^n \to \mathbb{R}^m$, $m = n - 1$, is a collection of guards such that, for $\alpha = (q_i, q_j)$, $\tilde{M}_\alpha = \{(t, x) : M_\alpha(t, x) = 0\}$ is a smooth codimension 1 submanifold of $\mathbb{R}^{n+1}$ and for all t $\tilde{M}_\alpha(t) = \{x : M_\alpha(t, x) = 0\}$, is a smooth codimension 1 $(q_i$ to $q_j)$ switching submanifold of $\mathbb{R}^n$. It is assumed that $\tilde{M}_\alpha(t) \cap \tilde{M}_\beta(t) = \emptyset$, for all $t \in \mathbb{R}$, $\alpha, \beta \in P$, $\alpha \neq \beta$. $\qquad\square$

2.2 Standing Assumptions (A1–A8)

A1 There exists $K_f < \infty$ and $L_f < \infty$ such that $\|f_{q_i}(x, u)\| \leq K_f$, $x \in \mathbb{R}^n$, $u \in U$, $q_i \in Q$. and $\|f_{q_i}(x_1, u) - f_{q_i}(x_2, u)\| \leq L_f \|x_1 - x_2\|$, $x_1, x_2 \in \mathbb{R}^n$, $u \in U$, $q_i \in Q$.

A2 The matrix $\frac{\partial M_{q_i q_j}}{\partial x}(t, x)$ has full rank for all $x \in \mathbb{R}^n$ and all $q_i, q_j \in Q$.

A3 $f_{q_i}(x, u_1)$ and $f_{q_j}(x, u_2)$ are transversal to $\tilde{M}_{q_i q_j}$ for all $x \in \mathbb{R}^n$, $u_1, u_2 \in U$, $q_i, q_j \in Q$.

A4 $\|\frac{\partial M_{q_i q_j}}{\partial x}\| \leq K_1 < \infty$ for all $(t, x) \in \mathbb{R} \times \mathbb{R}^n$ and for all $q_i, q_j \in Q$. $\|\frac{\partial M_{q_i q_j}}{\partial t}\| \leq K_2 < \infty$ for all $(t, x) \in \mathbb{R} \times \mathbb{R}^n$, $q_i, q_j \in Q$.

Definition 2. A hybrid (system) time trajectory is a strictly increasing (finite or infinite) sequence of times $\tau = (t_0, t_1, t_2, \dots)$ or equivalently, a sequence of non-empty half open intervals $\tau = ([t_0, t_1), [t_1, t_2), \dots)$.
A hybrid (system) switching (event) sequence is a (finite or infinite) sequence $(\tau, \sigma) = ((t_0, \sigma_0), (t_1, \sigma_1), (t_2, \sigma_2), \dots)$ of pairs of times and discrete input events where τ is a hybrid time trajectory, $\sigma_0 = id$, $\sigma_i \in \Sigma$, $i \geq 1$, and where σ is called a location schedule.
A hybrid (system) input trajectory is a triple $I_{\mathbb{H}} \triangleq (\tau, \sigma, u)$ defined on a half open interval $[t_0, T), T \leq \infty$, where (τ, σ) is a hybrid switching sequence and $u \in \mathcal{U}$. $\qquad\square$

Definition 3. A hybrid state trajectory is a triple (τ, q, x) consisting of a hybrid time trajectory $\tau = (t_0, t_1, t_2, \dots)$, an associated sequence of discrete states $q = (q_0, q_1, q_2, \dots)$, and a sequence $x = (x_{q_0}, x_{q_1}, x_{q_2}, \dots)$ absolutely continuous and hence almost everywhere differentiable functions of time taking values in $\mathbb{R}^n$, such that $x_{q_j} : [t_j, t_{j+1}) \to (q_j, \mathbb{R}^n)$. $\qquad\square$

Definition 4. A hybrid system execution $e_{\mathbb{H}} = (\tau, \sigma, u, q, x)$ for the hybrid system $\mathbb{H}$ is a hybrid input trajectory (τ, σ, u), defined over an interval $[t_0, T)$, together with a hybrid state trajectory (τ, q, x) defined over and interval $[t_0, T') \subset [t_0, T)$, which satisfies the following conditions:

(i) (continuous dynamics)

$$CS : \qquad \frac{d}{dt} x_{q_j}(t) = f_{q_j}(x_{q_j}(t), u(t)), \qquad a.e. \ t \in [t_j, t_{j+1}), \qquad (2)$$

i.e. $x_{q_j}(\cdot)$ is an absolutely continuous function such that $\dot{x}_{q_j}(t) = f_{q_j}(x_{q_j}(t), u(t))$, a.e. $t \in [t_j, t_{j+1})$,

(ii) (controlled discrete dynamics)

In the hybrid execution $e_{\mathbb{H}}$ *consider the hybrid switching time* t_i, $i \geq 1$, *at which the left limit* $\lim_{t \uparrow \uparrow t_i} x_{q_{i-1}}(t) = x^*(t_i)$ *exists. A controlled discrete transition occurs at* $t = t_i$ *if there exists a discrete control input* $\sigma_i \in \Sigma_c$ *for which*

$$DSC: \qquad \Gamma_c(q_{i-1}, \sigma_i(t_i)) \equiv \Gamma_c(q_{i-1}, \sigma_i) = q_i, \qquad (t_i, \sigma_i) \in (\tau, \sigma), \quad (3)$$

with $q_{i-1} \neq q_i$ *and* $x_{q_i}(t_i) = x^*(t_i)$. *In this case* t_i *is a* controlled switching time.

(iii) (autonomous discrete dynamics)

In the hybrid execution $e_{\mathbb{H}}$, *at the switching time* t_i, $i \geq 1$, *the limit from the left at* t_i *exists and satisfies* $\lim_{t \uparrow \uparrow t_i} x_{q_{i-1}}(t) = x^*(t_i)$. *A discrete transition occurs at* $t = t_i$ *if*

$$DSU: \qquad M_{q_{i-1}, q_i}(t_i, x^*(t_i)) = 0, \qquad t_i \in \tau, \tag{4}$$

where $M_{q_{i-1}, q_i}(t, x) = 0$ *defines a switching manifold. Such a transition, denoted by* Γ_u, *corresponds to an element* $\sigma_i \in \Sigma_u$. *In this case* t_i *is an* autonomous switching time. □

A5 For every $q_i, q_j \in Q$ there exists $\sigma_{ij} \in \Sigma_c$ such that $\Gamma_c(q_i, \sigma_{ij}) = q_j$.

A6 (Non-Zeno condition) There exists $T_r > 0$ such that if t_s is a switching time then $t_0 < t_s - T_r$, $t_f > t_s + T_r$ and there is no other switching time in the interval $[t_s - T_r, t_s + T_r]$.

A7 A switching time is either controlled, or autonomous, but not both.

A8 The initial state $(x_0 \underset{\triangle}{=} x(t_0), q_0) \in \mathbb{H}$ is such that at initial time $t_0 \in \mathbb{R}$, $M_{q_0 q_j}(t_0, x_0) \neq 0$, $q_j \in Q$.

A hybrid system $\mathbb{H}$ and an initial hybrid state (q_0, x_0) satisfying assumptions A1–A8 with time invariant switching manifolds possesses a unique hybrid execution; this existence and uniqueness result is given its complete statement and proved in [5], [8], [9].

2.3   The Hybrid Optimal Control Problem

Let $l_{q_i} : \mathbb{R}^n \times U \to \mathbb{R}$, denote a *loss function* for each $q_i \in Q$, satisfying the following assumptions:

A9 There exist $K_l < \infty$ and $L_l < \infty$ such that $|l_{q_i}(x, u)| \leq K_l$, $x \in \mathbb{R}^n$, $u \in U$, $q_i \in Q$, and $|l_{q_i}(x_1, u) - l_{q_i}(x_2, u)| \leq L_l \|x_1 - x_2\|$, $x_1, x_2 \in \mathbb{R}^n$, $u \in U$, $q_i \in Q$.

Let $S_{\mathbb{H}} = ((t_0, \sigma_0), (t_1, \sigma_1), \dots, (t_L, \sigma_L))$ or $S_{\mathbb{H}} = ((t_0, q_0), (t_1, q_1), \dots, (t_L, q_L))$ be a hybrid switching sequence. Let $I_{\mathbb{H}} = (S_{\mathbb{H}}, u)$, $u \in \mathcal{U}$ be a hybrid input trajectory. Then for given initial and final times t_0 and t_f initial hybrid state $h_0 = (q_0, x_0)$ the hybrid system $\mathbb{H}$ has a well defined execution. We define the hybrid cost function as:

$$J(t_0, h_0; I_{\mathbb{H}}) \triangleq \sum_{i=0}^{L} \int_{t_i}^{t_{i+1}} l_{q_i}(x_{q_i}(s), u(s))\, ds + g(x_{q_L}(t_f)), \tag{5}$$

where

$$\dot{x}_{q_i}(t) = f_{q_i}(x_{q_i}(t), u(t)), \quad a.e.\ t \in [t_i, t_{i+1}), \quad i = 0, 1, \ldots, L,$$
$$h_0 = (q_0, x_{q_i}(t_0)) = (q_0, x_0),$$
$$x_{q_i}(t_i) = \lim_{t \uparrow t_i} x_{q_{i-1}}(t), \quad i = 1, 2, \ldots, L+1, \quad \text{and}$$
$$t_{L+1} = t_f,$$

and where

A10 $|g(x)| \le K_g$, $x \in \mathbb{R}^n$, $L_g < \infty$. $g \in C^k(\mathbb{R}^n : \mathbb{R}_+)$, $k \ge 1$.

Proposition 1. *([8], [9]) Under Assumption A6, if t_f is finite then L is finite and $L \le \lfloor (t_f - t_0)/T_r \rfloor$.*

Given the system $\mathbb{H}$ with continuous dynamics (2) and discrete dynamics (3, 4), loss functions $\{l_q, q \in Q\}$, initial and final times, t_0, t_f, and the initial hybrid state $h_0 = (q_0, x_0)$, the *hybrid optimal control problem* (HOCP(t_0, t_f, h_0)) is to find a hybrid input trajectory $I_{\mathbb{H}}^0$ such that hybrid cost function (5) is minimized. In Theorem 1 below we consider the case $g \equiv 0$, where the final continuous state x_f is fixed; it employs the following strong small time local controllability hypothesis which is not found in [7], [14].

Definition 5. *(Strong Small Time Local Controllability (SSTLC)) The system (CS) satisfies the SSTLC property (with respect to $\mathcal{U}$) at $x_0 \in \mathbb{R}^n$ if for all sufficiently small $T > 0$ and all sufficiently small neighborhoods $B_\epsilon(x_0) \triangleq \{x \in \mathbb{R}^n : \|x - x_0\| < \epsilon\}$, there exists $\delta = \delta(\epsilon) < \epsilon$ such that for any $x, y \in B_\delta(x_0)$ there is an admissible input function $u(\cdot) \in \mathcal{U}$ such that $\phi(t, x, u) = y$ for some t, $0 \le t \le T$, which satisfies $\phi(s, x, u) \in B_\epsilon(x_0)$, $0 \le s \le t$. The system (CS) is said to be Strong Small Time Locally Controllable (with respect to $\mathcal{U}$) if the SSTLC property holds at all $x_0 \in \mathbb{R}^n$.* □

Theorem 1. *([8], [9] after [7]) Consider a hybrid system $\mathbb{H}$ satisfying assumptions A1-A6, and an HOCP$(t_0, x_0, q_0; t_f, x_f, q_f)$. Let a switching schedule S^0, an admissible input function $u^0 \in \mathcal{U}$ and the resulting continuous state trajectory x^0 be optimal and assume that the continuous system in each location satisfies the SSTLC property, then*

(i) there exists a (continuous to the right), piecewise absolutely continuous adjoint process λ^0 satisfying

$$\dot{\lambda}^0 = -\frac{\partial H_{q_i}}{\partial x}(x^0, \lambda^0, u^0), \quad a.e.\ t \in (t_{s_i}, t_{s_{i+1}}), \quad i \in \{0, 1, 2, \ldots, |S^0|\},$$

where the following boundary value conditions hold with $\lambda^0(t_0)$ and $\lambda^0(t_f)$ free:

(a) if t_{s_i} is a controlled switching time then $\lambda^0(t_{s_i}-) \equiv \lambda^0(t_{s_i}) = \lambda^0(t_{s_i}+)$, $i \in \{0, 1, 2, \ldots, |S^0|\}$,

(b) if t_{s_i} is an autonomous switching time satisfying $M_{q_k,q_j}(x(t_{s_i}), t_{s_i}) = 0$ then

$$\lambda^0(t_{s_i}-) \equiv \lambda^0(t_{s_i}) = \lambda^0(t_{s_i}+) + \left. \frac{\partial M_{q_k,q_j}}{\partial x} p \right|_{t=t_{s_i}}$$

for some $p \in \mathbb{R}^m$, where $q(t) = \begin{cases} q_k & t \in (t_{s_{i-1}}, t_{s_i}) \\ q_j & t \in (t_{s_i}, t_{s_{i+1}}), \end{cases}$

(ii) the Hamiltonian minimization conditions are satisfied, i.e.

(a) $H_{q_i}(x^0(t), \lambda^0(t), u^0(t)) \leq H_{q_i}(x^0(t), \lambda^0(t), u)$, $\forall u \in U$, $t \in [t_{s_i}, t_{s_{i+1}})$, $i \in \{0, 1, 2, \ldots, |S^0|\}$

(b) $H_{q_i}(x^0(t), \lambda^0(t), u^0(t)) \leq H_{q_k}(x^0(t), \lambda^0(t), u^0(t))$, $t \in [t_{s_i}, t_{s_{i+1}})$, $k \in \{0, 1, 2, \ldots, |S^0|\}$.

(iii) Let $H(t) \underline{\Delta} H_{q_i}(t)$, $t \in [t_{s_i}, t_{s_{i+1}})$, $i \in \{0, 1, 2, \ldots, |S^0|\}$. If t_{s_i} is a controlled switching time then the following Hamiltonian continuity conditions hold at $t = t_{s_i}$

$$H(t_{s_i}-) \equiv H_{q_{i-1}}(t_{s_i}-) = H_{q_{i-1}}(t_{s_i}) = H_{q_i}(t_{s_i}) = H_{q_i}(t_{s_i}+)$$
$$\equiv H(t_{s_i}+),$$

uniquely defining $H(t_{s_i})$, and

(iv) if t_{s_i} is an autonomous switching time satisfying $M_{q_i,q_j}(x(t_{s_i}), t_{s_i}) = 0$ then the following transversality condition holds at $t = t_{s_i}$

$$H(t_{s_i}) \equiv H_{q_i}(t_{s_i}) = H_{q_i}(t_{s_i}+) \equiv H(t_{s_i}+) = H_{q_{i-1}}(t_{s_i}-) + \left. \frac{\partial M_{q_k,q_i}}{\partial t} p \right|_{t=t_{s_i}}$$

$$\equiv H(t_{s_i}-) + \left. \frac{\partial M_{q_k,q_i}}{\partial t} p \right|_{t=t_{s_i}}.$$

In case there are no autonomous switchings the SSTLC controllability hypothesis can be omitted.

3 Hybrid Trajectory Optimization Algorithms

Based on Theorem 1, we formulate the following algorithm for optimizing the location switching times τ and associated continuous controls u for a given location switching schedule σ.

3.1 HMP[MAS] (Multiple Autonomous Switchings) Algorithm

For simplicity we present the single autonomous switching case (see Comment 2 below).

1. Algorithm Initialization: Fix $0 < \epsilon_1 \ll 1$, $0 < \epsilon_2 \ll 1$, $0 < \epsilon_f \ll 1$ and $0 \le \mu \le 1$. Let (t_s, x_s) be a nominal switching time-state pair such that $t_0 < t_s < t_f$. Set the iteration counter $k = 0$. Set $t_s^k = t_s$ and. $x_s^k = x_s$. Compute the optimal control functions $u_1^k(t)$, $0 \le t < t_s$ and $u_2^k(t)$, $t_s \le t \le t_f$. Compute the associated state and costate trajectories and Hamiltonians over the two intervals $[0, t_s^k]$ and $[t_s^k, t_f]$, with the terminal state pairs (x_0, x_s^k) and (x_s^k, x_f) respectively. Also compute the new total cost $J^k(t_s^k, x_s^k)$.

2. Increment k by 1. Compute $\frac{\partial M}{\partial x}(t_s^{k-1}, x_s^{k-1})$ and $\frac{\partial M}{\partial t}(t_s^{k-1}, x_s^{k-1})$.

3. Set $\eta_k \triangleq \left\| \begin{pmatrix} H_1^k(t_s^{k-1}) - H_2^k(t_s^{k-1}) \\ \lambda_2^k(t_s^{k-1}) - \lambda_1^k(t_s^{k-1}) \end{pmatrix} - \begin{pmatrix} \frac{\partial M}{\partial t}(t_s^{k-1}, x_s^{k-1}) \\ \frac{\partial M}{\partial x}(t_s^{k-1}, x_s^{k-1}) \end{pmatrix} p^k \right\|^2$
$+ \left\| M(t_s^{k-1}, x_s^{k-1}) \right\|^2.$

Set $Q_k \triangleq \begin{pmatrix} \frac{\partial M}{\partial t}(t_s^{k-1}, x_s^{k-1}) \\ \frac{\partial M}{\partial x}(t_s^{k-1}, x_s^{k-1}) \end{pmatrix}$ and compute the unique minimizing argu-

ment $p^k \in \mathbb{R}^m$ of η_k given by $p^k = (Q_k^T Q_k)^{-1} Q_k^T \begin{pmatrix} H_1^k(t_s^{k-1}) - H_2^k(t_s^{k-1}) \\ \lambda_2^k(t_s^{k-1}) - \lambda_1^k(t_s^{k-1}) \end{pmatrix}$.

4. Set $t_s^k = t_s^{k-1} - \epsilon_1 \left(H_1^k(t_s^{k-1}) - H_2^k(t_s^{k-1}) - \frac{\partial M}{\partial t}(t_s^{k-1}, x_s^{k-1}) p^k \right)$
$- \epsilon_1 \frac{\partial M}{\partial t}(t_s^{k-1}, x_s^{k-1}) M(t_s^{k-1}, x_s^{k-1}).$

5. Set $x_s^k = x_s^{k-1} - \epsilon_2 \left(\lambda_2^k(t_s^{k-1}) - \lambda_1^k(t_s^{k-1}) - \frac{\partial M}{\partial x}(t_s^{k-1}, x_s^{k-1}) p^k \right)$
$- \epsilon_2 \frac{\partial M}{\partial x}(t_s^{k-1}, x_s^{k-1}) M(t_s^{k-1}, x_s^{k-1}).$

6. Compute the optimal control functions $u_1^k(t)$, $0 \le t < t_s$ and $u_2^k(t)$, $t_s \le t \le t_f$. Compute the associated state and costate trajectories and Hamiltonians over the two intervals $[0, t_s^k]$ and $[t_s^k, t_f]$ with the terminal state pairs (x_0, x_s^k) and (x_s^k, x_f) respectively. Next, compute the new total cost $J^k(t_s^k, x_s^k)$.

7. If $\mu(J^{k-1}(t_s^{k-1}, x_s^{k-1}) - J^k(t_s^k, x_s^k)) + (1 - \mu)\eta_k < \epsilon_f$ then STOP; else go to Step 2.

Comments on HMP[MAS].

1. Since there is no switching cost, the function $J(t_s, x_s)$ is continuous but not necessarily differentiable at $(t_s^{\text{opt}}, x_s^{\text{opt}})$ (see [8], [9]). The expressions $\left(H_1^k(t_s^{k-1}) - H_2^k(t_s^{k-1}) - \frac{\partial M}{\partial t}(t_s^{k-1}, x_s^{k-1}) p^k \right)$ and $\left(\lambda_2^k(t_s^{k-1}) - \lambda_1^k(t_s^{k-1}) - \frac{\partial M}{\partial x}(t_s^{k-1}, x_s^{k-1}) p^k \right)$ approximate $\frac{\partial J^{\text{opt}}}{\partial t}(t_s^{k-1}, x_s^{k-1})$ and $\frac{\partial J^{\text{opt}}}{\partial x}(t_s^{k-1}, x_s^{k-1})$, respectively, in the neighbourhood of $(t_s^{\text{opt}}, x_s^{\text{opt}})$ where $M(t_s^{\text{opt}}, x_s^{\text{opt}}) = 0$ (see [2], [8], [9]). Hence their use in Steps 3 and 4 where we note that on $\{M(t, x) = 0\}$ their approximation of $\frac{\partial J^{\text{opt}}}{\partial x}$ and $\frac{\partial J^{\text{opt}}}{\partial x}$ guarantees that the steps in 3, 4 are in the correct direction.

2. Algorithm 3.1 can be generalized to the multiple autonomous switchings case in a straightforward manner. This is possible because of assumption A6 and because by the assumption on switching manifolds they never intersect. The algorithm can also be specialized to the controlled switchings case by skipping Step 2 and setting $p^k = 0$ in Steps 3 and 4.
3. The optimal control functions in Steps 0 nd 5 of the algorithm can be computed using the HHADP methodology which is an extension of the Hierarchically Accelerated Dynamic Programming (HADP) methodology (see [10], [8], [9]) to continuous time continuous state systems.
4. We observe that, as for HMP[MAS], the recently proposed hybrid control algorithms (see [13], [14]) repeatedly compute the optimal controls.
5. Let $\delta z_s^k \triangleq \begin{pmatrix} \delta t_s^k \\ \delta x_s^k \end{pmatrix} = \begin{pmatrix} t_s^k - t_s^{k-1} \\ x_s^k - x_s^{k-1} \end{pmatrix}$ and $\gamma_k \triangleq \begin{pmatrix} H_1^k(t_s^{k-1}) - H_2^k(t_s^{k-1}) \\ \lambda_2^k(t_s^{k-1}) - \lambda_1^k(t_s^{k-1}) \end{pmatrix}$.

Assume that at iteration k (t_s^{k-1}, x_s^{k-1}) is in the switching manifold, i.e. $M(t_s^{k-1}, x_s^{k-1}) = 0$. Then by Taylor series expansion:

$$M(t_s^k, x_s^k) = \frac{\partial M^T}{\partial t}(t_s^{k-1}, x_s^{k-1})\delta t_s^k + \frac{\partial M^T}{\partial x}(t_s^{k-1}, x_s^{k-1})\delta x_s^k + o(\|\delta z_s^k\|)$$

$$= Q_k^T \delta z_s^k + o(\|\delta z_s^k\|). \tag{6}$$

We note Q_k has full rank by assumption A2. The update equations in Steps 2, 3, 4 (setting $\epsilon_1 = \epsilon_2 = \epsilon$) are $\delta z_k = -\epsilon(\gamma_k - Q_k p^k)$. The analytic minimization of η_k with respect to p^k yields $p^k = (Q_k^T Q_k)^{-1} Q_k^T \gamma_k$ and this implies that $Q_k^T \delta z_s^k = -\epsilon Q_k^T(\gamma_k - Q_k p^k) = 0$. (This corresponds to the fact that the vector difference of γ_k and its orthogonal projection on the span $\mathrm{Sp}(Q_k)$ of the columns of Q_k, i.e. the normals to the switching manifold $\{M = 0\}$, is orthogonal to $\mathrm{Sp}(Q_k)$.) Hence Equation 6 implies:

Lemma 1. *Let $\epsilon_1 = \epsilon_2 = \epsilon$. At any iteration k in the Algorithm HMP[MAS], if (t_s^{k-1}, x_s^{k-1}) is such that $M(t_s^{k-1}, x_s^{k-1}) = 0$ then $M(t_s^k, x_s^k)$ is of $o(\|\delta z_s^k\|)$, i.e. to first order, δz_s^k lies in the tangent space $Q_k^\perp$ to the switching manifold $\{M = 0\}$.*

We state the convergence properties of the algorithm HMP[MAS] in Proposition 2 below whose proof mimics that of the convergence of the interior penalty method for equality constrained finite dimensional optimization problems [1].

3.2   General Results for Penalty Function Methods

Given a fixed initial state $x(0) = x_0$, assumption A1 implies that $\|x(t)\| \leq \|x_0\| + K_1 t_f$, $0 \leq t \leq t_f$. Hence if t_f is finite then the set $S_{x_0} \triangleq \{(t, x) \in [0, t_f] \times \mathbb{R}^n : \|x\| \leq \|x_0\| + K_1 t_f\} = [0, t_f] \times \{x \in \mathbb{R}^n : \|x\| \leq \|x_0\| + K_1 t_f\}$ is compact. Let us set $z \triangleq (t, x)$ and let $S \triangleq cl\{z \in S_{x_0} : M(z) \equiv M(t, x) = 0\}$. Notice that if $(t_s, x_s) \in S$ then $x(x_0, t_s) = x_s$. Clearly all switching time-state pairs lie in S; so assuming a switching time exists in the interval $[0, t_f]$, S is a nonempty compact set and S can be made a complete metric space by endowing it with the metric $d(z_1, z_2) \triangleq \|z_1 - z_2\|$.

In Steps 0 and 5 of Algorithm HMP[MAS], since the (global) optimal cost in each location is optimal with respect to that location, the cost function J, as well as the error term η_k in Step 2, are functions of z_s. We treat the problem of minimizing $J(\cdot)$ with the constraint $\eta_k = 0$ via penalty function methods. Define a penalty function $R(z_s, r) \triangleq J(z_s) + r\eta(z_s) \triangleq J(z_s) + r(\|\gamma(z_s) - Q(z_s)p(z_s)\|^2 + \|M(z_s)\|^2) = J(z_s) + r(\|\gamma(z_s) - (Q^T(z_s)Q(z_s))^{-1}Q^T(z_s)\gamma(z_s)\|^2 + \|M(z_s)\|^2)$, where $z_s \triangleq (t_s, x_s)$, γ is defined above and J, γ and Q are computed at z_s as in Steps 2 and 3 of the Algorithm HMP[MAS].

To discuss general penalty function methods we consider the continuous functions $J, \eta : \mathbb{R}^n \to \mathbb{R}$ and the compact set S. (J, η, S in this section need not be identified with J, η, S in Section 3.1.)

Define a function $\psi(r) \triangleq \inf_{z \in S} \{J(z) + r\eta(z)\}$. Then in view of the compactness of S and the continuity of $J(\cdot)$, and $\eta(\cdot)$ it is clear that for each r there exists z_r in S such that $\psi(r) = \inf_{z \in S} \{J(z) + r\eta(z)\} = J(z_r) + r\eta(z_r)$.

Lemma 2. *([8], [9] after [1]) (i)* $\inf_{z \in S} \{J(z) : \eta(z) = 0\} \geq \sup_{r \geq 0} \psi(r)$; *(ii) (a)* $\eta(z_r)$ *is a decreasing function of* r, *(b)* $J(z_r)$ *is an increasing function of* r, *(c)* $\psi(r)$ *is an increasing function of* r.

Theorem 2. *([8], [9] after [1])*

$$\inf_{z \in S} \{J(z) : \eta(z) = 0\} = \sup_{r \geq 0} \psi(r) = \lim_{r \to \infty} \psi(r).$$

Proof. Since $\psi(r)$ is an increasing function of r, $\sup_{r \geq 0} \psi(r) = \lim_{r \to \infty} \psi(r)$.

We next show that $\lim_{r \to \infty} \eta(z_r) = 0$ by showing that for every $\epsilon > 0$ there is $r_\epsilon \in \Re$ such that, for all $r \geq r_\epsilon$, $\eta(z_r) \leq \epsilon$. Let $z_0 \in S$ be a feasible point, i.e. $\eta(z_0) = 0$ and let $\epsilon > 0$. Further, for $r = 1$, let $z_1 = \operatorname{argmin}_{z \in S} \{J(z) + \eta(z)\}$ (i.e. in this case $r = 1$). Finally take r to be such that $r \geq \frac{1}{\epsilon}|J(z_1) - J(z_0)| + 2$. Then, since $r > 1$, by Lemma 2 (ii)(b), $J(z_r) \geq J(z_1)$. In order to obtain a contradiction, assume that $\eta(z_r) > \epsilon$. Then $r\eta(z_r) > r\epsilon \geq |J(z_1) - J(z_0)| + 2\epsilon$. Then by Lemma 2,

$$\inf_{z \in S} \{J(z) : \eta(z) = 0\} \geq \psi(r) = J(z_r) + r\eta(z_r)$$
$$\geq J(z_1) + r\eta(z_r)$$
$$> J(z_1) + |J(z_1) - J(z_0)| + 2\epsilon$$
$$> J(z_1) + J(z_0) - J(z_1) + 2\epsilon$$
$$> J(z_0)$$

which is a contradiction. Hence $\eta(z_r) \leq \epsilon$ for such an r. Since ϵ is arbitrary, this shows that $\lim_{r \to \infty} \eta(z_r) = 0$.

Let $\{r_l : l \in \mathbb{Z}_1\}$ be a sequence tending to ∞, and let $\{z_{r_k}\}$ be a convergent subsequence of the infinite sequence $\{z_{r_l}\} \subset S$. Let $\{z_{r_k}\}$ converge to $\bar{z} \in S$.

Then

$$\sup_{r \geq 0} \psi(r) \geq \psi(r_k) = J(z_{r_k}) + r_k \eta(z_{r_k}) \geq J(z_{r_k}),$$

which by continuity of J implies that $\sup_{r \geq 0} \psi(r) \geq J(\bar{z})$.

Similarly, continuity of η implies that $\lim_{r_k \to \infty} \eta(z_{r_k}) = \eta(\bar{z}) = 0$. This shows that $\bar{z}$ is feasible. Again from Lemma 2

$$\inf_{z \in S} \{ J(z) : \eta(z) = 0 \} \geq \sup_{r \geq 0} \psi(r) \geq \sup_{r_k \to \infty} (J(z_{r_k}) + r_k \eta(z_{r_k})) \geq J(\bar{z}).$$

However, since $\inf_{z \in S} \{ J(z) : \eta(z) = 0 \} \leq J(\bar{z})$ we must have equality throughout in the above expression and hence $J(\bar{z}) = \sup_{r \geq 0} \psi(r) = \lim_{r \to \infty} \psi(r)$. Also since $0 \leq r_k \eta(z_{r_k}) \leq \sup_{r \geq 0} \psi(r) - J(z_{r_k})$ and since $\lim_{r_k \to \infty}(\sup_{r \geq 0} \psi(r) - J(z_{r_k})) = J(\bar{z}) - J(\bar{z}) = 0$ we must have $\lim_{r_k \to \infty} r_k \eta(z_{r_k}) = 0$. □

3.3 Convergence Analysis of Algorithm HMP[MAS]

Theorem 2 above is not immediately applicable to the convergence analysis of the Algorithm HMP[MAS]. Let us identify $J(z_k)$ here with $J^k(z_s^k)$ in Step 5 of the algorithm. Then the missing link is provided by the following key assumptions.

A11 There is a unique optimizing switching time-state pair $z_s^0 \triangleq (t_s^0, x_s^0) \in S$.

A12′ At the kth iteration, at Steps 3, 4 and 5, the Algorithm HMP[MAS] computes $z_k = \arg\min_{z \in S} \{ J(z) + r_k \eta(z) \}$, where the sequence $\{ r_k \}_{k=1}^{\infty}$ is a strictly increasing sequence of positive numbers such that $\lim_{k \to \infty} r_k = \infty$.

With these assumptions we may apply Theorem 2 to the Algorithm HMP[MAS] and immediately obtain the following result:

Proposition 2. ([8], [9]) *Under the standing assumptions and assumptions A11, A12′ the Algorithm HMP[MAS] generates a sequence $\{ z_k : k \geq 1 \}$ which converges to z_s^0.*

It is seen that assumption A12′ may be too restrictive for applications since it is unlikely that HMP[MAS] minimizes $J(z_k) + r_k \eta(z_k)$ at iteration k. We replace A12′ by the weaker assumption A12 as follows:

A12 z_k, $J(z_k)$ computed by Steps 3, 4 and 5 of Algorithm HMP[MAS] at iteration k are such that: $J(z_k) + r_k \eta(z_k) \leq \inf_{z \in S} \{ J(z) + r_k \eta(z) \} + \alpha_k$, where $\{ \alpha_k \}_{k \in \mathbb{Z}}$ is a sequence of positive numbers such that $\lim_{k \to \infty} \alpha_k = 0$.

Proposition 3. ([8], [9]) *Under the standing assumptions and assumptions A11, A12 HMP[MAS] generates a sequence $\{ z_k : k \geq 1 \}$ which converges to z_s^0 satisfying:*

$$J(z_s^0) = \inf_{z \in S} \{ J(z) : \eta(z) = 0 \} = \sup_{r \geq 0} \psi(r) = \lim_{r \to \infty} \psi(r).$$

Proof. The first equality follows by the continuity of $J(\cdot)$ and assumption A11. By assumption A12 the point computed at iteration k, z_k in S, is such that

$$J(z_k) + r_k\eta(z_k) \leq \inf_{z \in S}\{J(z) + r_k\eta(z)\} + \alpha_k.$$

Hence the hypotheses of Ekeland's theorem [6] are satisfied and so there is z_k^* in S such that at each iteration k, $\|z_k - z_k^*\| \leq \sqrt{\alpha_k}$ and z_k^* minimizes $G(z_k) = J(z_k) + r_k\eta(z_k) + \sqrt{\alpha_k}\|z_k - z_{r_k}^*\|$. Hence as k goes to infinity, the sequences $\sqrt{\alpha_k}$ and $\|z_k - z_k^*\|$ approach zero and by Theorem 2 the desired convergence result follows. $\square$

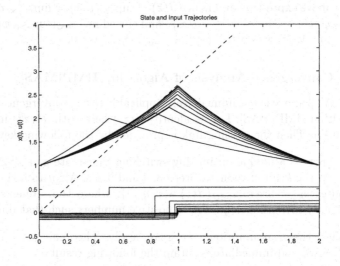

Fig. 1. Convergence to the Optimal Trajectory: single autonomous switching case

Example 1: To illustrate the Algorithm HMP[MAS] we consider a system which successively occupies the locations q_1 and q_2 and which has one switching manifold defined by $M(x,t) = x - et = 0$ ($e = 2.7183...$). The dynamics in q_1, q_2 are given by: $\dot{x} = x + xu$, $\dot{x} = -x + xu$, $t_0 = 0$, $t_f = 2$, $x(0) = 1$, $x(2) = 1$. The cost function to be minimized is: $J(u) = \dfrac{1}{2}\displaystyle\int_0^2 u^2(s)\,ds$.

Starting with the initial guess $t_s = 0.5$, $x_s = 2$, Figure 1 shows the convergence of $\{t_s^k, x_{s_1}^k\}_{k=1}^\infty$, to the unique optimal switching time $t_s = 1$ and state $x_s = e$. The unique optimal control in this case is $u^0 \equiv 0$ resulting in optimal cost $J^0 = 0$. The computation was performed using Matlab 6.0 on a Pentium III 550 MHz machine with 128MB of SDRAM running a Redhat Linux 6.2 operating system. It took 105.98 seconds of CPU time.

3.4   HMP[MCS] (Multiple Controlled Switchings, Fixed Schedule) Algorithm

1. Algorithm Initialization: Fix the H-tolerance $0 < h \ll 1$, λ-tolerance $0 < l \ll 1$, minimum location residence time $0 < T_r \ll 1$, $0 < \epsilon_1 \ll 1$, $0 < \epsilon_2 \ll 1$. Set the iteration counter k to 0. Let S^{N^0} be a given switching schedule and $\bar{u}^0$ a nominal control resulting in a nominal trajectory $\bar{x}^0$. Set the total cost $J^0(S^{N^0}, \bar{x}^0) = \infty$.

2. Increment k by 1. Compute the optimal controls $u_{q_i}^k(\cdot)$, the resulting state $x_{q_i}^k(\cdot)$, the resulting costate $\lambda_{q_i}^k(\cdot)$ and the Hamiltonian functions $H_{q_i}^k(t) = \lambda_{q_i}^k(t)f_{q_i}(x^k(t), u^k(t)) + l_{q_i}(x^k(t))$, in each location for $i = 0, 1, \dots, |S^{N^0}|$, where $|S^{N^0}|$ denotes the cardinality of the set S^{N^0}. Also compute the cost in each location $J_{q_i}^k$. If $J^k = \sum_{i=0}^{|S^{N^0}|} J_{q_i}^k \geq J^{k-1}$ then STOP.

3. Compute the difference of Hamiltonians $H_{q_i}^k(t_{s_i}^k) - H_{q_{i+1}}^k(t_{s_i}^k)$ at each switching time $t_{s_i}^k$.

4. If $k > 1$ then
   for each $i \in \{1, 2, \dots, |S^{N^0}| - 1\}$
   if $|H_{q_i}^k(t_{s_i}^k) - H_{q_{i+1}}^k(t_{s_i}^k)| > h$ and
   $(H_{q_i}^k(t_{s_i}^k) - H_{q_{i+1}}^k(t_{s_i}^k))(H_{q_i}^{k-1}(t_{s_i}^{k-1}) - H_{q_{i+1}}^{k-1}(t_{s_i}^{k-1})) > 0$ then
   $t_{s_i}^k = t_{s_i}^{k-1} - \epsilon_1(H_{q_i}^k(t_{s_i}^k) - H_{q_{i+1}}^k(t_{s_i}^k))$;
   else $t_{s_i}^k = t_{s_i}^{k-1}$;
   end if
   end for
   end if.

5. If $k > 1$ then
   for each $i \in \{1, 2, \dots, |S^{N^0}| - 1\}$
   if $\|\lambda_{q_{i+1}}^k(t_{s_i}^k) - \lambda_{q_i}^k(t_{s_i}^k)\| > l$ and
   $\left(\lambda_{q_{i+1}}^k(t_{s_i}^k) - \lambda_{q_i}^k(t_{s_i}^k)\right)^T \left(\lambda_{q_{i+1}}^k(t_{s_i}^k) - \lambda_{q_i}^k(t_{s_i}^k)\right) > 0$ then
   $x^k(t_{s_i}^k) = x^{k-1}(t_{s_i}^{k-1}) - \epsilon_2\left(\lambda_{q_{i+1}}^k(t_{s_i}^k) - \lambda_{q_i}^k(t_{s_i}^k)\right)$;
   else $x^k(t_{s_i}^k) = x^{k-1}(t_{s_i}^{k-1})$;
   end if
   end for
   end if.

6. If all the switching time differences satisfy $t_{s_{i+1}}^k - t_{s_i}^k > T_r$ then accept the new switching times; else, if $t_{s_i}^k$ is such that $t_{s_{i+1}}^k - t_{s_i}^k \leq T_r$, then compute the costs $\int_{t_{s_i}}^{t_{s_{i+1}}} l_{q_{i-1}}(x^k(t), u^k(t))dt$ and $\int_{t_{s_i}}^{t_{s_{i+1}}} l_{q_{i+1}}(x^k(t), u^k(t))dt$, $i \in \{1, 2, \dots, |S^{N^0}| - 1\}$, in locations q_{i-1} and q_{i+1} respectively and replace the location q_i by whichever location on either side gives lower cost and by either location whenever they give an equal cost.

7. If the criteria in Steps 4, 5, 6 all fail then STOP; else go to Step 2.

A rigorous analysis similar to that for algorithm HMP[MAS] establishes the convergence of algorithm HMP[MCS] (see [8], [9]).

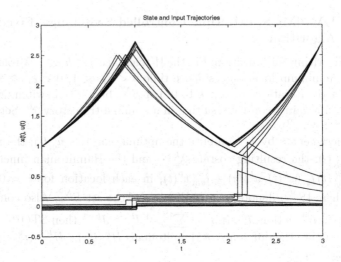

Fig. 2. Convergence to the Optimal Trajectory: multiple controlled switchings case

Example 2: To illustrate the Algorithm HMP[MCS] we consider a system which successively occupies the locations q_1, q_2 and q_3 and which has two controlled switchings. The dynamics in q_1, q_2, q_3 are given by:
$$\dot{x} = x + xu, \quad \dot{x} = -x + xu, \quad \dot{x} = x + u, \quad t_0 = 0, \ t_f = 3, \quad x(0) = 1, \ x(3) = e.$$
The cost function to be minimized is: $J(u) = \dfrac{1}{2} \displaystyle\int_0^3 u^2(s)\,ds$.

Starting with the initial guess $t_{s_1} = 0.8$, $x(t_{s_1}) = 2.5$, $t_{s_2} = 2.2$, $x(t_{s_2}) = 0.8$, Figure 2 shows the convergence of $\{z_{s_2}^k\}_{k=1}^\infty = \{(t_{s_1}^k, x_{s_1}^k), (t_{s_2}^k, x_{s_2}^k)\}_{k=1}^\infty$ to the unique optimal switching times $t_{s_1} = 1$, $t_{s_2} = 2$ and states $x_{s_1} = e$ and $x_{s_1} = 1$. The unique optimal control in this case is $u^0 \equiv 0$ resulting in optimal cost $J^0 = 0$. The computation was performed using Matlab 6.0 on a Pentium III 550 MHz machine with 128MB of SDRAM running a Redhat Linux 6.2 operating system. It took 152.43 seconds of CPU time.

4   Combinatoric Search for Locally Optimal Schedules

Algorithms HMP[MAS] and HMP[MCS] may be embedded in the so-called HMP[Comb] (see [8], [9]) algorithm class; this extends the HMP class with combinatorial search algorithms which find (combinatorially local) optimal switching schedules and their associated locally optimal switching times and control inputs.

Let $Q = 1, 2, \ldots, M$ be a list of locations. Let $s_0 = (q_0, q_1, \ldots, q_{N-1})$, where $q_0, q_1, \ldots, q_{N-1}$ are not necessarily distinct, be an ordered list from Q. Then a *k-neighbourhood* of s_0, denoted $N_k(s_0)$, $k \le N$, is defined to be the set of all lists $S \triangleq \{(p_0, p_1, \ldots, p_{N-1}) : p_i \in Q, i = 0, 1, \ldots, N-1\}$ which differ from s_0 in at most k places, i.e. they have a *Hamming distance* k or less from s_0. Given an initial sequence s_0, a *locally k-optimal solution* is the one that is best among all $N_k(s_0)$ sequences.

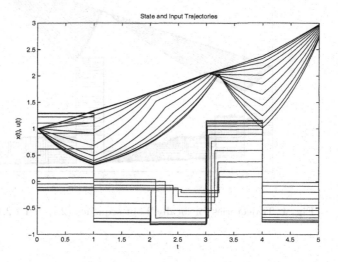

Fig. 3. Trajectories for locally 2-opt sequence (2,1,1,2,1).

Since a location schedule is a list of locations with associated switching times, the problem of finding an optimal schedule given a fixed number of locations is a combinatorial optimization problem with the added complexity of optimizing the switching times and associated state values (and implicitly the continuous controls). Such problems are hard to solve globally since in the worst case combinatoric search has exponential time complexity (see e.g. [11]); despite this, a local heuristic search can often efficiently find a (combinatorially local) hybrid optimal control law and its associated cost.

Example 3: In an application of HMP[Comb] to a combinatoric extension of Example 2 we consider the case of three locations, i.e. $Q = \{1, 2, 3\}$, and modify the cost function to include a terminal cost g (to illustrate the case $\lambda = \text{grad}(g)$ at the terminal time, see [8], [9]).

$$J(u) = \frac{1}{2}(x(5) - e)^2 + \frac{1}{2}\int_0^5 u^2(s)\,ds.$$

Now consider the following two cases:

(i) Starting with
$s_0^1 = \{(t_0, q_0), (t_1, q_1), \dots, (t_{N-1}, q_{N-1})\} = \{(0, 1), (1, 1), (2, 1), (3, 1), (4, 1)\}$
the algorithm generates $\sum_{i=0}^{2} \binom{5}{i} 2^i = 51$ sequences in $N_2(s_0^1)$ and executes

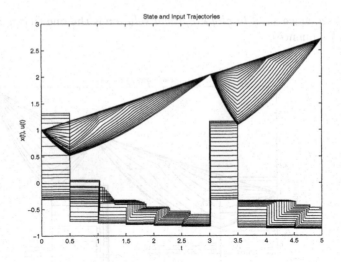

Fig. 4. Trajectories for locally 2-opt sequence (2,1,1,1,1,1,2,1,1,1).

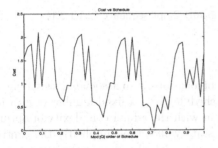

Fig. 5. Costs in $N_2(1,1,1,1,1)$.   Fig. 6. Costs in $N_2(1,1,1,1,1,1,1,1,1,1)$.

HMP[MCS] on each one of them. Figure 3 shows the execution of Algorithm HMP[MCS] on the locally optimal sequence. The initial state trajectory is the top one and the final state trajectory is the bottom one.

(ii) In this case, starting with

$s_0^2 = \{(0,1),(0.5,1),(1,1),(1.5,1),(2,1),(2.5,1),(3,1),(3.5,1),(4,1),(4.5,1)\}$

the algorithm generates $\sum_{i=0}^{2}\binom{10}{i}2^i = 201$ sequences in $N_2(s_0^2)$ and executes HMP[MCS] on each one of them as shown in Figure 4.

For the purpose of illustration, each string in $N_2(s_0^i)$, $i = 1, 2$, is converted to a unique corresponding ternary number as follows: if $s = (q_0, q_1, \ldots, q_{N-1})$ where $q_i \in \{1, 2, 3\}$, $i = 0, 1, \ldots N - 1$, then its ternary representation is $\sum_{j=0}^{N-1}(q_j -$

1)$3^{(N-1-j)}$. For Example 3 these numbers have been normalized and are plotted against the corresponding costs as shown in Figures 5 and 6.

We note the stability of the overall procedure in the sense that locally optimal 10-time slot location sequence (Figure 3) consists simply of lengthened segments of the locally optimal 5-time slot sequence (Figure 4).

References

1. Bazaraa, M.S., C.M. Shetty, C.M.: Nonlinear programming theory and algorithms. John Wiley & Sons, New York (1979)
2. Berkovitz, L.D.: Variational methods in problems of control and programming. J. Math. Anal. Appl. Vol. 3, (1961) 145–169
3. Branicky, M.S.: Studies in Hybrid Systems: Modeling, Analysis, and Control. PhD thesis, Department of Electrical Engineering and Computer Science, Massachusetts Institute of Technology, Cambridge, MA (1995)
4. Broucke, M., Benedetto, M.D.D., Gennaro, S.D., Sangiovanni-Vincentelli, A.: Theory of optimal control using bisimulations. Proceedings of the third international workshop, Hybrid Systems: Computation and Control. Springer-Verlag. Pittsburgh, CA (2000) 89–102
5. Caines, P.E.: Notes on Hybrid Systems. Technion & McGill University (2001)
6. Ekeland, I.: Nonconvex minimization problems. Bull. Amer. Math. Soc. Vol. 1, No. 3 (1979) 443–474
7. Riedinger, P., Kratz, F., Iung, C., Zanne, C.: Linear Quadratic Optimization of Hybrid Systems. Proceedings of the 38th IEEE Conference on Decision and Control, Phoenix, AZ (1999) 3059–3064
8. Shaikh, M.S.: Optimal Control of Hybrid Systems: Theory and Algorithms. PhD thesis, in preparation, Department of Electrical and Computer Engineering, McGill University (2002)
9. Shaikh, M.S., Caines, P.E.: Trajectory Optimization for Hybrid Control Systems. ECE Research Report, McGill University (2002)
10. Shen, G., Caines, P.E.: Hierarchically accelerated dynamic programming for finite state machines. IEEE Transactions on Automatic Control, (2002) 271–283
11. Papadimitriou, C.H., Steiglitz, K.: Combinatorial Optimization: Algorithms and Complexity. Prentice-Hall, Inc. Englewood Cliffs, NJ, (1982)
12. Sussmann, H. A maximum principle for hybrid optimal control problems Proceedings of the 38th IEEE Conference on Decision and Control, Phoenix, AZ, pp.425–430, (1999)
13. Xu, X., Antsaklis, P.J.: An approach for solving general switched linear quadratic optimal control problems. Proceedings of the 40th IEEE Conference on Decision and Control, Orlando, FL (2001) 2478–2483
14. Xu, X., Antsaklis, P.J.: An approach to optimal control of switched systems with internally forced switchings. Proceedings of the American Control Conference, Anchorage, AK (2002) 148–153

Efficient Representation and Computation of Reachable Sets for Hybrid Systems

Olaf Stursberg[1,2] and Bruce H. Krogh[2]

[1] Process Control Laboratory (CT-AST)
University of Dortmund, 44221 Dortmund, Germany
olaf.stursberg@uni-dortmund.de
[2] Carnegie Mellon University
Pittsburgh, PA 15213-3890, USA
krogh@ece.cmu.edu

Abstract. Computing reachable sets is an essential step in most analysis and synthesis techniques for hybrid systems. The representation of these sets has a deciding impact on the computational complexity and thus the applicability of these techniques. This paper presents a new approach for approximating reachable sets using *oriented rectangular hulls* (ORHs), the orientations of which are determined by singular value decompositions of sample covariance matrices for sets of reachable states. The orientations keep the over-approximation of the reachable sets small in most cases with a complexity of low polynomial order with respect to the dimension of the continuous state space. We show how the use of ORHs can improve the efficiency of reachable set computation significantly for hybrid systems with nonlinear continuous dynamics.

Keywords. Convex Hull, Hybrid Dynamic Systems, Hyperrectangles, Model Checking, Polyhedra, Singular Value Decomposition.

1 Introduction

Research on hybrid systems (HSs) has led to a variety of methods for verification of properties, such as safety or liveness (e.g., [1,2,3,4]), and controller synthesis (e.g., [5,6,7,8,9,10]). For the vast majority of these methods, a common step is to compute approximations for the set of reachable states in the continuous state space. Typically, the state space is either partitioned into a finite number of subsets and an (approximate) evaluation of the continuous dynamics reveals which elements of the partition are reachable, or the continuous dynamics are used to propagate the reachable set iteratively from the set of initial states. In both cases the reachable sets are used to determine which discrete transitions are possible and to check if the given property is fulfilled or violated (possibly for specific control inputs).

The geometry chosen to represent reachable sets has a crucial effect on the efficiency of the whole procedure. Usually, the more complex the geometry of the representation is: (i) the more costly is the storage of the sets, (ii) the more

O. Maler and A. Pnueli (Eds.): HSCC 2003, LNCS 2623, pp. 482–497, 2003.

difficult it is to perform operations like union and intersection, and (iii) the more elaborate is the computation of new reachable sets, but (iv) the better the approximation of the actual set of reachable states for the HS. Choosing the geometry has to be a compromise between these impacts.

Several approaches have been proposed in the literature to over-approximate reachable sets by unions of convex objects of simple geometry such as hyperrectangles [11,12,13], polyhedra obtained from convex hull computations [3,14], and ellipsoids [15,16]. Each of these representations has strengths and weaknesses. Hyperrectangles have the advantage that they are easy to represent and the number of faces grows only linearly with the dimension, but a large number of boxes (i.e., a small grid) must be used to assure the approximations are not overly conservative. Polyhedra can give arbitrarily close approximations to convex sets, but the number of faces and vertices can grow prohibitively large and, as shown in [17,18], the computation of polyhedra by convex hull routines becomes intractable for large sets of points in higher dimensions. Ellipsoids are attractive because the representation grows quadratically with the dimension of the continuous space. However, many ellipsoids may be needed to represent reachable sets with sufficient accuracy, and intersections and unions of ellipsoids are not ellipsoids.

This paper proposes an alternative that combines the geometrical simplicity of hyperrectangles with an orientation derived from the true reachable set rather than being fixed to the state-space axes. For a given number of points obtained from the evaluation of the dynamics, a preferred orientation is determined by the singular value decomposition (SVD) of the corresponding covariance matrix. Using this orientation, the smallest hyperrectangle that encloses all points is computed, giving as *oriented hyperrectangular hull* (ORH). When these geometrical objects are used as building blocks for the reachable set, a suitable compromise between computational complexity, approximation accuracy, and the ability to compute intersections and unions is often obtained.

In the following sections, we first identify the steps of reachability algorithms for hybrid systems for which the set representation has a crucial impact. We also explain in more detail in which cases previously proposed approaches have disadvantages with respect to efficiency. Then the concept of the ORH is introduced, and the complexity of ORH computations is discussed. Finally we show for one specific instance of reachability algorithms that the use of ORHs can reduce the computational costs drastically while retaining sufficient approximation accuracy.

2 Set Representation in Reachability Analysis of Hybrid Systems

2.1 Reachable Sets of Hybrid Systems

Throughout the paper we refer to the following definition of hybrid systems. The discussion of reachable set representation applies as well to other variations of this model that appear in literature.

Definition 1. *Syntax of a Hybrid Automaton HA*
The hybrid automaton $HA = (Z, z_0, X, X_0, inv, T, g, j, f)$ contains:

- *the finite set of locations Z with an initial location $z_0 \in Z$;*
- *the continuous state space $X \subseteq \mathbb{R}^n$, and an initial continuous set $X_0 \subseteq X$;*
- *the invariant function $inv : Z \to 2^X$ that assigns an invariant $inv(z) \subseteq X$ to each location $z \in Z$; for convenience we require that $X_0 \subseteq inv(z_0)$;*
- *the set of discrete transitions $T \subseteq Z \times Z$;*
- *the guard function $g : T \to 2^X$ that assigns a guard set $g(t) \subseteq X$ to each transition $t = (z_1, z_2) \in T$;*
- *the jump function $j : T \times X \to 2^X$ that assigns a jump set $j(t, x) \subseteq X$ to each pair $t \in T$ and $x \in g(t)$;*
- *and the flow function $f : Z \to (X \to \mathbb{R}^n)$ assigns a continuous vector field $f(z)$ to each location $z \in Z$. The continuous evolution in z is determined by the ODE $\dot{\chi}(t) = f(z, \chi(t))$ for which we assume that a unique solution exists for each $\chi(0) \in inv(z)$.* ◇

Definition 2. *Runs and the Reachable Set of HA*
Let $S = \bigcup_{z \in Z} \bigcup_{x \in inv(z)} (z, x)$ denote the set of hybrid states (z, x) of a hybrid automaton HA. Then, each possible run of HA is a sequence $\sigma = \{s_0, s_1, s_2, \dots\}$, iff:

- *the initial hybrid state is $s_0 = (z_0, x_0)$, with $x_0 \in X_0$,*
- *and each pair of consecutive states $(s_i, s_{i+1}) \in \sigma$ with $s_i = (z_i, x_i)$ and $s_{i+1} = (z_{i+1}, x_{i+1})$ satisfies:*
  - *either (discrete transition) $(z_i, z_{i+1}) \in T$, $x_i \in g((z_i, z_{i+1}))$, and $x_{i+1} \in j((z_i, z_{i+1}), x_i)$;*
  - *or (continuous evolution) $z_i = z_{i+1}$ and there exists $\chi : [0, \tau] \to X$, $\tau \in \mathbb{R}^{>0}$ such that $x_i = \chi(0)$, $\dot{\chi}(t) = f(z_i, \chi(t))$, $\chi(t) \in inv(z_i)$ for $t \in [0, \tau]$, and $x_{i+1} = \chi(\tau)$.*

If Σ is the set of all possible runs of HA, the reachable set is defined by $R = \{s \mid \exists \sigma \in \Sigma : s \in \sigma\} \subseteq S$, i.e., R contains all hybrid states that are elements of at least one run σ. ◇

2.2   Computation of Reachable Sets

In order to point out where the set representation plays a role in computing the reachable set R of HA, we consider the general reachability procedure shown in Fig. 1. Starting from the initial set S_0, R is computed iteratively.[1] In each step k those hybrid states D are added to R that are reached in the current step but were not reached before. We leave open at this point what exactly defines a step – it could be a specified time increment, space increment, or, e.g., a consecutive pair of continuous evolution and discrete transition. The operator *Reach* computes the set of states that are reachable in one step according to the semantics given in Def. 2. While the structure of this algorithm appears to be very simple, a concrete implementation leads to the following issues:

---

[1] The well known decidability results for hybrid automata (see, e.g., [19,20]) imply this procedure might not terminate.

$$\textbf{given:}\ S_0 = \{z_0\} \times X_0$$
$$k = 0,\ D = S_0,\ R = \emptyset$$
$$\texttt{WHILE}\ D \neq \emptyset$$
$$k = k + 1$$
$$R = R \cup D$$
$$S_k = Reach(D)$$
$$D = S_k \setminus R$$
$$\texttt{END}$$

Fig. 1. High-level algorithm for computing the reachable set R iteratively (S_0: initial set, S_k: set of states reachable within one step k, D: set of states that is reached the first time in step k).

(a) In the general case when D is an infinite set of hybrid states, the operator $Reach(D)$ requires the evaluation of an infinite number of behaviors of HA. If the ODEs cannot be solved analytically, one has to fall back to numerical (yet conservative) approximations of $Reach(D)$.

(b) The sets S_k are in general non-convex (even if analytical solutions of the ODEs exist). In order to store the reachable sets efficiently, they have to be approximated by objects of simple geometry (usually convex sets).

(c) Computing R, S_k, and D requires efficient implementations of operations like set intersection, set union, and set subtraction. Note in this context that computing $Reach(D)$ involves checking whether transition guards are enabled and applying the jump function.

In order to cope with problems (a) and (b), most of the existing algorithms compute a series of convex objects that over-approximate S_k. These algorithms include the computation of convex hulls for finite sets of points (e.g., see [14, 13]). The resulting polyhedra represent either an intermediate or the final result for approximating S_k. The choice of the geometry for the objects that establish S_k has a crucial impact on the accuracy of the approximation as well as on the storage requirements. As an example, Fig. 2 illustrates three alternatives for hulls of a given set of points determined to be reachable from the set D. The differences in accuracy and the effort to store the objects (hyperrectangle: a matrix in $\mathbb{R}^{n \times 2}$; hyperellipsoid: a matrix in $\mathbb{R}^{n \times (n+1)}$; convex hull: a matrix in $\mathbb{R}^{q \times (n+1)}$ where q is the number of faces) are apparent.

With respect to problem (c), the efficient applicability of the set operations is another important criterion in choosing suitable objects for the set representation. For convex polyhedra, the result of intersection, union and subtraction is itself a set of of convex polyhedra and standard routines exist. If hyperellipsoids are chosen to represent R, D, and S_k, these operations do not yield hyperellipsoids and an additional approximation step is required to obtain an ellipsoidal approximation.

The effort to compute the hull also plays a dominant role when making the decision for a specific geometric object. In particular, if S_k has a complex shape, the approximation accuracy usually requires that S_k be the union of several

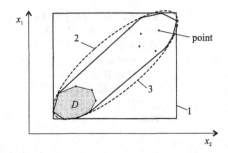

Fig. 2. Different types of hulls for a set of points encountered while computing $S_k =$ $Reach(D)$: 1 - hyperrectangle (axes-parallel), 2 - hyperellipsoid, 3 - convex hull.

small convex sets. The number of hull computations then becomes very large and it can be observed that the time spent on this step is a substantial portion of the overall computation time. This calls for an efficient procedure to compute the hull. Since existing reachability algorithms are limited to low-dimensional systems due to their complexity, the hull computation should especially scale well with the dimension n of the state space and the number of points in each step.

A last important criterion is the numerical stability. We have found that convex hull algorithms encounter difficulties if the set of points to be enclosed lies in a lower-dimensional subspace. Usually they return a convex hull that is 'bloated' to full dimension (i.e. some points are perturbed) or a lower-dimensional set that comprises a higher number of faces than necessary. With respect to an efficient set representation, it is certainly desirable to have a procedure that generates a hull of minimal dimension and a minimal number of faces.

3   Set Representation by Oriented Rectangular Hulls

This section first introduces the ORH as an alternative to the types of sets discussed in the previous section. We then describe the advantages of the ORH with respect to the criteria listed above.

3.1   Definition of the ORH

We begin with some basic definitions and notation. Let x be vector of continuous variables defined in the Euclidean space $\mathbb{R}^{n \times 1}$. A *half-space* is given by $S := \{x \mid c \cdot x \leq d, \ c \in \mathbb{R}^{1 \times n}, \ d \in \mathbb{R}\}$. For a given half-space S, let $B = \{x \mid c \cdot x = d\}$ denote the corresponding *bounding hyperplane*. If the intersection of a finite set $S = \{S_1, \dots, S_q\}$ of half-spaces with pairwise different normal vectors c is non-empty and bounded in $\mathbb{R}^n$, it determines a convex *polyhedron* $P := \{x \mid \exists S : x \in S_j \ \forall \ S_j \in \mathcal{S}\}$. The corresponding set of bounding hyperplanes is denoted by $\mathcal{B}$.

Let $\mathcal{X} = \{x^1, x^2, \dots, x^p\}$ be a finite set of vectors in $\mathbb{R}^{n \times 1}$. A polyhedron P is called a *polyhedral hull* of $\mathcal{X}$, denoted by $PH(\mathcal{X})$, iff $x^i \in P$ for all $x^i \in \mathcal{X}$, $i \in \{1, \dots, p\}$.

Given a polyhedral hull $PH(\mathcal{X})$, the set of *vertices* of PH is denoted by $\mathcal{V} = \{v_1, \ldots, v_r\}$, where each vertex $v := \{x \mid \exists\, \mathcal{B}' \subseteq \mathcal{B}, |\mathcal{B}'| \geq n,\ x \in \mathbb{R}^n :\ x \in B_j\ \forall\ B_j \in \mathcal{B}'\}$ is determined by the intersection of at least n bounding hyperplanes.

The polyhedral hull PH is called a *convex hull*, denoted by $CH(\mathcal{X})$, iff $\mathcal{V} \subseteq \mathcal{X}$ applies. A convex hull CH is called a *rectangular hull*, denoted by $RH(\mathcal{X})$, iff S is the intersection of $q = 2 \cdot n$ half-spaces such that for each $S_j = \{x \mid c_j \cdot x \leq d_j\}$: (i) there exists an $S_{k \neq j} = \{x \mid c_k \cdot x \leq d_k\}$ with $c_j = -c_k$, and (ii) for each $S_{i \neq j, i \neq k} \in S$, $\langle c_j, c_i^T \rangle = 0$. Let $\mathcal{E} = \{e_1, \ldots, e_n\}$ be the set of directions of the axes of $\mathbb{R}^n$, i.e., $e_i = (0^{1 \times i-1}, 1, 0^{1 \times n-i})$, $i \in \{1, \ldots, n\}$. In the special case that for the normal vector c of each half-space of S there exists an $e_i \in \mathcal{E}$ with $\langle \pm e_i, c^T \rangle = 0$, we call $RH(\mathcal{X})$ an *axes-parallel rectangular hull*, denoted by $ARH(\mathcal{X})$.

The attractive feature of a rectangular hull $RH(\mathcal{X})$ is that the number of bounding hyperplanes increases only linearly with n and is independent of p, the number of points it encloses. The definition of $RH(\mathcal{X})$ does not, however, specify an orientation of the hull (i.e, of the choice of the normal vectors), except of the special case of $ARH(\mathcal{X})$. For the latter, it is easy to imagine a set of points for which the axes-parallel orientation is not suitable in the sense of a tight enclosure of $\mathcal{X}$ (see Fig. 2). To overcome this problem, we now introduce an efficient procedure for choosing the parameters c and d of the halfspaces defining $RH(\mathcal{X})$.

The principle is to derive the orientation from the distribution of the points within the space $\mathbb{R}^n$. The elements of $\mathcal{X}$ are interpreted as p sampled evaluations of the dynamics of HA. The arithmetic mean of the samples $x^m = \frac{1}{p} \sum_{i=1}^{p} x^i$ is chosen as the origin of a set of translated samples: $\overline{\mathcal{X}} = \{\overline{x}^1, \ldots, \overline{x}^p\}$, $\overline{x}^i = x^i - x^m$. To characterize the distribution of $\overline{\mathcal{X}}$ we define the sample covariance matrix as follows.

Given the set $\overline{\mathcal{X}}$ of p translated samples of the vector of n continuous variables x, the sampling matrix is denoted by:

$$\overline{X} = \begin{pmatrix} \overline{x}_{1,1} & \cdots & \overline{x}_{1,p} \\ \vdots & \ddots & \vdots \\ \overline{x}_{n,1} & \cdots & \overline{x}_{n,p} \end{pmatrix} \tag{1}$$

where $\overline{x}_{i,j} = x_i^j - x_i^m$ is the j-th sample of the i-th variable. For two components of the translated state vector, $\overline{x}_i = x_i - x_i^m$ and $\overline{x}_k = x_k - x_k^m$, the *sample covariance* is defined as:

$$Cov(\overline{x}_i, \overline{x}_k) = \frac{1}{p-1} \sum_{j=1}^{p} \overline{x}_{i,j} \cdot \overline{x}_{k,j}. \tag{2}$$

In the context of reachable set computations for hybrid systems, the correlation of two variables x_i, x_k (resulting in $Cov(\overline{x}_i, \overline{x}_k) \neq 0$) follows from the fact that $\mathcal{X}$ is obtained from the evaluation of coupled ODEs to generate x_i, x_k.

The *sample covariance matrix*, which represents the distribution of $\mathcal{X}$ in $\mathbb{R}^n$, is then written as:

$$Cov(\bar{x}) = \begin{pmatrix} Cov(\bar{x}_1, \bar{x}_1) & \cdots & Cov(\bar{x}_1, \bar{x}_n) \\ \vdots & \ddots & \vdots \\ Cov(\bar{x}_n, \bar{x}_1) & \cdots & Cov(\bar{x}_n, \bar{x}_n) \end{pmatrix} = \frac{1}{p-1} \cdot \overline{X} \cdot \overline{X}^T. \tag{3}$$

To obtain a suitable orientation for a rectangular hall $RH(\mathcal{X})$ from $Cov(\bar{x})$, we use the technique known as *principal component analysis* (PCA) in literature. As described in the early publications [21,22,23], PCA usually aims at finding the dominating correlations between large sets of variables for given large sets of data. By considering the dominating correlations only, the original data can be represented by a small yet meaningful set of variables (the principal components). In our setting however, we use PCA to derive an orientation to define a particular $RH(\mathcal{X})$ for $\mathcal{X}$. The orientation is obtained from the *singular value decomposition* of $Cov(\bar{x})$, given by

$$Cov(\bar{x}) = U \cdot \Sigma \cdot V^T, \tag{4}$$

where $U \in \mathbb{R}^{n \times n}$ and $V \in \mathbb{R}^{n \times n}$ are unitary matrices. If $r = rank(Cov(\bar{x}))$, the matrix of singular values is

$$\Sigma = \begin{pmatrix} \Sigma_r & 0^{r \times n-r} \\ 0^{n-r \times r} & 0^{n-r \times n-r} \end{pmatrix}, \text{ with } \Sigma_r = diag(\sigma_1, \ldots, \sigma_r) \in \mathbb{R}^{r \times r}, \tag{5}$$

and the *singular values* σ are ordered such that $\sigma_1 \geq \ldots \geq \sigma_r > 0.$[2]

Since $Cov(\bar{x})$ is symmetric, $U = V$. If we write $U = [U_r, U_{n-r}]$ with $U_r \in \mathbb{R}^{n \times r}$ and $U_{n-r} \in \mathbb{R}^{n \times n-r}$, the columns of U_r define an orthonormal basis of the r-dimensional subspace that contains all points in $\mathcal{X}$. We use the directions defined by this basis to determine the orientation of $RH(\mathcal{X})$:

Definition 3. Oriented Rectangular Hull
Let $\mathcal{X} = \{x^1, x^2, \ldots, x^p\}$ be a given set of samples, $\overline{\mathcal{X}}$ the set of translated samples with a covariance matrix $Cov(\bar{x}) = U \cdot \Sigma \cdot V^T$. We write $U_{\bullet,i}$ to denote the i-th column of U. The oriented rectangular hull, denoted $ORH(\mathcal{X})$, is the rectangular hull $RH(\mathcal{X})$ defined by the set $\mathcal{S} = \{S_1, S_2, \ldots, S_{2 \cdot n}\}$ of halfspaces such that for a $\varepsilon \in \mathbb{R}^{\geq 0}$ and $\forall\, i \in \{1, \ldots, n\}$:

− $\exists\, S_j \in \mathcal{S}$: $S_j = \{x \mid U_{\bullet,i}^T \cdot x \leq \max_{\bar{x} \in \overline{\mathcal{X}}} \{U_{\bullet,i}^T \cdot \bar{x}\} + U_{\bullet,i}^T \cdot x^m + \varepsilon\}$, and:

− $\exists\, S_k \in \mathcal{S}$: $S_k = \{x \mid -U_{\bullet,i}^T \cdot x \leq -\min_{\bar{x} \in \overline{\mathcal{X}}} \{U_{\bullet,i}^T \cdot \bar{x}\} - U_{\bullet,i}^T \cdot x^m + \varepsilon\}$

⋄

Note that for a rank deficiency ($i > r$), the two halfspaces S_j and S_k lead to a hull ORH that is 'flat' in the direction of $U_{\bullet,i}$ (if $\varepsilon = 0$). If a full dimensional hull is deemed to be numerically more stable within the computation of $S_k = Reach(D)$, a small tolerance $\varepsilon > 0$ can be chosen.

---

[2] It can be shown that the singular values are given by $\sigma_i = \sqrt{\lambda_i}$, where λ_i, $i = 1, \ldots, r$, are the nonzero eigenvalues of $Cov(\bar{x}) \cdot Cov(\bar{x})^T$, which are all real and non-negative.

3.2 Assessment of ORH

The criteria for assessing hulls, as listed at the end of Sec. 2, are now applied to ORHs. Figure 3 shows four distributions of points in $\mathbb{R}^2$ and the corresponding ORHs. It is apparent that, if the distribution of points has a preferred orientation (upper row of figures), one of the axes of ORH represents the corresponding direction (determined by $U_{\bullet,1}$). If all points lie in a lower-dimensional subspace (as in Fig. 3.b), the expansion in the null space is just given by $2 \cdot \varepsilon$. If the distribution of points is completely symmetric with respect to x^m (i.e., two or more singular values are identical), the orthonormal basis U_r is not uniquely defined, and an additional criterion should be employed. For the points shown in Fig. 3.c, both rectangles correspond to a valid singular value decomposition of $Cov(\overline{x})$. To obtain the solution marked by the solid line, which is clearly the better solution (and equivalent to the convex hull), the additional requirement is that the vertices of ORH coincide with the given points. The point set in Fig. 3.c does not have a visible preferred orientation either, but has a random distribution. It is not obvious, however, that a rectangular hull with a more suitable orientation exists.

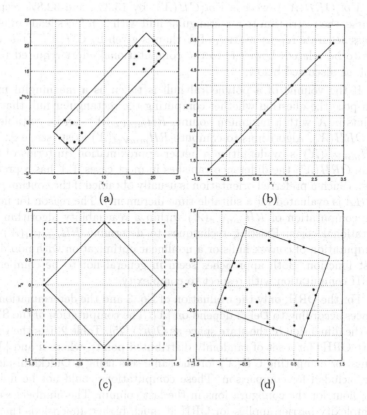

Fig. 3. Oriented rectangular hulls for different example sets of points.

Table 1. Volumes of different polyhedral hulls for the example sets in Fig. 3 (with $\varepsilon = 0$ for Fig. 3.b).

Fig. 3:	(a)	(b)	(c)	(d)
$ORH(\mathcal{X})$	152.99	0	3.13	3.20
$CH(\mathcal{X})$	134.99	0	3.13	2.41
$ARH(\mathcal{X})$	400.00	17.64	6.25	3.28

In order to assess the accuracy of representing $\mathcal{X}$ by an ORH, we compare its volume $Vol(ORH(\mathcal{X}))$ to that of other types of polyhedral hulls. The volume may seem to be a questionable measure for accuracy since polyhedral hulls of completely different shape can have the same volume. However, relating $Vol(ORH(\mathcal{X}))$ to the volume of the convex hull $Vol(CH(\mathcal{X}))$ gives some estimation for the degree by which $ORH(\mathcal{X})$ overapproximates the set $\mathcal{X}$. This is true since $CH(\mathcal{X})$ is by definition the exact polyhedral hull that contains $\mathcal{X}$. Table 1 shows the volumes of $ORH(\mathcal{X})$, $CH(\mathcal{X})$, and $ARH(\mathcal{X})$ for the four cases chosen in Fig. 3. In the two cases with non-symmetrical distribution of points (a, d), $Vol(ORH(\mathcal{X}))$ exceeds $Vol(CH(\mathcal{X}))$ by 13.3%, and 32.8% respectively. Of course, the restriction to a rectangular hull with $2 \cdot n$ faces leads in most cases to a less accurate representation of $\mathcal{X}$ than is given by $CH(\mathcal{X})$. This disadvantage has to be related, however, to the computational effort required to obtain the hull, as discussed below.

If the volume of a polyhedral hull is taken as a meaningful measure, one can pose the question whether computing the rectangular hull that encloses all points in $\mathcal{X}$ with a minimum volume $RH_{minVol}(\mathcal{X})$ can be suitable alternative to $ORH(\mathcal{X})$. Algorithms to compute $RH_{minVol}(\mathcal{X})$ exist (see, e.g., [24]). While $RH_{minVol}(\mathcal{X})$ is by definition a better approximation (in terms of the volume) than $ORH(\mathcal{X})$, the difference vanishes in most cases if $\mathcal{X}$ has a preferred direction. (Such a preferred orientation is usually obtained if the continuous dynamics of HA is evaluated for a suitable time increment). The reason for not proposing the computation of $RH_{minVol}(\mathcal{X})$ within a reachability algorithm is the computational costs: Existing techniques to determine $RH_{minVol}(\mathcal{X})$ involve the computation of convex hulls or a nonlinear optimization with non-differentiable cost function. Both approaches seem in general not to be competitive to the ORH computation with respect to complexity.

For the ORH, only the evaluation of Eq. 3 and the determination of the half-spaces according to Def. 3 depend on $|\mathcal{X}|$. The computation of the SVD depends on the dimension of the state space as $O(n^3)$ [25]. Table 2 lists the times to compute ORHs for a set of randomly distributed points, where n and $|\mathcal{X}|$ vary. The times for computing $CH(\mathcal{X})$ for the same sets using a Quickhull-algorithm [26] are included for comparison. These computations could not be finished within one hour for the configurations in the last column. The numbers show that the complexity barrier applies for ORH at much higher dimensions than for convex hulls, and that the number of points affects the ORH computation much less

Table 2. Computation times. The shown values are the mean CPU-times in seconds of 5 experiments each. (Implementation: Matlab; Machine: Pentium III, 700MHz).

$|\mathcal{X}| = 20, n :$	2	4	6	8	10	12
$ORH(\mathcal{X})$	0.05	0.06	0.08	0.17	1.81	77.4
$CH(\mathcal{X})$	0.05	0.62	8.80	93.61	$> 10^3$	–
$n = 5, |\mathcal{X}| :$	20	40	60	80	100	1000
$ORH(\mathcal{X})$	0.06	0.06	0.06	0.06	0.07	0.53
$CH(\mathcal{X})$	2.42	9.20	28.41	51.09	87.55	–

than they effect the computation of $CH(\mathcal{X})$. Although not included in the table, it should be noted that the computation of ellipsoid containing a given set of points involves the solution of optimization problems [27].

In order to asses the storage requirements, we note that an ORH is determined by $C \cdot x \leq d$, with matrices $C \in \mathbb{R}^{2 \cdot n \times n}$ and $d \in \mathbb{R}^{2 \cdot n}$. (In the case of rank deficiency, $2 \cdot (n - r)$ inequalities can be replaced by $n - r$ equalities.) Therefore, the amount of data to be stored grows quadratically with the dimension n and is independent of $|\mathcal{X}|$. In comparison, the number of inequalities required to define $CH(\mathcal{X})$ depends on the number of vertices determining the convex hull, and can be significantly higher even for low dimensions (e.g., for the points in Fig. 3.d). As mentioned in Sec. 2.2, hyperellipsoids can be represented by $(x - b)^T \cdot C \cdot (x - b) \leq d$, $C \in \mathbb{R}^{n \times n}$, $d \in \mathbb{R}^n$, $b \in \mathbb{R}^n$, i.e., the required memory also grows quadratically with n.

As for the suitability of a particular type of hull for operations like intersection, union, and set subtraction, the complexity of all these operations crucially depends on the number of faces of a polyhedral hull, or the dimensions of C and c specifying ellipsoids respectively. Hence, the discussion above for the required memory applies when assessing the complexity of set operations. Note that union and set subtraction can lead to non-convex results, and thus an approximating step is required to yield a set that is of the same type as the original sets.

Finally, the issue of handling lower-dimensional sets deserves a comment. When applying convex hull algorithms, we have observed that existing approaches lead to difficulties if all points in $\mathcal{X}$ are in a lower-dimensional subspace. Most algorithms perturb the points slightly to compute a full dimensional convex hull first, and then the result is projected onto the original lower-dimensional space. The consequence is a hull that contains identical rows in the C- and d-matrix, and extra vertices. These identical rows can cause numerical problems in many operations. A remedy for this problems is to first transform $\mathcal{X}$ into the lower-dimensional space, compute a convex-hull in this space, and to transform the vertices back into full dimension. The ORH computation does not require the projection into a lower-dimensional space. As given in Def. 3, the concept of transforming into a space of appropriate dimension is implicit, and the tolerance ε can be chosen to control the effects of numerical errors.

4   Oriented Rectangles in Reach Set Computations

4.1   Reachability Computation Based on ORH

This section describes for one specific instance of reachable set algorithms what the impact of the set representation is, and shows that the use of ORH can be favorable. Referring to the algorithm in Fig. 1, we now assume that a step (denoted by k) is given by a continuous evolution followed by a discrete transition. The operator $S_k = Reach(D)$ first determines the set of hybrid states which are reachable from states in D by continuous evolution until a transition is enabled, and then applies the transition. The first step must conservatively compute all possible evolutions starting from D. We here employ the algorithm used in the tool CHECKMATE, as described in [28]. This algorithm can be written as follows:

$$
\begin{aligned}
&\textbf{given: } D, \triangle T \in \mathbb{R} \\
&S_k = \emptyset \\
&Z_D = \{z \mid z \in Z : s = (z,x) \in D\} \\
&\textbf{FOR ALL } z \in Z_D \\
&\quad Q = \{x \mid \exists\, s = (z,x) \in D\} \\
&\quad G = Q \\
&\quad \textbf{WHILE } G \cap inv(z) \neq \emptyset \\
&\qquad V = evolve\_vertices(z, G, \triangle T) \\
&\qquad H = determine\_hull(G, V) \\
&\qquad G = bloat\_hull(z, H) \\
&\qquad Q = Q \cup (G \cap inv(z)) \\
&\quad \textbf{END} \\
&\quad S_Q = \{s \mid \exists x \in Q : s = (z,x) \in S) \\
&\quad S_{trans} = execute\_transition(S_Q) \\
&\quad S_k = S_k \cup S_Q \cup S_{trans} \\
&\textbf{END}
\end{aligned}
$$

Fig. 4. A high-level algorithm to compute the set $S_k = Reach(D)$.

The set Z_D denotes the locations that correspond to D. Q is the set of continuous states x that form a subset of D together with a particular $z \in Z_D$, and it is given as convex polyhedral set.[3] Starting from Q, the part of the invariant $inv(z)$ is computed which is reachable by continuous evolution. Let G be a set of continuous states that is initialized to Q. The computation then involves three phases that are applied stepwise until the current location invariant is completely left. The function $evolve\_vertices$ first simulates the vertices of G for a given timestep $\triangle T$. The result is the set V of vertices. A function $determine\_hull$ then computes a polyhedral hull H containing V and all vertices of G. This is

---

[3] Here we assume for simplicity that Q is one polyhedral object. In general it can be a list of polyhedral sets and the WHILE-loop has to be applied to each of these.

the point where the choice between convex hull, ORH, or another polyhedral hull has to be made. The third step, denoted by a function *bloat_hull*, expands H such that all trajectories emerging from G are completely contained in the bloated hull. This is achieved by pushing the faces of H outwards by solving the following optimization problem: Let $\mathcal{B}$ again be the set of bounding hyperplanes of the hull H. Then, the solution of:

$$\max_{\substack{\chi(0) \in G \\ \tau \in [0, \Delta T]}} \{c \cdot \chi(t)\} \quad \text{s.t.} \quad \chi(t) = \chi(0) + \int_0^\tau f(z, \chi(\tau)) \cdot d\tau \qquad (6)$$

for every bounding hyperplane $B = \{x \mid c \cdot x = d\} \in \mathcal{B}$ leads to a *bloated hull* that entirely contains the set of points reachable from G within the timestep ΔT. It is important to note that one optimization is carried out for each bounding hyperplane of the hull, and that the orientations of B (determined by the vectors c) are obtained from the hull computation. It is thus obvious that the chosen type of hull plays a key role in determining the computation required to construct the approximation for the reachable set.

The result of the bloating operation (or more precisely, the part which is inside of $inv(z)$) is added to Q. By repeating this three-phase procedure until $G \cap inv(z) = \emptyset$ applies, the subset of $inv(z)$ that is reachable from the initial Q is conservatively approximated.[4] The function *execute_transition* determines which outgoing transitions of z are enabled. This step includes computing the intersection of Q with the corresponding transition guards. Applying the jump function (see Def. 1) to these intersections leads then to the hybrid state set S_{trans}. S_Q is the set of hybrid states that are formed by $z \in Z_D$ and the final set Q. The sets S_{trans} and S_Q are added to S_k at the end of each cycle of the FOR-loop. When this loop terminates, S_k is the returned.

4.2   Example: Van der Pole System

We illustrate the algorithm by the example of Van der Pole equations with an additional clock variable:

$$Z = \{z_1, z_2, z_3\}, \quad z_0 = z_1, \quad X = \mathbb{R}^3, \quad X_0 = [0.6, 0.9] \times [0.6, 0.9] \times 0, \qquad (7)$$

$$inv(z_1) = [-2, 2] \times [-2, 2] \times [0, 9], \quad inv(z_2) = [2, 5] \times [-2, 2] \times [0, 12],$$

$$inv(z_3) = [-2, 2] \times [-2, 2] \times [9, 12]$$

$$T = \{(z_1, z_2), (z_1, z_3)\},$$

$$g((z_1, z_2)) = 2 \times [-2, 2] \times [0, 9], \quad g((z_1, z_3)) = [-2, 2] \times [-2, 2] \times 9,$$

$$j((z_1, z_2), x) = x, \quad j((z_1, z_3), x) = x,$$

$$f(z_1) = (x_2, \frac{x_2}{5} \cdot (x_1^2 - 1) - x_1, 1)^T, \quad f(z_2) = f(z_3) = (0, 0, 0)^T$$

---

[4] Conservativeness is achieved under the assumptions for Eq. 6 that the optimization leads to the global optimum and that the continuous trajectory $\chi(t)$ is exactly computable. In practice, both are achieved within a specified tolerance.

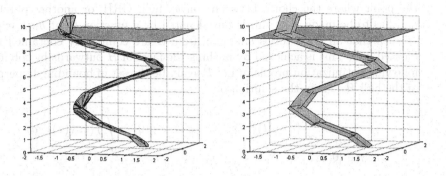

Fig. 5. Reachable set for the 3-dim. Van der Pole system ($\triangle T = 1$): left – convex hulls, right – oriented rectangular hulls.

For this system we have posed the verification problem whether the location z_2 is reachable from the initial hybrid set specified by z_0 and X_0. The reachable set is shown in Fig. 5 for two different choices of hulls (i.e., two different functions *determine_hull*). The set of grey-shaded polyhedra in the left figure is the result obtained with convex hull approximation, while the right figure shows the result using ORH. The plane at $x_3 = 9$ (vertical axis) corresponds to the guard $g((z_1, z_3))$. The figures reveal that the reachable set approximation is slightly larger when the ORH is used, but the result is not significantly different from the result using the convex hull. It is also apparent that the number of bounding hyperplanes for each set G is large if convex hulls are used (i.e., each segment of the reachable set is a hull with several faces), while six bounding hyperplanes suffice in each step in the ORH case. Hence, the number of optimizations according to Eq. 6 carried out in each step is considerably lower using ORHs.

Table 3 shows computation times for the two alternatives in comparison for different timesteps $\triangle T$. In order to evaluate the computational complexity for varying dimensions of this example, we have introduced further clock variables. This means that continuous variables x_4 and x_5 with dynamics as for x_3 are defined (and the sets X and X_0, as well as the invariants and guards are extended accordingly). The results in Table 3 show that for a fixed dimension a reduction

Table 3. Computation times in seconds for the Van der Pole system for varying dimensions n and timesteps $\triangle T$. (Implementation: Matlab; Machine: Pentium IV, 1.5GHz).

n :	3	3	3	4	4	4	5	5	5
$\triangle T$:	1	0.6	0.2	1	0.6	0.2	1	0.6	0.2
$ORH(\mathcal{X})$	82.7	116.8	335.1	119.9	183.7	561.84	198.4	297.6	855.4
$CH(\mathcal{X})$	214.4	434.0	1051.4	559.9	1140.5	2689.5	1483.8	3257.8	$> 5 \cdot 10^4$

of the timestep increases the CPU-times roughly linearly (a constant overhead is required for model compilation etc.). For a constant Δt, the CPU-time for the use of convex hulls leads to a quick increase with the dimension and prohibits the verification for dimension much larger than $n = 5$ for this example. An increase is also observed for the use of ORH, but for the same configurations the computation time is considerably smaller.

5   Conclusions

Set representation is a crucial component of reachable set algorithms for hybrid systems. Among the different options for defining hulls of point sets $\mathcal{X}$, the oriented rectangular hulls have been identified as a choice that (a) is efficiently computable, (b) can be stored with small memory requirements, (c) is suitable for operations like set intersection, union, and subtraction, (d) can represent $\mathcal{X}$ with sufficient accuracy in many cases, (e) scales favorably (over convex hulls) with the dimension and the cardinality of $\mathcal{X}$, and (f) can lead to considerable computational savings due to the relatively small number of bounding hyperplanes when used in reachability algorithms. Although the latter point has been demonstrated only for one specific algorithm, the advantages should be similar for other procedures in which the geometry of the hulls determines the computational effort.

The ORH represents a good approximation of point sets $\mathcal{X}$ particularly when $\mathcal{X}$ has a preferred orientation. Since $\mathcal{X}$ is obtained from simulating the hybrid systems over a time span ΔT, a straightforward approach is to choose ΔT such that $\mathcal{X}$ has a preferred orientation (if at all possible for the given dynamics). Our current work aims at addressing this issue. One approach is to simulate until the decomposition of the covariance matrix leads to singular values that differ to a specified extent. The value of $\Delta T \in \mathbb{R}$ would then be adjusted to the evolution of the hybrid system. This modification would not only eliminate the difficult task of finding a suitable timestep ΔT, but would also avoid the cases in which a missing preferred orientation of $\mathcal{X}$ leads to poor accuracy of the $ORH(\mathcal{X})$ (in comparison to $CH(\mathcal{X})$).

Acknowledgment. This research has been financially supported in part by the U.S. Army Research Office and the U.S. Defense Advanced Projects Research Agency.

References

1. Alur, R., Courcoubetis, C., Halbwachs, N., Henzinger, T.A., Ho, P.H., Nicollin, X., Olivero, A., Sifakis, J., Yovine, S.: The algorithmic analysis of hybrid systems. Theoretical Computer Science **138** (1995) 3–34
2. Bemporad, A., Morari, M.: Verification of hybrid systems via mathematical programming. In: Hybrid Systems: Computation and Control. Volume 1569 of LNCS., Springer (1999) 31–45

3. Greenstreet, M.R., Mitchell, I.: Reachability analysis using polygonal projections. In: Hybrid Systems: Computation and Control. Volume 1569 of LNCS., Springer (1999) 103–116
4. Asarin, E., Bournez, O., Dang, T., Maler, O.: Approximate reachability analysis of piecewise-linear dynamical systems. In: Hybrid Systems – Computation and Control. Volume 1790 of LNCS., Springer (2000) 20–31
5. Wong-Toi, H.: The synthesis of conbtrollers for linear hybrid automata. In: Proc. 36th IEEE Conf. Decision and Control. (1997) 4607–4612
6. Cury, J., Krogh, B., Niinomi, T.: Synthesis of supervisory controller for hybrid systems based on approximating automata. IEEE Transaction on Automatic Control **43** (1998) 564–569
7. Asarin, E., Bournez, O., Dang, T., Maler, O., Pnueli, A.: Effective synthesis of switching controllers for linear systems. Proc. of the IEEE **88** (2000) 1011–1025
8. Tomlin, C., Lygeros, J., Sastry, S.: A game theoretic approach to controller design for hybrid systems. Proc. of the IEEE **88** (2000) 949–970
9. Xia, H., Pang, Y., Trontis, A., Spathopoulos, M.: Eventuality synthesis for controlled linear automata. In: Proc. American Control Conf. (2002) 160–165
10. Mitchell, I., Bayen, A., Tomlin, C.: Computing reachable sets for continuous dynamic games using level set methods. IEEE Trans. on Automatic Control (2003) to appear
11. Bournez, K., Maler, O., Pnueli, A.: Orthogonal polyhedra: Representation and computation. In: Hybrid Systems: Computation and Control. Volume 1569 of LNCS., Springer (1999) 46–60
12. Puri, A., Borkar, V., Varaiya, P.: ϵ-approximations of differential inclusions. In: Hybrid Systems III. Volume 1066 of LNCS., Springer (1996) 363–376
13. Stursberg, O.: Analysis of switched continuous systems based on discrete approximation. In: Proc. 4th Int. Conf. on Automation of Mixed Processes. (2000) 73–78
14. Chutinan, A., Krogh, B.: Verification of infinite-state dynamic systems using approximate quotient transition systems. IEEE Trans. on Automatic Control **46** (2001) 1401–1410
15. Botchkarev, O., Tripakis, S.: Verification of hybrid systems with linear differential inclusions using ellipsoidal approximations. In: Hybrid Systems: Computation and Control. Volume 1790 of LNCS., Springer (2000) 73–88
16. Kurzhanski, A., Varaiya, P.: Ellipsiodal techniques for reachability analysis. In: Hybrid Systems: Computation and Control. Volume 1790 of LNCS., Springer (2000) 202–214
17. Chazelle, B.: An optimal convex hull algorithm in any fixed dimension. Discrete Comput. Geom. **10** (1993) 377–409
18. Avis, D., Bremner, D., Seidel, R.: How good are convex hull algorithms? Comput. Geom.: Theory and Appl. **7** (1997) 265–301
19. Henzinger, T.A., Kopke, P.W., Puri, A., Varaiya, P.: What's decidable about hybrid automata? Journ. Computer and System Sciences **57** (1998) 94–124
20. Lafferriere, G., Pappas, G.J., Yovine, S.: A new class of decidable hybrid systems. In: Hybrid Systems: Computation and Control. Volume 1569 of LNCS., Springer (1999) 137–151
21. Pearson, K.: On lines and panes of closest fit to systems of points in space. Phil. Mag. **6** (1901)
22. Hotelling, H.: Analysis of a complex of statistical variables into principal components. J. Educ. Psychol. **24** (1933) 417–441
23. Jolliffe, I., ed.: Principal Component Analysis. Series in Statistics. Springer (1986)

24. Barequet, G., Har-Peled, S.:   Efficiently approximating the minimum-volume bounding box of a point set in three dimensions. J. of Algorithms **38** (2001) 99–109
25. Klema, V.C., Laub, A.J.: The singular value decomposition: its computation and some applications. IEEE Trans. on Automatic Control **25** (1980) 164–176
26. Barber, C., Dobkin, D., Huhdanpaa, H.: The quickhull algorithm for convex hulls. ACM Trans. on Mathematical Software **22** (1996) 469–483
27. Vandenberghe, L., Boyd, S., Wu, S.: Determinant maximization with linear matrix inequalities. SIAM Journ. Matrix Analysis and Applications **19** (1998) 499–533
28. Chutinan, A., Krogh, B.H.: Computational techniques for hybrid system verification. IEEE Trans. on Automatic Control **48** (2003)

Model Checking LTL over Controllable Linear Systems Is Decidable

Paulo Tabuada and George J. Pappas

Department of Electrical and Systems Engineering
University of Pennsylvania
Philadelphia, PA 19104
{tabuadap,pappasg}@seas.upenn.edu

Abstract. The use of algorithmic verification and synthesis tools for hybrid systems is currently limited to systems exhibiting simple continuous dynamics such as timed automata or rectangular hybrid systems. In this paper we enlarge the class of systems amenable to algorithmic analysis and synthesis by showing decidability of model checking Linear Temporal Logic (LTL) formulas over discrete time, controllable, linear systems. This result follows from the construction of a language equivalent, finite abstraction of a control system based on a set of finite observations which correspond to the atomic propositions appearing in a given LTL formula. Furthermore, the size of this abstraction is shown to be polynomial in the dimension of the control system and the number of observations. These results open the doors for verification and synthesis of continuous and hybrid control systems from LTL specifications.

1 Introduction

Hybrid systems are a powerful modeling paradigm for large-scale, complex systems where interaction between discrete and continuous components occurs. Due to highly nontrivial interaction between discrete and continuous components, one would like to have automatic tools for the analysis and synthesis of such systems. Unfortunately, existing tools only address classes of systems with very simple continuous dynamics, such as timed automata [2], multi-rate automata [1] or rectangular hybrid systems [25,13].

The main contribution of this paper is to show that algorithmic approaches are also possible for larger classes of continuous dynamics. In particular, we show that given a specification described by a Linear Temporal Logic (LTL) formula φ, it is possible to construct a language equivalent finite abstraction of a discrete time, controllable, linear system based on the formula φ. This construction immediately implies that model checking a specification formula φ over a linear system is decidable as it can be performed on the finite abstraction. Furthermore, these results also open the doors for automatic controller synthesis of linear systems from LTL specifications. Combining automatic synthesis for continuous systems with existing tools for discrete systems [16,18,19,11] will eventually lead to automatic synthesis for hybrid systems.

O. Maler and A. Pnueli (Eds.): HSCC 2003, LNCS 2623, pp. 498–513, 2003.

Automatic analysis and synthesis of hybrid systems began with the seminal work of Alur and Dill on timed automata [2]. Subsequent extensions lead to multi-rate automata [1] and rectangular hybrid automata [25,13] which lies on the decidability boundary [14]. Different classes of dynamics for which finite abstractions exist were introduced in [17] by combining tools from logic and linear dynamical systems. See also [3] for a survey of these methods. Nonlinear dynamics were considered in [6], and bisimulation based on foliations transverse to the nonlinear flow were introduced. A different kind of dynamics, simple planar differential inclusions, was considered in [4] where it was shown that qualitative analysis of system trajectories is decidable by making use of unique topological properties of the plane.

Our approach differs from all the above in that we consider *control* systems instead of dynamical systems. It is the use of control that allows to modify[1] the trajectories of the system into a form which admits a finite representation. Hence, our results are closer to synthesis than verification problems. Another important difference is that we consider continuous control systems in discrete time as opposed to continuous time. Synthesis for hybrid systems using logic has already been considered in [22], however the logic is not used to model the specifications but rather to motivate the development of the synthesis procedures as well as to prove several facts regarding the proposed algorithms. Other synthesis techniques include supervisory control based on approximate finite abstractions [9], invariants for the continuous dynamics [28], convexity properties of affine systems [12] and mixed integer linear programming [5].

The construction of the finite abstraction of a given control system is performed in two steps, each exploiting in a fundamental way the ability to shape the system trajectories by appropriate choices of control. First, we show that (by the use of control) we can transform any discrete time, controllable, linear system into a canonical form, which induces a quotient system on a denumerable state space, namely $\mathbb{Z}^n$. If the observations are also compatible with the quotient, we have a bisimilar quotient. This first step depends crucially on the controllability of the original system. The second step further abstracts the quotient system into a finite, language equivalent system based on a finite set of observations. The finiteness of this abstraction is again a consequence of the controllability properties of the original control system.

The outline of this paper is the following. We revisit transition systems in Section 2 and discuss the relation between linear control systems and transition systems in Section 3. Section 4 shows how a denumerable (but not finite, however) bisimulation of a control system can be obtained. This bisimulation can be further reduced to a language equivalent finite abstraction. This is described in Section 5, where the main contribution of the paper is also presented. For space reasons no proofs are presented and the interested reader is referred to [29].

---

[1] We note that the results in [4] can also be given a control interpretation. The authors prove a normal form for the edge crossing trajectories (edge signatures) by showing that for any system trajectory, there is another with the same qualitative properties but with a special structure. This new trajectory can then be though as the result of applying a suitable control law. However, our results are not restricted to planar systems.

2   Transition Systems

Given a set S (finite or not), we denote by S^ω the set of all infinite strings formed by elements of S. An element of S^ω is of the form $\alpha = \alpha_1 \alpha_2 \ldots$ and we identify it with the map $\alpha : \mathbb{N} \to S$ by setting $\alpha(1) = \alpha_1$, $\alpha(2) = \alpha_2$, etc. The main object used in this work are transition systems:

Definition 1. *A transition system with observations is a tuple $T = (Q, L, \longrightarrow, O, h)$, where:*

- Q *is a (possibly infinite) set of states,*
- L *is a (possibly infinite) set of labels,*
- $\longrightarrow \subseteq Q \times L \times Q$ *is a transition relation,*
- O *is a (possibly infinite) set of observations,*
- $h : Q \to O$ *is a map assigning to each $q \in Q$ an observation $h(q) \in O$.*

We say that T is finite when Q, L, O are finite, and infinite otherwise. We will usually denote by $q \xrightarrow{l} q'$ a triple (q, l, q') belonging to $\longrightarrow$. As we will only use transition systems with observations, we shall refer to them simply as transition systems. Transition systems define subsets of O^ω, also called languages:

Definition 2. *Given a transition system $T = (Q, L, \longrightarrow, O, h)$, we say that $\gamma \in O^\omega$ is an observed string of T if there exists a pair of infinite strings $(\alpha, \beta) \in Q^\omega \times L^\omega$ such that $\alpha(i) \xrightarrow{\beta(i)} \alpha(i+1)$ and $\gamma(i) = h(\alpha(i))$ for every $i \in \mathbb{N}$. The collection of all observed strings is denoted by $\mathbf{L}(T)$ and defines the language of the transition system.*

Given transition systems T_1 and T_2 with the same observation space, we say that T_1 is language equivalent to T_2 when $\mathbf{L}(T_1) = \mathbf{L}(T_2)$. For later use we introduce also the Pre operator. Given a state $q \in Q$, we denote by $\mathrm{Pre}(q)$ the set of states in Q that can reach q in one step, that is:

$$\mathrm{Pre}(q) = \{q' \in Q \; : \; q' \xrightarrow{l} q \text{ for some } l \in L\}$$

We extend Pre to sets $Q' \subseteq Q$ in the usual way:

$$\mathrm{Pre}(Q') = \bigcup_{q' \in Q'} \mathrm{Pre}(q')$$

Finally, we recursively define $\mathrm{Pre}^i(Q')$ by:

$$\begin{aligned} \mathrm{Pre}^1(Q') &= \mathrm{Pre}(Q') \\ \mathrm{Pre}^i(Q') &= \mathrm{Pre}(\mathrm{Pre}^{i-1}(Q')) \end{aligned} \tag{1}$$

2.1   Transition Systems as LTL Models

Linear temporal logic (LTL) provides a succinct and formal way of representing temporal properties of dynamical and control systems. In this section we briefly describe the syntax and semantics of LTL.

Specification formulas are built from atomic propositions belonging to a finite set $\mathcal{P}$ and are recursively defined by:

- **true, false**, p and $\neg p$ are LTL formulas for all $p \in \mathcal{P}$;
- if φ_1 and φ_2 are LTL formulas, then $\varphi_1 \wedge \varphi_2$ and $\varphi_1 \vee \varphi_2$ are LTL formulas;
- if φ_1 and φ_2 are LTL formulas, then $\bigcirc\varphi_1$ and $\varphi_1 \mathcal{U} \varphi_2$ are LTL formulas.

The operator $\bigcirc$ is read as "next", with the meaning that the formula it precedes will be true in the next time step. The second operator $\mathcal{U}$ is read as "until" and the formula $\varphi_1 \mathcal{U} \varphi_2$ specifies that φ_1 must hold until φ_2 holds.

We shall interpret LTL formulas over observed sequences of transition systems. We consider that the set of observations O is defined by $\mathcal{P} \cup \{\tau\}$ for some element $\tau \notin \mathcal{P}$. This allows to use LTL formulas to specify the sequences of observations. The special symbol τ is used to represent observations not corresponding to any atomic proposition. LTL formulas are now interpreted over sequences of observations $\gamma : \mathbb{N} \to O$ as follows:

For any $p \in \mathcal{P}$, LTL formulas φ_1, φ_2, and $i \in \mathbb{N}$:

- $\gamma(i) \models p$ iff $p = \gamma(i)$,
- $\gamma(i) \models \varphi \wedge \varphi_2$ iff $\gamma(i) \models \varphi_1$ and $\gamma(i) \models \varphi_2$,
- $\gamma(i) \models \varphi \vee \varphi_2$ iff $\gamma(i) \models \varphi_1$ or $\gamma(i) \models \varphi_2$,
- $\gamma(i) \models \bigcirc\varphi_1$ iff $\gamma(i+1) \models \varphi_1$,
- $\gamma(i) \models \varphi_1 \mathcal{U} \varphi_2$ iff $\exists j \geq i$ such that for all k, $0 \leq k < j$ $\gamma(k) \models \varphi_1$ and $\gamma(j) \models \varphi_2$.

Finally we say that a sequence γ satisfies formula φ iff $\gamma(0) \models \varphi$.

In Section 3 we will associate a transition system with a given control system. Such association will enable the use of LTL as a specification mechanism for control systems through the use of the associated transition system.

2.2   Relationships between Transition Systems

We now review some relationships between transition systems. The interested reader may which to consult [8,20] for a detailed discussion these and other related concepts. We start by introducing simulation and bisimulation relations [21, 24].

Definition 3 (Simulation and Bisimulation). *Let* $T_1 = (Q_1, L_1, \longrightarrow_1, O, h_1)$ *and* $T_2 = (Q_2, L_2, \longrightarrow_2, O, h_2)$ *be transition systems and* $R \subseteq Q_1 \times Q_2$ *a relation. Relation* R *is a simulation relation from* T_1 *to* T_2 *if* $(q_1, q_2) \in R$ *implies:*

- *if* $q_1 \xrightarrow{l_1}_1 q_1'$, *there exists* $q_2' \in Q_2$, $l_2 \in L_2$ *such that* $q_2 \xrightarrow{l_2}_2 q_2'$ *and* $(q_1', q_2') \in R$,
- $h(q_1) = h(q_2)$.

Relation R *is a bisimulation relation between* T_1 *and* T_2 *if* R *is a simulation relation from* T_1 *to* T_2 *and* R^{-1} *is a simulation relation from* T_2 *to* T_1.

We note that in the previous definition we require the observation spaces of T_1 and T_2 to be the same. Furthermore, we only require T_2 to match transitions in T_1 with transitions having equal observations but not necessarily equal labels as we are only interested in the observed behavior.

We now review several important consequences of bisimulation relations:

Theorem 1. *Let* $T_1 = (Q_1, L_1, \longrightarrow_1, O, h_1)$ *and* $T_2 = (Q_2, L_2, \longrightarrow_2, O, h_2)$ *be transition systems and* $R \subseteq Q_1 \times Q_2$ *a bisimulation relation between* T_1 *and* T_2. *Then, they are language equivalent, that is, the following equality holds:*

$$\mathbf{L}(T_1) = \mathbf{L}(T_2)$$

Language equivalence is important as it ensures that properties expressible in LTL are preserved:

Theorem 2 ([27,10]). *Let* T_1 *and* T_2 *be two language equivalent transition systems. Then, any LTL formula interpreted over observed sequences is satisfied by* T_1 *iff it is satisfied by* T_2.

Combining Corollary 1 with Theorem 2 we conclude that bisimilarity preserves properties expressible in LTL, however bisimilarity also preserves properties expressible in other temporal logics such as CTL, CTL* and μ-calculus [8].

3   Linear Control Systems as Transition Systems

Control systems can be seen as specifying infinite transition systems. In this section we will see how to extract such transition systems from linear control systems:

Definition 4. *A discrete time, linear control system* $\Sigma = (A, B)$ *is a controlled, discrete dynamical system defined by:*

$$x(t+1) = Ax(t) + Bu(t) \tag{2}$$

with $x(t) \in \mathbb{R}^n$, $A \in \mathbb{Q}^{n \times n}$, $B \in \mathbb{Q}^{n \times m}$, $u(t) \in \mathbb{R}^m$ *and* $t \in \mathbb{N}$.

The vector x describes the state of the system which can be influenced by the inputs u through the controlled dynamics (2). Although in control theory [26] it is customary to define A as an element of $\mathbb{R}^{n \times n}$ and B as an element of $\mathbb{R}^{n \times m}$, we consider only rational entries since any computer implementation of the results presented in this paper requires computable or decidable fields. The number n is the dimension of the control system.

In this paper we consider discrete time, controllable, linear systems. A control system is controllable if every point in the state space is reachable from any other point in the state space. Such property can be effectively decided through Kalman's rank condition which asserts that a control system $\Sigma = (A, B)$ is controllable iff the matrix $[B \ AB \ \dots \ A^{n-2}B \ A^{n-1}B]$ is full row rank [26].

Given a linear control system $\Sigma = (A, B)$ we can construct a transition system T_Σ defined by:

$$T_\Sigma = (\mathbb{R}^n, \mathbb{R}^m, \longrightarrow, O, h)$$

with $\longrightarrow \subseteq \mathbb{R}^n \times \mathbb{R}^m \times \mathbb{R}^n$ given by $x \xrightarrow{u} x'$ iff $x' = Ax + Bu$.

The observation space O and observation map h are not defined by Σ. The nature of O and h will be determined in the next sections. We note that T_Σ is only one of the possible embeddings, described in [23], of control systems in the class of transition systems.

4   Controllable Linear Systems and Their Denumerable Bisimulations

The main contribution of this paper is to provide a decidability result obtained through the computation of a finite abstraction of T_Σ for a given discrete time, controllable, linear system Σ and finite set of observations O. This finite abstraction will be constructed through several intermediate steps, the first one being the extraction of a bisimulation with denumerable state space from T_Σ. This will be achieved by transforming the control system into a normal form which immediately suggests how to obtain such a denumerable bisimulation.

We consider a discrete time, controllable, linear system $\Sigma = (A, B)$ and transform it to a special form called Brunovsky normal form [26]:

Definition 5 (Brunovsky normal form). *Consider a linear control system of dimension n with m inputs defined by the pair of matrices (A, B) and let $k = (k_1, k_2, \dots, k_r)$ be a sequence of integers satisfying:*

$$k_1 \geq k_2 \geq \dots \geq k_r \quad and \quad k_1 + k_2 + \dots + k_r = n \qquad (3)$$

We say that the pair (A, B) is in Brunovsky normal form if matrices A and B are of the following form:

$$A = \begin{bmatrix} A_{k_1} & 0 & \dots & 0 \\ 0 & A_{k_2} & \dots & 0 \\ \vdots & \vdots & \ddots & \vdots \\ 0 & 0 & \dots & A_{k_r} \end{bmatrix} \quad B = \begin{bmatrix} b_{k_1} & 0 & \dots & 0 & 0 \dots 0 \\ 0 & b_{k_2} & \dots & 0 & 0 \dots 0 \\ \vdots & \vdots & \ddots & \vdots & \vdots \ddots \vdots \\ 0 & 0 & \dots & b_{k_r} & 0 \dots 0 \end{bmatrix} \qquad (4)$$

where matrix A is partitioned in r^2 blocks while matrix B is partitioned in mr blocks. Each block A_{k_i} and b_{k_i} are of the form:

$$A_{k_i} = \begin{bmatrix} 0 & 1 & 0 & \cdots & 0 \\ 0 & 0 & 1 & \cdots & 0 \\ \vdots & \vdots & \vdots & \ddots & \vdots \\ 0 & 0 & 0 & \cdots & 1 \\ \alpha_1^i & \alpha_2^i & \alpha_3^i & \cdots & \alpha_{k_i}^i \end{bmatrix} \qquad b_{k_i} = \begin{bmatrix} 0 \\ 0 \\ \vdots \\ 0 \\ 1 \end{bmatrix} \tag{5}$$

where $\lambda^{k_i} - \alpha_{k_i}^i \lambda^{k_i-1} - \ldots - \alpha_2^i \lambda - \alpha_1^i$ is the characteristic polynomial[2] of A_{k_i}.

Any controllable linear system can be effectively transformed to Brunovsky normal form by a change of state coordinates as asserted by the following result:

Theorem 3 ([7,15]). *For every controllable linear system, there exists a unique sequence of integers $k = (k_1, k_2, \ldots, k_r)$ satisfying (3) and an invertible linear transformation $P \in \mathbb{Q}^{n \times n}$ such that the pair (PAP^{-1}, PB) is in Brunovsky normal form.*

In addition to state transformation P, we consider also a feedback transformation determining new inputs u' from inputs u and state x as follows:

$$\begin{bmatrix} u_1' \\ u_2' \\ \vdots \\ u_m' \end{bmatrix} = \begin{bmatrix} u_1 + \alpha_1^1 x_1 + \alpha_2^1 x_2 + \ldots + \alpha_{k_1}^1 x_{k_1} \\ u_2 + \alpha_1^2 x_{k_1+1} + \alpha_2^2 x_{k_1+2} + \ldots + \alpha_{k_2}^2 x_{k_1+k_2} \\ \vdots \\ u_m + \alpha_1^r x_{n-k_r+1} + \alpha_2^r x_{n-k_r+2} + \ldots + \alpha_{k_r}^r x_n \end{bmatrix} \tag{6}$$

where we assumed $m = r$, which corresponds to the requirement that columns of matrix B are linearly independent and constitutes no loss of generality. Such assumption will be used throughout the paper. Combining state transformation P with feedback transformation (6) we obtain the invertible transformation U : $\mathbb{R}^n \times \mathbb{R}^m \to \mathbb{R}^n \times \mathbb{R}^m$ defined by:

$$\begin{bmatrix} x' \\ u' \end{bmatrix} = U \begin{bmatrix} x \\ u \end{bmatrix} = \begin{bmatrix} P & \mathbf{0}_{n \times m} \\ V & \mathbf{I}_{m \times m} \end{bmatrix} \begin{bmatrix} x \\ u \end{bmatrix} \tag{7}$$

where $\mathbf{0}_{n \times m}$ is a $n \times m$ matrix of zeros, $\mathbf{I}_{m \times m}$ is the $m \times m$ identity matrix and V is a matrix where each row v_i is of the form:

$$v_i = \begin{bmatrix} \mathbf{0}_{1 \times (k_1+k_2+\ldots+k_{i-1})} & \alpha_1^i & \alpha_2^i & \cdots & \alpha_{k_i}^i & \mathbf{0}_{1 \times (k_{i+1}+\ldots+k_r)} \end{bmatrix} \tag{8}$$

Note that, as it was the case for P, transformation U is also invertible and has rational entries. The control system $\Sigma' = (A', B')$ obtained from Σ by

---

[2] The characteristic polynomial of a square matrix A is given by $\det(A - \lambda I)$, where I is the identity matrix. Note that since A has rational entries, the coefficients α_j^i are also rational.

transformation U has state space $\mathbb{R}^n$ with coordinates $x' = Px$, input space $\mathbb{R}^m$ with coordinates u' defined by (6) and is of the form:

$$x'(t+1) = A'x'(t) + B'u'(t) \tag{9}$$

where the pair (A', B') is defined by block matrices with the format (4), but where each block is of the form:

$$A'_{k_i} = \begin{bmatrix} 0 & 1 & 0 & \dots & 0 \\ 0 & 0 & 1 & \dots & 0 \\ \vdots & \vdots & \vdots & \ddots & \vdots \\ 0 & 0 & 0 & \dots & 1 \\ 0 & 0 & 0 & \dots & 0 \end{bmatrix} \qquad b'_{k_i} = \begin{bmatrix} 0 \\ 0 \\ \vdots \\ 0 \\ 1 \end{bmatrix} \tag{10}$$

We now see that the effect of feedback (6) was to cancel out the last line of the matrices A'_{k_i}. This has the effect of rendering these matrices nilpotent and can only be achieved by means of control. This fact marks the departure of the presented results from existing techniques for dynamical systems, where no inputs are available to modify the system dynamics. We shall refer to the form (9), (10) as the *shift register* form. This name is justified by the representation of control system (9) presented in Figure 1. In the control literature, the use of feedback transformations of the form (6) is usually referred to as *deadbeat control*, see for example, [26], Section 1.3, for a quick introduction to digital control.

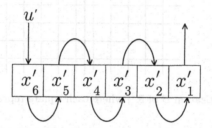

Fig. 1. Representation of a discrete time system in shift register form as a shift register for $n = 6$ and $m = 1$.

Control systems Σ and Σ' are related by the invertible transformation U which has the following immediate consequence for the transition systems they define:

Proposition 1. *Let $T_\Sigma = (\mathbb{R}^n, \mathbb{R}^m, \longrightarrow_\Sigma, O, h_\Sigma)$ be the transition system defined by a discrete time, controllable, linear system Σ of dimension n with m inputs, let Σ' be the shift register form of Σ and $T_{\Sigma'} = (\mathbb{R}^n, \mathbb{R}^m, \longrightarrow_{\Sigma'}, O, h_{\Sigma'})$ the corresponding transition system. Given any observation map $h_{\Sigma'} : \mathbb{R}^n \to O$ for $T_{\Sigma'}$, the choice of observation map $h_\Sigma = h_{\Sigma'} \circ P$ for T_Σ renders T_Σ bisimilar to $T_{\Sigma'}$ with respect to the relation $R \subseteq \mathbb{R}^n \times \mathbb{R}^n$ defined by:*

$$R = \{(x, x') \in \mathbb{R}^n \times \mathbb{R}^n \ : \ Px = x'\}$$

Proposition 1 is not surprising since Σ and Σ' are isomorphic via the invertible linear transformation U. However, this result paves the way to the introduction of a new transition system, bisimilar to $T_{\Sigma'}$, but with state space $\mathbb{Z}^n$. The new state space $\mathbb{Z}^n$ is obtained from $\mathbb{R}^n$ through the following quantization:

$$\mathcal{B} = \bigcup_{z \in \mathbb{Z}^n} B^\delta(z)$$

where the blocks $B^\delta(z)$ are defined for any $\delta \in \mathbb{Q}^+$ by:

$$B^\delta(z) = \{x \in \mathbb{R}^n \ : \ \delta z_i - \delta/2 < x'_i \leq \delta z_i + \delta/2 \qquad i = 1, 2, \ldots, n\}$$

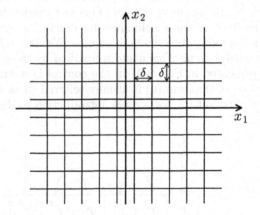

Fig. 2. Quantization $\mathcal{B}$ of $\mathbb{R}^2$, where each square represents a block $B^\delta(z)$.

The quantization induced by $\mathcal{B}$ defines the new state space by identifying each block $B^\delta(z) \subset \mathbb{R}^n$ with the point $z \in \mathbb{Z}^n$. This identification is given by the quantization map $h_\mathcal{B} : \mathbb{R}^n \to \mathbb{Z}^n$, where the ith component $h_{\mathcal{B}i}$ of $h_\mathcal{B}$ is defined by:

$$h_{\mathcal{B}i}(x') = \left\lfloor \frac{x'_i}{\delta} + \frac{1}{2}\mathrm{sgn}(\frac{x'_i}{\delta}) \right\rfloor \tag{11}$$

In the previous expression, $\lfloor a \rfloor$ denotes the floor map, returning the integer part of a while sgn denotes the sign map defined by:

$$\mathrm{sgn}(a) = \begin{cases} -1 \text{ if } a < 0 \\ 1 \text{ if } a \geq 0 \end{cases}$$

For the sake of exposition, we now assume that $n = 2$ and $m = 1$, as this will allow to represent graphically the next steps of the construction. For $n = 2$,

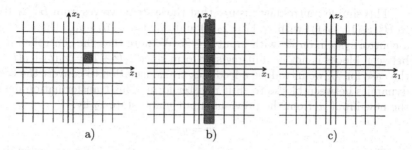

Fig. 3. Controlled evolution on the space of blocks. The left figure represents the initial state $B^\delta(2,1)$ at $t = 0$. The middle figure illustrates the reachable set in one step from the initial condition, while the right figure represents the set reached for input $w = 2$.

the quantization defined by $\mathcal{B}$ divides the plane in a square grid of resolution δ as displayed in Figure 2. We now introduce a control system on $\mathbb{Z}^2$, which we shall denote by Γ, such that T_Γ will be bisimilar to $T_{\Sigma'}$ under suitably defined[3] observations. The construction of Γ exploits the fact that, the shift register form of Σ' induces a well defined controlled dynamics between blocks of the quantization $\mathcal{B}$. This means that, under appropriate inputs, blocks will move into other blocks of the grid.

To illustrate the main idea of the construction process, consider all the points $(x_1', x_2') \in B^\delta(z_1, z_2)$ for some $(z_1, z_2) \in \mathbb{Z}^2$. These points (x_1', x_2') are represented in Figure 3a) for $(z_1, z_2) = (2,1)$ and satisfy at $t = 0$:

$$\delta z_2 - \delta/2 < x_2'(0) \le \delta z_2 + \delta/2$$

Since control system Σ' is in shift register form, $x_1'(1) = x_2'(0)$, that is:

$$\delta z_2 - \delta/2 < x_1'(1) \le \delta z_2 - \delta/2 \tag{12}$$

This shows that, after one time step, all the points in block $B^\delta(z_1, z_2)$ will be contained in the vertical strip displayed in Figure 3b) and defined by (12). To have a well defined controlled dynamics between blocks, we only need to ensure that $x_2'(1)$ will, in fact, be contained in a interval of length δ. However, this can easily be achieved with the control law:

$$u'(t) = x_2'(t) + \delta y(t), \quad y \in \mathbb{Z} \tag{13}$$

The following computations show that $x_2'(1)$ will also lie on a interval of length δ:

$$
\begin{aligned}
\delta z_2 - \delta/2 &< x_2'(0) \le & \delta z_2 + \delta/2 \\
\delta z_2 + \delta y(0) - \delta/2 &< x_2'(0) + \delta y(0) \le \delta z_2 + \delta y(0) + \delta/2 \\
\hline
\delta(z_2 + y(0)) - \delta/2 &< x_2'(1) \le & \delta(z_2 + y(0)) + \delta/2
\end{aligned}
$$

---

[3] Recall that Proposition 1 holds for any observation map $h_{\Sigma'}$.

This simple control law ensures that the system evolves from $B^\delta(z_1(0), z_2(0))$ to $B^\delta(z_1(1), z_2(1))$ with $z_1(1) = z_2(0)$ and $z_2(1) = z_2(0) + y(0)$ therefore defining a control system on $\mathbb{Z}^2$ with input $y \in \mathbb{Z}$. We note that the controlled dynamics between blocks is not in shift register form since $z_2(t+1) = z_2(t) + y(t)$. As was the case for Σ, we introduce a feedback transformation to convert the controlled dynamics between blocks to shift register form. This transformation determines the new input w from the previous input y and state z_2 by:

$$w = y + z_2 \tag{14}$$

The previous argument used for the construction of the controlled dynamics between blocks can be extended for any n and m resulting in control system Γ defined by:

$$z(t+1) = A'z(t) + B'w(t)$$

for $z \in \mathbb{Z}^n$ and $w \in \mathbb{Z}^m$. Transition system $T_{\Sigma'}$ can now be related to transition system T_Γ defined by control system Γ:

Theorem 4. *Let $T_{\Sigma'} = (\mathbb{R}^n, \mathbb{R}^m, \longrightarrow_{\Sigma'}, O, h_{\Sigma'})$ be the transition system defined by control system Σ' and let $T_\Gamma = (\mathbb{Z}^n, \mathbb{Z}^m, \longrightarrow_\Gamma, O, h_\Gamma)$ be the transition system defined by control system Γ. Given any observation map $h_\Gamma : \mathbb{Z}^n \to O$ for T_Γ, the choice of observation map $h_{\Sigma'} = h_\Gamma \circ h_B$ for $T_{\Sigma'}$ renders $T_{\Sigma'}$ bisimilar to T_Γ with respect to the relation $R^\delta \subseteq \mathbb{R}^n \times \mathbb{Z}^n$ defined by:*

$$R^\delta = \left\{ (x', z) \in \mathbb{R}^n \times \mathbb{Z}^n \ : \ h_B(x') = z \right\} \tag{15}$$

In practice it is not necessary to compute T_Γ to obtain a finite abstraction of T_Σ. Instead, we compute the finite abstraction directly from Σ as described in the next section. However, the introduction of T_Γ greatly simplifies the presentation of the forthcoming results.

5   Language Equivalent Finite Abstractions

In this section we further restrict the set of observations O to be finite. We consider a finite set $S \subset \mathbb{Z}^n$ on the state space of T_Γ and define the observation space O to be:

$$O = S \cup \{\tau\} \tag{16}$$

for some $\tau \notin S$. The set S is identified with the finite set of atomic propositions $\mathcal{P}$ appearing in a given LTL specification formula. Finiteness of observations, and the shift register form of Γ will now allow to obtain a language equivalent, finite abstraction of T_Γ. This finite abstraction requires the following subsets of the state space, defined for any $a \in S$:

$$C_0^a = \{a\}$$
$$C_1^a = \mathrm{Pre}(C_0^a) \backslash S$$
$$C_2^a = \mathrm{Pre}(C_1^a) \backslash S$$
$$\vdots$$
$$C_{k_1}^a = \mathrm{Pre}(C_{k_1-1}^a) \backslash S$$

These sets have some properties that are fundamental to define the finite abstraction of T_Γ:

Proposition 2. *For any $0 \le i \le k_1$ and $a \in S$, the sets C_i^a are nonempty.*

Proposition 3. *For any $a \in S$, $b \in \mathbb{Z}^n$ there exists a $c \in C_{k_1}^a$ such that $b \in \mathrm{Pre}(c)$.*

Proposition 3 is the heart of the finite abstraction construction. It shows that, if it is possible to go from a state z to a state a without visiting S, then it is possible to do so in no more than $k_1 + 1$ steps. This bound on the number of steps implies a finite bound on the number of states necessary to encode the controlled dynamics between states in S and hence finiteness of the abstraction.

We now have all the necessary ingredients to construct a finite transition system $T_\Delta = (Q, L, \longrightarrow_\Delta, O, h_\Delta)$ defined by:

$$Q = S \times \{0, 1, 2, \ldots, k_1\} \tag{17}$$
$$L = \{1\} \tag{18}$$
$$O = S \cup \{\tau\} \tag{19}$$
$$h_\Delta((a, i)) = \begin{cases} a \text{ if } i = 0 \\ \tau \text{ if } i \ne 0 \end{cases} \tag{20}$$

It remains to define the transition relation $\longrightarrow_\Delta \subseteq Q \times L \times Q$. We proceed as follows:

$$((a, k_1), 1, (a, k_1)) \in \longrightarrow_\Delta \quad \text{for any } a \in S, \tag{21}$$
$$((a, i), 1, (a, i-1)) \in \longrightarrow_\Delta \quad \text{for any } a \in S \text{ and any } 1 \le i \le k_1, \tag{22}$$
$$((a, 0), 1, (b, 0)) \in \longrightarrow_\Delta \quad \text{for any } a, b \in S \text{ such that } a \in \mathrm{Pre}(b), \tag{23}$$
$$((a, 0), 1, (b, i)) \in \longrightarrow_\Delta \quad \text{for any } a, b \in S \text{ such that } a \in \mathrm{Pre}(c)$$
$$\text{for some } c \in C_i^b, \ 1 \le i \le k_1 - 1, \tag{24}$$
$$((a, 0), 1, (b, k_1)) \in \longrightarrow_\Delta \quad \text{for any } a, b \in S. \tag{25}$$

Intuitively, we retain from T_Γ all the states $a \in S$ in the form $(a, 0) \in Q$, as well as all the transitions between these states. However, to capture the controlled dynamics between states not in S, only k_1 states of additional memory are required for each $a \in S$ and these states are encoded by the states $(a, i) \in Q$ for $1 \le i \le k_1$.

The finite transition system T_Δ obtained through the previous construction is language equivalent to the infinite transition system T_Γ as asserted in the next result:

Theorem 5. *Let $T_\Delta = (Q, L, \longrightarrow_\Delta, O, h_\Delta)$ be the finite transition system obtained from $T_\Gamma = (\mathbb{Z}^n, \mathbb{Z}^m, \longrightarrow_\Gamma, O, h_\Gamma)$ by the previous construction and consider the observation space $O = S \cup \{\tau\}$ and the observation maps:*

$$h_\Gamma(z) = \begin{cases} z \text{ if } z \in S \\ \tau \text{ if } z \notin S \end{cases} \qquad h_\Delta((z, i)) = \begin{cases} z \text{ if } i = 0 \\ \tau \text{ if } i \ne 0 \end{cases}$$

Transition systems T_Γ and T_Δ are language equivalent.

Transition system T_Δ has $(k_1 + 1)|S|$ states, which shows that in the worst case the size of T_Δ grows linearly with the dimension of the control system. The size of T_Δ is also linear in the number of observables, which is natural, as the observed dynamics is also encoded in T_Δ. Furthermore, the size of T_Δ is independent of the grid resolution δ considered in the previous section. This is another important factor contributing for the scalability of the proposed results.

As our main result asserts decidability of model checking, we start by showing that the computation of T_Δ from Σ can be performed in a finite number of steps:

Lemma 1. *Let $\Sigma = (A, B)$ be a discrete time, controllable, linear system and consider a finite set of observations $O = S \cup \{\tau\}$, where $\tau \notin S$ and elements in S denote subsets of $\mathbb{R}^n$ of the form $P^{-1}h_B^{-1}(h_B(Px))$, $x \in \mathbb{R}^n$ and h_B^{-1} denoting the set valued inverse of h_B. Then, constructing T_Δ from Σ can be performed in a finite number of steps.*

The main contribution of the paper is now obtained by combining Proposition 1 with Theorems 4 and 5, and Lemma 1. Intuitively the result follows from the ability to effectively construct T_Δ and from the fact that T_Σ is language equivalent to T_Δ under the appropriate observations.

Theorem 6. *Let Σ be a discrete time, controllable, linear system on $\mathbb{R}^n$ and φ any LTL formula where each atomic proposition denotes a subset of $\mathbb{R}^n$ of the form $P^{-1}h_B^{-1}(h_B(Px))$, $x \in \mathbb{R}^n$ and h_B^{-1} denoting the set valued inverse of h_B. Then, determining if T_Σ satisfies φ is decidable.*

The previous result can also be summarized in the following diagram:

$$T_\Sigma \xrightarrow{bisimilar} T_{\Sigma'} \xrightarrow{bisimilar} T_\Gamma \xrightarrow{lang.\ eq.} T_\Delta$$

where the relationships between the several transition systems are represented. As bisimilarity implies language equivalence and language equivalence preserves LTL formulas, the previous figure shows that deciding if T_Σ is a model for a LTL formula is equivalent to decide if T_Δ is a model for the same formula. However, such translation between models is accompanied by an appropriate translation of the sets denoted by the atomic propositions. To see this, consider the following diagram representing the relation between the observation spaces of the several transitions systems:

$$\mathbb{R}^n \xrightarrow{P} \mathbb{R}^n \xrightarrow{h_B} \mathbb{Z}^n \xrightarrow{h_\Gamma} S \cup \{\tau\}$$

We now see that an atomic proposition denoting a set of the form $P^{-1}h_B^{-1}(h_B(Px))$ for T_Σ is mapped by P to a set of the form $PP^{-1}h_B^{-1}(h_B(Px)) = h_B^{-1}(h_B(x'))$ for $T_{\Sigma'}$ and since this set is a quantization block, the quantization map h_B now transforms it to an element $h_B(x') = z \in \mathbb{Z}^n$. The finite set S is chosen so as to capture every $z \in \mathbb{Z}^n$ which is the image of a set in $\mathbb{R}^n$ denoted by an atomic proposition. Therefore observed sequences of transition system T_Δ represent sequences of atomic propositions interleaved with sequences of the element τ, denoting that no atomic proposition is satisfied.

The above discussion shows that there is a tradeoff between the decidability result of Theorem 6 and the requirement of having atomic propositions denoting sets of the special form $P^{-1}h_{\bar{B}}^{-1}(h_B(Px))$. These sets are hypercubes skewed by the linear transformation P^{-1}, where the amount of linear distortion caused by P^{-1} is determined by the controllability properties of Σ. Nevertheless, these sets can be arbitrarily scaled by properly adjusting the resolution parameter δ and used to model any other set as a union of such skewed hypercubes.

6 Discussion

Theorem 6 shows that given a discrete time, controllable, linear system Σ, and a LTL formula φ with adequate atomic propositions, we can effectively decide if T_Σ is a model for φ. However, this result is far more interesting and important for control design than for verification. From the assumption of controllability, we know that every state is reachable from any other state, which somewhat reduces the interest in verification questions. Furthermore, we have used several times, in a fundamental way, the fact that control inputs u take values in an unbounded set, namely $\mathbb{R}^m$. This makes somewhat difficult to interpret the action of u as the environment or as a disturbance acting on the system. Nevertheless, these results seem extremely promising at the level of control design. Given a specification formula φ, one can determine the intersection of the language satisfying φ with the language of transition system T_Δ in the form of a Buchi automaton. Such automaton can then be refined to define a controller for T_Σ. This allows to design controllers for all the specifications expressible in LTL thereby enriching the class of specifications (and respective controller designs) usually used in control theory. We note that, although the system is assumed to be controllable, not every specification is achievable by the system. Even the simple formula $\varphi_1 \, \mathcal{U} \, \varphi_2$ may represent an unachievable specification as the system may need to leave the set denoted by atomic proposition φ_1 in order to reach the set denoted by φ_2.

Acknowledgments. The authors greatly acknowledge Salvatore La Torre, P. Madhusudan and Rajeev Alur for their guidance among many automata theoretic ramifications of temporal logic. This research was partially supported by the NSF Information Technology Research grant CCR01-21431 and NSF CAREER CCR-01-32716.

References

1. R. Alur, C.Courcoubetis, N. Halbwachs, T.A. Henzinger, P.H. Ho, X. Nicollin, A.Olivero, J. Sifakis, and S. Yovine. Hybrid automata: An algorithmic approach to specification and verification of hybrid systems. *Theoretical Computer Science*, 138:3–34, 1995.
2. R. Alur and D.L. Dill. A theory of timed automata. *Theoretical Computer Science*, 126:183–235, 1994.
3. Rajeev Alur, Thomas A. Henzinger, Gerardo Lafferriere, and George J. Pappas. Discrete abstractions of hybrid systems. *Proceedings of the IEEE*, 88:971–984, 2000.

4. E. Asarin, G. Schneider, and S. Yovine. On the decidability of the reachability problem for planar differential inclusions. In M. D. Di Benedetto and A. Sangiovanni-Vincentelli, editors, *Hybrid Systems: Computation and Control*, volume 2034 of *Lecture Notes in Computer Science*, pages 89–104. Springer-Verlag, 2001.

5. A. Bemporad and M.Morari. Control of systems integrating logic, dynamics and constraints. *Automatica*, 35(3):407–427, 1999.

6. Mireille Broucke. A geometric approach to bisimulation and verification of hybrid systems. In Fritz W. Vaandrager and Jan H. van Schuppen, editors, *Hybrid Systems: Computation and Control*, volume 1569 of *Lecture Notes in Computer Science*, pages 61–75. Springer-Verlag, 1999.

7. P. Brunovsky. A classification of linear controllable systems. *Kybernetika*, 6(3):173–188, 1970.

8. Edmund M. M. Clarke, Doron Peled, and Orna Grumberg. *Model Checking*. MIT Press, 1999.

9. J.E.R. Cury, B.H. Krogh, and T. Niinomi. Synthesis of supervisory controllers for hybrid systems based on approximating automata. *IEEE Transactions on Automatic Control : Special Issue on Hybrid Systems*, 43(4):564–568, April 1998.

10. E. A. Emerson. *Handbook of Theoretical Computer Science*, volume B, chapter Temporal and modal logic, pages 995–1072. Elsevier Science, 1990.

11. E. A. Emerson and E. M. Clarke. Using branching time temporal logic to synthesize synchronization skeletons. *Science of Computer Programming*, 2:241–266, 1982.

12. L.C.G.J.M. Habets and J. H. van Schuppen. Control of piecewise-linear hybrid systems on simplices and rectangles. In M. D. Di Benedetto and A. Sangiovanni-Vincentelli, editors, *Hybrid Systems: Computation and Control*, volume 2034 of *Lecture Notes in Computer Sience*, pages 261–274. Springer-Verlag, 2001.

13. T.A. Henzinger and R. Majumdar. Symbolic model checking for rectangular hybrid systems. In S. Graf, editor, *TACAS 2000: Tools and algorithms for the construction and analysis of systems*, Lecture Notes in Computer Science, New-York, 2000. Springer-Verlag.

14. Thomas A. Henzinger, Peter W. Kopke, Anuj Puri, and Pravin Varaiya. What's decidable about hybrid automata? *Journal of Computer and System Sciences*, 57:94–124, 1998.

15. R. E. Kalman. Kronecker invariants and feedback. In L. Weiss, editor, *Ordinary Differential Equations*, pages 459–471. Academic Press, New York, 1972.

16. Orna Kupferman, P. Madhusudan, P. S. Thiagarajan, and Moshe Y. Vardi. Open systems in reactive environments: Control and synthesis. In *Proceedings of the 11th International Conference on Concurency Theory*, volume 1877 of *Lecture Notes in Computer Science*, pages 92–107. Springer-Verlag, 2000.

17. Gerardo Lafferriere, George J. Pappas, and Shankar Sastry. O-minimal hybrid systems. *Mathematics of Control, Signals and Systems*, 13(1):1–21, March 2000.

18. P. Madhusudan and P.S. Thiagarajan. Branching time controllers for discrete event systems. *Theoretical Computer Science*, 274:117–149, March 2002.

19. Z. Manna and P. Wolper. Synthesis of communication processes from temporal logic specifications. *ACM Transactions on Programming Languages and Systems*, 6:68–93, 1984.

20. K. L. McMillan. *Symbolic Model Checking*. Kluwer Academic Publishers, 1993.

21. R. Milner. *Communication and Concurrency*. Prentice Hall, 1989.

22. T. Moor and J. M. Davoren. Robust controller synthesis for hybrid systems using modal logic. In M. D. Di Benedetto and A. Sangiovanni-Vincentelli, editors, *Hybrid Systems: Computation and Control*, volume 2034 of *Lecture Notes in Computer Science*. Springer-Verlag, 2001.

23. George J. Pappas. Bisimilar linear systems. *Automatica*, 2001. To appear.
24. D.M.R. Park. *Concurrency and automata on infinite sequences*, volume 104 of *Lecture Notes in Computer Science*. Springer-Verlag, 1980.
25. A. Puri and P. Varaiya. Decidability of hybrid systems with rectangular inclusions. In *Computer Aided Verification*, pages 95–104, 1994.
26. Eduardo D. Sontag. *Mathematical Control Theory*, volume 6 of *Texts in Applied Mathematics*. Springer-Verlag, New-York, 2nd edition, 1998.
27. Colin Stirling. *Handbook of logic in computer science*, volume 2, chapter Modal and Temporal Logics, pages 477–563. Oxford University Press, 1992.
28. J.A. Stiver, X.D. Koutsoukos, and P.J. Antsaklis. An invariant based approach to the design of hybrid control systems. *International Journal of Robust and Nonlinear Control*, 11(5):453–478, 2001.
29. Paulo Tabuada and George J. Pappas. Finite bisimulations of controllable linear systems. *Theoretical Computer Science*, January 2003. Submitted, available at www.seas.upenn.edu/~tabuadap.

Approximate Reachability for Linear Systems*

Ashish Tiwari

SRI International,
333 Ravenswood Ave,
Menlo Park, CA, U.S.A
tiwari@csl.sri.coma
Tel/Fax:+1.650.859.4774/2844

Abstract. We describe new techniques to construct, and subsequently refine, over-approximations of the reachability sets for linear dynamical systems. Our approach extracts information from real eigenvectors and more generally, from certain vectors in the primary decomposition, to generate suitable invariants of the system and can be used in conjunction with other reachability computation methods. We also describe experimental results from using this technique inside the qualitative abstraction tool [18], where it helps to generate refined abstractions of hybrid systems with linear continuous dynamics. We illustrate this on a collision-avoidance example from automobile cruise control problem, which was handled completely automatically by our tool.

1 Introduction

Establishing safety properties of hybrid and dynamical systems is one of the most interesting, but equally challenging, problem for formal methods. With the increased embedding of digital controllers inside physical devices, such as automobiles and aircraft, the need for automated tools and techniques for formal analysis and verification has become more pressing. Exhaustive testing via simulation is, in most cases, neither possible nor practical.

Reachability and safety are now being recognized as central problems in designing controllers. While issues related to stability and controllability are well-studied, there are not many results on computing the reachable set of hybrid systems. Known classes of hybrid systems for which reachability problem is decidable are timed automata [2], multirate automata [1], rectangular hybrid automata [16,8], and certain subclasses of linear hybrid systems [12]. The most general decidability result [12] enforces stringent conditions on the continuous dynamics, where the matrix representing the linear dynamics is required to be diagonalizable with certain restricted kinds of eigenvalues. Moreover, the reach set computation algorithm uses the decision procedure for real closed fields to perform quantifier elimination on large and complex formulas, which is quite impractical.

---

* Research supported in part by DARPA under the MoBIES program administered by AFRL under contract F33615-00-C-1700 and NASA Langley Research Center contract NAS1-00108 to Rannoch Corporation.

O. Maler and A. Pnueli (Eds.): HSCC 2003, LNCS 2623, pp. 514–525, 2003.

One natural question then is whether we can relax the conditions and get an over-approximation of the reach set efficiently. So, for instance, if only a subset of eigenvalues of a linear system are rational, then can we still say something about the set of reachable states of the system? What about non-rational eigenvalues? Furthermore, can we get better over-approximations as more and more eigenvalues turn out to be rationals? This paper presents techniques that answer these questions in the affirmative.

The basic idea proposed in this paper is that real eigenvectors can be used to construct linear forms (over the state variables of the dynamical system), whose value can be bounded for all reachable states. For linear systems with nonreal complex eigenvalues, certain vectors from the (invariant) subspaces of a primary decomposition can be used for the same purpose. This gives sound upper bounds of the reach sets that are relatively easy to compute and use, in conjunction, with most other methods and tools for reachability computation. The computation of these over-approximations of the reach set is completely symbolic and does not require any numerical calculations [6,5,11,15] or the use of computationally expensive quantifier elimination procedure for the real-closed fields [4,10,13]. The techniques are applicable whenever there exists a real eigenvalue or a complex eigenvalue with nonpositive real part. The results can be incrementally applied if more than one eigenvalue satisfies either of these two conditions.

The linear forms generated from eigenvector information have been used to generate refined abstractions using the automated qualitative abstraction tool [18]. The qualitative abstraction technique [18] was developed to generate sound, discrete, and finite state abstractions of hybrid systems by fully preserving the mode change logic, while preserving just enough of the continuous behavior. The continuous dynamics were projected onto qualitative dynamics of the signs of certain intelligently chosen saturated set of polynomials [18]. For systems that were presented using only polynomials (possibly non-linear), the method was completely automated using a decision procedure for the (quantifier-free fragment of) real closed fields. The abstraction procedure uses thousands of calls to this decision procedure with small and simple formulas, in a failure-tolerant way. In many cases, the abstractions generated by our tool were found to be too weak to prove the properties of interest. This is because success crucially depends upon the choice of the seed polynomial set which is used to construct the abstraction. The new results in this paper provide a way to automatically generate the "correct" set of seed polynomials for modes with linear dynamics.

An important feature of the incorporation of the eigenvector information in the abstraction procedure is that the eigenvectors do not need to be *explicitly* computed. They can be represented using symbolic coefficients and these symbolic coefficients can be constrained using algebraic equations. The abstraction algorithm treats the symbolic coefficients as parameters. With this improvement, our abstraction based approach for proving safety properties can now automatically handle several non-trivial systems. In this paper, we describe a collision avoidance example from automobile cruise control problem.

1.1 Preliminaries: Linear Continuous Dynamical Systems

A *linear (continuous dynamical) system* CS is a tuple $(X, Init, A)$ where X is a finite set of variables interpreted over the reals $\mathbb{R}$, $\mathbf{X} = \mathbb{R}^X$ is the set of all valuations of the variables X, $Init \subseteq \mathbf{X}$ is the set of initial states, and $A \in \mathbb{Q}^{n \times n}$ is the matrix which constrains the dynamics of CS by the differential equation $\dot{x} = Ax$. Since interest is in computational feasibility, the matrix A is assumed to contain rational entries.

The semantics, $[[CS]]$, of a linear system $CS = (X, Init, A)$ over an interval $I = [t_0, t_1] \subseteq \mathbb{R}$ is a collection of mappings $x : I \mapsto \mathbf{X}$ satisfying (i) the initial condition: $x(t_0) \in Init$, and (ii) the continuous dynamics: for all $t \in [t_0, t_1]$, $\dot{x}(t) = Ax(t)$. In case the interval I is left unspecified, it is assumed to be the interval $[0, \infty)$.

We say that a state $s \in \mathbf{X}$ is *reachable* in a continuous dynamical system CS if there exists a function $x \in [[CS]]$ such that $s = x(t)$ for some $t \in I$. The set, $Reach(CS)$, is defined as the set of all reachable states of the system CS.

The problem of computing the exact reachability set $Reach(CS)$ for a given dynamical system CS is intractable in general. However, for purposes of verification of safety properties, it often suffices to compute an *over-approximation* (or superset) of the reachable set of states—if the over-approximation does not intersect a set of bad states, then the original system will never reach a bad state. Note that the linear continuous dynamical systems we consider here are autonomous, that is, they have no inputs.

The reachability set computation problem has been shown to be decidable for a subclass of linear continuous dynamical systems. In particular, if the set $Init$ of initial states is algebraic and either (1) A is a nilpotent matrix (that is, $A^m = 0$ for some $m \geq 0$), or (2) A is a diagonalizable matrix with rational eigenvalues, or (3) A is a diagonalizable matrix with purely imaginary eigenvalues of the form ir with $r \in \mathbb{Q}$, then the set $Reach(CS)$ can be computed exactly [13]. In fact, this decidability result was established for systems with inputs from a certain restricted set.

Let $CS = (X, Init, A)$ be a linear system. Then the set $[[CS]]$ contains all mappings $x(t)$ defined by $x(t) = e^{At}s$, where $s \in Init$ and the matrix exponential e^{At} is defined by the series $e^{At} = \sum_{k=0}^{\infty} \frac{t^k}{k!} A^k$. Therefore, the set of reachable states is

$$Reach(CS) = \{s \in \mathbb{R}^n : \exists t, s_0. \, (t \geq 0 \, \wedge \, s_0 \in Init \, \wedge \, s = e^{At}s_0)\}.$$

Example 1 (Collision Avoidance in Cruise Control). Consider a part of the leader control developed in [7] and also discussed in [17]. The control is applied during safety-critical situations when the inter-vehicle distance is small, or the relative velocity between vehicles is large. Let gap, v_f, v, and a respectively represent the gap between the two cars, the velocity of the leading car, and the velocity and acceleration of the rear car.

$$\dot{v} = a, \quad \dot{a} = -3a - 3(v - v_f) + (gap - (v + 10)), \quad \dot{gap} = v_f - v.$$

Formally, this describes a linear dynamical system with $X = \{v, v_f, a, gap\}$. Assuming the variable v_f is a parameter (unchanging symbolic constant), the dynamics can be written as $\dot{x} = Ax + B$, where

$$A = \begin{bmatrix} 0 & 0 & 1 & 0 \\ 0 & 0 & 0 & 0 \\ -4 & 3 & -3 & 1 \\ -1 & 1 & 0 & 0 \end{bmatrix} \qquad B = \begin{bmatrix} 0 \\ 0 \\ -10 \\ 0 \end{bmatrix}$$

By a change of variables, $rgap \leftarrow gap - 10$, we get $\dot{x} = Ax$, where $x = [v, v_f, a, rgap]^T$. The set $Init$ of initial states is left unspecified. We have also not formalized invariant sets here, but we will use bounds on the acceleration and other state variables later in the analysis. For a given set of possible initial states, the problem is to verify that the rear car would never collide with the car in front, that is, always $gap > 0$, or $rgap > -10$. It can be easily verified that the matrix A does not satisfy any of the three conditions specified above and hence, this example falls out of the class of systems for which reachability is known to be decidable.

2   Linear Systems with Real Eigenvalues

Let $CS = (X, Init, A)$ be a linear system with $A \in \mathbb{Q}^{n \times n}$. If λ is a real eigenvalue of A and $c = [c_1, \ldots, c_n]^T$ is an eigenvector of A^T corresponding to λ, then we consider the linear form $p = c^T x$, where x is the vector of state variables X. The derivative of this linear form over the state variables is

$$\dot{p} = c^T \dot{x} = c^T Ax = (A^T c)^T x = (\lambda c)^T x = \lambda p,$$

and hence, the value of this linear form over any trajectory of CS is given by $p(t) = e^{\lambda t} p(0)$, where $p(0)$ is the value of p in an initial state of CS. Since $\lambda \in \mathbb{R}$, therefore, the components c_i of c are also reals. Therefore, an over-approximation of the reachable states is given by the formula

$$\exists t, s_0.\ (t \geq 0 \wedge c^T x = e^{\lambda t} c^T s_0 \wedge s_0 \in Init).$$

Doing an approximate quantifier elimination, we notice that the value of $c^T x(t)$ will either (i) monotonically increase or decrease while remaining sign-invariant (if $\lambda > 0$), or (ii) asymptotically converge to 0 (if $\lambda < 0$), or (iii) remain constant (if $\lambda = 0$). We formally state this in Theorem 1.

Theorem 1. *Let $CS = (X = \{x_1, \ldots, x_n\}, Init, A)$ be a linear dynamical system with the matrix $A \in \mathbb{Q}^{n \times n}$. Let λ be a real eigenvalue of the matrix A^T, $c = [c_1, c_2, \ldots, c_n]^T$ be a corresponding eigenvector (of A^T), and $p = c_1 x_1 + c_2 x_2 + \cdots + c_n x_n = c^T x$ be the corresponding linear form.*

Then, the components c_i of the eigenvector c are all real. If d_{min} and d_{max} denote, respectively, the minimum and maximum values in the set $\{c^T x(0) : x(0) \in Init\}$, then

(i) if $\lambda > 0$, then the linear form p is sign invariant for CS; more specifically, if $d_{min} > 0$, then $p \geq d_{min}$ always, if $d_{max} < 0$, then $p \leq d_{max}$ always, and if $d_{min} = d_{max} = 0$, then $p = d$ always;
(ii) if $\lambda < 0$, then the value of the linear form p asymptotically converges to 0; more specifically, it is always true that $\min\{0, d_{min}\} \leq p \leq \max\{0, d_{max}\}$; and
(iii) if $\lambda = 0$, then the linear form p is an invariant function for CS, that is, it is always the case that $p = p(0)$.

Theorem 1 gives a method to generate over-approximations of the reach set. It can be applied repeatedly, using different eigenvectors and the corresponding linear forms, to give several different formulas which over-approximate the reach set, and the conjunction (set intersection) of these formulas (sets) will still be an over-approximation. In particular, the more real eigenvalues the matrix A has, the more refined reach set computation will result. This points to the results in [13] where the exact reach set is shown to be computable when matrix A has exactly n rational eigenvalues. The exact connection will be explored in Section 3.

Representation and Computability Issues. Theorem 1 gives a way to generate formulas representing over-approximations of the reach set whenever matrix A has a real eigenvalue. But, for purposes of computing, we need finite representations of the real eigenvalue λ and the eigenvector c. We use polynomials for this purpose and we show below (Proposition 2) that this representation suffices.

Definition 1. *A real number $\alpha \in \mathbb{R}$ is algebraic over a commutative ring K if it is a zero of some polynomial in $K[X]$. If the base ring K is unspecified, then it is assumed to be the field of rationals $\mathbb{Q}$.*

The vector space generated by a finite set of algebraic numbers (over $\mathbb{Q}$) is finite-dimensional (over the field $\mathbb{Q}$). The following facts on algebraic numbers are well known.

Proposition 1. *If $\alpha \in \mathbb{R}$ is algebraic over $\mathbb{Q}[\beta]$, where β is algebraic over $\mathbb{Q}$, then α is algebraic over $\mathbb{Q}$. Furthermore, the set of algebraic numbers is closed under addition, subtraction, multiplication, and division. If α is an algebraic number over K, then so is $c\alpha$ and $\alpha + c$ for any constant $c \in K$.*

The following is an obvious observation about eigenvectors.

Proposition 2. *The components of an eigenvector c of a matrix $A \in \mathbb{Q}^{n \times n}$ corresponding to an eigenvalue λ are algebraic over $\mathbb{Q}[\lambda]$. Since λ is algebraic, so are the components of c.*

The fact that the eigenvalue is algebraic and that the eigenvectors have algebraic components (Proposition 2) is crucial since it implies that the linear form p can be expressed in terms of polynomials *over* $\mathbb{Q}$, and hence, effectively represented in a computational tool. In fact, the polynomials representing the coefficients of the eigenvector can be easily obtained, since they are solutions of $A^T c = \lambda c$.

Example 2. Consider the linear system of Example 1. The characteristic polynomial for A, $\lambda(\lambda^3+3\lambda^2+4\lambda+1)$, has exactly two real zeros. The nonzero real eigenvalue, denoted by λ, lies between $-1/3$ and $-1/4$. Now, if $c = [c_1, c_2, c_3, c_4]^T$ is an eigenvector of A^T corresponding to λ, then $A^T c = \lambda c$. We assume, without loss of generality, that $c_4 = 1$, and hence we get an eigenvector $[c_1, c_2, c_3, 1]^T$ where c_1, c_2 and c_3 satisfy the equations $c_3 = \lambda$, $c_1 = \lambda^2 + 3\lambda$, and $c_2 = -c_1 - 1$. Therefore, the linear form corresponding to this eigenvector, $p = c_1 v - (c_1+1)v_f + c_3 a + rgap$, asymptotically converges to 0 as the linear system evolves (by Theorem 1).

Suppose the deceleration of the car under maximum braking is $-2(m/s^2)$, that is, $a > -2$ is specified as an invariant. If initially $p > 0$, then we can prove that $rgap > -10$ always. This follows from the fact that the formula

$$p \geq 0 \;\wedge\; rgap = -10 \;\wedge\; v - v_f > 0 \;\wedge\; a > -2$$

is unsatisfiable under the condition that $-1/3 < \lambda < -1/4$. Note that for collision to occur, it should be the case that $v - v_f > 0$. This analysis was automatically done by our abstraction and model-checking tool, see Section 4.

In case $p < 0$ initially, if $rgap_0, v_0, a_0$ denote the values of variables at $t = 0$ and $rgap, v, a$ denote the values at a later time, then $rgap_0 - c_1 v_f + c_1 v_0 - v_f + c_3 a_0 < rgap - c_1 v_f + c_1 v - v_f + c_3 a$. Assuming initially $8v_0 - 9gap_0 + 21 < 0$, then we can again establish collision avoidance for these initial states by observing that the formula

$$p_0 < p \;\wedge\; v > 0 \;\wedge\; 8v_0 - 9gap_0 + 21 < 0$$

is unsatisfiable assuming the invariants $a < 5 \;\wedge\; a > -2 \;\wedge\; -8/9 < c_1 < -11/16$.

Note that this approach also provides a way to *synthesize* switching laws that guarantee safety: for example, if the car switches into this control mode only when $p > 0$ *OR* $(p < 0$ *AND* $8v - 9gap + 21 < 0)$ is true, then collision avoidance is guaranteed.

2.1   Linear Systems with Complex Eigenvalues

Let $CS = (X, Init, A)$ be a linear system with $A \in \mathbb{Q}^{n \times n}$. If A has a real eigenvalue λ, then we can use Theorem 1 to generate useful reachability information using the eigenvalue λ and the corresponding eigenvector of A^T. We now discuss generalizations of this theorem that would allow similar kind of information to be extracted from non-real eigenvalues of A as well.

Suppose $ch(y)$ is the characteristic polynomial of matrix A^T. Since A is a rational matrix, the polynomial $ch(y)$ has rational coefficients. In general, the polynomial $ch(A)$ can be factored over the field of reals, as

$$ch(y) \;=\; \Pi_i(y - \lambda_i).\Pi_j(y^2 + a_j y + b_j),$$

where $\lambda_i, a_j, b_j \in \mathbb{R}$, $a_j \neq 0$ and $4b_j > a_j^2$. In Section 2 we extracted reachability information out of factors of the first kind. In this section, we will do the same with factors of the second kind.

Let $y^2 + ay + b$ be a factor of the characteristic polynomial of A, where $a, b \in \mathbb{R}$ and $a \neq 0, 4b > a^2$. Let W denote the null space of the transformation $(A^T)^2 + aA^T + bI$, that is,

$$W = \{c : ((A^T)^2 + aA^T + bI)c = 0\}.$$

If λ is a complex root of $y^2 + ay + b$ and c is a complex eigenvector of A^T corresponding to λ, then clearly, c is in W. In fact, since $A^T \in \mathbb{Q}^{n \times n}$, $a \in \mathbb{R}$, and $b \in \mathbb{R}$, it follows that there exist vectors $c \in \mathbb{R}^n$ (over the reals) in the subspace W. We note that W is a subspace of some component in the primary decomposition (induced by A^T) and W is invariant under A^T [9].

Let $c \in \mathbb{R}^n$ be a nonzero vector in W. Consider the linear form $p = c^T x$ over the state variables corresponding to this vector. Clearly, this linear form satisfies the equation $\ddot{p} + a\dot{p} + bp = 0$, as

$$\ddot{p} + a\dot{p} + bp = c^T \ddot{x} + ac^T \dot{x} + bc^T x = c^T A^2 x + ac^T Ax + bc^T x$$
$$= c^T(A^2 + aA + bI)x = (((A^T)^2 + aA^T + bI)c)^T x = 0$$

Therefore, solving the differential equation for p gives

$$p = e^{-at/2}(p(0)\cos(Dt) + \frac{ap(0) + 2p'(0)}{2D}\sin(Dt)), \quad \text{where } D = \frac{\sqrt{4b - a^2}}{2},$$

where $p(0)$ and $p'(0)$ are the initial values of the linear form and its derivative, respectively. Again, using an approximate quantifier elimination procedure, we get the following result.

Theorem 2. *Let* $CS = (X, Init, A)$ *be a linear dynamical system with* $A \in \mathbb{Q}^{n \times n}$. *Let* $y^2 + ay + b$ *be a factor of the characteristic polynomial of* A *with* $a, b \in \mathbb{R}$, $a^2 < 4b$. *Let* $c = [c_1, c_2, \ldots, c_n]^T$ *be a nonzero real vector in the set* W *(defined as above with respect to the factor* $y^2 + ay + b$*), and* $p = c_1 x_1 + c_2 x_2 + \cdots + c_n x_n = c^T x$ *be the corresponding linear form. Then, the components* c_i *of the vector* c *are all real and if* $a \geq 0$ *then*

$$-(d_1^2 + d_2^2)^{1/2} \leq p \leq (d_1^2 + d_2^2)^{1/2}$$

where $d_1 = max\{|c^T x_0| : x_0 \in Init\}$ *and* $d_2 = (max\{2|c^T \dot{x}_0| : x_0 \in Init\} + d_1 a)/(4b - a^2)^{1/2}$.

The condition $a > 0$ is a necessary condition for stability. Note that we do not require that the real part of *every* eigenvalue be negative, but only that the real part of *some* eigenvalue be nonpositive for applying Theorem 2 and obtaining bounds on the reach set.

Finally, we note that the real numbers a and b are both algebraic. This is because if λ_1 and λ_2 are the two (complex) roots of $y^2 + ay + b$, then $a = \lambda_1 + \lambda_2$ and $b = \lambda_1\lambda_2$. But λ_1 and λ_2 are algebraic (roots of the characteristic polynomial) and hence, a and b are algebraic too (using Proposition 1).

Example 3. Consider the linear system from Example 1. In Example 2, we used
the real root of the characteristic polynomial $y^3 + 3y^2 + 4y + 1$. The other two
roots of the characteristic polynomial are the roots of the polynomial $y^2 + (3 + \lambda)y + (\lambda^2 + 3\lambda + 4)$, or equivalently $y^2 + (3 + \lambda)y - 1/\lambda$, where λ is the real root. The
equation $((A^T)^2 + (\lambda + 3)A^T - (1/\lambda)I)c = 0$ has two solutions $c = [-\lambda, \lambda, 1, 0]^T$
and $c = [1/\lambda, -(1 + \lambda)/\lambda, 0, 1]^T$. Since $\lambda + 3 > 0$, Theorem 2 is applicable.
Consider the linear form $p_2 = 1/\lambda v - ((1 + \lambda)/\lambda)v_f + rgap$ corresponding to the
latter solution. For simplicity, assume that the initial conditions are given by
$1/\lambda(v - v_f) - v_f + rgap = 0$, so that $d_1 = 0$. Now, assuming $|a| < 1 \wedge |rgap| <
4 \wedge |v_f| < 20$ initially, we get $B < 12$. Thus, we get the following over-
approximation of the reach set: $-12 < p_2 < 12$. This can be used to prove
collision avoidance under the assumption that v_f is at least 10.

2.2   Unifying the Results

Let matrix A be such that (a) there are k linear forms $p_1, p_2, \ldots, p_k$, as in
Section 2, corresponding to real eigenvalues $\lambda_1, \ldots, \lambda_k$; and (b) there are l linear
forms $q_1, q_2, \ldots, q_l$, as in Section 2.1, corresponding to complex eigenvalue pairs
$a_1 \pm ib_1, \ldots, a_m \pm ib_m$. (The linear forms corresponding to quadratic factors of
the characteristic polynomial from Section 2.1 can also be thought of as linear
forms corresponding to the roots of the quadratic factor.) Putting the results
in Sections 2 and 2.1 together, we get the following expression for (an over-
approximation of) the set of reachable states,

$$\exists t \geq 0. \ (\bigwedge_{i=1}^{k} p_i(t) = p_i(0)e^{\lambda_i t}) \wedge \tag{1}$$

$$(\bigwedge_{i=1}^{l} q_i(t) = e^{a_i t}(q_i(0)cos(b_i t) + \frac{\dot{q}_i(0) - q_i(0)a_i}{b_i}sin(b_i t))) \tag{2}$$

In the previous sections, we have over approximated the reach set by distributing
the existential quantifier over the conjunctions and treating each equation in
the formula above separately. But, there are other ways to simplify the above
formula and obtain stronger upper-bounds on the reach set, without attempting
to perform exact quantifier elimination on it. As a simple example, if linear
forms p_1 and p_2 correspond to the same real eigenvalue λ_i, then we can deduce
the invariant $p_2(0)p_1 = p_1(0)p_2$ for the system. This can be used to further
strengthen the approximate reachable set produced using Theorems 1 and 2.
The efficient extraction and use of these optimizations will be further studied in
the future. Note that if λ_i's (and a_i and b_i's) are rational, then the representation
of the eigenvalues and computation with the eigenvectors becomes much easier.

3   Characterizing the Approximations

The approximate reachability techniques described in this paper are, in a sense,
dual to the exact reachability computation techniques in [13] owing to the follow-

ing facts: (i) eigenvectors of A^T are central in our approach, whereas eigenvectors of A were crucial in [13]; (ii) knowledge about *all* eigenvectors/eigenvalues is required in [13], while our approach can be incrementally used even in the presence of partial knowledge of the eigenvectors; and (iii) eigenvalues are required to be either all rational or all imaginary with rational imaginary components in [13], whereas we derive successively better over-approximations using any mix of eigenvalues of the matrix A.

One natural question is how close can one get to exact reachability sets using our techniques, especially in the case when the stronger conditions of [13] are satisfied. We address this question next.

Consider the case when A is diagonalizable with rational eigenvalues $\lambda_1, \lambda_2,\ldots,\lambda_n$, that is, $A = UDU^{-1}$, where D is a diagonal matrix with entries $\lambda_1, \ldots, \lambda_n$ on its diagonal and U is the matrix with eigenvectors of A as its columns. Now, the solution to the differential equation $\dot{x} = Ax$ is $x(t) = Ue^{Dt}U^{-1}x(0)$ where $x(0) \in Init$ is an initial state of the system. Therefore, the *exact* reach set is given by

$$\exists t \geq 0.\ x(t) = Ue^{Dt}U^{-1}x(0) \ \wedge \ x(0) \in Init$$
$$\Leftrightarrow \exists t \geq 0.\ U^{-1}x(t) = e^{Dt}U^{-1}x(0) \ \wedge \ x(0) \in Init$$
$$\Leftrightarrow \exists t \geq 0.\ P(t) = e^{Dt}P(0) \ \wedge \ P(0) \in U^{-1}Init$$
$$\Leftrightarrow \exists t \geq 0.\ P(t) - [e^{\lambda_1 t}p_1(0),\ e^{\lambda_2 t}p_2(0), \ldots, e^{\lambda_n t}p_n(0)]^T \ \wedge \ P(0) \in U^{-1}Init$$

Here we have assumed that $p_1, \ldots, p_n$ are the linear forms defined by $p_i(t) = w_i^T x(t)$, where w_i^T is the i-th row of matrix U^{-1} and P is the (row) vector consisting of these linear forms. The notation $U^{-1}Init$ denotes the set of all vectors obtained by transforming vectors in $Init$ by U^{-1}.

Note that the expressions in the vector P are exactly the linear forms that are computed in our approach. This is because

$$A^T = (U^{-1})^T D^T U^T = (U^{-1})^T D U^T$$

and therefore, since w_i^T is the i-th row of U^{-1}, w_i is the i-th column of $(U^{-1})^T$, or the eigenvector of A^T corresponding to the eigenvalue λ_i. Thus, the difference between [13] and our approach for this restricted class of systems is (i) we work in the space obtained by applying the transformation U^{-1}, and (ii) we use the following logical inference rule to *simplify* the quantifier elimination problem,

$$\exists t.(\phi_1(t) \ \wedge \ \phi_2(t)) \Rightarrow \exists t.\phi_1(t) \ \wedge \ \exists t.\phi_2(t)$$

Clearly, the right-hand side formula is *weaker* than the left-hand side formula, and hence applying this results in an *over-approximation* of the reach set. Thus, the exact reach set formula above is approximated in our approach to

$$\bigwedge_{i=1}^{n} (\exists t \geq 0.\ p_i(t) = e^{\lambda_i t}p_i(0) \ \wedge \ p_i(0) \in (U^{-1}Init)|_i)$$

and then we apply even further approximations to *completely eliminate* the need for quantifier elimination (as in the statements of Theorems 1 and 2). The significance of our results is for the cases when the result of [13] are either not applicable or impractical.

4   Integrating with the Hybrid System Abstraction Tool

We have integrated the ideas presented in this paper with our qualitative abstraction tool for hybrid systems [18]. In effect, the linear forms corresponding to real eigenvalues or complex eigenvalue pairs are used as "seed polynomials" that are used to define the abstract state space. In the case when the linear form corresponds to a real eigenvalue (Section 2), our abstraction tool can automatically infer the conclusions of Theorem 1 and implicitly use it to create finer abstractions.

The abstraction tool views a hybrid automata as a suitable composition of component modes, where each mode is just a continuous dynamical system. Abstraction of a hybrid automaton model is performed compositionally by abstracting the dynamics in individual modes using a possibly different set of polynomials for different modes. The polynomials for each mode are generated from the specification, for example, the guards of all outgoing transitions from that mode. In light of the new observations presented here, we can now add additional seed polynomials in modes with linear continuous dynamics. The individual continuous dynamical system components interact in an hybrid automaton through discrete transitions. In the presence of strong assumptions on these transitions—for example, see the assumptions in the definition of o-minimality [12]—the abstraction can be done compositionally without inducing any additional approximations.

The current version of our abstraction tool makes no assumption that the dynamics are linear and does not implement any specific optimizations for this case. However, it can still deduce the facts given in Theorem 1 if it is given the correct set of seed polynomials. Following up on Example 2, the polynomial $c_1 v - (c_1 + 1)v_f + c_3 a + rgap$ can be given to the system by adding c_1 and c_3 as (dummy) parameters and specifying, as invariant Inv, the two equations satisfied by c_1 and c_3, as in Example 2. In the experiments that we carried out, we also added, as additional invariants Inv, the facts that $-1/3 < \lambda < -1/4, -8/9 < c_1 < -11/16$ and $a > -2$ (thus limiting the maximum deceleration of the rear car). Now, given this information, the abstraction tool automatically identifies that for the given dynamical system,

$$d/dt(rgap - c_1 v_f + c_1 v - v_f + c_3 a) = \lambda(rgap - c_1 v_f + c_1 v - v_f + c_3 a)$$

for some *negative* real number λ. Though the generation of the eigenvectors is not currently automated in our tool, it can easily be done and is left for future development.

If the initial condition of the system are specified as

$$(rgap - c_1 v_f + c_1 v - v_f + c_3 a > 0) \wedge rgap > -10$$

or any other expression which is *stronger* than this (that is, entails a subset of the initial states specified by the above formula), and the invariants are specified as described above, then the tool automatically constructs a finite state discrete transition system abstraction of the dynamical system against which the collision avoidance property is validated. This proves collision avoidance for the original dynamical system and in fact, it gives a condition that should be true of the initial states for which we are guaranteed to not collide with the car in front. Thus, if the initial state region was a subset of the more general one described here, our tool would still successfully prove collision avoidance.

5   Conclusion

In this paper we have presented new techniques to compute over-approximations of the reach set for linear dynamical systems. It is applicable to any system where the matrix A either has a real eigenvalue or a complex eigenvalue with nonpositive real part. This does not preclude the possibility of some other eigenvalues having positive real parts. Thus, our techniques can handle systems with mixed (reals and imaginary) eigenvalues unlike results by Lafferriere et. al. [3, 13]. The approximate reachability is, in many cases, sufficient to establish safety properties of the system. Our method integrates naturally with our qualitative abstraction tool. The tool uses a decision procedure for the quantifier-free theory of reals in a failure-tolerant mode. This means that even if the decision procedure fails (due to a lack of sufficient memory or time), the procedure can still be used (without compromising soundness).

The technique for generating over approximations of the reach sets can be integrated with most of the other tools and techniques for performing reachability computation. It can be viewed as an incremental approach to using the results of [3,13] in practice—it eliminates the need for the use of computationally expensive quantifier elimination procedure for real closed fields, and it also relaxes the stringent conditions required by these other results.

In this work, we have used eigenvectors and certain vectors in the invariant subspaces of a primary decomposition to generate seed polynomials for qualitatively abstracting linear dynamical system. Finding a good set of initial seed polynomials for other classes of systems would be a topic for future research. In the future, we also wish to investigate more intelligent heuristics for eliminating quantifiers from Formula 2 and using them for synthesizing switching laws.

Acknowledgements. The author wishes to thank Prof. Gaurav Khanna (Long Island University) and the anonymous reviewers for their helpful comments.

References

[1] R. Alur, C. Courcoubetis, N. Halbwachs, T. A. Henzinger, P.-H. Ho, X. Nicollin, A. Olivero, J. Sifakis, and S. Yovine. The algorithmic analysis of hybrid systems. *Theoretical Computer Science*, 138(3):3–34, 1995.

[2] R. Alur and D. Dill. A theory of timed automata. *Theoretical Computer Science*, 126:183–235, 1994.

[3] Rajeev Alur, Tom Henzinger, Gerardo Lafferriere, and George J. Pappas. Discrete abstractions of hybrid systems. *Proceedings of the IEEE*, 88(2):971–984, July 2000.

[4] H. Anai and V. Weispfenning. Reach set computations using real quantifier elimination. In M. D. Di Benedetto and A. L. Sangiovanni-Vincentelli, editors, *HSCC*, volume 2034 of *Lecture Notes in Computer Science*, pages 63–76. Springer, 2001.

[5] A. Chutinan and B. H. Krogh. Verification of polyhedral-invariant hybrid automata using polygonal flow pipe approximations. In Vaandrager and van Schuppen [19], pages 76–90.

[6] T. Dang and O. Maler. Reachability analysis via face lifting. In T. A. Henzinger and S. Sastry, editors, *HSCC*, volume 1386 of *LNCS*, pages 96–109. Springer, 1998.

[7] D. Godbole and J. Lygeros. Longitudinal control of the lead car of a platoon. *IEEE Transactions on Vehicular Technology*, 43(4):1125–35, 1994.

[8] T. A. Henzinger, P. W. Kopke, A. Puri, and P. Varaiya. What's decidable about hybrid automata? *Journal of Computer and System Sciences*, 57:94–124, 1998. A preliminary version appeared in the *Proc. of the 27th Annual ACM Symposium on Theory of Computing (STOC 1995)*, pp. 373–382.

[9] K. Hoffman and R. Kunze. *Linear Algebra*. Prentice-Hall, second edition, 1971.

[10] M. Jirstrand. Algebraic methods for modeling and design in control. Licentiate thesis LIU-TEK-LIC-1996:05 Linköping Studies in Science and Technology. Thesis No 540, Department of Electrical Engineering, Li, 1996.

[11] A. B. Kurzhanski and P. Varaiya. Ellipsoidal techniques for reachability analysis. In Lynch and Krogh [14], pages 202–214.

[12] G. Lafferriere, G. J. Pappas, and S. Yovine. A new class of decidable hybrid systems. In Vaandrager and van Schuppen [19], pages 137–151.

[13] G. Lafferriere, G. J. Pappas, and S. Yovine. Symbolic reachability computations for families of linear vector fields. *J. Symbolic Computation*, 32(3):231–253, 2001.

[14] N. A. Lynch and B. H. Krogh, editors. *Hybrid Systems: Computation and Control, Third International Workshop, HSCC 2000, Proceedings*, volume 1790 of *LNCS*. Springer, 2000.

[15] I. Mitchell and C. Tomlin. Level set methods for computation in hybrid systems. In Lynch and Krogh [14].

[16] A. Puri and P. Varaiya. Decidability of hybrid systems with rectangular differential inclusions. In D. L. Dill, editor, *Computer Aided Verification, CAV*, volume 818 of *LNCS*, pages 95–104. Springer Verlag, 1994.

[17] A. Puri and P. Varaiya. Driving safely in smart cars. In *Proceedings of the 1995 American Control Conference*, 1995.

[18] A. Tiwari and G. Khanna. Series of abstractions for hybrid automata. In C. Tomlin and M. R. Greenstreet, editors, *HSCC*, volume 2289 of *Lecture Notes in Computer Science*, pages 465–478. Springer, 2002.

[19] F. W. Vaandrager and J. H. van Schuppen, editors. *Hybrid Systems: Computation and Control, Second International Workshop, HSCC'99, Proceedings*, volume 1569 of *Lecture Notes in Computer Science*. Springer, 1999.

Observability of Linear Hybrid Systems*

René Vidal[1], Alessandro Chiuso[2], Stefano Soatto[3], and Shankar Sastry[1]

[1] Department of EECS, University of California, Berkeley CA 94720, USA
   Phone: (510) 643-2382, Fax: (510) 642-1341, rvidal@eecs.berkeley.edu
[2] Dipartimento di Ingegneria dell'Informazione, Università di Padova, Italy
   Phone: +39-049-8277709, Fax: +39-049-8277699, chiuso@dei.unipd.it
[3] Department of CS, University of California, Los Angeles CA 90095, USA
   Phone: (310) 825-4840, Fax: (310) 794-5056, soatto@ucla.edu

Abstract. We analyze the observability of the continuous and discrete states of continuous-time linear hybrid systems. For the class of jump-linear systems, we derive necessary and sufficient conditions that the structural parameters of the model must satisfy in order for filtering and smoothing algorithms to operate correctly. Our conditions are simple rank tests that exploit the geometry of the observability subspaces. For linear hybrid systems, we derive weaker rank conditions that are sufficient to guarantee the uniqueness of the reconstruction of the state trajectory, even when the individual linear systems are unobservable.

1 Introduction

Observability refers to the study of the conditions under which it is possible to uniquely infer the state of a dynamical system from measurements of its output. For discrete-event systems, the definition of current-location observability was proposed in [12] as the property of being able to estimate the location of the system after a finite number of steps. A similar definition was given in [11] together with a polynomial test for observability, the so-called current-location tree, which depends on properties of the nodes of a finite state machine associated with the discrete-event system. For continuous systems with linear dynamics, it is well known that the observability problem can be reduced to that of analyzing the rank of the so-called *observability matrix*. This is the well known Popov-Belevic-Hautus rank test for linear systems [10]. For nonlinear systems with smooth dynamics, different definitions of observability have been proposed. We refer interested readers to [8] and references therein for a recent comparison of different definitions of observability. For hybrid systems, most of the previous work has concentrated on the areas of modeling, stability, controllability and verification (see previous workshop proceedings). Relatively little attention, however, has been devoted to the study of the observability of both the continuous and discrete states of a hybrid system.

* Research supported by grants ONR N00014-00-1-0621, NSF STC "CENS" and ECS0200511, European Project RECSYS, MIUR National Project *Identification and Adaptive Control of Industrial Systems* and Italian Space Agency.

O. Maler and A. Pnueli (Eds.): HSCC 2003, LNCS 2623, pp. 526–539, 2003.
© Springer-Verlag Berlin Heidelberg 2003

1.1   Prior Work

To the best of our knowledge, the first attempt to characterize the observability of hybrid systems can be found in [15], where a definition of observability is proposed. [14] gives conditions for the observability of a particular class of linear time-varying systems where the system matrix is a linear combination of a basis with respect to time-varying coefficients. [6] addresses the observability and controllability of switched linear systems with known and periodic transitions. [13] gives a condition for the observability of switched linear systems in terms of the existence of a discrete state trajectory. [3] proposes the notion of incremental observability for piecewise affine systems. Such a notion requires the solution of a mixed-integer linear program in order to be tested. [16] derives necessary and sufficient conditions for the observability of discrete-time jump-linear systems. The conditions can be tested using simple simple rank tests on the structural parameters of the model. [5] derives different rank tests for the weak observability of jump-Markov linear systems. [9] gives observability conditions for stochastic linear hybrid systems in terms of the covariances of the outputs.

A problem related to observability that has been recently considered is the design of observers for linear hybrid systems. [1] considers the case in which the discrete state is known and proposes a Luenberger observer for the continuous state. [2] combines location observers with Luenberger observers to design a hybrid observer that identifies the discrete location in a finite number of steps and converges exponentially to the continuous state.

1.2   Contributions

In this paper we study the observability of a class of linear hybrid systems known as jump- (or switched-) linear systems, *i.e.*, systems whose evolution is determined by a collection of linear models with *continuous state* $x_t \in \mathbb{R}^n$ connected by switches among a number of *discrete states* $\lambda_t \in \{1, 2, \dots, N\}$. In Section 2 we introduce a notion of observability for jump-linear systems. We define the observability index ν of a jump-linear system and use it to derive rank conditions that the structural parameters of the model must satisfy in order for filtering and smoothing algorithms to operate correctly. We show that the state trajectory is observable if and only if the pairwise intersection of different observable subspaces is trivial. We also show that the switching times are observable if and only if the difference between any pair of observability matrices is nonsingular. The rank conditions we derive are simpler than their discrete-time counterparts [16] and can be thought of as an extension of the Popov-Belevic-Hautus rank test for linear systems. Our conditions only depend on the geometry of the observability subspaces, and therefore they are applicable also to the case of hybrid models where the switching mechanism depends on the continuous state. In Section 3 we derive weaker rank conditions that guarantee the observability of a linear hybrid system, even if the individual linear systems are unobservable. In this case, observability is gained by requiring that the output switches at least once in the given observability interval. Section 4 concludes the paper with a discussion about the role of the inputs in the observability of the discrete state.

2   Observability of Jump-Linear Systems

We consider a class of continuous-time hybrid systems known as jump-linear systems, *i.e.*, systems whose evolution is determined by a collection of linear models with *continuous state* $x_t \in \mathbb{R}^n$ connected by switches of a number of *discrete states* $\lambda_t \in \{1, 2, \ldots, N\}$. The evolution of the continuous state x_t is described by the linear system

$$\dot{x}_t = A(\lambda_t)x_t \tag{1}$$
$$y_t = C(\lambda_t)x_t, \tag{2}$$

where $A(k) \in \mathbb{R}^{n \times n}$ and $C(k) \in \mathbb{R}^{p \times n}$, for $k \in \{1, 2, \ldots, N\}$. The evolution of the discrete state λ_t can be modeled, for instance, as an irreducible Markov chain governed by the transition map $\pi(t) \doteq P(\lambda_{t+1}|\lambda_t)$ or, as we do here, as a deterministic but unknown input that is piecewise constant, right-continuous and finite-valued[1]. Furthermore, we assume that the hybrid system admits no Zeno executions. More specifically, we assume that the switching times $\{t_i, i \geq 1\}$ are separated by at least $\tau > 0$; that is, we assume that $t_{i+1} - t_i \geq \tau > 0$. Having a minimum separation τ between consecutive switches is not a strong assumption to make, since τ can be arbitrarily small, as long as it is constant and positive.

Given a jump-linear system $\Sigma = \{A(k), C(k); k = 1, \ldots, N\}$, we focus our attention on how to infer the state of the system $\{x_t, \lambda_t\}$ from the output $\{y_t\}$. The simplest instance of this problem can be informally described as follows. Assume that we are given the model parameters $A(\cdot), C(\cdot)$ and that Σ evolves starting from an (unknown) initial condition (x_{t_0}, λ_{t_0}). Given the output $\{y_t\}$ in the interval $[t_0, t_0+T]$, is it possible to reconstruct the continuous state trajectory x_t and the discrete state trajectory λ_t uniquely?

If the sequence of discrete states $\lambda_{t_0}, \lambda_{t_1}, \ldots, \lambda_{t_0+T}$ is known, then the output of the system between two consecutive jumps can be written explicitly in terms of the model parameters $A(\cdot), C(\cdot)$, and the initial value of the continuous state x_{t_0} as

$$y_t = \begin{cases} C(\lambda_{t_0})e^{A(\lambda_{t_0})(t-t_0)}x_{t_0} & t \in [t_0, t_1) \\ C(\lambda_{t_1})e^{A(\lambda_{t_1})(t-t_1)}e^{A(\lambda_{t_0})(t_1-t_0)}x_{t_0} & t \in [t_1, t_2) \\ \vdots & \vdots \end{cases} \tag{3}$$

We thus propose the following notions of indistinguishability and observability.

---

[1] Most of the literature on hybrid systems restricts the switching mechanism of the discrete state to depend on the value of the continuous state. While this is generally sensible in the study of stability, it could be a significant restriction to impose in the context of filtering and identification. Therefore, our model is more general from an observability point of view, since it imposes no restriction on the mechanism that governs the transitions between discrete states. The conditions we derive are therefore sufficient for systems with state-dependent transitions.

Definition 1 (Indistinguishability). *We say that the states $\{x_{t_0}, \lambda_t\}$ and $\{\bar{x}_{t_0}, \bar{\lambda}_t\}$ are* **indistinguishable** *on the interval $t \in [t_0, t_0 + T]$ if the corresponding outputs in free evolution $\{y_t\}$ and $\{\bar{y}_t\}$ are equal. We use $\{x_{t_0}, \lambda_{t_0}, \ldots, \lambda_{t_0+T}\}$ instead of $\{x_{t_0}, \lambda_t\}$ to denote the state when the switching times are known. We denote the set of states which are indistinguishable from $\{x_{t_0}, \lambda_t\}$ as $\mathcal{I}(x_{t_0}, \lambda_t)$.*

Definition 2 (Observability). *We say that a state $\{x_{t_0}, \lambda_t\}$ is* **observable** *on $t \in [t_0, t_0 + T]$ if $\mathcal{I}(x_{t_0}, \lambda_t) = \{x_{t_0}, \lambda_t\}$. When any admissible state is observable, we say that the model Σ is* **observable**.

Remark 1. Notice that we have defined observability in terms of the initial continuous state x_{t_0} and the discrete state evolution λ_t rather than in terms of the hybrid state evolution $\{x_t, \lambda_t\}$. This is because if $A(\cdot)$, x_{t_0} and λ_t are known, then x_t is automatically determined, similarly to (3).

2.1 Observability of the Initial State

We first analyze the conditions under which we can determine x_{t_0} and $\lambda_t = \lambda_{t_0}$ for $t \in [t_0, t_1)$ uniquely, *i.e.*, before a switch occurs. We have that $\{x_{t_0}, \lambda_{t_0}\}$ is indistinguishable from $\{\bar{x}_{t_0}, \bar{\lambda}_{t_0}\}$ if and only if

$$C(\lambda_{t_0})e^{A(\lambda_{t_0})(t-t_0)}x_{t_0} = C(\bar{\lambda}_{t_0})e^{A(\bar{\lambda}_{t_0})(t-t_0)}\bar{x}_{t_0} \qquad \text{for } t \in [t_0, t_1). \qquad (4)$$

After expanding both sides in Taylor series about t_0, the indistinguishability condition can be written as

$$y_{t_0}^{(k)} = C(\lambda_{t_0})A(\lambda_{t_0})^k x_{t_0} = C(\bar{\lambda}_{t_0})A(\bar{\lambda}_{t_0})^k \bar{x}_{t_0} \qquad \text{for } k \geq 0. \qquad (5)$$

If we let $\mathcal{O}_\infty(\lambda_{t_0})$ and $\mathcal{O}_\infty(\bar{\lambda}_{t_0})$ be the infinite-dimensional extended observability matrices of the pairs $(A(\lambda_{t_0}), C(\lambda_{t_0}))$ and $(A(\bar{\lambda}_{t_0}), C(\bar{\lambda}_{t_0}))$, respectively, then the indistinguishability condition can be compactly written as

$$\mathcal{O}_\infty(\lambda_{t_0})x_{t_0} = \mathcal{O}_\infty(\bar{\lambda}_{t_0})\bar{x}_{t_0}. \qquad (6)$$

Therefore, the initial state $\{x_{t_0}, \lambda_{t_0}\}$ is observable if and only if the rank condition $\text{rank}([\mathcal{O}_\infty(\lambda_{t_0}) \ \mathcal{O}_\infty(\bar{\lambda}_{t_0})]) = 2n$ holds. It turns out that, as in the linear systems case, we can restrict our attention to finite-dimensional observability matrices, because the *extended joint observability matrix* $\mathcal{O}_\infty(k, k') \triangleq [\mathcal{O}_\infty(k) \ \mathcal{O}_\infty(k')]$ equals the extended observability matrix of the $2n$-dimensional system defined by

$$A(k, k') = \begin{bmatrix} A(k) & 0 \\ 0 & A(k') \end{bmatrix} \quad \text{and} \quad C(k, k') = [C(k) \ C(k')].$$

Hence, we define the *joint observability index* of systems k and k' as the minimum integer $\nu(k, k')$ such that the rank of the finite-dimensional joint observability matrix $\mathcal{O}_j(k, k') \triangleq [\mathcal{O}_j(k) \ \mathcal{O}_j(k')]$, where

$$\mathcal{O}_j(k) = [C(k)^T \ (C(k)A(k))^T \ \cdots \ (C(k)A(k)^{j-1})^T]^T, \qquad (7)$$

stops growing. Thus, we can rephrase the indistinguishability condition in terms of the largest joint observability index $\nu \triangleq \max_{k \neq k'}\{\nu(k, k')\} \leq 2n$ as

$$\mathcal{Y}_\nu(t_0) \triangleq \begin{bmatrix} y_{t_0} \\ \dot{y}_{t_0} \\ \vdots \\ y_{t_0}^{(\nu-1)} \end{bmatrix} = \mathcal{O}_\nu(\lambda_{t_0})x_{t_0} = \mathcal{O}_\nu(\bar{\lambda}_{t_0})\bar{x}_{t_0}. \tag{8}$$

From this equation we derive the following condition on the observability of the initial state $\{x_{t_0}, \lambda_{t_0}\}$.

Lemma 1 (Observability of the initial state). *If $t_1 - t_0 \geq \tau > 0$, then the initial state $\{x_{t_0}, \lambda_{t_0}\}$ is observable if and only if for all $k \neq k' \in \{1, \ldots, N\}$ we have* $\mathrm{rank}([\mathcal{O}_\nu(k)\ \mathcal{O}_\nu(k')]) = 2n$. *Furthermore, the initial state is given by*

$$\lambda_{t_0} = \{k : \mathrm{rank}([\mathcal{O}_\nu(k)\ \mathcal{Y}_\nu(t_0)]) = n\} \quad and \quad x_{t_0} = \mathcal{O}_\nu(\lambda_{t_0})^\dagger \mathcal{Y}_\nu(t_0), \tag{9}$$

where $M^\dagger = (M^T M)^{-1} M^T$.

We illustrate the applicability of Lemma 1 with the following example.

Example 1 (Two observable linear systems give an unobservable hybrid system). Consider the one-dimensional jump-linear system composed of the two linear systems

$$\begin{aligned} \dot{x} = 0 \\ y = c_1 x \end{aligned} \quad \text{and} \quad \begin{aligned} \dot{x} = 0 \\ y = c_2 x \end{aligned}, \tag{10}$$

where $c_1 \neq 0$, $c_2 \neq 0$ and $c_1 \neq c_2$. We observe that the initial state of each linear system is observable, but the initial state of the jump-linear system is not: One can set the initial condition of system 1 to x_0 and the initial condition of system 2 to $c_1 x_0/c_2$ and obtain identical outputs. That is, states $\{x_0, 1\}$ and $\{c_1 x_0/c_2, 2\}$ are indistinguishable. Notice that in this example the rank-$2n$ condition is violated, because $\mathrm{rank}([c_1\ c_2]) = 1 < 2$.

Remark 2 (Observability subspaces). Notice that the rank-$2n$ condition implies that each linear system $(A(k), C(k))$ must be observable, because it implies that $\mathrm{rank}(\mathcal{O}_\nu(k)) = n$ for all $k \in \{1, \ldots, N\}$. In addition, if we denote the range of $\mathcal{O}_\nu(k)$ as the observability subspace associated with linear system k, then the rank-$2n$ condition implies that the intersection of the observability subspaces of each pair of linear systems must be trivial. In fact, the set of unobservable states can be directly obtained from the intersection of the observability subspaces. One could therefore introduce a notion of distance between models using the angles between the observability subspaces, similarly to [4].

2.2   Observability of the First Switching Time

Lemma 1 provides conditions for the observability of the initial state $\{x_{t_0}, \lambda_{t_0}\}$. We are now interested in the observability of $\{x_{t_0}, \lambda_t\}$ for $t \in [t_0, t_1]$. Since λ_t is a piecewise constant function, we only need to concentrate on the conditions under which the first switching time, t_1, can be uniquely determined. The output of the jump-linear system is given by

$$y_t = \begin{cases} C(\lambda_{t_0})e^{A(\lambda_{t_0})(t-t_0)}x_{t_0} & t \in [t_0, t_1) \\ C(\lambda_{t_1})e^{A(\lambda_{t_1})(t-t_1)}e^{A(\lambda_{t_0})(t_1-t_0)}x_{t_0} & t \in [t_1, t_2) \end{cases} \qquad (11)$$

and we want to determine if it is possible to also write the output as

$$y_t = \begin{cases} C(\lambda_{t_0})e^{A(\lambda_{t_0})(t-t_0)}x_{t_0} & t \in [t_0, \bar{t}_1) \\ C(\lambda_{\bar{t}_1})e^{A(\lambda_{\bar{t}_1})(t-\bar{t}_1)}e^{A(\lambda_{t_0})(\bar{t}_1-t_0)}x_{t_0} & t \in [\bar{t}_1, t_2) \end{cases} \qquad (12)$$

Without loss of generality, assume that $\bar{t}_1 > t_1$ and consider the output y_t in the interval $[t_1, \bar{t}_1)$. We observe that t_1 is indistinguishable if and only if for $t \in [t_1, \bar{t}_1)$

$$C(\lambda_{t_0})e^{A(\lambda_{t_0})(t-t_1)}e^{A(\lambda_{t_0})(t_1-t_0)}x_{t_0} = C(\lambda_{t_1})e^{A(\lambda_{t_1})(t-t_1)}e^{A(\lambda_{t_0})(t_1-t_0)}x_{t_0}. (13)$$

After expanding both sides in Taylor series about t_1, the indistinguishability condition can be written as

$$y_{t_1}^{(k)} = C(\lambda_{t_0})A(\lambda_{t_0})^k x_{t_1} = C(\lambda_{t_1})A(\lambda_{t_1})^k x_{t_1} \qquad \text{for } k \geq 0. \qquad (14)$$

As before, then the indistinguishability condition can be compactly written in terms of the extended observability matrices as

$$\mathcal{O}_\nu(\lambda_{t_0})x_{t_1} = \mathcal{O}_\nu(\lambda_{t_1})x_{t_1}. \qquad (15)$$

Hence, t_1 is indistinguishable when the difference between the observability matrices $\mathcal{O}_\nu(\lambda_{t_0}) - \mathcal{O}_\nu(\lambda_{t_1})$ is singular. Since this could happen for any pair of observability matrices, in order for t_1 to be observable, we need to ensure that the difference of any pair of observability matrices is nonsingular. We therefore have the following Lemma on the observability of the first switching time.

Lemma 2 (Observability of the first switching time). *If $t_1 - t_0 \geq \tau > 0$, then the first switching time is observable if and only if for all $k \neq k' \in \{1, \ldots, N\}$ we have $\mathrm{rank}(\mathcal{O}_\nu(k) - \mathcal{O}_\nu(k')) = n$. Furthermore, the first switching time can be recovered as the time instance at which the output y_t is not C^∞, i.e.,*

$$t_1 = \min\{t > t_0 : \mathcal{Y}_\nu(t^-) \neq \mathcal{Y}_\nu(t^+)\}. \qquad (16)$$

Remark 3 (Continuous reset map). Notice that if the continuous reset is different from the identity map, then the switching times can be found by looking at the discontinuities of y_t directly, with no need for higher-order derivatives of y_t.

Remark 4 (Unobservable subspaces). Notice that if a continuous state x is unobservable for linear systems k and k', then $\mathcal{O}_\nu(k)x = \mathcal{O}_\nu(k')x = 0$, hence $(\mathcal{O}_\nu(k)-\mathcal{O}_\nu(k'))x = 0$. Therefore, the rank-$n$ condition $\mathrm{rank}(\mathcal{O}_\nu(k)-\mathcal{O}_\nu(k')) = n$ implies that the intersection of the null-spaces of any pair of observability matrices, *i.e.*, the intersection of the unobservable subspaces, must be trivial. While this observation is irrelevant for the observability of a jump-linear system, because each linear system has to be observable (See Remark 2), it will be quite important for uniquely reconstructing the state trajectory of unobservable jump-linear systems, as we will discuss in Section 3.

2.3   Observability of Jump-Linear Systems

Once x_{t_0}, λ_{t_0} and t_1 have been determined, we just repeat the process for the remaining jumps. The only difference is that x_{t_i}, $i \geq 1$, will be given. However, since λ_{t_0} is originally unknown, we still need to check the rank-$2n$ condition of Lemma 1 for any pair of extended observability matrices in order for x_{t_0} and λ_{t_0} to be uniquely recoverable. Therefore, since the rank-$2n$ condition $\mathrm{rank}([\mathcal{O}_\nu(k) \ \mathcal{O}_\nu(k')]) = 2n$ implies the rank-n condition $\mathrm{rank}(\mathcal{O}_\nu(k)-\mathcal{O}_\nu(k')) = n$, we have the following theorem on the observability of jump-linear systems.

Theorem 1 (Observability of jump-linear systems). *If for all $i \geq 0$ we have $t_{i+1} - t_i \geq \tau > 0$, then $\{x_{t_0}, \lambda_t\}$ is observable on $t \in [t_0, t_0 + T]$ if and only if for all $k \neq k' \in \{1, \ldots, N\}$ we have $\mathrm{rank}([\mathcal{O}_\nu(k) \ \mathcal{O}_\nu(k')]) = 2n$. Furthermore, the state trajectory can be uniquely recovered as*

$$\lambda_{t_0} = \{k : \mathrm{rank}([\mathcal{O}_\nu(k) \ \mathcal{Y}_\nu(t_0)]) = n\}, \tag{17}$$

$$x_{t_0} = \mathcal{O}_\nu(\lambda_{t_0})^\dagger \mathcal{Y}_\nu(t_0), \tag{18}$$

$$t_i = \min\{t > t_{i-1} : \mathcal{Y}_\nu(t^-) \neq \mathcal{Y}_\nu(t^+)\}, \tag{19}$$

$$\lambda_{t_i} = \{k : \mathrm{rank}([\mathcal{O}_\nu(k) \ \mathcal{Y}_\nu(t_i)]) = n\}. \tag{20}$$

Remark 5 (Observability of discrete-time jump-linear systems). Notice that the rank conditions of Theorem 1 are simpler than their discrete-time counterparts. In discrete time, it is possible that a switch occurs at time t_i but its effect in the output appears some time steps after t_i. In that case, in order to guarantee observability, additional rank constraints need to be imposed, for example the $A(\cdot)$ matrices must be nonsingular and they cannot commute. We refer interested readers to [16] for more details about the discrete-time case.

Remark 6 (Observability of jump-linear systems in terms of observability operators). The rank constraints of Theorem 1 can also be expressed in terms of observability operators. For example, let $\mathcal{L}(k) : \mathbb{R}^n \to \mathcal{C}^\infty_{[0,\tau]}$ be defined as

$$x \mapsto y(t) = [\mathcal{L}(k)x](t) \triangleq C(k)e^{A(k)t}x \quad \text{for} \quad t \in [0, \tau]. \tag{21}$$

Also let the adjoint observability operator $\mathcal{L}^*(k) : C^\infty_{[0,\tau]} \to \mathbb{R}^n$ be defined as

$$\xi(\cdot) \mapsto x = \mathcal{L}^*(k)\xi \triangleq \int_0^\tau e^{A(k)^T(\tau-s)} C(k)^T \xi(s)\, ds \quad \text{for} \quad \xi(\cdot) \in C^\infty_{[0,\tau]}. \quad (22)$$

Then a linear hybrid system is observable if and only if for all $k \neq k' \in \{1, \dots, N\}$ the range of the operator $\mathcal{L}(k) \times \mathcal{L}(k')$ is $2n$-dimensional. This implies that $Range(\mathcal{L}(k)) \cap Range(\mathcal{L}(k')) = 0$ and that $\mathcal{L}(k) - \mathcal{L}(k')$ is injective. Then one can reconstruct the state trajectory by orthogonally projecting the output onto the range of these observability operators. More specifically, one can determine the initial discrete state λ_{t_0} by looking at k such that

$$y(t) - \left[\mathcal{L}(k)(\mathcal{L}^*(k)\mathcal{L}(k))^{-1}\mathcal{L}^*(k)y\right](t) = 0 \quad \forall t \in [0,\tau), \quad \tau \leq t_1.$$

Given λ_{t_0}, the initial continuous x_{t_0} can be determined as

$$x_{t_0} = (\mathcal{L}^*(\lambda_{t_0})\mathcal{L}(\lambda_{t_0}))^{-1}\mathcal{L}^*(\lambda_{t_0})y(t).$$

Similarly, the first switching time, t_1, can be determined as the first time instant $t > t_0$ such that

$$y(t) - \left[\mathcal{L}(\lambda_{t_0})(\mathcal{L}^*(\lambda_{t_0})\mathcal{L}(\lambda_{t_0}))^{-1}\mathcal{L}^*(\lambda_{t_0})y\right](t) \neq 0.$$

The same argument applies for the subsequent discrete states and switching times.

Remark 7. For ease of exposition and in order to make the connection with the discrete-time case, we have chosen to state our results in terms of derivatives of the output. Nevertheless, when it comes to doing computations and quantifying errors, working with grammians may turn out to be more convenient. Just to mention one point, in practice one needs to quantify "how far" two linear systems are and how this affects the estimation of the initial state and of the discrete sequence in the presence of "noise". If one considers, for instance, L^2 distances in the output spaces $d_{[0,\tau]}(k) = \int_0^\tau \|y(t) - [\mathcal{L}(k)(\mathcal{L}^*(k)\mathcal{L}(k))^{-1}\mathcal{L}^*(k)y](t)\|^2\, dt$ then a natural way to measure the distance between two systems is by looking at the subspace angles between observability subspaces, as suggested in [4]. In fact, assume that $y(t)$ has been generated by system 1 and we measure $d_{[0,\tau]}(2)$ then it holds that $d_{[0,\tau]}(2) \geq \|y\|^2 \sin^2(\theta_{min})$ where θ_{min} is the smallest canonical angle between $Range(\mathcal{L}(1))$ and $Range(\mathcal{L}(2))$. Investigating these issues will be the subject of future research.

Remark 8 (Role of the input in the observability of the discrete state). The notion of observability we have proposed does not depend on the input. This is consistent with the standard theory for linear systems. However, identifying the discrete state of a jump-linear system is equivalent to a system identification problem, where the class of possible models is restricted to a finite set. Unlike observability, identifiability – even for linear systems – does depend on the input[2], and therefore the input ought to play a role in the identification of linear hybrid systems. We discuss this further in Section 4.

---

[2] This fact was pointed out to us by Prof. Claire Tomlin (personal communication).

3   Observability of Linear Hybrid Systems

Theorem 1 gives *necessary and sufficient* conditions for the observability of a class of linear hybrid systems known as jump-linear systems. Since the theorem imposes no restriction on the mechanism that governs the transitions between discrete states, the conditions of Theorem 1 remain *sufficient* for other classes of linear hybrid systems in which the switching mechanism depends on the value of the continuous state, e.g. piecewise affine systems, as long as there is a minimum separation $\tau > 0$ between consecutive switches. This is because, given a linear hybrid system $\mathcal{H}$, one can always associate with it a jump-linear systems Σ that abstracts the discrete behavior as well as the interaction between discrete and continuous states defined by the guards and invariants. Then, if the jump-linear system Σ is observable, so is the linear hybrid system $\mathcal{H}$.

However, the conditions of Theorem 1 are not *necessary* for the observability of a linear hybrid system. In fact, there are cases in which the associated jump-linear system is itself unobservable (in the sense of Definition 2), yet it is possible to uniquely reconstruct the state trajectory from a particular output[3]. Intuitively, this happens when the linear hybrid system switches from an unobservable state for system k to an observable one for system k', as we illustrate in the following example. (See [3] for additional examples in discrete-time).

Example 2 (Unique reconstruction from two unobservable linear systems). Consider a two-dimensional linear hybrid system composed of the two linear systems

$$\dot{x} = \begin{bmatrix} 1 & 0 \\ 0 & 2 \end{bmatrix} x \qquad\qquad \dot{x} = \begin{bmatrix} 1 & 0 \\ 0 & 2 \end{bmatrix} x$$

$$\text{and} \tag{23}$$

$$y = \begin{bmatrix} 1 & 0 \end{bmatrix} x \qquad\qquad y = \begin{bmatrix} 0 & 1 \end{bmatrix} x \;.$$

Let $t_0 = 0$, $T = 2$, $x_0 = [0, 1]^T$ and assume that there is a single switch from system 1 to system 2 at time $t_1 = 1$. Then $\nu = 2$,

$$x_t = \begin{bmatrix} 0 \\ 1 \end{bmatrix} e^{2t}, \quad y_t = \begin{cases} 0 & t \in [0, 1) \\ e^{2t} & t \in [1, 2) \end{cases}, \quad \mathcal{O}_2(1) = \begin{bmatrix} 1 & 0 \\ 1 & 0 \end{bmatrix} \quad \text{and} \quad \mathcal{O}_2(2) = \begin{bmatrix} 0 & 1 \\ 0 & 2 \end{bmatrix}.$$

In this example, both linear systems are unobservable and the initial condition lies in the unobservable subspace of system 1. Also notice that the rank-$2n$ condition is violated, since rank($[\mathcal{O}_2(1) \;\; \mathcal{O}_2(2)]$) = 2 < 4, thus Lemma 1 does not apply. However, the first switching time can be uniquely recovered, because the rank-n condition of Lemma 2 holds since rank($\mathcal{O}_2(2) - \mathcal{O}_2(1)$) = 2. In fact, y_t is discontinuous at $t_1 = 1$. Furthermore, one can uniquely reconstruct x_{t_0}, λ_{t_0} and λ_{t_1}, because the unobservable subspace of system 1 is observable for system 2 and vice-versa. We make this more precise in the rest of this Section.

---

[3] Notice that this is impossible for linear systems. A linear system is either observable, in which case one can uniquely reconstruct the state for any given nonzero output, or it is unobservable, in which case for any output there are always infinitely many possible state trajectories generating it.

Following Example 2, in this section we derive weaker sufficient conditions under which one can uniquely reconstruct the state trajectory of a linear hybrid system given a particular output. We show how this can be done despite the individual linear systems being unobservable or the output of the system being zero during a switching interval. We start by assuming that we know the number and location of the switching times in the interval $[t_0, t_0 + T]$. According to our discussion in the previous section, this is equivalent to assuming that for all $k \neq k' \in \{1, \ldots, N\}$ we have $\text{rank}(\mathcal{O}_\nu(k) - \mathcal{O}_\nu(k')) = n$. Notice that this rank-$n$ condition does not require the individual linear systems to be observable. Now, from the indistinguishability condition

$$\mathcal{Y}_\nu(t_0) = \mathcal{O}_\nu(\lambda_{t_0})x_{t_0} = \mathcal{O}_\nu(\bar{\lambda}_{t_0})\bar{x}_{t_0}, \tag{24}$$

we have that the initial discrete state is indistinguishable whenever the intersection of any pair of observability subspaces is nontrivial, which happens if

$$\text{rank}([\mathcal{O}_\nu(k) \ \mathcal{O}_\nu(k')]) < \text{rank}(\mathcal{O}_\nu(k)) + \text{rank}(\mathcal{O}_\nu(k')). \tag{25}$$

We thus have the following:

1. If $\mathcal{Y}_\nu(t_0) \neq 0$, then the discrete state λ_{t_0} can be uniquely recovered provided that the intersection of any pair of observability subspaces is trivial. That is, for all $k \neq k' \in \{1, \ldots, N\}$ we must have

$$\text{rank}([\mathcal{O}_\nu(k) \ \mathcal{O}_\nu(k')]) = \text{rank}(\mathcal{O}_\nu(k)) + \text{rank}(\mathcal{O}_\nu(k')). \tag{26}$$

   In this case we have

$$\lambda_{t_0} = \{k : \text{rank}([\mathcal{O}_\nu(k) \ \mathcal{Y}_\nu(t_0)]) = \text{rank}(\mathcal{O}_\nu(k))\}. \tag{27}$$

   Notice that we do not need $\mathcal{O}_\nu(k)$ to be full rank, hence the rank-$2n$ condition may be violated here.

2. If $\mathcal{Y}_\nu(t_0) \neq 0$ and $t_1 > t_0 + T$, i.e., if there is no switch during the observability window, then the continuous state can be uniquely recovered if and only if each linear system is observable, i.e., if for all $k \in \{1, \ldots, N\}$ we have $\text{rank}(\mathcal{O}_\nu(k)) = n$. Let λ_{t_0} be defined as in (27), then we have

$$x_{t_0} = \mathcal{O}_\nu(\lambda_{t_0})^\dagger \mathcal{Y}_\nu(t_0). \tag{28}$$

   This means that, if there is no switch, then we *do* need every system to be observable, hence the rank-$2n$ condition has to be in effect.

3. If $\mathcal{Y}_\nu(t_0) \neq 0$ and $t_1 < t_0 + T$, i.e., if at least one switch occurs during the observability window, then the continuous state may *not* be uniquely recovered from the output in the interval $[t_0, t_1)$, but one may still be able to uniquely recover it from the output on the whole interval $[t_0, t_0 + T]$. Loosely speaking, we need to find a condition such that the part of x_{t_0} that is not observable on $[t_0, t_1)$ becomes observable on $[t_1, t_0 + T]$. For example, imagine that there is only one switch at time t_1. Then we have that

$$\begin{bmatrix} \mathcal{O}_\nu(\lambda_{t_0}) \\ \mathcal{O}_\nu(\lambda_{t_1})e^{A(\lambda_{t_0})(t_1-t_0)} \end{bmatrix} x_{t_0} = \begin{bmatrix} \mathcal{Y}_\nu(t_0) \\ \mathcal{Y}_\nu(t_1) \end{bmatrix}. \tag{29}$$

Therefore, in order to determine x_{t_0} uniquely we need

$$\text{rank}\begin{bmatrix} \mathcal{O}_\nu(\lambda_{t_0}) \\ \mathcal{O}_\nu(\lambda_{t_1})e^{A(\lambda_{t_0})(t_1-t_0)} \end{bmatrix} = n. \tag{30}$$

This rank condition is trivially satisfied, because the null-space of $\mathcal{O}_\nu(\lambda_{t_0})$ is $e^{A(\lambda_{t_0})}$-invariant and we have assumed that $\text{rank}(\mathcal{O}(\lambda_{t_1}) - \mathcal{O}(\lambda_{t_0})) = n$ in order for t_1 to be observable (See Remark 4).

More generally, if there are j switches, $t_1, t_2, \ldots t_j$, on the interval $[t_0, t_0+T]$, $\mathcal{Y}_\nu(t_i) \neq 0$ for $i = 0, 1, \ldots, j$, and the corresponding sequence of discrete states $\lambda_{t_0}, \lambda_{t_1}, \ldots, \lambda_{t_j}$ can be uniquely recovered similarly to (27), then the initial continuous state x_{t_0} can be uniquely recovered from

$$\begin{bmatrix} \mathcal{O}_\nu(\lambda_{t_0}) \\ \mathcal{O}_\nu(\lambda_{t_1})e^{A(\lambda_{t_0})(t_1-t_0)} \\ \vdots \\ \mathcal{O}_\nu(\lambda_{t_j})e^{A(\lambda_{t_{j-1}})(t_j-t_{j-1})} \ldots e^{A(\lambda_{t_0})(t_1-t_0)} \end{bmatrix} x_{t_0} = \begin{bmatrix} \mathcal{Y}_\nu(t_0) \\ \mathcal{Y}_\nu(t_1) \\ \vdots \\ \mathcal{Y}_\nu(t_j) \end{bmatrix}. \tag{31}$$

Notice again that the matrix on the left is full rank thanks to the rank-n condition $\text{rank}(\mathcal{O}_\nu(k) - \mathcal{O}_\nu(k')) = n$.

4. If $\mathcal{Y}_\nu(t_0) = 0$, then we cannot compute λ_{t_0} from (27). However, the rank constraint in (30) guarantees that $\mathcal{Y}_\nu(t_1) = \mathcal{O}_\nu(\lambda_{t_1})e^{A(\lambda_{t_0})(t_1-t_0)}x_{t_0} \neq 0$. Therefore, we can solve for λ_{t_1} uniquely similarly to (27). Given λ_{t_1}, the rank-n condition $\text{rank}(\mathcal{O}_\nu(k) - \mathcal{O}_\nu(k')) = n$ guarantees that λ_{t_0} can be uniquely determined as

$$\lambda_{t_0} = \{k : \text{rank}\begin{bmatrix} \mathcal{O}_\nu(k) & 0 \\ \mathcal{O}_\nu(\lambda_{t_1}) & \mathcal{Y}_\nu(t_1) \end{bmatrix} = \text{rank}\begin{bmatrix} \mathcal{O}_\nu(k) \\ \mathcal{O}_\nu(\lambda_{t_1}) \end{bmatrix}\}. \tag{32}$$

More generally, whenever the output is zero in an interval $[t_i, t_{i+1})$, i.e., whenever $\mathcal{Y}_\nu(t_i) = 0$, we must have that $\mathcal{Y}_\nu(t_{i+1}) \neq 0$ from which we can uniquely recover $\lambda_{t_{i+1}}$ as in (27). Given $\lambda_{t_{i+1}}$ one can uniquely determine λ_{t_i} as in (32). Then we are back into the situation of step 3 in which the discrete sequence is known, hence x_{t_0} can be uniquely recovered from (31).

We summarize our discussion in the following Theorem.

Theorem 2 (Observability of linear hybrid systems). *Consider a linear hybrid system $\mathcal{H}$ such that the switching times satisfy $t_{i+1} - t_i \geq \tau \; \forall i \geq 0$, and let $\Sigma = \{A(k), C(k); k = 1, \ldots, N\}$ be the associated jump-linear system. We have the following.*

1. ***Observability of the switching times:*** *If the difference between any pair of observability matrices is nonsingular; that is, if*

$$\text{for all } k \neq k' \in \{1, \ldots, N\} \text{ we have } \text{rank}(\mathcal{O}_\nu(k) - \mathcal{O}_\nu(k')) = n, \tag{33}$$

then the switching times can be uniquely recovered as the time instances at which the output y_t is not C^∞, that is

$$t_i = \min\{t > t_{i-1} : \mathcal{Y}_\nu(t^-) \neq \mathcal{Y}_\nu(t^+)\}. \tag{34}$$

We denote by j the total number of switches in the interval $[t_0, t_0 + T]$.

2. **Observability of the discrete state trajectory:** *If in addition the intersection of the observability subspaces of any pair of observability matrices is trivial, that is if for all $k \neq k' \in \{1, \ldots, N\}$ we have*

$$\text{rank}([\mathcal{O}_\nu(k) \; \mathcal{O}_\nu(k')]) = \text{rank}(\mathcal{O}_\nu(k)) + \text{rank}(\mathcal{O}_\nu(k')), \qquad (35)$$

then the discrete state trajectory can be uniquely recovered as follows:
a) For the switching times t_i such that $\mathcal{Y}_\nu(t_i) \neq 0$, obtain the discrete state similarly to (27) as

$$\lambda_{t_i} = \{k : \text{rank}([\mathcal{O}_\nu(k) \; \mathcal{Y}_\nu(t_i)]) = \text{rank}(\mathcal{O}_\nu(k))\}. \qquad (36)$$

b) For the switching times t_i such that $\mathcal{Y}_\nu(t_i) = 0$,
– Compute $\lambda_{t_{i+1}}$ similarly to (36) as

$$\lambda_{t_{i+1}} = \{k : \text{rank}([\mathcal{O}_\nu(k) \; \mathcal{Y}_\nu(t_{i+1})]) = \text{rank}(\mathcal{O}_\nu(k))\}. \qquad (37)$$

– Compute λ_{t_i} similarly to (32) as

$$\lambda_{t_i} = \{k : \text{rank} \begin{bmatrix} \mathcal{O}_\nu(k) & 0 \\ \mathcal{O}_\nu(\lambda_{t_{i+1}}) & \mathcal{Y}_\nu(t_{i+1}) \end{bmatrix} = \text{rank} \begin{bmatrix} \mathcal{O}_\nu(k) \\ \mathcal{O}_\nu(\lambda_{t_{i+1}}) \end{bmatrix} \}. \qquad (38)$$

3. **Observability of the initial continuous state:** *Under the conditions stated before, the initial value of the continuous state can be uniquely recovered as*

$$x_{t_0} = \begin{bmatrix} \mathcal{O}_\nu(\lambda_{t_0}) \\ \mathcal{O}_\nu(\lambda_{t_1})e^{A(\lambda_{t_0})(t_1-t_0)} \\ \vdots \\ \mathcal{O}_\nu(\lambda_{t_j})e^{A(\lambda_{t_{j-1}})(t_j-t_{j-1})} \cdots e^{A(\lambda_{t_0})(t_1-t_0)} \end{bmatrix}^\dagger \begin{bmatrix} \mathcal{Y}_\nu(t_0) \\ \mathcal{Y}_\nu(t_1) \\ \vdots \\ \mathcal{Y}_\nu(t_j) \end{bmatrix}. \qquad (39)$$

Example 3 (Unique reconstruction of the state of a linear hybrid system composed of two unobservable linear systems). Consider the two-dimensional linear hybrid system of Example 2, where $t_0 = 0$, $t_1 = 1$, $T = 2$, $x_0 = [0, 1]^T$ and

$$\begin{aligned} \dot{x} &= \begin{bmatrix} 1 & 0 \\ 0 & 2 \end{bmatrix} x & \dot{x} &= \begin{bmatrix} 1 & 0 \\ 0 & 2 \end{bmatrix} x & x_t &= \begin{bmatrix} 0 \\ 1 \end{bmatrix} e^{2t} & y_t &= \begin{cases} 0 & t \in [0, 1) \\ e^{2t} & t \in [1, 2) \end{cases}. \qquad (40) \\ y &= \begin{bmatrix} 1 & 0 \end{bmatrix} x & y &= \begin{bmatrix} 0 & 1 \end{bmatrix} x \end{aligned}$$

In this example we have $\nu = 2$,

$$\mathcal{O}_2(1) = \begin{bmatrix} 1 & 0 \\ 1 & 0 \end{bmatrix}, \quad \mathcal{O}_2(2) = \begin{bmatrix} 0 & 1 \\ 0 & 2 \end{bmatrix}, \quad \mathcal{Y}_2(0) = \begin{bmatrix} 0 \\ 0 \end{bmatrix} \quad \text{and} \quad \mathcal{Y}_2(1) = \begin{bmatrix} e^2 \\ 2e^2 \end{bmatrix}. (41)$$

Therefore, both linear systems are unobservable and the initial condition lies in the null-space of $\mathcal{O}_2(1)$. Also notice that the rank-$2n$ condition is violated, since $\text{rank}([\mathcal{O}_2(1) \; \mathcal{O}_2(2)]) = 2 < 4$, thus Lemma 1 does not apply. However, we have $\text{rank}(\mathcal{O}_2(1) - \mathcal{O}_2(2)) = 2$, thus t_1 can be uniquely recovered, because y_t is discontinuous at $t_1 = 1$. Also $\text{rank}([\mathcal{O}_2(1) \; \mathcal{O}_2(2)]) = \text{rank}(\mathcal{O}_2(1)) + \text{rank}(\mathcal{O}_2(2)) = 1 + 1 = 2$, thus $\lambda_{t_i} = 2$ can be uniquely recovered, because $\text{rank}([\mathcal{O}_2(1) \; \mathcal{Y}_2(1)]) = 2 \neq 1$ while $\text{rank}([\mathcal{O}_2(2) \; \mathcal{Y}_2(1)]) = 1 = 1$. Given t_1 and λ_{t_1}, one can estimate $\lambda_{t_0} = 1$ uniquely from (38), and $x_{t_0} = [0, 1]^T$ uniquely from (39).

4   Conclusions, Discussion, and Open Issues

We have presented an analysis of the observability of the continuous and discrete states of linear hybrid systems. For jump-linear systems, we demonstrated that under mild assumptions one can derive necessary and sufficient conditions that the structural parameters of the model must satisfy in order to guarantee the observability of the system. Our characterization is simple and intuitive and sheds light on the geometry of the observability subspaces generated by the output of a jump-linear system. For linear hybrid systems, we derived weaker rank conditions that guarantee the uniqueness of the reconstruction of the state trajectory, even if the individual linear systems are unobservable. In this case, observability is gained by requiring that the given output switches at least once in the observability interval. Although the conditions we have derived are sufficient for the observability of linear hybrid systems in which the switching mechanism depends on the value of the continuous state, e.g. piecewise affine systems, in the near future we expect to obtain weaker conditions that are also necessary.

An important issue that we did not addressed is concerned with characterizing the set of observationally equivalent models. In linear systems theory, this is done elegantly by the Kalman decomposition, which partitions the state space into orthogonal subspaces. Future work will address a characterization of this set for linear hybrid models.

Other aspects which remains to be investigated are the effect of measured inputs on the observability. The analysis we have carried out in the first part of the paper is limited to the case where the system evolves starting from some initial state with no driving input. The conditions we have derived, therefore, involve only the matrices $A(\cdot)$ and $C(\cdot)$. As we have anticipated in Remark 8, this is only part of the story. In fact, estimating the discrete state can be interpreted as the identification of a model within a finite number of possible models, and from a finite set of data. Therefore, unfortunately, one cannot use asymptotic results since, by assumption, switches occur in finite time. Instead, conditions on the input, such as persistence of excitation, that play a crucial role in system identification, will likely play an important role in the observability of hybrid systems too. For instance, let us consider a simple example where $N = 2$ and the two linear systems have *identical* $A(\cdot)$ and $C(\cdot)$ matrices, but different input-to-state coefficients (say for instance that $B(1) = 2B(2)$). Assume that the system is excited with white Gaussian noise. It is easy to prove that as the discrete state jumps from system 1 to system 2, the variance of the state increases and so does the variance of the output. Therefore, one should be able to detect a jump even though the $A(1) = A(2)$ and $C(1) = C(2)$, and hence the two models are indistinguishable according to our definition. This very simple example should caution the reader that a sensible definition of observability ought to also involve the input matrices (B, D). One may be tempted to give observability conditions in terms of the covariances of the outputs, but again this does not appear promising for at least two reasons. First, one can never compute good approximations of stationary covariances from finite sequences of data (in between switches). Second, well-known results [7] show that the output covariance of a jump-Markov linear system can be realized with a finite-dimensional ARMA model, and therefore covariance data are not sufficient to guarantee identifiability. The quest for different statistics (for instance, higher-order functions of the data) is worth investigating for this problem.

References

[1] A. Alessandri and P. Coletta. Design of Luenberger observers for a class of hybrid linear systems. In *Hybrid Systems: Computation and Control*, volume 2034 of *LNCS*, pages 7–18. Springer Verlag, 2001.

[2] A. Balluchi, L. Benvenuti, M. Di Benedetto, and A. Sangiovanni-Vincentelli. Design of observers for hybrid systems. In *Hybrid Systems: Computation and Control*, volume 2289 of *LNCS*, pages 76–89. Springer Verlag, 2002.

[3] A. Bemporad, G. Ferrari, and M. Morari. Observability and controllability of piecewise affine and hybrid systems. *IEEE Transactions on Automatic Control*, 45(10):1864–1876, October 2000.

[4] K. De Cock and B. De Moor. Subspace angles and distances between ARMA models. In *Proc. of Mathematical Theory of Networks and Systems*, 2000.

[5] E. Costa and J. do Val. On the detectability and observability for continuous-time Markov jump linear systems. In *Proc. of IEEE Conference on Decision and Control*, 2001.

[6] J. Ezzine and A. H. Haddad. Controllability and observability of hybrid systems. *International Journal of Control*, 49(6):2045–2055, 1989.

[7] C. Francq and J. Zakoïan. Stationarity of multivariate Markov-switching ARMA models. *Journal of Econometrics*, 102:339–364, 2001.

[8] J. Hespanha, D. Liberzon, and E. Sontag. Nonlinear observability and an invariance principle for switched systems. In *Proc. of IEEE Conference on Decision and Control*, pages 4300–4305, 2002.

[9] I. Hwang, H. Balakrishnan, and C. Tomlin. Observability criteria and estimator design for stochastic linear hybrid systems. In *Proc. of European Control Conference*, 2003. Submitted.

[10] T. Kailath. *Linear Systems*. Prentice Hall, 1980.

[11] C. Özveren and A. Willsky. Observability of discrete event dynamic systems. *IEEE Transactions on Automatic Control*, 35:797–806, 1990.

[12] P. Ramadge. Observability of discrete-event systems. In *Proc. of IEEE Conference on Decision and Control*, pages 1108–1112, 1986.

[13] A. Sun, S. S. Ge, and T. H. Lee. Controllability and reachability criteria for switched linear systems. *Automatica*, 38:775–786, 2002.

[14] F. Szigeti. A differential algebraic condition for controllability and observability of time varying linear systems. In *Proc. of IEEE Conference on Decision and Control*, pages 3088–3090, 1992.

[15] J. K. Tugnait. Adaptive estimation and identification for discrete systems with Markov jump parameters. *IEEE Transactions on Automatic Control*, 27(5):1054–1065, 1982.

[16] R. Vidal, A. Chiuso, and S. Soatto. Observability and identifiability of jump linear systems. In *Proc. of IEEE Conference on Decision and Control*, pages 3614–3619, 2002.

Results and Perspectives on Computational Methods for Optimal Control of Switched Systems*

Xuping Xu[1] and Panos J. Antsaklis[2]

[1] Department of Electrical and Computer Engineering,
Penn State Erie, Erie, PA 16563, USA,
Xuping-Xu@psu.edu
[2] Department of Electrical Engineering,
University of Notre Dame, Notre Dame, IN 46556, USA,
antsaklis.1@nd.edu

Abstract. This paper surveys some of the recent progresses on computational methods for optimal control of switched systems. A general model of switched system that allows externally forced switching (EFS) and internally forced switching (IFS) is first introduced and two important classes of optimal control problems are formulated. After a brief review of some relevant theoretical results, we present the idea of two stage optimization. Based on the theoretical results and two stage optimization, we then survey computational methods based on discretization, and computational methods not based on discretization. Comments are made on the merits and restrictions of each method.

1 Introduction

Switched systems are a particular class of hybrid systems consisting of several subsystems and a switching law specifying the active subsystem at each time instant. Examples of switched systems can be found in chemical processes, automotive systems, and electrical circuit systems, to name a few.

Recently, optimal control problems of hybrid and switched systems have attracted researchers from various fields in science and engineering, due to the problems' significance in theory and application. The available results on such problems include theoretical and computational ones. The available theoretical results usually extend the classical maximum principle or dynamic programming to such problems. As to the computational results, researchers have taken advantage of efficient nonlinear optimization techniques and high-speed computers to develop efficient numerical methods for such problems.

This paper surveys some of the recent progresses on computational methods for optimal control problems of switched systems. Such problems are difficult to

---

* The partial support of the National Science Foundation (NSF ECS99-12458 & CCR01-13131), and of the DARPA/ITO-NEST Program (AF-F30602-01-2-0526) is gratefully acknowledged.

O. Maler and A. Pnueli (Eds.): HSCC 2003, LNCS 2623, pp. 540–555, 2003.

solve, due to the involvement of switchings of subsystem dynamics. The recent decade has seen some breakthrough in the development of efficient computational methods for such problems. However, the literature results are often based on different models and differ in problem formulations and approaches. Therefore, it is necessary to call for an overview of these results under a unified framework.

In this paper, we first propose a general model of switched system that includes externally forced switching (EFS) and internally forced switching (IFS) and formulate EFS and IFS optimal control problems. Such formulations then serve as unified frameworks for our survey. After a brief review of some relevant theoretical results, we present the idea of two stage optimization for EFS problems where stage 1 seeks optimal continuous input and stage 2 seeks optimal switching sequence. Extensions of the two stage optimization to IFS problems are also mentioned. Based on the theoretical results and two stage optimization, we survey two classes of computational methods — those based on discretization and those not based on discretization. Several methods based on discretization and methods for discrete-time problems are overviewed and their merits and restrictions are indicated. We then report recent developments of computational methods not based on discretization for stage 1 optimization in which a prespecified sequence of active subsystems is given. We point out that a stage 1 problem can further be decomposed into stage 1(a), which is a conventional optimal control problem that seeks the optimal cost given a switching sequence, and stage 1(b), which is a nonlinear optimization problem that seeks the optimal switching instants. Stage 1(b) poses difficulties because it is hard to obtain the information of the derivatives of the stage 1(a) optimal cost with respect to the switching instants. To address these difficulties, we finally overview two methods which can find approximations and accurate values of the derivative values, respectively.

2 Problem Statement

2.1 Switched Systems

A switched system consists of several subsystems and a switching law. A switching usually takes place when a certain event signal is received. An event signal may be an external signal (generated exogenously) or an internal signal generated when an internal condition for the states, inputs and/or time evolution is satisfied. In the sequel, we call a switching triggered by an external event an externally forced switching (EFS) and a switching triggered by an internal event an internally forced switching (IFS).

Definition 1. *A* **switched system** *is a 3-tuple* $S = (\mathcal{D}, \mathcal{F}, \mathcal{L})$ *where*
- $\mathcal{D} = (I, E)$ *is a directed graph indicating the discrete mode structure of the system.* $I = \{1, 2, \cdots, M\}$ *is the set of indices for subsystems.* E *is a subset of* $I \times I - \{(i, i) | i \in I\}$ *which contains the valid events. If an event* $e = (i_1, i_2)$ *takes place, the system switches from subsystem* i_1 *to* i_2. *Furthermore* $E = E_E \cup E_I$ (E_E *and* E_I *may not be disjoint) where* E_E *is the external event set and* E_I *is the internal event set.*

- $\mathcal{F} = \{f_i : X_i \times U_i \to \mathbb{R}^n | i \in I\}$ *where* f_i *describes the vector field for the i-th subsystem* $\dot{x} = f_i(x, u)$. *Here* $X_i \subseteq \mathbb{R}^n$ *and* $U_i \subseteq \mathbb{R}^m$ *are respectively the state and control constraint sets for the i-th subsystem.*
- $\mathcal{L} = \mathcal{L}_E \cup \mathcal{L}_I$ *provides logic constraints that relate the continuous state and mode switchings. Here* $\mathcal{L}_E = \{\Lambda_e | \Lambda_e \subseteq \mathbb{R}^n, \emptyset \neq \Lambda_e \subseteq X_{i_1} \cap X_{i_2}, e = (i_1, i_2) \in E_E\}$ *corresponds to the external events; only when* $x \in \Lambda_e$ *for* $e = (i_1, i_2)$, *an EFS from subsystem* i_1 *to* i_2 *is possible. Also here* $\mathcal{L}_I = \{\Gamma_e | \Gamma_e \subseteq \mathbb{R}^n, \emptyset \neq \Gamma_e \subseteq X_{i_1} \cap X_{i_2}, e = (i_1, i_2) \in E_I\}$ *corresponds to the internal events; when subsystem* i_1 *is active and the state trajectory intersects* Γ_e *for* $e = (i_1, i_2)$, *the event* $e = (i_1, i_2)$ *must be triggered and the system is forced to switch to subsystem* i_2.   □

For a switched system, the presence of switchings makes the behavior of the system more complicated than that of conventional systems. In particular, the evolution of the continuous and discrete states will leave us with a timed sequence of active subsystems that is defined as a switching sequence as follows.

Definition 2. *A* **switching sequence** σ *in* $[t_0, t_f]$ *is a timed sequence* $\sigma = ((t_0, i_0), (t_1, i_1), \cdots, (t_K, i_K))$, *where* $0 \leq K < \infty$, $t_0 \leq t_1 \leq \cdots \leq t_K \leq t_f$, *and* $i_k \in I$ *for* $0 \leq k \leq K$.   □

A switching sequence σ defined above indicates that the system starts from subsystem i_0 at t_0, and switches to subsystem i_k from subsystem i_{k-1} at t_k for $1 \leq k < K$. Subsystem i_k will remain active in $[t_k, t_{k+1})$. For a switched system to be well-behaved, we generally exclude the undesirable *Zeno phenomenon*, i.e., infinitely many switchings in finite amount of time. The pairs (t_k, i_k)'s in σ can be classified into two categories — those corresponding to EFS denoted by (t_k^E, i_k^E), and those corresponding to IFS denoted by (t_k^I, i_k^I). By distinguishing EFS and IFS, we can define the EFS sequence $\sigma_E = ((t_0, i_0), (t_1^E, i_1^E), \cdots, (t_{K_1}^E, i_{K_1}^E))$ and the IFS sequence $\sigma_I = ((t_0, i_0), (t_1^I, i_1^I), \cdots, (t_{K_2}^I, i_{K_2}^I))$. The combination of σ_E and σ_I gives us the overall switching sequence $\sigma \stackrel{\triangle}{=} \sigma_E \cup \sigma_I$ (here $K_1 + K_2 = K$).

Given a switched system, the overall exogenous control input is a pair (σ_E, u). Along with the evolution of $x(t)$, an IFS sequence σ_I will be generated implicitly. σ_E and σ_I then lead to the overall σ. Given initial pair $(x(t_0), i_0)$, an exogenous input pair (σ_E, u) is said to be *valid* if the evolution of the system under it generates a nonblocking state trajectory $x(t)$ and a nonZeno σ.

Remark 1. For switched systems in Definition 1, the continuous state does not exhibit jumps at switching instants. We propose this framework due to two reasons. First, in many applications such as some chemical processes, there are no state jumps at switchings. Second, analysis and design of switched systems without jumps usually require simpler notations and are more amenable to rigorous study as opposed to systems with jumps. Therefore, we mainly focus on systems without jumps in this paper. However, we note that many methods reported in the paper can actually be extended to problems with jumps.   □

Remark 2. If we let all subsystems be discrete-time systems, we can similarly define discrete-time switched systems.   □

2.2   Optimal Control Problems

Although general optimal control problems can be formulated for switched systems with both EFS and IFS, notations would be complicated and results would be difficult to obtain. Hence, we choose to study two important classes of problems, i.e., optimal control problems for systems with EFS only (EFS Problems), and problems for systems with IFS only (IFS Problems). In doing so, the objective of overviewing available results can be fulfilled, because most of the available literature results are on computational methods for one of these two classes of problems. In the following, we call a valid (σ_E, u) (or u for IFS problems) *admissible* if the corresponding $x(t)$ meets the terminal manifold.

Problem 1 (EFS Problem). Consider a switched system S with EFS only. Find an admissible control pair (σ_E, u) (u is piecewise continuous) such that x departs from a given initial state $x(t_0) = x_0$ at the given initial time t_0 and meets an $(n - l_f)$-dimensional smooth manifold S_f at t_f (t_f is free) and

$$J = \psi\big(x(t_f)\big) + \int_{t_0}^{t_f} L\big(x(t), u(t)\big) \, dt + \sum_{1 \leq k \leq K} \delta\big(x(t_k), i_{k-1}, i_k\big)$$

is minimized (here K is the number of switchings in σ_E). $\qquad\qquad \square$

Problem 2 (IFS Problem). Consider a switched system S with IFS only. Find an admissible $u(t)$ (u is piecewise continuous) such that x departs from a given initial state $x(t_0) = x_0$ at the given initial time t_0 and meets an $(n - l_f)$-dimensional smooth manifold S_f at t_f (t_f is free) and

$$J = \psi\big(x(t_f)\big) + \int_{t_0}^{t_f} L\big(x(t), u(t)\big) \, dt + \sum_{1 \leq k \leq K} \delta\big(x(t_k), i_{k-1}, i_k\big)$$

is minimized (here K is the number of switchings in σ_I). $\qquad\qquad \square$

Remark 3. Problems 1 and 2 are formulated as general Bolza problems with terminal cost ψ, running cost $\int_{t_0}^{t_f} L \, dt$, and switching cost δ. In the sequel, we assume that f_i, ψ, L, and δ are smooth enough (e.g., twice continuously differentiable). In the results we will overview, various additional assumptions may be imposed. For example, for the convenience of developing numerical methods, problems with fixed t_f are sometimes studied. In fact, a free-final-time problem can always be transcribed into a fixed-final-time one by introducing additional state variables (see page 101 in [30]). $\qquad\qquad \square$

Remark 4. Problems 1 and 2 are different due to the different exogenous inputs. Such difference makes the two problems different in many aspects when we develop computational methods. In fact, the implicit generation of σ_I makes the IFS problem more difficult. $\qquad\qquad \square$

3   An Overview of Some Theoretical Results

In this section, we briefly overview some basic theoretical results that can help understand Problems 1 and 2 and can serve as foundations for the development of various computational methods.

The Maximum Principle

[28] is an early paper on continuous-time optimal control problems for a class of hybrid systems in which transitions of discrete state are triggered by the continuous state (an IFS problem). The main results in [28] include a version of MP. In particular, it is proved that the costate satisfies some jump conditions at the switching instants. Another early paper [25] studies problems akin to IFS Problem 2 and reports conditions for the existence of optimal solutions for problems with two subsystems.

More general optimal control problems for hybrid systems with switchings and jumps have recently been reported in [20,26]. [20] introduces a general hybrid system model similar to Definition 1 except for the jumps. Due to the general hybrid systems model, even analysis of the existence of solutions is quite involved (and additional assumptions must be made). Hence [20] then focuses on two special classes of problems and proves a version of MP. In [26], optimal control problems for hybrid systems with a similar formulation to that of [20] are studied. The optimal control problems studied there are more like EFS problems. Several versions of MP are then given there, including a nonsmooth version.

More recent results on EFS problems have been reported in [23,24]. A version of MP is proposed for problems with running cost only. The MP is specifically applied to time optimal control problems and linear quadratic problems.

The MPs proposed in the above papers usually provide necessary conditions with no specific sequence of active subsystems assumed. This introduces a problem formed by a continuous-time mixed differential algebraic equation (DAE) and an integer programming problem, which is not amenable for numerical computations. However, in Section 4.2, after introducing the two stage optimization method, we will state a version of MP for a given sequence of active subsystems that only involves DAE and can be used for numerical methods.

The Dynamic Programming

Similar to conventional optimal control, DP can be used to derive the HJB equation for Problems 1 and 2. Detailed derivations of HJB equations for various formulations of optimal control problems for switched systems and systems with impulse effect and costs for switchings can be found in [37]. Following the ideas in [37], a version of HJB for EFS Problem 1 without cost for switchings is derived in [29], under additional assumptions $X_i = \mathbb{R}^n$, $U_i = \mathbb{R}^m$, $\Lambda_e = \mathbb{R}^n$. To briefly reiterate the result, we define

$$V^{*i}(x,t) \triangleq \min_{\text{admissible } (\sigma_E, u)'s} \left\{ \psi(x(t_f)) + \int_t^{t_f} L(x(\tau), u(\tau)) \, d\tau \right\}$$

where $x(\tau)$ is equal to x at time instant $\tau = t$. If $V^{*i}(x,t) \in C^1[t_0, t_f]$, then we have the following HJB equation

$$\min \left\{ \min_{j \in \{i' | (i,i') \in E_E\}} \left\{ V^{*j}(x,t) \right\} - V^{*i}(x,t), \; V_t^{*i}(x,t) + \min_{u \in \mathbb{R}^m} \left\{ L(x,u) \right. \right.$$
$$\left. \left. + V_x^{*i}(x,t) f_i(x,u) \right\} \right\} = 0 \tag{1}$$

The DP method and HJB equation can be useful in developing methods utilizing value functions. (1) is very difficult to solve analytically. One way to solve it is to discretize the continuous time and state spaces and then apply backward searching methods to solve the discretized problem. However, combinatorial explosion problems may arise as the discretization level becomes finer.

A result closely related to DP is the derivation of the generalized quasi-variational inequalities (GQVI's) reported in [5]. The hybrid DP developed in [12] is also relevant in this regard.

4 Two Stage Optimization

4.1 Two Stage Optimization Formulation

Problem 1 requires the solution of a valid optimal pair (σ_E^*, u^*) such that
$$J(\sigma_E^*, u^*) = \min\nolimits_{\text{admissible } (\sigma_E, u)'s} J(\sigma_E, u). \tag{2}$$
In [29], a lemma is given which proposes a way to formulate (2) into a two stage optimization problem. With only slight modifications, we can rewrite the lemma to be applicable to Problem 1 as follows.

Lemma 1. *For Problem 1, if*

(a). an admissible optimal solution (σ_E^*, u^*) exists and
(b). for any given EFS sequence σ_E for which at least one continuous input u exists so that (σ_E, u) is admissible, there exists a corresponding admissible $u^* = u_{\sigma_E}^*$ such that the function $J_{\sigma_E}(u) \triangleq J(\sigma_E, u)$ is minimized,

then the following equation holds

$$\min_{\text{ad. } (\sigma_E, u)'s} J(\sigma_E, u) = \min_{\sigma \in \{\sigma_E | \exists u, (\sigma_E, u) \text{ is ad.}\}} \min_{u \in \{u | (\sigma_E, u) \text{ is ad.}\}} J(\sigma_E, u). \tag{3}$$

Here 'ad.' stands for 'admissible'.   □

The right hand side of (3) needs twice the minimization processes. This implies that the following two stage optimization method can be applied.

A Two Stage Optimization Method

Stage 1. Fixing σ, solve the inner minimization problem (or claim that σ_E is invalid, i.e., no u exists for the given σ_E such that (σ_E, u) is admissible).
Stage 2. Regarding the optimal cost for each valid σ_E as a function
$$J_1 = J_1(\sigma_E) = \min\nolimits_{u \in \{u | (\sigma_E, u) \text{ is admissible}\}} J(\sigma_E, u),$$
minimize J_1 with respect to all valid σ_E's.   □

In [29], under the assumptions $X_i = \mathbb{R}^n$, $U_i = \mathbb{R}^m$, $\Lambda_e = \mathbb{R}^n$, and t_f being given, we implement the above method by the following more detailed algorithm.

Algorithm 1 (A Two Stage Algorithm).

Stage 1. (a). Fix the total number of switchings to be K and the sequence of active subsystems and let the minimum value of J with respect to u be a function of the K switching instants, i.e., $J_1 = J_1(t_1, \cdots, t_K)$ for $K \geq 0$ ($t_0 \leq t_1 \leq \cdots t_K \leq t_f$). Find J_1. ($J_1 = \infty$ when no admissible pair (σ_E, u) can be found.)

(b). Minimize J_1 with respect to $t_1, \cdots, t_K$.

Stage 2. (a). Vary the sequence of active subsystems to find an optimal solution under K switchings.

(b). Vary the value of K to find an optimal solution for Problem 1.   □

In the following, when we mention stage 1 optimization, we actually refer to stage 1 in Algorithm 1. In practice, many problems only require the solutions of optimal continuous inputs and optimal switching instants for stage 1 optimization in which a prespecified sequence of active subsystems is given. We will focus on such stage 1 optimization in the rest of this section.

IFS problems are more difficult due to the additional constraint that x must be in the set $\Gamma_{(i_1, i_2)}$ when the system switches from subsystem i_1 to i_2. Moreover, the switching instants can depend on the continuous input in a complicated way. In [31], an extension of the algorithm for EFS problems to stage 1 optimization of IFS problems is proposed (in the case that the switching set is a hypersurface).

Method 1 (A Method for IFS Problems)

1. Denote in a redundant fashion that an optimal solution to the IFS problem contains both an optimal continuous input and an optimal switching sequence (starting at subsystem i_0), i.e., regard an IFS problem as an EFS problem with additional state constraints at the switching instants. Solve the corresponding EFS problem.
2. Verify the validity of the solution for the IFS problem (i.e., if the system under the continuous input can evolve validly and generate the corresponding switching sequence).   □

The decomposition of the problem into two stages and the conceptual Algorithm 1 are still applicable to step 1 in the above method. Such an extension must address the additional requirement that the system's state is restricted to a switching hypersurface at each switching instant.

4.2 More on Stage 1 Optimization

Now we concentrate on stage 1 optimization. Note that many real world problems are in fact stage 1 optimization problems. For example, the speeding-up of a power train only requires switchings from gear 1 to 2 to 3 to 4. As can be seen from Algorithm 1, stage 1 can be further decomposed into two sub-steps (a) and (b). Stage 1(a) is in essence a conventional optimal control problem which seeks the minimum of J with respect to u under a given switching sequence $\sigma = ((t_0, i_0), (t_1, i_1), \cdots, (t_K, i_K))$. We denote the corresponding optimal cost as a function $J_1(\hat{t})$, where $\hat{t} \triangleq (t_1, t_2, \cdots, t_K)^T$. Stage 1(b) is in essence a constrained nonlinear optimization problem

$$\min_{\hat{t}} J_1(\hat{t})$$
$$\text{subject to } \hat{t} \in T \tag{4}$$

where $T \triangleq \{\hat{t} = (t_1, \cdots, t_K)^T | t_0 \leq t_1 \leq \cdots \leq t_K \leq t_f\}$.

Stage 1(a)

For stage 1(a) where a switching sequence $\sigma = ((t_0, i_0), (t_1, i_1), \cdots, (t_K, i_K))$ is given, finding $J_1(\hat{t})$ for the corresponding $\hat{t}$ is a conventional optimal control problem. In stage 1(a), we need to find an optimal continuous input u and the corresponding minimum J. In order to find solutions for stage 1(a) problems, computational methods must be adopted in most cases. Most of the available numerical methods for unconstrained conventional optimal control problems with fixed end-time can be used. See [16,21] for surveys of computational methods. It is not difficult to use the calculus of variations techniques (see e.g. [13]) to prove the following necessary conditions.

Theorem 1 (Necessary Conditions for Stage 1(a)). *Consider the stage 1(a) problem for Problem 1. Assume subsystem k is active in $[t_{k-1}, t_k)$ for $1 \leq k \leq K$ and subsystem $K+1$ in $[t_K, t_f]$. Let u be a piecewise continuous input such that x departs from a given initial state $x(t_0) = x_0$ and meets $S_f = \{x | \phi_f(x) = 0, \phi_f : \mathbb{R}^n \to \mathbb{R}^{l_f}\}$ at t_f. In order that u be optimal, it is necessary that there exists a vector function $p(t) = [p_1(t), \cdots, p_n(t)]^T$, $t \in [t_0, t_f]$, such that*

(a). For almost any $t \in [t_0, t_f]$ the state equation $\frac{dx(t)}{dt} = \left(\frac{\partial H}{\partial p} (x(t), p(t), u(t)) \right)^T$ and costate equation $\frac{dp(t)}{dt} = -\left(\frac{\partial H}{\partial x} (x(t), p(t), u(t)) \right)^T$ hold. Here $H(x, p, u) \triangleq L(x, u) + p^T f_k(x, u)$, if $t \in [t_{k-1}, t_k)$ ($k = K+1$ if $t \in [t_K, t_f]$).

(b). For almost any $t \in [t_0, t_f]$, the stationarity condition $0 = \left(\frac{\partial H}{\partial u} (x(t), p(t), u(t)) \right)^T$ holds.

(c). At t_f, the function p satisfies $p(t_f) = \left(\frac{\partial \psi}{\partial x} (x(t_f)) \right)^T + \left(\frac{\partial \phi_f}{\partial x} (x(t_f)) \right)^T \lambda$, where λ is an l_f-dimensional vector.

(d). At any t_k, $k = 1, 2, \cdots, K$, we have $p(t_k-) = p(t_k+)$. □

In general, it is difficult or even impossible to find an analytical expression of $J_1(\hat{t})$ using the above conditions. The reason is that conditions (a)-(d) present a two point boundary value differential algebraic equation (DAE) that, in most cases, cannot be solved analytically. However, the above DAE can be solved efficiently using many numerical methods (e.g., shooting methods and collocation methods). Note that Theorem 1 can also be extended to IFS problems if a pre-specified sequence of active subsystems is given and each set Γ_e is a hypersurface. The only difference in the IFS case is that the costate will have discontinuous jumps at the switching instants (see [28,31] for more details).

Stage 1(b)

In stage 1(b), we need to solve the constrained nonlinear optimization problem (4) with simple constraints. Computational methods for the solution of such problems are abundant in the nonlinear optimization literature. For example, feasible direction methods and penalty function methods are two commonly used classes of methods. These methods use the information of first-order derivative $\frac{\partial J_1}{\partial \hat{t}}$ and even second-order derivative $\frac{\partial^2 J_1}{\partial \hat{t}^2}$ (see [4,17] for details).

Finally in this section, we should point out that [9,10] independently propose a conceptual method of hierarchical decomposition similar to stage 1(a) and 1(b) for a class of hybrid systems optimal control problems under the assumption of a given sequence of active subsystems. The problems are motivated by previous works in manufacturing systems [6,18,19] but the formulation is more general. Both IFS and EFS problems can be formulated. The method decomposes the solution of such problems into two levels. The lower level is a conventional optimal control problem seeking an optimal continuous input and the higher level is a nonlinear optimization problem seeking initial and final states (since they are not prespecified in the problem formulations in [9,10]) and the optimal time durations.

5   Computational Methods Based on Discretization

Now we will look at specific computational methods for Problems 1 and 2. The first class of computational methods are based on discretization of the original problem, or discretization of some continuous conditions. The benefits of using discretization-based methods are two fold. First, such methods are usually not restricted to stage 1. Second, since such methods are usually directly built on nonlinear programming methods, general constraints can be dealt with and both EFS and IFS problems can be handled within a unified framework.

5.1   Methods Based on Discretization

A discretization-based method in line with the two stage optimization in Section 4 is reported in [27]. An EFS problem with running cost and switching cost is considered, assuming no state, continuous input, and switching set constraints. The subsystem dynamics and the cost functional are discretized to obtain a discrete-time problem. The cost functional becomes

$$J\big(i(0),\cdots,i(N-1),u(0),\cdots,u(N-1)\big) = \sum_{j=0}^{N}\Big(L\big(x(j),u(j)\big)+\delta(j)\Big)$$

where the switching cost δ is 0 if no switching occurs during the time interval $[t(j),t(j+1))$. A discrete-time version of the two stage optimization then is

$$J_{opt} = \inf_{i(0),\cdots,i(N-1)\in I}\ \inf_{u(0),\cdots,u(N-1)\in\mathbb{R}^m}\ J\big(i(0),\cdots,i(N-1),u(0),\cdots,u(N-1)\big).$$

$$(5)$$

It can be seen that (5) can be solved in two stages. For a given discrete sequence of active subsystems $\big(i(0),\cdots,i(N-1)\big)$ (denoted as i in the following), denote

$$J_1(i,x(0)) = \inf_{u(0),\cdots,u(N-1)\in\mathbb{R}^m}\ J\big(i(0),\cdots,i(N-1),u(0),\cdots,u(N-1)\big) \quad (6)$$

subject to the discretized system equation. (6) is a classic discrete-time optimal control problem. The optimal hybrid control is achieved by

$$J_{opt} = \inf_i J_1\big(i,x(0)\big). \quad (7)$$

One disadvantage of solving (7) to find the optimal i is that it is enumerative.

Another approach based on discretization is reported in [11,12], in which free-final-time EFS problems with running and switching costs are studied. Instead of directly discretizing the optimal control problem, the authors first introduces a set of piecewise C^1 functions V_i's and forms inequalities of Bellman type. It is then proved that for every given initial condition (x_0, i_0), $V_{i_0}(x_0)$ gives a lower bound on the cost for optimally bringing the system from (x_0, i_0) to the given (x_f, i_f). To simplify the notation, let us assume that all $X_i = X$ and $U_i = U$. The inequalities can then be written as

$$0 \leq \frac{\partial V_i(x)}{\partial x} f_i(x, u) + L(x, u), \; \forall x \in X, u \in U, i \in I$$
$$0 \leq V_{i_1}(x) - V_{i_2}(x) + \delta(x, i_1, i_2), \; \forall x \in \Lambda_{(i_1, i_2)}, \; i_1, i_2 \in I, \; i_1 \neq i_2$$
$$0 = V_{i_f}(x_f)$$

For the above equations, a set of value functions $V_i(x)$ is involved, with i being the index of the initial active subsystem. Note that the result of a maximization of $V_i(x)$ is always identical to the optimal cost for the corresponding initial (x, i). In order to utilize a computer to solve the above inequalities and maximize $V_{i_0}(x_0)$, a straightforward approach is to grid the state space and inequalities to be met at a set of uniformly distributed points. Such a discretization method leads to a lower bound V_i which is a good approximation of the optimal cost. A suboptimal feedback control law can then be obtained as $u(x, i) = \text{argmin}_{u \in U} \left\{ \frac{\partial V_i}{\partial x} f_i(x, u) + L(x, u) \right\}$ and $i(t) = \text{argmin}_{(i(t^-), i) \in E_E | x \in \Lambda_{(i(t^-), t)}} \left\{ V_i(x) + \delta(x, i(t^-), i) \right\}$.

A closely related paper which also utilizes Bellman type inequalities is [22]. The paper focuses on piecewise linear quadratic optimal control and uses linear matrix inequalities (LMIs) to solve the maximization problems.

As can be seen from the above discussions, discretization-based methods are capable of dealing with problems with constraints. Today's efficient nonlinear optimization solvers can even provide us with solutions of global optima or solutions close to them. However, the solutions thus obtained may not be accurate enough in terms of their continuous counterparts.

5.2   Discrete-Time Problems

Since discrete-time problems are closely related to discretization methods, here we briefly mention some results related to our discussions.

[14] utilizes a discrete-time DP approach for quadratic full information EFS optimal control problems for systems with stochastic linear subsystems. In the discrete-time setting, the optimal value function can be expressed as a quadratic function of the continuous state and the optimal continuous input can be expressed in state feedback form. The optimal switching sequence is found by backward iteration. The main result in [14] is a method for efficient pruning of the backward search tree to avoid combinatoric explosion. The idea of the algorithm is to make sure that pruned sequences would have resulted in a higher cost than those remaining after the pruning. Although this result is proposed in stochastic settings, it may be extended to deterministic cases.

An early result on discrete-time IFS problems is reported in [15]. In [15], an IFS optimal control problem for a discrete-time switched system is studied. The switching of the subsystems depends on the continuous state as well as the current active subsystem. For each i, it is assumed that $\Gamma_{(i,j)}$, $j \in I$ do not overlap (expect for the shared boundaries) and cover the state space $\mathbb{R}^n$ (Here $\Gamma_{(i,i)}$ is understood as the set where the system stays at subsystem i). An iterative algorithm using constrained differential dynamic programming, which is similar to that for IFS problems proposed in Section 4, is proposed. Assume an initial $(x(0), i(0))$ is given. An initial guess of $u(k)$, $k = 0, \cdots, N-1$, is chosen and then the corresponding state trajectory $x(k)$ and the active subsystem sequence $i(k)$ can be computed. Now regard the sequence of active subsystems as a constraint and solve a constrained optimal control problem. Accept the result if no resultant state $x(k)$ lies on the boundary of some switching set. Otherwise, according to certain termination rules, either accept the result or perturb the active subsystem sequence constraint and repeat the constrained optimization.

One of the very nice modeling frameworks for hybrid systems is the mixed logical dynamical (MLD) systems [1], which describes discrete-time switched and hybrid systems as follows

$$x(k+1) = Ax(k) + B_1 u(k) + B_2 \delta(k) + B_3 z(k) \tag{8}$$
$$E_2 \delta(k) + E_3 z(k) \le E_1 u(k) + E_4 x(k) + E_5 \tag{9}$$

where $x \in \mathbb{R}^{n_c} \times \{0,1\}^{n_l}$ is a vector of continuous and binary states, $u \in \mathbb{R}^{m_c} \times \{0,1\}^{m_l}$ are the continuous and binary inputs, $\delta \in \{0,1\}^{r_l}$ and $z \in \mathbb{R}^{r_c}$ represent auxiliary binary and continuous variables respectively, which are introduced when transforming logic relations into mixed-integer linear inequalities.

Based on that modeling framework, [2] studies optimal control problems which require the minimization of a weighted l_1/∞-norm of the tracking error and the input trajectory over a finite horizon. The problem is motivated by the requirement of designing a stabilizing model predictive controller. The overall optimal control problem subject to constraints (8)-(9) can then be regarded as a multiparametric mixed-integer linear programming (MILP) problem. If the optimal control problem uses performance criteria based on quadratic norms, a recent result in [3] shows that the optimal control for the finite time optimal control problem is a time-varying piecewise affine state feedback control law. Such optimal control law can be computed by means of dynamic programming and multiparametric quadratic programming. Note that the benefit of using an MLD framework is that there is no need to distinguish the optimization of continuous and discrete inputs (i.e., stages 1 and 2). However, such result can only be obtained for a class of discrete-time problems with linear subsystems.

6   Computational Methods Not Based on Discretization

As mentioned in Section 5, solutions obtained by discretization-based methods may not be accurate enough in terms of their continuous counterparts. Recently, some results that do not rely on discretization have been reported. In particular, many of these results are developed for stage 1 of Algorithm 1. The ideas of these results are based on the observation that stages 1(a) and 1(b) can be solved separately and iteratively. The following conceptual algorithm describes such an iterative method and provides a formal framework for the optimization methods in the sequel.

Algorithm 2 (A Conceptual Algorithm for Stage 1 Optimization).

(1). Set the iteration index $j = 0$. Choose an initial $\hat{t}^j$.

(2). By solving an optimal control problem (i.e., stage (a)), find $J_1(\hat{t}^j)$.

(3). Find $\frac{\partial J_1}{\partial t}(\hat{t}^j)$ (and $\frac{\partial^2 J_1}{\partial t^2}(\hat{t}^j)$ if second-order method is to be used).

(4). Use some feasible direction method to update $\hat{t}^j$ to be $\hat{t}^{j+1} = \hat{t}^j + \alpha^j d\hat{t}^j$ (here $d\hat{t}^j = -\left(\frac{\partial J_1}{\partial t}(\hat{t}^j)\right)^T$ or $d\hat{t}^j = -\left(\frac{\partial^2 J_1}{\partial t^2}(\hat{t}^j)\right)^{-1}\left(\frac{\partial J_1}{\partial t}(\hat{t}^j)\right)^T$ and the stepsize α^j is chosen using the Armijo's rule [4]). Set the iteration index $j = j + 1$.

(5). Repeat Steps (2), (3), (4) and (5), until a prespecified termination condition is satisfied (e.g. the norm of the projection of $\frac{\partial J_1}{\partial t}(\hat{t}^j)$ on any feasible direction is smaller than a given small number ϵ). □

Note that following the similar two stage decomposition idea, [9,10] also independently come up with iterative solution methods similar to Algorithm 2. It should be noted that the key difficulty of Algorithm 2 lies in the computation of $\frac{\partial J_1}{\partial t}(\hat{t}^j)$ (and $\frac{\partial^2 J_1}{\partial t^2}(\hat{t}^j)$) in step (3). In [9], it is proposed that the lower level problems be solved analytically first and then the result is substituted into high level to seek the optimal switching instants. However, we should point out that it is not always possible to derive analytical solutions to the lower level optimal control problems. This is evident from the fact that only few classes of conventional optimal control problems possess closed form solutions. Even for the case of linear quadratic (LQ) problems, we do not have the closed form solutions [35]. Therefore it is necessary to devise optimization methods that do not require the explicit expression of J_1 as a function of t_k's. In [32,34,35], the authors noticed that stage 1(b) (i.e., higher level) is a nonlinear optimization problem that can be optimized if we know the derivatives of the cost with respect to the switching instants. Instead of seeking closed form solutions to stage 1(a), we only need accurate values of the derivatives in order to carry out stage 1(b) optimization. Here we will survey two methods of computing these derivatives. In the following, we assume that $X = \mathbb{R}^n$, $U_i = \mathbb{R}^m$, $\Lambda_e = \mathbb{R}^n$, $S_f = \mathbb{R}^n$, and there is no switching cost in the problem formulation.

6.1 Method Based on Direct Differentiations of Value Functions

The first method was reported in [34] that approximates the derivatives by direct differentiations of value functions. Consider stage 1 optimization where the number of switchings is K and the order of active subsystems is $1, 2, \cdots, K, K+1$. We need to find an optimal switching instant vector $\hat{t} = (t_1, \cdots, t_K)^T$ and an optimal control input u.

Given a nominal $\hat{t}$ and a nominal u, we denote the corresponding cost as a value function (which is not necessarily optimal)

$$V^0\big(x(t_0), t_0, t_1, \cdots, t_K\big) = \psi\big(x(t_f)\big) + \int_{t_0}^{t_1} L(x, u)\, dt + \cdots + \int_{t_K}^{t_f} L(x, u)\, dt$$

where the superscript 0 is to indicate that the starting time for evaluation is t_0. Similarly, we can define the value function at the k-th switching instant as

$$V^k\big(x(t_k), t_k, t_{k+1}, \cdots, t_K\big) = \psi\big(x(t_f)\big) + \int_{t_k}^{t_{k+1}} L(x, u)\, dt + \cdots + \int_{t_K}^{t_f} L(x, u)\, dt.$$

The idea of the method is to approximate $\frac{\partial J_1}{\partial t}$ and $\frac{\partial^2 J_1}{\partial t^2}$ by $\frac{\partial V^0}{\partial t}$ and $\frac{\partial^2 V^0}{\partial t^2}$, respectively.

The explicit expressions of $\frac{\partial V^0}{\partial \hat{t}}$ and $\frac{\partial^2 V^0}{\partial \hat{t}^2}$ are derived in [34]. They are

$$V^0_{t_k} = L^{k-} - L^{k+} + V^{k+}_x(f^{k-} - f^{k+}),$$

$$V^0_{t_k t_k} = (f^{k-} - f^{k+})^T V^{k+}_{xx}(f^{k-} - f^{k+}) - (V^{k+}_x f^{k+}_x + L^{k+}_x)(f^{k-} - f^{k+}) + \left(V^{k+}_x(f^{k-}_x\right.$$
$$\left. -f^{k+}_x) + L^{k-}_x - L^{k+}_x\right)f^{k-} + (V^{k+}_x f^{k-}_u + L^{k-}_u)\dot{u}^{k-} - (V^{k+}_x f^{k+}_u + L^{k+}_u)\dot{u}^{k+},$$

$$V^0_{t_k t_l} = \left(V^{l+}_x(f^{l-}_x - f^{l+}_x) + (f^{l-} - f^{l+})^T V^{l+}_{xx} + L^{l-}_x - L^{l+}_x\right)A(t_l, t_k)(f^{k-} - f^{k+}).$$

where we write a function with a superscript $k-$ (resp. $k+$) whenever it is evaluated at t_k and the nominal values $x(t_k)$, $u(t_k-)$ (resp. t_k and the nominal values $x(t_k)$, $u(t_k+)$) (see [34] for details). Note here $A(t_l, t_k)$ is the state transition matrix for the variational time-varying equation $\dot{y}(t) = \frac{\partial f(x(t), u(t))}{\partial x}y(t)$ for $y(t), t \in [t_k, t_l]$; here f corresponds to the active subsystem vector field at each time instant and u, x are the current nominal input and state. Also note here $\dot{u}^{k-} \triangleq \frac{du(t_k-)}{dt}$ and $\dot{u}^{k+} \triangleq \frac{du(t_k+)}{dt}$.

Furthermore, a modified and more efficient version of the method is reported in [34] for EFS problems with linear subsystems and general quadratic costs.

6.2   Method Based on Parameterization of the Switching Instants

As opposed to approximations in [34], a method is proposed in [32,35] to obtain accurate values of the derivatives of J_1. The method is based on solving boundary value differential algebraic equations (DAEs). Such DAEs are similar to those for conventional optimal control problems, except for more equations due to the differentiations with respect to the switching instants (regarded as parameters).

To illustrate the method and make notation clear, let us concentrate on the case of two subsystems where subsystem 1 is active in the interval $t \in [t_0, t_1)$ and subsystem 2 is active in the interval $t \in [t_1, t_f]$ (t_1 is the switching instant to be determined). We also assume that $S_f = \mathbb{R}^n$ (for general S_f, we can introduce Lagrange multipliers as in Theorem 1 and develop similar method). It was shown in [32,35] that the stage 1 problem can be transcribed into the following equivalent problem.

Problem 3 *(An Equivalent Problem)*. For a system with dynamics

$$\frac{dx(\tau)}{d\tau} = \begin{cases} (x_{n+1} - t_0)f_1(x, u), & \text{for } \tau \in [0, 1), \\ (t_f - x_{n+1})f_2(x, u), & \text{for } \tau \in [1, 2], \end{cases}$$

find optimal parameter x_{n+1} and $u(\tau)$, $\tau \in [0, 2]$ such that the cost functional

$$J = \psi(x(2)) + \int_0^1 (x_{n+1} - t_0)L(x, u)\ d\tau + \int_1^2 (t_f - x_{n+1})L(x, u)\ d\tau$$

is minimized. Here t_0, t_f and $x(0) = x_0$ are given. x_{n+1} is a parameter which corresponds to the switching instant t_1. The independent time variable τ has the following relationship to the original time variable t

$$t = \begin{cases} t_0 + (x_{n+1} - t_0)\tau, & 0 \le \tau < 1, \\ x_{n+1} + (t_f - x_{n+1})(\tau - 1), & 1 \le \tau \le 2. \end{cases} \qquad \square$$

Based on the equivalent Problem 3, we now develop a method for deriving accurate numerical value of $\frac{dJ_1}{dt_1}$. First note that for Problem 3, the optimal x and u will be functions in x_{n+1}. Also note that

$$J_1(x_{n+1}) = \psi(x(2, x_{n+1})) + \int_0^1 (x_{n+1} - t_0)L(x, u)\ d\tau + \int_1^2 (t_f - x_{n+1})L(x, u)\ d\tau.$$

Differentiating J_1 with respect to x_{n+1} provides us with

$$\frac{dJ_1}{dx_{n+1}} = \frac{\partial \psi\left(x(2,x_{n+1})\right)}{\partial x} \frac{\partial x(2,x_{n+1})}{\partial x_{n+1}} + \int_0^1 \left(L(x,u) + (x_{n+1} - t_0)(\frac{\partial L}{\partial x} \frac{\partial x}{\partial x_{n+1}}\right.$$
$$\left. + \frac{\partial L}{\partial u} \frac{\partial u}{\partial x_{n+1}})\right) d\tau + \int_1^2 \left(-L(x,u) + (t_f - x_{n+1})(\frac{\partial L}{\partial x} \frac{\partial x}{\partial x_{n+1}} + \frac{\partial L}{\partial u} \frac{\partial u}{\partial x_{n+1}})\right) d\tau.$$

Therefore, what we need to know are the values of x, u, $\frac{\partial x}{\partial x_{n+1}}$, $\frac{\partial u}{\partial x_{n+1}}$. In [32,35], it was shown that their values for $\tau \in [0,2]$ can be obtained by solving a two point boundary value DAE formed by the parameterized state, costate, stationarity equations (in order to make exposition brief, we do not list them here but refer the readers to Theorem 1), the boundary and continuity conditions

$$x(0, x_{n+1}) = x_0,$$
$$p(2, x_{n+1}) = \left(\frac{\partial \psi}{\partial x}\left(x(2,x_{n+1})\right)\right)^T.$$

for Problem 3 and their derivatives with respect to the parameter x_{n+1}.

For each given x_{n+1}, the DAE can be solved using numerical methods. Assume we have solved the above DAE and obtained the optimal $x(\tau, x_{n+1})$, $p(\tau, x_{n+1})$ and $u(\tau, x_{n+1})$, we can then obtain the value of the derivative $\frac{dJ_1}{dx_{n+1}}$. Using this method, we can address general problems involving nonlinear systems and cost functionals. This method is also applicable to the case of more than one switchings and to the computation of higher order derivatives. Moreover, for EFS problems with linear subsystems and general quadratic costs, the burden of solving DAE can be relieved and one only needs to solve a set of ODEs formed by the Riccati equations and their differentiations with respect to the switching instants. A preliminary result of applying this method to IFS problem based on Method 1 discussed at the end of Section 4.1 is also reported in [31,35].

6.3 Results for Switched Autonomous Systems

When each subsystem is autonomous (i.e., with no continuous input), stage 1 problem becomes a nonlinear optimization problem and J becomes a function of the switching instants. The method in Section 6.1 can still be applied to similar stage 1 problems where a prespecified sequence of active subsystems is given. Because u is absent, it is shown in [33] that accurate values of $\frac{\partial J_1}{\partial t}$ and $\frac{\partial^2 J_1}{\partial t^2}$ can be obtained. The result has been extended to hybrid autonomous systems with state jumps [36]. Closely related papers are [7,8] that present closed-loop solutions to a special class of problems, i.e., infinite horizon problems for switched linear autonomous systems. However, there are some differences between the results in [7,8] and [33,36]. First, [33,36] deal with finite horizon problems with nonlinear subsystems, and with costs which are not necessarily quadratic, while [7,8] deal with infinite horizon problems with linear subsystems and quadratic costs. Moreover, the result in [33,36] can be applied to reachability problems, while the result in [7,8] fits better for stability problems.

7 Conclusion

In this paper, we have surveyed some recent results on computational methods for optimal control of switched systems. In particular, we formally formulate the problems and discussed in detail the two stage optimization. Computational methods based on discretization and computational methods not based on discretization are surveyed. We have aimed at providing an overview of general results and ideas. For technical details, the reader may consult the reference listed below. Despite the results reported here, it can be seen that the subject is still largely open and we are far from total understanding and complete solution of such problems. Each result we presented usually imposes several additional assumptions so that a specific method can be developed. There are many future research directions which we can pursue. For example, even stage 1 optimization for problems with state and input constraints has not been solved yet. By solving this problem, applications to real-world processes can be greatly expanded. From the paper, it can also be seen that very few results are available for efficient optimization of the number and the order of active subsystems. This can be a very challenging problem that our continuous methods may no longer be capable of handling. Moreover, extensions of the surveyed methods to general hybrid systems can also provide us with many new results. In all, the subject of computational methods for optimal control problems of switched and hybrid systems is an exciting open area that deserves more attention and can stimulate the development of hybrid system theory and application.

References

1. A. Bemporad and M. Morari. Control of systems integrating logic, dynamics, and constraints. *Automatica*, 35(3):407–427, March 1999.
2. A. Bemporad, F. Borrelli, and M. Morari. Optimal controllers for hybrid systems: stability and piecewise linear explicit form. *Proc. 39th IEEE CDC*, 1810–1815, 2000.
3. A. Bemporad, F. Borrelli, and M. Morari. On the optimal control law for linear discrete time hybrid systems. *HSCC 2002, LNCS* 2289, 105–109, Springer, 2002.
4. D.P. Bertsekas. Nonlinear Programming, Second Edition. Athena Scientific, 1999.
5. M.S. Branicky, V.S. Borkar, and S.K. Mitter. A unified framework for hybrid control: model and optimal control theory. *IEEE Trans. on AC*, 43(1):31–45, January 1998.
6. C.G. Cassandras, D.L. Pepyne, and Y. Wardi. Optimal control of a class of hybrid systems. *IEEE Trans. on AC*, 46(3):398–415, March 2001.
7. A. Giua, C. Seatzu, and C. Van Der Mee. Optimal control of autonomous linear systems switched with a pre-assigned finite sequence. *Proc. 2001 IEEE ISIC*, 144–149, 2001.
8. A. Giua, C. Seatzu, and C. Van Der Mee. Optimal control of switched autonomous linear systems. *Proc. 40th IEEE CDC*, 2472–2477, 2001.
9. K. Gokbayrak and C.G. Cassandras. A hierarchical decomposition method for optimal control of hybrid systems. *Proc. 39th IEEE CDC*, 2472–2477, 2000.
10. K. Gokbayrak and C.G. Cassandras. Hybrid controllers for hierarchically decomposed systems. *HSCC 2000, LNCS* 1790, 117–129, Springer, 2000.
11. S. Hedlund and A. Rantzer. Optimal control of hybrid system. *Proc. 38th IEEE CDC*, 3972–3977, 1999.
12. S. Hedlund and A. Rantzer. Convex dynamic programming for hybrid systems. *IEEE Trans. on AC*, 47(9):1536–1540, September 2002.
13. F.L. Lewis. Optimal Control. Wiley Interscience, 1986.

14. B. Lincoln and B.M. Bernhardsson. Efficient pruning of search trees in LQR control of switched linear systems. *Proc. 39th IEEE CDC*, 1828–1833, 2000.

15. J. Lu, L. Liao, A. Nerode, and J.H. Taylor. Optimal control of systems with continuous and discrete states. *Proc. 32nd IEEE CDC*, 2292–2297, 1993.

16. B. Ma. An improved algorithm for solving constrained optimal control problems. Ph.D. Thesis, University of Maryland, 1994.

17. S.G. Nash and A. Sofer. Linear and Nonlinear Programming. McGraw-Hill, 1996.

18. D.L. Pepyne and C.G. Cassandras. Modeling, analysis, and optimal control of a class of hybrid systems. *DEDS: Theory and Applications*, Vol. 8, 175–201, 1998.

19. D.L. Pepyne and C.G. Cassandras. Optimal control of hybrid systems in manufacturing. *Proceedings of the IEEE*, 88(7):1108–1123, July 2000.

20. B. Piccoli. Hybrid systems and optimal control. *Proc. 37th IEEE CDC*, 13–18, 1998.

21. E. Polak. An historical survey of computational methods in optimal control. *SIAM Review*, 15(2):553–584, April 1973.

22. A. Rantzer and M. Johansson. Piecewise linear quadratic optimal control. *IEEE Trans. on AC*, 45(4):629–637, April 2000.

23. P. Riedinger, F. Kratz, C. Iung, and C. Zanne. Linear quadratic optimization for hybrid systems. *Proc. 38th IEEE CDC*, 3059–3064, 1999.

24. P. Riedinger, C. Zanne, and F. Kratz. Time optimal control of hybrid systems. *Proc. 1999 ACC*, 2466–2470, 1999.

25. T.I. Seidman. Optimal control for switching systems. *Proc. 21st Annual Conf. on Infor. Sci. and Sys.*, 485–489, 1987.

26. H.J. Sussmann. A maximum principle for hybrid optimal control problems. *Proc. 38th IEEE CDC*, 425–430, 1999.

27. L.Y. Wang, A. Beydoun, J. Cook, J. Sun, and I. Kolmanovsky. Optimal hybrid control with applications to automotive powertrain systems. *LNCIS* 222, 190–200, Springer, 1997.

28. H.S. Witsenhausen. A class of hybrid-state continuous-time dynamic systems. *IEEE Trans. on AC*, 11(2):161–167, April 1966.

29. X. Xu and P.J. Antsaklis. Optimal control of switched systems: new results and open problems. *Proc. 2000 ACC*, 2683–2687, 2000.

30. X. Xu. Analysis and design of switched systems. Ph.D. Thesis, University of Notre Dame, August 2001. Also available at: http://ece.bd.psu.edu/~xu/

31. X. Xu and P.J. Antsaklis. An approach to optimal control of switched systems with internally forced switchings. *Proc. 2002 ACC*, 148–153, 2002.

32. X. Xu and P.J. Antsaklis. An approach to switched sytems optimal control based on parameterization of the switching instants. *Proc. 15th IFAC World Congress*, 2002.

33. X. Xu and P.J. Antsaklis. Optimal control of switched autonomous systems. *Proc. 41st IEEE CDC*, 4401–4406, 2002.

34. X. Xu and P.J. Antsaklis. Optimal control of switched systems via nonlinear optimization based on direct differentiations of value functions. *Int. J. of Control*, 75(16/17):1406–1426, 2002.

35. X. Xu and P.J. Antsaklis. Optimal control of switched systems based on parameterization of the switching instants. *IEEE Trans. on AC*, accepted, 2002.

36. X. Xu and P.J. Antsaklis. Optimal control of hybrid autonomous systems with state jumps. *The 2003 ACC*, submitted, 2002.

37. J. Yong. Systems governed by ordinary differential equations with continuous, switching and impulse controls. *Appl. Math. Optim.*, 20:223–235, 1989.

Author Index

Lecture Notes in Computer Science

For information about Vols. 1–2532

please contact your bookseller or Springer-Verlag

Vol. 2570: M. Jünger, G. Reinelt, G. Rinaldi (Eds.), Combinatorial Optimization – Eureka, You Shrink!. Proceedings, 2001. X, 209 pages. 2003.

Vol. 2571: S.K. Das, S. Bhattacharya (Eds.), Distributed Computing. Proceedings, 2002. XIV, 354 pages. 2002.

Vol. 2572: D. Calvanese, M. Lenzerini, R. Motwani (Eds.), Database Theory – ICDT 2003. Proceedings, 2003. XI, 455 pages. 2002.

Vol. 2574: M.-S. Chen, P.K. Chrysanthis, M. Sloman, A. Zaslavsky (Eds.), Mobile Data Management. Proceedings, 2003. XII, 414 pages. 2003.

Vol. 2575: L.D. Zuck, P.C. Attie, A. Cortesi, S. Mukhopadhyay (Eds.), Verification, Model Checking, and Abstract Interpretation. Proceedings, 2003. XI, 325 pages. 2003.

Vol. 2576: S. Cimato, C. Galdi, G. Persiano (Eds.), Security in Communication Networks. Proceedings, 2002. IX, 365 pages. 2003.

Vol. 2578: F.A.P. Petitcolas (Ed.), Information Hiding. Proceedings, 2002. IX, 427 pages. 2003.

Vol. 2580: H. Erdogmus, T. Weng (Eds.), COTS-Based Software Systems. Proceedings, 2003. XVIII, 261 pages. 2003.

Vol. 2581: J.S. Sichman, F. Bousquet, P. Davidsson (Eds.), Multi-Agent-Based Simulation II. Proceedings, 2002. X, 195 pages. 2003. (Subseries LNAI).

Vol. 2583: S. Matwin, C. Sammut (Eds.), Inductive Logic Programming. Proceedings, 2002. X, 351 pages. 2003. (Subseries LNAI).

Vol. 2585: F. Giunchiglia, J. Odell, G. Weiß (Eds.), Agent-Oriented Software Engineering III. Proceedings, 2002. X, 229 pages. 2003.

Vol. 2586: M. Klusch, S. Bergamaschi, P. Edwards, P. Petta (Eds.), Intelligent Information Agents. VI, 275 pages. 2003. (Subseries LNAI).

Vol. 2587: P.J. Lee, C.H. Lim (Eds.), Information Security and Cryptology – ICISC 2002. Proceedings, 2002. XI, 536 pages. 2003.

Vol. 2588: A. Gelbukh (Ed.), Computational Linguistics and Intelligent Text Processing. Proceedings, 2003. XV, 648 pages. 2003.

Vol. 2589: E. Börger, A. Gargantini, E. Riccobene (Eds.), Abstract State Machines 2003. Proceedings, 2003. XI, 427 pages. 2003.

Vol. 2590: S. Bressan, A.B. Chaudhri, M.L. Lee, J.X. Yu, Z. Lacroix (Eds.), Efficiency and Effectiveness of XML Tools and Techniques and Data Integration over the Web. Proceedings, 2002. X, 259 pages. 2003.

Vol. 2591: M. Aksit, M. Mezini, R. Unland (Eds.), Objects, Components, Architectures, Services, and Applications for a Networked World. Proceedings, 2002. XI, 431 pages. 2003.

Vol. 2592: R. Kowalczyk, J.P. Müller, H. Tianfield, R. Unland (Eds.), Agent Technologies, Infrastructures, Tools, and Applications for E-Services. Proceedings, 2002. XVII, 371 pages. 2003. (Subseries LNAI).

Vol. 2593: A.B. Chaudhri, M. Jeckle, E. Rahm, R. Unland (Eds.), Web, Web-Services, and Database Systems. Proceedings, 2002. XI, 311 pages. 2003.

Vol. 2594: A. Asperti, B. Buchberger, J.H. Davenport (Eds.), Mathematical Knowledge Management. Proceedings, 2003. X, 225 pages. 2003.

Vol. 2595: K. Nyberg, H. Heys (Eds.), Selected Areas in Cryptography. Proceedings, 2002. XI, 405 pages. 2003.

Vol. 2597: G. Păun, G. Rozenberg, A. Salomaa, C. Zandron (Eds.), Membrane Computing. Proceedings, 2002. VIII, 423 pages. 2003.

Vol. 2598: R. Klein, H.-W. Six, L. Wegner (Eds.), Computer Science in Perspective. X, 357 pages. 2003.

Vol. 2599: E. Sherratt (Ed.), Telecommunications and beyond: The Broader Applicability of SDL and MSC. Proceedings, 2002. X, 253 pages. 2003.

Vol. 2600: S. Mendelson, A.J. Smola, Advanced Lectures on Machine Learning. Proceedings, 2002. IX, 259 pages. 2003. (Subseries LNAI).

Vol. 2601: M. Ajmone Marsan, G. Corazza, M. Listanti, A. Roveri (Eds.) Quality of Service in Multiservice IP Networks. Proceedings, 2003. XV, 759 pages. 2003.

Vol. 2602: C. Priami (Ed.), Computational Methods in Systems Biology. Proceedings, 2003. IX, 214 pages. 2003.

Vol. 2604: N. Guelfi, E. Astesiano, G. Reggio (Eds.), Scientific Engineering for Distributed Java Applications. Proceedings, 2002. X, 205 pages. 2003.

Vol. 2606: A.M. Tyrrell, P.C. Haddow, J. Torresen (Eds.), Evolvable Systems: From Biology to Hardware. Proceedings, 2003. XIV, 468 pages. 2003.

Vol. 2607: H. Alt, M. Habib (Eds.), STACS 2003. Proceedings, 2003. XVII, 700 pages. 2003.

Vol. 2609: M. Okada, B. Pierce, A. Scedrov, H. Tokuda, A. Yonezawa (Eds.), Software Security – Theories and Systems. Proceedings, 2002. XI, 471 pages. 2003.

Vol. 2611: S. Cagnoni, J.J. Romero Cardalda, D.W. Corne, J. Gottlieb, A. Guillot, E. Hart, C.G. Johnson, E. Marchiori, J.-A. Meyer, M. Middendorf, G.R. Raidl (Eds.), Applications of Evolutionary Computing. Proceedings, 2003. XXI, 708 pages. 2003.

Vol. 2612: M. Joye (Ed.), Topics in Cryptology – CT-RSA 2003. Proceedings, 2003. XI, 417 pages. 2003.

Vol. 2614: R. Laddaga, P. Robertson, H. Shrobe (Eds.), Self-Adaptive Software: Applications. Proceedings, 2001. VIII, 291 pages. 2003.

Vol. 2615: N. Carbonell, C. Stephanidis (Eds.), Universal Access. Proceedings, 2002. XIV, 534 pages. 2003.

Vol. 2616: T. Asano, R. Klette, C. Ronse (Eds.), Geometry, Morphology, and Computational Imaging. Proceedings, 2002. X, 437 pages. 2003.

Vol. 2618: P. Degano (Ed.), Programming Languages and Systems. Proceedings, 2003. XV, 415 pages. 2003.

Vol. 2619: H. Garavel, J. Hatcliff (Eds.), Tools and Algorithms for the Construction and Analysis of Systems. Proceedings, 2003. XVI, 604 pages. 2003.

Vol. 2620: A.D. Gordon (Ed.), Foundations of Software Science and Computational Structures. Proceedings, 2003. XII, 441 pages. 2003.

Vol. 2621: M. Pezzè (Ed.), Fundamental Approaches to Software Engineering. Proceedings, 2003. XIV, 403 pages. 2003.

Vol. 2622: G. Hedin (Ed.), Compiler Construction. Proceedings, 2003. XII, 335 pages. 2003.

Vol. 2623: O. Maler, A. Pnueli (Eds.), Hybrid Systems: Computation and Control. Proceedings, 2003. XII, 558 pages. 2003.

Vol. 2626: J.L. Crowley, J.H. Piater, M. Vincze, L. Paletta (Eds.), Computer Vision Systems. Proceedings, 2003. XIII, 546 pages. 2003.